PETERSON'S®

MASTER THE™
SSAT® & ISEE®

About Peterson's®

Peterson's has been your trusted educational publisher for more than 50 years. It's a milestone we're quite proud of as we continue to offer the most accurate, dependable, high-quality educational content in the field, providing you with everything you need to succeed. No matter where you are on your academic or professional path, you can rely on Peterson's for its books, videos, online information, expert test-prep tools, the most up-to-date education exploration data, and the highest quality career success resources—everything you need to achieve your education goals. For our complete line of products, visit **www.petersons.com.**

For more information, contact Peterson's, 4380 S. Syracuse St., Suite 200, Denver, CO 80237; 800-338-3282 Ext. 54229; or visit us online at **www.petersons.com.**

Kelsie McWilliams, Editorial Project Manager; Lacey N. Smith, Content Editor; Peter Giebel, Managing Editor; Jennifer Baker, Editor; Michelle Galins, Book Designer

ISBN-13: 978-0-7689-4579-9

Printed in the United States of America

10 9 8 7 6 5 4 3 2 1   24 23 22

Tenth Edition

CONTENTS

Part I: Preparing for the Exams

CONTENTS

Part IV: Quantitative and Nonverbal Skills

CONTENTS

PART V: Strategies for Writing Essays

PART VI: Practice Tests

CONTENTS

Peterson's Updates and Corrections:

Check out our website at **www.petersonsbooks.com/updates-and-corrections/** to see if there is any new information regarding the test and any revisions or corrections to the content of this book. We've made sure the information in this book is accurate and up to date; however, the test format or content may have changed since the time of publication.

Credits

Excerpt from "Dada Manifesto" by Hugo Ball (1916)

Excerpt from "The Sculptor's Funeral" by Willa Cather (1905)

Review of "What Science Tells Us about the Mood-Boosting Effects of Indoor Plants" by Lala Tammoy Das from *Washington Post* (June 2022)

Excerpt from "My Escape from Slavery" by Frederick Douglass (1881)

Review of "How Advertisers Convinced Americans They Smelled Bad" by Sarah Everts from *Smithsonian Magazine* (August 2012)

"Snowy Mountains" by John Gould Fletcher (1922)

Excerpt from "The Prophet" by Kahlil Gibran (1923)

Review of "Do Trees Talk to Each Other?" by Richard Grant from *Smithsonian Magazine* (March 2018)

"The Slave Mother" by Frances Ellen Watkins Harper (1854)

Excerpt from *In Ghostly Japan* by Lafcadio Hearn (1899)

Excerpt from "By Your Response to Danger" by Jenny Holzer (1980–1982)

"The Spring and the Fall" by Edna St. Vincent Millay (1923)

Review of "How People Learn: Brain, Mind, Experience, and School: Expanded Edition" by National Research Council (2000)

Review of "Overview – SSRI Antidepressants" by UK National Health Service (February 2021)

BEFORE YOU BEGIN

OVERVIEW

Why You Should Use This Book

How This Book Is Organized

What to Study

How to Use This Book

Special Study Features

An Important Note for Eighth and Ninth Graders

Top 10 Ways to Raise Your Score

Peterson's® Publications

Give Us Your Feedback

You're Well on Your Way to Success

WHY YOU SHOULD USE THIS BOOK

Peterson's *Master the*™ *SSAT*® *& ISEE*® is designed by test experts and educators to fully prepare you for test-day success, regardless of which entrance exam you're preparing to take. Take a look at everything on offer in this comprehensive guide to the SSAT and ISEE (Upper Level).

ESSENTIAL TEST INFORMATION

We take the stress out of planning for your entrance exam by providing all the information you'll need before the big day in one place—including how to decide which test is right for you, how to register, where to go, and even what to bring on the day of the exam. We've got you covered!

COMPREHENSIVE COVERAGE OF THE SSAT AND ISEE TEST FORMATS

After using this book, you'll know the structure and format of your exam from start to finish and have all the information you'll need for success on either exam.

THOROUGH TEST TOPIC REVIEW

You'll get a thorough review of *every topic* tested on the SSAT and ISEE. Not only will there be few surprises on test day, but you'll also have the confidence of knowing that you're thoroughly prepared to tackle the exam. We even include a boatload of advice on how to tailor your study approach to address your unique learning needs.

PLENTY OF REALISTIC TEST QUESTION PRACTICE

Every topic chapter in this book contains realistic practice with questions just like those you'll encounter during the actual exam. In addition, you can customize your preparation based on your target test. Take a full-length diagnostic exam for either the SSAT or the ISEE to help you determine your strengths and weaknesses and target your study time effectively. Once you're nearing your exam date, build your confidence by taking a full-length practice exam for either the SSAT or the ISEE, which you can use to strengthen your test-taking skills and get comfortable with the timing and pace of the actual exams. There's no better way to practice for the big day!

EXPERT TIPS, ADVICE, AND STRATEGIES

Our test prep professionals and veteran educators know what it takes to get a top score on the SSAT and ISEE—you'll get the expert tools that have proven to be effective on exam day, putting you a step ahead of the test-taking competition. Consider this your inside edge as you prepare to conquer your entrance exam!

We know that doing well on your exam is important, both to you and your family—and we're here to help you through every step of your journey. Consider this book your all-in-one test preparation package to get you through the entrance exam and on your way to the school of your choice.

HOW THIS BOOK IS ORGANIZED

This book has all the answers to your questions about the SSAT and the ISEE. It contains up-to-date information, hundreds of practice questions, and solid test-taking advice. Here's how you can use it to get your best high school entrance exam score and get into the secondary school of your choice.

A Breakdown of This Book

Part I: Preparing for the Exams	Part I contains answers to all your questions about the SSAT and the ISEE. You'll learn what kinds of questions to expect and how they look, how the tests are scored, and numerous study skills and learning strategies to help you make the most of your prep time.
Part II: Diagnosing Strengths and Weaknesses	Part II provides you the opportunity to try your hand at sample questions from both exams. This section contains one diagnostic test for the SSAT and one diagnostic test for the ISEE. The diagnostic test can show you where your skills are strong and where to focus your study time. We recommend taking it early on in your exam prep journey. Use your results from the diagnostic test to help you pinpoint which chapters might be most helpful to you.
Part III: Verbal Skills	Part III covers the verbal ability and reading comprehension sections of the exams. In these chapters, you'll learn how to approach synonym, analogy, and sentence completion questions. You'll also learn strategies for how to read passages and answer different kinds of questions about them, including vocabulary questions.
Part IV: Quantitative and Nonverbal Skills	Part IV covers topics that you should expect to see on the quantitative sections of your exam. Here, you can get a refresher on basic math, algebra, and geometry. You'll also learn strategies for answering quantitative ability and quantitative comparison questions.
Part V: Strategies for Writing Essays	Part V walks you through the essay component of the exam. Remember that this section is unscored, but it's still important to do your best. You'll learn strategies for how to approach different kinds of prompts and how to plan, improve, and revise your writing.
Part VI: Practice Tests	Part VI contains two practice tests, one each for the SSAT and ISEE. Toward the end of your exam prep journey, take at least one to see your improvement since taking the diagnostic test. Use your results to focus on any last-minute prep.

WHAT TO STUDY

Parts III through V of this book provide content for you to review. Use the table below to determine which chapters to study for your test.

WHAT TO STUDY FOR THE SSAT AND ISEE		
Chapter/Topic	SSAT	ISEE
Chapter 7: Synonyms	✔	✔
Chapter 8: Verbal Analogies	✔	
Chapter 9: Sentence Completion		✔
Chapter 10: Reading Comprehension	✔	✔
Chapter 11: Basic Mathematics	✔	✔
Chapter 12: Algebra	✔	✔
Chapter 13: Geometry	✔	✔
Chapter 14: Quantitative Ability	✔	✔
Chapter 15: Quantitative Comparisons		✔
Chapter 16: Essay Writing	✔	✔
Chapter 17: Writing Mechanics	✔	✔

HOW TO USE THIS BOOK
Diagnostic Test Method

A diagnostic test is a test that helps you understand your strengths and weaknesses on the exam. It "diagnoses" the skills that need the most improvement.

One way to use this book is to start by taking a diagnostic test. Part II contains two full-length diagnostic tests that contain the kinds of questions you are likely to see on the actual exam. Depending on which exam you plan on taking, use either the SSAT (Chapter 5) or the ISEE (Chapter 6). This test will make it easier to determine the best use of your exam prep, since you can allot your available practice time according to your needs.

Once you've taken your diagnostic test, score yourself to see your strengths and weaknesses. How did you do? For instance, if you scored well on math but poorly on verbal skills, then you can count math as a strength. Your verbal skills, on the other hand, will need some work. Rank the different sections in terms of your strongest and weakest skills.

Use your ranking list to develop your study plan. Your plan should prioritize boosting your weaker skills. You don't need to spend as much time brushing up on your strengths. However, you should still plan to spend some time on "strong skills" exercises—just to stay in shape.

Once you've got a study plan, put it to work. Read the introduction to your test in Part I. Then, focus on improving your weaker skills by studying the sections

 TIP

If you take both the diagnostic test and practice test for your exam of choice and still want more practice, consider going back and using the diagnostic or practice test for the other exam covered in this book. The SSAT and ISEE are not identical but are similar enough that practice for one should still help you with the other.

in Parts III through V. After you've reviewed the content sections, take a practice test in Part VI. This test should show an improvement in your score!

Front-to-Back Method

Another way to use this book is the front-to-back method. In this method, you work through the book the way it is organized.

Start at Part I and carefully read through the introductory section on your exam. This will help you understand the exam and how it's scored. Next, take a diagnostic test in Part II. Then, study the content sections in Parts III, IV, and V. Focus on the sections that relate to your exam. If you know your stronger and weaker skills, you might devote extra time to sections where you need the most improvement.

After you've reviewed the content, take a practice test in Part VI. Taking a practice test will help you be more prepared on exam day. Even if you somehow don't improve your score between the diagnostic test and practice test, the process of taking each can itself help increase your score. This is because you become more familiar with the test format each time you try, which increases your confidence.

After you complete each test, review your answers with the explanations provided. If you still don't understand how to answer a certain question, consider asking a teacher for help. A review session with a friend might prove helpful too.

 NOTE

Peterson's offers a variety of test-prep materials so you can get more practice on the SSAT and ISEE. For more information, go to **www.petersons.com/testprep/high-school-entrance-exams.**

SPECIAL STUDY FEATURES

Peterson's *Master the™ SSAT® & ISEE®* was designed to be easy to use so that you can locate the information you need. It includes several features to make your preparation easier.

Overview

Each review chapter begins with an overview listing the topics that will be covered in the chapter. You know immediately where to look for a topic that you need to work on.

Summing It Up

Each chapter ends with a point-by-point summary that captures the most important concepts in the chapter.

Test Yourself Exercises

In some chapters, you'll find Test Yourself exercises that are designed to help you practice question types or specific concepts. Use these practice exercises to ensure that you understand key concepts as they are introduced.

Knowledge Checks

At the end of most chapters, you'll find a Knowledge Check, which is a short quiz designed to test your understanding of the concepts presented throughout the chapter. Set a timer and try to complete the Knowledge Check in the time allotted so that you can see how you might perform on the actual exam. In some chapters, like Chapter 16: Essay Writing, you'll find sample prompts or other test information in place of a traditional Knowledge Check.

Bonus Information

In addition, be sure to look out for helpful notes, tips, and alerts throughout the book.

- **NOTES**: highlight critical information about the format of the SSAT and the ISEE.
- **TIPS**: draw your attention to valuable concepts, advice, and shortcuts for tackling the tests or your study time.
- **ALERTS**: Whenever you need to be careful of a common pitfall or test taker trap, you'll find an *Alert*. This information reveals and helps eliminate the wrong turns many people take on the exam.

QR Codes

Throughout this book, you'll find QR codes that link to supplemental video content. These videos are designed to provide you with focused lessons on specific topics. If you find yourself struggling with a specific concept, look for a QR code in the section or chapter for additional instruction.

AN IMPORTANT NOTE FOR EIGHTH AND NINTH GRADERS

You may find that some of the test questions that appear on the SSAT or ISEE are extremely difficult or cover material that you have not yet been exposed to. This is intentional. Keep in mind that the same upper-level exam is administered to students in grades 8, 9, 10, and 11. However, your final score will only be compared to the scores of other students in your grade. When the Secondary School Admission Test Board and the Educational Records Bureau send admission officers your scores, they'll include information that allows your score to be compared to all students in your grade who have taken the test in the past three years. No one expects you to compete against older students, so don't worry if you encounter vocabulary questions that seem too advanced or math concepts that you haven't mastered yet in school. It won't be held against you. Besides, because you're working with this book, you'll be better prepared to deal with those tough questions when you take the real test!

TOP 10 WAYS TO RAISE YOUR SCORE

When it comes to taking your entrance exam, some test-taking skills will help you more than others. There are concepts you can learn, techniques you can follow, and tricks you can use that will help you to perform your very best. Here are our picks for the top 10 ways to raise your score:

01 Regardless of which plan you will follow, get started by reading Part I to familiarize yourself with the test formats.

02 Make sure you understand the information in Chapter 4 on effective learning and studying. Apply it as you work through this book.

03 Use the QR codes throughout the book to see things explained in video form.

04 Make sure to complete the practice exercises in each chapter you read.

05 Revisit challenging chapters and their summaries.

06 After you have completed all the study sections, take a practice test. See how your scores have improved and identify any areas you might need to review again.

07 If you have the time, you might find it beneficial to take the diagnostic and practice test for the other exam. For example, if you're required to take the SSAT, you might also test yourself with the ISEE exam.

08 During the last phase of your study, review the practice tests.

09 The night before your exam, RELAX. You'll be prepared.

10 The morning of your exam, make sure you have everything you need for your test, and don't bring anything you're not allowed to have with you. Eat a balanced breakfast that morning and take time to breathe and focus your mind before the exam.

PETERSON'S® PUBLICATIONS

Peterson's publishes a full line of books—career preparation, education exploration, test prep, and financial aid. Peterson's books are available for purchase online at **www.petersons.com**. Sign up for one of our online subscription plans and you'll have access to our entire test prep catalog of more than 150 exams *plus* instructional videos, flashcards, interactive quizzes, and more! Our subscription plans allow you to study as quickly as you can or as slowly as you'd like. For more information, and access to practice for high school entrance exams like the SSAT and ISEE, go to **www.petersons. com/testprep/high-school-entrance-exams**.

GIVE US YOUR FEEDBACK

We welcome any comments or suggestions you may have about this publication. Your feedback will help us make educational dreams possible for you—and others like you.

YOU'RE WELL ON YOUR WAY TO SUCCESS

Remember that knowledge is power. By using this book, you will be studying the most comprehensive guide available.

The first step to acing your high school entrance exam is to know the structure and format of the exam you're going to take inside and out, including all the basics you need to know.

We know you're eager to get to the test practice and review, but taking the time to develop a thorough understanding of the exam from top to bottom will give you a real advantage—and put you ahead of the test-taking competition. In Part I, we'll go carefully through each exam—the SSAT and the ISEE—and guide you through each step so you'll be confident and prepared for test day success. Let's get started!

PART I

PREPARING FOR THE EXAMS

1 | All about the Exams

2 | All about the Secondary School Admission Test (SSAT)

3 | All about the Independent School Entrance Exam (ISEE)

CHAPTER

All about the Exams

ALL ABOUT THE EXAMS

OVERVIEW

Five Common High School Entrance Exams

What Is the Secondary School Admission Test (SSAT)?

What Is the Independent School Entrance Exam (ISEE)?

Test Day Strategies

Summing It Up

There are several types of high school entrance exams, so knowing which one you are going to take is important. In this chapter, we'll provide an overview of five of the exams. We'll focus on the Secondary School Admission Test (SSAT) and the Independent School Entrance Exam (ISEE), but we'll also briefly cover the Test for Admission into Catholic High Schools (TACHS), the High School Placement Test (HSPT), and the Specialized High School Admissions Test (SHSAT). That's a lot of different tests (and acronyms), but we'll help you figure out which one applies to you and how you can use this book to study for what's on your exam. Throughout this book, the first page of each chapter will include a legend that tells you which tests the chapter is relevant to; at a glance, you'll be able to see if the content covered in the chapter is on the exam you are going to take.

As a result of the COVID-19 pandemic, all the tests covered here now offer a remote testing option. The protocol for online remote testing varies depending on the exam. Make sure that you fully understand the system requirements, code of conduct, and testing protocol for the remote testing option for the exam you plan to take.

FIVE COMMON HIGH SCHOOL ENTRANCE EXAMS

High school entrance exams are standardized tests. Independent, parochial, religious-affiliated, and specialized public high schools use scores on these exams to help them make their admissions decisions. There are a number of widely used standardized high school exams. The best known of these are the following:

SSAT

The Secondary School Admission Test (SSAT) is an entrance exam that can be taken by students as part of their application to a private high school. The Upper Level of the SSAT is offered to students applying for grades 9 through 12. The SSAT lasts about 3 hours and 10 minutes, including two 10-minute breaks. The test is broken into the following sections: Quantitative (Math), Verbal, Reading, an unscored Writing Sample, and an unscored Experimental section, which includes a mix of verbal, reading, and math questions. Your score will be based on the number of questions you answer correctly. One point is given for each correctly answered question. An incorrect answer results in a loss of one quarter of a point. Scores are reported in percentile ranks, which means that your score will be weighed against the performance of others in the same grade who have taken the test. The SSAT is offered in both online and paper testing formats, and each format follows the same rules, guidelines, and timing requirements.

ISEE

The Independent School Entrance Exam (ISEE) is an entrance exam that can be taken by students as part of their application to a private high school. The ISEE is offered in both online and paper testing formats, and each format follows the same rules, guidelines, and timing requirements. The Upper Level of the ISEE exam is offered to students applying for grades 9 through 12. The ISEE lasts about 2 hours and 40 minutes, not including two 5- to 10-minute breaks. This exam is broken into five parts: Verbal Reasoning, Quantitative Reasoning, Reading Comprehension, Mathematics Achievement, and an Essay component. There are no penalties for incorrect answers. Scores are reported in percentile ranks, so your performance on the exam will be weighed against the performance of other students in the same grade as you who took the exam over the past three years.

TACHS

The Test for Admission into Catholic High Schools (TACHS) is the entrance test for eighth grade students who want to attend a Catholic high school in the Diocese of Brooklyn/Queens or Archdiocese of New York City. In 2021 and 2022, the Catholic High Schools of Long Island (Diocese of Rockville Center) used an online TACHS exam in lieu of the Catholic High School Entrance Exam (CHSEE), so this may be the case going forward as well. The TACHS is a multiple-choice exam that lasts about 2 hours, including time to give directions. If you are currently in the eighth grade and plan to attend a Catholic high school in this area, you'll take the TACHS exam as part of your admissions application. If, however, you plan to enter a school in this area as a tenth, eleventh, or twelfth grader, you don't need to take the TACHS. Instead, you'll apply directly to the high school you wish to attend.

HSPT

The High School Placement Test (HSPT) is part of the admissions process for many Catholic high schools. The HSPT is a multiple-choice, 298-question exam designed to test your reading, mathematics, verbal, quantitative, and language skills. There's also an optional forty-question test in either science, mechanical aptitude, or religion. The exam takes about 2 hours and 30 minutes; along with your school records, your HSPT score will be sent to the high schools you're applying to so they can make an admissions decision.

SHSAT

The Specialized High School Admissions Test (SHSAT) is open to students in grades 8 and 9 who reside in New York City and who want to apply to enroll in a local Catholic high school. The test consists of two sections: an English Language Arts section and a Math section. English language learners will also be given a glossary with word-to-word translations of mathematics terms, but these glossaries do not include definitions. You will have 180 minutes to complete the test, and you can divide your time between both the English Language Arts section and the Math section however you want.

Which Exam Should I Take?

Contact the admissions offices of all schools to which you are applying and ask which exam each school requires or will accept. Ask also for the cutoff dates by which your scores must be received by the school. Find out if the school has made special arrangements for testing its applicants on a specific date at a convenient location.

If I Have a Choice of Exams, How Do I Choose?

If all your schools will accept scores from either the SSAT or the ISEE, you can choose based on convenience of testing date and location. Or, if you began your preparations early enough and have tried a sample of various exams, such as the two in this book, you can choose the exam with which you feel more comfortable. You can get lists of testing locations, dates, registration deadlines, and fees along with official test descriptions, official sample questions, and registration forms by writing or calling or by visiting the website for the tests you're considering taking.

WHAT IS THE SECONDARY SCHOOL ADMISSION TEST (SSAT)?

The SSAT is an entrance exam that can be taken by students as part of their application to a private high school. The Upper Level of the SSAT exam is offered to students applying for grades 9 through 12. The SSAT lasts about 3 hours and 10 minutes, including two 10-minute breaks. The SSAT is broken into the following sections: Quantitative (Math), Verbal, Reading, an unscored Writing Sample, and an unscored Experimental section, which includes a mix of verbal, reading, and math questions.

SSAT TEST STRUCTURE		
Section	Number of Questions	Duration
Writing Sample (unscored)	1	25 minutes
Break		10 minutes
Quantitative (Part 1)	25	30 minutes
Reading	40	40 minutes
Break		10 minutes
Verbal	60	30 minutes
Quantitative (Part 2)	25	30 minutes
Experimental (unscored)	16	15 minutes

Along with your school records, your SSAT score is sent to the schools that you're applying to so that they can make an admissions decision. You are allowed to take the SSAT multiple times, depending on which format of the test you are taking. For computer-based SSAT exams, you may take a combined total of 2 SSAT at Home or Prometric Test Center tests per testing year (August 1 through July 31). For paper-based SSAT exams, you may take up to 5 Upper Level Standard tests plus 1 Flex test.

How to Register

To register, you'll need to create an account on the SSAT website. Once you've created an account, you'll be able to log in and select "My Testing" and then "Register for a Test." You'll be able to select which testing option you prefer, find a test date that works with your schedule, and locate a test center if needed.

Testing Locations and Fees

There are three ways to take the SSAT:

1

On Paper at a Test Center: You can register to take the SSAT on paper at a test center. Between October and April, there are six Saturday sessions offered for the paper-based SSAT, and you can take the Upper Level Standard SSAT up to 5 times per year. In addition to these test dates, you also have the option of taking one Flex SSAT per year. The Flex SSAT is a standard paper-based SSAT test offered outside of the fixed test dates. Open Flex test sessions are available to the general public at a test center, and closed Flex test sessions are administered by an educational consultant to an individual or small group of students. The Upper Level Standard paper option and the open Flex option require a $165 registration fee. The Flex option with an educational consultant is available for a $240 registration fee.

2

Online at a Prometric Test Center: You can also register to take the SSAT online in a group setting at a Prometric Test Center, where the test will be proctored in person. The fee for this testing option is $235. Students are permitted to take a total of two combined Prometric and SSAT at Home tests per testing year.

3 **At Home:** You can register to take the SSAT online from your home. There are numerous designated testing dates offered for the SSAT at Home. Free equity tech kits are offered for students who do not have a device capable of running the SSAT at Home. The registration fee for this option is $255. Students are permitted to take a total of two combined Prometric and SSAT at Home tests per testing year.

Depending on which option you register for, you may also be able to reschedule your exam for a fee. For more information, visit the SSAT website.

Online Testing Protocol

To complete the SSAT at Home, you will first want to schedule your test. Once you've registered, you must check your computer, internet connection, and testing area at least three to four days in advance of the test. You should be able to complete the SSAT at Home on a laptop or desktop Mac or PC, but make sure that you have a microphone, speakers, webcam, and a reliable internet connection. You will need to be able to show your testing environment to your test proctor to ensure that you are compliant with testing requirements. Chrome is the preferred browser for running the SSAT at Home. The test is not compatible with mobile devices, such as a tablet, phone, or Chromebook.

Next, you'll want to run a system check; if your system check passes, you will be directed to install the secure browser, which is how you will access and complete the SSAT at Home. If you are retaking the SSAT at Home and already have the browser installed, you may need to uninstall and reinstall it on your computer. If your devices are not compatible for any reason, you can request a free equity kit from SSAT. Be sure to request a kit well in advance of your test date, as it may take several weeks for your kit to arrive.

In preparation for test day, check your internet connection to ensure that everything is running smoothly and quickly. During the test, keep your laptop or computer plugged in to ensure that your computer is fully charged while you're taking the exam. It's important that you take the test in a comfortable and quiet location with adequate lighting. Minimize any distractions by silencing notifications and alerts on your computer and your phone. Do not bring any headphones or earbuds to your test. Visit the SSAT's website for more information on device and room requirements.

Exam Accommodations

Students who need accommodations on the SSAT should wait to register for a test date until after they are approved for any accommodations. Students must submit documentation of their disability to receive accommodations. Allow up to two weeks for the SSAT to review and process your request. For more information, visit **ssat.org/testing/accommodations/guide-for-students**.

What to Bring

If you're taking the SSAT at Home, then only the following items are permitted:

 One No. 2 pencil

 A clear water bottle

 Two pieces of scrap paper

If you're taking the SSAT at a test center, then you should bring the following items:

 Your admission ticket (log in to your SSAT account and click "Print Ticket")

 Three No. 2 pencils with erasers (do NOT bring mechanical pencils or pens)

 A clear plastic water bottle with your name on it

 Snacks in a clear plastic bag with your name on it

There are several prohibited items that you cannot bring or use during your test session if you are taking the exam at a test center. If you do bring these items to the test center, you will be required to leave them in an area for prohibited items until the test is over:

 Personal devices, such as cell phones, watches, fitness trackers, and media players

 Backpacks, bags, purses, and large jewelry

 Coats and hats

 Books, erasers, mechanical pencils, notes or paper, pens, and rulers

You cannot bring a calculator unless you have been approved for an accommodation that allows you to use one. If you have opted to take the SSAT at a Prometric Test Center, you may also be required to show proof of vaccination against COVID-19. Contact your individual test center for details.

How the Test Is Scored

The Quantitative, Verbal, Reading, and Experimental sections consist of multiple-choice questions with five possible answers. Students will be scored based on the number of questions they answer correctly. You receive one point for each correct answer, but you will lose one quarter of a point for each incorrect answer. As such,

only guess if you are confident that you can eliminate at least two wrong answers. Scores are reported in percentile ranks, so your performance on the exam will be weighed against the performance of other students in the same grade as you who have taken the exam. The Writing Sample section is not scored. The schools you are applying to will receive a copy of your score report along with your essay.

Format and Focus

The SSAT is offered in both online and paper testing formats, and each format follows the same rules, guidelines, and timing requirements. If you opt for the paper format of the exam, you can take the test at school, at an office, or at a testing center. Depending on your needs and preferences, you may find it more convenient to test at your local school or at an office in a smaller group environment. If you go to a testing center, a parent or guardian is required to stay at the testing center for the duration of your exam. If you opt for the online testing format, you can take the SSAT from home.

The SSAT is broken into the following sections: Quantitative (Math), Verbal, Reading, an unscored Writing Sample, and an unscored Experimental section, which includes a mix of verbal, reading, and math questions. The exam only consists of multiple-choice questions with five answer options, except the Writing Sample component, which requires a written response. For the Writing Sample component of the exam, you will be given a pair of essay prompts, a pair of creative writing prompts, or a combination of each. You will be asked to choose one and write a short essay or story response in 25 minutes. The Writing Sample section of the SSAT serves two purposes. First, you can showcase your personality to the schools to which you are applying. Second, you can demonstrate your writing skills, specifically your ability to organize and express your thoughts and ideas.

The Quantitative (Math) section consists of 50 questions, given in two 30-minute sections on the exam. These questions test your ability in arithmetic, algebra, and geometry, as well as other topics. You are not permitted to use a calculator on this section of the exam.

On the Reading Comprehension section of the exam, you will have 40 minutes to answer 40 questions. There will be both argumentative and narrative passages ranging from approximately 200 to 400 words in length. Reading comprehension passages are taken from sources such as literary fiction; the humanities, including biography, art, and poetry; science, including anthropology, astronomy, and medicine; and social studies, including history, sociology, and economics. Questions may ask you to identify the main idea, find details, make inferences, define words, determine the author's purpose and tone, evaluate arguments, and make predictions based on information in the text.

On the Verbal Reasoning portion of the exam, you will have 30 minutes to answer 60 questions. The Verbal Reasoning section will include synonym and analogy items. For synonym items, you will be given a word and will be asked to select the word that means most nearly the same from among five answer choices. For verbal analogy items, you will be given a comparison and asked to determine the logical relationship between the words by selecting the word that best completes the analogy.

The Experimental section on the exam is unscored and is designed to test future questions for the SSAT.

WHAT IS THE INDEPENDENT SCHOOL ENTRANCE EXAM (ISEE)?

The ISEE is an entrance exam that can be taken by students as part of their application to a private high school. The Upper Level of the ISEE exam is offered to students applying for grades 9 through 12. The ISEE lasts about 2 hours and 40 minutes, not including two 5- to 10-minute breaks. The ISEE is broken into five parts: Verbal Reasoning, Quantitative Reasoning, Reading Comprehension, Mathematics Achievement, and an unscored Essay component. On the ISEE, there are no penalties for incorrect answers, so you'll want to answer every question, even if you need to guess.

ISEE TEST STRUCTURE		
Section	**Number of Questions**	**Duration**
Verbal Reasoning	40	20 minutes
Quantitative Reasoning	37	35 minutes
Break		5–10 minutes
Reading Comprehension	36	35 minutes
Mathematics Achievement	47	40 minutes
Break		5–10 minutes
Essay	1	30 minutes

Along with your school records, your ISEE score is sent to the principals of the schools that you're applying to so that they can make an admissions decision. You can take the ISEE up to three times in a 12-month admission cycle. However, the test can only be taken once per season: fall (August to November), winter (December to March), and spring/summer (April to July).

How to Register

There are two ways to register for the ISEE:

1 Online—Visit erblearn.org/families/isee-registration/ to register online. This is the preferred method of registration, as there is no waiting involved. After you have completed your registration, you can have your confirmation instantly emailed to you. Be sure to bookmark your confirmation email for easy reference on test day.

2 By Phone—Students, parents, and guardians can also register for the ISEE by calling 1-800-446-0320. To register by phone, you'll need to pay a $30 fee. To avoid the fee, register for the ISEE online instead.

Testing Locations and Fees

There are four ways to take the ISEE:

1 At Home: You can register to take the ISEE online from your home. The test will be administered remotely by either your school for a $150 fee or by the Educational Records Bureau (ERB) for a $200 fee.

2 At School: You can register to complete the ISEE in a school setting alongside other students taking the same exam level. The test is administered in person and can be taken in either a paper or online format. You can register for the online test up to 3 days in advance for a fee of $150, but you must register at least three weeks in advance for the paper exam. Late registration and walk-in registration options are available for the paper format of the exam at a cost of $180 and $190, respectively.

3 In Office: You can take the ISEE in a professional educational testing office either individually or in a small group setting. For this format, the test is administered in person and is offered in either a paper or online format. If you opt for the group testing option, the fee is $210, and if you opt for the individual testing option, the fee is $240.

4 At a Prometric Test Center: You can also register to take the ISEE in a group setting at a Prometric Test Center, where the test will be administered in person and offered in an online format. The fee for this testing option is $210, and you can only register online, not by phone.

Depending on which option you register for, you may also be able to reschedule or cancel your exam for a fee. For more information, visit the ERB website.

Online Testing Protocol

To complete the ISEE at home, you will need to carefully read the ISEE at Home Family Guide at least a week before your test date. The guide can be found on the ERB website at **erblearn.org/families/isee-at-home/getting-started/**. Then, you will need to download the secure ISEE testing browser, which you will need in order to access your test and complete the practice session. Next, check your device compatibility at least three days before your test date. Personal computers, Macs, and iPads all support at-home testing for the ISEE. You'll also need to have a built-in or separate webcam and microphone so that your proctor can monitor your testing environment during the exam. Finally, be sure to check in to your exam at least 15 minutes before your test's scheduled start time.

When checking in, you'll need to enter your session number, which is sent to you via email or text between one day and one hour before the start time for your test. Be sure to check your email client's spam folder. You should also have your Verification Letter handy—you should have received this letter in the mail, but you can also find a copy in your online account. The Verification Letter contains your ISEE ID, which you will need in order to check in for your exam. Next, you'll need to provide some form of identification. You can use a birth certificate, social security card, driver's license, school ID, etc. If you encounter any issues during the exam, consult the ERB's FAQs page for answers and solutions to common problems.

In preparation for test day, make sure that your internet connection is strong and reliable so that everything runs smoothly during your exam. During the test, keep your laptop or computer plugged in to ensure that your computer is fully charged. Make sure that your testing location is quiet and has adequate lighting, and don't forget to silence any notifications and alerts on your computer to minimize distractions. Visit the ISEE's website for more information on device and room requirements.

Exam Accommodations

Students who need accommodations on the ISEE should wait to register for a test date until after they have received an accommodations decision via email. Students must provide documentation of their disability to receive accommodations. This process can take up to two weeks once your request has been received, and any accommodations are valid for up to 15 months from the date of approval. Once you are approved for your accommodations, you can register for a test online, but please note that not all accommodations are available for at-home testing. For more information, visit **erblearn.org/families/isee-accommodations/**.

What to Bring

If you're taking the ISEE at home, at school, or at a testing office (not a Prometric Testing Center), then it is recommended that you bring the following items:

 Verification Letter

 Student Identification

 Snacks, which can only be consumed during test breaks

 Paper testing materials (if you are taking the test in a paper format), such as four sharpened No. 2 pencils, four erasers, and two black or blue ballpoint pens

Students are not permitted to bring any books, papers, rulers, mobile devices, Bluetooth headphones or earbuds, or smart watches to their examination room. You cannot use a calculator unless you have been approved for an accommodation that allows you to use one. If you are taking the ISEE at a Prometric Test Center, you may also be required to show proof of vaccination against COVID-19. Be sure to contact your individual test center for details.

How the Test Is Scored

The Verbal Reasoning, Quantitative Reasoning, Reading Comprehension, and Mathematics Achievement sections consist of multiple-choice questions with four possible answers. Students will be scored based on the number of questions they answer correctly, with no penalties for incorrect answers. Scores are reported in percentile ranks, so your performance on the exam will be weighed against the performance of other students in the same grade as you who took the exam over the past three years. The Essay section is not scored. The schools you are applying to will receive a copy of your score report along with your essay.

Format and Focus

The ISEE consists of five sections: Verbal Reasoning, Quantitative Reasoning, Reading Comprehension, Mathematics Achievement, and an Essay component. The exam only consists of multiple-choice questions, except the Essay component, which requires a written response. On the Verbal Reasoning portion of the exam, you will have 20 minutes to answer 40 questions. The Verbal Reasoning section will include vocabulary and sentence completion items. For vocabulary items, you will be given a word and asked to select a synonym for that word from four answer options. For sentence completion items, you will be asked to fill in one or two blanks within a sentence; you will be given four pairs of words and you must choose the pair that best completes the sentence.

On the Quantitative Reasoning section, which is one of two math sections on the exam, you will have 35 minutes to answer 37 questions. The emphasis of this section is on your ability to think and reason mathematically, so very few calculations will be required. Instead, you will likely be using logic and reason to solve problems, analyze and interpret data, compare and contrast quantities, and other tasks.

On the Reading Comprehension section of the exam, you will have 35 minutes to answer 36 questions. There will be six passages on topics such as history, science, literature, and contemporary life. Questions may ask you to identify the main and supporting ideas, make inferences, define words, identify the structure of the passage, and interpret literary elements within the passage.

The Mathematics Achievement section of the exam tests your mathematical abilities on a variety of topics, including numbers and operations, algebra, geometry, measurement, data analysis and probability, and problem solving. For this section of the exam, you will have 40 minutes to answer 47 questions. In contrast to the Quantitative Reasoning section, you will need to perform calculations to determine the correct answer to certain problems on this part of the exam. The good news is that you do not have to memorize any conversion factors; if required, they will be given to you in the question. You cannot use a calculator and you won't be given scratch paper for the paper format of the exam, but you can write in the test booklet.

For the Essay component of the exam, you will be given a prompt and asked to write a short essay in 30 minutes. The Essay section of the ISEE serves two purposes. First, you can showcase your personality to the schools to which you are applying. Second, you can demonstrate your writing skills, specifically your ability to organize and express your thoughts and ideas. The essay prompts focus on topics that allow you to talk more about yourself, including your interests, your strengths, and your goals. On the exam, you can use a piece of scratch paper to create a short outline for your response before you start drafting.

Test Day Strategies

You may find it helpful to keep the following strategies in mind for the actual test day.

1 **Be prepared**. Research what you will need to bring or have with you on test day. The night before, make sure you have everything you need in one place. Decide on the outfit you will wear. Be comfortable but look put together.

2 **Eat smart**. Plan to eat a balanced meal before your exam. Have something with a combination of healthy fats, protein, and carbohydrates. Avoid caffeine if it makes you jittery and avoid sugary items that will spike your energy level—it won't last, and you'll be worse for it as you work through your exam.

3 **Focus only on the test.** Don't plan any other activities on test day or attempt to squeeze the test in between other plans.

4 **Arrive rested, relaxed, and on time.** Plan to arrive a little bit early. Leave plenty of time for any unexpected delays. This still applies if you're taking the test from home: get set up early.

5 **If the test is proctored, ask questions if there are any instructions you do not understand.** Make sure that you know exactly what to do. In the test room, the proctor will provide the instructions you must follow when taking the examination. If something is unclear, ask for clarification.

6 **Follow instructions exactly during the examination.** Do not begin until you are told to do so. Stop as soon as you are told to stop. Any infraction of the rules can be considered cheating.

7 **Maintain a positive attitude.** Remain calm—you know yourself best and which strategies or techniques will help you ease any test anxiety. Remember that a can-do attitude creates confidence, and confidence is key.

SUMMING IT UP

- Students can take the Secondary School Admission Test (SSAT) as part of their application to a private high school.

  - The Upper Level of the SSAT is offered to students applying for grades 9 through 12.

  - The duration of the SSAT is about 3 hours and 10 minutes, including two 10-minute breaks.

  - The exam is broken into the following sections: Quantitative (Math), Verbal, Reading, an unscored Writing Sample, and an unscored Experimental section, which includes a mix of verbal, reading, and math questions.

  - Students are scored based on the number of questions they answer correctly.

  - You receive one point for each correct answer, but you will lose one quarter of a point for each incorrect answer. We recommend guessing only when you can eliminate at least two answers.

- Students can take the Independent School Entrance Exam (ISEE) as part of their application to a private high school.

  - The Upper Level of the ISEE exam is offered to students applying for grades 9 through 12.

  - The duration of the ISEE is about 2 hours and 40 minutes, not including two 5- to 10-minute breaks.

  - There are five parts on the ISEE: Verbal Reasoning, Quantitative Reasoning, Reading Comprehension, Mathematics Achievement, and an unscored Essay component.

  - On the ISEE, there are no penalties for incorrect answers, so be sure to answer every question, even if you need to guess.

- Make sure that you know which exam you're taking, how to register for it, the format and focus of the test, how to take the test online (if applicable), and how your exam is scored.

- To prepare for the exam, make sure you get enough rest the night before, wear comfortable but presentable clothing, eat a well-balanced breakfast, and budget plenty of time for the test.

CHAPTER

SSAT Format and Questions

SSAT FORMAT AND QUESTIONS

OVERVIEW

What to Expect on the SSAT

The Writing Sample

Quantitative Ability Questions

Reading Ability Questions

Verbal Ability Questions

Summing It Up

WHAT TO EXPECT ON THE SSAT

On the SSAT, there are four sections designed to test your verbal and quantitative abilities and your reading comprehension. Additionally, you will be asked to write a short, unscored essay on an assigned topic—this essay will serve as a writing sample for any schools that require the SSAT. The SSAT also includes an experimental section, which consists of six verbal, five reading, and five quantitative questions. These questions are unscored, but they are designed to test out future questions for the SSAT, so your responses can help other students who are taking the exam in the future.

In this chapter, we provide a brief overview of each section on the test along with sample questions. By learning about the different sections and question types, you can go into the SSAT confident that you're prepared and ready to do your best. Throughout this book, we will cover the sections of the exam and the different question types in depth. This will give you an opportunity to familiarize yourself with the different sections of the exam and to practice answering the different types of questions so that you know what to expect on exam day.

THE WRITING SAMPLE

At the beginning of the SSAT, you will have 25 minutes to create a writing sample on a given topic. You will be given an essay prompt, a creative writing story prompt, or a combination of both options. This section is not scored, but it is duplicated and sent to each school as a sample of your ability to express yourself in writing under the same conditions as all other candidates for admission to the school. If you are taking a test online, you will be able to type your writing sample; otherwise, plan on using the lined space provided to you on paper. The directions for both the essay and story will look something like this:

> **Directions:** Read the prompts, choose the one that interests you the most, and plan your essay or story before writing. Write a legible response on the paper provided.

If you opt to write the essay, you will generally be given an essay topic that allows you to take a position for or against a given topic. Alternatively, the prompt may be more personal and open-ended, allowing you to express your thoughts on a given topic. Here are two example SSAT essay prompts. The first is a more general topic that requires you to take a position, and the second is more personal and open-ended. Try to organize and write an essay on each of these topics.

> **Topic:** Bad things always happen in threes.
>
> Do you agree or disagree with this statement? Support your position with examples from your own experience, the experience of others, current events, or your own existing knowledge.
>
> **Topic:** Describe a time in your life where you encountered an obstacle. What was the obstacle, and were you able to overcome it? Why or why not?

If you end up with a story prompt instead of an essay, you will be given 1–2 prompts to choose from to start your story. Usually, these will include a personal and general option for a first sentence of your story. The main difference between an essay and a story is that rather than choosing a position and defending it, you'll need to set the scene, develop plot, reach a climax, and then bring everything to a resolution. In both cases, it's important that your writing have a clear beginning, middle, and end, but this is especially important if you are writing a story.

Here is a sample prompt for the story option.

EXAMPLE:

Topic: Consider the following two statements.

A: I didn't know when I woke up that morning that it would be the first day of the rest of my life.

B: They finished packing the car and then they were off.

Write a story using one of these two statements as the first sentence. Be sure your story has a clear beginning, middle, and end.

In preparation for the writing sample section of the SSAT, consult Chapter 16: Essay Writing and Chapter 17: Writing Mechanics for further tips and strategies to help you deliver your best writing on exam day.

QUANTITATIVE ABILITY QUESTIONS

The SSAT tests your quantitative ability in two 25-question mathematics sections for a total of 50 mathematics questions in all. Each section measures your ability to answer questions on topics such as arithmetic, elementary algebra, geometry, and other quantitative concepts. You'll have 30 minutes for each section of 25 questions. You will not be able to use a calculator.

The directions are the same for both quantitative sections. Here are four sample SSAT quantitative ability questions showing the range of mathematical questions. Try each of these on your own before you read the explanation that accompanies it.

EXAMPLES:

Directions: Read the question, work out your answer, and select the best option.

1. $\frac{1}{4}$% of 1,500 =

   A. 60

   B. 15

   C. 7.50

   D. 3.75

   E. 1.50

The correct answer is D. $\frac{1}{4}$% written as a decimal is 0.0025. (1,500)(0.0025) = 3.75. You could have done this problem in your head by thinking: 10% of 1,500 is 150; 1% of 1,500 is 15; $\frac{1}{4}$ of 1% = 15 ÷ 4 = 3.75.

2. If a survey shows that K percent of dogs are brown, the number of dogs that are not brown per 100 dogs is

   A. 100 – K.

   B. 1 – K.

   C. K – 100.

   D. 100 ÷ K.

   E. K ÷ 100.

The correct answer is A. *Percent* means "out of 100." If K percent of dogs are brown, then K out of 100 are brown. The remainder of dogs, 100 – K, are not brown.

3. A piece of wood 35 feet, 6 inches long was used to make 4 shelves of equal length. The length of each shelf is

    A. 9 feet, $1\frac{1}{2}$ inches.

    B. 8 feet, $10\frac{1}{2}$ inches.

    C. 8 feet, $1\frac{1}{2}$ inches.

    D. 7 feet, $10\frac{1}{2}$ inches.

    E. 7 feet, $1\frac{1}{2}$ inches.

The correct answer is B. First convert the feet to inches. 35 feet, 6 inches = 420 inches + 6 inches = 426 inches. 426 ÷ 4 = 106.5 inches per shelf = 8 feet, $10\frac{1}{2}$ inches per shelf.

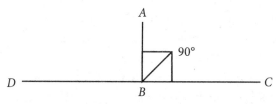

4. Angle *ABD* is a(n)

    A. straight angle and contains 180°.

    B. acute angle and contains 35°.

    C. obtuse angle and contains 360°.

    D. right angle and contains 45°.

    E. right angle and contains 90°.

The correct answer is E. Angle *ABC* and angle *ABD* are supplementary angles. Since angle *ABC* = 90°, angle *ABD* must also equal 90° (180° − 90° = 90°). A right angle contains 90°.

Part IV of this book contains the chapters that address mathematical topics, so be sure to review them in preparation for the quantitative questions on the SSAT.

ALERT

Note that the directions ask you to choose the best answer. There may be several answers that are partially correct but only one that is completely correct. You should always read all the answer choices before you make your final selection.

READING ABILITY QUESTIONS

The SSAT measures your ability to read quickly and to understand what you read by asking you questions about given reading passages. The 40 questions in the SSAT reading comprehension section are based on 8–10 reading passages, with each passage ranging in length from approximately 200–400 words. You have 40 minutes to complete this section of the exam, which means you have about 4–5 minutes per passage and set of questions. Here is a sample SSAT reading passage followed by four questions. Read the passage and try answering the questions on your own before reading the explanations.

EXAMPLE:

Directions: Read each passage carefully and then answer the questions that follow. For each question, decide based on the details of the passage which one of the choices best answers the question.

Roller derby got its start in the 1930s and has since evolved to form a culture all its own. While it might not seem revolutionary by today's standards, roller derby played a critical role in evolving American assumptions about the capabilities of women as athletes. For one, roller derby was and remains an aggressive, high-impact, full-contact sport in which players are <u>prone</u> to injury due to the very physical nature of competition. While roller derby is primarily associated with women today, it afforded men and women equal opportunities at its outset, leveling the playing field between men and women as athletes. The rules and expectations were the same for both, meaning that women participants in roller derby were considered true equals of their male counterparts.

In roller derby, two teams each skate laps around a track for two 30-minute intervals called "jams." While a roller derby team consists of fifteen skaters, each team only has five players on the track at a time—one "jammer" designated by a star on their helmet and four blockers who help protect the jammer. To score points for their team, the jammer must lap members of the other team, meaning complete a full loop to pass them on the track. This means that blockers are uniquely tasked with both offense and defense, since they must assist their own jammer in lapping opposing teams while also blocking the opposing jammer from passing them. As a result of all the jostling and jockeying to pass, derby is known for its physical skirmishes, a trait reflected in the colorful nicknames of derby participants such as "Helmet-Bash Heidi" and "Debbie Destructor."

1. As used in paragraph 1, the underlined term *prone* most nearly means

   A. vulnerable.

   B. resistant.

   C. accustomed.

   D. avoidant.

   E. forgetful.

The correct answer is A. Vocabulary-in-context questions appear frequently on the SSAT. Remember to address the word in the context in which it appears. The context from paragraph 1 indicates that you are looking for a word that means something like "likely to occur," "frequent," or "inclined." You also have a context clue that the word must fit with the adverb form of *to*. Of your options, *vulnerable (to)* is the nearest in meaning to *prone (to)* and fits the context of the passage.

2. During a "jam," how many jammers are on the track?

   A. 1

   B. 2

   C. 4

   D. 5

   E. 15

The correct answer is B. This is an inference question that also asks you about supporting details. While the answer is not stated directly in the passage, you can figure it out based on the information you are given. Paragraph 2 notes that during a jam, each team has one jammer and four blockers on the track. Since there are two teams, you can infer that there are two jammers on the track during each jam. Don't be distracted by numbers that appear in the passage but do not answer the question, such as 15 (choice E), which refers to the number of players on a team, or 4 (choice C), which refers to the number of blockers for each team.

3. The author's primary purpose in this passage is to

   A. analyze the historical impact of roller derby.

   B. discuss some of the most impactful roller derby athletes.

   C. clarify how roller derby got its start.

   D. explain how roller derby is played and why its emergence was important.

   E. justify continued funding of roller derby leagues.

The correct answer is D. Questions about the author's purpose are related to questions about the passage's main idea. In this case, the author wrote the passage to explain how roller derby is played and why its emergence was important.

4. The author's tone in this passage can be described as

   A. praising.

   B. skeptical.

   C. straightforward.

   D. sarcastic.

   E. judgmental.

The correct answer is C. Tone questions are asking you about the way the author communicates the information in the passage. Since the author has a generally positive or neutral view of their topic in this passage, you can eliminate choices that communicate a negative tone, like *skeptical* (choice B), *sarcastic* (choice D), and *judgmental* (choice E). Of the two options left, *straightforward* does a better job of communicating the direct and informative tone of the passage than does *praising* (choice A).

For a more in-depth analysis of the question types in the reading comprehension section and how to master them, see Chapter 10: Reading Comprehension.

VERBAL ABILITY QUESTIONS

The SSAT measures your verbal ability with two question types: synonyms and analogies. The verbal section consists of 60 questions total; 30 of these questions are synonyms and 30 are analogies. You'll have 30 minutes to answer all 60 questions.

Synonym Questions

A synonym is a word with the same meaning or nearly the same meaning as another word. SSAT synonym questions ask you to choose the best synonym for a question word that is written in capital letters. Here are two sample SSAT synonym questions. Try each one on your own; then read the explanation that accompanies it.

EXAMPLES:

Directions: The first half of the questions in this section covers synonyms. Each question consists of one word followed by five words or phrases. You are to select the one word or phrase whose meaning is closest to the word in CAPITAL letters.

1. NOVICE
   - **A.** competitive
   - **B.** clumsy
   - **C.** aged
   - **D.** beginner
   - **E.** impulsive

The correct answer is D. A novice is a beginner, someone without experience. You may recognize the root of *novel*, meaning "new," a clue to the definition.

2. CONVOY
   - **A.** hearse
   - **B.** voyage
   - **C.** group
   - **D.** motorized
   - **E.** opponent

The correct answer is C. A convoy is a group traveling together for protection or convenience. You have probably seen convoys of military vehicles traveling single file.

For more strategies on how to deal with synonyms in both verbal questions and when they appear in the reading comprehension section, see Chapter 7: Synonyms.

Verbal Analogies

Verbal analogy questions ask you to match up pairs of words that are related in the same way. Each question starts with a word pair. Your job is to find or create another pair of words that is related in the same way as the first pair. Here are two sample SSAT analogy questions. Try each one on your own before reading the explanation that accompanies it.

EXAMPLES:

> **Directions:** The second half of the questions in this section covers analogies. These questions ask you to find relationships between words. For each question, select the answer choice that best completes the meaning of the sentence.

1. Lid is to box as cork is to

    A. float.

    B. bottle.

    C. wine.

    D. beverage.

    E. stopper.

The correct answer is B. The relationship is one of purpose. The purpose of a lid is to close a box; the purpose of a cork is to close a bottle.

2. Poison is to death as

    A. book is to pages.

    B. music is to violin.

    C. kindness is to cooperation.

    D. life is to famine.

    E. nothing is to something.

The correct answer is C. This is a cause-and-effect relationship. Poison may lead to death; kindness may lead to cooperation. Neither outcome is a foregone conclusion, but both are equally likely. Choice B offers a reversed relationship.

We discuss analogy questions in greater detail in Chapter 8: Verbal Analogies.

SUMMING IT UP

- At the beginning of the SSAT, you must write a 25-minute writing sample following a given prompt.
- The SSAT measures quantitative ability in two sections covering topics such as arithmetic, elementary algebra, geometry, and other concepts.
- The reading comprehension section tests your ability to read quickly and understand what you read. The answers to the reading comprehension questions are based on information either directly stated or implied in the passages.
- The SSAT measures verbal ability with two question types: synonyms and analogies.

NOTES

CHAPTER

ISEE FORMAT
AND QUESTIONS

ISEE FORMAT AND QUESTIONS

OVERVIEW

What to Expect on the ISEE

Verbal Reasoning Questions

Quantitative Reasoning Questions

Reading Comprehension Questions

Mathematics Achievement Questions

The Essay Question

Summing It Up

WHAT TO EXPECT ON THE ISEE

The ISEE uses five question types to test your verbal and quantitative abilities and your achievement in mathematics and reading comprehension. Additionally, the unscored essay section acts as a writing sample for any schools that require the ISEE. This chapter will describe each section and provide examples of questions that could appear in each. By familiarizing yourself with the questions, you'll know what to expect and you won't have any unpleasant surprises when you begin the exam, even if the format ends up looking slightly different than what you planned for. Each of the question types on the ISEE are also covered in depth in different chapters throughout this book, so you have everything you need right here to be prepared to do your best on the exam.

VERBAL REASONING QUESTIONS

The ISEE measures your verbal reasoning ability with two question types: synonyms and sentence completions. The verbal reasoning test consists of 40 questions, usually split evenly between the two question types. You'll have 20 minutes to complete this section of the exam.

Synonym Questions

A synonym is a word with the same meaning or nearly the same meaning as another word. ISEE synonym questions ask you to choose the best synonym for a capitalized word. Here are two sample ISEE synonym questions. Try each one on your own; then, read the explanation that accompanies it.

EXAMPLES:

Directions: Each question in this section consists of a word in capital letters followed by four answer choices. Select the one word that is most nearly the same in meaning as the word in capital letters.

1. TENANT

   A. occupant

   B. landlord

   C. owner

   D. farmer

The correct answer is A. The word *tenant* most commonly refers to a renter, so *occupant* is the best choice. The tenant is never the landlord. The owner may well be an occupant, but unless the owner occupies on a very temporary basis, they are not considered a tenant. A tenant farmer lives on and cultivates the land of another.

2. CALCULATED

   A. multiplied

   B. added

   C. answered

   D. figured out

The correct answer is D. Calculating may well include multiplying or adding to arrive at the answer, but not all calculations need be mathematical. To figure out is to calculate.

We cover synonym questions in greater depth in Chapter 7: Synonyms.

Sentence Completion Questions

Just as the name implies, sentence completions are fill-in-the-blank questions. ISEE sentence completion questions may have one or two blanks. Your job is to choose from among the answer choices the word or words that best fit each blank. The directions for ISEE sentence completion questions look something like this:

Directions: Each question in this section is made up of a sentence with one or two blanks. One blank indicates that one word is missing. Two blanks indicate that two words are missing. Each sentence is followed by four answer choices. Select the word or pair of words that best completes the meaning of the sentence as a whole.

Here are two sample ISEE sentence completion questions: a one-blank question and a two-blank question. Try each one on your own before reading the explanation that accompanies it.

EXAMPLES:

1. Utility is not _____, for the usefulness of an object changes with time and place.

   A. planned

   B. practical

   C. permanent

   D. understandable

The correct answer is C. If the usefulness of an object changes, then that usefulness is not permanent.

2. A string of lies had landed her in such a hopeless _____ that she didn't know how to _____ herself.

   A. status ... clear

   B. pinnacle ... explain

   C. confusion ... help

   D. predicament ... extricate

The correct answer is D. A "hopeless predicament" is an idiomatic expression meaning "impossible situation." This is a reasonable position for one to be in after a string of lies. The second blank is correctly filled with a term that implies that she couldn't get out of the mess she had created.

We cover sentence completion questions in greater depth in Chapter 9: Sentence Completion.

QUANTITATIVE REASONING QUESTIONS

On the ISEE, you'll encounter two math sections: quantitative reasoning and mathematics achievement. The first math section on the ISEE is the quantitative reasoning section. This section of the exam tests your understanding of quantitative concepts and your ability to apply those concepts with two question types: word problems and quantitative comparisons. You'll have 35 minutes to answer 37 questions. These questions test how you think mathematically, meaning your ability to reason through a math problem by estimating numbers, using logic, comparing and contrasting quantities, analyzing and interpreting numerical data and graphs, calculating probability, understanding and applying measurements, and more.

Word Problems

Here are two sample ISEE multiple-choice quantitative ability questions. Try each of these on your own before you read the explanation that accompanies it.

 ALERT -

Note that the directions ask you to choose the best answer. There may be several answer choices that are almost right, but only one that is completely correct. You should always read every answer choice before making your final selection.

Directions: Each question in this section consists of a word problem followed by four answer choices. You may write in your test booklet; however, you may be able to solve many of these problems in your head. Next, look at the four answer choices given and select the best answer.

1. If $A^2 + B^2 = A^2 + X^2$, then B equals

    A. $\pm X$

    B. $X^2 - 2A^2$

    C. $\pm A$

    D. $A^2 + X^2$

The correct answer is A. Subtract A^2 from both sides of the equation: $B^2 = X^2$, therefore $B = \pm X$.

2. How much time is there between 8:30 a.m. today and 3:15 a.m. tomorrow?

    A. $17\frac{3}{4}$ hours

    B. $18\frac{1}{2}$ hours

    C. $18\frac{2}{3}$ hours

    D. $18\frac{3}{4}$ hours

The correct answer is D. 12:00 = 11:60

From 8:30 a.m. until noon today: 11:60 − 8:30 = 3:30
3 hrs. and 30 min.

From noon until midnight: 12 hours

From midnight until 3:15 a.m.: 3 hrs. 15 min.

Total: 3 hrs. 30 min. + 12 hrs. + 3 hrs. 15 min. = 18 hrs. 45 min. = $18\frac{3}{4}$ hours

Quantitative Comparisons

ISEE quantitative comparisons are probably not like any other math question you've ever seen. These questions present you with two quantities, one in Column A and one in Column B. Your job is to decide whether one quantity is greater, whether the two quantities are equal, or whether no comparison is possible. There are always four answer choices for this question type, and they are always the same. You can expect the directions to resemble the following.

Directions: All questions in this section are quantitative comparisons between the quantities shown in Column A and Column B. Using the information given in each question, compare the quantity in Column A to the quantity in Column B, and select the correct comparison from the answer choices:

(A) The quantity in Column A is greater.

(B) The quantity in Column B is greater.

(C) The two quantities are equal.

(D) The relationship cannot be determined from the information given.

Remember the following information as you tackle quantitative comparison questions.

- For some questions, information concerning one or both of the quantities to be compared is centered above the entries in the two columns.
- Symbols that appear in both columns represent the same thing in Column A as in Column B.
- Letters such as x, n, and k are symbols for real numbers.
- All figures are accurately drawn to scale unless otherwise noted.

Here are two sample ISEE quantitative comparison questions. Try each of these on your own before you read the explanation that accompanies it.

1.

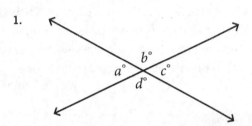

NOTE: Figure not drawn to scale.

Column A	**Column B**
$180 - a$	$d + c - b$

The correct answer is D. Since we do not know if $a > b$ or $a < b$, the relationship cannot be determined.

2.

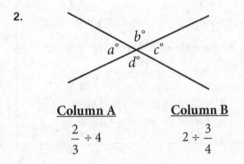

Column A	**Column B**
$\dfrac{2}{3} \div 4$	$2 \div \dfrac{3}{4}$

The correct answer is B. To divide by a fraction, we multiply by the reciprocal of the fraction.

$$\frac{2}{3} \div 4 = \frac{2}{3} \times \frac{1}{4} = \frac{2}{12} \quad \text{vs.} \quad 2 \div \frac{3}{4} = \frac{2}{1} \times \frac{4}{3} = \frac{8}{3}$$

Therefore, Column A > Column B.

Part IV of this book contains chapters on math topics that will help you address any question type that might come up in this section of the ISEE.

READING COMPREHENSION QUESTIONS

The ISEE measures your ability to read actively and to understand what you read by asking you questions about passages you are given. The 36 questions in the reading comprehension section of the ISEE are based on six passages of approximately 200–400 words each, though occasionally one might be even shorter. Because the ISEE is interested in both your level of reading and your ability to comprehend material from the sciences and from social studies, some of the content of the reading passages is based on science and social studies. You may also see humanities passages covering the arts and literature, including poems or excerpts from literary texts, as well as passages on contemporary life.

Here are samples of two shorter ISEE reading passages, each followed by two questions. The first passage is a social studies passage and the second is a science-based passage. Read each passage and try to answer the questions on your own before you read the explanations.

EXAMPLE:

Directions: Answer the questions on the basis of what is <u>stated</u> or <u>implied</u> in the passage.

A large proportion of the people who are behind bars are not convicted criminals but are people who have been arrested and are being held until their trial in court. Experts have often pointed out that this detention system does not operate fairly. For instance, a person who can afford to pay bail usually will not get locked up. The theory of the bail system is that the person will make sure to show up in court when they are expected to show; otherwise, their bail will be forfeited, meaning the person will lose the money they put up. Sometimes, a person who can show that they are a stable citizen with a job and a family will be released on "personal recognizance" (without bail). The result is that the well-to-do, the employed, and those with families can often avoid the detention system. The people who do wind up in detention tend to be the poor, the unemployed, the single, and the young.

1. According to the preceding passage, people who are put behind bars

   A. are almost always dangerous criminals.

   B. include many innocent people who have been arrested by mistake.

   C. are often people who have been arrested but have not yet come to trial.

   D. are all poor people who tend to be young and single.

   The correct answer is C. The answer to this question is directly stated in the first sentence. Choice B might be possible, but it is neither stated nor implied by the passage. The word *all* in choice D makes it an incorrect statement.

2. Suppose that two people were booked on the same charge at the same time and that the same bail was set for both of them. Person 1 was able to put up bail and they were released. Person 2 was not able to put up bail and was held in detention. The writer of the passage would most likely feel that this result is

   A. unfair because it does not have any relation to guilt or innocence.

   B. unfair because Person 1 deserves severe punishment.

   C. fair because Person 1 is obviously innocent.

   D. fair because the law should be tougher on poor people than on the rich.

   The correct answer is A. You can infer this attitude from the tone of the passage.

Fire often travels inside the partitions of a burning building. Many partitions contain wooden studs for support, but the studs leave a space that fire can pass through. Therefore, flames may spread from the bottom to the upper floors through the partitions. Sparks from a fire in the upper part of a partition may fall and start a fire at the bottom. Some signs that a fire is spreading inside a partition are: (1) blistering paint, (2) discolored paint or wallpaper, or (3) partitions that feel hot to the touch. If any of these signs is present, the partition must be opened up to look for the fire. Finding cobwebs inside the partition is one sign that fire has not spread through the partition.

3. Fires can spread inside partitions because

    A. there are spaces between studs inside of partitions.

    B. fires can burn anywhere.

    C. partitions are made out of materials that burn easily.

    D. partitions are usually painted or wallpapered.

    The correct answer is A. This statement of fact is made in the second sentence.

4. If a firefighter sees the paint on a partition beginning to blister, they should first

    A. wet down the partition.

    B. check the partitions in other rooms.

    C. chop a hole in the partition.

    D. close windows and doors and leave the room.

    The correct answer is C. As the passage states, blistering paint is a sign that fire is spreading inside a partition. The passage goes on to say that if this sign is present, the firefighter must open the partition to look for the fire, usually by chopping a hole in it.

We cover reading comprehension questions in greater depth in Chapter 10: Reading Comprehension.

NOTE

In ISEE reading comprehension questions, the answers will always be either directly stated or implied in the passage. Some questions may require you to make inferences, but all the information you need to do so will be in the passage. You can think of it as an open-book test!

MATHEMATICS ACHIEVEMENT QUESTIONS

The second mathematics section on the ISEE measures your mathematics achievement by asking you to answer math questions that relate to:

- Numbers and operations
- Algebraic concepts
- Geometry
- Measurement
- Data analysis and probability

The mathematics achievement test consists of 47 multiple-choice questions, each with four answer options to choose from, which you must answer in 40 minutes. For certain questions, you will need to perform calculations to find the correct answer. You will not have to memorize conversions in the US standard system for the exam; they will be provided as needed in the question. You will, however, need to know conversions within the same unit in the metric system, such as the conversion between meters and millimeters. For the paper exam, you will be able to write in your test booklet. If you are taking the test on a computer, you can have up to 4 sheets of scratch paper with you along with two pens and/or two pencils.

Here are four sample ISEE mathematics achievement questions. Try each of these on your own before you read the explanation that accompanies it.

EXAMPLES:

Directions: Each question is followed by four suggested answers. Read each question and then decide which one of the four suggested answers is best.

1. If $\frac{3}{4}$ of a class is absent and $\frac{2}{3}$ of those present leave the room, what fraction of the original class remains in the room?

   A. $\frac{1}{4}$

   B. $\frac{1}{8}$

   C. $\frac{1}{12}$

   D. $\frac{1}{24}$

The correct answer is C. If $\frac{3}{4}$ are absent, $\frac{1}{4}$ are present. If $\frac{2}{3}$ of the $\frac{1}{4}$ present leave, $\frac{1}{3}$ of the $\frac{1}{4}$ remain.

$\frac{1}{3} \times \frac{1}{4} = \frac{1}{12}$ remain in the room.

2. A cog wheel having 8 cogs plays into another cog wheel having 24 cogs. When the small wheel has made 42 revolutions, how many has the larger wheel made?

   A. 10

   B. 14

   C. 16

   D. 20

The correct answer is B. The larger wheel is 3 times the size of the smaller wheel, so it makes $\frac{1}{3}$ the revolutions: $42 \div 3 = 14$.

3. 75% of 4 is the same as what percent of 9?

   A. 25

   B. $33\frac{1}{3}$

   C. 36

   D. 40

The correct answer is B. 75% of 4 = 3

$3 = 33\frac{1}{3}$ % of 9

4. If $\frac{1}{2}$ cup of spinach contains 80 calories and the same amount of peas contains 300 calories, how many cups of spinach have the same caloric content as $\frac{2}{3}$ cup of peas?

   A. $\frac{2}{5}$

   B. $1\frac{1}{3}$

   C. 2

   D. $2\frac{1}{2}$

The correct answer is D. $\frac{1}{2}$ cup spinach = 80 calories

$\frac{1}{2}$ cup peas = 300 calories

1 cup peas = 600 calories

$\frac{2}{3}$ cup peas = 400 calories

$400 \div 80 = 5$ half cups of spinach

$= 2\frac{1}{2}$ cups of spinach

Part IV of this book contains numerous chapters that can help you address quantitative questions like those found in this section of the ISEE.

THE ESSAY QUESTION

At the end of each ISEE testing session, you will have 30 minutes to write an essay on an assigned subject. This essay is not scored. However, it is duplicated and sent to each school as a sample of your ability to express yourself in writing under the same conditions as all other candidates for admission to the school. The prompt will include a contemporary topic and ask the test taker to respond to a situation. This situation could be personal, community-based, or global in nature.

Depending on whether you take the paper-based version of the test or the at-home, computer-based version of the test, you'll have different instructions for the essay section. If you are taking the ISEE at a testing site and on paper, you'll need to write your essay in the test booklet. If you are taking the test at home, then you'll be able to type your essay, and you can spell check your essay.

Here is a sample ISEE essay topic, also called a "prompt." Try to organize and write an essay on this topic.

EXAMPLE:

Directions: You will have 30 minutes to plan and write an essay on the following topic. Do not write on another topic. An essay on another topic is not acceptable.

The essay is designed to give you an opportunity to show how well you can write. You should try to express your thoughts clearly. How well you write is much more important than how much you write, but you need to say enough for a reader to understand what you mean.

You will probably want to write more than a short paragraph. You should also be aware that a copy of your essay will be sent to each school that will be receiving your test results. Please write or print so that your writing may be read by someone who is not familiar with your handwriting.

You may make notes and plan your essay in the space provided. Allow enough time to copy the prompt onto the first two lines of your answer sheet. Please remember to write your response in blue or black pen. Again, you may use cursive writing or you may print.

Topic: An exchange student from another country has just entered your school. What will you tell this student about student life at your school?

Chapter 16: Essay Writing contains a more comprehensive look at the kinds of essay questions that could come up on the ISEE, while Chapter 17: Writing Mechanics can help you brush up on critical grammar and writing skills that will be necessary to put your best foot forward on the essay.

SUMMING IT UP

- The ISEE measures verbal reasoning with two question types: synonyms and sentence completions.
- The ISEE tests quantitative reasoning with two question types: word problems and quantitative comparisons.
- The ISEE measures reading ability with reading comprehension questions based on information that is either directly stated or implied in the passages.
- The ISEE measures mathematics achievement in five areas: numbers and operations, algebraic concepts, geometry, measurement, and data analysis and probability.
- At the end of each ISEE test, you must write a 30-minute essay on an assigned subject.

 NOTES

CHAPTER

Strategies and Skills for Learning Effectively

STRATEGIES AND SKILLS FOR LEARNING

OVERVIEW

What Is Learning and How Does It Work?

Learning Effectively

Techniques and Strategies for Active and Effective Studying

Study Time Surveys

Summing It Up

Whether someone is an expert in astrophysics, algebra, English grammar, social media, or dog grooming, they possess traits that are common to most if not all experts. Research says that experts are different than most people not because of their intellect but because they've built a set of skills that take full advantage of how humans learn.

Learning *how* to learn isn't something we are exposed to every day. That may vary from school to school, classroom to classroom, and even student to student, but in general, more time is spent on what we're trying to learn rather than how to learn it well.

To help you get the most out of this book, this chapter contains tips and strategies to help put you in an expert mindset as you prepare for your exam. We'll look at ideas related to what learning is and how it works so that you can make choices that help you both learn more and study more efficiently.

NOTE ------------------------------

This chapter is all about learning and studying effectively. There's a lot to take in here, so don't be afraid to take it in a section at a time. You can also set a reminder to revisit this information as you work through this book to make sure you're preparing for your test in the best way possible.

WHAT IS LEARNING AND HOW DOES IT WORK?

What does it mean to learn something? What even is *learning*? In school, learning is the acquisition, formation, and application of knowledge. You do this through lectures, readings, and studying. But you're also learning any time your ideas, behaviors, beliefs, skills, and/or attitudes change. The process of changing any of those things is often about practice. Changing who you are and how you think isn't something you do lightly, though. More than likely, you want to have as much control over that process as possible so that you can become exactly who you need to be to accomplish what you want.

There are some things that you need only experience once to learn well; for example, the wisdom behind the label "HOT! DO NOT TOUCH!" becomes pretty clear after you lean on a glowing stove. Your first encounter with a spider (harmless or not) may have "taught" you that every trip to a dark and dusty closet could be a life-or-death ordeal. Perhaps there are simply things that stick easily—you learned how to spell *restaurant* one time and have never had to think about it again. Other times, there are concepts that just don't seem to stick. Maybe you can't remember the differences between mean, median, and mode. Maybe you can't remember all the rules for comma usage. For whatever reason, those things may not be cemented into your thinking the same way other things are. So, what do you do when you need some of the "slippery" knowledge to stick around?

Well, according to recent findings from the fields of psychology and neurobiology, learning is about making changes to a physical system: your brain. When you're acquiring information, your brain cells (neurons) are "firing." Moreover, when neurons fire together, they "wire" together, leading to the creation or modification of "pathways" throughout your brain. On the surface, it might seem like cementing tricky information in your memory requires little more than creating a neural pathway to store it in memory; however, creating those neural pathways is not a perfect process. You have all sorts of routines that already have well-developed pathways, and they may have to change (or resist change) to accommodate something new. Then there's everything your body might be going through when learning—sleep deprivation, dehydration, distraction, and more. It might be hard to lock in new information at first, but the more you practice with a pathway, the more efficient that pathway becomes.

NOTE ------------------------------

The description of memory used in this chapter is referred to as the Atkinson-Shiffrin model. It suggests that most of the time, human memory works like saving a file on a computer. You enter the information, choose to save it, and then can access it later.

Your brain is a complex organ and learning is not a direct route from A to B. Instead, it's a pathfinding process that requires time and energy. To better understand it, we can try to think about learning as a sequence of basic processes and conditions. Let's start with memory.

The Memory Process

You are constantly bombarded with sensory information, and you don't remember most of it. In fact, only a tiny fraction of what you experience every day is stored for later use. To understand why, think of memory as a series of steps taking place within different kinds of memory. You have several different forms of memory: sensory memory (meaning information you retain long enough for your senses to recognize and identify it), short-term memory (STM), and long-term memory (LTM). Remembering something requires use of all three. The process itself starts with sensing and transforming information and ends with you retrieving it from the vast storage of your long-term memory.

Encoding

To start the process of memory, your brain takes in information through your senses. Anything you touch, taste, hear, see, or smell flashes in your sensory memory. Though your brain ignores most of these experiences, this is happening constantly. However, if you pay attention to something, you kick-start a memory transfer process. What would have been a fleeting moment in your sensory memory has now moved into your short-term memory. Your STM is all about what your mind is currently working with and only concerns information you've focused in on within the last 60 seconds or so.

You then hold the information in your short-term memory and encode the info—change it into something usable to your mind. After this manipulation, you might find that you can now recall it later. All of this constitutes a process called encoding. Sometimes remembering things feels automatic, but most of the time, to keep things from being forgotten almost immediately, you need to focus on the information and change it into a new form through an encoding process.

Once upon a time, people had to memorize each other's phone numbers, a process that, for most, meant saying the numbers again and again under their breath. That's not a bad way of encoding because it can work. It has the person see the numbers then work with those numbers in STM. By repeating them (acoustic encoding),

TYPES OF MEMORY

SENSORY MEMORY

- High-capacity
- 2–3 seconds long
- Information must be brought in by senses

SHORT-TERM MEMORY

- 5–9 items
- Usually lasts no longer than 60 seconds
- Information must be selected with attention

LONG-TERM MEMORY

- Nearly unlimited capacity
- A day to an entire lifetime
- Information must be encoded, stored, and maintained

TIP

Pause regularly throughout this chapter to check that you understand how learning works and the choices that can make your learning more effective.

the digits then might be stored for retrieval in long-term memory. The key word, though, is *might*. There's never a guarantee that things will transfer—at least not perfectly.

Yet, if you're trying to remember something, you want to increase the chance of that happening as much as possible. Repetition (what's called "rehearsal") is necessary, but just hearing or picturing info is a shallow form of processing. You can encode more effectively by processing information deeply—which requires thinking about the meaningful characteristics of the information you're trying to encode (what's called semantic encoding).

For instance, instead of trying to memorize the individual numbers that make up the phone number, someone could think of the digits as forming a "chunk." Chunking is the process of looking at information as meaningful wholes rather than individual pieces. The average limit for short-term memory is seven items, so by grouping things into chunks, your STM can hold more at one time. Say someone gave you a phone number with the following starting digits: 718-5050. Instead of trying to remember each digit individually, the information could be divided into meaningful chunks: 718 is a New York area code, 5050 reminds you of a "fifty/fifty" chance at something. Instead of six individual items, you now have two chunks in memory, each connected to a semantic characteristic to help you remember. Rehearsing works if you can't think of any way to chunk information, but chunking is usually a more efficient way to memorize.

You can chunk in all sorts of ways. For another example, each sequence could be visualized as a series of strange images: imagine the 7 is a construction crane that builds a radio tower, 1, which then falls through a pair of pink sprinkled donuts, 8, and so on. That stream of images is distinct and will probably stick in your memory, no matter how whimsical it seems. If the digits were like another number you already knew, connecting it to that prior knowledge would also make recall easier later on. All those moments of processing, or "recoding," make encoding more effective, creating better conditions for the next stages of memory.

Before moving on, rehearse the process of encoding: after you're exposed to information, you have to select info with your attention and then encode it by changing or repeating its form in your short-term memory.

Multiple conditions lead to better encoding, especially if information is:

- distinct (or odd) in the context of what you're experiencing
- connected with strong emotions or prior knowledge
- visualized in your mind's eye
- processed for its meaning and not just its superficial qualities (what it looks like, sounds like, etc.)
- received in multiple different forms (auditory, visual, haptic)
- chunked into more manageable and meaningful parts

MULTI-STORE MODEL OF MEMORY

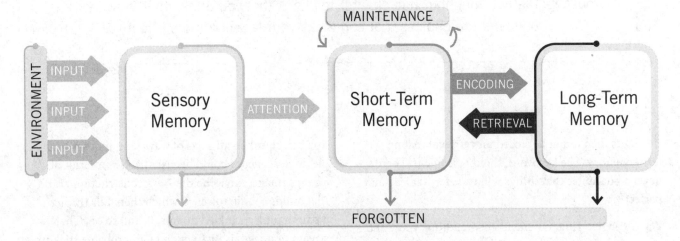

Storage

As information moves through different forms of memory and encoding, it goes through the process of storage. Storage is all about getting information to persist in your memory. To do that, it must pass through each form of memory. You know that at the start of the memory process, information moves from your sensory memory (a few seconds long but high volume) to your short-term memory (less than a minute and very limited in its capacity). In your short-term memory, you do some encoding, and then, the hope is, information starts to travel into your long-term memory (something that may have a near infinite capacity). Some

form of storage is happening in each of those different memory spaces and is aided by rehearsal (selection and repetition).

Essentially, storage is when your brain is rewiring to accommodate the information you've just encoded. This often requires some maintenance (saying it to yourself, picturing it again, etc.) to send that signal. Storage is not a perfect process. Not everything survives the trip from your STM to your LTM. It all depends on memory traces, little biochemical changes to the brain's structure. Those traces, like anything that occurs in a physical system, may have flaws and can even be impacted by your current mood or mindset. That said, the greater the repetition of signals through the newly forming neural pathways, the greater the chance that the information will take hold in your LTM—which is the key to the next step in the process.

NOTE

Look up "memory palaces" to see how people with even average memories can remember incredible amounts of information. Clemens Mayer, a World Memory Champion, once used the memory palace technique to memorize and recall 1,040 random digits in a half-hour.

Retrieval

Once information has been stored to your long-term memory, it's ready for retrieval. Retrieval is the act of accessing your stored memories. Sometimes, retrieval feels involuntary, like when you hear someone mutter a phrase and suddenly you're humming the chorus to a song you haven't heard in years. Retrieval is often considered the true purpose and power of memory. After all, what would be the point of encoding and storing information if we couldn't use it when we needed to?

NOTE

A survey in 2021 found data to suggest that every month more than half of Americans have to reset at least five of their online passwords. How could that be? Often, people select a new password but maybe don't pay attention to it, so it's forgotten. Or it gets encoded poorly so that it's only stored as a weak memory. When it comes time to retrieve it, it's not all there (was there capitalization, numbers, an exclamation point?). But if a password is used frequently, it can be maintained and stored more effectively for later recall.

As such, the goal is to gain control over what's accessible in long-term memory. You want to be able to retrieve the information you want when you need it. So how do you do that? Let's use a simple metaphor: your memory is a garden. Once you've got the seeds and planted them, you need to periodically walk through, pull some weeds, and water what you care about. Some things just won't survive when left on their own.

For strong retrieval, you must periodically revisit the information that's important for your goals. To do that, you have to pull information from your long-term memory into your short-term memory and rehearse it. That retrieval should be done periodically (soon after learning, multiple times per week, and over longer intervals). Tending to memory is a crucial step that many learners skip in their learning process. Students just like you assume that because they were exposed to it (encoding) and maybe felt like they remember

it (storage), that they can actually use it (retrieval). Often, because the interval between memorization and retrieval is too great and leads to forgetting, they can't.

For the most part, the more often and thoroughly you retrieve, the more engrained information becomes. By repeatedly walking that pathway in your brain, you make it easier to traverse in the future. As you'll see later in this chapter, you need to take the time to actively quiz yourself on what you need to remember. However, that's just one part of the process because learning doesn't end with memory.

Learning Is about Understanding

Learning is about acquiring knowledge, but to use knowledge you've acquired, you have to understand it. What "understanding" is or exactly how it works in the brain is still a foggy concept, but what scientists *can* identify is what some of the outcomes of understanding are. If someone understands something, they might be able to execute a procedure, express the relationships between different topics, or state why something works the way that it does. In effect, understanding means that someone can execute another task as a result of the knowledge acquired.

In those outcomes, a person is using various facts, ideas, concepts, and processes and connecting them together. That network may be present because of how they initially learned the information or because of

NOTE

Look into a process called interleaving to see how switching between different topics while studying can actually improve your memory of the different materials.

what they chose to do with their knowledge. Remember that neurons that fire together wire together. To build up your network of neural pathways and expand your capacity for learning, you can activate different pathways at the same time.

Activation of more parts of the brain depends on the use of higher-level cognitive processes. Those higher-level processes include the following and more:

- setting goals
- identifying what information is important and what's not
- organizing information
- using information in different situations
- adapting behavior to new situations
- evaluating understanding
- determining relationships between ideas

By thinking about what you know and using higher-level cognition to process your learning, you're working to create those new connections. Those connections

lead not only to better recall but also to even better understanding, which you can think of as expertise. It may all sound like a paradox: to reach understanding, you must try to understand. Yet it seems to work because it leads to a cycle of thinking that compounds what you know, how well you know it, and what you can do with your knowledge.

All of this is to say that while you may be able to remember certain things sometimes, true mastery requires more than just memory. You need to take steps that allow you to access and apply information when you need it.

LEARNING EFFECTIVELY

Now that you know a bit about how learning works, let's examine some of the ways you can learn effectively. Learning is supported by all sorts of activities. That said, you can probably guess that not all learning strategies and study techniques are equally effective for all learners. Some methods are going to support how your brain works and others aren't. Since all brains create neural networks differently, the strategies that work best for one person may also differ from those that work well for another.

This is where we can start thinking about experts again. In general, experts are experts because they approach learning differently. Experts are always trying to build upon their skills and expand their knowledge. That means that they're always trying to acquire new strategies and improve on their old ones. In fact, research indicates that one of the key differences between experts and other learners is that experts frequently reflect on their learning to make changes to how they learn.* In many ways, experts process learning differently than the way most are taught to learn in school. Experts are both strategic and deep learners. That means they're persistent, creative, reflective, and highly active. To get more from your learning, strive to activate these same expert traits.

In the following sections, you'll see that effective learning and studying is supported by the following choices:

*Citation: National Research Council. *How People Learn: Brain, Mind, Experience, and School: Expanded Edition.* Washington, DC: National Academies Press, 2000.

1. Practicing metacognition to make meaningful decisions about studying

2. Being active rather than passive while studying

3. Using higher-level thinking to connect ideas

4. Alternating between focused and diffused modes of thinking

5. Adopting a growth mindset

Active vs. Passive Learning

Research shows that when most learners are preparing for a test, they use a strategy called *rereading*. Calling it a "strategy" is generous for what is just looking over notes or a textbook, something students then do again and again, on repeat, until they're either too tired to continue or run out of time. Students who do this believe that simply recognizing the material on the page means they'll be able to both remember and understand it later. Educators have taken to calling this situation an illusion of competence—students feel like they know it, but when it comes time to use it, that knowledge is nowhere to be found.

This is just one of many examples of what's called "passive learning." Passive learning, or passive studying, occurs any time a student tries to absorb the information in front of them without injecting intention and energy. The problem stems from the belief that people will perfectly remember and understand a topic after watching a video or reading something for the first time. By default, there's no activity in that passive process. Nothing is created and no choices are being made, so usually, no neural pathways are being formed to store information in memory. Furthermore, rereading a chapter or rewatching a video multiple times doesn't really change that. Rereading will serve neither the purpose nor the mechanics of learning without an active process to accompany it. Yes, repetition is important for memory, but it needs to be made more efficient and effective through "active" processes.

You learned earlier that learning is a top-down process, meaning that to remember information well and approach understanding, you must also make choices for your learning. You need to actively select what

To learn more about active vs. passive learning, scan this QR code.

you're going to remember, organize that information, and build upon it. You must engage both your memory and your thinking.

Just like watching someone dance or play a game doesn't necessarily make you better at either of those things, you are unlikely to expand your knowledge simply by staring at a page in a book. You need to be active to convert learning to understanding.

While working through this book, consider the following ways to learn actively:

1. Plan out your work time

2. Preview the chapter or section

3. Connect information to your prior knowledge

4. Read strategically

5. Take some form of notes

6. Create something to study from

7. Work for sustained, focused periods free of distractions

8. Test yourself regularly and intensely

9. Take periodic breaks during studying to reflect on and connect ideas

10. Review often (multiple times per week)

11. Assess whether your studying is working and what you can do differently

All that activity will come from multiple practices: planning, evaluating, and reviewing (metacognition), practicing higher-level thinking, alternating between different modes of thinking, maintaining an all-around practice of a growth mindset, and using a variety of

effective study strategies. The combination of those behaviors is the best way to be active and support how you actually learn.

Metacognition

One major part of active learning is something called metacognition. It's a practice of thinking about your thinking. Research shows that metacognition is one of the top three traits among people we would call experts—people who know a lot in a particular field but continue to build on their knowledge all the time.

To start thinking about what metacognition is, let's think through a scenario. Imagine you're training for a marathon. Your ultimate goal is to go 26.2 miles, but that doesn't mean you're going to put on your running gear, head out your front door, and take off at a dead sprint on day one.

Instead, you'll make a plan. You'll set up a training schedule. You'll train for different periods of time and in different conditions. You'll have some short routes and some longer ones. Eventually, once you've built some stamina, you'll give that marathon-length route a try. Perhaps you'll find yourself at only a quarter of the way wheezing and panting, but perhaps not. Regardless, you'll take that trial as an opportunity to evaluate what's working in your training routine and what's not. Then, you'll modify what you're doing to get the gains you're looking for.

That process of planning, monitoring, and evaluating is called metacognition. It's a cycle of thinking that helps people perform better and is a crucial part of effective learning.

Let's see the cycle in action in an educational setting. Imagine Ivan. He's a typical student. He studies when he has tests, but sports, clubs, friends, and family can

Scan this QR code to learn more about metacognition.

Three Essential Steps to Metacognition

STEP 1 — PLAN
What do I know and what will I do to build on that knowledge?

STEP 2 — EVALUATE
How well am I doing while I'm learning and what can I do differently?

STEP 3 — REVIEW
What do I still need to work on and how can I guarantee that I'm prepared?

routinely get in the way of studying as much as he might say he should. Sometimes, he's also just not in the mood.

Ivan just learned that he failed his last math test. He's always been strong in the subject, but this semester has felt harder. On top of that, Ivan knows that if he fails another test, his grade point average is going to slip.

Instead of wallowing in his bad grade, though, Ivan pushes himself to think: "Why did I fail?" He evaluates his studying process and how he got to this point. Ivan thinks to himself, "Well, I only started studying the night before the test. I didn't give myself a lot of time. And I know that the more time I have to review, the better I remember things." Ivan pushes himself to dig deeper, thinking to himself, "I also wasn't remembering things while studying. I recognized things on the page, but I didn't test myself. All I really did was look over my notes."

Ivan now knows that the way he studied just didn't work for him and that he needs to do something different going forward. He's thinking about his thinking and making some informed decisions about what he

knows works for him. Ivan is practicing metacognition.

Ivan now thinks, "Next time, I need to start studying earlier. I also need to watch videos about the topics in the chapters instead of just reading. I know that I have an easier time remembering and understanding when I watch something to engage my visual learning style and then write down my ideas in my own words. From the class syllabus, I also know that the next test is about something I don't understand at all. I'm going to need to study more and be active."

That's Ivan's starting point. Because he plans to start studying earlier (Step 1), he can also take time to evaluate the progress of his studying as he goes (Step 2). After evaluating his strategies, Ivan can then make changes to serve his current level of understanding (Step 3).

At some point, Ivan might think, "The videos definitely help, but I'm still having trouble remembering all of this information. I need to make some flashcards, draw things out, and do some practice questions too." Ivan might engage in similar thought processes as he evaluates his strategies for individual problems, quizzes, videos, or even an entire textbook chapter.

NOTE

Did you know that there's an amount of stress that's good for you? Eustress is moderate stress that helps you perform better. Exactly how much stress that is varies from person to person. Finding that stressful sweet spot, though, will actually help you perform better in all sorts of circumstances. However, if your stress level goes too high or too low, your performance can suffer.

At the same time, during Ivan's new and improved study sessions, he also needs to ask himself questions such as "Do I understand this?" He might realize, "I actually don't get this. I know the terms and individual parts, but I don't think I could explain it if someone asked me to. I need to go through it again, do something differently, or even try another resource."

When Ivan's test comes around and he improves, he will have built himself a working framework for how to approach not only his next unit test but also tests in his other courses. Through metacognition, Ivan will have figured out how to self-direct his learning to achieve better results.

Metacognition is, thus, thinking about thinking. It's not the WHAT of learning; it's the HOW. Learning is not just what you know but how you know what you know. Remember, plan your studying, evaluate what's working and what's not as you go, and review what you know and what you need to do differently next time.

Keep in mind that to practice metacognition, you're trying to:

- See beyond the subject matter—not just the what of learning but the how
- Know what effective learning strategies are and demonstrate curiosity for learning how to do them
- Understand your personal strengths and weaknesses—how you learn and how your brain works
- Identify the limits of your knowledge—what you know, how well you know it, and what you still need to learn

NOTE

Metacognition requires thinking about your thinking before, during, and after you study. It's all about making good choices that suit how you learn.

Higher-Level Thinking

The thoughts you have can be divided into higher-level and lower-level thinking. We can say that the lowest level of thinking is gathering information. Gathering can mean either remembering something or simply finding it online or on a page. Higher-level thinking still requires you to gather, but it also necessitates some degree of understanding.

For example, imagine you were asked to do the following tasks:

Task 1: List the colors of a standard Rubik's cube

Task 2: Explain the relationship between the different colors on a Rubik's cube

Task 3: Demonstrate how to solve a Rubik's cube

Task 4: Design a new device that is similar to a Rubik's cube

If you were to perform those tasks, what kinds of thinking would each of them require?

Task 1 asks for the colors of a standard Rubik's cube. You can accomplish that task either by recalling the colors or pointing to them on an actual cube. Task 2, though, requires you to not only know the colors but also understand how they're positioned; that's going to require more thought. Task 3 then complicates the situation even further by asking you to solve a Rubik's cube; while there are methods for doing that, it requires significant knowledge and practice to do so. The complexity of your thinking while demonstrating such knowledge is dramatically higher. Task 4 requires even more thinking; to design a new device, you'd need to have complete knowledge of how the original puzzle works and be able to devise a method of solving whatever new contraption you come up with to know that it can indeed be done. That's a powerful combination of memory, understanding, and creativity all used to achieve a specific result.

Each of those tasks demands increasingly complex levels of thinking to be completed. Tellingly, it's those higher levels of thinking that people aspire to when beginning a new hobby or preparing for a test—recall, comprehend, create.

How does that help you, though? Well, if you can perform those different actions (recalling, comprehending, creating something new) with a topic, then you have some degree of mastery over said topic. If you can't perform higher-level thinking tasks on a topic, then you likely don't yet have mastery of the topic, which in the case of exam prep means you're probably not yet prepared for your test.

Additionally, just as you're making connections between ideas, so too are you forming connections in your brain. The greater the number of connections, the more engrained that information is in your brain's structure, which translates to greater expertise and recall ability.

The table given here has a sample of some of the different actions that you might be expected to take with a topic and the different levels of thinking. The level of thinking increases from left to right.

These action words are those that teachers often use to create objectives for a class or unit. They know that if a student can perform the higher-level verbs by the end of the term, then the student has mastered the related topics. If you can't perform the higher-level actions, then it means that you may need to do more to remember or understand a topic—more studying, different study strategies, etc.

The levels of thinking that you'll need to apply on your tests tend to be more limited because of the nature of multiple-choice questions. However, being able to practice the higher levels of thinking and pushing yourself there in your studying—especially for entirely new topics—isn't going to hurt you on the test. In fact, it can only help.

For the tests in this book, you'll need to remember what a fraction is or be able to identify from different word roots. You'll also need to apply rules for operations with fractions in word problems or figure out unknown vocabulary using your knowledge of word parts. You won't need to perform every level of

LEVELS OF THINKING AND EXAMPLE VERBS*					
Remember	**Understand**	**Apply**	**Analyze**	**Evaluate**	**Create**
Define	Compare	Demonstrate	Combine	Assess	Compose
Gather	Discuss	Estimate	Debate	Judge	Design
List	Explain	Implement	Experiment	Monitor	Generate
Recognize	Paraphrase	Modify	Illustrate	Recommend	Produce
Select	Translate	Use	Predict	Test	Transform

*Adapted from Anderson, L.W., & Krathwohl, D.R. (Eds.) (2001). *A taxonomy for learning, teaching, and assessing: A revision of Bloom's taxonomy of educational objectives.* New York: Longman.

thinking with every concept, but you should take the time when you're studying to check that you not only remember the information but can also use it in different ways. You should also check to make sure you can apply different types of knowledge, such as the range of skills related to reading comprehension, in a variety of contexts.

Focused and Diffused Thinking

Just as your thoughts can be divided into different levels, they can be used in different modes too. Let's consider two of those modes when it comes to learning things: focused and diffused.

When you're reading or trying to work through a problem, you're in your focused mode. That mode kicks on any time you're really concentrating to try to figure something out. In that mode, your thinking is traveling the pathways that exist in your brain, the ones that you've used in the past. Those pathways become more refined and more efficient with use.

Alternatively, you've got your diffused mode. This mode is what was just active whenever you catch your mind wandering. The diffused mode of thinking turns on when you're doing things that don't require that much attention. You likely experience it when you go for a walk, take a shower, or play a song you've played many times before. In the diffused mode, your brain is great at making connections. You might have some

epiphany about how two things are related or figure out a new way to do something.

Those modes represent two very different ways of thinking that serve very different purposes. One is for getting things done (focused). The other is for making surprising connections (diffused). When you're dealing with a new topic, you might get stuck in that laser-focused thinking mode because your thoughts are being forced to travel the pathways your brain already has built. If the situation is similar enough to something you've done before, you might figure it out. But if it's truly new information or a new way of thinking, then your existing chunks aren't going to be enough. They're going to keep you from seeing what's new. To fix that, you're going to need to let your mind wander off the beaten path to form some new connections.

There are plenty of stories of famous inventors and artists hacking their brains to come up with new ideas. People like Thomas Edison and Salvador Dalí figured out that their brains were at their most creative right before they fell asleep. Supposedly, Thomas Edison used to sit in a chair while holding a piece of metal in his hand. Beneath his hand, he would position a plate. He would then close his eyes and as soon as he started to drift off, he would drop the metal, letting it fall onto the plate with a loud clatter. The sound would stir him awake and he would use his brain's creative state to ease him through a difficult problem or give him a glimpse of some potential invention.

NOTE

Setting strict time limits for your work and breaks can improve not only your motivation and attention but also trigger that diffused state of mind when you step away. The Pomodoro technique is one such method. It has you work in short, concentrated bursts with short breaks in between. Give it a try: Choose your task. Set a 25-minute timer. Work on that task and nothing else until the timer expires. Take a 5-minute break. For every four 25-minute periods, take a 15–30 minute break. Keep that up until you're done for the day. See how it can improve your productivity and focus.

Even just closing your eyes—taking a long blink—can help you step away from your current mode of thinking and allow your mind to, potentially, forge new connections. Sometimes, you're going to need to give your mind a larger incentive to switch modes than that. Sometimes, you need to take an actual break.

When you're trying to learn something new, if you feel like you're running into a wall, you should do something that allows your brain to focus less and wander more. To initiate that mode of thinking, you can try the following:

- Go for a walk
- Take a shower
- Exercise
- Draw
- Listen to instrumental music
- Take a nap
- Dance to a favorite song

However, this doesn't mean taking breaks every few minutes. Your breaks need to come after intense active studying. Studying that doesn't require energy won't do you any good. You need to alternate between your focused and diffused thinking. When you get back from your break, whether you had some grand epiphany or not, switch back to focused thinking and practice retrieval (see what you can remember without

NOTE

Not everything will get you into a relaxed state for your diffused thinking to take over. Choose things that are easy for your brain and free of stress. While things like playing a video game or hopping on social media for a few minutes might be good rewards for hard work, they're not going to let your mind wander.

looking back at the material) and some higher-level thinking, and then review to make sure you're remembering correctly and that you actually understand. Your diffused mode of thinking is a great asset, but spending too much time in that aimless state will stall your learning.

Adopting a Growth Mindset

Learning new things is hard. You're trying to internalize a wealth of information, develop new skills, and change behaviors. In short, you're trying to grow. There are all sorts of barriers to your improvement, though. One that we must contend with every day is our attitude or mindset. Our beliefs tend to impact what we do and how we do it, and if we're stuck in the mindset that we can't do something or are no good at it, we usually don't even try.

Here's the reality: we don't grow when we avoid doing the hard things, and no one gets better by not practicing.

With practice, though, you can be a math person, a better writer, a better reader, or a better thinker. But, like everything, it requires work. Just like it takes you time to improve at a sport, build muscle at the gym, play a new song on an instrument, or make skillful drawings, your brain requires time and repetition to build expertise for academic topics.

While your brain is trying to grow, you need to frame what you're doing with growth in mind. Say to yourself, "I'm struggling now, but I'll keep getting better. I just need to keep working." From there, you get to make the critical decisions that can help you overcome frustration and continue to learn.

Take those that say, "I'm just not a math person." They think that because math has been hard that it will always be hard. Despite what you may have heard, math ability is not limited by "talent" or "gifts." Persistence is the key to long-term math success. Sooner or later, even someone who may be naturally "good at math" has to work hard to succeed. For some people, that need starts earlier than for others. But if you're one of those people, that doesn't mean you can fall into the trap of a fixed mindset.

The real secret to learning is that perseverance is more important than intelligence. High intelligence may make things seem easier for a while, but sooner or later, everyone hits a wall. The difference between good learners and those who struggle is what happens when they reach what feels like a breaking point.

In recent years, a mountain of research has emerged showing that your intellectual abilities are not fixed. You can and will improve when you use awareness of your growth potential to make better decisions. It sounds too simple, but students who know that their abilities can change then recognize the importance of effort. That belief in effort translates to better performance over time.

When you're aware that growth is always possible, it's harder to make excuses for how you can't or won't improve. If you know that your mindset matters and is your primary limiting factor, that awareness forces you to acknowledge the importance of practice and persistence. In doing so, you then have to decide whether you'll study the right way or "easy way," which by now you know is more ineffective than easy.

To learn more adopting a growth mindset instead of a fixed mindset, scan this QR code.

Understand that someone with a growth mindset may still say "I'm not good at math" or "I can't do this. . .", but they'll always end those sentences with the word *yet*. You can say it right now: "I can't do some things in math. . . yet." Then, make it about what you can be: "With practice, I can be a better reader or a better writer or student or thinker." Once you understand that it is only a matter of time and effort, you can make decisions that help you perform better. You don't need to resign yourself to the silly (and untrue!) idea that you'll never improve, grow, or change. You may not be a "math person" or a "great learner" now, but know that you can be.

TECHNIQUES AND STRATEGIES FOR ACTIVE AND EFFECTIVE STUDYING

There are several approaches to studying that check the boxes for effective and active learning. Here, we suggest a few that can help you maximize your retention and encourage understanding. Some work for when you first read through a chapter or watch a video. Others are techniques that require intense retrieval and higher-level thinking. They all ask you to recall information and form relationships in different ways. With many of these techniques you'll spend more time up front creating something, but then you'll have a new resource on hand that you can use to test yourself.

You'll see that some of these strategies and techniques have you complete similar tasks. Try to experiment with different ones, even merging some together, to

TIP

Read through this information now, but return here after you complete your diagnostic test and identify what areas you'll need to work on. Mark strategies that you think you'll want to try when you start studying.

Scan this QR code for more information on active learning strategies.

suit your preferences but also capitalize on your own strengths and weaknesses as well as your knowledge of how learning works. Each item is accompanied by an explanation of what it is, how it should be done, and why it can help you be a more effective and efficient learner.

SQ3R

What Is It?

SQ3R is a strategic reading technique. It stands for **S**urvey, **Q**uestion, **R**ead, **R**ecite, **R**eview. It is a five-step process that has you preview what you're going to read before you read it and review once you're done. To get the most out of a book chapter or section, you can prime yourself to identify what is most important or what you're less familiar with. You can then check your understanding at the end to make sure you took away the key points.

How Do You Do It?

Break down your reading of a chapter or section into five distinct steps:

1. **Survey:** Preview the entire chapter, reading section headings and examining graphics, captions, and the text's structure.

2. **Question:** Generate questions based on the information you surveyed.

3. **Read:** Read through the text.

4. **Recite:** Recite information from the text and try to answer your questions.

5. **Review:** Review the chapter or section to check your understanding and retention of what you read.

Why Does It Help?

SQ3R makes reading easier. By approaching reading as a multi-part process, you reduce the burden of having to try to learn everything in a single shot. By taking steps to find the purpose of a text (survey), identify points of confusion (questioning), read, retrieve key information (recite), and generate a cohesive summary of the text (review), you've done a lot to maximize encoding and improve understanding of what you read.

Mind Maps

What Is It?

Mind maps are diagrams that illustrate the relationships between different ideas. They can be used to represent the topic of a book, a mathematical or scientific concept, an entire field of study, and more. A mind map makes use of text, images, and colors to depict and relate different characteristics or parts of a topic to one another. Imagine it like a tree: a major topic branches off into minor topics, all with their own detailed leaves.

How Do You Do It?

Draw and/or label the main topic of the map in the center of a document. From the central topic, place subtopics in the space around the main topic. For the subtopics, provide important details, categories, characteristics, views, etc. Use color, arrows, images, and other diagramming features to add greater detail.

An example of a mind map for the topic of ecology.

Why Does It Help?

A mind map helps you identify the key features of a topic while developing spatial and logical relationships between said features. Mind maps capitalize on the brain's strong visual capacity while also asking you to retrieve, organize, and connect information—all higher-level processes that reinforce retention and understanding.

Feynman Technique

What Is It?

Richard Feynman was a Nobel prize-winning physicist. He was a true expert who made incredible discoveries in the field and was always looking to learn more. Feynman is credited with developing a widely used study strategy called the Feynman technique. The Feynman technique is all about identifying, refining, and communicating what you know. Your goal is to create a short document that communicates a complex topic in a way that anyone reading it can understand.

How Do You Do It?

List the topic in question at the top of a sheet of paper or blank document on your computer or phone. Describe the topic in terms that could be understood by almost anyone. Be sure to identify what it is, how it works, why it works that way, why it is important, or what topics it is connected to. Avoid using technical terms and jargon. After completing a paraphrase, reread what you wrote. Identify any gaps in your understanding and consult other resources as necessary. Continue to revise your paraphrase until the topic is absolutely clear—you both remember and understand the topic and could teach it to someone else. You can even share the document with others to see if they understand what you wrote. Use any feedback to revise.

Why Does It Help?

If you can teach someone something, that usually means that you understand it completely. Not only does this technique force you to go through the process of retrieving and translating information (a form of higher-level thinking), but it also creates a resource that you can use to test yourself in the future.

Practice Testing

What Is It?

If your goal in studying is to do well on a test, then the best thing that you can do to supplement your preparation is to take practice tests that feel like the real thing. This strategy is likely why you're using this book. But as you might infer from the earlier sections of this chapter, just doing practice questions isn't quite enough. You can get more out of practice tests when you take time to make a plan for how you'll complete them, evaluate your performance as you're working, and review how well you did after finishing. This method of practice testing is all about injecting more opportunities for active learning.

How Do You Do It?

Find practice questions, set a timer, review your test-taking strategies, and take the test. Once you finish, check your score and record it so you can track your performance over time. Then ask yourself the following questions:

- How well did I do?
- How well did I use my time?
- What kinds of questions were harder?
- What kinds of questions did I miss?
- Why did I miss those questions?
- Were there any topics with which I consistently struggled?
- What can I do differently to improve for my next test?

Take the time to answer those questions thoroughly and determine what's next for your study process before you take your next test.

Why Does It Help?

Time and time again, research has shown that taking practice tests has a significant impact on future test performance. That's largely the result of the "practice effect" wherein practicing for a test with similar material will lead to gains. It's intuitive, but many students either skip the step (not knowing where to find practice tests) or think they're done once they check their scores. You need to assess your strengths and weaknesses and use that information to make choices for what you need to do differently next time (study more, read questions more slowly, etc.). If you don't take the time to think through those metacognitive questions, you might miss an opportunity to change something in your studying that just isn't working. Remember, you need to reflect. Your answers to those reflection questions are going to put you in a better position to make decisions that will help you do better next time.

Self-Questioning

What Is It?

Self-questioning asks you to create your own questions or problems based on the facts, concepts, and applications of the topics you're learning.

How Do You Do It?

You know that thinking has multiple different levels and that it is essential that you be able to remember information. Once you can remember information, you need to construct meaning—or develop relationships between different topics. After you understand something, you need to be able to apply it—or use information in different situations.

- First, pick topics with which you struggle.
- Then, start asking questions that require defining, listing, or identifying different ideas (e.g., define mean, median, and mode).
- Next, ask questions that compare, summarize, or classify ideas (e.g., comparing usage of different punctuation).
- Finally, pursue higher-level thinking by responding to, using, judging, or generating applications for the ideas (e.g., developing practice word problems).

Why Does It Help?

Those three kinds of "thinking" encompass the cognitive processes required by most tests. As such, if you can develop and answer questions that demand those tasks, you know that you're prepared for your assessment. Know that this strategy is very similar to practice testing. When practice tests are unavailable or inaccessible, you can try to make some of your own.

Cornell Notes

What Is It?

The Cornell method is a multi-step note-making process. It asks you to take, review, and revise your notes while also turning them into a method for self-quizzing. While most students typically take notes and then stuff them away for later, the Cornell method asks that you practice retrieval as soon after note-taking as possible. Once you've reviewed, you go through the process of revising your notes, making questions, and writing a summary. You then have a study resource you can refer to rather than having to consult a book chapter or video again.

How Do You Do It?

There are lots of variations on the Cornell note-taking method, but the following outlines the basic process of the method's structure and usage:

1. Format a document into two columns (1/3 of the page for the left column, 2/3 of the page for the right) with space for a topic name at the top of the document and a gap of roughly two inches at the bottom of the document.

2. While reading, watching a video, or listening to a lecture, record short, complete sentences in the right-hand column that describe the topic of the reading/video/lecture. After finishing the source material, reread what you wrote—this should happen as soon after recording has finished as possible.

3. Mark places where more information may be needed or any places of confusion. Add details that you may recall.

4. Then, in the left-hand column, record questions (either from the materials or ones that you generate) that may be answered by the information in the right-hand column.

5. Cover the right-hand column in some way and answer the self-generated questions without looking at the noted information. Check your accuracy and mark questions that you're unable to answer effectively.

6. Once you've completed that initial quizzing, use the gap at the bottom of the page to write a summary that describes the topic of the notes.

7. Revisit this document to study: read the summary and then answer the questions in the left-column while covering up the notes column.

Why Does It Help?

Revisiting information soon after your first exposure is a critical step that many students neglect, and skipping that step contributes to poor memory storage. A good note-making process will encourage you to both revisit notes soon after taking them and regularly revisit them to maintain retention. As described previously, the Cornell method has a built-in system of review in the form of questions and a format that allows you to easily quiz yourself on the content of the notes without a partner. At the same time, the summary creates a quick reference point so that you can get the gist of a topic without having to fully reread the entire set of notes.

ADEPT (in Reverse)

What Is It?

ADEPT is actually a common teaching strategy for introducing a new concept. It stands for **A**nalogy, **D**iagram, **E**xample, **P**lain English Definition, **T**echnical Definition. By presenting information in that order, students tend to encode more easily. However, it can also be used in the reverse to work through different levels of thinking for a concept. If you work through ADEPT in reverse, you go from simple recalling to understanding and even applying.

How Do You Do It?

To make use of ADEPT as a studying technique, do the following:

1. Select your topic.
2. Recall and write out the technical definition.
3. Paraphrase it into plainer English.
4. Create an example of the topic in action.
5. Draw a diagram to make it visual.
6. Create an analogy to compare the topic to something else.

If any of those steps prove difficult, consult your resources again to clarify the definition and your understanding of the topic. Like the Feynman technique, you can then use this resource to test your memory and understanding later on.

Why Does It Help?

New topics often require complex thinking, but you can breach the complexity of a new topic by starting with the basics and changing the way you look at the information. By bridging knowledge you already have in the analogy stage, you can also forge new connections. That process can then break down the barriers between what you know and what you're trying to learn. By moving through different types of communication for a new or complex topic, your higher-level thinking skills must grapple with examining a new idea from multiple perspectives. That serves to expand understanding and reinforce your memory.

STUDY TIME SURVEYS

You now know a lot more than you probably did when you started this chapter about what learning is, how learning works, and what will make your studying more effective. But, as you know, there's a big difference between being exposed to information and actually making use of it.

As you work through this book, you'll need to use what you've started to learn here to make your learning more effective in the other chapters. To assist with that goal, the following are surveys you can use when you study to determine whether you're doing everything you can to make your learning as active and effective as possible.

Studying for Results

You know that your studying needs to meet certain criteria to serve how learning works. Ask yourself the following as you work through this book:

- Are you being active when you study? Are you retrieving information from your memory, creating study tools, and practicing higher-level thinking?
- Are you practicing metacognition? Are you planning, evaluating, and reviewing your performance regularly (before, during, and after studying)?
- Are you taking breaks to practice diffused thinking? Are you engaging your diffused thinking when learning new things to help forge new connections between different parts of your brain?

- Are you practicing a growth mindset? Are you tracking your progress, maintaining effort, and developing a positive attitude about your ability to change?

Metacognition Questions

Throughout the various stages of studying, you need to think through the following questions to practice metacognition.

BEFORE STUDYING

- Have you previewed what you're going to be learning?
- Have you reviewed your prior knowledge about the topic?
- Can you connect the topic to something else?
- Do you know what you need to focus on?
- What strategies will you use?
- How will you test yourself?

DURING STUDYING

- What can you remember?
- What do you understand?
- What still doesn't make sense?
- How are you performing on the exercises?
- Is there anything you can do differently right now?

AFTER STUDYING

- What did you learn?
- What do you still need to work on?
- What will you do differently next time?
- How can you review between now and the next time you study?

SUMMING IT UP

- Learning is all about changing your brain. If you study in different ways, you're going to develop more connections between different memories and concepts, making them easier to access.

- Your memory has three stages: encoding (receiving the information), storage (keeping the information), and retrieval (recalling the information). Certain choices and situations make encoding more effective, but retrieval is the most important part of memory. Retrieve often and rigorously.

- Practice active studying, not passive studying. If you're not testing yourself (retrieving information), creating something when studying, or reflecting on what you understand and what you don't, then you're not getting the most out of your study time.

- Use metacognition to plan what you'll study and how you'll do it (what strategies or techniques you'll use), evaluate how well you're doing as you're practicing or working on different topics, and, at the end of your session, review what you learned and what strategies seemed to work and which ones didn't.

- Thinking occurs at different levels, and expertise with a topic means that you remember it, understand it, and can apply that knowledge in different situations. The more you practice that higher-level thinking, the more readily accessible information will be in your mind.

- Intense study sessions will help you grow, but when dealing with new material, it's also important to take breaks to let your brain sort things out. Make use of your diffused thinking for new topics, especially in math. If you feel like you're hitting a wall, go for a walk, listen to some music, or take a brief rest to see what insights you have when you confront the material again.

- Adopt a growth mindset. Just because you can't do something now doesn't mean you won't be able to do it in the future. If ever you find yourself saying "I can't. . ." always finish that sentence with "yet." Then, make a plan for how to improve and execute it.

- Return to this chapter throughout your time with this book to reflect on whether you're learning as effectively as you can.

PART II

DIAGNOSING STRENGTHS AND WEAKNESSES

CHAPTER

SSAT (UPPER LEVEL)
DIAGNOSTIC TEST

SSAT (UPPER LEVEL) DIAGNOSTIC TEST

DIAGNOSTIC TEST

This diagnostic test is designed to help you recognize your strengths and weaknesses. The questions cover information from all the different sections of the SSAT. Use the results to help guide and direct your study time.

ANSWER SHEET: SSAT (UPPER LEVEL) DIAGNOSTIC TEST

Part I: Writing Sample

Lined pages provided within test.

Part II: Multiple Choice

Section 1: Quantitative (Math)

1. Ⓐ Ⓑ Ⓒ Ⓓ Ⓔ
2. Ⓐ Ⓑ Ⓒ Ⓓ Ⓔ
3. Ⓐ Ⓑ Ⓒ Ⓓ Ⓔ
4. Ⓐ Ⓑ Ⓒ Ⓓ Ⓔ
5. Ⓐ Ⓑ Ⓒ Ⓓ Ⓔ
6. Ⓐ Ⓑ Ⓒ Ⓓ Ⓔ
7. Ⓐ Ⓑ Ⓒ Ⓓ Ⓔ

8. Ⓐ Ⓑ Ⓒ Ⓓ Ⓔ
9. Ⓐ Ⓑ Ⓒ Ⓓ Ⓔ
10. Ⓐ Ⓑ Ⓒ Ⓓ Ⓔ
11. Ⓐ Ⓑ Ⓒ Ⓓ Ⓔ
12. Ⓐ Ⓑ Ⓒ Ⓓ Ⓔ
13. Ⓐ Ⓑ Ⓒ Ⓓ Ⓔ
14. Ⓐ Ⓑ Ⓒ Ⓓ Ⓔ

15. Ⓐ Ⓑ Ⓒ Ⓓ Ⓔ
16. Ⓐ Ⓑ Ⓒ Ⓓ Ⓔ
17. Ⓐ Ⓑ Ⓒ Ⓓ Ⓔ
18. Ⓐ Ⓑ Ⓒ Ⓓ Ⓔ
19. Ⓐ Ⓑ Ⓒ Ⓓ Ⓔ
20. Ⓐ Ⓑ Ⓒ Ⓓ Ⓔ
21. Ⓐ Ⓑ Ⓒ Ⓓ Ⓔ

22. Ⓐ Ⓑ Ⓒ Ⓓ Ⓔ
23. Ⓐ Ⓑ Ⓒ Ⓓ Ⓔ
24. Ⓐ Ⓑ Ⓒ Ⓓ Ⓔ
25. Ⓐ Ⓑ Ⓒ Ⓓ Ⓔ

Section 2: Reading

1. Ⓐ Ⓑ Ⓒ Ⓓ Ⓔ
2. Ⓐ Ⓑ Ⓒ Ⓓ Ⓔ
3. Ⓐ Ⓑ Ⓒ Ⓓ Ⓔ
4. Ⓐ Ⓑ Ⓒ Ⓓ Ⓔ
5. Ⓐ Ⓑ Ⓒ Ⓓ Ⓔ
6. Ⓐ Ⓑ Ⓒ Ⓓ Ⓔ
7. Ⓐ Ⓑ Ⓒ Ⓓ Ⓔ
8. Ⓐ Ⓑ Ⓒ Ⓓ Ⓔ
9. Ⓐ Ⓑ Ⓒ Ⓓ Ⓔ
10. Ⓐ Ⓑ Ⓒ Ⓓ Ⓔ

11. Ⓐ Ⓑ Ⓒ Ⓓ Ⓔ
12. Ⓐ Ⓑ Ⓒ Ⓓ Ⓔ
13. Ⓐ Ⓑ Ⓒ Ⓓ Ⓔ
14. Ⓐ Ⓑ Ⓒ Ⓓ Ⓔ
15. Ⓐ Ⓑ Ⓒ Ⓓ Ⓔ
16. Ⓐ Ⓑ Ⓒ Ⓓ Ⓔ
17. Ⓐ Ⓑ Ⓒ Ⓓ Ⓔ
18. Ⓐ Ⓑ Ⓒ Ⓓ Ⓔ
19. Ⓐ Ⓑ Ⓒ Ⓓ Ⓔ
20. Ⓐ Ⓑ Ⓒ Ⓓ Ⓔ

21. Ⓐ Ⓑ Ⓒ Ⓓ Ⓔ
22. Ⓐ Ⓑ Ⓒ Ⓓ Ⓔ
23. Ⓐ Ⓑ Ⓒ Ⓓ Ⓔ
24. Ⓐ Ⓑ Ⓒ Ⓓ Ⓔ
25. Ⓐ Ⓑ Ⓒ Ⓓ Ⓔ
26. Ⓐ Ⓑ Ⓒ Ⓓ Ⓔ
27. Ⓐ Ⓑ Ⓒ Ⓓ Ⓔ
28. Ⓐ Ⓑ Ⓒ Ⓓ Ⓔ
29. Ⓐ Ⓑ Ⓒ Ⓓ Ⓔ
30. Ⓐ Ⓑ Ⓒ Ⓓ Ⓔ

31. Ⓐ Ⓑ Ⓒ Ⓓ Ⓔ
32. Ⓐ Ⓑ Ⓒ Ⓓ Ⓔ
33. Ⓐ Ⓑ Ⓒ Ⓓ Ⓔ
34. Ⓐ Ⓑ Ⓒ Ⓓ Ⓔ
35. Ⓐ Ⓑ Ⓒ Ⓓ Ⓔ
36. Ⓐ Ⓑ Ⓒ Ⓓ Ⓔ
37. Ⓐ Ⓑ Ⓒ Ⓓ Ⓔ
38. Ⓐ Ⓑ Ⓒ Ⓓ Ⓔ
39. Ⓐ Ⓑ Ⓒ Ⓓ Ⓔ
40. Ⓐ Ⓑ Ⓒ Ⓓ Ⓔ

Section 3: Verbal

1. Ⓐ Ⓑ Ⓒ Ⓓ Ⓔ
2. Ⓐ Ⓑ Ⓒ Ⓓ Ⓔ
3. Ⓐ Ⓑ Ⓒ Ⓓ Ⓔ
4. Ⓐ Ⓑ Ⓒ Ⓓ Ⓔ
5. Ⓐ Ⓑ Ⓒ Ⓓ Ⓔ
6. Ⓐ Ⓑ Ⓒ Ⓓ Ⓔ
7. Ⓐ Ⓑ Ⓒ Ⓓ Ⓔ
8. Ⓐ Ⓑ Ⓒ Ⓓ Ⓔ
9. Ⓐ Ⓑ Ⓒ Ⓓ Ⓔ
10. Ⓐ Ⓑ Ⓒ Ⓓ Ⓔ
11. Ⓐ Ⓑ Ⓒ Ⓓ Ⓔ
12. Ⓐ Ⓑ Ⓒ Ⓓ Ⓔ
13. Ⓐ Ⓑ Ⓒ Ⓓ Ⓔ
14. Ⓐ Ⓑ Ⓒ Ⓓ Ⓔ
15. Ⓐ Ⓑ Ⓒ Ⓓ Ⓔ

16. Ⓐ Ⓑ Ⓒ Ⓓ Ⓔ
17. Ⓐ Ⓑ Ⓒ Ⓓ Ⓔ
18. Ⓐ Ⓑ Ⓒ Ⓓ Ⓔ
19. Ⓐ Ⓑ Ⓒ Ⓓ Ⓔ
20. Ⓐ Ⓑ Ⓒ Ⓓ Ⓔ
21. Ⓐ Ⓑ Ⓒ Ⓓ Ⓔ
22. Ⓐ Ⓑ Ⓒ Ⓓ Ⓔ
23. Ⓐ Ⓑ Ⓒ Ⓓ Ⓔ
24. Ⓐ Ⓑ Ⓒ Ⓓ Ⓔ
25. Ⓐ Ⓑ Ⓒ Ⓓ Ⓔ
26. Ⓐ Ⓑ Ⓒ Ⓓ Ⓔ
27. Ⓐ Ⓑ Ⓒ Ⓓ Ⓔ
28. Ⓐ Ⓑ Ⓒ Ⓓ Ⓔ
29. Ⓐ Ⓑ Ⓒ Ⓓ Ⓔ
30. Ⓐ Ⓑ Ⓒ Ⓓ Ⓔ

31. Ⓐ Ⓑ Ⓒ Ⓓ Ⓔ
32. Ⓐ Ⓑ Ⓒ Ⓓ Ⓔ
33. Ⓐ Ⓑ Ⓒ Ⓓ Ⓔ
34. Ⓐ Ⓑ Ⓒ Ⓓ Ⓔ
35. Ⓐ Ⓑ Ⓒ Ⓓ Ⓔ
36. Ⓐ Ⓑ Ⓒ Ⓓ Ⓔ
37. Ⓐ Ⓑ Ⓒ Ⓓ Ⓔ
38. Ⓐ Ⓑ Ⓒ Ⓓ Ⓔ
39. Ⓐ Ⓑ Ⓒ Ⓓ Ⓔ
40. Ⓐ Ⓑ Ⓒ Ⓓ Ⓔ
41. Ⓐ Ⓑ Ⓒ Ⓓ Ⓔ
42. Ⓐ Ⓑ Ⓒ Ⓓ Ⓔ
43. Ⓐ Ⓑ Ⓒ Ⓓ Ⓔ
44. Ⓐ Ⓑ Ⓒ Ⓓ Ⓔ
45. Ⓐ Ⓑ Ⓒ Ⓓ Ⓔ

46. Ⓐ Ⓑ Ⓒ Ⓓ Ⓔ
47. Ⓐ Ⓑ Ⓒ Ⓓ Ⓔ
48. Ⓐ Ⓑ Ⓒ Ⓓ Ⓔ
49. Ⓐ Ⓑ Ⓒ Ⓓ Ⓔ
50. Ⓐ Ⓑ Ⓒ Ⓓ Ⓔ
51. Ⓐ Ⓑ Ⓒ Ⓓ Ⓔ
52. Ⓐ Ⓑ Ⓒ Ⓓ Ⓔ
53. Ⓐ Ⓑ Ⓒ Ⓓ Ⓔ
54. Ⓐ Ⓑ Ⓒ Ⓓ Ⓔ
55. Ⓐ Ⓑ Ⓒ Ⓓ Ⓔ
56. Ⓐ Ⓑ Ⓒ Ⓓ Ⓔ
57. Ⓐ Ⓑ Ⓒ Ⓓ Ⓔ
58. Ⓐ Ⓑ Ⓒ Ⓓ Ⓔ
59. Ⓐ Ⓑ Ⓒ Ⓓ Ⓔ
60. Ⓐ Ⓑ Ⓒ Ⓓ Ⓔ

Section 4: Quantitative (Math)

1. Ⓐ Ⓑ Ⓒ Ⓓ Ⓔ
2. Ⓐ Ⓑ Ⓒ Ⓓ Ⓔ
3. Ⓐ Ⓑ Ⓒ Ⓓ Ⓔ
4. Ⓐ Ⓑ Ⓒ Ⓓ Ⓔ
5. Ⓐ Ⓑ Ⓒ Ⓓ Ⓔ
6. Ⓐ Ⓑ Ⓒ Ⓓ Ⓔ
7. Ⓐ Ⓑ Ⓒ Ⓓ Ⓔ

8. Ⓐ Ⓑ Ⓒ Ⓓ Ⓔ
9. Ⓐ Ⓑ Ⓒ Ⓓ Ⓔ
10. Ⓐ Ⓑ Ⓒ Ⓓ Ⓔ
11. Ⓐ Ⓑ Ⓒ Ⓓ Ⓔ
12. Ⓐ Ⓑ Ⓒ Ⓓ Ⓔ
13. Ⓐ Ⓑ Ⓒ Ⓓ Ⓔ
14. Ⓐ Ⓑ Ⓒ Ⓓ Ⓔ

15. Ⓐ Ⓑ Ⓒ Ⓓ Ⓔ
16. Ⓐ Ⓑ Ⓒ Ⓓ Ⓔ
17. Ⓐ Ⓑ Ⓒ Ⓓ Ⓔ
18. Ⓐ Ⓑ Ⓒ Ⓓ Ⓔ
19. Ⓐ Ⓑ Ⓒ Ⓓ Ⓔ
20. Ⓐ Ⓑ Ⓒ Ⓓ Ⓔ
21. Ⓐ Ⓑ Ⓒ Ⓓ Ⓔ

22. Ⓐ Ⓑ Ⓒ Ⓓ Ⓔ
23. Ⓐ Ⓑ Ⓒ Ⓓ Ⓔ
24. Ⓐ Ⓑ Ⓒ Ⓓ Ⓔ
25. Ⓐ Ⓑ Ⓒ Ⓓ Ⓔ

PART I: WRITING SAMPLE

25 Minutes

Directions: Read the topics, choose the one that interests you the most, and plan your essay or story before writing. Write a legible essay on the paper provided.

Topic A: Consider the following two statements.

A: To reduce the accident rate, the state legislature should pass a proposal to raise the minimum driving age from 16 to 18.

B: A person's relationships with their family members are more important than their relationships with their friends.

Choose one of the statements, then determine if you agree or disagree with the statement. Support your position with examples from your own experience, the experience of others, current events, or from knowledge you've gained.

Topic B: Consider the following two statements.

A: I could feel the feeling building in my stomach—something big was about to happen.

B: A peaceful and eerie silence hung in the air.

Write a story using one of these two statements as the first sentence. Be sure your story has a clear beginning, middle, and end.

_____

_____

_____

_____

_____

_____

_____

_____

_____

PART II: MULTIPLE CHOICE

Section 1: Quantitative (Math)

25 Questions—30 Minutes

Directions: Calculate the answer to each of the following questions. Select the answer choice that is best and mark the appropriate letter on your answer sheet.

1. $1\dfrac{1}{2} + 0.750 + 0.1010 =$

   A. 1.001

   B. 2.051

   C. 2.055

   D. 2.351

   E. 2.551

2. Evaluate: $\dfrac{2^{12}}{2^{8}}$.

   A. 2

   B. 8

   C. 16

   D. 120

   E. 220

3. $503.384 \div 62.3 =$

   A. 7.08

   B. 7.68

   C. 8.08

   D. 9.08

   E. 10.08

4. Evaluate: $\dfrac{1\dfrac{3}{4} - \dfrac{1}{8}}{\dfrac{1}{8}}$.

   A. 1

   B. 2

   C. 12

   D. 13

   E. 14

5. $2.01 \div 1.02 =$

   A. 0.507

   B. 1.83

   C. 1.97

   D. 2.0001

   E. 3.03

6. $-3 - [(2 - 1) - (3 + 4)] =$

   A. 12

   B. 6

   C. 3

   D. -6

   E. -9

7. $3003 - 699 =$

   A. 2,294

   B. 2,304

   C. 2,314

   D. 2,404

   E. 2,414

8. If $a = 5$ and $b = \dfrac{1}{5}$, what is the value of a when expressed in terms of b?

   A. $25b$

   B. $20b$

   C. $5\dfrac{1}{5}b$

   D. $5b$

   E. $\dfrac{1}{25}b$

9. 140% of 70 is

A. 0.98.

B. 9.8.

C. 98.

D. 150.

E. 9,800.

10. 5 gallons   2 quarts   1 pint

   −1 gallon   3 quarts

A. 2 gal. 2 qt. 1 pt.

B. 2 gal. 6 qt. 2 pt.

C. 3 gal. 3 qt. 1 pt.

D. 4 gal. 3 qt. 1 pt.

E. 4 gal. 9 qt. 1 pt.

11. In the fraction $\dfrac{xy}{z}$, if the value of z is doubled and the value of x is halved, the value of the fraction is

A. multiplied by 4.

B. decreased by $\dfrac{1}{2}$.

C. increased by $\dfrac{1}{2}$.

D. doubled.

E. divided by 4.

12. 20 is 8% of

A. 1.60

B. 160

C. 200

D. 250

E. 400

13. How much larger than 80 is 100?

A. 18%

B. 20%

C. 25%

D. 35%

E. 40%

14. If $\dfrac{3}{8}$ inches on a scale drawing is equivalent to one foot at full scale, what distance on the drawing will stand for 40 inches?

A. $\dfrac{1}{8}$ inches

B. $\dfrac{7}{8}$ inches

C. $1\dfrac{1}{4}$ inches

D. $2\dfrac{1}{3}$ inches

E. $8\dfrac{8}{9}$ inches

15. $6 \div \dfrac{1}{3} + \dfrac{2}{3} \times 9 =$

A. $\dfrac{2}{3}$

B. 11

C. 24

D. 54

E. 168

16. If $x - 3 < 12$, x may be

A. less than 15

B. greater than 16

C. equal to 15

D. less than 18

E. equal to 18

17. If $a = 9$, $b = 2$, and $c = 1$, what is the value of $\sqrt{a + 3b + c}$?

A. 16

B. 7

C. 6

D. 4

E. 2

18. The average of –10, 6, 0, –3, and 22 is

    A. 4

    B. 3

    C. 2

    D. –3

    E. –6

19. In the fraction $\dfrac{1}{\Delta - 2}$, Δ can be replaced by all of the following EXCEPT:

    A. +3

    B. +2

    C. 0

    D. –1

    E. –2

20. 0.10101 ÷ 10 is equivalent to

    A. 0.0010101

    B. 0.0100

    C. 0.010101

    D. 0.1001

    E. 1.0101

21. David walked from his home to town, a distance of 5 miles, in 1 hour. The return trip took 2 hours because he made several stops along the way. What was his average rate of speed (in miles per hour) for the entire walk?

    A. $\dfrac{3}{10}$ mph

    B. $1\dfrac{1}{2}$ mph

    C. $1\dfrac{2}{3}$ mph

    D. $3\dfrac{1}{3}$ mph

    E. 4 mph

22. 7 is to 21 as $\dfrac{2}{3}$ is to

    A. 3

    B. 2

    C. $\dfrac{4}{3}$

    D. 1

    E. $\dfrac{5}{9}$

23. If $n = \sqrt{85}$, then

    A. $9 > n > 8$

    B. $n = 9.5$

    C. $10 > n > 9$

    D. $8 < n < 9$

    E. $n^2 > 100$

24.

The sum of which points on the number line above would be equal to zero?

    A. B, D, E, I

    B. C, D, G, H

    C. A, C, F, I

    D. D, E, F, G

    E. B, C, H, I

25. How many fourths are there in $\dfrac{5}{6}$?

    A. $\dfrac{5}{24}$

    B. $\dfrac{7}{12}$

    C. $1\dfrac{1}{2}$

    D. 2

    E. $3\dfrac{1}{3}$

END OF SECTION.
IF YOU HAVE ANY TIME LEFT, GO OVER YOUR WORK IN THIS SECTION ONLY.
DO NOT WORK IN ANY OTHER SECTION OF THE TEST.

Section 2: Reading

40 Questions—40 Minutes

Directions: Read each passage carefully. Then decide which of the possible responses is the best answer to each question. Mark the appropriate space on your answer sheet.

Questions 1–5 refer to the following passage.

In 1963, when anthropologists first came upon the archaeological site in Turkey now known as Göbekli Tepe, their initial analysis was that the limestone slabs jutting up from the ground were grave markers. Decades passed on the assumption that the site was little more than a cemetery abandoned sometime during the medieval period. Then, in 1994, a German archaeologist named Klaus Schmidt came upon the so-called cemetery and began looking closer on the suspicion that there might be more to it. To say that he was right is a <u>gargantuan</u> understatement.

What Schmidt ended up uncovering is Göbekli Tepe, an ancient gathering space, potentially religious in nature, and what is now widely considered to be the oldest human monument in the world. The discoveries researchers have made and continue to make at Göbekli Tepe, which is Turkish for "belly hill," are proof of the earliest stirrings of human civilization. The site is at least 11,000 years old, making it millennia older than some of the human monuments previously thought to be the oldest in the world, such as Stonehenge and the Great Pyramid of Giza.

The most astounding thing about the human-like stone figures and other carvings erected at Göbekli Tepe is that they predate the invention of pottery and metal tools, making it difficult to conceive how prehistoric humans were able to produce such a volume of artifacts with stone tools alone. Moreover, discoveries made at the site offer insights into how early hunter-gatherers may have first started settling more permanently around findable landmarks.

Because the dig site at Göbekli Tepe has revealed animal bones from wild species rather than domesticated animals, anthropologists have concrete evidence that the monument was likely the product of a collaboration between nomadic peoples. This assertion is supported by the labor required to create a monument of this size during the Neolithic era and the fact that no other evidence of plant or animal domestication could be found at the site. Schmidt proposes that the site could have been a sacred meeting space for far-flung nomadic tribes, likely meaning it would have been used for feasts and other gatherings. It is even possible that this very site was the first of its kind ever created.

1. As used in paragraph 1, the underlined word *gargantuan* most nearly means

   A. ridiculous.

   B. minor.

   C. major.

   D. tiny.

   E. enormous.

2. Klaus Schmidt's 1994 discovery about Göbekli Tepe was important to anthropologists because it

   A. demonstrated that Neolithic hunter-gatherers had been raising animals at the site.

   B. showed that Göbekli Tepe was the first monument ever created using metal tools.

   C. proved that Neolithic hunter-gatherers had already begun collaborating on monuments as early as 11,000 years ago.

   D. turned out to be a medieval cemetery, with lots to reveal about life during that period.

   E. contained animal bones from wild species that had never been seen before.

3. Based on the information in the passage, we know for sure that Göbekli Tepe is older than

   A. Lascaux Cave.

   B. the Palace of Knossos.

   C. Tell es-Sultan.

   D. Tell Qaramel.

   E. Stonehenge.

4. We can infer from the passage that

   A. if archaeologists discover a similar site that is even older than Göbekli Tepe, they will want to study it closely.

   B. if archaeologists discover a similar site that is even older than Göbekli Tepe, it will prove that Göbekli Tepe is older than they once thought.

   C. Göbekli Tepe is without a doubt the first monument ever created by Neolithic humans.

   D. Göbekli Tepe was never meant to be a religious gathering space.

   E. Neolithic hunter-gatherers never ended up settling in Turkey.

5. Which of the following words does *not* describe the author's tone in this passage?

   A. Informative

   B. Objective

   C. Subjective

   D. Detached

   E. Formal

Questions 6–10 refer to the following passage.

Most music today has some kind of electronic element. Whether it's pop, rock, hip-hop, techno, dance, country, or any other musical genre, electronic instrumentation using synthesizers and computers is an increasingly common feature of the musical soundscape. That's why it's such a surprise that so many people have never heard of the Grammy-winning electronic music pioneer Wendy Carlos, who is one of the most influential composers of the modern age.

One of the instruments that Carlos helped make famous was the Moog synthesizer. Back in 1968, she released an album called *Switched-On Bach* on which she translated the music of classical composer Johann Sebastian Bach for the Moog. Few people had used electronic sounds to compose music before that point, so hearing Bach in this new way made Carlos a sensation. Furthermore, the success of the album made the Moog synthesizer one of the <u>definitive</u> sounds of the 1970s, as everyone who's anyone started using it in their music. Later, producers like the Italo-disco legend Giorgio Moroder and the German band Kraftwerk would help popularize genres centered on the synthesizer sound, creating a ripple effect that still resonates today; everyone from Jay-Z to Coldplay has made modern songs directly influenced by these early electronic sounds. Many music historians would argue that without Wendy Carlos' influence, music might sound completely different today.

In the 1980s, Carlos went on to lend her signature electronic compositions to films like Stanley Kubrick's *The Shining* and Disney's *Tron*, and she has continued making electronic music well into the 21st century. In 2005, for her contributions to both electronic music and issues of social equality, Carlos was awarded a Lifetime Achievement Award by the Society for Electro-Acoustic Music in the United States.

6. As used in paragraph 2, the underlined term *definitive* most nearly means
   A. disappointing.
   B. quintessential.
   C. forgotten.
   D. mysterious.
   E. exciting.

7. Which is the best title for this passage?
   A. "Wendy Carlos: Electronic Music Icon"
   B. "The Rise of Disco Music"
   C. "Electronic Music in American Society"
   D. "The Power of the Moog"
   E. "What Is a Synthesizer?"

8. One place we can see Wendy Carlos' influence on music today is through the
   A. use of computer-based beats in rap and pop music.
   B. numerous music schools she founded.
   C. continued popularity of Johann Sebastian Bach.
   D. many bands she started.
   E. sound of synthesizers.

9. This passage is intended to
   A. persuade.
   B. inform.
   C. amuse.
   D. critique.
   E. analyze.

10. The first sentence of paragraph 2 notes that Wendy Carlos "translated the music of classical composer Johann Sebastian Bach for the Moog." An equivalent idea of translation would be a
    A. medical interpreter in the US translating what a doctor has said for a Japanese speaker.
    B. child figuring out what their grandparent really means by saying a certain old-fashioned proverb.
    C. friend saying "I'm fine" but actually being very angry.
    D. film using captions to show what someone speaking another language is saying.
    E. dance company creating a hip-hop dance version of a famous ballet.

Questions 11–14 refer to the following passage.

Astronomers around the world contributing to the Event Horizon Telescope (EHT) collaboration celebrated in May 2022 when they achieved the impressive feat of finally capturing an image of Sagittarius A* (Sgr A*), the supermassive black hole at the center of the Milky Way. While it may shock some to learn that there is a black hole so close to home, scientists have long suspected there was such an object in the center of our galaxy. They based these <u>suppositions</u> about Sgr A* (which is pronounced "sadge-ay-star") on their observation of gases and objects orbiting that spot at the center of the Milky Way.

A research team working for the EHT produced the image by creating a composite of observations taken using an entire network of radio telescopes positioned around the globe. Of course, given the nature of black holes, the image of Sgr A* isn't a picture of the black hole itself so much as a representation of all the light that bends around it. Think of the negative of a print photograph—by seeing how light moves around this massive object, you can see a representation of the object by way of the negative space the light's edges reveal. Thus, the image shows a bright ring around a supermassive object that astronomers can presume is indeed Sgr A*.

EHT is also known for another image of a black hole; namely, what is often called the first image of a black hole ever. The 2019 image shows M87*, a black hole in the Messier 87 galaxy. Though much further away than Sgr A*, M87* is a much steadier black hole to observe than Sgr A*, which is surrounded by rapidly moving gases that make it hard to create a clear image. According to EHT, at least 300 researchers representing more than 80 worldwide institutes collaborated to develop advanced new tools capable of accounting for the difficulties in detecting Sgr A*. Their achievement is a momentous illustration of the possibilities fostered by worldwide scientific collaboration and a monumental discovery about the nature of our home galaxy.

11. As used in paragraph 1, the underlined term *suppositions* most nearly describes

   A. guesses.
   B. non-sequiturs.
   C. realities.
   D. statements.
   E. facts.

12. A logical way for the passage to continue in a hypothetical paragraph 4 would be to

   A. discuss why Pluto is no longer considered a planet.
   B. explain which other celestial bodies exist in the Milky Way.
   C. discuss the process the EHT collaboration used to create the advanced new instruments they needed to make an image of Sgr A*.
   D. explain how the EHT was founded and why.
   E. offer a biography of the scientist who first theorized the existence of Sgr A*.

13. In which galaxy would you find the black hole known as M87*?

   A. Milky Way
   B. Messier Way
   C. Messier 87
   D. Sagittarius-A
   E. Event Horizon

14. Which of the following would *not* make a good title for the passage?

   A. "Collaboration in Science: The Story of Sgr A*"
   B. "The World's First Image of Sgr A*"
   C. "Capturing an Image of a Black Hole in the Milky Way"
   D. "The EHT's Collaboration to Capture Black Hole Images"
   E. "A History of Black Holes"

Questions 15–19 refer to the following passage.

Georg Wilhelm Friedrich Hegel (1770–1831) is one of the most prominent German philosophers of all time. Though his dense works are notorious for giving today's philosophy students headaches, his complex ideas were so revolutionary that they founded the basis of most modern philosophy, including serving as inspiration to prominent thinkers like Karl Marx, Søren Kierkegaard, and Michel Foucault. Hegel developed a way of thinking known as the dialectic, which involved investigating how contradictions between two seemingly true things, termed a "thesis" and "antithesis," can reveal an even higher level of truth. The process of thinking through both the contradiction between thesis and antithesis and its implications was known as the "Hegelian dialectic." Students of Hegelian philosophy embrace the idea that engaging in dialectical thinking helps advance world knowledge over time.

Hegel's most illustrative example of the dialectic involves the idea of power. The conceptual example is often termed the "master/slave dialectic," and it describes a dialectical thought process in which one imagines the power dynamic that would exist between an enslaved person and the person who enslaves them. Sometimes also referred to as the "Lordship and Bondage" dialectic, the concept is essentially that the two cannot exist without the other. To elaborate, let's call the "thesis" the idea that a person cannot be enslaved without another person forcing them to do so. No one would choose to be a slave, most likely, so they can only become one if someone else <u>exerts</u> power over them. Meanwhile, let's call the "antithesis" the idea that the person who forces another person to be their slave cannot feel that sense of power over another without a person to force into slavery. Their existence as "master" over a slave only happens so long as the slave exists. Therefore, the power of one does not exist without the antithetical power of the other. This master/slave dialectic is thus meant to reveal a greater truth about the nature of power.

15. The purpose of paragraph 1 is to

   A. explain the master/slave dialectic.

   B. introduce Hegel and the concept of dialectical thinking.

   C. criticize Michel Foucault and other philosophers who followed Hegel.

   D. give a background on Hegel's early years.

   E. provide a history of Enlightenment era philosophy.

16. As used in paragraph 2, the underlined term *exerts* most nearly means

   A. creates.

   B. eliminates.

   C. hides.

   D. gathers.

   E. expends.

17. Based on the passage, we can infer that

   A. no one read Hegel anymore after the 19th century.

   B. a thesis and an antithesis are important to philosophy.

   C. power dynamics, such as those between master and slave, do not contain contradictions.

   D. Karl Marx used dialectical thinking when developing his philosophical writings.

   E. people find Hegel to be a very approachable philosopher to read.

18. What does the author mean by saying Hegel's works "[give] today's philosophy students headaches" in paragraph 1?

   A. Hegel's books are heavy and hard to carry.

   B. Hegel is notorious for being difficult to read and understand.

   C. Hegel can only be read in old tomes written in a tiny, old-fashioned font.

   D. People find Hegel exceptionally boring and aren't interested in him.

   E. People find Hegel's ideas morally offensive.

19. How might you characterize the primary contradiction of the master/slave dialectic?

   A. Power can be both given and taken away.

   B. No one wants to be the boss, but someone has to be.

   C. No one wants to be a slave, yet some people are enslaved.

   D. Power is also weakness.

   E. Neither the slave nor the master can exist without the other.

Questions 20–23 refer to the following passage.

Australia is known for its biodiversity, including a wide array of marsupials. While kangaroos, wallabies, and koalas are familiar to most people, there are other marsupials, like the Tasmanian devil, the wallaroo, and the bandicoot, that tend to be less understood outside of the land down under. One example of a lesser-known marsupial is the quokka. Sometimes called the "happiest animal in the world" due to its almost teddy bear-like appearance, these friendly, small, native Australian marsupials have round, <u>stout</u> bodies. They usually grow to be about 16–21 in. (40–54 cm) long and have coarse, brownish-grey fur.

A quokka's most charming feature is its face; with round ears and a habit of looking like they're grinning from ear-to-ear, quokkas always seem happy to make your acquaintance. This appearance is matched by a tendency to trust and be curious about humans—a tendency that has conservationists exerting great effort to remind tourists that it's still best not to feed or interact too closely with these wild animals! Nonetheless, visitors to quokka habitats like Rottnest Island, home of the largest quokka population in Australia due to its lack of predators, have been known to pose for pictures with the smiling animals.

Unfortunately, quokkas are considered a vulnerable species. For one, deforestation from commercial development and logging has contributed to slowly declining quokka populations. Climate change, urbanization, and other environmental factors have displaced many animals from their own traditional habitats, meaning that new predators, like foxes, have moved into areas where quokkas used to safely roam. Attacks from domestic animals like dogs and cats also pose a threat to quokkas, as do humans, who will sometimes cruelly (and illegally) hunt them for sport. Habitat loss from natural events like wildfires also threatens quokkas and will continue to do so as the climate changes.

To support the development of a more robust quokka population in the future, conservationists are taking numerous measures, including using baiting techniques to curtail introduced predator populations, pushing for environmental protection measures, and monitoring existing quokka populations for changes.

20. As used in paragraph 1, the underlined term *stout* most nearly means

    A. plump.

    B. thin.

    C. agile.

    D. stiff.

    E. angular.

21. Which of the following is *not* identified as a marsupial in the passage?

    A. Tasmanian Devil

    B. Koala

    C. Wallaby

    D. Fox

    E. Bandicoot

22. It is hard to get tourists to stop taking pictures with quokkas on Rottnest Island because

    A. quokkas are friendly and curious about humans, so they willingly approach tourists.

    B. quokkas are so rarely seen that people risk it to get a photo.

    C. a social media challenge to take a selfie with a quokka popularized the practice.

    D. there are too many tourists on Rottnest Island for authorities to keep them away.

    E. tourists to Rottnest Island are mostly there to hunt quokkas.

23. The main purpose of this passage is to

    A. inform the reader about what quokkas are, how they're threatened, and what sort of conservation efforts are being made to support them.

    B. discuss why quokkas are considered the happiest marsupial on the planet.

    C. examine why people don't pay as much attention to quokkas as koalas.

    D. determine why tourists are particularly interested in visiting Rottnest Island.

    E. persuade the reader that quokkas are the most interesting marsupial in Australia.

Questions 24–27 refer to the following passage.

All over the world, people gather for festivals to celebrate events, mark holidays, create community, and engage in shared cultural traditions. The tendency toward festival-style gathering is common across human cultures, meaning that the world is full of beautiful festival traditions. However, cultures vary, so just as there are certain types of celebrations that appear over and over, like weddings and harvest festivals, there are others that are truly <u>singular</u>.

One such singular festival is the Nakizumo Baby Crying Festival, an annual event that takes place in Tokyo, Japan. Translated into English, *Nakizumo* means "Naki Sumo," which is a hint as to what occurs at this unorthodox event. Namely, two sumo wrestlers enter a ring, each carrying a baby. The objective is to be the first sumo wrestler to get your opponent's baby to cry while also soothing your own baby to keep them from crying. Contests like this go on throughout the festival's events.

While this may seem a bit wacky from an outsider perspective, the event is steeped in a nearly 400-year-old tradition. Specifically, the festival is linked with the long-held Japanese belief that getting a baby to have a hard cry will help ensure they stay healthy. One related saying, "Naku-ko wa sodatsu," translates to "the child who cries grows up," meaning that the Japanese see crying as essential for childhood development. There are also some regions of Japan that share further beliefs about crying babies, such as the idea that the sound of a baby's cry can ward off evil spirits.

You might think that it's easy enough to get a baby to cry during this festival, but it can actually be quite tough when the festival atmosphere is laidback and celebratory. Babies tend to pick up on the energy around them, so they aren't always fast to cry when everyone around them is having fun. When this happens, the sumo wrestlers must resort to other measures to bring on the waterworks, such as startling the babies with loud sounds, donning scary costumes and masks, and contorting their faces into grimaces. It's a battle of the tears, and whoever makes a baby cry first (or loudest, if both babies start at once) wins!

24. As used in paragraph 1, the underlined term *singular* most nearly means

   A. lonely.

   B. common.

   C. unique.

   D. unremarkable.

   E. mysterious.

25. The festival described in the passage is based primarily on a centuries-old belief that

   A. babies are afraid of sumo wrestlers.

   B. sumo wrestlers aren't good at handling babies.

   C. babies need to cry to grow up healthy.

   D. babies need to cry for their parents to have good luck.

   E. to scare off evil spirits, it's good to get a baby to cry.

26. The purpose of paragraph 4 is to

   A. describe the folkloric beliefs behind the Nakizumo Baby Crying Festival.

   B. introduce the concept of cultural festivals generally.

   C. explain how the Nakizumo Baby Crying Festival got its name.

   D. illustrate what sumo wrestlers do when neither baby will cry.

   E. estimate the economic impact of the festival on the surrounding region.

27. The phrase "bring on the waterworks" as used in paragraph 4 most likely refers to

   A. getting a baby to start crying.

   B. getting a sumo wrestler to start crying.

   C. dumping a bucket of water on a baby.

   D. dumping a bucket of water on a sumo wrestler.

   E. getting the crowd to pretend to cry.

Questions 28–32 refer to the following passage.

Over the course of the 20th century, the American suburb evolved from do-it-yourself homes on plots of land at the end of urban rail lines to the most dominant form of prefabricated housing development in the United States. In their current form, American suburbs are modeled on what Harvard professor Dolores Hayden has termed "sitcom suburbs." Emerging in the period immediately following WWII, Hayden suggests that most of today's suburban housing development is fashioned on the early suburbs that became a shared visual idea of "suburbia" for Americans through their reflection in the sitcoms of early television.

One of the most influential developers during this period was William J. Levitt. His company, Levitt & Sons, built a suburban housing development called Levittown outside New York City between 1947 and 1951. They pioneered a prefabrication model for quickly and efficiently constructing identical houses on similar sized lots, allowing them to sell for low prices. Once this model proved successful, they created additional Levittowns across the country and other developers began mimicking their model. Levittown solidified the <u>distinctive</u> look associated with suburbia today: individual homes in a row of individual lots with grass-filled front yards, a space to park your car, and if you're lucky, a white picket fence.

However, the fences weren't the only things white about the sitcom suburbs. The Levittown housing covenants explicitly forbade people of color, Jews, and single women from buying homes. Once an African American family did eventually move into a Levittown in Pennsylvania in the 1950s, they were harassed and threatened to the point where Martin Luther King, Jr. got involved to advocate on their behalf. On top of that, the National Housing Act of 1934 had made it standard practice to follow the then newly created Federal Housing Administration's (FHA) guidelines for issuing mortgage loans, which were in turn informed by the FHA's racially biased practice of redlining.

Redlining was a formalized process to help banks make determinations about mortgage applications. From 1934 onward, maps were created to divide every major city in the US into sections based on a neighborhood's suitability for housing. Under redlining, neighborhoods with large communities of color were drawn in "red," deeming them least desirable. People consequently couldn't get favorable mortgages for homes in redlined areas, yet they were the only areas with racial covenants that allowed certain populations (mainly people of color) to live there. White families were thus free to take part in expanding suburbanization in any neighborhood they wished, while families of color were largely left out and forced to remain in their redlined neighborhoods, where it remained difficult for them to get favorable mortgages. Therefore, understanding how redlining contributed to housing segregation along racial lines is critical for understanding the generational wealth gaps that are a tangible measure of racial inequality today.

28. With which of the statements below would the author of this passage likely agree?

    A. There were no real negative side effects of redlining.

    B. William J. Levitt had little influence over the suburbanization of the US.

    C. Mortgage lending is generally a neutral process free from discrimination.

    D. Families of color did not often experience the effects of redlining.

    E. Redlining made it much harder for families of color to move to the suburbs than it was for white families.

29. Dolores Hayden termed mid-20th century suburban development in the US "sitcom suburbs" because

    A. she had seen this style of suburban development in a sitcom.

    B. early sitcoms reinforced the appearance of Levittown-style developments as ideal.

    C. suburbs had appeared on television shows before they ever appeared in real life.

    D. the word "sitcom" describes prefabricated housing developments.

    E. sitcoms were used to advertise housing developments.

30. The author's tone in this passage can best be described as

    A. belligerent.

    B. farcical.

    C. sentimental.

    D. analytical.

    E. resigned.

31. If a neighborhood was "redlined," what did this mean?

    A. Banks considered the neighborhood a more desirable place to issue mortgages.

    B. Banks issued more mortgages to that neighborhood than any other.

    C. Banks considered the neighborhood a less desirable place to issue mortgages.

    D. No housing developments were allowed in these neighborhoods.

    E. Only white families were allowed to get mortgages in these neighborhoods.

32. Which of the following brief quotations shows the author appealing to credibility?

    A. "In their current form, American suburbs evolved from what Harvard professor Dolores Hayden has termed 'sitcom suburbs.'"

    B. "One of the most influential developers during this period was William J. Levitt."

    C. "Once this model proved successful, they created additional Levittowns across the country and other developers began mimicking their model."

    D. "The Levittown housing covenants explicitly forbade people of color, Jews, and single women from buying homes."

    E. "From 1934 onward, maps were created to divide every major city in the US into sections based on a neighborhood's suitability for housing."

Questions 33–36 refer to the following passage.

And the priestess spoke again and said: Speak to us of **Reason and Passion**.

And he answered, saying:

Your soul is oftentimes a battlefield, upon which your reason and your judgment wage war against your passion and your appetite.

Would that I could be the peacemaker in your soul, that I might turn the <u>discord</u> and the rivalry of your elements into oneness and melody.

But how shall I, unless you yourselves be also the peacemakers, nay, the lovers of all your elements?

Your reason and your passion are the rudder and the sails of your seafaring soul.

If either your sails or your rudder be broken, you can but toss and drift, or else be held at a standstill in mid-seas. For reason, ruling alone, is a force confining; and passion, unattended, is a flame that burns to its own destruction.

Therefore let your soul exalt your reason to the height of passion, that it may sing;

And let it direct your passion with reason, that your passion may live through its own daily resurrection, and like the phoenix rise above its own ashes.

I would have you consider your judgment and your appetite even as you would two loved guests in your house.

Surely you would not honour one guest above the other; for he who is more mindful of one loses the love and the faith of both.

Excerpt from "The Prophet" by Kahlil Gibran (1923)

33. As used in the passage, the underlined term *discord* most nearly means

A. agreement.
B. disagreement.
C. harmony.
D. melody.
E. trepidation.

34. By calling reason and passion "the rudder and the sails of your seafaring soul," the author means that

A. no one should pay attention to their passions, only their reason.
B. no one knows how to master their reason and passion.
C. reason and passion are two different mechanisms for guiding your choices and they work best separately.
D. reason and passion are two different mechanisms for guiding your choices and they work best together.
E. reason and passion will pull you in two different directions.

35. Of the following quotations from the passage, which is *not* an example of figurative language?

    A. "Your soul is oftentimes a battlefield. . ."

    B. ". . . your reason and your judgment wage war against your passion and your appetite."

    C. ". . . passion, unattended, is a flame that burns to its own destruction."

    D. ". . . and like the phoenix rise above its own ashes."

    E. "For he who is more mindful of one loses the love and the faith of both."

36. We can infer from the passage that

    A. the "Prophet" named in the title of the work excerpted is the unnamed figure to whom the priestess speaks.

    B. the priestess is not interested in learning about reason and passion.

    C. this work is intended for children.

    D. this work is intended for religious ceremonies.

    E. passion is more vital to human life than reason.

Questions 37–40 refer to the following passage.

On 6 June 1822, French Canadian fur trade voyageur Alexis St. Martin was accidentally shot in the stomach at an American Fur Company store on Michigan's Mackinac Island. The blast left a gaping wound in St. Martin's abdomen. St. Martin eventually recovered from the gruesome accident, but the wound never closed completely, leaving a small permanent opening in his stomach wall. His surgeon, William Beaumont, began monitoring gastric secretions through this opening in St. Martin's body. Beaumont, who would later become known as the father of gastric physiology, would attach various types of food to a string and suspend them through the hole. Later he would pull out the string to see what portion of the food had been digested. During these experiments, Beaumont noticed that St. Martin's mood seemed to affect how quickly he digested food. When St. Martin was irritable, for instance, food broke down more slowly.

These early observations provided the first clues of crosstalk between the brain and the gut. Researchers later called this communication system the gut–brain axis. Over the years, studies have revealed that the brain influences the gastrointestinal (GI) tract through several mechanisms. Yet, only recently have scientists recognized the importance of a third component to the gut–brain axis: the trillions of bacteria, viruses, archaea, and eukaryotes that make up the gut microbiome. In little more than a decade, researchers have uncovered compelling associations between gut bacteria and a host of neurological disorders and psychiatric conditions. These include depression, anxiety, autism spectrum disorders (ASDs), and Parkinson's disease.

Most of the early research on the microbiome–gut–brain axis has been conducted in rodents. Germ-free mice—which are born in sterile conditions and free of all microorganisms—are popular for gut flora research because scientists can inoculate the mice with specific microbes and watch what happens. Experiments with germ-free mice have yielded intriguing clues about the possible influence of the gut microbiome on behavior and neurodevelopment. However, it is still unclear whether these findings are relevant to humans. Now, additional researchers are beginning to probe the connection in humans. Outside neuroscience, gut microbiome research in laboratory animals and humans is changing the way some environmental health scientists view the effects of environmental exposures on neurodevelopment and brain chemistry. From the moment of birth—and possibly even earlier—our microbiomes begin to develop. There is evidence that a healthy gut microbiome is important for brain development.

37. The passage indicates that the reason germ-free mice are desirable for gut-microbiome experiments is because

   A. scientists can isolate different microbes and test what effects they have.

   B. mice microbiomes have a lot in common with human microbiomes.

   C. it's ethically questionable to experiment on humans.

   D. they share a lot of DNA with humans and can provide clues to our microbiomes.

   E. their microbiomes respond to inputs in the same way.

38. Based on the passage, which of the following statements most accurately captures the relevance of rodent gut-microbiome experiments to humans?

   A. Rodent gut-microbiome experiments can provide clues, but scientists are still not certain how the results will apply to human health.

   B. Rodent gut-microbiome experiments can mimic the human microbiome with a high degree of accuracy.

   C. Experiments on germ-free mice artificially introduce microbes into the gut and are therefore not relevant to humans, who naturally host microbes.

   D. Findings from gut-microbiome experiments on rodents are not applicable to humans because of their vastly different brain size.

   E. It is impossible for rodent gut-microbiome experiments to yield results that would be relevant to human DNA.

39. The passage mentions all the following components of the gut microbiome EXCEPT:

   A. Viruses

   B. Bacteria

   C. Algae

   D. Archaea

   E. Eukaryotes

40. The author's main purpose in providing the anecdote about Alexis St. Martin in the first paragraph is to

   A. show the history of microbiome experiments before discussing the present day.

   B. create a sense of drama that highlights the importance of the topic.

   C. cause the reader to feel pity for St. Martin, to make them care more about the topic.

   D. demonstrate the ethical issues that surround the microbiome experiments.

   E. amuse the reader with the story of an interesting person.

SSAT (UPPER LEVEL) DIAGNOSTIC TEST

END OF SECTION.
IF YOU HAVE ANY TIME LEFT, GO OVER YOUR WORK IN THIS SECTION ONLY.
DO NOT WORK IN ANY OTHER SECTION OF THE TEST.

Section 3: Verbal

60 Questions—30 Minutes

Directions: Each question shows a word in CAPITAL letters followed by five words or phrases. Choose the word or phrase with the meaning most similar to that of the word in CAPITAL letters. Mark the appropriate space on your answer sheet.

1. DETER
    A. halt
    B. steer
    C. sting
    D. turn
    E. discourage

2. HOSTILE
    A. friendly
    B. unfriendly
    C. suspicious
    D. indifferent
    E. doubtful

3. UTILIZE
    A. make use of
    B. utilities
    C. modernize
    D. sing
    E. undo

4. ABDICATE
    A. resign
    B. explain
    C. remorse
    D. disprove
    E. control

5. PROMINENT
    A. disturbing
    B. secret
    C. outstanding
    D. extravagant
    E. surreptitious

6. BOUNDARY
    A. hovel
    B. limit
    C. opening
    D. map
    E. seam

7. ILLITERATE
    A. unable to vote
    B. unmanageable
    C. sickly
    D. unable to read
    E. unclean

8. ORATOR
    A. professor
    B. poet
    C. speaker
    D. ear
    E. student

9. CORROBORATE

   A. confirm

   B. understand

   C. cooperate

   D. agree

   E. disagree

10. RATIFY

   A. delete

   B. consider

   C. approve

   D. examine

   E. assess

11. PERILOUS

   A. careless

   B. conniving

   C. irregular

   D. estranged

   E. hazardous

12. STATIONARY

   A. paper

   B. moving

   C. immobile

   D. position

   E. mobile

13. TRANSCRIBE

   A. copy

   B. illustrate

   C. circulate

   D. request

   E. author

14. PROFICIENT

   A. well-known

   B. professional

   C. adept

   D. practice

   E. prolific

15. DECEIVE

   A. rearrange

   B. mislead

   C. pretend

   D. stun

   E. examine

16. AGILE

   A. strong

   B. similar

   C. anxious

   D. rested

   E. nimble

17. DURATION

   A. area

   B. temptation

   C. term

   D. wait

   E. former

18. AMBIGUOUS

   A. unclear

   B. adhere

   C. aspire

   D. afflict

   E. certain

19. PREROGATIVE

    A. command
    B. choice
    C. prerequisite
    D. conviction
    E. haggard

20. INTRIGUING

    A. business
    B. furtive
    C. mystery
    D. fascinating
    E. boorish

21. CLANDESTINE

    A. overt
    B. dated
    C. exclusive
    D. fortunate
    E. secret

22. BOUNTEOUS

    A. elastic
    B. industrious
    C. abundant
    D. mutinous
    E. energetic

23. DIVERGE

    A. annoy
    B. change course
    C. stay
    D. analyze
    E. distract

24. BENIGN

    A. gentle
    B. blessed
    C. initial
    D. virulent
    E. malignant

25. CAUCUS

    A. dispersal
    B. corpse
    C. meeting
    D. partnership
    E. cosmetic

26. DISSEMINATE

    A. collate
    B. strip
    C. collect
    D. disagree
    E. spread

27. CHAGRIN

    A. delight
    B. alter
    C. embarrass
    D. wreck
    E. anger

28. VALOR

    A. courage
    B. disclosure
    C. treason
    D. hate
    E. foreboding

29. NONCHALANT

A. interested

B. caring

C. impoverished

D. indifferent

E. persecuted

30. LIAISON

A. permission

B. laziness

C. scarf

D. remedy

E. association

Directions: The following questions ask you to find relationships between words. Read each question, then choose the answer that best completes the meaning of the sentence. Mark the appropriate space on your answer sheet.

---

31. Beg is to borrow as offer is to

A. lender.

B. bank.

C. lend.

D. repay.

E. security.

32. Lazy is to inert as resist is to

A. refuse.

B. reply.

C. respond.

D. active.

E. insist.

33. Cylinder is to circle as pyramid is to

A. sphere.

B. point.

C. triangle.

D. angle.

E. height.

34. Crocodile is to reptile as kangaroo is to

A. amphibian.

B. marsupial.

C. opossum.

D. canine.

E. tail.

35. Milliliter is to quart as

A. pound is to gram.

B. millimeter is to yard.

C. inch is to yard.

D. pint is to quart.

E. foot is to yard.

36. Destroy is to demolish as

A. win is to lose.

B. candid is to secret.

C. amend is to change.

D. establish is to abolish.

E. attempt is to succeed.

37. Plaintiff is to defendant as

A. plain is to ordinary.

B. lawyer is to courtroom.

C. professor is to college.

D. complain is to complainant.

E. prosecute is to defend.

38. Fundamental is to frivolous as

A. fantasy is to fiction.

B. nonfiction is to fact.

C. regulation is to rule.

D. truth is to nonsense.

E. strange is to common.

39. Wild is to wolf as domestic is to

    A. dog.

    B. coyote.

    C. pet.

    D. cat.

    E. animal.

40. Hammer is to carpenter as

    A. awl is to cobbler.

    B. computer is to printer.

    C. saw is to timber.

    D. author is to typewriter.

    E. scale is to musician.

41. Subject is to predicate as senator is to

    A. congress.

    B. president.

    C. capitol.

    D. representative.

    E. senate.

42. Pungent is to odor as

    A. intense is to emotion.

    B. pervade is to atmosphere.

    C. infect is to spread.

    D. proverb is to paragraph.

    E. resent is to denial.

43. Exploit is to adventure as

    A. rule is to governor.

    B. safari is to expedition.

    C. school is to field trip.

    D. attack is to hunt.

    E. chase is to escape.

44. Spread is to scatter as separate is to

    A. integrate.

    B. distribute.

    C. reap.

    D. group.

    E. displace.

45. Exuberant is to mood as adroit is to

    A. proficient.

    B. adept.

    C. hand.

    D. dexterous.

    E. movement.

46. Defiance is to opposition as exertion is to

    A. expert.

    B. vigor.

    C. endeavor.

    D. restraint.

    E. challenge.

47. Food is to nutrition as light is to

    A. watt.

    B. bulb.

    C. electricity.

    D. reading.

    E. vision.

48. Perpetuity is to impermanence as interminable is to

    A. impertinent.

    B. brief.

    C. incessant.

    D. eternal.

    E. occasional.

49. Erratic is to predictable as exorbitant is to

    A. reasonable.

    B. productive.

    C. absorbent.

    D. small.

    E. implicit.

50. Comment is to speech as

    A. question is to answer.

    B. exclamation is to statement.

    C. written is to spoken.

    D. prose is to essay.

    E. note is to letter.

51. Flammable is to inflammable as

    A. persistent is to important.

    B. opportune is to inopportune.

    C. relevant is to incoherent.

    D. truculent is to intrusion.

    E. impartial is to disinterested.

52. Tailor is to pattern as builder is to

    A. architect.

    B. contractor.

    C. foundation.

    D. construct.

    E. blueprint.

53. Impeach is to dismiss as

    A. arraign is to indict.

    B. accuse is to charge.

    C. imprison is to jail.

    D. plant is to sow.

    E. absent is to present.

54. Speedy is to greyhound as

    A. wool is to lamb.

    B. shark is to voracious.

    C. clever is to fox.

    D. mammal is to whale.

    E. fin is to fish.

55. Exhale is to lung as

    A. exhume is to corpse.

    B. pump is to heart.

    C. think is to brain.

    D. perspire is to skin.

    E. taste is to tongue.

56. Celebrate is to birth as

    A. grieve is to death.

    B. announce is to birthday.

    C. crime is to penalty.

    D. joy is to lament.

    E. party is to graduation.

57. Recommend is to urge as

    A. request is to plead.

    B. refuse is to deny.

    C. harass is to bother.

    D. cajole is to insult.

    E. apply is to receive.

58. Weeping is to tears as breathing is to

    A. air.

    B. lungs.

    C. nose.

    D. mouth.

    E. carbon dioxide.

59. Plane is to air pocket as

   A. vehicle is to rut.

   B. hangar is to airport.

   C. ground is to sky.

   D. safety is to danger.

   E. horse is to reins.

60. Arbitrate is to dispute as

   A. solve is to mystery.

   B. regard is to problem.

   C. exacerbate is to problem.

   D. organize is to labor.

   E. management is to union.

END OF SECTION.
IF YOU HAVE ANY TIME LEFT, GO OVER YOUR WORK IN THIS SECTION ONLY.
DO NOT WORK IN ANY OTHER SECTION OF THE TEST.

Section 4: Quantitative (Math)

25 Questions—30 Minutes

> **Directions:** Each question below is followed by five possible answers. Select the one that is best and mark the appropriate letter on your answer sheet

1. In 2 hours, the minute hand of a clock rotates through an angle of

    A. 60°.

    B. 90°.

    C. 180°.

    D. 360°.

    E. 720°.

2. Which of the following fractions is less than one third?

    A. $\dfrac{22}{63}$

    B. $\dfrac{4}{11}$

    C. $\dfrac{15}{46}$

    D. $\dfrac{33}{98}$

    E. $\dfrac{102}{303}$

3.

    The length of each side of the square above is $\dfrac{2x}{3} + 1$. What is the perimeter of the square?

    A. $\dfrac{8x}{3} + 4$

    B. $\dfrac{8x + 4}{3}$

    C. $\dfrac{2x}{3} + 4$

    D. $\dfrac{2x}{3} + 16$

    E. $\dfrac{4x}{3} + 2$

4. *The diagram shows a cube.*

    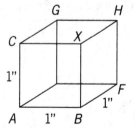

    The distance from A to X is

    A. 2 inches.

    B. $\sqrt{3}$ inches.

    C. $\sqrt{2}$ inches.

    D. 1 inch.

    E. $\dfrac{1}{\sqrt{2}}$ inches.

5. A motorist travels 120 miles to their destination at an average speed of 60 miles per hour and returns to the starting point at an average speed of 40 miles per hour. What is the average speed for their entire trip?

   A. 53 miles per hour

   B. 52 miles per hour

   C. 50 miles per hour

   D. 48 miles per hour

   E. 45 miles per hour

6. A snapshot measures $2\frac{1}{2}$ inches by $1\frac{7}{8}$ inches. It is to be enlarged so that the longer dimension will be 4 inches. The length of the enlarged shorter dimension will be

   A. $2\frac{1}{2}$ inches.

   B. $2\frac{5}{8}$ inches.

   C. 3 inches.

   D. $3\frac{3}{8}$ inches.

   E. $3\frac{5}{8}$ inches.

7. The largest circle possible is cut out of a piece of tin in the shape of a square 6 inches on a side. Which of the following is closest in value to the ratio of the area of the circle to the area of the original square?

   A. $\frac{4}{5}$

   B. $\frac{2}{3}$

   C. $\frac{3}{5}$

   D. $\frac{7}{9}$

   E. $\frac{1}{4}$

8. If the outer diameter of a metal pipe is 2.84 in. and the inner diameter is 1.94 in., what is the thickness of the metal?

   A. 0.45 in.

   B. 0.90 in.

   C. 1.42 in.

   D. 1.94 in.

   E. 2.39 in.

9. A sportswriter, Twyla, claims that her football predictions are accurate 60% of the time. During football season, a fan kept records and found that Twyla was inaccurate for a total of 16 games, although she did maintain her 60% accuracy. For how many games was Twyla accurate?

   A. 5

   B. 15

   C. 24

   D. 40

   E. 60

10. In a certain boys' camp, 30% of the boys are from New York State and 20% of these are from New York City. What percent of the boys in the camp are from New York City?

   A. 60%

   B. 50%

   C. 33%

   D. 10%

   E. 6%

11.

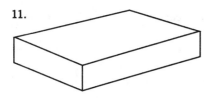

A unit block for construction is 1 × 2 × 3 inches. What is the number of whole blocks required to cover an area 1 foot long by $1\frac{1}{4}$ feet wide with *one layer* of blocks?

A. 30 blocks

B. 60 blocks

C. 72 blocks

D. 90 blocks

E. 180 blocks

12. If the number of square inches in the area of a circle is equal to the number of inches in its circumference, the diameter of the circle is

A. 4 inches.

B. 2 inches.

C. 1 inch.

D. π inches.

E. 2π inches.

13. The least common multiple of 20, 24, and 32 is

A. 240

B. 480

C. 960

D. 1,920

E. 15,360

14. If $9x + 5 = 23$, the numerical value of $18x + 5$ is

A. 46

B. 41

C. 38

D. 36

E. 32

15. When the fractions $\frac{2}{3}, \frac{5}{7}, \frac{8}{11}$, and $\frac{9}{13}$ are arranged in ascending order of size, the result is

A. $\frac{8}{11}, \frac{5}{7}, \frac{9}{13}, \frac{2}{3}$.

B. $\frac{5}{7}, \frac{8}{11}, \frac{2}{3}, \frac{9}{13}$.

C. $\frac{2}{3}, \frac{8}{11}, \frac{5}{7}, \frac{9}{13}$.

D. $\frac{2}{3}, \frac{9}{13}, \frac{5}{7}, \frac{8}{11}$.

E. $\frac{9}{13}, \frac{2}{3}, \frac{8}{11}, \frac{5}{7}$.

16. If a cubic inch of a metal weighs 2 pounds, a cubic foot of the same metal weighs

A. 8 pounds.

B. 24 pounds.

C. 96 pounds.

D. 288 pounds.

E. 3,456 pounds.

17. A micromillimeter is defined as one millionth of a millimeter. A length of 17 micromillimeters may be represented as

A. 0.00017 mm

B. 0.000017 mm

C. 0.0000017 mm

D. 0.00000017 mm

E. 0.000000017 mm

18. To find the radius of a circle with a circumference of 60 inches,

A. multiply 60 by π.

B. divide 60 by 2π.

C. divide 30 by 2π.

D. divide 60 by π and extract the square root of the result.

E. multiply 60 by $\frac{\pi}{2}$.

19. A carpenter needs four boards, each 2 feet 9 inches long. If wood is sold only by the foot, how many feet must he buy?

    A. 9

    B. 10

    C. 11

    D. 12

    E. 13

20. The approximate distance in feet, S, that an object falls in t seconds when dropped from a height can be found by using the formula $S = 16t^2$. In 8 seconds, the object will fall

    A. 256 feet.

    B. 1,024 feet.

    C. 1,084 feet.

    D. 2,048 feet.

    E. 15,384 feet.

QUESTIONS 21 AND 22 REFER TO THE FOLLOWING GRAPH.

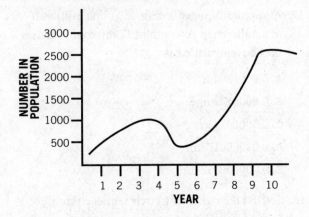

21. During which years did the population increase at the fastest rate?

    A. Years 1–3

    B. Years 4–5

    C. Years 5–7

    D. Years 7–9

    E. Years 9–10

22. During which year did the size of the population decrease the most?

    A. Years 1–3

    B. Years 4–5

    C. Years 5–7

    D. Years 7–9

    E. Years 9–10

23. The number of landline telephones in Adelaide, Australia, is 48,000. If this represents 12.8 telephones per 100 people, the population of Adelaide to the nearest thousand is

    A. 128,000

    B. 375,000

    C. 378,000

    D. 556,000

    E. 575,000

24. One person can load a truck in 25 minutes, a second can load it in 50 minutes, and a third can load it in 10 minutes. How long would it take the three together to load the truck?

    A. $5 \dfrac{3}{11}$ minutes

    B. $6 \dfrac{1}{4}$ minutes

    C. $8 \dfrac{1}{3}$ minutes

    D. 10 minutes

    E. $28 \dfrac{1}{3}$ minutes

25. Event A occurs every 4 minutes, event B every 6 minutes, and event C every 15 minutes. If they occur simultaneously at noon, when is the next time all three events will occur together again?

    A. 1 p.m.

    B. 1:30 p.m.

    C. 3 p.m.

    D. 6 p.m.

    E. 12 a.m.

END OF SECTION.
IF YOU HAVE ANY TIME LEFT, GO OVER YOUR WORK IN THIS SECTION ONLY.
DO NOT WORK IN ANY OTHER SECTION OF THE TEST.

ANSWER KEYS AND EXPLANATIONS

Part I: Writing Sample

Here is an example of a well-written response to each prompt.

PROMPT 1

The proposal to raise the minimum licensing age from 16 to 18 should be rejected for a number of reasons. There are no solid statistics proving that teenage drivers are the primary cause of the accidents that they are involved in, so the 16- and 17-year-old age group should not automatically be penalized for those accidents. Furthermore, for many young people, use of a car is an absolute necessity, so punishing teen drivers by taking away their privileges will cause more problems than it solves.

Legislators should ask themselves why 16- to 18-year-old drivers tend to be involved in accidents. I think that the main cause of these accidents is lack of experience. If a study were made, I suspect that it would show that new drivers of any age tend to have accidents. Raising the licensing age would only raise the age of drivers involved in accidents, not prevent the possibility of newer drivers getting in more accidents. A better cure might be driving education programs that stress judgment on the road and a requirement for a longer period of driving under supervision before licensing. That way, new drivers of any age would be better prepared for the demands of the road once driving.

Raising the driving age would also create a real financial hardship for some teenagers and their families. Working parents sometimes have to rely on their teens to use the car to accomplish household tasks, such as picking up groceries, running errands, or transporting younger siblings to and from school. Other teens have part-time jobs in locations that can be reached only by car or which require use of their car, such as delivering pizzas. Still others need their cars to be able to participate in sports and activities—if they didn't have a way to transport themselves to and from practice, they would likely have to drop out of the activities that mean so much to them.

Attempting to solve the accident problem by age-restricting licenses more than they are doesn't actually solve the problem. In fact, in some ways, it could even worsen it. People who need to drive will likely do so anyway, including teenagers. Doing so without benefit of driver education or the testing that is required for getting that license would be far less safe than having programs to teach teens to drive safely. Therefore, the 16-year minimum should be retained, though it would be fair to insist all new drivers get more training.

PROMPT 2

A peaceful and eerie silence hung in the air. Luz and I had never once been in a fight this big, but it had been two days and she still wasn't speaking to me. You could cut the tension in our shared bedroom with a knife. I looked over at Luz lying on her belly on the bed, reading a mystery novel like she always was. Every time she turned the page, it was like she was trying to make the paper sound angry.

"Are we ever going to talk about what happened?!" I finally blurted out, causing Luz to jump a little from being startled. She slowly took off her reading glasses, placed them gently on the bedside table, and turned to face me.

"Well, Marta, what do you want to talk about?" Her lips were pursed into a thin line and her grey eyes half-squinted at me. It was clear she wasn't going to make things easy.

"Look, I shouldn't have ruined your sleepover by getting into an argument with you in front of your friends. That was your party and I made it all about me. I'm sorry." Luz's eyes began to soften, so I thought it safe to press my luck. "At the same time, you shouldn't have told dad my big secret." In an instant, Luz's cheeks were red with anger again.

"You shouldn't have asked me to keep a secret that big!" She was referring, of course, to my plan to move out without telling dad. Living with him was becoming unbearable since mom died, so I thought I had a better chance of being happy if I lived with our aunt. At least, then I wouldn't be reminded of mom all the time. Dad didn't know and I didn't want him to find out until I got to Aunt Lucia's and convinced her to let me stay. Lost in thought about my plan, I barely noticed that Luz had started crying.

"This isn't about the sleepover, is it?" I asked, gently, watching my sister push a tear away from her cheek.

"You're not the only one who misses mom, you know," Marta responded, the sound of a lump in her throat still obvious. "But what am I supposed to do if you leave? We're sisters. Sisters are supposed to stick it out together."

With that, she threw an arm around me and wrapped me into a hug so tight that I thought she was going to put me in a sleeper hold. To be honest, I hadn't thought about how Luz would feel if I left. I figured since she kept to herself and her books, she wouldn't even notice me gone. I decided then and there that I would be there for my sister, even if it meant sharing a cramped bedroom a little longer.

Part II: Multiple Choice

Section 1: Quantitative (Math)

1. D	**6.** C	**11.** E	**16.** A	**21.** D
2. C	**7.** B	**12.** D	**17.** D	**22.** B
3. C	**8.** A	**13.** C	**18.** B	**23.** C
4. D	**9.** C	**14.** C	**19.** B	**24.** A
5. C	**10.** C	**15.** C	**20.** C	**25.** E

1. **The correct answer is D.** Rename $1\frac{1}{2}$ as the decimal 1.5 and add.

$$
\begin{array}{r}
1.5 \\
0.750 \\
\underline{0.1010} \\
2.3510
\end{array}
$$

2. **The correct answer is C.** When dividing numbers having the same base, simply subtract the exponents.

$$\frac{2^{12}}{2^{8}} = 2^{12-8} = 2^{4} = 16$$

3. **The correct answer is C.**

$$
\begin{array}{r}
8.08 \\
62.3\overline{)503.384} \\
\underline{4{,}984} \\
4{,}984 \\
\underline{4{,}984} \\
0
\end{array}
$$

4. **The correct answer is D.** Simplify the numerator of the fraction, and then divide.

$$\frac{1\frac{3}{4} - \frac{1}{8}}{\frac{1}{8}} = \frac{1\frac{6}{8} - \frac{1}{8}}{\frac{1}{8}}$$

$$= \frac{1\frac{5}{8}}{\frac{1}{8}} = 1\frac{5}{8} \times \frac{8}{1}$$

$$= \frac{13}{8} \times \frac{8}{1} = 13$$

5. **The correct answer is C.**

$$
\begin{array}{r}
1.970 \\
1.02\overline{)2.010000} \\
\underline{102} \\
990 \\
\underline{918} \\
720 \\
\underline{714} \\
60
\end{array}
$$

6. **The correct answer is C.** Begin working with the innermost parentheses and work your way out.

$$-3 - \left[(2-1) - (3+4) \right]$$
$$= -3 - \left[(1) - (7) \right]$$
$$= -3 - \left[-6 \right]$$
$$= -3 + 6$$
$$= 3$$

7. **The correct answer is B.** This is a good problem to do in your head. Mentally subtract 700 from 3,003 and get 2,303. Then look at the answers carefully and note that only choice B is close to your estimate.

$$
\begin{array}{r}
3{,}003 \\
\underline{-\ 699} \\
2{,}304
\end{array}
$$

8. **The correct answer is A.** The problem states that $a = 5$ and $b = \frac{1}{5}$; $\frac{1}{5}$ is $\frac{1}{25}$ of 5. Therefore, the value of a expressed in terms of b is $25 \times \frac{1}{5} = 5$ or $25b$.

9. **The correct answer is C.** This is a good problem to do in your head. Note that 10% of 70 is 7. 140%, then, is 14×7, or 98.

10. **The correct answer is C.** Borrow a gallon and add it to 2 quarts. Rewrite the problem. Remember that you borrowed.

$$\begin{array}{cccc}
 & 4 \text{ gallons} & 6 \text{ quarts} & 1 \text{ pint} \\
- & 1 \text{ gallon} & 3 \text{ quarts} & \\
\hline
 & 3 \text{ gallons} & 3 \text{ quarts} & 1 \text{ pint}
\end{array}$$

11. **The correct answer is E.** By doubling the denominator of a fraction, we actually divide it by 2. By halving one of the factors in the numerator, we also halve the value of the fraction. By doing both, we have actually divided the original value by 4. Plug in some values for x, y, and z, and try this.

12. **The correct answer is D.** This is a good problem to estimate. Since 8% is slightly less than $\frac{1}{12}$, you can multiply 20 by 12 to approximate the answer. Note that 250 is close enough to your 240 estimate. To be precise:

$$20 \div 0.08 = 0.08\overline{)20.00}$$

with long division giving quotient 250. (16, 40, 40, 0)

13. **The correct answer is C.** 100 is 20 larger than 80. 20 is one fourth, or 25%, of 80.

14. **The correct answer is C.** 40 inches equals $3\frac{1}{3}$ feet. Since $\frac{3}{8}$ in. on the drawing equals 1 foot at full scale, then:

$$3\frac{1}{3} \text{ feet} = 3\frac{1}{3} \times \frac{3}{8}$$
$$= \frac{10}{3} \times \frac{3}{8}$$
$$= \frac{10}{8}$$
$$= 1\frac{1}{4} \text{ in.}$$

15. **The correct answer is C.** Bracket the multiplication and division first and solve the problem.

$$\left(6 \div \frac{1}{3}\right) + \left(\frac{2}{3} \times 9\right)$$
$$= 18 + 6$$
$$= 24$$

16. **The correct answer is A.** Since $x - 3 < 12$, x can be any number less than 15.

17. **The correct answer is D.** Substitute the values into the expression.

$$\sqrt{9 + 3(2) + 1}$$
$$= \sqrt{9 + 6 + 1}$$
$$= \sqrt{16}$$
$$= 4$$

18. **The correct answer is B.** To find the average, find the sum of the addends and divide that sum by the number of addends.

$$-10 + 6 + 0 + -3 + 22 = 15$$
$$15 \div 5 = 3$$

19. **The correct answer is B.** By substituting +2 for the triangle, the denominator of the fraction becomes zero. A denominator of zero is undefined in mathematics.

20. **The correct answer is C.** Move the decimal point one place to the left and insert a zero in the newly created decimal place.

$$0.10101 \div 10 = 0.010101$$

21. **The correct answer is D.** The formula for rate is rate = distance ÷ time. In this problem, rate = 10 miles ÷ 3 hours, or $3\frac{1}{3}$ miles per hour.

22. **The correct answer is B.** 7 is one third of 21, and $\frac{2}{3}$ is one third of 2. As a proportion:

$$\frac{7}{21} = \frac{\frac{2}{3}}{x}$$

23. **The correct answer is C.** The square root of 85 is between 9, whose square is 81, and 10, whose square is 100.

24. **The correct answer is A.** $-6 + -2 + 0 + 8 = 0$

25. **The correct answer is E.** Simply divide $\frac{5}{6}$ by $\frac{1}{4}$.

$$\frac{5}{6} \div \frac{1}{4} = \frac{5}{6} \times \frac{4}{1}$$
$$= \frac{20}{6} = 3\frac{1}{3}$$

Section 2: Reading Comprehension

1. E	9. B	17. D	25. C	33. B
2. C	10. E	18. B	26. D	34. D
3. E	11. A	19. E	27. A	35. E
4. A	12. C	20. A	28. E	36. A
5. C	13. C	21. D	29. B	37. A
6. B	14. E	22. A	30. D	38. A
7. A	15. B	23. A	31. C	39. C
8. A	16. E	24. C	32. A	40. A

1. **The correct answer is E.** The word *gargantuan* means "enormous, vast, or massive."

2. **The correct answer is C.** Klaus Schmidt's 1994 insights on Göbekli Tepe proved that Neolithic hunter-gatherers had begun collaborating on monuments to be used as gathering spaces before they ever began settling land more permanently for crops and cattle. This insight shifted paradigms about the history of Neolithic humans. Close reading of the passage reveals details that contradict all the other statements. The discovery at the site of fossils from primarily wild species contradicts the idea that hunter-gatherers were raising animals at Göbekli Tepe (choice A), and there is no mention of the wild animals discovered being novel species (choice E). The passage also says the site was constructed prior to the advent of metal tools (choice B) and that while it was long thought to be a medieval cemetery (choice D), Schmidt's discovery upended that assumption.

3. **The correct answer is E.** If you're an archaeology savant, then you may know that Lascaux Cave (choice A) and Tell Qaramel (choice D) are both older than Göbekli Tepe and would have then been able to eliminate them right away. However, don't get distracted by what is seemingly a trick question about history. Instead, think of this as a close reading question—only Stonehenge is mentioned in the passage, so it's the only answer you can support based on the passage alone.

4. **The correct answer is A.** The passage's main idea is that the discovery of the monument at Göbekli Tepe was a major revelation for the world's understanding of Neolithic early humans. It stands to reason, then, that if anthropologists and archaeologists were to happen upon an even older monument with similar features, it would be even bigger news than Göbekli Tepe was. Such a discovery would not necessarily change insights about Göbekli Tepe's age (choice B). Since such a discovery is still possible (since there is no way of knowing that all the world's archaeological sites have already been discovered), there is no way to say without a doubt that Göbekli Tepe is for sure the oldest (choice C). The details of the passage contradict choice D, since Schmidt *did* think it was possible that Göbekli Tepe was used for religious gatherings. There is nothing in the passage to suggest that choice E is true.

5. **The correct answer is C.** *Informative* (choice A), *detached* (choice D), and *formal* (choice E) are all words that describe an objective (choice B) tone, meaning one that is unprejudiced and fact-based. *Subjective* (choice C) is the opposite of *objective*; it means "biased, prejudiced, or dependent on personal opinion." Even if you didn't recognize that the author's tone in this passage is primarily informative, you could use a process of elimination to find the adjective least like the others.

6. **The correct answer is B.** Something that is definitive can also be described as quintessential, meaning "an ideal example of something." Contextually,

the passage is saying that the Moog synthesizer sound was typical of 1970s music and recognizable as such.

7. **The correct answer is A.** A good title for this passage might be "Wendy Carlos: Electronic Music Icon." This theme occurs throughout the passage. Choices B and D focus on small details of the passage that do not encompass the main point, while choice C is too vague and choice E is not representative of the topics discussed in the passage.

8. **The correct answer is A.** This question is asking you to make an inference based on the information in the passage. We know from the details provided that Wendy Carlos had a huge influence on today's music and that she was known for using computers and electronic instruments. You may have also spotted references to the rapper Jay-Z and the pop band Coldplay. These context clues help to provide supporting information to conclude that the use of computer-based beats in rap and pop music is an example of Carlos' influence on later music. Even when the context makes things clear, ensure that the other answers aren't more logical; neither choice B nor choice D is supported by the passage, and Bach is famous enough that he would have likely remained popular even without Carlos' influence (choice C). Choice E is too vague to adequately address the scope of the question.

9. **The correct answer is B.** The author describes the passage's subject in a matter of fact, straightforward way, which means that *inform* is the most apt choice. While the argument might persuade (choice A) someone to believe Wendy Carlos is an interesting figure, that is not the main purpose of the passage. Furthermore, there is no attempt to amuse the reader (choice C) or to critique Carlos or her music (choice D). With a stretch, it might seem possible that the author is analyzing (choice E) Carlos' influence, but in an analysis, you would likely see the author go into greater detail than we do in this informative biographical summary.

10. **The correct answer is E.** Every answer given provides an example of something either being

translated or needing translation—your job is to figure out which matches the context used in the passage. The passage describes Carlos taking Bach's original music and creating an electronic version of the same compositions using a Moog synthesizer. The answer that best matches is choice E, since a dance company using a famous choreographer's ballet and doing a hip-hop interpretation of it would be a very similar act of translation. Reading between the lines of what someone is saying (choices B and C) and making something understandable across language barriers (choices A and D) are two different concepts of translation that are valid, but which do not match the context here.

11. **The correct answer is A.** Suppositions are guesses, hypotheses, hunches, or presumptions.

12. **The correct answer is C.** The overarching purpose of the passage is to discuss what the EHT collaboration is and how they managed to make an image of Sgr A*. Since the question asks you to consider how the author might build on what is discussed in paragraph 3, you should first revisit paragraph 3 to get a sense of what would logically come next. Paragraph 3 focuses on the EHT collaboration itself, their prior achievement of photographing M87*, and the idea that—to create the Sgr A* image—they had to invent more advanced instruments. It would make the most sense for the next paragraph to discuss how exactly they did that, so choice C is the only answer that follows a logical sequence with paragraph 3.

13. **The correct answer is C.** As the passage states, "The 2019 image shows M87*, a black hole in the Messier 87 galaxy."

14. **The correct answer is E.** The title "A History of Black Holes" is too broad to address the main idea of the passage.

15. **The correct answer is B.** The purpose of paragraph 1 is to introduce Hegel and the concept of dialectical thinking so that in paragraph 2, the author can go on to explain the master/slave dialectic (choice A). None of the other answers appear in the passage.

16. **The correct answer is E.** To exert means to "expend, apply, or utilize."

17. **The correct answer is D.** The passage states that Hegel's ideas were a big influence on Karl Marx. The passage also states that dialectical thinking was central to Hegelian philosophy. Therefore, one can infer that if Marx was drawing on Hegel's philosophy, he must have also been engaged in dialectical thinking. Don't get distracted by answers that seem true simply because they reference other things from the passage; choices C and E are contradicted by the details of the passage, choice B is too vague to make sense as an inference, and choice A has no relation to the contents of the passage.

18. **The correct answer is B.** Saying that the works give students headaches is a figurative way of saying that Hegel is difficult to read and understand.

19. **The correct answer is E.** As the passage states, "Sometimes also referred to as the 'Lordship and Bondage' dialectic, the concept is essentially that the two cannot exist without the other."

20. **The correct answer is A.** *Stout* means "plump, fat, burly, or heavy."

21. **The correct answer is D.** While foxes are mentioned in the passage, it's not because they are identified as marsupials. Rather, they are identified as introduced predators for quokkas. Foxes are placental mammals rather than marsupials.

22. **The correct answer is A.** The passage discusses both how quokkas are naturally human-curious creatures with seemingly friendly appearances and how it's difficult for conservationists to get tourists to stop taking photos with them. You can thus infer that this is happening because the quokkas are facilitating the practice by willingly approaching tourists. The passage does not say anything about quokkas rarely being seen (choice B), a social media challenge spawning the practice (choice C), or Rottnest Island being overrun by tourists (choice D). While it does mention humans hunting quokkas illegally (choice E), there is not enough detail to infer that that is the primary reason most tourists visit Rottnest Island.

23. **The correct answer is A.** This is an informative passage focused on characteristics of quokkas as well as the various factors that affect conservation efforts for quokka populations. While the passage does discuss how the quokka came to be called the happiest marsupial on the planet (choice B) and the details may persuade the reader that quokkas are the most interesting marsupial in Australia (choice E), this is not the main purpose of the passage. There is no attempt to examine why koalas get more attention (choice C) or address the motivations of tourists to Rottnest Island (choice D).

24. **The correct answer is C.** If something is singular, that means it is unique, unusual, or exceptional.

25. **The correct answer is C.** As the passage states, "the festival is linked with the long-held Japanese belief that getting a baby to have a hard cry will help ensure they stay healthy." The key word in the question is *primarily*; while the passage does mention that some regions believe a baby's cry can ward off evil spirits (choice E), this is not the primary belief behind the festival.

26. **The correct answer is D.** The purpose of paragraph 4 is to illustrate what sumo wrestlers do when they can't get a baby to cry during the festival. Most of the other choices discuss the topics of other paragraphs, such as the introduction to the concept of cultural festivals (choice B) in paragraph 1, the explanation of the festival's name (choice C) in paragraph 2, and the description of the folklore behind the festival (choice A) in paragraph 3. The economic impact of the festival (choice E) is never addressed.

27. **The correct answer is A.** The phrase "bring on the waterworks" is commonly used to refer to getting someone to cry, so you can eliminate choices C, D, and E. Active reading of the passage will reveal that it's the babies who must cry in this contest, not the sumo wrestlers holding them.

28. **The correct answer is E.** While the first part of this passage is primarily informative, it takes a turn for the argumentative in the final paragraph. Specifically, the author makes a clear assertion that the negative impacts of redlining made it

harder for families of color to accumulate generational wealth and participate in the suburbanization process. You can eliminate choices A and D since the author clearly believes redlining had a negative effect on families of color. Similarly, choice C cannot be true if there were negative impacts for families of color seeking mortgages. Choice B is false because the second paragraph implies that the opposite was true.

29. **The correct answer is B.** At the end of the first paragraph, the passage states Hayden's suggestion that "the suburban model upon which most of today's development is fashioned became a shared visual idea of 'suburbia' for Americans through [its] reflection in the sitcoms of early television." Choices A and C both suggest that the sitcom ideal came before the housing developments, which is backwards. Choice D is false. Choice E may be true to some degree, but it is not mentioned in this passage.

30. **The correct answer is D.** The author of this passage takes time to critically analyze various aspects of the issue of redlining and racial discrimination during mid-20th century suburbanization. In addition to *analytical*, one might use the terms *informative*, *argumentative*, or *critical* to define the author's tone. The author does make a point at the end to suggest that something should be done (people should develop a better understanding of redlining), so while *resigned* (choice E) might have seemed right, it doesn't fit as well as *analytical*.

31. **The correct answer is C.** The maps used to divide cities into sections based on their suitability for mortgages involved using a literal red pen to draw lines around the neighborhoods deemed least suitable for mortgage lending. Therefore, choices A and B represent the opposite of the truth. Choice D is false because there was still housing development that occurred in redlined neighborhoods; it was just harder to do so without access to favorable financial backing to sell newly built homes. Choice E is false because while white people could have chosen to try for mortgages in redlined

neighborhoods, the issue isn't who could apply in redlined areas so much as who was restricted from applying anywhere else.

32. **The correct answer is A.** Sometimes also called an "appeal to ethics," an author appeals to credibility when they show how the information they are using comes from an expert with relevant knowledge. By pointing out that Dolores Hayden is a professor at Harvard University who has written on the passage's topic, the author is demonstrating that they have used trustworthy, reliable research to craft their argument.

33. **The correct answer is B.** The term *discord* refers to "a disagreement, lack of harmony, or general strife."

34. **The correct answer is D.** The author uses the metaphor of the rudder and sails to show that reason and passion are two mechanisms for "steering" one's destiny that work best when they work together. If a ship's rudders and sails don't work in concert, the ship is not likely to go anywhere. This is the author's figurative way of saying that reason and passion must work together.

35. **The correct answer is E.** The only answer that does not contain a piece of figurative language like a simile (choice D), metaphor (choices A and C), or personification (choice B) is choice E.

36. **The correct answer is A.** We can infer from the passage that a priestess figure is speaking to a masculine figure (identified as "he" in the poem) who is sharing wisdom with an audience. Since the title of the work is "The Prophet," it would make sense to infer that the prophet is the unnamed person to whom the priestess identified in the excerpt is speaking. There is no evidence in this passage to support choices C and D, and the details of the passage contradict choices B and E.

37. **The correct answer is A.** In the final paragraph, the passage states that germ-free mice are "popular for gut flora research because scientists can inoculate the mice with specific microbes and watch what happens." There are not enough details in the passage to support any of the other choices.

38. **The correct answer is A.** Support for this answer can be found in paragraph 3, which states "experiments with germ-free mice have yielded intriguing clues about the possible influence of the gut microbiome on behavior and neurodevelopment. However, it is still unclear whether these findings are relevant to humans." Choice A basically restates this information in different words.

39. **The correct answer is C.** This question is asking you to look for the exception: algae is never mentioned in the passage. While algae can be categorized as a eukaryote, which *is* mentioned, it is not a component of the gut microbiome indicated by the passage.

40. **The correct answer is A.** The anecdote discusses a historical example of a doctor performing an experiment and finding a connection between mood and the stomach, stating that "Beaumont noticed that St. Martin's mood seemed to affect how quickly he digested food." Just after providing the story, the author adds: "These early observations provided the first clues of crosstalk between the brain and the gut." Therefore, the author explicitly states why they have used this anecdote, which is to set up the idea that doctors have historically noticed a brain-gut connection, before diving into more current research on the topic.

Section 3: Verbal

1. E	11. E	21. E	31. C	41. D	51. E
2. B	12. C	22. C	32. A	42. A	52. E
3. A	13. A	23. B	33. C	43. B	53. A
4. A	14. C	24. A	34. B	44. B	54. C
5. C	15. B	25. C	35. B	45. E	55. D
6. B	16. E	26. E	36. C	46. E	56. A
7. D	17. C	27. C	37. E	47. E	57. A
8. C	18. A	28. A	38. D	48. B	58. E
9. A	19. B	29. D	39. A	49. A	59. A
10. C	20. D	30. E	40. A	50. E	60. A

1. **The correct answer is E.** The verb *deter* means to "discourage a person or group from doing something."

2. **The correct answer is B.** The word *hostile* means "antagonistic or unfriendly."

3. **The correct answer is A.** To utilize means to "make practical use" (of something).

4. **The correct answer is A.** To abdicate means to "resign" or "formally give up (something)," such as a royal title.

5. **The correct answer is C.** The adjective *prominent* describes something that is noticeable, sticking out, or outstanding.

6. **The correct answer is B.** A boundary is a border, so *limit* is the nearest synonym.

7. **The correct answer is D.** *Illiterate* means "unable to read."

8. **The correct answer is C.** The term *orator* means "one who speaks."

9. **The correct answer is A.** To corroborate something, such as a testimony or alibi, means to strengthen, support, or confirm that thing.

10. **The correct answer is C.** The verb *ratify* means "give official sanction to" or "approve."

11. **The correct answer is E.** Something that is perilous is dangerous or risky. The word *hazardous* is the most similar in meaning.

12. **The correct answer is C.** The term *stationary* means "immobile" or "not movable." It is the adjective form of the noun *station*. Choice A refers to the homophone *stationery*.

13. **The correct answer is A.** The verb *transcribe* means "write out in full" or "make a recording (of what was said)."

14. **The correct answer is C.** If someone is described as proficient, that means they are adept, competent, or skilled.

15. **The correct answer is B.** To deceive means to lie or otherwise make a person believe that which is not true. The word *mislead* implies leading astray, so it's the most similar in meaning.

16. **The correct answer is E.** Synonyms for the adjective *agile* include *nimble, light,* and *spry.*

17. **The correct answer is C.** *Duration* describes the time that a thing continues or lasts. The word *term* has the most similar meaning.

18. **The correct answer is A.** *Ambiguous* can mean either "having two meanings" or "being vague and uncertain." The prefix *ambi-* means "both" and implies that two or more possible interpretations of something might be correct, meaning none are certain. The word *unclear* is the closest in meaning to *ambiguous.*

19. **The correct answer is B.** A prerogative is a right, privilege, or special advantage. The word *choice* is closest in meaning.

20. **The correct answer is D.** If something is intriguing, that means it is fascinating and excites curiosity or interest.

21. **The correct answer is E.** The adjective *clandestine* describes something that is secret or surreptitious, usually for some illicit reason or purpose.

22. **The correct answer is C.** The word *bounteous* means "plentiful, generous, or abundant."

23. **The correct answer is B.** To diverge is to "move off in different directions" or "become different." In other words, to change course.

24. **The correct answer is A.** The adjective *benign* means "good-natured, kindly, or harmless." The word *gentle* is similar in meaning. When applied to a tumor, *benign* means "harmless" in the manner opposed to *malignant*, which means "life-threatening."

25. **The correct answer is C.** A caucus is a meeting of people with similar goals, usually a group of people from within a larger group, such as a congress.

26. **The correct answer is E.** The verb *disseminate* means "to scatter widely." The word *spread* is similar in meaning.

27. **The correct answer is C.** The word *chagrin* describes embarrassment or humiliation.

28. **The correct answer is A.** The term *valor* describes courage or bravery.

29. **The correct answer is D.** The adjective *nonchalant* describes something or someone indifferent or "without enthusiasm."

30. **The correct answer is E.** A liaison is a connection or "linking up." *Association* is a synonym.

31. **The correct answer is C.** The relationship is not of precise synonyms, but it is close. Both *beg* and *borrow* have to do with *ask for* and *take*. Both *offer* and *lend* have to do with *give*. *Repay* also has to do with *give*, but it implies a previous activity not implied in the relationship of *beg* and *borrow*.

32. **The correct answer is A.** One who is lazy is inert. One who resists is one who refuses. The relationship is one of characteristics or even synonyms.

33. **The correct answer is C.** A circle is the base of a cylinder; a triangle is the base of a triangular pyramid. This is a part-to-whole relationship. Note that the actual statement of the analogy is whole-to-part.

34. **The correct answer is B.** This is a true part-to-whole analogy. A crocodile is part of a larger group, reptiles. A kangaroo is part of a larger group, marsupials.

35. **The correct answer is B.** This is another part-to-whole relationship. A quart is roughly equivalent to a liter, and a milliliter is one-thousandth of a liter. A yard is roughly equivalent to a meter, and a millimeter is one-thousandth of a meter. Choice A reverses the relationship. The other choices do not move from metric to imperial measures.

36. **The correct answer is C.** The relationship is one of true synonyms. *Demolish* is a synonym for *destroy* and *change* is a synonym for *amend*.

37. **The correct answer is E.** *Plaintiff* and *defendant* are the opposite of each other, which reflects an antonym relationship. *Prosecute* is to *defend* reflects the correct opposing relationship.

38. **The correct answer is D.** In neither set are the terms true antonyms, but they clearly have opposite connotations. *Truth* is to *nonsense* reflects the same relationship. While choice E also offers opposite connotations, the order of the terms is reversed. Remember, order in word relationships matters.

39. **The correct answer is A.** *Wild* describes a characteristic of a wolf as *domestic* describes a characteristic of both a dog and a cat. You must narrow further to choose the best answer. *Dog* is the domestic counterpart of *wolf*, so *dog* creates the best analogy.

40. **The correct answer is A.** This is a purpose relationship. A hammer is a tool used by a carpenter;

an awl is a tool used by a cobbler. Choice D reverses the order of tool and its user.

41. **The correct answer is D.** This is a part-to-part relationship. Both *subject* and *predicate* describe parts of a sentence; both *senator* and *representative* describe parts of a congress. Choice A is incorrect because a senator's relationship to a congress is that of part-to-whole.

42. **The correct answer is A.** This is an association relationship. *Pungent* is an adjective used to describe a degree of odor. *Intense* is an adjective used to describe a degree of emotion.

43. **The correct answer is B.** The analogy is based on synonyms. *Exploit* and *adventure* are synonyms. So are *safari* and *expedition*.

44. **The correct answer is B.** *Spread* and *scatter* are synonyms, so we are looking for two words that reflect the same relationship, which is *separate* and *distribute*.

45. **The correct answer is E.** The relationship is one of association or characteristic. *Exuberant* is an adjective used to describe mood; *adroit* is an adjective used to describe movement.

46. **The correct answer is E.** Opposition leads to defiance; challenge leads to exertion. The actual statement of the analogy is effect and its cause.

47. **The correct answer is E.** This is a true cause-and-effect relationship. Food helps one acquire nutrition; light helps one acquire vision.

48. **The correct answer is B.** The relationship is that of true antonyms. The false choices are synonyms or partial antonyms.

49. **The correct answer is A.** This is a relationship of antonyms. *Exorbitant* and *reasonable* are antonyms.

50. **The correct answer is E.** This may be either a part-to-whole relationship or an analogy of degree. When considered as a part-to-whole relationship, a comment is part of a speech, and a note is part of a letter. When evaluated as an analogy of degrees, a comment is much shorter than a speech and a note is much shorter than a letter.

51. **The correct answer is E.** Be careful. *Flammable* and *inflammable* are synonyms; both mean easily inflamed. *Disinterested* means "impartial."

52. **The correct answer is E.** This is a purpose relationship. A tailor follows a pattern to construct a piece of clothing; a builder follows a blueprint to construct a building.

53. **The correct answer is A.** The relationship is sequential. An impeachment (accusation) comes before a dismissal. An arraignment (accusation) comes before an indictment (placement of charges).

54. **The correct answer is C.** The relationship is of characteristic to animal. Speedy is to greyhound as clever is to fox. While a shark is voracious, choice B reverses the relationship to one of animal to characteristic.

55. **The correct answer is D.** All choices except A involve the activity of a bodily organ, so you must think further. Both *exhalation* and *perspiration* involve giving off something from within the body.

56. **The correct answer is A.** You celebrate a birth; you grieve over a death. The analogy states the effect and its cause.

57. **The correct answer is A.** This is an analogy of degree. To urge is to "passionately recommend"; to plead is to "passionately request." Choice B offers synonyms of equal degree; choice C reverses the order.

58. **The correct answer is E.** This is a cause-and-effect relationship. When one weeps, one gives off tears; when one breathes, one gives off carbon dioxide.

59. **The correct answer is A.** The relationship is hard to categorize but hopefully easy to spot. An air pocket makes a plane bounce; a rut has the same effect on a vehicle.

60. **The correct answer is A.** This is a verb-to-noun relationship. *Arbitrate* describes what one does to a dispute; *solve* describes what must be done to a mystery.

Section 4: Quantitative (Math)

1. E	6. C	11. A	16. E	21. D
2. C	7. D	12. A	17. B	22. B
3. A	8. A	13. B	18. B	23. B
4. C	9. C	14. B	19. C	24. B
5. D	10. E	15. D	20. B	25. A

1. **The correct answer is E.** In one hour, the minute hand of a clock goes around in a complete circle. In two hours, it revolves through two circles. Because each circle consists of 360°, two revolutions equal 720°.

2. **The correct answer is C.** A fraction is less than $\frac{1}{3}$ if three times the numerator is less than the denominator. Of the fractions listed, only $\frac{15}{46}$ has a numerator that is less than $\frac{1}{3}$ of the denominator.

3. **The correct answer is A.** The figure is a square, so all four sides are equal in length. The perimeter is the sum of the lengths of the four sides. Each side is $\frac{2x}{3}+1$.

   The sum, then, is:

   $$\left(\frac{2x}{3}+1\right) + \left(\frac{2x}{3}+1\right) + \left(\frac{2x}{3}+1\right) + \left(\frac{2x}{3}+1\right)$$

   $$=\frac{8x}{3}+4$$

   You could also multiply $\frac{2x}{3}+1$ by 4 for the same result.

4. **The correct answer is C.** The face of the cube is a square, 1 by 1. Use the Pythagorean theorem to find the length of the diagonal of the square.

   $$c^2 = a^2 + b^2$$
   $$c^2 = 1^2 + 1^2$$
   $$c^2 = 2$$
   $$c = \sqrt{2}$$

5. **The correct answer is D.** The average speed for the entire trip is the total distance (240 miles) divided by the total time (5 hours), which yields 48 mph.

6. **The correct answer is C.** This is a proportion problem. Set up the proportion as follows:

   $$\frac{2\frac{1}{2}}{4} = \frac{1\frac{7}{8}}{?}$$

   Substitute x for ?: $\dfrac{2\frac{1}{2}}{4} = \dfrac{1\frac{7}{8}}{x}$

   Cross-multiply: $\dfrac{2\frac{1}{2}}{4} \diagup\!\!\!\!\diagdown \dfrac{1\frac{7}{8}}{x}$

   $$=2\frac{1}{2}x = 4 \cdot 1\frac{7}{8}$$

   To better make sense of them, change your mixed fractions to improper fractions. First the left side:

   $$2\frac{1}{2}x = \frac{5}{2}x$$

   Then the right:

   $$4 \cdot 1\frac{7}{8} = 4 \cdot \frac{15}{8} = \frac{60}{8}$$

   Divide both sides by the coefficient of x and calculate:

   $$\frac{5}{2}x = \frac{60}{8}$$
   $$x = \frac{60}{8} \div \frac{5}{2}$$
   $$x = \frac{60}{8} \cdot \frac{2}{5}$$
   $$x = 3$$

7. **The correct answer is D.** To find the ratio of the area of the circle to the area of the square, first find the area of each. Note that the diameter of the circle equals the width of the square.

Area of the square:

$$6 \times 6 = 36 \text{ sq. in.}$$

Area of circle:

$$\pi 3^2 = 9\pi = 9 \times \frac{22}{7} = \frac{198}{7} \approx 28 \text{ sq. in.}$$

Ratio of the area of the circle to the area of the square:

$$\frac{28}{36} = \frac{7}{9}$$

8. **The correct answer is A.** The difference is 0.90 inches, but the outside diameter consists of two thicknesses of metal (one on each side). Therefore, the thickness of the metal is $0.90 \div 2 = 0.45$ inches.

9. **The correct answer is C.** If 60% of the games were predicted accurately, 40% of the games were predicted inaccurately. Let x = games played.

$$0.40x = 16$$
$$x = 40 \text{ games played}$$
$$40 - 16 = 24 \text{ games won}$$

Therefore, Twyla was accurate for 24 games.

10. **The correct answer is E.** Thirty percent of the boys are from New York State, and 20% of them (0.20 of them) are from New York City. Therefore, 6% (0.20×0.30) of the boys in the camp are from New York City.

11. **The correct answer is A.** An area 1 foot long by $1\frac{1}{4}$ feet wide is $12'' \times 15''$, or 180 square inches in area. Each block is 6 square inches in area. Therefore, the number of blocks needed is $\frac{180}{6} = 30$ blocks. The height of each block is irrelevant to the solution of the problem.

12. **The correct answer is A.** The area of a circle is equal to πr^2. The circumference of a circle is equal to πd. If the number of inches in each are equal, then $\pi d = \pi r^2$, or the diameter equals the square of the radius. The only value for which the diameter can equal the square of the radius is a diameter of 4 inches.

13. **The correct answer is B.** The LCM is found by rewriting each number in prime factorization and finding the product of each unique prime factor. 2^2 and 2^3 are not selected because each is a factor of 2^5.

$$20 = 2^2 \times 5$$
$$24 = 2^3 \times 3$$
$$32 = 2^5$$
$$\text{LCM} = 5 \times 3 \times 2^5 = 480$$

Trial and error can also give you this answer.

14. **The correct answer is B.** If $9x + 5 = 23$, then $9x = 18$, and $x = 2$. Therefore, $18x + 5$ equals $18(2) + 5 = 41$.

15. **The correct answer is D.** Fractions are most easily compared by comparing cross-products. Start by comparing $\frac{2}{3}$ with $\frac{5}{7}$. The product of 3 and 5 is 15. The product of 7 and 2 is 14. Therefore, $\frac{5}{7}$ is larger than $\frac{2}{3}$. Continue this process with the other fractions to be compared.

$$\frac{5}{7} \times \frac{8}{11}, \text{ note } \frac{8}{11} > \frac{5}{7} \text{ and also } \frac{8}{11} > \frac{2}{3}$$
$$\frac{8}{11} \times \frac{9}{13}, \text{ note } \frac{8}{11} > \frac{9}{13}$$
$$\frac{2}{3} \times \frac{9}{13}, \text{ note } \frac{9}{13} > \frac{2}{3} \text{ and also } \frac{9}{13} < \frac{5}{7}$$

Therefore, $\frac{2}{3} < \frac{9}{13} < \frac{5}{7} < \frac{8}{11}$.

16. **The correct answer is E.** A cubic foot contains $12'' \times 12'' \times 12''$, or 1,728 cubic inches. If each cubic inch weighs two pounds, the substance weighs $2 \cdot 1,728$ or 3,456 pounds.

17. **The correct answer is B.** 17 millionths in decimals is 0.000017. The number of places to the right of the decimal point is equal to the number of zeros in the whole number. 17,000,000 has six zeros.

18. **The correct answer is B.** Because the circumference of a circle is equivalent to π times the diameter, the circumference is also equal to π times twice the radius. Divide the circumference by 2π.

19. **The correct answer is C.** Four boards, each 2'9" long, total 11 feet. The carpenter must buy 11 feet of wood.

20. **The correct answer is B.** Find the answer to this problem by substituting the values given into the formula.

$$S = 16t^2$$

$$S = 16(8)^2 = 16(64) = 1,024 \text{ feet}$$

21. **The correct answer is D.** The graph is steepest between years 7 and 9. The population was approximately 1,000 in Year 7 and increased to over 2,500 by Year 9.

22. **The correct answer is B.** The size of the population was quite constant from Year 3 to Year 4 and decreased from Year 4 to Year 5 from almost 1,000 to 500. Notice that the population was the same in Year 3 as in Year 7.

23. **The correct answer is B.** By knowing how many landline telephones are in Adelaide (48,000), and how many serve each group of 100 in the population (12.8), we can find how many groups of 100 are in the population.

48,000 telephones ÷ 12.8 telephones per 100 of population = 3,750 groups of 100 in the population.

3,750 × 100 = 375,000 people

24. **The correct answer is B.** The first person does $\frac{1}{25}$ of the job in 1 minute. The second person does $\frac{1}{50}$ of the job in 1 minute. The third person does $\frac{1}{10}$ of the job in 1 minute. Together $\frac{1}{25} + \frac{1}{50} + \frac{1}{10} = \frac{8}{50}$ or $\frac{4}{25}$ of the job in 1 minute. This is $\frac{25}{4}$ minutes for the entire job, or $6\frac{1}{4}$ minutes.

25. **The correct answer is A.** To find the number of minutes that must pass before the events next occur simultaneously, calculate the least common multiple of 4, 6, and 15. The LCM is 60 minutes. If the events last occurred together at noon, the next occurrence will thus be 60 minutes later, or at 1 p.m.

SCORE YOURSELF

Check your answers against the answer keys. Count the number of answers you got right and the number you got wrong.

SELF-SCORING		
Section	**No. Right**	**No. Wrong**
Quantitative (Math)		
Reading Comprehension		
Verbal		

Now calculate your raw scores:

Quantitative (Math):   (_____) $- \left(\dfrac{1}{4}\right)$ (_____) = (_____)
                              No. Right   No. Wrong   Raw Score

Reading Comprehension: (_____) $- \left(\dfrac{1}{4}\right)$ (_____) = (_____)
                              No. Right   No. Wrong   Raw Score

Verbal: (_____) $- \left(\dfrac{1}{4}\right)$ (_____) = (_____)
                              No. Right   No. Wrong   Raw Score

ANSWERS: SSAT (UPPER LEVEL) DIAGNOSTIC TEST

Now check your Raw Score against the conversion charts to get an idea of the range in which your test scores fell:

RAW SCORE CONVERSION CHART			
Raw Score	**Quantitative (Math)**	**Reading Comprehension**	**Verbal**
60			800
55			800
50	800		779
45	782		752
40	755	800	725
35	725	722	698
30	698	692	671
25	668	662	644
20	641	632	617
15	614	602	590
10	584	572	563
5	557	542	533
0	530	512	506
−5 or lower	500	500	500

Remember:

- The same exam is given to students in grades 8 through 11. You are not expected to know what you have not been taught.

- You will be compared only to students in your own grade. Use your scores to plan further study if you have time.

NOTES

CHAPTER

ISEE (UPPER LEVEL)
DIAGNOSTIC TEST

ISEE (UPPER LEVEL) DIAGNOSTIC TEST

DIAGNOSTIC TEST

This diagnostic test is designed to help you recognize your strengths and weaknesses. The questions cover information from all the different sections of the ISEE. Use the results to help guide and direct your study time.

ANSWER SHEET: ISEE (UPPER LEVEL) DIAGNOSTIC TEST

Section 1: Verbal Reasoning

1. Ⓐ Ⓑ Ⓒ Ⓓ   11. Ⓐ Ⓑ Ⓒ Ⓓ   21. Ⓐ Ⓑ Ⓒ Ⓓ   31. Ⓐ Ⓑ Ⓒ Ⓓ
2. Ⓐ Ⓑ Ⓒ Ⓓ   12. Ⓐ Ⓑ Ⓒ Ⓓ   22. Ⓐ Ⓑ Ⓒ Ⓓ   32. Ⓐ Ⓑ Ⓒ Ⓓ
3. Ⓐ Ⓑ Ⓒ Ⓓ   13. Ⓐ Ⓑ Ⓒ Ⓓ   23. Ⓐ Ⓑ Ⓒ Ⓓ   33. Ⓐ Ⓑ Ⓒ Ⓓ
4. Ⓐ Ⓑ Ⓒ Ⓓ   14. Ⓐ Ⓑ Ⓒ Ⓓ   24. Ⓐ Ⓑ Ⓒ Ⓓ   34. Ⓐ Ⓑ Ⓒ Ⓓ
5. Ⓐ Ⓑ Ⓒ Ⓓ   15. Ⓐ Ⓑ Ⓒ Ⓓ   25. Ⓐ Ⓑ Ⓒ Ⓓ   35. Ⓐ Ⓑ Ⓒ Ⓓ
6. Ⓐ Ⓑ Ⓒ Ⓓ   16. Ⓐ Ⓑ Ⓒ Ⓓ   26. Ⓐ Ⓑ Ⓒ Ⓓ   36. Ⓐ Ⓑ Ⓒ Ⓓ
7. Ⓐ Ⓑ Ⓒ Ⓓ   17. Ⓐ Ⓑ Ⓒ Ⓓ   27. Ⓐ Ⓑ Ⓒ Ⓓ   37. Ⓐ Ⓑ Ⓒ Ⓓ
8. Ⓐ Ⓑ Ⓒ Ⓓ   18. Ⓐ Ⓑ Ⓒ Ⓓ   28. Ⓐ Ⓑ Ⓒ Ⓓ   38. Ⓐ Ⓑ Ⓒ Ⓓ
9. Ⓐ Ⓑ Ⓒ Ⓓ   19. Ⓐ Ⓑ Ⓒ Ⓓ   29. Ⓐ Ⓑ Ⓒ Ⓓ   39. Ⓐ Ⓑ Ⓒ Ⓓ
10. Ⓐ Ⓑ Ⓒ Ⓓ   20. Ⓐ Ⓑ Ⓒ Ⓓ   30. Ⓐ Ⓑ Ⓒ Ⓓ   40. Ⓐ Ⓑ Ⓒ Ⓓ

Section 2: Quantitative Reasoning

1. Ⓐ Ⓑ Ⓒ Ⓓ   11. Ⓐ Ⓑ Ⓒ Ⓓ   21. Ⓐ Ⓑ Ⓒ Ⓓ   31. Ⓐ Ⓑ Ⓒ Ⓓ
2. Ⓐ Ⓑ Ⓒ Ⓓ   12. Ⓐ Ⓑ Ⓒ Ⓓ   22. Ⓐ Ⓑ Ⓒ Ⓓ   32. Ⓐ Ⓑ Ⓒ Ⓓ
3. Ⓐ Ⓑ Ⓒ Ⓓ   13. Ⓐ Ⓑ Ⓒ Ⓓ   23. Ⓐ Ⓑ Ⓒ Ⓓ   33. Ⓐ Ⓑ Ⓒ Ⓓ
4. Ⓐ Ⓑ Ⓒ Ⓓ   14. Ⓐ Ⓑ Ⓒ Ⓓ   24. Ⓐ Ⓑ Ⓒ Ⓓ   34. Ⓐ Ⓑ Ⓒ Ⓓ
5. Ⓐ Ⓑ Ⓒ Ⓓ   15. Ⓐ Ⓑ Ⓒ Ⓓ   25. Ⓐ Ⓑ Ⓒ Ⓓ   35. Ⓐ Ⓑ Ⓒ Ⓓ
6. Ⓐ Ⓑ Ⓒ Ⓓ   16. Ⓐ Ⓑ Ⓒ Ⓓ   26. Ⓐ Ⓑ Ⓒ Ⓓ   36. Ⓐ Ⓑ Ⓒ Ⓓ
7. Ⓐ Ⓑ Ⓒ Ⓓ   17. Ⓐ Ⓑ Ⓒ Ⓓ   27. Ⓐ Ⓑ Ⓒ Ⓓ   37. Ⓐ Ⓑ Ⓒ Ⓓ
8. Ⓐ Ⓑ Ⓒ Ⓓ   18. Ⓐ Ⓑ Ⓒ Ⓓ   28. Ⓐ Ⓑ Ⓒ Ⓓ
9. Ⓐ Ⓑ Ⓒ Ⓓ   19. Ⓐ Ⓑ Ⓒ Ⓓ   29. Ⓐ Ⓑ Ⓒ Ⓓ
10. Ⓐ Ⓑ Ⓒ Ⓓ   20. Ⓐ Ⓑ Ⓒ Ⓓ   30. Ⓐ Ⓑ Ⓒ Ⓓ

Section 3: Reading Comprehension

1. Ⓐ Ⓑ Ⓒ Ⓓ
2. Ⓐ Ⓑ Ⓒ Ⓓ
3. Ⓐ Ⓑ Ⓒ Ⓓ
4. Ⓐ Ⓑ Ⓒ Ⓓ
5. Ⓐ Ⓑ Ⓒ Ⓓ
6. Ⓐ Ⓑ Ⓒ Ⓓ
7. Ⓐ Ⓑ Ⓒ Ⓓ
8. Ⓐ Ⓑ Ⓒ Ⓓ

9. Ⓐ Ⓑ Ⓒ Ⓓ
10. Ⓐ Ⓑ Ⓒ Ⓓ
11. Ⓐ Ⓑ Ⓒ Ⓓ
12. Ⓐ Ⓑ Ⓒ Ⓓ
13. Ⓐ Ⓑ Ⓒ Ⓓ
14. Ⓐ Ⓑ Ⓒ Ⓓ
15. Ⓐ Ⓑ Ⓒ Ⓓ
16. Ⓐ Ⓑ Ⓒ Ⓓ

17. Ⓐ Ⓑ Ⓒ Ⓓ
18. Ⓐ Ⓑ Ⓒ Ⓓ
19. Ⓐ Ⓑ Ⓒ Ⓓ
20. Ⓐ Ⓑ Ⓒ Ⓓ
21. Ⓐ Ⓑ Ⓒ Ⓓ
22. Ⓐ Ⓑ Ⓒ Ⓓ
23. Ⓐ Ⓑ Ⓒ Ⓓ
24. Ⓐ Ⓑ Ⓒ Ⓓ

25. Ⓐ Ⓑ Ⓒ Ⓓ
26. Ⓐ Ⓑ Ⓒ Ⓓ
27. Ⓐ Ⓑ Ⓒ Ⓓ
28. Ⓐ Ⓑ Ⓒ Ⓓ
29. Ⓐ Ⓑ Ⓒ Ⓓ
30. Ⓐ Ⓑ Ⓒ Ⓓ
31. Ⓐ Ⓑ Ⓒ Ⓓ
32. Ⓐ Ⓑ Ⓒ Ⓓ

33. Ⓐ Ⓑ Ⓒ Ⓓ
34. Ⓐ Ⓑ Ⓒ Ⓓ
35. Ⓐ Ⓑ Ⓒ Ⓓ
36. Ⓐ Ⓑ Ⓒ Ⓓ

Section 4: Mathematics Achievement

1. Ⓐ Ⓑ Ⓒ Ⓓ
2. Ⓐ Ⓑ Ⓒ Ⓓ
3. Ⓐ Ⓑ Ⓒ Ⓓ
4. Ⓐ Ⓑ Ⓒ Ⓓ
5. Ⓐ Ⓑ Ⓒ Ⓓ
6. Ⓐ Ⓑ Ⓒ Ⓓ
7. Ⓐ Ⓑ Ⓒ Ⓓ
8. Ⓐ Ⓑ Ⓒ Ⓓ
9. Ⓐ Ⓑ Ⓒ Ⓓ
10. Ⓐ Ⓑ Ⓒ Ⓓ

11. Ⓐ Ⓑ Ⓒ Ⓓ
12. Ⓐ Ⓑ Ⓒ Ⓓ
13. Ⓐ Ⓑ Ⓒ Ⓓ
14. Ⓐ Ⓑ Ⓒ Ⓓ
15. Ⓐ Ⓑ Ⓒ Ⓓ
16. Ⓐ Ⓑ Ⓒ Ⓓ
17. Ⓐ Ⓑ Ⓒ Ⓓ
18. Ⓐ Ⓑ Ⓒ Ⓓ
19. Ⓐ Ⓑ Ⓒ Ⓓ
20. Ⓐ Ⓑ Ⓒ Ⓓ

21. Ⓐ Ⓑ Ⓒ Ⓓ
22. Ⓐ Ⓑ Ⓒ Ⓓ
23. Ⓐ Ⓑ Ⓒ Ⓓ
24. Ⓐ Ⓑ Ⓒ Ⓓ
25. Ⓐ Ⓑ Ⓒ Ⓓ
26. Ⓐ Ⓑ Ⓒ Ⓓ
27. Ⓐ Ⓑ Ⓒ Ⓓ
28. Ⓐ Ⓑ Ⓒ Ⓓ
29. Ⓐ Ⓑ Ⓒ Ⓓ
30. Ⓐ Ⓑ Ⓒ Ⓓ

31. Ⓐ Ⓑ Ⓒ Ⓓ
32. Ⓐ Ⓑ Ⓒ Ⓓ
33. Ⓐ Ⓑ Ⓒ Ⓓ
34. Ⓐ Ⓑ Ⓒ Ⓓ
35. Ⓐ Ⓑ Ⓒ Ⓓ
36. Ⓐ Ⓑ Ⓒ Ⓓ
37. Ⓐ Ⓑ Ⓒ Ⓓ
38. Ⓐ Ⓑ Ⓒ Ⓓ
39. Ⓐ Ⓑ Ⓒ Ⓓ
40. Ⓐ Ⓑ Ⓒ Ⓓ

41. Ⓐ Ⓑ Ⓒ Ⓓ
42. Ⓐ Ⓑ Ⓒ Ⓓ
43. Ⓐ Ⓑ Ⓒ Ⓓ
44. Ⓐ Ⓑ Ⓒ Ⓓ
45. Ⓐ Ⓑ Ⓒ Ⓓ
46. Ⓐ Ⓑ Ⓒ Ⓓ
47. Ⓐ Ⓑ Ⓒ Ⓓ

Section 5: Essay

Lined pages provided within test.

SECTION 1: VERBAL REASONING

40 Questions—20 Minutes

> **Directions:** Each question is made up of a word in capital letters followed by four choices. Choose the one word that is most nearly the same in meaning as the word in capital letters and mark its letter on your answer sheet.

1. FEINT

   A. fool

   B. proclaim

   C. penalize

   D. scavenge

2. PEER

   A. officer

   B. beginner

   C. equal

   D. patient

3. TRITE

   A. unskilled

   B. common

   C. unlikely

   D. ignorant

4. AMIABLE

   A. forgetful

   B. friendly

   C. strange

   D. great

5. GRIMACE

   A. sneer

   B. grindstone

   C. journal

   D. treasure

6. COMPELLED

   A. calculated

   B. combined

   C. collected

   D. forced

7. ALLY

   A. opponent

   B. passage

   C. friend

   D. preference

8. SOLICIT

   A. consent

   B. comfort

   C. request

   D. help

9. REFUTE

   A. demolish

   B. postpone

   C. disprove

   D. assist

10. EXPLICIT

    A. ambiguous

    B. clearly stated

    C. give information about

    D. to blow out

ISEE (UPPER LEVEL) DIAGNOSTIC TEST

11. RETAIN

  A. pay out

  B. play

  C. keep

  D. inquire

12. CORRESPONDENCE

  A. letters

  B. files

  C. testimony

  D. response

13. LEGITIMATE

  A. democratic

  B. legal

  C. genealogical

  D. underworld

14. DEDUCT

  A. conceal

  B. understand

  C. subtract

  D. terminate

15. EGRESS

  A. extreme

  B. extra supply

  C. exit

  D. high price

16. HORIZONTAL

  A. marginal

  B. in a circle

  C. left and right

  D. up and down

17. CONTROVERSY

  A. publicity

  B. debate

  C. revolution

  D. revocation

18. PREEMPT

  A. steal

  B. empty

  C. preview

  D. appropriate

19. PER CAPITA

  A. for an entire population

  B. by income

  C. for each person

  D. for every adult

20. OPTIONAL

  A. not required

  B. infrequent

  C. choosy

  D. for sale

Directions: Each of the following questions is made up of a sentence containing one or two blanks. The sentences with one blank indicate that one word is missing. Sentences with two blanks have two missing words. Each sentence is followed by four choices. Choose the one word or pair of words that will best complete the meaning of the sentence as a whole and mark the letter of your choice on your answer sheet.

21. Custom has so _____ our language that we can _____ only what has been said before.

    A. improved ... repeat

    B. changed ... understand

    C. constrained ... say

    D. dominated ... hear

22. A few of the critics _____ the play, but in general they either disregarded or ridiculed it.

    A. discredited

    B. criticized

    C. denounced

    D. appreciated

23. There were numerous _____ in her spelling test.

    A. explanations

    B. arguments

    C. errors

    D. excuses

24. Because of his _____ nature, he often acts purely on impulse.

    A. stoic

    B. reflective

    C. passionate

    D. wistful

25. A prospective job candidate ought to be _____ by the _____ of their contributions.

    A. controlled ... intelligence

    B. justified ... number

    C. examined ... wealth

    D. judged ... caliber

26. We seldom feel _____ when we are allowed to speak freely, but any _____ of our free speech brings anger.

    A. silenced ... celebration

    B. grateful ... restriction

    C. scholarly ... understanding

    D. exploited ... gratitude

27. The worse team lost because it had many players who, though not completely _____, were also not really _____.

    A. qualified ... agile

    B. clumsy ... incompetent

    C. amateurish ... dexterous

    D. ungraceful ... incapable

28. Although the _____ of the legislature become law, the exact _____ of the law is the result of judicial interpretation.

    A. ideas ... enforcement

    B. bills ... wording

    C. works ... punishment

    D. words ... meaning

29. Since movies have become more _____, many people believe television to be _____.

    A. helpful ... utilitarian

    B. expensive ... necessary

    C. common ... inadequate

    D. costly ... useless

30. Spores are a form of life that remain _____ until environmental conditions exist in which they can become _____.

    A. inactive ... vibrant

    B. hidden ... dangerous

    C. suppressed ... visible

    D. controlled ... rampant

31. The spirit of science is always trying to lead people to the study of _____ and away from the spinning of fanciful theories.

    A. tradition

    B. order

    C. legalities

    D. literature

32. My uncle has a _____ bomb shelter behind his house where he keeps homemade canned goods.

    A. submersive

    B. subterranean

    C. inexorable

    D. virtual

33. The fame of the author does not _____ the quality of their works. We must avoid equating success with infallibility.

    A. prejudice

    B. assure

    C. dignify

    D. extol

34. The mechanisms that develop hatred in humans are most potent, since there is more _____ than _____ in the world.

    A. tolerance ... prejudice

    B. joy ... rapture

    C. love ... hatred

    D. strife ... tranquility

35. Mining is often called a _____ industry, since it neither creates nor replenishes what it takes.

    A. robber

    B. ecology

    C. natural

    D. evil

36. The problem of landing astronauts on Mars is of such _____ that it makes going to the moon seem _____.

    A. complexity ... helpful

    B. certainty ... problematic

    C. magnitude ... basic

    D. docility ... effortless

37. To be _____, a theatrical setting must resemble _____.

    A. believable ... home

    B. effective ... reality

    C. reasonable ... beauty

    D. respectable ... ideas

38. During his speech, the candidate eagerly _____ rage among the _____ crowd.

    A. fomented ... hateful

    B. distilled ... docile

    C. indicted ... inquisitive

    D. assuaged ... elitist

39. Errors in existing theories are discovered, and the theories are either _____ or _____.

    A. improved ... obeyed

    B. removed ... followed

    C. altered ... discarded

    D. explained ... excused

40. In observing the _____ society of the ant, the scientist can learn much about the more _____ society of man.

A. hostile ... evil

B. elementary ... complicated

C. plain ... homogeneous

D. unadorned ... unsophisticated

END OF SECTION.
IF YOU HAVE ANY TIME LEFT, GO OVER YOUR WORK IN THIS SECTION ONLY.
DO NOT WORK IN ANY OTHER SECTION OF THE TEST.

ISEE (UPPER LEVEL) DIAGNOSTIC TEST

SECTION 2: QUANTITATIVE REASONING

37 Questions—35 Minutes

Note: You may assume that all figures accompanying Quantitative Reasoning questions have been drawn as accurately as possible EXCEPT when it is specifically stated that a particular figure is not drawn to scale. Letters such as *x*, *y*, and *n* stand for real numbers. The Quantitative Reasoning Test includes two types of questions. There are separate directions for each type of question.

Directions: For questions 1–19, work each problem in your head or in the margins of the test booklet. Mark the letter of your answer choice on the answer sheet.

1. Which pair of values for *x* and ☐ will make the following statement true?

   $2x \,\square\, 8$

   A. (6, <)

   B. (4, >)

   C. (0, <)

   D. (–3, >)

2. Complete the following statement:

   $7(3 \times \underline{\hspace{1cm}}) + 4 = 2{,}104$

   A. 10

   B. 10 + 2

   C. 10^2

   D. 10^3

3. 0.5% is equal to

   A. 0.005

   B. 0.05

   C. $\dfrac{1}{2}$

   D. 0.5

4. A scalene triangle has

   A. two equal sides.

   B. two equal sides and one right angle.

   C. no equal sides.

   D. three equal sides.

5. If $a - 2b = -7$, then which expression is equal to *a*?

   A. $2b - 7$

   B. $2b + 7$

   C. $-2b + 7$

   D. $-2b - 7$

6. A millimeter is what part of a meter?

   A. $\dfrac{1}{10}$

   B. $\dfrac{1}{100}$

   C. $\dfrac{1}{1{,}000}$

   D. $\dfrac{1}{10{,}000}$

7. What is the least common denominator for $\dfrac{2}{3}, \dfrac{1}{2}, \dfrac{5}{6},$ and $\dfrac{7}{9}$?

   A. 36

   B. 32

   C. 24

   D. 18

8. Find the area of a triangle whose dimensions are $b = 14$ inches, $h = 20$ inches.

   A. 140 square inches

   B. 208 square inches

   C. 280 square inches

   D. 288 square inches

9. What is the difference between $(4 \times 10^3) + 6$ and $(2 \times 10^3) + (3 \times 10) + 8$?

   A. 168

   B. 1,968

   C. 3,765

   D. 55,968

10. The set of common factors for 30 and 24 is

   A. {1, 2, 3, 6}

   B. {1, 2, 3, 4, 6}

   C. {1, 2, 4, 6}

   D. {1, 2, 4, 6, 12}

11.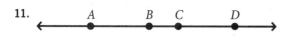

   $\overline{AC} \cap \overline{BD}$ is equal to

   A. $\overline{BC}$

   B. $\overline{BD}$

   C. $\overline{AC}$

   D. $\overline{AD}$

12. What is the value of the expression

   $\dfrac{2\left(2^3 + 2^2\right)}{4(8+2)}$?

   A. $\dfrac{3}{10}$

   B. $\dfrac{3}{5}$

   C. $\dfrac{1}{2}$

   D. $\dfrac{2}{3}$

13. The board shown below is 6 feet long, 4 inches wide, and 2 inches thick. One-third of it will be driven into the ground. How much surface area remains above ground?

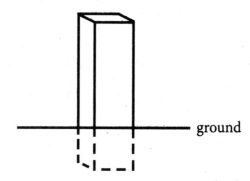

   A. About 4 sq. ft.

   B. Slightly less than 5 sq. ft.

   C. Slightly more than 5 sq. ft.

   D. About 8 sq. ft.

14. Mitchell can run M miles in H hours. A faster runner, Naya, can run N miles in L hours. Which equation expresses the difference in their rates?

   A. $\dfrac{M-N}{H}$

   B. $MH - HL$

   C. $\dfrac{HN}{M-L}$

   D. $\dfrac{N}{L} - \dfrac{M}{H}$

15. If Minhi is x years old now and her sister is 3 years younger, then 5 years from now her sister will be what age?

   A. $x + 5$ years

   B. $x + 3$ years

   C. $x + 2$ years

   D. 8 years

16. In the figure below, the largest possible circle is cut out of a square piece of tin. The area of the remaining piece of tin, in square inches, is approximately

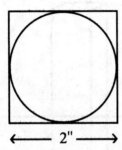

← 2" →

A. 0.14

B. 0.75

C. 0.86

D. 3.14

17. A square has an area of 49 sq. in. The number of inches in its perimeter is

A. 7

B. 14

C. 28

D. 98

18. If an engine pumps G gallons of water per minute, then the number of gallons pumped in half an hour may be found by

A. taking one half of G.

B. dividing 60 by G.

C. multiplying G by 30.

D. dividing 30 by G.

19. Two cars start from the same point at the same time. One drives north at 20 miles per hour and the other drives south on the same straight road at 36 miles per hour. How many miles apart are they after 30 minutes?

A. Less than 10

B. Between 10 and 20

C. Between 20 and 30

D. Between 30 and 40

Directions: For questions 20–37, two quantities are given—one in Column A and the other in Column B. In some questions, additional information concerning the quantities to be compared is centered above the entries in the two columns. Compare the quantities in the two columns, and mark your answer sheet as follows:

A. The quantity in Column A is greater.

B. The quantity in Column B is greater.

C. The two quantities are equal.

D. The relationship cannot be determined from the information given.

20.

$$s = 1$$
$$t = 3$$
$$a = -2$$

Column A	**Column B**
$[5a(4t)]^3$	$[4a(5s)]^2$

21. $\qquad 4 > x > -3$

Column A	**Column B**
$\dfrac{x}{3}$	$\dfrac{3}{x}$

22.

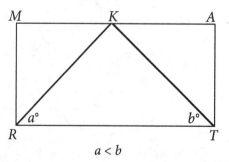

$$a < b$$

Column A	**Column B**
KR	KT

23.

Column A	**Column B**
$\dfrac{2}{3} + \dfrac{3}{7}$	$\dfrac{16}{21} - \dfrac{3}{7}$

24.

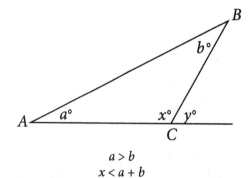

$$a > b$$
$$x < a + b$$

Column A	**Column B**
$a + b$	y

25. $\qquad y = $ an odd integer

Column A	**Column B**
The numerical value of y^2	The numerical value of y^3

26.

Column A	**Column B**
$(8 + 6) \div [3 - 7(2)]$	$(6 + 8) \div [2 - 7(3)]$

27.

Column A	**Column B**
Three fourths of $\dfrac{9}{9}$	$\dfrac{9}{9} \times \dfrac{3}{4}$

28.

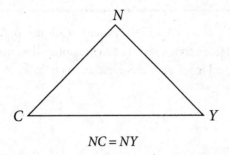

$$NC = NY$$
$$\angle N > \angle C$$

Column A	Column B
NC	CY

29.

Column A	Column B
$\dfrac{1}{\sqrt{9}}$	$\dfrac{1}{3}$

30.

Column A	Column B
$5\left(\dfrac{2}{3}\right)$	$\left(\dfrac{5}{3}\right)2$

31.

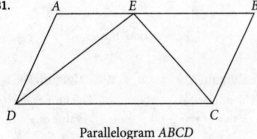

Parallelogram $ABCD$

E is a point on $\overline{AB}$

Column A	Column B
Area of $\triangle DEC$	Area of $\triangle AED$ + Area $\triangle EBC$

32. $x = -1$

Column A	Column B
$x^3 + x^2 - x + 1$	$x^3 - x^2 + x - 1$

33.

Column A	Column B
The edge of a cube whose volume is 27	The edge of a cube whose total surface area is 54

34.

Column A	Column B
$\dfrac{\frac{1}{2}+\frac{1}{3}}{\frac{2}{3}}$	$\dfrac{\frac{2}{3}}{\frac{1}{2}+\frac{1}{3}}$

35.

Column A	Column B
Area of a circle whose radius is x^3	Area of a circle whose radius is $3x$

36.

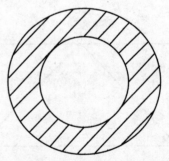

Radius of larger circle = 10

Radius of smaller circle = 7

Column A	Column B
Area of shaded portion	Area of smaller circle

37. $a < 0 < b$

<u>Column A</u>   <u>Column B</u>

a^2

$$\frac{b}{2}$$

END OF SECTION.
IF YOU HAVE ANY TIME LEFT, GO OVER YOUR WORK IN THIS SECTION ONLY.
DO NOT WORK IN ANY OTHER SECTION OF THE TEST.

SECTION 3: READING COMPREHENSION

36 Questions—35 Minutes

> **Directions:** Each reading passage is followed by questions based on its content. Answer the questions based on what is stated or implied in the passage. On your answer sheet, mark the letter of the answer you choose.

Questions 1–6 refer to the following passage.

Born in Pakistan on July 12, 1997, Malala Yousafzai was still just a teenager when she started changing the world. Often known simply as "Malala," this young activist took the world by storm when she survived an assassination attempt at the tender age of 15, then went on to tell her story to rally for change and publicly support the right for all girls in the world to receive an education.

When Malala was growing up, the Pakistani Taliban instituted a prohibition on educating girls. As the daughter of an activist and educator, Malala's family supported her when she decided to oppose this prohibition and go to school despite the Taliban's threats. She was only 11 when she gave her first speech in defense of girls' education at a protest. The speech was titled "How Dare the Taliban Take Away My Basic Right to Education?" and because press was in attendance, it got published throughout Pakistan. During this time, the Taliban was routinely attacking girls for attending school, bombing schools that dared to educate girls, and actively restricting women from playing an equal role in society.

Despite the danger her activism posed, Malala continued to oppose the Taliban's restrictions, blogging for the BBC under an assumed name and making television appearances. While her efforts were recognized in many ways, including her receiving Pakistan's first ever National Youth Peace Prize (which was later renamed the National Malala Peace Prize in her honor), it didn't protect her from being targeted by the Taliban. Malala was shot in the head by a gunman from the Pakistani Taliban on October 9, 2012, when walking home from school.

Miraculously, Malala survived this brutal attack and it only made her more dedicated to her cause. Following this heinous assault, a wave of worldwide protests in support of Malala also led Pakistan to adopt its first Right to Education Bill ensuring Pakistani girls' access to education. Since then, Malala has received numerous accolades for the activist work she continues to pursue. Her most notable award is the Nobel Peace Prize, which she received in 2014 at the age of 17, making her the youngest person to ever receive this award. To share her side of the story, Malala also wrote a <u>memoir</u> entitled *I Am Malala: The Girl Who Stood Up for Education and Was Shot by the Taliban* in 2013.

1. As used in paragraph 4, the underlined term *memoir* most nearly means

   A. biography.

   B. autobiography.

   C. news article.

   D. play.

2. Which of the following statements best expresses a central tenet of Malala Yousafzai's activism?

   A. The Taliban does not support Pakistani teachers enough.

   B. The quality of education in Pakistan is subpar.

   C. Pakistani girls are the only girls whose education is threatened this severely.

   D. All girls around the world deserve an education.

3. Which of the following is *not* mentioned as one of the ways the Pakistani Taliban targeted education?

   A. Attacking girls on their way to attend school

   B. Restricting women from societal roles that would allow them to impact education

   C. Bombing schools that allowed girls to attend

   D. Restricting students from choosing which school they wish to attend

4. Of the following quotations from the passage, which depicts a metaphor?

   A. "…to go to school despite the Taliban's threats."

   B. "…bombing schools that dared to educate girls…"

   C. "…it only made her more dedicated to her cause."

   D. "…a wave of worldwide protests in support of Malala…"

5. The passage states that Malala wrote articles for the BBC under an assumed name. What can you infer would be the reason Malala chose to disguise her name?

   A. Since Malala was from Pakistan, she needed to assume a British identity to write for a British publication.

   B. The BBC asked her to do so to avoid drawing attention to the articles.

   C. As a young person, she assumed the identity of an older person to be taken seriously.

   D. Malala wanted to protect herself from the Pakistani Taliban, who would use the articles to target her further.

6. How might you categorize the genre of writing used in this passage?

   A. Fictional

   B. Narrative

   C. Expository

   D. Persuasive

ISEE (UPPER LEVEL) DIAGNOSTIC TEST

The Spring and the Fall

In the spring of the year, in the spring of the year,
I walked the road beside my dear.
The trees were black where the bark was wet.
I see them yet, in the spring of the year.
He broke me a bough of the blossoming peach
That was out of the way and hard to reach.

In the fall of the year, in the fall of the year,
I walked the road beside my dear.
The rooks went up with a <u>raucous</u> trill.
I hear them still, in the fall of the year.
He laughed at all I dared to praise,
And broke my heart, in little ways.

Year be springing or year be falling,
The bark will drip and the birds be calling.
There's much that's fine to see and hear
In the spring of a year, in the fall of a year.
'Tis not love's going hurts my days,
But that it went in little ways.

—Edna St. Vincent Millay (1923)

Questions 7–12 refer to the following passage.

7. Which of the following best represents the rhyme scheme in the first stanza?

   A. AABACC

   B. ABABCC

   C. ABCBAC

   D. ABCABC

8. As used in the poem's second stanza, the underlined term *raucous* most nearly means

   A. soft.

   B. harsh.

   C. high-pitched.

   D. low-pitched.

9. What does the poet mean by saying "the bark will drip" in the third stanza?

   A. Everything seems surreal when you're in love.

   B. After a year, the trees will have contracted a disease.

   C. The wetness of the bark will make it look like it's dripping.

   D. Pieces of bark will fall off the trees.

10. What inference can you make based on the last two lines of the poem?

   A. The lovers are in a big fight.

   B. The poet's lover has proposed marriage.

   C. It took a year for the two people in the poem to fall in love.

   D. The poet is still sad about a breakup.

11. In the second stanza of the poem, the poet's lover

   A. hits them.

   B. criticizes things the poet likes.

   C. curses at them.

   D. cries and apologizes.

12. How might you describe the poem's overall theme?

   A. Love is mysterious, and no one can understand how it works.

   B. People who break your heart aren't worth the time you spend missing them.

   C. While love may come and go, time continues to pass and changes all things slowly.

   D. It is better to love for a short time than not at all.

Questions 13–18 refer to the following passage.

A certain question has plagued zoologists for years now: How did giraffes end up with such long necks? One of the reasons that scientists find this question intriguing is that long necks are not necessarily helpful to giraffes. For example, their vascular systems must work overtime to get all that blood pumping up and down the great distance between their hearts and brains. This is wildly inefficient because of the large amount of energy required simply to maintain blood pressure. Therefore, scientists have long assumed that there must be a specific reason that giraffes have this trait; otherwise, the species would have likely evolved to have more efficient features.

The most widely accepted theory has been that giraffes evolved this way to reach leaves on higher and higher trees, an adaptation that would have been crucial when drought or overgrazing meant lower foliage was picked over. While this seems like a straightforward theory, there's a catch—research has shown that giraffes don't necessarily go for the highest foliage they can reach, often seeming perfectly content to munch on lower-hanging leaves. Another theory suggests that the length of the neck was a way for male giraffes to attract mates, but female giraffes have the same average neck length as males, so this has also largely been considered speculation.

By analyzing various archeological specimens of an ancient giraffoid (meaning "giraffe-like") creature with a helmet-shaped protrusion on its forehead that have been discovered in China over the last few decades, scientists believe they now have a new clue about how giraffes got their long necks. The ancient creature, named *Discokeryx xiezhi* after the term for a unicorn figure from Chinese folklore, *xhiezhi*, likely used this hard forehead protrusion to headbutt others of its kind when competing for mates.

Consequently, scientists studying *Discokeryx xiezhi* fossil specimens believe it possible that giraffes' long necks evolved because male-male combat between ancient giraffoid creatures became more intense and involved more of the neck over time. While the search for high foliage likely did still play some role in helping giraffes evolve long necks, the fossils suggest that as fighting between males became more complex, natural selection favored animals with the longest and strongest necks. While there are some zoologists who are still skeptical of this theory, it adds new fodder to the discussion about how today's giraffes ended up with the features they have now.

13. Which statement best reflects the main idea of this passage?

   A. Archaeologists need to work harder to find more giraffoid fossils.

   B. No one will ever know why giraffes have long necks.

   C. Male giraffes do not necessarily have longer necks than female giraffes.

   D. Fossil evidence from ancient giraffoid specimens can provide clues about today's giraffes.

14. The author's purpose in paragraph 2 is to

   A. speculate as to why zoologists are interested in giraffe neck length.

   B. clarify common theories about giraffe neck length that have been debated by zoologists so far.

   C. convince the reader that new fossil evidence shatters old theories.

   D. criticize those who support one theory about giraffe neck length over another.

15. The ancient giraffoid creature known as *Discokeryx xhiezhi* borrows its name from a(n)

   A. famous giraffe at the Beijing Zoo.

   B. archaeologist who was instrumental in identifying the specimen.

   C. bone found in its jaw.

   D. unicorn figure in Chinese folklore.

16. As used in paragraph 3, the underlined term *protrusion* most nearly means

   A. wound.

   B. muscle.

   C. bone.

   D. bump.

17. Which of the following terms most nearly describes the author's tone?

   A. Resigned

   B. Informative

   C. Laudatory

   D. Hypercritical

18. We can infer from the passage that

   A. scientists will continue to debate theories about giraffe neck length.

   B. scientists will stop debating giraffe neck length.

   C. giraffes will evolve to have shorter necks over time.

   D. most zoologists are not interested in discussing giraffe neck length.

Questions 19–24 refer to the following passage.

My free life began on the third of September, 1838. On the morning of the fourth of that month, after an anxious and most perilous but safe journey, I found myself in the big city of New York, a FREE MAN—one more added to the mighty throng which, like the confused waves of the troubled sea, surged to and fro between the lofty walls of Broadway. Though dazzled with the wonders which met me on every hand, my thoughts could not be much withdrawn from my strange situation. For the moment, the dreams of my youth and the hopes of my manhood were completely fulfilled. The bonds that had held me to "old master" were broken. No man now had a right to call me his slave or assert mastery over me. I was in the rough and tumble of an outdoor world, to take my chance with the rest of its busy number. I have often been asked how I felt when first I found myself on free soil. There is scarcely anything in my experience about which I could not give a more satisfactory answer. A new world had opened upon me. If life is more than breath

and the "quick round of blood," I lived more in that one day than in a year of my slave life. It was a time of joyous excitement which words can but tamely describe. In a letter written to a friend soon after reaching New York, I said: "I felt as one might feel upon escape from a den of hungry lions." Anguish and grief, like darkness and rain, may be depicted; but gladness and joy, like the rainbow, defy the skill of pen or pencil. During ten or fifteen years I had been, as it were, dragging a heavy chain which no strength of mine could break; I was not only a slave, but a slave for life. I might become a husband, a father, an aged man, but through all, from birth to death, from the cradle to the grave, I had felt myself doomed. All efforts I had previously made to secure my freedom had not only failed but had seemed only to rivet my fetters the more firmly, and to render my escape more difficult. <u>Baffled</u>, entangled, and discouraged, I had at times asked myself the question, May not my condition after all be God's work, and ordered for a wise purpose, and if so, Is not submission my duty? A contest had in fact been going on in my mind for a long time, between the clear consciousness of right and the plausible make-shifts of theology and superstition. The one held me an <u>abject</u> slave—a prisoner for life, punished for some transgression in which I had no lot nor part; and the other counseled me to manly endeavor to secure my freedom. This contest was now ended; my chains were broken, and the victory brought me unspeakable joy.

Excerpt from "My Escape from Slavery" by Frederick Douglass (1881)

19. Which of the following quotations from the passage does *not* contain figurative language?

A. "… one more added to the mighty throng which, like the confused waves of the troubled sea, surged to and fro between the lofty walls of Broadway."

B. "I lived more in that one day than in a year of my slave life."

C. "It was a time of joyous excitement …"

D. "I felt as one might feel upon escape from a den of hungry lions."

20. As used in the passage, the underlined term *baffled* most nearly means

A. entertained.

B. shy.

C. perplexed.

D. anticipatory.

21. Where did Frederick Douglass first go after his free life began?

A. Washington, D.C.

B. Boston

C. Philadelphia

D. New York City

22. What might you logically expect to come next in the narrative?

A. Information on what Douglass did during his first few weeks as a free man

B. The story of how, when, and where Douglass was born

C. A historical background on slavery

D. Data on how many people escaped slavery in the years leading up to the Civil War

23. What might be the best alternate title for this passage?

A. "My Victory"

B. "All About Frederick Douglass"

C. "September 1838"

D. "Thoughts from a Newly Free Man"

24. As used in the passage, the underlined term *abject* most nearly means

A. rejected by his peers.

B. without pride or dignity.

C. lost and alone.

D. in a state of disillusionment.

Questions 25–30 refer to the following passage.

Scholars study the phenomenon of collective memory to better understand how groups of people remember and engage with the past. Collective memory refers to the experiences and memories that are shared by a group of people and passed down through generations. In the United States, there are many public memorials to commemorate a variety of important events, like the 9/11 Memorial in New York City or the USS Arizona Memorial in Pearl Harbor, Hawaii. Memorials provide insight into how a country collectively remembers people and events and how those events have shaped history and national identity.

Sometimes, people disagree on how a certain event or experience should be commemorated. Most war memorials in the United States pay tribute to those who served and died in war with towering white columns or heroic sculptures depicting the strength and bravery of service members. However, the Vietnam Veterans Memorial, designed by American architect Maya Lin, broke the mold. Lin's winning design for the memorial consisted of two black granite walls, partially buried in the earth, that meet at a 125-degree angle to form a "V" shape. More than 58,000 names are etched into the walls, commemorating those who died in the war. The black granite has a mirror-like effect, so people looking at the wall can see their own reflections.

The Vietnam War was controversial in and of itself, and the memorial was no different. The design for the memorial did not <u>overtly</u> celebrate the war effort but rather encouraged viewers to draw their own conclusions about the reality of the war. Many people protested the memorial's message, or lack thereof, and a more traditional bronze statue depicting three soldiers was added to the entrance of Lin's Vietnam War memorial. For many, the Vietnam War was a source of shame; for others, it was still important to acknowledge the sacrifice made by those who fought.

Now, the Vietnam Veterans Memorial is viewed as a groundbreaking and deeply moving structure. In the past, war had been seen as a necessary evil, one that required sacrifice and heroism in the face of death and destruction. But American attitudes toward war have changed, and we often question the necessity and purpose of modern-day conflicts. Accordingly, our collective memory, the way we decide to commemorate the experience of war, has also changed, prompting us to reimagine our country's relationship to war.

25. As used in paragraph 3, the underlined term *overtly* most nearly means

A. directly.

B. indirectly.

C. formally.

D. informally.

26. The author's tone in this passage can most accurately be described as

A. compliant.

B. playful.

C. mournful.

D. objective.

27. The purpose of paragraph 2 is to

   A. discuss what made the Vietnam Veterans Memorial so controversial.

   B. explain what collective memory is.

   C. describe the appearance of the Vietnam Veterans Memorial in detail.

   D. introduce the concept of a commemorative memorial.

28. Which of the following is *not* one of that reasons that Maya Lin's design for the memorial was regarded as "groundbreaking and deeply moving"?

   A. The memorial is in the shape of a V and partially buried in the ground, evoking a headstone.

   B. Lin didn't follow the typical "mold" for creating a war memorial.

   C. A traditional bronze statue of soldiers graces the memorial's entrance.

   D. There are more than 58,000 names etched into the walls to commemorate the fallen.

29. Collective memory can be described as a(n)

   A. art theory used to create impactful commemorative memorials.

   B. way of thinking that involves preserving memories as best as possible.

   C. memory that is a composite of images one remembers, rather than a specific incident.

   D. shared experience of remembering within a group of people or across generations.

30. What can you infer is true about the Vietnam Veterans Memorial?

   A. Lin hoped that all who saw the memorial would come away with the same message.

   B. Some people consider the memorial to be too large and showy.

   C. It would look much better if it were white instead of black.

   D. There are people who do not like the memorial because it does not celebrate the war effort more explicitly.

Questions 31–36 refer to the following passage.

Invasive species can wreak havoc on ecosystems, and the emerald ash borer is no exception. Emerald ash borers are brightly colored wood-boring beetles that only attack ash trees. Native to Asia, the emerald ash borer was first located in the United States in 2002 when it was spotted in Michigan. The insect likely made its way over to the US by hitching a ride on a shipping crate or in wooden packing materials.

Emerald ash borers are an invasive species in the US and Canada, killing up to 99% of ash trees in their path. While adult emerald ash borers don't do much damage, the larvae feed on the inner bark, making it difficult for the trees to get the proper nutrients. Signs of an emerald ash borer infestation include D-shaped exit holes, woodpecker feeding holes, bark deformities, yellowing foliage, and more.

The most recent data suggest that emerald ash borers have been spotted in at least 35 states. In states where emerald ash borers are widespread, there are often restrictions on the transport of firewood between counties since this is how the insects are likely to spread. Residents with ash trees are encouraged to vaccinate their trees against emerald ash borer infestation or else risk losing their trees to the invasive beetle. In areas where infestation is likely or even <u>inevitable</u>, some cities and counties are taking preemptive action by either vaccinating trees or replacing ash trees with more resilient native species. It's important that residents in affected areas keep an eye out for emerald ash borers or other invasive species and notify the proper authorities of any sightings.

31. The best title for this passage would be

    A. "Emerald Ash Borers: An Invasive Species"

    B. "What's an Invasive Species?"

    C. "Invasive Species of Michigan"

    D. "Signs of Infestation"

32. According to the passage, in how many US states have emerald ash borers been identified?

    A. 20

    B. 25

    C. 30

    D. 35

33. From this passage, we can infer that

    A. once emerald ash borers are present in a forest, it is very difficult to save the ash trees in their path.

    B. the best solution to invasive species like the emerald ash borer is to never plant ash trees again.

    C. conservationists are overdoing it on trying to combat the emerald ash borer.

    D. conservationists are not interested in combatting the emerald ash borer.

34. As used in paragraph 3, the underlined word *inevitable* most nearly means

    A. predictable.

    B. unpredictable.

    C. complicated.

    D. unavoidable.

35. Which piece of information, if added to paragraph 2, would *not* serve the author's purpose?

    A. Statistics on how large an area an emerald ash borer infestation can destroy in a single week.

    B. A detailed description of how an ash tree looks before and after an infestation.

    C. A diagram showing the difference between an adult emerald ash borer and their larvae.

    D. The author's story about a time they held an emerald ash borer in their hand.

36. What is the overall tone of the passage?

    A. Explanatory

    B. Apologetic

    C. Macabre

    D. Witty

END OF SECTION.
IF YOU HAVE ANY TIME LEFT, GO OVER YOUR WORK IN THIS SECTION ONLY.
DO NOT WORK IN ANY OTHER SECTION OF THE TEST.

SECTION 4: MATHEMATICS ACHIEVEMENT

47 Questions—40 Minutes

Directions: Each question is followed by four answer choices. Choose the correct answer to each question and mark the corresponding letter on your answer sheet.

1. A square measures 8 inches on one side. By how much will the area be increased if its length is increased by 4 inches and its width decreased by 2 inches?

   A. 14 sq. in.

   B. 12 sq. in.

   C. 10 sq. in.

   D. 8 sq. in.

2. $r = 35 - (3 + 6)(-n)$

   $n = 2$

   $r =$

   A. 53

   B. 17

   C. −17

   D. −53

3. $(3 + 4)^3 =$

   A. 1

   B. 91

   C. 343

   D. 490

4. Which value is *not* equal to $\dfrac{4}{9}$?

   A. $\dfrac{2}{4.5}$

   B. 0.4444444

   C. $\dfrac{9}{18}$

   D. $0.\overline{4}$

5. Aluminum bronze consists of copper and aluminum, usually in the ratio of 10:1 by weight. If an object made of this alloy weighs 77 pounds, how many pounds of aluminum does it contain?

   A. 7

   B. 7.7

   C. 10

   D. 70

6. How many boxes 2 inches × 3 inches × 4 inches can fit into a carton 2 feet × 3 feet × 4 feet?

   A. 100

   B. 144

   C. 1,000

   D. 1,728

7. A clerk can add 40 columns of figures an hour by using an adding machine and 20 columns of figures an hour without using an adding machine. What is the total number of hours it will take the clerk to add 200 columns of figures if $\dfrac{3}{5}$ of the work is done by machine and the rest without the machine?

   A. 6 hours

   B. 7 hours

   C. 8 hours

   D. 9 hours

8. Mr. Griffin makes a weekly salary of $750 plus 7% commission on his sales. What will his income be for a week in which he makes sales totaling $4,725?

   A. $1,425.00

   B. $1,275.00

   C. $1,080.75

   D. $783.07

9. Solve for x: $x^2 + 5 = 41$

   A. ± 6

   B. ± 7

   C. ± 8

   D. ± 9

10. Two rectangular boards each measuring 5 feet by 3 feet are placed together to make one large board. How much shorter will the perimeter be if the two long sides are placed together than if the two short sides are placed together?

    A. 2 feet

    B. 4 feet

    C. 6 feet

    D. 8 feet

11. If a plane travels 1,000 miles in 5 hours 30 minutes, what is its average speed in miles per hour?

    A. $181\dfrac{9}{11}$

    B. $191\dfrac{1}{2}$

    C. 200

    D. 215

12. Two years ago, a company purchased 500 dozen pencils at 40 cents per dozen. This year, only 75 percent as many pencils were purchased as were purchased two years ago, but the price was 20 percent higher than the old price. What was the total cost of pencils purchased by the company this year?

    A. $180

    B. $187.50

    C. $240

    D. $257.40

13. An adult's mini golf ticket costs twice as much as a child's ticket. If a family of three children and two adults can play mini golf for $49, what is the cost of an adult ticket?

    A. $7

    B. $10

    C. $12

    D. $14

14. Solve for x: $\dfrac{x}{2} + 36 = 37.25$

    A. 2.5

    B. 3.5

    C. 12.5

    D. 18.5

15. A group of 6 people raised $690 for charity. One of the people raised 35% of the total. What was the amount raised by the other 5 people?

    A. $448.50

    B. $241.50

    C. $89.70

    D. $74.75

16. Which expression is equivalent to the expression $(y + 5)(y - 1)$?

    A. $y^2 - 5$

    B. $y^2 + 4$

    C. $y^2 - 4y - 5$

    D. $y^2 + 4y - 5$

17. If the scale on a blueprint is $\frac{1}{4}$ inch = 1 foot, give the blueprint dimensions of a room that in real-life measures 29 feet long and 23 feet wide.

    A. $6\frac{3}{4}$" × 6"

    B. $7\frac{1}{4}$" × $5\frac{1}{2}$"

    C. $7\frac{1}{4}$" × $5\frac{3}{4}$"

    D. $7\frac{1}{2}$" × $5\frac{1}{2}$"

18. Find the area of a rectangle with a length of 176 feet and a width of 79 feet.

    A. 13,904 sq. ft.

    B. 13,854 sq. ft.

    C. 13,804 sq. ft.

    D. 13,304 sq. ft.

19. $63 \div \frac{1}{9} =$

    A. 7

    B. 56

    C. 67

    D. 567

20. With an 18% discount, Jarrod was able to save $13.23 on a coat. What was the original price of the coat?

    A. $69.75

    B. $71.50

    C. $73.50

    D. $74.75

21. If it takes three people 56 minutes to fill a trench 4' × 6' × 5' and two of the people work twice as rapidly as the third, how many minutes will it take the two faster people alone to fill this trench?

    A. 70 minutes

    B. 60 minutes

    C. 50 minutes

    D. 40 minutes

22. Population figures for a certain area show there are $1\frac{1}{2}$ times as many umarried men as unmarried women in the area. The total unmarried population is 18,000. There are 1,122 married couples with 756 children. How many unmarried men are there in the area?

    A. 3,000

    B. 6,000

    C. 9,000

    D. It cannot be determined from the information given.

23. If a vehicle is to complete a 20-mile trip at an average rate of 30 miles per hour, it must complete the trip in

    A. 20 minutes.

    B. 30 minutes.

    C. 40 minutes.

    D. 50 minutes.

24. Solve for x: $2x^2 + 3 = 21$

    A. ± 3

    B. ± 5

    C. ± 9

    D. ± 10

25. Find the area of a circle whose diameter is 6".

    A. 29.26

    B. 28.26

    C. 27.96

    D. 27.26

26. The scale on a map is $\frac{1}{8}$" = 25 miles. If two cities are $3\frac{7}{8}$" apart on the map, what is the actual distance between them?

    A. 31 miles

    B. 56 miles

    C. 675 miles

    D. 775 miles

27. A house was valued at $500,000 and insured for 80% of that amount. Find the yearly premium if it is figured at $0.45 per hundred dollars of value.

   A. $1,580.00

   B. $1,670.24

   C. $1,800.00

   D. $1,920.00

28. If a certain job can be performed by 18 clerks in 26 days, the number of clerks needed to perform the job in 12 days is

   A. 24 clerks.

   B. 30 clerks.

   C. 39 clerks.

   D. 52 clerks.

29. $72.61 \div 0.05 =$

   A. 1.45220

   B. 14.522

   C. 145.220

   D. 1,452.20

30. A car dealer sold three different makes of used cars. The price of the first make was $4,200, the second $4,800, and the third $5,400. The total sales were $360,000. If three times as many of the third car were sold as the first, and twice as many of the second make were sold than the first, how many cars of the third make were sold?

   A. 15

   B. 24

   C. 36

   D. It cannot be determined by the information given.

31. One third of the number of people attending a football game were admitted at the full price of admission. How many people paid full price if the gate receipts were $42,000?

   A. 2,800 people

   B. 3,500 people

   C. 5,000 people

   D. It cannot be determined by the information given.

32. 7 days 3 hours 20 minutes – 4 days 9 hours 31 minutes =

   A. 2 days 17 hours 49 minutes

   B. 2 days 17 hours 69 minutes

   C. 3 days 10 hours 49 minutes

   D. 3 days 10 hours 69 minutes

33. Find the area of a triangle whose dimensions are $b = 12'$, $h = 14'$.

   A. 168 sq. ft.

   B. 84 sq. ft.

   C. 42 sq. ft.

   D. 24 sq. ft.

34. Increased by 150%, the number 72 becomes

   A. 108

   B. 170

   C. 180

   D. 188

35. Which equation represents the statement four times a certain number divided by three, minus six, equals two?

   A. $\dfrac{4n}{3} - 6 = 2$

   B. $4n^2 - 6 = 2$

   C. $4n^2 \div 3 - 6 = 2$

   D. $\left(\dfrac{1}{4}n \div 3\right) - 6 = 2$

36. If $14x - 2y = 32$ and $x + 2y = 13$, then $x =$

   A. 8

   B. 5

   C. 4

   D. 3

37. An ordinary die is thrown. What are the odds that it will come up 1?

   A. $\dfrac{1}{4}$

   B. $\dfrac{1}{6}$

   C. $\dfrac{1}{8}$

   D. $\dfrac{1}{12}$

38. Which is the longest time?

   A. 25 hours

   B. 1,440 minutes

   C. 1 day

   D. 3,600 seconds

39. Two cars are 550 miles apart, both traveling on the same straight road toward each other. If one travels at 50 miles per hour, the other at 60 miles per hour, and they both leave at 1 p.m., what time will they meet?

   A. 4 p.m.

   B. 4:30 p.m.

   C. 5:45 p.m.

   D. 6 p.m.

40. Write 493 in expanded form, using exponents.

   A. $(4 \times 10^3) + (9 \times 10^2) + (3 \times 10)$

   B. $(4 \times 10^2) + (9 \times 10) + 3$

   C. $(4 \times 10^2) + (9 \times 10) - 7$

   D. $(4 \times 10^1) + (9 \times 10) + 3$

41. If 10 workers earn \$5,400 in 12 days, how much will 6 workers earn in 15 days?

   A. \$10,500

   B. \$5,400

   C. \$4,050

   D. \$2,025

42. The scale of a particular map is $\dfrac{3}{8}" = 5$ miles. If the distance between points A and B is $4\dfrac{1}{2}"$ on the map, what is the distance in actuality?

   A. 12 miles

   B. 36 miles

   C. 48 miles

   D. 60 miles

43. Find the diameter of a circle whose area is 78.5 sq. in.

   A. 25 feet

   B. 10 feet

   C. 25 inches

   D. 10 inches

44. If $ab + 4 = 52$, and $a = 6$, then $b =$

   A. 4

   B. 8

   C. 21

   D. 42

45. If $\dfrac{2}{3}$ of a jar is filled with water in 1 minute, how many minutes longer will it take to fill the remainder of the jar?

   A. $\dfrac{1}{4}$

   B. $\dfrac{1}{3}$

   C. $\dfrac{1}{2}$

   D. $\dfrac{2}{3}$

46. A group left on a trip at 8:50 a.m. and reached its destination at 3:30 p.m. How long, in hours and minutes, did the trip take?

    A. 3 hours 10 minutes

    B. 4 hours 40 minutes

    C. 5 hours 10 minutes

    D. 6 hours 40 minutes

47. A square is changed into a rectangle by increasing its length 10% and decreasing its width 10%. Its area

    A. remains the same.

    B. decreases by 10%.

    C. increases by 1%.

    D. decreases by 1%.

END OF SECTION.
IF YOU HAVE ANY TIME LEFT, GO OVER YOUR WORK IN THIS SECTION ONLY.
DO NOT WORK IN ANY OTHER SECTION OF THE TEST.

SECTION 5: ESSAY

30 Minutes

Directions: You will have 30 minutes to plan and write an essay on the following topic. Do not write on another topic. An essay on another topic is not acceptable.

The essay is designed to give you an opportunity to show how well you can write. You should try to express your thoughts clearly. How well you write is much more important than how much you write, but you need to say enough for a reader to understand what you mean.

You will probably want to write more than a short paragraph. You should also be aware that a copy of your essay will be sent to each school that will be receiving your test results. Please write or print so that your writing may be read by someone who is not familiar with your handwriting.

You may make notes and plan your essay. Allow enough time to copy the prompt onto the first two lines of your answer sheet. Please remember to write your response in blue or black pen. Again, you may use cursive writing or you may print.

Topic: If you could spend an afternoon with any author, living or dead, with whom would you spend it? What would you talk about?

ANSWER KEYS AND EXPLANATIONS

Section 1: Verbal Reasoning

1. A	9. C	17. B	25. D	33. B
2. C	10. B	18. D	26. B	34. D
3. B	11. C	19. C	27. C	35. A
4. B	12. A	20. A	28. D	36. C
5. A	13. B	21. C	29. B	37. B
6. D	14. C	22. D	30. A	38. A
7. C	15. C	23. C	31. B	39. C
8. C	16. C	24. C	32. B	40. B

1. **The correct answer is A.** To feint is to "deceive or make a pretense of." The word *fool* has nearly the same meaning.

2. **The correct answer is C.** The term *peer* describes "someone or something that is of equal standing to another."

3. **The correct answer is B.** *Trite* means "boring from too much use." *Commonplace* is a synonym of *trite*, so the word that is closest in meaning is *common*.

4. **The correct answer is B.** *Amiable* means "friendly, sociable, and congenial."

5. **The correct answer is A.** A grimace is "a facial expression of disgust or displeasure." A sneer expresses scorn or contempt.

6. **The correct answer is D.** To compel is to force.

7. **The correct answer is C.** The term *ally* describes "another with a common purpose, an associate, or a helper." A friend is an ally. Be careful not to confuse *ally* with *alley*. An alley is a passage.

8. **The correct answer is C.** To solicit means to "approach with a request or plea."

9. **The correct answer is C.** To refute is to "disprove" or "show something to be false."

10. **The correct answer is B.** *Explicit* means "distinct, observable, or clearly stated."

11. **The correct answer is C.** To retain means to hold on or keep.

12. **The correct answer is A.** The term *correspondence* describes either "an exchange of letters" or the letters themselves. *Correspondence* can also mean an agreement or conformity. However, this is not the correct meaning based on the answer options given.

13. **The correct answer is B.** *Legitimate* means "conforming to the law" or "abiding by the rules." The word *legal* is closest in meaning.

14. **The correct answer is C.** The verb *deduct* means "to subtract." The word with a meaning closer to "understand" is *deduce*.

15. **The correct answer is C.** *Egress* means "the way out." *Exit* is the closest synonym.

16. **The correct answer is C.** *Horizontal* means "parallel to the horizon" or "left-to-right."

17. **The correct answer is B.** The meaning of the term *controversy* is "an exchange of opposing opinions or arguments." The word *debate* is closest in meaning.

18. **The correct answer is D.** To preempt is to "seize before anyone else can" or "appropriate." Note that the term does not imply dishonesty, just speed or privilege.

19. **The correct answer is C.** *Per capita* literally means "for each head," therefore "for each person."

20. **The correct answer is A.** Optional means either "not required" or "left to one's choice."

21. **The correct answer is C.** The sense of the sentence calls for a word with a negative connotation in

the first blank; therefore, we need consider only choices C and D. Of these choices, *constrained . . . say*, choice C, is the better completion.

22. **The correct answer is D.** Since it is stated that most critics disregarded or ridiculed the play, the few critics remaining must have done the opposite and appreciated the work.

23. **The correct answer is C.** The context here implies the correct answer must be something that occurs on a test. The correct choice is *errors*.

24. **The correct answer is C.** One who acts purely on impulse is most likely to have a *passionate* (emotional or intense) nature.

25. **The correct answer is D.** When evaluating a potential new hire, the term for the measure by which the candidate should be judged is *caliber*, meaning "the degree of ability or merit of one's work or achievements."

26. **The correct answer is B.** Freedom of speech is something we take for granted, so we do not feel grateful when allowed to exercise this freedom; however, we do become angry when any restriction (limit) is imposed on our right to speak freely.

27. **The correct answer is C.** The qualities attributed to the players on the worse team must be opposites for comparison and adjectives for parallelism within the sentence. *Amateurish*, which means not professional, and *dexterous*, which means skilled or nimble, make up the only choice that meets both requirements.

28. **The correct answer is D.** It is the function of the legislature to write laws (their words become law). It is the function of the judiciary to interpret the words of the law (to determine their meaning).

29. **The correct answer is B.** Movies and television are both media of entertainment. The sentence compares the two media in terms of their cost, stating that many people believe television (which is inexpensive after the initial investment in the set) is necessary because movies have become so expensive (and therefore out of reach for many people).

30. **The correct answer is A.** The context of the sentence calls for two words that are opposites and that can both be applied to life forms. Spores are the tiny particles in certain plants that act as seeds in the production of new plants. These spores remain dormant or inactive until the proper conditions exist to render them vigorous or vibrant, thus creating a new generation of plants.

31. **The correct answer is B.** The completion needed is a word that is opposite in meaning to "the spinning of fanciful theories." Of the choices given, *order* best fulfills this requirement.

32. **The correct answer is B.** *Subterranean* is a synonym for *underground*. It is the only choice given with a meaning that suits the sentence.

33. **The correct answer is B.** The second sentence provides the clue to the meaning of the first. If success does not mean infallibility (certainty), then the fame of an author does not assure the quality of their work.

34. **The correct answer is D.** The completion here demands words that are opposites. In addition, the first blank requires a word that would promote hatred. Only *strife*, meaning "conflict," and *tranquility*, meaning "peace," fulfill these requirements and complete the meaning of the sentence.

35. **The correct answer is A.** Since mining takes away without replacing what it takes, it may be called a robber industry. Given these characteristics, mining might also be considered evil, but *robber* is the most specific adjective to describe an industry that does not replenish what it takes.

36. **The correct answer is C.** This sentence presents two problems that are being compared in terms of the ease of their solution. The only choices that fulfill the requirements of such a comparison are *magnitude* and *basic*.

37. **The correct answer is B.** A theatrical setting serves to create a mood or a feeling of being in another time or place. If the setting is to be effective (to make the desired impression on the audience), it must have some semblance of reality.

38. **The correct answer is A.** The word *rage* is key for determining what pair of words we need. The only pair of words that makes sense is *fomented*, meaning "incited" or "instigated," and *hateful*.

39. **The correct answer is C.** When errors are discovered in existing theories, those theories must either be altered (changed) in light of the new information or they must be discarded altogether, if the new information renders the old theories false.

40. **The correct answer is B.** The sentence compares two different societies and therefore requires completions that are both parallel and opposite. *Elementary* (simple) and *complicated* (intricate) best meet these requirements.

Section 2: Quantitative Reasoning

1. C	9. B	17. C	25. D	33. C
2. C	10. A	18. C	26. B	34. A
3. A	11. A	19. C	27. C	35. D
4. C	12. B	20. B	28. B	36. A
5. A	13. A	21. D	29. C	37. D
6. C	14. D	22. A	30. C	
7. D	15. C	23. A	31. C	
8. A	16. C	24. C	32. A	

1. **The correct answer is C.** If $x = 0$, then $2x < 8$ because $2(0) < 8$. None of the other pairs result in a true statement.

2. **The correct answer is C.** Substitute n for the blank space.

$$7(3 \times n) + 4 = 2,104$$
$$7(3n) + 4 = 2,104$$
$$21n + 4 = 2,104$$
$$21n = 2,100$$
$$n = 100 \text{ or } 10^2$$

3. **The correct answer is A.** Since $1\% = 0.01$, one half of one percent is written 0.005.

4. **The correct answer is C.** A scalene triangle has no equal sides.

5. **The correct answer is A.** To solve for a, add $2b$ to both sides of the equation. This gives us $a = -7 + 2b$. We can reorder the expression to read $2b - 7$.

6. **The correct answer is C.** There are 1,000 millimeters in a meter.

7. **The correct answer is D.** The LCD is the smallest whole number that can be divided by each denominator. If we start with the number 18, we quickly see that each denominator is a factor of 18. Since 18 is the smallest whole number among the answer choices given, we know that this is the LCD.

8. **The correct answer is A.** The area of a triangle is found by using

$$A = \frac{1}{2}bh$$
$$A = \frac{1}{2} \times 14 \times 20$$
$$= 140 \text{ sq. in.}$$

9. **The correct answer is B.**

$$(4 \times 10^3) + 6 = 4,006$$
$$(2 \times 10^3) + (3 \times 10) + 8 = 2,038$$

The difference is 1,968.

10. **The correct answer is A.** The set of factors for 24 is: {1, 2, 3, 4, 6, 8, 12, 24}

The set of factors for 30 is: {1, 2, 3, 5, 6, 10, 15, 30}

The set of common factors is: {1, 2, 3, 6}

11. **The correct answer is A.** The intersection of the two line segments is the place they overlap. Note that they overlap in the interval marked $\overline{BC}$.

12. **The correct answer is B.** Perform the calculations, using the order of operations: PEMDAS. First, perform the calculations in parentheses:

$$\frac{2(2^3 + 2^2)}{4(8 + 2)} = \frac{2(2^3 + 2^2)}{4(10)}$$

Next, perform calculations involving exponents:

$$\frac{2\left(2^3+2^2\right)}{4(10)}=\frac{2(8+4)}{4(10)}$$

$$=\frac{2(12)}{4(10)}$$

Now, perform multiplication and division:

$$\frac{2(12)}{4(10)}=\frac{24}{40}=\frac{3}{5}$$

13. **The correct answer is A.** One third of the board will be driven into the ground, leaving 4 feet exposed. The exposed part of the board has 5 faces: two faces 4 feet long by 4 inches wide; two faces 4 feet long by 2 inches wide; and one face (the end) 2 inches by 4 inches. Because the answer choices are in units of square feet, we will calculate in square feet:

$$2\times4\times\frac{1}{3}=\frac{8}{3}\text{ or }2\frac{2}{3}\text{ sq. ft.}$$

$$2\times4\times\frac{1}{6}=\frac{8}{6}\text{ or }1\frac{1}{3}\text{ sq. ft.}$$

$$1\times\frac{1}{3}\times\frac{1}{6}=\frac{1}{18}\text{ sq. ft.}$$

The sum is $4\frac{1}{18}$ sq. ft. of board remaining above ground.

14. **The correct answer is D.** Mitchell's rate is $\frac{M}{H}$ miles per hour. Naya's rate is $\frac{N}{L}$ miles per hour. We know Naya is faster, so the difference in their rates is written as $\frac{N}{L}-\frac{M}{H}$.

15. **The correct answer is C.** Minhi's age is x. Her sister's age is $x-3$. In 5 years, her sister's age will be $x-3+5=x+2$.

16. **The correct answer is C.**

The area of a square $=s^2$

The area of this square $=2^2=4$

The area of a circle $=\pi\bullet r^2$

$$\left(r=\frac{1}{2}d\right)(\pi=3.14)$$

The area of this circle $\pi\bullet1^2=\pi\bullet1=\pi$

The difference between the area of this square and the area of this circle is $4-3.14=0.86$

17. **The correct answer is C.**

Area of a square $=s^2$

$49=7^2$

One side $=7$ inches

$P=4s$

$P=4\times7=28$ inches

18. **The correct answer is C.** One half hour = 30 minutes, so you would multiply G by 30. Amount = rate (G) × time (30 minutes)

19. **The correct answer is C.** One car went 20 mph for $\frac{1}{2}$ hour = 10 miles. The other car went 36 mph for $\frac{1}{2}$ hour = 18 miles. Since they went in opposite directions, add the two distances to find the total number of miles apart. $10+18=28$

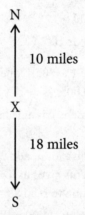

20. **The correct answer is B.**

$$\left[5a(4t)\right]^3=\left[-10(12)\right]^3$$

$$=(-120)^3$$

$$=\text{ negative answer}$$

$$\left[4a(5s)\right]^2=\left[-8(5)\right]^2$$

$$=(-40)^2$$

$$=\text{ positive answer}$$

A positive product is greater than a negative one.

21. **The correct answer is D.** Since x could be any non-zero value from 4 to –3, the values of the fractions are impossible to determine.

22. **The correct answer is A.** $a < b \therefore b > a$ (given).

    $\therefore KR > KT$ (in a triangle the greater side lies opposite the greater angle)

23. **The correct answer is A.**

    $$\frac{2}{3} + \frac{3}{7} = \frac{14}{21} + \frac{9}{21} = \frac{23}{21}$$

    $$\frac{16}{21} - \frac{3}{7} = \frac{16}{21} - \frac{9}{21} = \frac{7}{21}$$

24. **The correct answer is C.**

    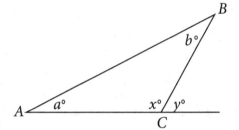

    $y = a + b$ (An exterior angle of a triangle is equal to the sum of the two interior remote angles.)

25. **The correct answer is D.** There is not enough information, as y could equal 1, which would make both quantities equal, or y could be greater than 1, which would make y^3 greater than y^2. If y were a negative integer, then y^2 would be greater than y^3.

26. **The correct answer is B.**

    $$(8+6) \div \left[3-7(2)\right]$$
    $$= (14) \div (-11)$$
    $$= \frac{14}{-11}$$
    $$(6+8) \div \left[2-7(3)\right]$$
    $$= (14) \div (-19)$$
    $$= \frac{14}{-19}$$

27. **The correct answer is C.**

    $$\frac{3}{4} \times \frac{9}{9} = \frac{3}{4} \qquad \frac{9}{9} \times \frac{3}{4} = \frac{3}{4}$$

28. **The correct answer is B.**

    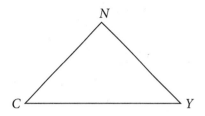

    $NC = NY$ (given)

    $\angle C = \angle Y$ (angles opposite equal sides are equal)

    $\angle N > C$ (given)

    $\angle N > \angle Y$ (substitution)

    $CY > NC$ (the greater side lies opposite the greater angle)

29. **The correct answer is C.**

    $$\frac{1}{\sqrt{9}} = \frac{1}{3}$$

30. **The correct answer is C.**

    $$5\left(\frac{2}{3}\right) = \frac{5}{1} \times \frac{2}{3} = \frac{10}{3}$$

    $$\left(\frac{5}{3}\right)2 = \frac{5}{3} \times \frac{2}{1} = \frac{10}{3}$$

31. **The correct answer is C.** A triangle inscribed in a parallelogram is equal in area to one half the parallelogram. Therefore, the area of $\triangle DEC$ equals the combined areas of $\triangle ADE$ and $\triangle EBC$.

32. **The correct answer is A.**

    $$x^3 + x^2 - x + 1$$
    $$= (-1)^3 + (-1)^2 - (-1) + 1$$
    $$= -1 + 1 + 1 + 1$$
    $$= 2$$

    $$x^3 - x^2 + x - 1$$
    $$= (-1)^3 - (-1)^2 + (-1) - 1$$
    $$= -1 - 1 - 1 - 1$$
    $$= -4$$

    Therefore, Column A is greater than Column B.

33. The correct answer is C.

$$e^3 = 27$$
$$e = 3$$
$$6e^2 = 54$$
$$e^2 = 9$$
$$e = 3$$

Therefore, Column A = Column B.

34. The correct answer is A.

First equation:

$$\frac{\frac{1}{2} + \frac{1}{3}}{\frac{2}{3}} = \frac{\frac{3+2}{6}}{\frac{2}{3}} = \frac{\frac{5}{6}}{\frac{2}{3}}$$

Multiply the numerator and denominator by $\frac{3}{2}$ and solve:

$$\frac{\frac{15}{12}}{1} = \frac{15}{12} = \frac{5}{4}$$

Second equation:

$$\frac{\frac{2}{3}}{\frac{1}{2} + \frac{1}{3}} = \frac{\frac{2}{3}}{\frac{3+2}{6}} = \frac{\frac{2}{3}}{\frac{5}{6}}$$

Multiply the numerator and denominator by $\frac{6}{5}$ and solve:

$$\frac{\frac{12}{15}}{1} = \frac{12}{15} = \frac{4}{5}$$

Since $\frac{5}{4} > \frac{4}{5}$, Column A is greater than Column B.

35. The correct answer is D. We cannot determine the areas of the circles unless the value of x is known.

36. The correct answer is A.

$$\begin{pmatrix} \text{Area of} \\ \text{shaded} \\ \text{portion} \end{pmatrix} = \begin{pmatrix} \text{Area of} \\ \text{larger} \\ \text{circle} \end{pmatrix} - \begin{pmatrix} \text{Area of} \\ \text{smaller} \\ \text{circle} \end{pmatrix}$$

$$= \pi\left(10^2\right) - \pi\left(7^2\right)$$
$$= 100\pi - 49\pi$$
$$= 51\pi$$

Since $51\pi > 49\pi$, Column A is greater than Column B.

37. The correct answer is D. A number smaller than 0 is a negative number, so a is a negative number. A negative number squared becomes a positive number. Without knowing absolute values of a and b, there is insufficient information to determine the answer to this question.

Section 3: Reading Comprehension

1. B	7. A	13. D	19. C	25. A	31. A
2. D	8. B	14. B	20. C	26. D	32. D
3. D	9. C	15. D	21. D	27. C	33. A
4. D	10. D	16. D	22. A	28. C	34. D
5. D	11. B	17. B	23. D	29. D	35. D
6. C	12. C	18. A	24. B	30. D	36. A

1. **The correct answer is B.** The word *memoir* describes a story someone tells about their own life. You can eliminate *news article* (choice C) and *play* (choice D) because while someone could tell their life story in these formats, there is not enough information in the passage to suggest any of these answers. Of the remaining two answers, *biography* (choice A) refers to someone's life story as told by another person, whereas *autobiography* (choice B) refers to a person's life story as told by themselves. Therefore, choice B is the closest in meaning to the word *memoir*.

2. **The correct answer is D.** The passage very clearly states its thesis that Malala "[told] her story to rally for change and publicly support the right for all girls in the world to receive an education." None of the other options are directly supported by the passage.

3. **The correct answer is D.** Choices B, C, and D are mentioned directly in the following quote: "The Taliban was routinely attacking girls for attending school, bombing schools that dared to educate girls, and actively restricting women from playing an equal role in society." By process of elimination, you can determine the answer is choice D; you can also confirm your answer because there are no details in the passage that address school choice.

4. **The correct answer is D.** A metaphor is a figure of speech that uses the nonliteral application of a word to make a point. The only answer option that contains a metaphor is choice D, since the word *wave* is being used nonliterally to express a sudden, large swell in the number of worldwide protests.

5. **The correct answer is D.** The only answer one can infer based on the details given in the passage is choice D. Since the passage states that the Taliban targeted those who criticized them, it would make logical sense for Malala to have hidden her name to make it easier to publish ideas that were critical of the Pakistani Taliban, something she was able to do because the BBC publishes outside of Pakistan.

6. **The correct answer is C.** Expository writing is that which is meant to inform, explain, or describe something to the reader. In this biographical expository passage, the goal is to inform the reader about who Malala Yousafzai is and why it's important to understand her role in world history.

7. **The correct answer is A.** Each letter in a rhyme scheme represents a different rhyming sound. The first line's end rhyme, *-ear*, is represented by A. Therefore, you can eliminate any rhyme scheme that doesn't have an A in the first, second, and fourth position to correspond with the lines that end in an *-ear* sound, so strike choices B, C, and D. Verify that your correct answer matches the rhyme scheme by ensuring that rhyme C, *-each*, is represented in the last two lines of the first stanza, which it is.

8. **The correct answer is B.** The term *raucous* means "harsh, loud, discordant, or dissonant."

9. **The correct answer is C.** This line from the third stanza calls back to the line in the first stanza that says, "the trees were black where the bark was wet." Since the line about how the bark will drip is meant to evoke the idea that all seasons return eventually, the reader can assume the dripping

bark is a reference to when wetness turns the bark black again in spring.

10. **The correct answer is D.** The poet states that "love's going" is less the thing that "hurts [their] days" so much as the fact that it happened over time, "in little ways." The line makes it clear that there was a romantic breakup, so you can eliminate any answer that doesn't reference one (choices A, B, and C).

11. **The correct answer is B.** The second stanza suggests that the lover "broke [the poet's] heart" by "[laughing] at all [the poet] dared to praise," so we can assume that the lover is criticizing things that matter to the poet.

12. **The correct answer is C.** In this poem, Edna St. Vincent Millay discusses the changing of the seasons in between discussing how a love evolved over time and changed "in little ways," much like the nature scenes she describes. Therefore, of the options given, choice C best represents the idea that time passing changes all things slowly, including love.

13. **The correct answer is D.** Choice D does the best job of summarizing the main idea. Choices A and B are too vague to address the passage's topic, while choice C points to a supporting detail mentioned in the passage but does not address the main idea.

14. **The correct answer is B.** The author's purpose in paragraph 2 is to clarify what the predominant theories on giraffe neck length have been up until recent fossil evidence provided new clues. While the way choice C is expressed uses hyperbole, it could still arguably be considered the topic of paragraph 3. There is no attempt by the author to speculate about people's interest in giraffes (choice A) or criticize those who support a given theory (choice D).

15. **The correct answer is D.** This detail question is asking you to read closely for an answer that is plainly stated at the end of paragraph 3. If you somehow missed that detail, a process of

elimination will reveal that none of the other answers were mentioned.

16. **The correct answer is D.** A protrusion, like a bump, is something that sticks out from a given surface.

17. **The correct answer is B.** The author's straightforward, informative tone in this passage is intended to relay a series of facts and findings without bias or judgment. *Resigned* (choice A) means something like "unhappily accepting," which is the opposite of the author's attitude toward the findings. *Hypercritical* (choice D) means something like "scornfully dismissive," so that would not be accurate here, nor is *laudatory* (choice C), which describes a tone of enthusiastic praise.

18. **The correct answer is A.** Since the new fossil evidence provides a compelling theory but does not actually settle the question of how giraffes evolved to have long necks, we can infer zoologists will continue to debate the question. Choice B expresses the opposite sentiment, while choice D expresses value judgments that are not within the scope of the passage. There is no evidence in the passage to support choice C.

19. **The correct answer is C.** Choice C is a direct statement that uses a simple adjective to give extra meaning to the noun *excitement*. You can find a simile, which is a figure of speech that makes a comparison using *like* or *as*, in choice A ("like the confused waves") and choice D ("as one might feel upon escape from a den of hungry lions"). Douglass may have meant the statement from choice B literally, but the phrase "more in that day one than in a year" implies a figure of speech called a hyperbole, which is an exaggerated statement that isn't meant to be taken literally.

20. **The correct answer is C.** *Baffled* means something like "totally perplexed or bewildered."

21. **The correct answer is D.** This straightforward question is posed to ensure you are reading closely. The only city mentioned in the passage is New York City. Remember that you can also look for

other context clues, such as the mention of Broadway, that point you to the correct answer.

22. **The correct answer is A.** After describing what it was like to be free for the first time, the reader can logically expect that Douglass' narrative will go on to describe how he spent his first few weeks as a free man. In a personal narrative, Douglass is highly unlikely to switch to a more informative tone, such as by giving a historical account (choice C) or sharing data on slavery (choice D). Information on Douglass' place and time of birth (choice B) is more likely to have come earlier in his narrative, if at all.

23. **The correct answer is D.** The best alternate title for "My Escape from Slavery" would be "Thoughts from a Newly Free Man." This title best encompasses all aspects of the excerpt provided. While "My Victory" (choice A) and "September 1838" (choice C) both point to ideas and themes from the narrative, they are too vague on their own to make adequate titles. Choice B does not adequately address the main idea of the passage.

24. **The correct answer is B.** Douglass viewed himself as abject, meaning "without pride or dignity," in his enslavement.

25. **The correct answer is A.** The adverb *overtly* is used to describe performing an action in a direct, definite, or obvious manner.

26. **The correct answer is D.** If an author writes in an objective tone, that means they are providing facts in a neutral, nonbiased manner, which is precisely what the author of this passage does. If you weren't sure what *objective* means, you could also use a process of elimination. There is nothing to suggest that the tone is playful (choice B). Nor is it written in a compliant (choice A) tone, as that wouldn't make sense for the type of writing presented. There may be an element of mournfulness (choice C) to the discussion of the memorial itself, but that would not be an accurate way to describe the tone of the overall passage.

27. **The correct answer is C.** The purpose of paragraph 2 is to offer a detailed description of the Vietnam Veterans Memorial's appearance and the design choices that went into installing it. The first paragraph in the passage discusses collective memory (choice B) and the concept of a commemorative memorial (choice D), while paragraph 3 touches on the controversy surrounding the memorial (choice A).

28. **The correct answer is C.** Paragraphs 2 and 3 mention all the given reasons as examples of why Lin's design was considered groundbreaking and moving except for one; the traditional bronze statue was added to the entrance to the memorial not to make it more groundbreaking but rather to quiet critics who said that Lin's design was not traditional enough.

29. **The correct answer is D.** As the passage directly states, "Collective memory refers to the experiences and memories that are shared by a group of people and passed down through generations."

30. **The correct answer is D.** The passage mentions both that the memorial has critics and that there are some who believe it is not direct enough in celebrating wartime efforts. Therefore, you can infer that the lack of celebration for wartime efforts is the reason that some do not like the memorial's design. None of the other responses offer inferences that can be supported by the details given.

31. **The correct answer is A.** This passage focuses specifically on the emerald ash borer and its status as an invasive species. Therefore, the most straightforward and direct title would be "Emerald Ash Borers: An Invasive Species." "Signs of Infestation" (choice D) is too vague and addresses only one aspect of the passage, while titles like "What's an Invasive Species?" (choice B) and "Invasive Species of Michigan" (choice C) both veer off topic.

32. **The correct answer is D.** You'll find this answer at the start of paragraph 3: "The most recent data suggest that emerald ash borers have been spotted in at least 35 states."

33. **The correct answer is A.** The passage states both that emerald ash borers destroy "up to 99% of ash trees in their path" and that the number of states they're found in is likely to increase. One can logically infer from this information that the emerald ash borer is very difficult to stop from spreading, making it very difficult to save trees caught in the path of an infestation. None of the other conclusions can be logically supported by explicit evidence from the passage.

34. **The correct answer is D.** Something that is inevitable is unavoidable.

35. **The correct answer is D.** Since this is an informative piece of writing on a scientific matter, any evidence related to furthering scientific understanding of the topic would be acceptable. The only answer that does *not* fit this description is choice D, the author's story about a time they held an emerald ash borer in their hand, which would be unlikely to further scientific understanding.

36. **The correct answer is A.** The only term that adequately describes the author's informative, direct tone is *explanatory*. None of the other terms make logical sense for a data-based passage on a scientific matter; *apologetic* (choice B) means "remorseful," *macabre* (choice C) means "frightening," and *witty* (choice D) means "funny."

Section 4: Mathematics Achievement

1. D	9. A	17. C	25. B	33. B	41. C
2. A	10. B	18. A	26. D	34. C	42. D
3. C	11. A	19. D	27. C	35. A	43. D
4. C	12. A	20. C	28. C	36. D	44. B
5. A	13. D	21. A	29. D	37. B	45. C
6. D	14. A	22. C	30. C	38. A	46. D
7. B	15. A	23. C	31. D	39. D	47. D
8. C	16. D	24. A	32. A	40. B	

1. **The correct answer is D.**

   Area = length × width

   Area of square:

   8 × 8 = 64 sq. in.

   Area of rectangle:

   (8 + 4)(8 − 2) = 12 × 6 = 72 sq. in.

   Solve as follows:

   72 − 64 = 8 sq. in.

2. **The correct answer is A.**

   $$r = 35 - (9)(-n)$$
   $$r = 35 - (9)(-2)$$
   $$r = 35 - (-18)$$
   $$r = 35 + 18$$
   $$r = 53$$

   When subtracting a negative number, change the sign of the subtrahend and proceed as in algebraic addition.

3. **The correct answer is C.** First perform the operation within the parentheses. To cube a number, multiply it by itself, three times.

   $$(3 + 4)^3 = (7)^3 = 7 \times 7 \times 7 = 343$$

4. **The correct answer is C.** The fraction $\frac{4}{9}$ is equivalent to the decimal number 0.4444444. The number 4 goes on infinitely, so it can be written as $0.\overline{4}$. The fraction $\frac{9}{18}$ reduces to $\frac{1}{2}$, so it is larger than $\frac{4}{9}$.

5. **The correct answer is A.** Copper and aluminum in the ratio of 10:1 means 10 parts copper to 1 part aluminum. Let x = weight of aluminum, so $10x$ = weight of copper. Solve as follows:

   $$10x + x = 77$$
   $$11x = 77$$
   $$x = 7$$

6. **The correct answer is D.**

   Volume = L × W × H

   Volume of 1 carton $= 2' \times 3' \times 4'$

   $= 24$ ft.^{3}

   Volume of 1 box $= 2'' \times 3'' \times 4''$

   $= 24$ in.^{3}

   1 cubic foot $= 12'' \times 12'' \times 12''$

   $= 1,728$ in.^{3}

   $$\frac{1,728 \times \overset{1}{\cancel{24}}}{\underset{1}{\cancel{24}}} = 1,728 \text{ boxes will fit in the carton}$$

7. **The correct answer is B.**

   $\frac{3}{5}$ (200 columns) = 120 columns

   120 columns by machine/40 columns per hour = 3 hours

   80 columns without machine/20 columns per hour = 4 hours

   Therefore, 3 hours + 4 hours = 7 hours to complete the job.

8. **The correct answer is C.** The total income is equal to 7% of the sales plus $750.

   7% of the sales is $4,725 × 0.07 = $330.75.

   $330.75 + $750 = $1,080.75

9. **The correct answer is A.**

$$x^2 + 5 = 41$$
$$x^2 = 41 - 5$$
$$x^2 = 36$$
$$x = \pm 6$$

10. **The correct answer is B.**

   Perimeter = $2l + 2w$

   If the two long sides are together, the perimeter will be:

$$5 + 3 + 3 + 5 + 3 + 3 = 22$$

   If the two short sides are together, the perimeter will be:

$$3 + 5 + 5 + 3 + 5 + 5 = 26$$

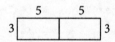

   Solve:

$$26 - 22 = 4 \text{ feet}$$

11. **The correct answer is A.**

$$5 \text{ hours } 30 \text{ minutes} = 5\frac{1}{2} \text{ hours}$$

$$1{,}000 \text{ miles} \div 5\frac{1}{2} \text{ hours}$$

$$= 1{,}000 \div \frac{11}{2}$$

$$= 1{,}000 \times \frac{2}{11}$$

$$= 181\frac{9}{11} \text{ mph}$$

12. **The correct answer is A.** 500 dozen @ $0.40 per dozen = purchase of two years ago

   75% of 500 dozen = 375 dozen pencils purchased this year

   20% of $0.40 = $0.08 increase in cost per dozen

   375 × $0.48 = $180 spent on pencils this year

13. **The correct answer is D.** A child's ticket costs x dollars. Each adult ticket costs twice as much, or $2x$ dollars. $2(2x) = 2$ adult tickets; $3x = 3$ children's tickets. Write a simple equation, and solve for x.

$$2(2x) + 3x = \$49$$
$$4x + 3x = \$49$$
$$7x = \$49$$
$$x = \$7$$

   $7 is the cost of a child's ticket; $14 is the cost of an adult's ticket.

14. **The correct answer is A.**

$$\frac{x}{2} + 36 = 37.25$$

$$\frac{x}{2} = 37.25 - 36$$

$$\frac{x}{2} = 1.25$$

$$x = 2.50$$

15. **The correct answer is A.**

   One person raised 35% of $690.

   $690 × 0.35 = $241.50.

   The remainder raised by the others was:

   $690 – 241.50 = $448.50

16. **The correct answer is D.** To determine the value of this expression, multiply the binomials using FOIL. Multiply the first, outer, inner, and last terms:

$$(y+5)(y-1) = y^2 - y + 5y - 5$$
$$= y^2 + 4y - 5$$

17. The correct answer is C. For the length, 29 feet would be represented by 29 units of $\frac{1}{4}$", resulting in $\frac{29}{4}$, or $7\frac{1}{4}$ inches. For the width, 23 feet would be represented by 23 units of $\frac{1}{4}$", resulting in $\frac{23}{4}$, or $5\frac{3}{4}$ inches.

18. The correct answer is A.

Area = length × width

= 176 ft. × 79 ft.

= 13,904 sq. ft.

19. The correct answer is D.

$$63 \div \frac{1}{9} = 63 \times \frac{9}{1} = 567$$

This is a good answer to estimate. By dividing a number by $\frac{1}{9}$, you are, in effect, multiplying it by 9. Only one of the suggested answers is close.

20. The correct answer is C. Rephrased, the problem is asking, "What number is $13.23 18% of?"

Solve accordingly. $13.23 ÷ 0.18 = $73.50.

21. The correct answer is A. Each fast worker is equivalent to two slow workers; therefore, the three workers are the equivalent of five slow workers. The whole job, then, requires 5 × 56 = 280 minutes for one slow worker. It also requires half that time, or 140 minutes, for one fast worker, and half as much again, or 70 minutes, for two fast workers.

22. The correct answer is C. Subtract from the total population of 18,000 the 756 children and the 2,244 married people:

18,000 – 756 – 2,244 = 15,000 single people

Because there are $1\frac{1}{2}$ times as many men as women, we know that 60% of the 15,000 single people are men, and 40% are women.

60% of 15,000 = 9,000

23. The correct answer is C. No calculations are needed here. Note that a 20-mile trip at 60 mph (which is 1 mile per minute) would take 20 minutes. Since the vehicle is traveling half as fast (30 mph), the 20-mile trip should take twice as long, or 40 minutes.

24. The correct answer is A.

$$2x^2 + 3 = 21$$
$$2x^2 = 21 - 3$$
$$2x^2 = 18$$
$$x^2 = 9$$
$$x = \pm 3$$

You should have been able to predict that x would be a small number, since, according to the equation, twice its square is no larger than 21.

25. The correct answer is B.

The area of a circle is $A = \pi r^2$

The radius equals $\frac{1}{2}$ the diameter.

Therefore, $r = 3$ and $\pi = \frac{22}{7}$ or 3.14.

$$A = \pi r^2$$
$$A = \pi (3)^2$$
$$A = 9\pi$$
$$A = 9(3.14)$$
$$A = 28.26 \text{ sq. in.}$$

26. The correct answer is D.

The scale is $\frac{1}{8}$" = 25 miles.

In $3\frac{7}{8}$" there are 31 units.

The distance is:

31 × 25 = 775 miles

27. The correct answer is C. The amount the house was insured for is 80% of $500,000, or $400,000. The insurance is calculated at 45¢ per hundred or $4.50 per thousand of value. Since there are 400 thousands of value, 400 × $4.50 per thousand equals the yearly premium of $1,800.

28. **The correct answer is C.** The size of the job can be thought of this way: 18 clerks working for 26 days do 18 × 26 or 468 clerk-days of work. To do 468 clerk-days of work in only 12 days would require 468 ÷ 12 = 39 clerks.

29. **The correct answer is D.** The digits are all alike, so you do not need to calculate. Move the decimal point of the divisor two places to the right; do the same for the dividend.

30. **The correct answer is C.** Solve this problem as you would any mixture-value problem. The numbers of cars sold are all related to the number of those sold for $4,200. If we call the number of $4,200 cars sold x, then it follows that:

The value of $4,200 cars sold is $4,200 • x

The value of $4,800 cars sold is $4,800 • $2x$

The value of $5,400 cars sold is $5,400 • $3x$

The sum of these values equals the total sales.

$$(\$4,200 \cdot x) + (\$4,800 \cdot 2x) + (\$5,400 \cdot 3x) = \$360,000$$
$$\$4,200x + \$9,600x + \$16,200x = \$360,000$$
$$\$30,000x = \$360,000$$
$$x = \$360,000 \div \$30,000$$
$$x = 12$$

Since $x = 12$ of the $4,200 cars, then $3x$, or 36, of the $5,400 model were sold.

31. **The correct answer is D.** There is not enough information to answer this problem. We must know how many attended the game to determine how many paid full price.

32. **The correct answer is A.** You must borrow one day's worth of hours and one hour's worth of minutes and rewrite the problem as follows:

	6 days	26 hr.	80 min.
−	4 days	9 hr.	31 min.
	2 days	17 hr.	49 min.

33. **The correct answer is B.** The formula for the area of a triangle is $A = \dfrac{1}{2}bh$. Plug in the numbers:

$$A = \frac{1}{2} \times 12 \times 14 = 84 \text{ sq. ft.}$$

34. **The correct answer is C.** This is a tricky question. It doesn't ask for 150% of 72, but rather to increase 72 by 150%. Since 150% of 72 = 108, we add 72 and 108 for the correct answer, which is 180.

35. **The correct answer is A.** Choice A is the correct numerical interpretation. Choice B is read as, "Four times the square of a certain number, minus 6, equals 2." Choice C is read as, "Four times the square of a number, divided by 3, minus 6, equals 2." Choice D is read as, "One fourth a given number, divided by 3, minus 6, equals 2."

36. **The correct answer is D.** Write down both equations and add them together.

$$14x - 2y = 32$$
$$+ \ \ x + 2y = 13$$
$$\overline{15x = 45}$$
$$x = 3$$

37. **The correct answer is B.** An ordinary die has six sides, each having a different number of dots. The chance of any face coming up is the same: $\dfrac{1}{6}$.

38. **The correct answer is A.** First, pick the two longest times, then compare them. 1,440 minutes and 25 hours are the longest periods. 25 hours contains 1,500 minutes.

39. **The correct answer is D.** The cars are traveling toward each other, so the distance between them is being reduced at 60 + 50 = 110 miles per hour. At a rate of 110 mph, 550 miles will be covered in 5 hours. If both cars left at 1 p.m., they should meet at 6 p.m.

40. **The correct answer is B.** 493 in expanded form is:

$$(4 \times 10^2) + (9 \times 10) + 3$$

Choice A is 4,930; choice C is 483; choice D is 133.

41. **The correct answer is C.** If 10 workers earn $5,400 in 12 days, each individual earns $540 in 12 days, or $45 per day. Therefore, 6 people working for 15 days at $45 per day will earn $4,050.

42. The correct answer is D. The map distance is $4\frac{1}{2}$" or $\frac{9}{2}$" or $\frac{36}{8}$". Each $\frac{3}{8}$" = 5 miles, and we know there are twelve $\frac{3}{8}$" units in $\frac{36}{8}$". Therefore, the twelve $\frac{3}{8}$" units correspond to 60 miles in actuality.

43. The correct answer is D. The area of a circle is found by $A = \pi r^2$. The radius is half the diameter. To find the diameter when the area is known, divide the area by π to find the square of the radius.

$$78.5 \div 3.14 = 25$$

Since the square of the radius is 25, we know the radius is 5, and the diameter is twice the radius, or 10 inches.

44. The correct answer is B. If $a = 6$, $ab + 4 = 52$ becomes $6b + 4 = 52$.

$$6b + 4 = 52$$
$$6b = 52 - 4$$
$$6b = 48$$
$$b = 8$$

45. The correct answer is C. If $\frac{2}{3}$ of the jar is filled in 1 minute, then $\frac{1}{3}$ of the jar is filled in $\frac{1}{2}$ minute. Since the jar is $\frac{2}{3}$ full, $\frac{1}{3}$ remains to be filled. The jar will be full in another $\frac{1}{2}$ minute.

46. The correct answer is D. First convert to a 24-hour clock.

$$3:30 \text{ p.m.} = 15:30 \text{ o'clock}$$
$$15:30 = 14:90$$
$$\underline{-8:50 = -8:50}$$
$$6:40 = 6 \text{ hours } 40 \text{ minutes}$$

To subtract a larger number of minutes from a smaller number of minutes, borrow 60 minutes from the hour to enlarge the smaller number.

47. The correct answer is D. Assign arbitrary values to solve this problem:

A square 10 ft. × 10 ft. = 100 sq. ft.

A rectangle 9 ft. × 11 ft. = 99 sq. ft.

$100 - 99 = 1$; $\frac{1}{100} = 1\%$

Section 5: Essay

Example of a well-written essay.

If I could spend an afternoon with any author, I would have a wonderful conversation with Jules Verne. I think of Jules Verne as the father of science fiction. We would talk about his books and why they make such good reading. I would tell him how much of his fiction has become fact. Then we would probably talk about recent science fiction and about the latest scientific and technological advances. Perhaps we would predict future developments.

The first book I would mention is my favorite, *Twenty Thousand Leagues Under the Sea*. I would ask Mr. Verne how he thought up the book and would tell him how much I admire his works and how I respect his imagination. Then I would tell him about submarines and submarine warfare and would describe all the deep sea explorations that I know about. It is hard to predict a conversation in advance, but *Around the World in Eighty Days* would certainly be a good next topic, and we might well consume the remainder of the afternoon with discussion of modern travel and of all the countries and cultures that can be visited today. For instance, I would ask him about the game *80 Days* based on his book. Since I have the game on my phone, I might even show him how to play it, if he's interested. I can only imagine what Verne might think seeing his own story translated into a modern-day video game!

No conversation with Jules Verne could conclude without mention of modern science fiction and of how predictive it might be. For instance, I wonder what Jules Verne would think of *Star Trek*. Finally, I would tell him about space exploration, moon landings, satellites, and all the exciting space work that is unfolding. Since none of this was around in his time, I suspect Verne would marvel at the feats of engineering humanity has achieved since he was imagining strange machines in his novels.

The prospect of a conversation with Jules Verne is very appealing. Even though I know it cannot happen, I could probably think of a dozen more things to share with him beyond what I've shared here. I would also want to give him space to ask me questions about our modern world—I'm sure he'd have as much to be curious about our world as I do about the incredible literary worlds he created.

SCORE YOURSELF

Scores on the ISEE are determined by comparing each student's results against all other students in their grade level who took that particular test. A scaled score is then calculated. You can use the following calculations to determine how well you did on this diagnostic test, but keep in mind that when you take the actual test, your score might vary.

ISEE SCORING			
Test	Raw Score ÷ No. questions	× 100	= %
Synonyms	÷ 20	× 100 =	%
Sentence Completions	÷ 20	× 100 =	%
Total Verbal Ability	÷ 40	× 100 =	%
Multiple-Choice Quantitative	÷ 19	× 100 =	%
Quantitative Comparisons	÷ 18	× 100 =	%
Total Quantitative Ability	÷ 37	× 100 =	%
Reading Comprehension	÷ 36	× 100 =	%
Mathematics Achievement	÷ 47	× 100 =	%

Remember:

- Scores are not reported as percentages. A low percentage may translate to a respectable scaled score.
- The same test is given to students in grades 8 through 11. Unless you have finished high school, you have not been taught everything on the test. You are not expected to know what you have not been taught.
- You will be compared only to students in your own grade.
- Use your scores to plan further study if you have time.

PART III
VERBAL SKILLS

CHAPTER

Synonyms

SYNONYMS

OVERVIEW

Understanding Synonym Questions

Strategies for Synonym Questions

Summing It Up

Knowledge Check: Synonyms

Answer Key and Explanations

UNDERSTANDING SYNONYM QUESTIONS

Synonym questions test your understanding of words. A synonym for a word is a word that means something similar. For example, *chilly* is a synonym for *cold*. Both words mean the same thing. Both the SSAT and ISEE test you with straightforward synonym questions. Understanding synonyms is also essential for other sections of the exam, such as the vocabulary questions you'll be asked in the reading section and other verbal question formats, such as sentence completions and analogies.

SSAT   ISEE

What Do Synonym Questions Look Like?

Here, we've included some examples to show you how synonym questions will likely be presented on the exam.

EXAMPLE:

Directions: Choose the word or phrase closest in meaning to the capitalized word.

1. PROFICIENT
   A. resentful
   B. amiable
   C. famous
   D. adept
   E. instructive

The correct answer is D. Someone who is proficient is particularly good at doing a certain task or activity. *Adept* is a synonym for *proficient*.

To learn more about synonyms, scan this QR code.

How Do I Answer Synonym Questions?

To answer synonym questions, follow these four steps:

Step 1: Carefully study the capitalized word. Determine whether you know the word or not. If you know the word, you're ahead of the game. If you don't know the word, you'll need to break it down to figure out what part of speech the word is and to approximate which of the answer choices is nearest in meaning. Later in this chapter, we'll outline additional strategies for how to answer the question if you don't know the answer.

Step 2: Eliminate responses that are obviously wrong. Sometimes, the answer choices will include antonyms, words that are the opposite of the given word. You can cross those options off right away.

Step 3: Use word analysis techniques to help you with difficult words. For example, the methods for analyzing roots, suffixes, and prefixes that we discuss in Chapter 10: Reading Comprehension can help you arrive at a general definition for the capitalized word and eliminate additional answer options.

Step 4: Try using the word in a sentence. Sometimes, it's helpful to think about the capitalized word and the answer options with context. How are these words used? What other words are often used with them? By creating sample sentences of your own, you can get closer to finding the synonym for the word.

EXAMPLES:

> **Directions:** Choose the word or phrase nearest in meaning to the capitalized word.

1. ELOQUENT

    A. verbose

    B. ignorant

    C. satisfactory

    D. undignified

    E. articulate

The correct answer is E. The word *eloquent* means "able to express oneself clearly and well." *Verbose* (choice A) means "using more words than needed" and is an antonym for *eloquent*. *Ignorant* (choice B) means "lacking knowledge or awareness," which is unrelated to the idea of expressing oneself well. *Satisfactory* (choice C) means "acceptable" and undignified (choice D) means "appearing foolish," so neither is a synonym for *eloquent*. *Articulate* is correct because it means "having the ability to speak fluently and coherently."

2. INFAMOUS

    A. well known

    B. poor

    C. disgraceful

    D. young

    E. cruel

The correct answer is C. The first word you see when you look at *infamous* is *famous*. *Famous* means well known. Because *in-*, meaning "not," is a negative prefix, you should be looking for a word with a negative relationship to the word *famous*. Knowing you need a negative word allows you to eliminate choice A, *well known*. Neither *poor* (choice B) nor *young* (choice D) are automatically synonymous with the idea of being "not well known." *Cruel* (choice E) means "willfully causing pain and suffering," and while someone can become infamous for being cruel, the two words do not mean the same thing. *Disgrace*, however, is a negative kind of fame. A person who behaves disgracefully is known for bad behavior and is thus *infamous*.

3. REMEDIAL

    A. class

    B. intermediate

    C. corrective

    D. isolated

    E. proficient

The correct answer is C. Upon seeing this question, one association you might recall is "remedial classes." That association can help you, but it can also lead you astray. *Remedial* is not synonymous with *class*. *Remedial* is an adjective—*class* is the noun it modifies. For example, students who are not reading at their grade level might receive remedial reading instruction in classes that are intended to improve their reading skills. Do you see the word *remedy* in *remedial*? You know that a remedy is a cure or correction for an ailment. If you combine all the information you now have, you can choose *corrective* as the word that most nearly means *remedial*.

STRATEGIES FOR SYNONYM QUESTIONS

Sometimes, you will encounter words that you just don't know. If you're taking the ISEE, then there is no penalty for incorrect answers, so you should use the strategies we outline here to make your best guess. On the SSAT, you lose a quarter of a point for each incorrect answer, so only guess if you've eliminated at least two wrong answers to increase your odds. Otherwise, you'll want to leave the answer blank.

In this section, we outline a few scenarios you might encounter when you're answering synonym questions or other questions that require you to guess the word that "most nearly" means the same as another.

Possibility #1

You know the meaning of the word, but none of the answer choices seems correct.

- Perhaps you misread the word. Are there other words that look like the word in the question? For example, did you mistake *stationary* for *stationery* or *principal* for *principle*?

- Perhaps you read the word correctly but accented the wrong syllable. Some words have alternative pronunciations with vastly different meanings. Consider *de-sert'* and *des'-ert*.

- Perhaps you are dealing with a single word that can be used as two different parts of speech and therefore has two entirely unrelated meanings. A *moor* (noun) is a boggy wasteland; to *moor* (verb) is to secure a ship or a boat in place; and the proper noun *Moor* refers to the Muslim conquerors of Spain.

- Perhaps the word appears as different parts of speech with numerous meanings and shades of meaning within each of these. *Fancy* (noun) can mean inclination, love, notion, whim, taste, judgment, or imagination. *Fancy* (verb) can mean to like, to imagine, and to think. *Fancy* (adjective) can mean whimsical, ornamental, and extravagant. Your task is to choose *one* of the choices that means the same as *one* of the meanings of the word *fancy*.

Possibility #2

You do not know the meaning of the word, but it appears to contain prefix, suffix, or root clues. Examine those clues to deduce your answer. For example, the word *maladapted* uses the prefix *mal-*, which means "bad" or "abnormal," so look for the best synonym of "badly or abnormally adapted." This technique would help you land on synonyms for *maladapted* like *unstable* or *defective*.

TIP

Examine the prefix, suffix, or root of the word to find clues to determine its meaning.

Possibility #3

You do not know the meaning of the word and can see no clues, but you have a feeling that the word has some specific positive or negative connotation. Play your hunch and choose a word with the same connotation.

Possibility #4

You are stumped. Guessing is a great option for the ISEE, but carries a risk of a lower score with the SSAT if the guess is incorrect. On the SSAT, we recommend guessing only when you can first eliminate at least two answers you're pretty sure are wrong. If you can eliminate two or more of the choices, you improve your odds of guessing correctly. Eliminate choices wherever you can, choose from the remaining options, and move on. There's no need to waste time on a question for which you cannot figure out the answer.

ALERT

On the SSAT, we recommend guessing when you can eliminate at least two answer choices that you believe are wrong. Narrowing it down to three potential answers increases your odds of being right enough that it's worth the guess.

Building Vocabulary Helps

All the previous suggestions can help you use clues to determine the meaning of words and find their synonyms. But many synonym questions give no clues at all. The best way to minimize the number of synonym questions that you simply cannot answer is to learn as many vocabulary words as you can.

One way to increase your vocabulary is to work with a dictionary when preparing for your exam. Another is to read everything you can in the weeks and months leading up to your exam. When you run into a word that's unfamiliar, look it up. If you run across a word you don't know while doing the practice exams, circle the word and look it up later. Look up words you find in the reading passages, new words from among the answer choices, words you find in the explanations, and words you meet in the study chapters. Looking up words for yourself and relating them to your own life is the best way to learn them. After defining a new word, write a sentence that creates a strong image. Your long-term memory excels with visual information, so creating images (especially those that are weird and wild) will help you more easily store the word and its meaning for later use.

We'll go into more depth with ways to expand your vocabulary in Chapter 10: Reading Comprehension. If you understand every word in this book, you are well on your way to a broad-based vocabulary and should be able to handle not only the synonym questions but the other verbal questions as well.

SUMMING IT UP

- When choosing an answer for a synonym question, first determine if you know the capitalized word or not. If you don't know the word, study the prefix, root word, and suffix to arrive at a general definition. You can do this for the answer choices as well.

- Eliminate obviously wrong answers—look for antonyms and words that are unrelated to the capitalized word.

- Try to use the word in a sentence to help you figure out what part of speech it is and what other words are often used alongside it. This can help you rule out words that are unrelated or identify words that have a similar connotation.

- When you think you know the meaning of the given word but can't find the answer, go back and check the following:

    ○ Did you misread the word?

    ○ Did you accent the wrong syllable?

    ○ Can the word be used as two different parts of speech?

    ○ Does the word have multiple meanings?

- On the SSAT, you will lose 1/4 point for every wrong answer. We recommend guessing only when you can eliminate two answers that you're pretty sure are wrong. That way, the 1 in 3 chance you have of guessing correctly is worth the risk. If you can eliminate more than 2 options, all the better!

- Remember, there are no penalties for guessing on the ISEE, so guess on every question.

- Consider connotation and the part of speech. If you try to guess, eliminate answers that you know are wrong and concentrate on using your vocabulary reasoning to make your best guess on the others.

KNOWLEDGE CHECK

SYNONYMS

20 Questions—10 Minutes

Directions: Choose the word or phrase closest in meaning to the CAPITALIZED word.

1. ENLIGHTEN
   - **A.** reduce
   - **B.** bleach
   - **C.** educate
   - **D.** absorb
   - **E.** obscure

2. AFFIRM
   - **A.** prove
   - **B.** validate
   - **C.** sign
   - **D.** stick
   - **E.** toughen

3. PARCH
   - **A.** boil
   - **B.** write
   - **C.** dry
   - **D.** steam
   - **E.** stroll

4. REFUGE
   - **A.** alibi
   - **B.** deny
   - **C.** church
   - **D.** reject
   - **E.** shelter

5. SKEPTIC
   - **A.** doubter
   - **B.** critic
   - **C.** heretic
   - **D.** opponent
   - **E.** scholar

6. TENUOUS
   - **A.** boring
   - **B.** impermanent
   - **C.** nervous
   - **D.** flimsy
   - **E.** strong-willed

7. MYTHICAL
   - **A.** ancient
   - **B.** religious
   - **C.** explanatory
   - **D.** imaginary
   - **E.** intriguing

8. ADULTERATE
   - **A.** cheat
   - **B.** age
   - **C.** shorten
   - **D.** idolize
   - **E.** dilute

9. OVATION
   A. speech
   B. applause
   C. egg dish
   D. misjudgment
   E. exaggeration

10. DIVERT
   A. submerge
   B. enjoy
   C. annoy
   D. focus
   E. deflect

11. SUPERFICIAL
   A. fantastic
   B. family ties
   C. thrifty
   D. unbelievable
   E. without depth

12. COMBATIVE
   A. honesty
   B. posture
   C. constructive
   D. correction
   E. argumentative

13. SPECTRUM
   A. range
   B. view
   C. variety
   D. magnifier
   E. idea

14. PERILOUS
   A. dangerous
   B. waterproof
   C. frightening
   D. poor
   E. perfect

15. BELLIGERENT
   A. warlike
   B. windy
   C. noisy
   D. passive
   E. endearing

16. RIFE
   A. nature
   B. widespread
   C. quarrelsome
   D. broken
   E. violent

17. TACIT
   A. understood
   B. sensitive
   C. sticky
   D. skillful
   E. mature

18. SHROUD
   A. cummerbund
   B. coffin
   C. veil
   D. wake
   E. mysterious

19. GREGARIOUS

A. haggling

B. sociable

C. quick

D. worm-like

E. surly

20. OBLITERATE

A. demonstrate

B. divest

C. entertain

D. annihilate

E. construct

ANSWER KEY AND EXPLANATIONS

1. C	5. A	9. B	13. A	17. A
2. B	6. B	10. E	14. A	18. C
3. C	7. D	11. E	15. A	19. B
4. E	8. E	12. E	16. B	20. D

1. **The correct answer is C.** *Enlighten* and *educate* both mean "to provide greater knowledge or understanding."

2. **The correct answer is B.** To affirm is to validate or confirm.

3. **The correct answer is C.** You may have heard the word *parched* as a synonym for *thirsty*. From that connotation, you could arrive at the correct answer, *dry*.

4. **The correct answer is E.** Someone who is seeking refuge is seeking sanctuary from something dangerous or threatening.

5. **The correct answer is A.** A skeptic is someone who doubts or questions conventional wisdom.

6. **The correct answer is B.** Something that is tenuous is impermanent.

7. **The correct answer is D.** The word *mythical* refers to something that is imaginary.

8. **The correct answer is E.** To adulterate something is to dilute it.

9. **The correct answer is B.** You are likely familiar with the idea of an audience giving someone a standing ovation. From this connotation, you could arrive at *applause* as a synonym for *ovation*.

10. **The correct answer is E.** To divert someone's attention is to deflect.

11. **The correct answer is E.** Something that is superficial lacks depth.

12. **The correct answer is E.** Someone who is combative is argumentative.

13. **The correct answer is A.** *Range* is a synonym for *spectrum*.

14. **The correct answer is A.** If someone is in a perilous situation, they are in danger.

15. **The correct answer is A.** A person who is belligerent is warlike or combative.

16. **The correct answer is B.** Rife is another way of saying widespread.

17. **The correct answer is A.** The word *tacit* means "something that is understood or implied without being explicitly said."

18. **The correct answer is C.** A shroud is also known as a veil.

19. **The correct answer is B.** Someone who is gregarious is considered sociable.

20. **The correct answer is D.** To obliterate something is to annihilate or destroy it.

CHAPTER

Verbal Analogies

VERBAL ANALOGIES

OVERVIEW

Types of Verbal Analogies

Strategies for Answering Analogy Questions

Summing It Up

Knowledge Check: Verbal Analogies

Answer Key and Explanations

SSAT   ISEE

Verbal analogy questions on the SSAT will test your ability to see relationships between words and apply those relationships accordingly. It is a test of your ability to think things through clearly and logically.

On the SSAT, verbal analogy questions typically follow this format: "[Word 1] is to [Word 2] as [Word 3] is to" and then you are given five answer choices. The answer you choose should be the "Word 4" that logically completes the sentence. Of the given answer choices, only one will best express a relationship to Word 3 that is similar to the relationship shown between Word 1 and Word 2. More advanced analogy questions may show you the relationship between Word 1 and Word 2 and then ask you to choose a pair of words with the same relationship.

To answer the question, you need to look at the relationship between the first two words and apply it to the third word and the answer options. The following is an example of how a verbal analogy question appears on the exam.

Deer is to fawn as goat is to

- **A.** chick.
- **B.** sheep.
- **C.** pup.
- **D.** kid.
- **E.** ram.

The correct answer is D. The word *deer* represents an adult stage of a *fawn*. To complete the analogy with *goat* as the first word, we need a term denoting a younger version of the animal in question. The word *kid* refers to a young goat.

Regardless of the form an analogy takes, the task is always the same: Define the relationship between two words and then apply that same relationship to a different set of words.

TYPES OF VERBAL ANALOGIES

This section of the test will depict a variety of relationships with its word pairs. The following table illustrates common types of relationships between words. Remember, some of these relationships may appear in a reversed form as well.

RELATIONSHIP	EXAMPLE
synonyms	ask : inquire
antonyms	long : short
homonyms	mail : male
location	Phoenix : Arizona
creator : creation	artist : painting
female : male	cow : bull
larger : smaller	lake : pond

RELATIONSHIP	EXAMPLE
noun : adjective	texture : coarse
cause : effect	negligence : accident
whole : part	chapter : paragraph
object : purpose or function	keyboard : type
object : user	camera : photographer
early stage : later stage	infant : adult
general : specific	vegetable : broccoli
more : less (degree)	arid : dry
verb : adjective	expand : large
measurement (e.g., time, distance, weight)	distance : mile
raw material : finished product	wood : bench
verb tense : verb tense	run : ran
singular noun : plural noun	child : children
subject pronoun : object pronoun	he : they
first-person pronoun : third-person pronoun	she : her
first-person pronoun : third-person pronoun	we : they
adjective : comparative adjective	good : better
adjective : superlative adjective	bad : worst

The following pages provide descriptions and sample questions for some of the most common analogy relationships: synonym/definition, antonyms, classification and function, and part-whole.

Synonym/Definition

Synonym analogies select words with the same or similar meanings. For example, *happy* and *glad* have the same meaning. The following synonym questions are similar to what you will see on your exam.

1. Interesting is to compelling as frightening is to

   A. afraid.

   B. fear.

   C. monster.

   D. charming.

   E. scary.

The correct answer is E. *Interesting* and *compelling* are synonyms, as are *scary* and *frightening*.

2. Enormous is to huge as muddy is to

   A. cavernous.

   B. clean.

   C. unclear.

   D. rocky.

   E. natural.

The correct answer is C. Something that is muddy is clouded or unclear.

3. Cradle is to crib as car is to

   A. airplane.

   B. automobile.

   C. stroller.

   D. bed.

   E. highway.

The correct answer is B. *Cradle* and *crib* are synonyms for places a baby sleeps. *Car* and *automobile* are also synonyms.

Antonyms

Antonyms are words that are opposite in meaning to the given word. For example, *cold* is the antonym for *hot*. The following antonym questions are similar to what you will see on your exam.

1. Seldom is to often as modern is to

   A. ancient.

   B. time.

   C. usually.

   D. era.

   E. contemporary.

The correct answer is A. *Seldom* and *often* are antonyms, as are *modern* and *ancient*.

2. Long is to short as wide is to

   A. tall.

   B. large.

   C. small.

   D. broad.

   E. narrow.

The correct answer is E. *Short* is the opposite of *long*, just as *wide* is the opposite of *narrow*.

3. Order is to chaos as discipline is to

   A. lawful.

   B. anarchy.

   C. fervor.

   D. containment.

   E. subject.

The correct answer is B. *Chaos* is the opposite of *order*, just as *anarchy* is the opposite of *discipline*.

Classification and Function

Classification and function analogy questions require you to create analogies expressing that terms are of a similar type, overlap in category, or share a functional relationship—either those that fulfill the same function or express a specific function. The following questions are similar to what you will encounter on your exam.

EXAMPLES:

1. Canoe is to sailboat as manual is to
   - A. flyer.
   - B. play.
   - C. textbook.
   - D. story.
   - E. operation.

The correct answer is C. A *canoe* and a *sailboat* are both watercrafts used for transportation, just as a *manual* and a *textbook* are both types of instructional books.

2. Candle is to flame as camera is to
   - A. photo.
   - B. portable.
   - C. phone.
   - D. flash.
   - E. apparatus.

The correct answer is A. A *candle* produces a *flame* just as a *camera* produces a *photo*.

3. Rose is to tulip as silver is to
   - A. metallic.
   - B. ring.
   - C. wood.
   - D. gold.
   - E. bell.

The correct answer is D. A *rose* and a *tulip* are both types of flowers, just as *silver* and *gold* are both types of metal.

4. Ceiling is to wall as television is to
   - A. telephone.
   - B. paper.
   - C. monitor.
   - D. floor.
   - E. book.

The correct answer is C. A *ceiling* and a *wall* are both used to support a building's structure. A *television* and a *monitor* are both devices used for viewing.

5. Argon is to gas as duck is to
   - A. swan.
   - B. avoid.
   - C. shirk.
   - D. bird.
   - E. feather.

The correct answer is D. *Argon* is a type of *gas*, just as a *duck* is a type of *bird*.

6. Hospital is to clinic as doctor is to
   - A. degree.
   - B. medic.
   - C. prescription.
   - D. clerk.
   - E. ambulance.

The correct answer is B. A *hospital* and a *clinic* are both medical facilities of greater and lesser degrees, just as a *doctor* and a *medic* are medical professionals of greater or lesser certification.

To learn more about analogies, scan this QR code.

Part-Whole

Part-Whole analogies (expressing either part-to-whole or whole-to-part relationships) compare a part of something to a whole or vice versa. The following part-whole questions are similar to what you will see on the actual exam.

EXAMPLES:

1. Book is to page as clock is to

   A. time.

   B. watch.

   C. tower.

   D. hand.

   E. minute.

The correct answer is D. A *page* is part of a *book*, just as a *hand* is part of a *clock*.

2. Line is to sketch as finger is to

   A. hand.

   B. knuckle.

   C. digit.

   D. glove.

   E. toe.

The correct answer is A. A *line* is one part of a whole *sketch*. A *finger* is a part of a *hand*.

3. Los Angeles is to California as Houston is to

   A. Dallas.

   B. Hollywood.

   C. city.

   D. Austin.

   E. Texas.

The correct answer is E. *Los Angeles* is a city in *California*, and *Houston* is a city in *Texas*.

STRATEGIES FOR ANSWERING ANALOGY QUESTIONS

Here, we'll outline a few steps for how to answer an analogy question.

STEP 1: Define the first set of words. Most often, you will know the meanings of both words, but if you're not sure, make a guess and move on to the next step.

STEP 2: Determine how those two words are related. Recall the different types of analogies we covered earlier in this chapter. As you look at the first two words in the analogy, it's important to get a clear understanding of how exactly the two words are related so that you know how to complete the pattern.

STEP 3: Now, use process of elimination to arrive at the best answer. Look at the third word in the analogy question and the five answer choices available. Start by crossing off the answers that you know are incorrect. Ideally, you will find a word that has the same relationship to the third word that the first set has.

STEP 4: If you have narrowed down the answers to two choices but can't decide which word best completes the analogy, then it's time to revisit the first pair of words and refine the relationship. Perhaps you initially believed the relationship was one of association, but upon closer inspection, you might realize that it is a cause-and-effect relationship.

STEP 5: If you have refined the relationship further, then re-examine the answer choices. Now that you have a better understanding of the analogy, this might mean revisiting answer choices you initially eliminated as incorrect. Look for the answer that would best complete the relationship you've identified. If you're unsure but you've narrowed it down to three choices, consider guessing. Otherwise, leave it blank—the SSAT penalizes for incorrect answers and you don't want to take a chance on a question for which you have less than a 1-in-3 shot shot of being correct.

The process of answering an analogy question consists of the following five steps:

1 Define the initial terms.

2 Describe the initial relationship.

3 Eliminate incorrect answers.

4 Refine the initial relationship, if necessary.

5 Choose the best of the remaining answer choices.

Defining Relationships to Eliminate Incorrect Answers

Let's look at how we can use the first and second steps to eliminate incorrect answer options. Remember, you should define the words first. Then, determine the relationship between them. As you undertake the second step, recall some of the analogies we covered earlier in this chapter. See if one relationship best describes the first pair of words in the analogy.

Let's take a look at an example to help illustrate this process.

EXAMPLE:

Brim is to hat as hand is to

   A. glove.

   B. finger.

   C. foot.

   D. arm.

   E. toe.

The correct answer is D. *Hand* is certainly associated with *glove* (choice A), but in no way is a hand part of a glove. *Hand* and *finger* (choice B) are certainly associated, and a *finger* is part of a *hand*. However, exercise caution here. Look again at the relationship of the first two words: *Brim* is a part of *hat*, or in other words, *hat* is the whole of which *brim* is a part. The relationship in choice B is the reverse of the relationship of the first two words. *Hand* is the whole and *finger* is the part. Your answer must maintain the same relationship in the same sequence as the original pair.

The relationship of *hand* and *foot* (choice C), and even less so that of *hand* and *toe* (choice E), is only one of association, not of part to whole. This answer is no more likely to be correct than choice A. In fact, because you have found two answers that have equal chances of being incorrect, you now know that neither of them is the answer you are looking for. There must be a best answer.

A *hand* is part of an *arm* in the same way that a *brim* is part of a *hat*. In other words, the *arm* is the whole of which a *hand* is a part in the same way that *hat* is the whole of which a *brim* is the part. Once you've spotted this, you're able to determine that *arm* is the best answer.

Identifying Parts of Speech to Determine Relationships

At the beginning of this chapter, we included a table to summarize the relationships commonly used in analogy questions along with corresponding examples. For some analogy questions, your ability to determine (Step 1) or refine (Step 4) the relationship depends on your knowledge of parts of speech. In this book, we cover the different parts of speech in Chapter 17: Writing Mechanics—knowing them will come in handy on multiple sections of the exam. For example, you may encounter an analogy with a noun and a corresponding adjective, like *sponge* and *absorbent* or *planet* and *round*. Some relationships will only consist of one part of speech, like *object* and *user*, which will both be nouns. Other relationships might contain an implied part of speech, like part-to-whole analogies, which will likely comprise pairs of nouns.

Let's look at a few examples where identifying parts of speech can help to determine or refine the relationship and arrive at the correct answer.

EXAMPLES:

1. Choose is to select as think is to

   A. contemplate.

   B. disagree.

   C. thought.

   D. careful.

   E. inquisitive.

The correct answer is A. These words will likely be familiar to you. The analogy presents a pair of verbs (*choose* and *select*) that are synonyms followed by another verb, *think*. This gives us direction when we go through the process of eliminating incorrect answers. While *thought* (choice C) can be both a noun and the past tense of *think*, it is not a synonym of *think*. *Contemplate* is both a verb and a synonym for *think*.

2. Goose is to geese as ox is to

   A. cow.

   B. oxen.

   C. elk.

   D. horns.

   E. mammal.

The correct answer is B. In this example, the correct answer should be a plural noun, since *goose* is the singular noun and *geese* is the plural form. *Ox* is a singular noun, and its irregular plural form is *oxen*.

3. Rabbit is to soft as cactus is to

   A. cacti.

   B. prickly.

   C. desert.

   D. green.

   E. hop.

The correct answer is B. *Rabbit* is a noun and *soft* is an adjective, so the correct answer must be an adjective that corresponds to the noun *cactus*. That leaves us with two options: *prickly* or *green*. Since the original analogy involves an adjective that describes the texture or feel of a rabbit, we need to select the option that describes the texture or feel of a cactus. The best answer that completes the analogy is *prickly*.

> **ALERT**
>
> Keep an eye out for answer choices that seem correct but are actually the reverse relationship of the first two words. This is one of the most common distractors used in verbal analogy answer options.

Using Parts of Speech to Refine the Relationship

Sometimes, you might be confronted with multiple answer choices that could each be correct. In this scenario, it likely means that your initial understanding of the analogy was too broad. To narrow your options further, you'll need to go back and refine the relationship between the first two words. Let's walk through an example of this scenario.

Consider an analogy that begins "letter is to word." Initially, you will probably think, "A letter is part of a word; therefore, the relationship is that of part-to-whole." If the relationship of the third word to any of the choices is also part-to-whole, then all is well. However, suppose the question looks like the following example.

EXAMPLE:

Letter is to word as song is to

- **A.** story.
- **B.** music.
- **C.** note.
- **D.** orchestra.
- **E.** musician.

The correct answer is C. Three choices offer an association relationship; however, you should attempt to refine your understanding of the relationship to be as specific as possible. No choice offers a whole of which a song might be a part (such as an opera). Therefore, you must return to the original pair of words and consider other relationships between *letter* and *word*. If *letter* refers to "written communication," rather than "letter of the alphabet," then a *word* is part of a *letter* and the relationship of the first to the second is the whole to a part. Then, the answer becomes clear: A *song* is the whole of which *note* is the part. The relationship of *song* and *note* is the same as that of *letter* and *word*.

TIP

Turn the analogy pairs into sentences to help see the connection. Then, fit the answer pairs into the same sentence until you find the one that works best.

Common Pitfalls in Answering Analogy Questions

Analogy questions also present many opportunities for error. Here are some of the most common pitfalls to avoid.

- **Reversal of sequence of the relationship:**
  - Part-to-whole is *not* the same as whole-to-part.
  - Cause-and-effect is *not* the same as effect to its cause.
  - Smaller to larger is *not* the same as larger to smaller.
  - Action to object is *not* the same as object to action.

- **Confusion of relationship:**
  - Part-to-part (*geometry* to *calculus*) with part-to-whole (*algebra* to *mathematics*)
  - Cause-and-effect (*fire* to *smoke*) with association (*hurricane* to *typhoon*)
  - Degree (*drizzle* to *downpour*) with antonyms (*dry* to *wet*)
  - Association (*walk* to *limp*) with synonyms (*eat* to *consume*)

- **Grammatical inconsistency:** The grammatical relationship of the first two words must be retained throughout the analogy. A wrong analogy would be *imprisoned* is to *convict* as *cage* is to *parrot*. While the meaningful relationship exists, the analogy is not parallel in construction. A correct analogy of this sort would have to read *prison* is to *convict* as *cage* is to *parrot*, or *imprisoned* is to *convict* as *caged* is to *parrot*. In analogy questions, you must create a pair that is both grammatically consistent with the first pair and shares a similar relationship.

- **Concentration on the meanings of words instead of on their relationships:** In this type of error, you see *gear* to *transmission*, and you think of *car* as the common relationship instead of spotting the part-to-part relationship; gears are part of the transmission. When looking for an analogy for the word *piston*, and the list of answers includes *car* and *engine*, you might pick *car* when the better answer is *engine*.

Remember: The key to answering analogy questions lies in the relationship between the first two words.

If you struggle with finding the relationship between the words of the initial pair, you might find it useful to mentally reverse their order. If this works, remember to mentally reverse the order of the third and fourth terms as well to maintain the relationship in your answer.

What if none of the answer pairs seems exactly right? Remember that the directions tell you to choose the <u>best</u> answer. The correct answer won't necessarily be a perfect fit, but it will work better than the other choices.

SUMMING IT UP

- Analogies are a test of your ability to identify logical relationships between words.
- Study and learn the different types of analogy relationships, with an emphasis on the following analogies: synonym/definition, antonym, classification and function, and part-whole.
- Follow the steps:
    1. Define the initial terms.
    2. Describe the initial relationship.
    3. Eliminate incorrect answers.
    4. Refine the initial relationship.
    5. Choose the best answer.
- Take note of common pitfalls in answering analogy questions:
    - Maintain the sequence of the original pair of words.
    - Avoid misidentifying similar types of relationships between words (e.g., cause-and-effect vs. association).
    - Maintain grammatical consistency across the pairs of words.
    - Focus on the relationship between words instead of their individual meanings.

KNOWLEDGE CHECK

VERBAL ANALOGIES

30 Questions—9 Minutes

> **Directions:** In the following questions, the first two words are related to each other in a certain way. The third and fourth words must be related to each other in the same way. Choose a word from among the five choices that is related to the third word in the same way that the second word is related to the first.

1. Gasoline is to petroleum as sugar is to
   A. sweet.
   B. oil.
   C. plant.
   D. cane.
   E. dessert.

2. Fly is to spider as mouse is to
   A. cat.
   B. rat.
   C. rodent.
   D. trap.
   E. cheese.

3. Volcano is to crater as chimney is to
   A. smoke.
   B. fire.
   C. pit.
   D. flue.
   E. stack.

4. Petal is to flower as fur is to
   A. coat.
   B. rabbit.
   C. warm.
   D. hairy.
   E. animal.

5. Retreat is to advance as timid is to
   A. bold.
   B. cowardly.
   C. fearful.
   D. shy.
   E. quiet.

6. Ledger is to accounts as journal is to
   A. pen.
   B. territory.
   C. book.
   D. observations.
   E. diary.

7. Picture is to see as speech is to
   A. view.
   B. enunciate.
   C. hear.
   D. soliloquize.
   E. speak.

8. Soprano is to high as bass is to
   A. guitar.
   B. instrument.
   C. low.
   D. bad.
   E. fish.

9. Addition is to addend as subtraction is to

   A. difference.

   B. sum.

   C. subtrahend.

   D. minus.

   E. division.

10. Famine is to hunger as drought is to

   A. crops.

   B. water.

   C. starvation.

   D. desert.

   E. thirst.

11. Acute is to chronic as temporary is to

   A. persistent.

   B. sick.

   C. pretty.

   D. narrow.

   E. timely.

12. Sleeves are to shirt as legs are to

   A. shoes.

   B. socks.

   C. hats.

   D. closets.

   E. slacks.

13. Chariot is to charioteer as automobile is to

   A. passenger.

   B. engine.

   C. motor.

   D. driver.

   E. highway.

14. Team is to league as player is to

   A. piano.

   B. team.

   C. tournament.

   D. football.

   E. school.

15. Honor is to citation as speeding is to

   A. citation.

   B. hurry.

   C. race.

   D. stop.

   E. slow

16. Stethoscope is to doctor as hose is to

   A. water.

   B. firefighter.

   C. firetruck.

   D. hydrant.

   E. garden.

17. *Hamlet* is to Shakespeare as telephone is to

   A. Bell.

   B. telegraph.

   C. smartphone.

   D. talk.

   E. cellular.

18. Distracting is to noise as soothing is to

   A. medicine.

   B. music.

   C. volume.

   D. bleeding.

   E. listening.

19. Year is to calendar as hour is to

    A. decade.

    B. minute.

    C. date.

    D. month.

    E. clock.

20. Superior is to inferior as skilled is to

    A. technical.

    B. unskilled.

    C. exterior.

    D. informed.

    E. talented.

21. Words are to books as notes are to

    A. songs.

    B. letters.

    C. pianos.

    D. fragrances.

    E. homework.

22. Pungent is to odor as shrill is to

    A. whisper.

    B. sound.

    C. piercing.

    D. shriek.

    E. annoying.

23. Present is to birthday as reward is to

    A. offer.

    B. medal.

    C. punishment.

    D. money.

    E. accomplishment.

24. Mouse is to mammal as lizard is to

    A. fish.

    B. scale.

    C. camouflage.

    D. reptile.

    E. pet.

25. Sky is to ground as ceiling is to

    A. floor.

    B. roof.

    C. top.

    D. plaster.

    E. above.

26. Food is to nutrition as light is to

    A. watt.

    B. bulb.

    C. electricity.

    D. illuminate.

    E. vision.

27. Actor is to play as musician is to

    A. guitarist.

    B. performer.

    C. instrument.

    D. concert.

    E. artist.

28. Square is to triangle as cube is to

    A. circle.

    B. line.

    C. ball.

    D. pyramid.

    E. shape.

29. Abacus is to calculator as propeller is to

   A. jet.

   B. airplane.

   C. mathematics.

   D. flight.

   E. movement.

30. Dizziness is to vertigo as fate is to

   A. adversity.

   B. order.

   C. destiny.

   D. pride.

   E. gift.

ANSWER KEY AND EXPLANATIONS

1. D	6. D	11. A	16. B	21. A	26. E
2. A	7. C	12. E	17. A	22. B	27. D
3. D	8. C	13. D	18. B	23. E	28. D
4. B	9. C	14. B	19. E	24. D	29. A
5. A	10. E	15. A	20. B	25. A	30. C

1. **The correct answer is D.** The relationship is that of the product to its source. *Gasoline* comes from *petroleum*; *sugar* comes from *cane*. Although you could argue that sugar also comes from a plant, cane is a more direct and specific relationship, much like the relationship between gasoline and petroleum.

2. **The correct answer is A.** The relationship is that of prey to hunter. The *fly* is hunted by the *spider*; the *mouse* is hunted by the *cat*. Refine this analogy to hunting (or eating) in order to solve it. If you were to consider only catching, then you would not be able to distinguish between the cat and the trap.

3. **The correct answer is D.** The relationship is functional. The *crater* contains the vent(s) for a *volcano*; the *flue* is the vent for a *chimney*.

4. **The correct answer is B.** The relationship is that of part-to-whole. A *petal* is part of a *flower*; *fur* is part of a *rabbit*. *Fur* might be part of a *coat*, but it is not part of every coat, so *rabbit* makes a better analogy.

5. **The correct answer is A.** The relationship is that of antonyms. *Retreat* is the opposite of *advance*; *timid* is the opposite of *bold*.

6. **The correct answer is D.** This analogy involves a functional relationship. A *ledger* stores and maintains accounts for *businesses*. A *journal* stores and maintains observations for *individuals*.

7. **The correct answer is C.** This is another variety of object-to-action relationship. You *see* a *picture*; you *hear* a *speech*.

8. **The correct answer is C.** The relationship is that of synonyms or definition. A *soprano* voice is *high*; a *bass* voice is *low*. While *bass* has multiple meanings, you must define the word in context of the relationship among the first two words.

9. **The correct answer is C.** The relationship is that of the whole to a part. The *addend* is one term of an *addition* problem; the *subtrahend* is one term of a *subtraction* problem.

10. **The correct answer is E.** This is a cause-and-effect relationship: *Famine* causes *hunger*, and *drought* causes *thirst*.

11. **The correct answer is A.** The relationship is that of antonyms. *Acute* means sudden and short; *chronic* means always present. *Temporary* is the opposite of *persistent*.

12. **The correct answer is E.** This is a part-to-whole relationship—*sleeves* are a part of a *shirt*. *Legs*, therefore, must be a part of the correct answer. Review the answer choices: *legs* are a part of *slacks*, which completes the analogy.

13. **The correct answer is D.** The relationship is that of object and actor. The *charioteer* drives the *chariot*; the *driver* drives the *automobile*. You must consider the action in this analogy in order to differentiate between *driver* and *passenger*.

14. **The correct answer is B.** The relationship is that of the part to the whole. The *team* is part of the *league*; the *player* is part of the *team*.

15. **The correct answer is A.** This analogy is probably more difficult than any you might encounter on the exam. The trick lies in the fact that *citation* has two distinct meanings. The relationship is that

of cause-to-effect. When you are to be *honored*, you receive a *citation*, which is a formal document describing your achievements. When you are stopped for *speeding*, you receive a *citation*, which is an official summons to appear in court.

16. **The correct answer is B.** The relationship is that of an object to its user. A *stethoscope* is used by a *doctor* and a *hose* is used by a *firefighter*.

17. **The correct answer is A.** This is a creation-creator relationship. *Shakespeare* is the creator (author) of *Hamlet*; the *telephone* is an invention of Alexander Graham *Bell*.

18. **The correct answer is B.** The relationship is that of effect to its cause. *Noise* is *distracting*; *music* is *soothing*.

19. **The correct answer is E.** This is a functional relationship. *Years* are measured on a *calendar*; *hours* are measured on a *clock*.

20. **The correct answer is B.** The relationship is one of antonyms. *Superior* is the opposite of *inferior*, and *skilled* is the opposite of *unskilled*.

21. **The correct answer is A.** This is a part-whole relationship. *Words* are parts of *books*; *notes* are parts of *songs*.

22. **The correct answer is B.** The relationship is that of an adjective to the noun it modifies. An *odor* may be described as *pungent*, though there are many other adjectives you could use. A sound may be described as *shrill*, though certainly not all sounds are shrill. *Shriek* is not the best answer because it not always a *shrill* sound.

23. **The correct answer is E.** This is a purpose relationship. The purpose of a *present* is to celebrate a *birthday*; the purpose of a *reward* is to celebrate an *accomplishment*.

24. **The correct answer is D.** The relationship is one of classification. A *mouse* is a *mammal*; a *lizard* is a *reptile*.

25. **The correct answer is A.** The relationship is one of antonyms. *Sky* is the opposite of *ground*; *ceiling* is the opposite of *floor*.

26. **The correct answer is E.** The relationship is that of cause-and-effect. *Food* promotes *nutrition*; *light* promotes *vision*.

27. **The correct answer is D.** This analogy highlights a part-to-whole relationship. An *actor* is a part of a *play* performance, and a *musician* is a part of a *concert* performance.

28. **The correct answer is D.** You might loosely state the relationship as four is to three. A *square* is a four-sided plane figure in relation to a *triangle*, which is a three-sided plane figure. A *cube* is a solid figure based on a square; a *pyramid* is a solid figure based on a triangle.

29. **The correct answer is A.** The relationship is sequential. An *abacus* is an earlier, more primitive *calculator*; a *propeller* is an earlier, less sophisticated means of propulsion than a *jet*.

30. **The correct answer is C.** The relationship is that of synonyms. *Vertigo* is *dizziness*; *destiny* is *fate*.

CHAPTER

Sentence Completions

SENTENCE COMPLETIONS

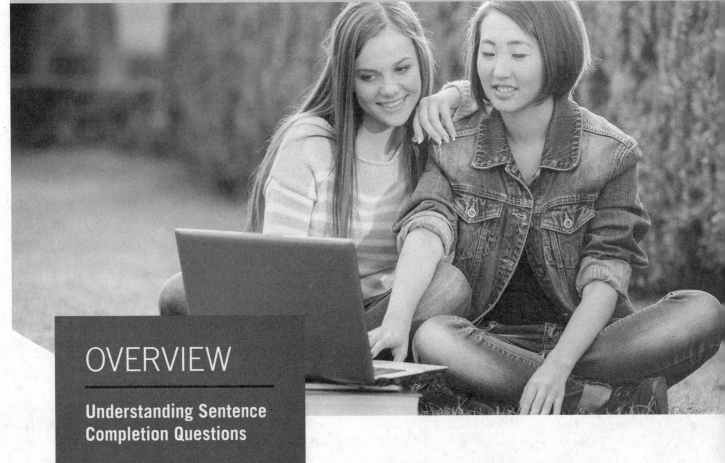

OVERVIEW

Understanding Sentence Completion Questions

Sentence Completion Strategies

Summing It Up

Knowledge Check: Sentence Completion

Answer Key and Explanations

UNDERSTANDING SENTENCE COMPLETION QUESTIONS

The ISEE contains a section on sentence completion questions, which are questions that test your knowledge of vocabulary, sentence structure, reading comprehension, and verbal logic simultaneously. In this kind of question, you are given a sentence that has one or more blanks. Four words or pairs of words are suggested to fill in the blank spaces. It's up to you to select the word or pair of words that will best complete the meaning of the sentence.

SSAT   ISEE

Here is an example of a sentence completion question.

EXAMPLE:

Those who believe in _____ are more prone to honesty.

A. integrity
B. intelligence
C. chance
D. calamity

In a typical sentence completion question, several of the choices *could* be inserted into the blank spaces. However, only one answer will complete the intended meaning of the sentence both grammatically and logically.

How Do I Answer Sentence Completion Questions?

The graphic below illustrates the six steps that will help you answer sentence completion questions.

Let's look at a few sentence completion examples to see how the six steps can help you choose the correct answer.

EXAMPLE:

It can be _____ and disheartening to look for a new job, especially given the long hours spent filling out applications.

A. courageous
B. elaborate
C. strenuous
D. elusive

Step 1: Read the sentence.

Step 2: Think of your own word to fill in the blank. You're looking for a word that completes the logic of the sentence, so you might come up with something like *difficult* or *exhausting*.

Sentence Completions: Getting It Right

1 Read the sentence carefully.

2 Guess the answer without looking at the answer choices.

3 Scan the answer choices for the word you guessed. If it or a synonym for it is there, mark it and go on. If it's not, go on to Step 4.

4 Examine the sentence for clues to the missing word.

5 Eliminate any answer choices that are ruled out by the clues.

6 Try the ones that are left and pick whichever is best.

Step 3: Look for *difficult* or *exhausting* in the answer choices. They're not there, but *strenuous* is. That's close, so mark it and go on.

Step 4: If you couldn't guess the word, take your clue from the word *disheartening* or the mention of the long hours that could be considered *tiring* or *annoying*. All point to a word associated with experiencing difficulty or negative emotions.

Step 5: Given those clues, you can eliminate *courageous* (choice A), which is a positive word, and *elaborate* (choice B), which is a neutral, emotionless adjective.

Step 6: Try the remaining choices in the sentence and you'll see that the word *strenuous* fits best because it makes more logical sense than *elusive*, which means "difficult to find or achieve."

Now, let's try those steps again, but this time, the question has two blanks. While this might seem more complicated, you will use the exact same techniques you would use to solve a question with one blank.

> **EXAMPLE:**
>
> Experienced teachers know that unruly teenagers usually become _____ if they are treated with _____ by those around them.
>
> **A.** angry … kindness
> **B.** calm … respect
> **C.** peaceful … abuse
> **D.** interested … medicine

Step 1: Read the sentence. This time, there are two blanks, and the missing words need to have some logical connection.

Step 2: Think of your own words to fill in the blanks. You might guess that the unruly teenagers will become *well-behaved* if they are treated with *consideration*.

Step 3: Now look for your guesses in the answer choices. They're not there, but you might note that *kindness* (choice A) and *respect* (choice B) are both like *consideration*.

Step 4: Go back to the sentence and look for clues. *Become* signals that the unruly teenagers will change their behavior. How that behavior changes will depend on how they are treated.

Step 5: You can eliminate choice A because a negative behavior change (*angry*) doesn't logically follow a positive treatment (*kindness*). Likewise, you can eliminate choice C because a *peaceful* behavior change is not likely to follow from *abuse*. Finally, you can eliminate choice D because *interested* and *medicine* have no logical connection—when you place them in the sentence, they do not form a coherent idea.

Step 6: The only remaining choice is B, which logically fits the sentence and must be the correct answer.

What Do I Do If I Don't Know the Definitions of My Answer Choices?

If you don't know the words, use context clues from the rest of the sentence to see if you can figure out what kind of word might fit. Perhaps you know that you are looking for a verb and can eliminate answers that are not verbs, or perhaps some of the words that you *do* know simply don't make logical sense in the sentence.

Sometimes, even if you don't know a word's meaning, reading the sentence to yourself with the answer choices substituted will show you which sentence sounds most logical based on sentences you've heard before. This is not the worst way to make a guess on a test like the ISEE, which does not penalize you for wrong choices.

Let's look at an example of a tough sentence completion question.

EXAMPLE:

Xiomara felt _____ when she was passed over for a promotion for the second time in a year.

A. trenchant

B. sagacious

C. indignant

D. contumacious

First, look for an answer choice that is a synonym for *hurt* or *offended*. Let's say, however, that you've never seen any of the word choices. Using your knowledge of root words and prefixes, you might be able to make an educated guess about what at least one of the words means. For instance, if you didn't know the meaning of the word *indignant*, you might reason that the prefix *in-* could mean something like *no* or *lacking*, since it appears in words like *inconsiderate* and *indecisive*, and that the "dign" at the center of *indignant* reminds you of the word *dignity*, so perhaps *indignant* means something like "lacking dignity." This reasoning would be very close—*indignant* means "aggrieved, resentful, or offended," which is how someone might feel if they were treated in a way that didn't feel dignified. Therefore, your educated guess that *indignant* is close to *offended* can help you arrive at the correct answer. Root words, prefixes, and suffixes are discussed in more depth in Chapter 10: Reading Comprehension.

SENTENCE COMPLETION STRATEGIES

There are a few different ways to break down sentence completion questions, particularly those that seem difficult to answer. Read through the strategies presented in this section, then practice them with the Knowledge Check at the end of this chapter. See which strategies prove most beneficial for your personal learning style and needs.

Think of Your Own Answer to Start

As we've stated before, it's important to think of your own potential answer before looking at the answer choices. Doing so simplifies your task to searching for synonyms in most cases. Practice with the following example.

EXAMPLE:

Zachariah was extremely _____ when he received a B on the exam, for he was almost certain he had gotten an A.

A. elated

B. dissatisfied

C. fulfilled

D. harmful

The correct answer is B. After reading the sentence, we know that Zachariah was not happy. Two words immediately come to mind as possible answers: *unhappy* and *disappointed*. Now, it's easier to spot that *dissatisfied* is the word that belongs in the blank.

Identify Clue Words

If you can't come up with the missing word immediately, look for clue words in the surrounding sentence. Clue words can tell you where the sentence is going. Is it continuing along one line of thought? If it is, you're looking for a word that supports that thought. Is it

changing direction in midstream? Then you're looking for a word that sets up a contrast between the thoughts in the sentence. Other adjectives or verbs in the sentence may give you clues about the missing word as well. Look for clues in the following example.

> **TIP**
>
> When you read the question to yourself, try substituting the word *blank* in your head for the missing word(s). "Hearing" the sentence in your mind with a substitute word sometimes helps you identify what should be in place of the blank.

EXAMPLE:

Though we had hoped to arrive on time, we were _____ by a delayed flight.

- **A.** assisted
- **B.** apprehended
- **C.** hindered
- **D.** preoccupied

The correct answer is C. Because this sentence starts with the word *though*, you have a clue that it is going to change direction. The word *delayed* is also a clue that the original hope of being on time was not fulfilled. *Hindered* is a synonym for *delayed*. The remaining word choices don't logically make sense in the sentence.

Pay Attention to the Flow of the Sentence

The missing word may be one that supports another thought in the sentence, so you need to look for an answer that goes with the flow of the sentence both grammatically and logically. Read the sentences to yourself and see which answer choices fit the sentence. You may be able to eliminate some that are obvious misfits. Let's practice on the following example.

EXAMPLE:

The service at the restaurant was so slow that by the time our meals had arrived we were _____.

- **A.** ravenous
- **B.** excited
- **C.** incredibly
- **D.** forlorn

The correct answer is A. Where is this sentence going? The restaurant service is very slow. That means you must wait a long time for your food, and the longer you wait, the hungrier you'll get. So, the word in the blank should be something that completes this train of thought. *Ravenous* means "very eager or greedy for food, satisfaction, or gratification." This is the best word choice to match the flow of the sentence. Note that an adjective is needed to complete the sentence. This immediately eliminates choice C because *incredibly* is an adverb. While *excited* and *forlorn* are adjectives, these words don't match the tone or the flow needed to complete the sentence.

Look for Blanks That Are "Pivots"

The missing word may be one that reverses a thought in the sentence, so you need to look for an answer that stands out from the rest or constitutes a pivot in the thought process.

EXAMPLE:

Advances in science have demonstrated that a fact that appears to contradict a certain theory may actually be _____ a more advanced formulation of that theory.

- **A.** incompatible with
- **B.** in opposition to
- **C.** consistent with
- **D.** eliminated by

The correct answer is C. Look at the logical structure of the sentence. The sentence has set up a contrast between what appears to be and what is actually true. This indicates that the correct answer will pivot and be the opposite of *contradict*. The choice *consistent with* provides this meaning. The other choices do not.

 ALERT

Remember that more than one answer can seem to make sense, but there is only one correct answer. Make your best guess based on the full meaning of the sentence.

Questions with Two Blanks Give You Two Ways to Get It Right

When there are two blanks in a sentence completion question, you have two ways to eliminate answer choices. You can start with either blank to eliminate choices that don't work, so pick the one that's easier for you. If you can eliminate just one of the words in a two-word answer choice, the whole choice becomes invalid, allowing you to toss it out and move on. Let's take a look at an example to help illustrate this technique.

EXAMPLE:

The Spanish dancer stamped her feet and _____ the rhythm with the click of her _____.

- **A.** ignored ... dice
- **B.** kept ... cutlery
- **C.** accented ... castanets
- **D.** diffused ... guitar

The correct answer is C. Let's focus on the second blank. Start by eliminating *guitar* (choice D) because a guitar does not click, which is a clue given in the sentence. This leaves *dice*, *cutlery*, and *castanets* as possible choices. It doesn't make much sense for a Spanish dancer to be holding dice or cutlery (unless the cutlery was a sword perhaps). But castanets are handheld percussion clapper instruments that make a clicking or clacking sound. Even if you aren't familiar with what castanets are, you can check to see if choice C is the correct answer by substituting both words from this answer choice in the given sentence.

SUMMING IT UP

- These six steps will help you as you work through sentence completions:

  1. Read the sentence carefully.

  2. Come up with your own guess for the word(s) to fill the blank(s).

  3. Scan the answer choices for the word you guessed or a synonym for it—if it's there, mark it and go on.

  4. If you still need help answering, examine the sentence for clues to the missing word.

  5. Use your clues and verbal reasoning to rule out any wrong answers.

  6. Try the answer choices that are left and pick whichever best fits.

- If you don't know any of the words in your answer choices, use your knowledge of vocabulary, word roots, prefixes, and suffixes to make your best guess. These are covered in more depth in Chapter 10: Reading Comprehension.

- You are not penalized for incorrect answers on the ISEE, so always make your best guess when you don't know.

- Always choose answers that flow both logically and grammatically with the rest of the sentence.

- Pay attention to context clues to determine if words match the ideas at the beginning of the sentence or constitute a pivot.

- On questions with two blanks, focus on one blank to start. You can eliminate any answer for which either blank is a mismatch.

SENTENCE COMPLETION

40 Questions—20 Minutes

> **Directions:** Each question is made up of a sentence with one or two blanks. One blank indicates that one word is missing. Two blanks indicate that two words are missing. Each sentence is followed by four answer choices. Select the one word or pair of words that best completes the meaning of the sentence as a whole.

1. His theory is not _____; it only sounds plausible to the uninformed because he _____ several facts and fails to mention the mountain of evidence that contradicts his ideas.

   A. tenable ... distorts

   B. pliable ... pursued

   C. predominant ... embellished

   D. sufficient ... invokes

2. Jimmy was so _____ as he approached his date's door that his hands were _____ and his knees shook.

   A. confident ... agitated

   B. impressed ... clean

   C. unhappy ... stiff

   D. nervous ... clammy

3. No one else could locate anything with his filing system because it was too _____.

   A. specific

   B. appropriate

   C. intense

   D. peculiar

4. When the last item on the _____ had been taken care of, the meeting was _____.

   A. roster ... called to order

   B. itinerary ... finalized

   C. table ... sequestered

   D. agenda ... adjourned

5. It has been predicted that the new _____ barring discrimination in employment on the basis of sexual orientation will dramatically _____ hiring practices.

   A. morality ... effect

   B. permissiveness ... reflect

   C. legislation ... affect

   D. rulings ... reset

6. The Navy scoured the area for over a month, but the _____ search turned up no clues.

   A. cursory

   B. fruitful

   C. present

   D. painstaking

7. Although her personality is sometimes _____, Deb is a conscientious worker and is _____ better treatment than she has received.

   A. pleasing ... conscious of

   B. abrasive ... entitled to

   C. gloomy ... eligible for

   D. cheerful ... granted

8. _____ manipulation of the stock market and other _____ practices in security sales resulted in the 1933 legislation for the control of security markets.

   A. Degenerate ... lucrative

   B. Economic ... useless

   C. Continual ... productive

   D. Unscrupulous ... unethical

9. The handbook _____ for beginners was written in an elementary style.

   A. bound

   B. intended

   C. paged

   D. critiqued

10. When a job becomes too _____, workers get _____, their attention wanders, and they start to make careless errors.

    A. diverse ... busy

    B. hectic ... lazy

    C. tedious ... bored

    D. fascinating ... interested

11. Because of her uncompromising stances on divisive issues, the candidate was unable to _____ broad support among the voters; however, the minority who did support her were exceptionally _____.

    A. alienate ... many

    B. survey ... divided

    C. cut across ... quiet

    D. amass ... loyal

12. The stranger's remarks were too _____ to be taken seriously.

    A. germane

    B. crucial

    C. pointed

    D. insipid

13. The head chef had been _____ in her preparations, so she knew dinner service would go _____.

    A. flawless ... upwards

    B. meticulous ... smoothly

    C. perilous ... effortlessly

    D. exactly ... tremendous

14. Since the course was not only _____ but also had a reputation for being extremely difficult, _____ students registered for it.

    A. enjoyable ... many

    B. required ... some

    C. useful ... practical

    D. optional ... few

15. The new secretary has a more businesslike manner than her _____ in the position.

    A. precedent

    B. ancestor

    C. successor

    D. predecessor

16. Because of the _____ hazard, regulations forbid the use of highly _____ materials in certain items such as camping gear and children's pajamas.

    A. health ... synthetic

    B. fire ... flammable

    C. drug ... inflammatory

    D. chemical ... flame-retardant

17. The _____ report was submitted, subject to such _____ as would be made before the final draft.

   A. preliminary ... revisions
   B. ubiquitous ... submissions
   C. ultimate ... editions
   D. committee's ... references

18. _____ action on the part of a passerby stabilized the victim before brain damage could occur.

   A. Physical
   B. Prompt
   C. Violent
   D. Delayed

19. As the workload _____, she _____ responsibility for many routine tasks to an assistant.

   A. evolved ... preserved
   B. changed ... handled
   C. increased ... delegated
   D. steadied ... abased

20. I wish I could guarantee that the machine is _____ reliable, but in truth, its performance is somewhat _____.

   A. invariably ... sporadic
   B. never ... skittish
   C. serially ... erratic
   D. consistently ... invincible

21. The food critic praised the sweet, fruity dessert as being nothing less than _____.

   A. surreal
   B. saccharine
   C. cloying
   D. succulent

22. A _____ in the diplomatic service, she had not yet _____ such a question of protocol.

   A. success ... dispatched
   B. volunteer ... avoided
   C. veteran ... battered
   D. novice ... encountered

23. Excessive fatigue can _____ be attributed to _____ working conditions such as poor lighting.

   A. inevitably ... archaic
   B. occasionally ... inadequate
   C. always ... obsolete
   D. never ... demoralizing

24. The company received a _____ from the government to help develop new sources of energy.

   A. reward
   B. compendium
   C. memorandum
   D. subsidy

25. The _____ with which the flight attendant calmed the anxieties and soothed the tempers of the travelers _____ by the delay was a mark of her experience.

   A. evasiveness ... angered
   B. reverence ... pleased
   C. facility ... inconvenienced
   D. mannerism ... destroyed

26. My annoying stepsister considers it her destiny in life to _____ me.

   A. perturb
   B. germinate
   C. perforate
   D. rebate

27. As the name of the prize winner was _____, the runner-up looked totally _____.

   A. extolled ... exonerated

   B. awarded ... devastated

   C. announced ... crestfallen

   D. proclaimed ... credulous

28. Today's students are encouraged to absorb facts rather than to apply _____, so education is becoming more _____.

   A. understanding ... regrettable

   B. intelligence ... invaluable

   C. knowledge ... passive

   D. formulas ... extensive

29. A human's survival is a result of mutual assistance, since humans are fundamentally _____ rather than _____.

   A. superior ... inferior

   B. cooperative ... competitive

   C. individualistic ... gregarious

   D. selfish ... stingy

30. Ancient Greeks were not only concerned with the development of the _____ but also felt training the body was of _____ importance.

   A. muscles ... equal

   B. psyche ... little

   C. mind ... utmost

   D. physical ... vital

31. Although for years _____ resources have been devoted to alleviating the problem, a satisfactory solution remains _____.

   A. natural ... costly

   B. adequate ... probable

   C. substantial ... elusive

   D. capital ... decisive

32. The strategic _____ of the burning buildings led the military investigator to conclude that the fires had been set in an act of _____.

   A. location ... arson

   B. insignificance ... sabotage

   C. stance ... sobriety

   D. discipline ... treason

33. The treaty cannot go into effect until it has been _____ by the Senate.

   A. considered

   B. debated

   C. ratified

   D. shelved

34. His _____ of practical experience and his psychological acuity more than _____ his lack of formal academic training.

   A. claims ... comprise

   B. background ... educate for

   C. brief ... account for

   D. wealth ... compensate for

35. Because I wanted to use a(n) _____, I looked the word up in the _____.

   A. synonym ... thesaurus

   B. homonym ... directory

   C. antonym ... encyclopedia

   D. pseudonym ... dictionary

36. You will have to speak to the head of the department; I am not _____ to give out that information.

   A. willing

   B. authorized

   C. programmed

   D. happy

37. Research in that field has become so _____ that researchers on different aspects of the same problem may be _____ each other's work.

A. secure ... bombarded with

B. partial ... surprised at

C. departmental ... inimical to

D. specialized ... unfamiliar with

38. She _____ the way things were done, but many of the _____ for which she broke ground were left to be fully realized by others.

A. disliked ... provocations

B. eliminated ... foundations

C. implemented ... buildings

D. revolutionized ... innovations

39. A change in environment is very likely to _____ a change in one's work habits.

A. affect

B. inflict

C. facilitate

D. elevate

40. A shift to greater use of _____ or inexhaustible resources in the production of power would slow the depletion of _____ fuel materials.

A. synthetic ... regional

B. natural ... chemical

C. renewable ... irreplaceable

D. unknown ... fossil

ANSWER KEY AND EXPLANATIONS

1. A	9. B	17. A	25. C	33. C
2. D	10. C	18. B	26. A	34. D
3. D	11. D	19. C	27. C	35. A
4. D	12. D	20. A	28. C	36. B
5. C	13. B	21. D	29. B	37. D
6. D	14. D	22. D	30. C	38. D
7. B	15. D	23. B	31. C	39. C
8. D	16. B	24. D	32. A	40. C

1. **The correct answer is A.** The first blank might be filled equally well by the first term of choice A or choice D; however, the coordinating conjunction *and* implies that the second blank must be filled with a negative action taken against the facts. *Distorts* is the best word here.

2. **The correct answer is D.** *Nervous* and *clammy* are the only word choices that make logical sense in the sentence.

3. **The correct answer is D.** If no one else could locate the material, you can be pretty sure that his filing system was peculiar.

4. **The correct answer is D.** The term *agenda* describes a list of items for consideration at a meeting. When the business is completed, one would typically adjourn the meeting.

5. **The correct answer is C.** The barring of discrimination is an official act, so only choices C or D could fill the first blank. Of the remaining choices, the second blank is best filled with the verb *affect*.

6. **The correct answer is D.** A search that lasts more than a month is most certainly a painstaking one.

7. **The correct answer is B.** The first blank calls for a negative trait to contrast with *conscientious*. Choices B and C might both be correct, but the phrase *entitled to* better fits the informality of the sentence. *Eligible for* implies a legal requirement.

8. **The correct answer is D.** The coordinating conjunction *and* in the compound subject requires that both words have the same connotation. Since

these acts led to the imposition of controls, we must assume that they were negative acts.

9. **The correct answer is B.** The style of a manual must be appropriate to the audience for which it is intended.

10. **The correct answer is C.** The key here is that the workers' attention wanders. Attention wanders when one is bored. One becomes bored when the work is tedious.

11. **The correct answer is D.** Only *amass* really makes sense in the first blank.

12. **The correct answer is D.** If the remarks couldn't be taken seriously, then they could be described as insipid, meaning they lacked quality or character.

13. **The correct answer is B.** Only the words *meticulous* and *smoothly* make sense both grammatically and logically.

14. **The correct answer is D.** The "not only ... but also" construction implies two complementary reasons why a subset of students might register for the course. Only choice D fits this requirement. A course that is both optional and very difficult will draw few registrants.

15. **The correct answer is D.** A predecessor is "someone who has previously occupied a position or office to which another has succeeded."

16. **The correct answer is B.** When examining the first word in each answer choice, only *health* and *fire* make sense in the first blank. Since synthetics are not in themselves a health hazard, but

flammable materials are a fire hazard, we know that choice B is the best answer.

17. **The correct answer is A.** The report was submitted before the final draft, so only the words *preliminary* (choice A) or *committee's* (choice D) can describe the report. Since a report is made subject to revisions, not subject to references, choice A is the best answer.

18. **The correct answer is B.** Since the action was taken before brain damage could occur, the best completion should imply speed. *Prompt* means "to move to action."

19. **The correct answer is C.** When a workload increases, routine tasks can be delegated to an assistant.

20. **The correct answer is A.** Only the words *invariable* and *sporadic* make sense both grammatically and logically for both blanks.

21. **The correct answer is D.** The word *praised* gives you a clue that you are looking for a positive word to describe a tasty dessert. *Succulent* is the best option you're given.

22. **The correct answer is D.** The words *not yet* imply that she was a novice in the diplomatic service, meaning she was new to it.

23. **The correct answer is B.** Excessive fatigue can often be attributed to factors other than inhospitable working conditions, but occasionally, inadequate working conditions are its cause.

24. **The correct answer is D.** Money offered by the government to incentivize completing a project is called a subsidy.

25. **The correct answer is C.** The blanks could be filled with choices A or C. However, extensive experience would lead to facility in soothing inconvenienced travelers, so choice C is logically the best answer.

26. **The correct answer is A.** Here, you are looking for a synonym for *annoy* and *perturb* does the trick.

27. **The correct answer is C.** The words *announced* and *crestfallen* are the only words that make grammatical and logical sense.

28. **The correct answer is C.** Absorption of facts is passive, as opposed to the more active mode of education, the application of knowledge.

29. **The correct answer is B.** As indicated by the words *rather than*, the sentence requires that the two words filling the blanks be opposites, so you can eliminate choice D. Since mutual assistance implies cooperation, choice B is the best answer.

30. **The correct answer is C.** The first blank requires a word that contrasts with *body*. Of the choices, *mind* best fulfills that requirement.

31. **The correct answer is C.** The sentence demands that the first blank be filled with a positive word while the second is filled with a less positive word. The words *substantial* and *elusive* best fit these requirements.

32. **The correct answer is A.** The words *location* and *arson* make the most logical and grammatical sense.

33. **The correct answer is C.** A treaty must be ratified to take effect.

34. **The correct answer is D.** The words in the blanks should contrast with the lack of formal academic training. A wealth of practical knowledge compensates for a lack of academic training.

35. **The correct answer is A.** A thesaurus is a book for finding synonyms.

36. **The correct answer is B.** All choices except C might be correct, but the imperative of "you will have to" implies that the authority to provide the information is not there.

37. **The correct answer is D.** No animosity is implied in this sentence, so the words *specialized* and *unfamiliar with* are the best fit.

38. **The correct answer is D.** Of the options, only innovations for which one breaks ground can be fully realized by others.

39. **The correct answer is C.** A change in environment makes a change in one's work habits more possible, so *facilitate* is the best answer since it means "make (an action or situation) easier or more likely."

40. **The correct answer is C.** Focus first on the second blank—you are looking for fuel materials that could be depleted, narrowing your choices to *synthetic* (choice A) and *renewable* (choice C). Of those two, only *renewable* makes sense when placed in the first blank.

CHAPTER

Reading Comprehension

READING COMPREHENSION

OVERVIEW

SSAT   ISEE

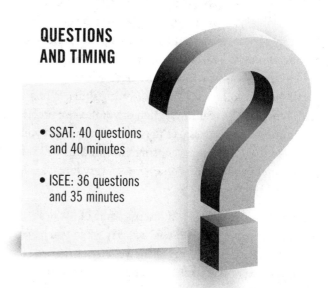

Both the SSAT and ISEE include sections on reading comprehension where you'll be presented with reading passages followed by a series of questions based on the text. The questions test not only how well you understand what you read on the surface but also how well you interpret the passage's meaning and the author's intent. These questions also test how well you draw conclusions based on what you've read.

To do well on the reading comprehension section of an exam, reading quickly is crucial—but so is comprehension. In this chapter, we'll go over the specifications of the reading sections on both the SSAT and ISEE; discuss strategies for improving reading comprehension, expanding your vocabulary, and approaching reading questions on timed exams; and discuss the different types of questions you'll encounter on the SSAT and ISEE and how to approach them.

UNDERSTANDING THE READING COMPREHENSION SECTION

In the reading sections of these tests, you'll be presented with passages and questions that test your ability to understand what you read. The questions are multiple-choice with either four (ISEE) or five (SSAT) answer choices. The passages could be about history, literature, science, art, economics, or lots of other topics. They may also be excerpts from literary texts, like poems, or historical texts, such as biographies.

On your exam day, the passages will include line numbers in the margin in case you are asked to look at a specific line or lines. Since test formats can change from year to year, this book includes questions with simple, standardized directions about where to locate parts of the text. For instance, a question might ask "According to paragraph 2…" as a way of telling you that the information you need is in the second paragraph of the passage. In poems, each "chunk" of the poem as separated by blank lines is called a stanza, so if a question asks about "stanza 3," you'll know that it's the third section of the poem.

QUESTIONS AND TIMING

- SSAT: 40 questions and 40 minutes

- ISEE: 36 questions and 35 minutes

The ISEE contains 6 passages followed by 6 questions each. The SSAT contains 8–10 passages followed by 3–6 questions each. That means you want to budget about 5–6 minutes (ISEE) or 4–5 minutes (SSAT) for each passage and its questions. This should be just enough time for you to actively read through the passage one time and then answer the questions. On longer passages, you may need to skim and scan to save time. You will almost assuredly *not* have enough time for rereading the passage unless you are a very speedy reader, so try to make the most of your limited reading time. On the SSAT, since you are penalized for wrong answers, skip any question for which you cannot eliminate at least two wrong answers before guessing. On the ISEE, you won't be penalized for wrong answers, so if you find yourself taking too long on a question, make your best educated guess and move on.

TIP

You should only need to read the entire passage a second time if you truly cannot answer multiple questions. Doing so will cost time, so try to answer what you can with one reading.

On both the SSAT and ISEE, passages will vary in length between approximately 200–400 words. They will also vary in difficulty, with some being readily accessible and others requiring more effort to understand. The same will be true of the questions themselves—some will be quite clear, while others will require you to flex your reasoning skills. When studying for the reading section of your exam, practice skimming longer passages to get the information you need without reading every single word. This will save you time if you should come across a very long passage on your exam.

Later in this chapter, we'll discuss some of the best strategies you can use to read actively when you have limited time on an exam. Then, we'll cover the types of questions you're likely to encounter and how to approach each. A key aspect of developing your reading abilities involves knowing what to look for while you read. If you know what topics test makers tend to ask about, you'll have a better chance of getting the information you need when actively reading.

While reading, ask yourself questions like:

- What is the author's main point, their tone, and their purpose for writing?
- What ideas are most important?
- What are important supporting details related to the main point?
- What is the purpose of each different section and how do they work together to form an overall idea?
- What words stand out to me?
- What do I already know about this topic?
- Is this a story or does it discuss an opinion? Does it inform me about a topic?
- What can I predict about this passage?

Practice asking and answering these questions as you read until looking for these things in a passage simply becomes how you actively read.

BUILDING YOUR VOCABULARY

Vocabulary and reading comprehension are closely related. You can't grow your vocabulary without reading, and you can't comprehend a text without a firm grasp of the words the author is using. Both for the reading section and other parts of your exam, such as writing and verbal ability, you'll need a strong vocabulary. Here are some ways you can build vocabulary expansion into any active reading you do to prepare for your exam.

Keep a Word Log

First off, read material that is more challenging. Check out magazines like *Scientific American*, *Newsweek*, *National Geographic*, and similar. Look over the *New York Times*, the *Washington Post*, the *Times of London*, and other well-regarded newspapers. You can even look ahead in some of your textbooks. The key is to find material with words that are new or unfamiliar to you.

Next, with pen in hand, write down the words that you don't understand. Instead of using a computer or mobile device, the act of writing something by hand actually helps you imprint the word into your memory. Once you have a good list of unfamiliar words, look up the definitions in a dictionary. Focus on learning a few words at a time so that you can learn them well. Sometimes, it can be helpful to start with a learner's dictionary, which will define a word in simpler language and provide more examples of how to use it in a sentence. Write down the definitions for the unfamiliar words. You can even go back to where you originally found the unfamiliar word and reread it to see how the now-familiar word is used in context.

Third, try to use the word yourself in a sentence or in conversation. Practice using the word by creating your own sentences and writing them down in a notebook. This will help you get a sense of how to use the word in different contexts while cementing the word and its meaning into your vocabulary. Take note of the contexts in which you often see or use a word. Getting

familiar with the topics and situations in which certain words are used will help you feel more confident and self-assured when you integrate new words into your vocabulary.

When keeping your word log, be sure to write down the new words you have learned as well as the words you want to learn. When you document the definition for a new word, include details like the part of speech, as well as any synonyms and antonyms, and give an example of how the word can be used in a sentence. You can also study the roots, prefixes, and suffixes of words, so you can apply all you know whenever you encounter a word that's unfamiliar. If a word has more than one meaning, you should include those as well. Here is an example of what an entry might look like.

ATTRITION: noun. 1. Sorrow for one's sins; 2. the act of wearing or grinding down by friction; 3. weakening or exhausting by constant harassment, abuse, or attack; 4. a reduction in numbers.

SYNONYMS: corrosion, erosion, degradation

ANTONYMS: buildup, growth, accumulation

SENTENCE: The attrition rate among social workers is high, due mainly to the long hours, difficult work, and low pay.

If it's not possible to keep a paper log of new words, a mobile device can be a valuable tool for taking notes. When you're at the grocery store or on the bus and you see or hear a word that is unfamiliar, you can write it down and look it up later. Some devices will let you use a stylus, so you can still write by hand. Mobile devices also have access to a dictionary, whether it's through an app or a web browser. Lastly, such devices can give you access to reading material like online magazines and newspapers, books, and research papers, especially things you wouldn't normally have easy access to.

Study Root Words, Prefixes, and Suffixes

You can increase your vocabulary—and your test score—by learning about the structure of words. This will help you figure out the meanings of unfamiliar words you come across in both the reading and verbal sections of your exam. Knowing what the parts of words mean is the key to deciphering words you've never seen before.

English words have recognizable parts that most often come from Latin or Greek. Generally, there are three basic types of word parts:

1. **Roots** are the basic elements of a word that determine its meaning. Most derive from Latin and Greek and must be combined with prefixes, suffixes, or both.

2. **Prefixes** attach to the beginning of a root word to alter its meaning or to create a new word.

3. **Suffixes** attach to the end of a root word to change its meaning, help make it grammatically correct in context, or form a new word. Suffixes often indicate whether a word is a noun, verb, adjective, or adverb.

Sometimes, depending on the word, it can be difficult to parse out whether a word part is a prefix or a root word. However, the key takeaway here is that certain word parts carry meaning that is recognizable no matter what the word is. Knowing the meaning of part of a word can help you infer the meaning of the word.

For more information on word parts, scan this QR code.

To aid you in your learning, we've compiled some frequently used prefixes, root words, and suffixes. These tables are by no means comprehensive, but they should help you get started on breaking down words you see often or encounter when reading.

COMMON PREFIXES

Prefix	Meaning	Example
Anti-	Against	Antifreeze, antibacterial
Bene-	Good	Benefit, benevolent
De-	Opposite	Deactivate, derail
Dis- Dys-	Not	Disagree, dysfunctional
En- Em-	Cover	Encode, embrace
Extra-	Beyond	Extraterrestrial, extracurricular
Fore-	Before	Forecast, forehead
Il- Im- In- Ir- Non- Un-	Not	Illegitimate, impossible, inexcusable, irregular, nonstop, nonsense, unable, undefined
Inter-	Between	Intergalactic, intermediary, interpret
Mal-	Bad, badly	Malicious, malnourished, malfunction
Mis-	Wrongly	Mistake, misinterpret, misnomer
Over-	Over, more, too much	Overlook, oversee, overachieve, overcast
Pre-	Before	Prefix, prevent, predict, prehistoric, prejudice
Re-	Again	Revision, reimagine, return
Trans-	Across	Transatlantic, transverse, transport

COMMON ROOTS

Root	Meaning	Example
Aqu Hydr	Water	Aqueous, aquarium, hydrate, hydrotherapy
Aud	Hear	Auditory, audio, audible
Biblio	Book	Bibliophile, bibliography
Chrono	Time	Chronological, chronology
Chrom	Color	Monochromatic, chromosome
Circ	Round	Circle, circus
Geo	Earth	Geography, geomagnetic
Juris	Law	Jurisdiction, jurisprudence
Junct	Join	Conjunction, juncture
Log Logue	Speaking, speech	Epilogue, eulogy, dialogue
Photo	Light	Photosynthesis, photography, photon
Scribe	Write	Describe, prescribe, inscribe
Sect	Cut	Dissect, sector
Volve	Roll, turn	Involve, evolve, revolve

To learn more about root words, scan this QR code.

COMMON SUFFIXES		
Suffix	Meaning	Example
-able -ible	Capable	Agreeable, collectible
-al	Pertaining to	Logical, magical, criminal
-ance -ence	Indicating a state or condition; indicating a process or action	Clearance, ignorance, evidence, patience
-ent	Causing, promoting, or doing an action; one who causes or does something	Different, absorbent, student, agent, deterrent
-fy -ize -ate -en	Cause to be	Classify, diversify, realize, contextualize, create, communicate, awaken, sharpen
-ious -ous	Characterized by; full of	Nutritious, delicious, simultaneous, nervous
-ism	Belief, act	Catholicism, plagiarism
-ity	State or quality of being	Enmity, ability, responsibility
-less	Without	Homeless, restless, countless
-let	Small	Booklet, piglet
-or -er -ist	A person who is or does something	Benefactor, investigator, driver, teacher, narcissist, chemist
-ship	Position held	Friendship, citizenship, allyship, ownership
-tion -sion -ment	Action or instance of something	Liberation, concentration, admission, decision, achievement, bereavement
-y	Quality of	Thirsty, wintry

STRATEGIES FOR GETTING IT RIGHT

There are a lot of different ways to approach a timed reading comprehension section like you'll find on the SSAT and ISEE to make sure you're setting yourself up for success. We suggest starting by performing the tips we provide here in the recommended order, but feel free to develop a different strategy that works for you personally. As you practice, see which aspects of reading exams you struggle with most: understanding passages, reading questions, getting through the passage in time, etc. Then, try and develop exam day strategies that suit your needs.

No matter how you practice, the skill you are developing is that of locating relevant information within a text you have just read. Practice making notes about the information you read as you go along, such as using key words to remember the topic of each paragraph. Remember, you only have roughly 4–5 minutes (SSAT) or 5–6 minutes (ISEE) per passage and question set. As a starting point, complete these steps in the following order to economize your time and maximize your chances of choosing correct answers:

Glance Quickly Through the Passage

Glance quickly through the passage to get the gist of what it's about. Look for key words or names that repeat, read the first and last sentence of the first and last paragraphs, and see if there are any concepts or terms that stand out. This part should be done fairly quickly.

Scan the Questions and Answer What You Can

Once you have a basic idea of what the passage is about, glance at the questions to see if there are any easier ones you can handle right away based on the little you've read so far. Main idea questions, for instance, may be possible to answer with just the first and last sentence of the first and last paragraphs. You can also

usually address vocabulary questions simply by reading the sentences that contain the word in question. It's possible that you'll be able to answer all the questions at this point and move on. However, if there are still some left, identify the topics of remaining questions so you can look for relevant details when you read. Your main goal when reading will be to locate where the answers can be found so you can read closer later when referring back to the question.

Actively Read the Passage One Time

Assuming you still have questions to answer, read actively but quickly through your passage one time. When you actively read, you focus less on reading every single word and more on catching key words, important ideas, and the purpose of each paragraph. Avoid reading the entire passage more than one time, as you will not likely have time to do so. Remember, your goal isn't to memorize every single fact in the passage; it will contain much more information than what you directly need. Instead, you are actively reading to locate the answers to your questions. Slow down and focus more when you find reading sections with relevant information, then speed through the parts that don't relate to your questions.

Draw Conclusions Based on Information in the Passage

Remember: while every question can be answered by information in the passage, not every answer will be explicitly stated in the passage. You might be asked to infer or predict something. Or you might be asked about something else an author won't usually state directly, like tone, mood, or point of view. When a question asks you what the author has implied or asks you about the tone of the passage, you must use what you've read to draw your own conclusions. Your goal may be to apply what the author has stated to lead you to a conclusion. To come to those ideas, you might ask yourself some analytical questions, like "What would I not understand had I not read this passage?" or "What conclusions can I draw that aren't stated directly but are still clear to me now that I've read?" In some situations, an "If/Then" construction can be a good way to do this: "If _____ is true/false, then…what comes next?"

Skip (SSAT) or Guess (ISEE) Questions You Can't Answer

You have so little time on the reading section that wasting it trying to decide on the answer to a single question won't benefit you much. If you're taking the SSAT, skip those questions and come back to

TIP

Don't waste your time on technical details or on information that the questions don't ask for. Practice skimming (reading quickly without absorbing every single word) and scanning (searching for relevant key words) rather than trying to catch every tiny detail.

them later if you have time. You will be penalized for wrong answers, so don't answer if you don't feel at least 60% sure of your answer, meaning you've eliminated at least two choices. For the ISEE, you need a different strategy; guesses don't count against you, so plan to make a guess and move on for any question that takes you longer than 30 seconds to answer.

Some Other Reminders and Advice

Here are a few other things to keep in mind if you want to tackle reading passages like a pro.

Predict the Answer after Reading the Question

After you read a question, make a prediction about what the answer should be based on what you know from the passage. If you see that answer or similar among the available choices, there's a good chance that it's correct.

Read All Your Answer Choices

Don't just mark down the first answer that seems correct. Instead, make sure you read each answer choice and eliminate those you know are wrong before choosing the *best* answer. Some answers may be similar and you need to evaluate each one before moving on.

Stick to the Passage

Avoid involving personal or emotional judgments when finding your answers. Even if you disagree with the author or spot a factual error in the passage, you must answer based on what's stated or implied in the text. Similarly, even if you have outside knowledge of a topic, answer based only on what's written in front of you. An answer can be true in the sense that it reflects something about the real world, but if it's not supported by the passage, it's wrong.

Eliminate Wrong Answers

There is only one right answer for each question, which means that there is a good reason why the right answer is correct and why each of the incorrect answers are wrong. Any answer that contradicts information in the passage (unless that's what the question is looking for) is incorrect, so you can eliminate it from consideration. After taking the steps to predict and read all the answer

choices, you should be able to narrow down your possible options. At that point, even if you haven't settled on one answer, you've done a lot of work to increase your likelihood of guessing correctly.

Don't Worry If You Don't Know the Topic

To put all test takers on a level playing field, test writers choose approachable reading passages on a variety of topics from the sciences, social sciences, and humanities. Some will be a little harder than others, but all are designed to be understandable to a general audience. You probably have not seen the reading material before, but you're not being tested on your knowledge of the topic. Instead, you're being tested on how well you can comprehend what you read and answer the questions accordingly.

For more tips on answering reading comprehension questions, scan this QR code.

Start with Your Strengths

If you have a choice, start with the passages you're interested in. If the topic or style appeals to you, you will probably go through the passage more quickly and find the questions easier to deal with. Doing so also maximizes your score, since you're focusing time on the passages you are likely to understand well enough to get the questions right. If you're not sure which passage types are easiest for you, pay attention when taking practice tests and then use that data to make decisions on exam day.

Personalize Your Approach

Everything we've laid out here is a basic template for how to approach reading questions, but no one knows you better than you. If a certain aspect of reading is harder for you, such as understanding questions or getting through the passages in time, figure out which of the strategies here you need to prioritize. Maybe you're the type of person who needs to closely read the questions first before reading a single word of the passage—this is a fine strategy, but it can also cost time, so when you're practicing, build your skimming and scanning skills to help make up that time. Maybe you're the type who needs to read more slowly but then can answer the questions quickly. Part of the benefit of practice is that you can figure out an approach that accounts for your strengths and weaknesses. See what impacts your score the most and make sure to time yourself when practicing so you can identify where you might need improvement before exam day.

 TIP

It's okay to approach reading passages in a unique way that supports your own strengths and weaknesses as a reader. When first practicing, time yourself by the passage and vary approaches to see which techniques best help you hit your target.

QUESTION TYPES (WITH PRACTICE!)

This section covers the types of questions you'll be asked on both the SSAT and ISEE. The SSAT questions offer five answer choices while the ISEE questions offer four. Throughout this chapter, example questions will resemble the five-question model, but don't worry if you are studying for the ISEE—with reading questions, you will use the same techniques to find correct answers regardless of how many answer choices you are given.

The six basic question types that the SSAT and ISEE use to evaluate reading ability test the following reading comprehension skills:

- Ability to identify the **main idea** of a text, including central themes or arguments and an author's overall purpose

- Comprehension of **supporting details** in the passage and the ability to identify information related to those details through active reading

- Word comprehension and the ability to define **vocabulary** words or phrases based on the context in which they are used within a passage

- Drawing **inferences** from ideas and details presented in the passage

- Identification of the author's **tone, style, and use of figurative language** such as simile, metaphor, hyperbole, personification, irony, and imagery as well as genre, mood, and point of view

- Understanding how a passage's **organization and logic** help an author meet their purpose

Not every question type will appear after each passage, but the bolded terms in the bullets correspond with the primary categories of evaluation indentified by test makers for the SSAT and ISEE. In the sections that follow, we'll discuss each of these categories, offer tips on how to address them, and give you a chance to practice your skills with real passages. Additionally, questions from any category may ask you to evaluate the author's argument or opinion, so we'll cover some strategies related to that as well. At the end of this section, you'll find a graphic model demonstrating how each question category relates to details from a single passage.

Main Idea Questions

The main idea of a passage is the primary point a passage is trying to make to readers. In argumentative writing, it will be the author's main opinion or argument. You can think of the main idea as the overall message an author is trying to send by writing a passage. Often, the quickest way to identify the main point is to read the first and last sentences of the first and last paragraphs of a passage. Otherwise, the main point should be evident after an active read-through.

QUESTIONS TO ASK YOURSELF: MAIN IDEA

- What is the author telling me?
- What does the author want me to take away from the passage?
- What would be a good title for this passage?
- Why did the author write this passage?
- If I had to summarize this passage in one sentence, what would it be?

Main idea questions will sometimes simply ask, "What is the main idea of this passage?" Other common types of main idea questions involve choosing an appropriate passage title or identifying the passage's overall purpose. No matter the approach, you can be prepared for any main idea question by trying to summarize the most important "takeaway" from the passage whenever you finish reading. Try and summarize what you just read in a single statement, such as by completing sentences like "This passage was about _____." or "The author wants the reader to know that _____." Having this main idea in mind should

make it easier to identify correct answers to both main idea questions and questions that are related to them, such as supporting detail questions and questions about organization and logic.

Addressing Main Idea Questions

One of the fastest ways to eliminate wrong answers to main idea questions is by looking for choices that are either too specific or too general. To demonstrate, let's say you read a passage and when you finish, you mentally summarize the main idea as follows: "This passage was about how squid develop over the course of their entire life." Then, you are faced with the following common type of main idea question.

EXAMPLE:

What might be the best title for this passage?

- A. "Squid Mating Habits"
- B. "How Baby Squid Develop"
- C. "The Life Cycle of Squid"
- D. "Animals of the Ocean"
- E. "The Evolution of Squid"

Since a passage's title should reflect its main idea, you are looking for the answer that is most like your summary of the passage's main idea. In this case, "The Life Cycles of Squid" (choice C) does the trick. Having already identified the main idea, the correct answer should hopefully stand out the second you read it. If it doesn't, remember to check for answers that are too vague or too specific. "Squid Mating Habits" (choice A) and "How Baby Squid Develop" (choice B) both reflect topics that relate to the life cycle of squid. These topics may even have been addressed in your passage, but they are too specific to encompass the main idea you identified, which included the stages of a squid's entire life. Meanwhile, "Animals of the Ocean" (choice D) is far too vague a title for a passage that talks about squid specifically.

Once you have eliminated options that are too specific or vague, the remaining incorrect answers will usually address something that either wasn't mentioned in the passage or that is slightly off topic from the passage. In this case, "The Evolution of Squid" (choice E) may be related to the main idea you identified, but not directly so, since the evolution of a species is different than its life cycle.

NOTE

Even if a test question doesn't use the words "main idea," it still might be asking for the main idea. If you have identified the main idea for yourself before you even get to the questions, then you shouldn't be caught off guard no matter how the question is phrased.

Addressing Questions about the Author's Purpose

One common subset of main idea questions specifically addresses the author's purpose. You might also be asked questions related to the author's purpose in certain paragraphs when you encounter questions on organization and logic. In short, the author's purpose is the reason the author has written the passage. While the main idea is about *what* is in the passage—the information the author wants you to know—the purpose is about *how* the author is presenting that information.

Scan this QR code for more information on answering main idea questions.

QUESTIONS TO ASK YOURSELF: AUTHOR'S PURPOSE

- Why did the author write the information they did in the way they did?

- What verbs would I use to describe what the author is doing in this passage?

- Is the author trying to convince me to believe something?

- Is the author making an argument for or against a particular thing or course of action?

- Is the author sticking to factual information?

- Is the author using any sources or pointing to any expert information to appeal to credibility?

- Is this written for a particular audience?

- Is the author telling me a story?

Questions that deal with the author's purpose are easy to spot because they usually contain the word *purpose*. The question might say, "The author's main purpose in this passage is to…" and then your task is to choose the answer that best matches how the author communicates the passage's main idea. An author's purpose can generally be expressed as a *to* + verb expression, with common author's purposes being to inform, explain, or argue. The following table provides a list of common verbs that are used to describe an author's purpose.

As with main idea questions, one of your best bets is to state for yourself what the author's purpose is whenever you finish reading a passage. Whatever verb you choose to describe the author's purpose (or a synonym for it) is likely to pop up in your answer options later.

COMMON VERBS TO DESCRIBE AN AUTHOR'S PURPOSE

Purpose Verbs	In a reading passage, this looks like the author...
inform educate teach	providing information to educate a reader on a topic, often (but not always) while gesturing to credible support.
persuade argue convince	convincing the reader to agree with an opinion or point of view.
amuse entertain	entertaining the reader with an interesting, inventive, or humorous topic.
compare contrast	showing the similarities or differences between ideas or known facts.
describe	using the five senses and other descriptive detail to portray the characteristics or qualities of a topic
explain (information) clarify break down	making an idea or issue clearer through description, details, or a breakdown of how something works or occurred.
discuss examine consider	examining different angles or perspectives of a topic or argument.
analyze evaluate assess	conducting a detailed analysis of numerous facts, quantities, or perspectives impacting an issue or topic, most often using credible support.
critique criticize	expressing disapproval for a topic, issue, or the perspective of another person.
praise celebrate	expressing approval for a topic, issue, or the perspective of another person.
tell narrate explain (as a story)	using a narrative (storytelling) approach to entertain, relay ideas, or explain a topic using figurative details.
quantify	employing statistics, facts, and other quantifiable data to "place a number" on something that is otherwise a concept.
summarize	providing a summary of a topic.

To illustrate, let's say you read a passage and you decide after reading that the author's purpose was to compare an alligator's typical diet with a crocodile's typical diet.

Therefore, you know you're looking for an answer that includes the word *compare* or whatever is closest to it. You are then given a seemingly vague question.

EXAMPLE:

The author's purpose in this passage is to

    A. praise.

    B. criticize.

    C. amuse.

    D. contrast.

    E. illustrate.

If you have already determined that the author's purpose is to compare, you will easily spot that choice D is the correct answer, since *contrast* is used as a synonym for *compare* when discussing an author's purpose. Sometimes, two answers may seem plausible. For instance, you might convince yourself that such a comparison illustrates (choice E) the difference between the animals' diets. However, always choose the answer that *best* expresses the author's purpose. *Contrast* is a more specific description of the author's purpose, which you determined was to compare the diets of two similar but different species.

TIP

If a question asks about the author's purpose, focus on the active verbs in the answer choices. Sometimes, you can automatically eliminate some incorrect choices by noting what the passage *didn't* do.

Test Yourself 1: Main Idea

Directions: Read the passage below and then answer the four main idea questions that follow. After you've selected each answer, read the answer explanations to check yourself.

Selective serotonin reuptake inhibitors, or SSRIs, are commonly known simply as "antidepressants," though they are not the only kind of antidepressant that exists. Compared with other antidepressants, SSRIs tend to cause fewer overall side effects in the general population, so they're one of the most commonly prescribed types. Most people who take SSRIs do so as treatment for depression, though others may do so in combination with forms of talk therapy related to generalized anxiety disorder, post-traumatic stress disorder (PTSD), obsessive-compulsive disorder (OCD), or other mental health afflictions.

Serotonin is a neurotransmitter found in serum and blood platelets. Common thinking around serotonin is that it's a "good mood" chemical that plays a vital role in regulating emotions, focus, and sleep—if you're feeling calm, happy, or at ease, it's probably because your serotonin levels are stable. In people with depression or other mental health concerns, it can be difficult to keep serotonin levels stable. When coupled with the fact that mental health disorders can also affect hormones, other neurotransmitters, and the body's physical sensations, it's clear why a medication that can help regulate serotonin would be beneficial. This is where SSRIs come in.

SSRIs work by ensuring the brain has enough serotonin even in individuals who have trouble keeping levels stable. According to the United Kingdom National Health Service (NHS), "After carrying a message, serotonin is usually reabsorbed by the nerve cells (known as 'reuptake'). SSRIs work by blocking ('inhibiting') reuptake, meaning more serotonin is available to pass further messages between nearby nerve cells." This explains the "R" and "I" in the term SSRIs; these types of drugs are reuptake inhibitors. Since there is less serotonin reuptake, more serotonin sticks around, making it easier to combat issues caused by decreased serotonin. While low serotonin isn't necessarily the cause of all mental health concerns treated by SSRIs, studies show that increasing serotonin levels is a positive therapeutic intervention for many. Though SSRIs aren't without their side effects, which the NHS notes include gastrointestinal issues, feelings of dizziness or blurred vision, and a suite of side effects related to reproductive wellness, for many who suffer from mental health struggles, the benefits of this type of therapy outweigh potential side effects.

Citation: National Health Service. 2021. "Overview - SSRI Antidepressants." *NHS.* February 15, 2021. https://www.nhs.uk/mental-health/talking-therapies-medicine-treatments/medicines-and-psychiatry/ssri-antidepressants/overview/.

Questions

1. What is the best title for this passage?

   A. "What is an Antidepressant?"

   B. "Are You Feeling Depressed?"

   C. "The Battle against Depression"

   D. "Antidepressants"

   E. "How SSRI Antidepressants Work"

2. The author's purpose in writing this passage is to

   A. narrate their experience taking SSRIs.

   B. praise SSRIs for being so effective.

   C. educate the reader about what SSRIs are and how they work.

   D. summarize scientific studies about the efficacy of SSRIs.

   E. evaluate the impact of SSRIs on individuals with depression.

3. Which of the following quotations does the best job summarizing the passage's main idea?

   A. "SSRIs tend to cause fewer overall side effects in the general population…" (Paragraph 1)

   B. "Most people who take SSRIs do so as treatment for depression…" (Paragraph 1)

   C. "If you're feeling calm, happy, or at ease, it's probably because your serotonin levels are stable." (Paragraph 2)

   D. "SSRIs work by ensuring the brain has enough serotonin even in individuals who have trouble keeping levels stable." (Paragraph 3)

   E. "…the benefits of this type of therapy outweigh potential side effects." (Paragraph 3)

4. The main idea of this passage is that SSRIs

   A. are safe for most individuals to take daily.

   B. work by inhibiting serotonin reuptake, thereby helping the brain retain more serotonin.

   C. produce numerous side effects, including gastrointestinal issues and dizziness.

   D. can be used to treat OCD, PTSD, and anxiety as well as depression.

   E. contribute to hormonal responses that can cause depression.

Answer Key and Explanations

1. **The correct answer is E.** The passage focuses specifically on SSRI antidepressants and how they work, so the best title for the passage is "How SSRI Antidepressants Work." Choice D is too vague, and the others don't suit the passage's main idea.

2. **The correct answer is C.** The author's purpose in this passage is to educate the reader about what SSRIs are and how they work.

3. **The correct answer is D.** Of the quotations given, the one that best summarizes the main idea reads "SSRIs work by ensuring the brain has enough serotonin even in individuals who have trouble keeping levels stable."

4. **The correct answer is B.** This passage is focused on how SSRIs work, so you need only identify which response concerns how SSRIs work.

NOTES

Supporting Detail Questions

Supporting details, or supporting ideas, are pieces of information that help the reader understand the author's main idea. Generally, they offer background or necessary context. These sentences might provide examples, facts, statistics, quotations, related stories, descriptions, or lots of other information to support the main idea and purpose. It's important to first understand the main idea and purpose so that you can then recognize the details that help support them.

On the SSAT and ISEE, questions about supporting details may not look like reading questions at all. Remember, though, these questions are on a reading exam, so they will never ask about anything you can't answer using the details of the reading passage alone. Don't be thrown off if you get a question that looks like it's from history, science, math, or any other subject besides reading. Instead, assume the question is asking about something you can answer by finding the relevant sentence(s) in the passage. Mentally noting things that stand out as key when you actively read will help you find relevant information for your questions later. For instance, if a name or word repeats often or if an entire paragraph is devoted to a related concept, there's a good chance that a supporting detail question will address it.

Supporting detail questions will look wildly different depending on the topic of the reading passage; in other words, don't expect to see something like "What are the supporting details in this passage?" Instead, detail questions on the SSAT and ISEE will ask you about the passage's content. For example, if the passage is informing you about five different types of pasta, a details question might ask, "Which of the following is *not* discussed as a type of pasta?" Or "In this passage, the author compares tortellini to…" It's your job to scan back through the passage and choose the right answer based on the details provided. You will never be asked a question about supporting details that requires you to have outside knowledge of a subject.

QUESTIONS TO ASK YOURSELF: SUPPORTING DETAILS

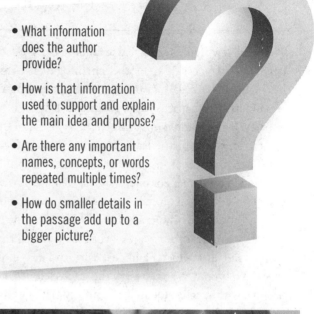

- What information does the author provide?

- How is that information used to support and explain the main idea and purpose?

- Are there any important names, concepts, or words repeated multiple times?

- How do smaller details in the passage add up to a bigger picture?

Test Yourself 2: Supporting Details

> **Directions:** Read the passage below and then answer the four supporting detail questions that follow. After you've selected each answer, read the answer explanations to check yourself.

There are few figures from Slavic folklore considered as formidable or intriguing as Baba Yaga. Loosely translated, her name is said to mean something like "Grandmother Witch," though this only partially encompasses her being. Baba Yaga is also a cannibal, goddess figure, fairy godmother, trickster, and villain, popping up in stories to terrorize heroes only to inadvertently provide them with the skills or items they require to complete their journey. Perhaps most importantly, Baba Yaga is a figure who symbolizes transformation, affording her further associations with birth, death, and transitional life phases like puberty.

There are numerous telltale characteristics that let you know Baba Yaga is in a story, even when she is not mentioned by name. For one, she lives in a hut in the woods that rests on chicken legs, which act like moveable stilts to hold the hut aloft. Because the house can move around the forest and turn itself in any direction, Baba Yaga is thought to always potentially be around the corner, giving her a frightening mystique. That's not her only means of transport, however, as she can also fly around using a mortar and pestle. Because she is associated with fertility, the mortar and pestle are said to symbolize her male and female sides. When travelling this way, she uses a broom to sweep away the tracks left behind; some scholars believe this is partially why we associate brooms with witches today. The primary way she threatens people is by kidnapping them and planning to eat them, though in most stories, they escape before she can feast.

One of the most famous stories that features Baba Yaga is called *Vasilisa the Beautiful,* and it is often considered the Slavic version of the Cinderella story. As in many stories that feature her, Baba Yaga first holds Vasilisa captive with the intention of cooking her for supper. Yet simply by being in Baba Yaga's hut surrounded by her magical objects, Vasilisa is able to obtain the burning magical light she needs to defeat her evil stepmother and stepsisters. Thus, while Baba Yaga first seems like a villain, threatening Vasilisa, it is Vasilisa's encounter with Baba Yaga that assures her eventual success. Vasilisa could not complete her heroic journey without getting unintentional help from Baba Yaga, which is why she is sometimes referred to as the "fairy godmother" of this Cinderella story.

Questions

1. Of the following, which is *not* a term used to describe Baba Yaga?

   A. Goddess

   B. Trickster

   C. Witch

   D. Vampire

   E. Villain

2. In the story *Vasilisa the Beautiful*, Vasilisa must visit Baba Yaga's hut to obtain a(n)

   A. magical light.

   B. skull.

   C. broom.

   D. vial of water.

   E. chicken's foot.

3. To get around, Baba Yaga travels by

   A. flying broomstick.

   B. mortar and pestle.

   C. teleportation.

   D. high-speed running.

   E. floating.

4. The passage states that Baba Yaga is associated with all the following EXCEPT:

   A. Birth

   B. Death

   C. Puberty

   D. Fertility

   E. Marriage

Answer Key and Explanations

1. **The correct answer is D.** Though vampires are indeed said to come partially from Slavic folklore, it is not one of the terms used to describe Baba Yaga.

2. **The correct answer is A.** As paragraph 3 states, "Yet simply by being in Baba Yaga's hut surrounded by her magical objects, Vasilisa is able to obtain the burning magical light she needs to defeat her evil stepmother and stepsisters."

3. **The correct answer is B.** As paragraph 2 states, in addition to having a moving hut that walks on chicken feet, "[Baba Yaga] can also fly around using a mortar and pestle."

4. **The correct answer is E.** The passage never mentions Baba Yaga being associated with marriage.

 NOTES

Vocabulary Questions

For this exam, you usually won't have to identify word definitions directly, as is common on other vocabulary tests. Instead, you're asked to identify a synonym for a word used in the passage that matches the context in which it was used in the passage. In this book, words that will pop up in vocabulary questions are underlined in the passage. Remember: a synonym is a word with the same meaning. You must consider how the word is used in the passage and then choose the word the most nearly matches that same contextual meaning.

On the SSAT and ISEE, questions about vocabulary will usually provide you with the word and the line number so you can go back and look at it in context. Then, you will be asked to choose the word that "most nearly means" the same thing. Sometimes, the question will present you with a short phrase instead of a single word, so don't be thrown off if you notice this. For instance, "in a little bit" is a perfectly suitable synonym for "soon," even if one is a phrase and the other a word.

QUESTIONS TO ASK YOURSELF: VOCABULARY

- What does this word mean?

- If I don't know this word, can I figure out its definition based on what the passage tells me?

- Which of these answer options means the same thing or something close?

- Can I eliminate answer options that I know the meaning of and which I know are incorrect answers?

ALERT

Vocabulary-in-context questions don't always ask for the most common meaning of a word. Instead of choosing the most common definition, look for the meaning that best fits the context in which the word was used in the passage.

Scan this QR code for more information on how to approach vocabulary questions.

Test Yourself 3: Vocabulary

Directions: Read the passage below and then answer the four vocabulary questions that follow. After you've selected each answer, read the answer explanations to check yourself.

The biggest of all species within the genus *Bathynomus* is the giant isopod, or *B. giganteus*. They may look like bugs, but giant isopods are not ocean insects. Rather, like crabs and shrimp, they're crustaceans. You might not expect a somewhat scary looking bottom dweller crustacean to get much love, but it seems the internet at large has given the giant isopod a new reputation. Thanks to the popularity of digital forms of communication like memes, the giant isopod has become recognizable to a wider swath of the general population, including a dedicated <u>subset</u> of isopod fans who insist these little guys are quite cute.

Giant isopods truly are sizable; their average length is between 7.5 and 14.2 inches, but scientists have found specimens as long as 2.5 feet! Their outer shells are usually brown or a pale lilac. Some researchers speculate that isopods evolved to be so massive to <u>withstand</u> the ocean's immense pressure. These carnivorous scavengers typically gorge themselves on the corpses of dead animals that fall to the ocean floor but are also adapted to forgo eating for long periods of time. One interesting adaptation isopods share with felines is what's called a tapeum, meaning a reflective layer toward the back of the eye that increases their ability to see in the dark. However, this only helps giant isopods so much—they have weak eyesight and often must depend on their antennae to <u>augment</u> their navigational abilities.

Their reproductive habits are quite <u>intriguing</u>. Giant isopod eggs are very large, and when a female is brooding, she will starve herself and bury herself in the sand to protect the eggs while conserving her own energy. When the juveniles finally emerge from the eggs, they look just like miniatures of adult giant isopods. As the isopod grows throughout its life, it will shed its exoskeleton each time it sizes up, like a Russian nesting doll in reverse. A giant isopod's body can, therefore, seemingly keep expanding forever, so long as it continues to feed and thrive.

Questions

1. As used in paragraph 1, the underlined word *subset* most nearly means

   A. team.

   B. portion.

   C. neighborhood.

   D. house.

   E. company.

2. As used in paragraph 2, the underlined word *withstand* most nearly means

   A. endure.

   B. prolong.

   C. avoid.

   D. create.

   E. ignore.

3. As used in paragraph 2, the underlined word *augment* most nearly means

   A. agree with.

   B. disagree with.

   C. camouflage.

   D. deflect.

   E. amplify.

4. As used in paragraph 3, the underlined word *intriguing* most nearly means

   A. fascinating.

   B. boring.

   C. intimidating.

   D. bothersome.

   E. indescribable.

Answer Key and Explanations

1. **The correct answer is B.** In paragraph 1, the term *subset* is used to refer to a portion of people from within a larger group (fans of giant isopods).

2. **The correct answer is A.** To withstand something—in this case, the ocean's pressure—means to endure, tolerate, or defy it.

3. **The correct answer is E.** The verb *augment* means "to amplify, strengthen, reinforce, or expand."

4. **The correct answer is A.** *Intriguing* means "fascinating, compelling, or stimulating."

NOTES

Inference Questions

You make an inference when you conclude something based on ideas in the passage. Generally, the answer won't be stated directly in the passage. Instead, you are looking for a reasonable conclusion that could be drawn from the information given. For instance, if the passage mentioned that field geologists often must spend long periods of time camping alone or in small groups, you could infer that camping skills are *most likely* a job requirement for field geologists even if the passage didn't say so directly. You don't have enough information to know if this is for sure the case, but it's a logical conclusion you could draw from what you read.

Inference questions are therefore asking you to "do something" with what you've just read. For example, you might be asked to make a prediction about what happens next or to compare ideas in the passage with each other. Similarly, you may also be asked to give an interpretation of what you've read or to identify a situation that is most like the one described in the passage. Additionally, questions might ask you to infer about the author's attitude or why characters make the choices they make.

Inference questions will sometimes be blunt and ask you, "Which of the following can you infer from this passage?" But these questions might also ask you things like "With which of these statements would the author of this passage most likely agree?" or "Based on this passage, what is the protagonist likely to do next?" They may also take the form of supporting detail questions, such as by asking you to identify which statement *might* be true in light of another detail from the passage. All of these are asking you to infer since the answer to the question is not in the passage—you can only make a logical prediction. Of all the reading comprehension abilities tested, this one relies the most on your critical thinking skills. You may have to think a little to find your answer, but remember that at their core, inference questions are asking what you can figure out from the information you've been given, so you shouldn't have to work super hard to make your answer fit.

QUESTIONS TO ASK YOURSELF: MAKING INFERENCES

- What do I know and what can I predict?
- How are ideas in the passage alike and different?
- What do I know about the characters present in the story and how they feel about the situation presented?
- What am I supposed to "get" that the author isn't saying directly?
- What might I understand to be true or false after reading this passage?

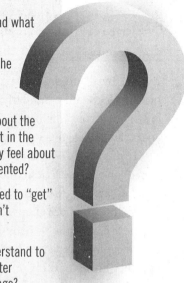

Test Yourself 4: Inferences

Directions: Read the passage below and then answer the four inference questions that follow. After you've selected each answer, read the answer explanations to check yourself.

Essentially all children are naturally endowed with curiosity, a sense of wonder about the world, and a need for nurturing and play. Similarly, almost all children around the world greet the first day of school with a mix of anticipation and trepidation. To ease these concerns and make the transition to schooling a little easier, different countries engage in a panoply of back-to-school traditions.

If you were a 6-year-old headed to your first day of school in Germany, you would likely do so with a giant paper cone in tow. These cones, called *Kindertüte*, are fun-filled goodie bags containing candy, toys, school supplies, and anything else a child might need to have a joyful first day. Even though the treats are nice, the Kindertüte are more about celebrating and communicating to children that they are entering a new stage of life. Japanese parents do something similar, gifting their children a new backpack and sometimes a new desk to use at home to mark the first day of school. As in Germany, these presents are intended to help the child understand that they are embarking on a new chapter in their development.

Many cultures mark the first day of school with a celebration. In Kazakhstan, children start school at the age of 7. Their first day is called Tyl Ishtar, which means "Initiation into Education," and to celebrate it, parents will invite family and friends to a giant feast at their home. During this feast, the school-bound child is expected to recite the names of their grandfathers going back seven generations to honor their ancestry. Other first day celebrations are more about giving children an opportunity to get to know one another. In Saudi Arabia, the first few days of school contain no lessons, instead giving children a chance to share food and play games. In parts of Indonesia, the first day is treated as an orientation to help children intentionally develop friendships meaningful enough to last through their schooling years.

Russia does something similar by kicking off school with a "Knowledge Day," except parents are also invited to participate alongside children. In front of the school building, the families celebrate and take pictures together, while students usually seek out their new teachers to offer them bouquets of flowers. In Vietnam, family and friends gather on the first day of school, and it is considered a nationwide celebration in that country. On that day, students perform songs for any and all citizens who have gathered.

Questions

1. From this passage, we can infer that

   A. children do not start school until after age 7 in Japan.

   B. there are no back-to-school traditions in the United States.

   C. Japanese and German children are culturally considered more mature once school starts.

   D. children in Japan are commonly homeschooled.

   E. starting school is not considered that important in Germany.

2. From paragraph 3, we can infer that

   A. children in both Kazakhstan and Indonesia start school at age 7.

   B. children's friendships aren't considered meaningful in Kazakhstan.

   C. children's friendships aren't considered meaningful in Indonesia.

   D. families in Kazakhstan have traditionally followed a patriarchal structure.

   E. families in Indonesia have traditionally followed a matriarchal structure.

3. From this passage, we can infer that

   A. around the world, children do not always start school at the same age.

   B. around the world, children always start school at the same age.

   C. Russian families take the first day of school more seriously than families in other countries do.

   D. Russian students have more respect for their teachers than students in other places do.

   E. Vietnam has a "Knowledge Day" on the first day of school.

4. From paragraph 4, we can infer that

   A. Russian people who don't have children may still celebrate the first day of school.

   B. Vietnamese people who don't have children may still celebrate the first day of school.

   C. the first day of school is like any other day in Vietnam.

   D. the first day of school is like any other day in Russia.

   E. school is year-round in both Vietnam and Russia.

Answer Key and Explanations

1. **The correct answer is C.** Paragraph 2 mentions how both Japan and Germany consider the start of school an important life stage transition for children. Consequently, it would be logical to infer that the start of school is considered an advancement in a child's maturity in these cultures.

2. **The correct answer is D.** On the first day of school, children in Kazakhstan are expected to honor their ancestors by reciting the names of their grandfathers going back seven generations. Since they are expected to recite the names of grand*fathers*, we can infer that families in Kazakhstan have traditionally followed a patriarchal structure.

3. **The correct answer is A.** In different parts of the passage, you are told that German children start school at 6 while children in Kazakhstan start at 7. Therefore, you can infer that around the world, children do *not* always start school at the same age.

4. **The correct answer is B.** Paragraph 4 states that the first day of school is considered a national celebration in Vietnam, so you can infer that even those who don't have children may still celebrate on the first day of school.

Questions on Style, Tone, and Language Use

Style, tone, and language use are all related in that they focus on the word choices an author makes to best fulfill their purpose. On the SSAT and ISEE, questions tend to focus most on an author's tone as well as their use of figurative language and different writing styles to communicate.

Questions on an Author's Tone or Mood

The term *tone* describes both an author's attitude toward the topic and the attitude they assume in writing about it. In fictional or literary narratives, such as poems or short stories, tone is more often described as mood. Questions about tone might provide you with

QUESTIONS TO ASK YOURSELF: STYLE, TONE, AND LANGUAGE USE

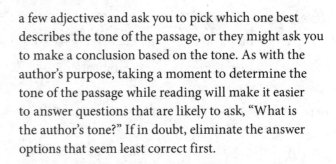

- How does the author feel about this topic?

- What would I say the genre or style of this passage is?

- What do the author's word choices communicate to the reader about their stance on the topic or their tone?

- What position is the author taking in this passage?

- How does the author use language for comparisons, descriptions, or meaning?

- What sort of non-literal language exists in the passage to communicate figurative ideas?

- What are the different methods the author uses to make their ideas and point of view clear?

a few adjectives and ask you to pick which one best describes the tone of the passage, or they might ask you to make a conclusion based on the tone. As with the author's purpose, taking a moment to determine the tone of the passage while reading will make it easier to answer questions that are likely to ask, "What is the author's tone?" If in doubt, eliminate the answer options that seem least correct first.

Questions on Point of View

An author's point of view is their position, opinion, belief, or angle regarding a topic. For example, an author might be for or against an idea, or an author might be stating ideas from personal experience. They may also be taking a position or making an argument from a particular perspective. These questions can sometimes look like main idea questions since they also concern the primary argument or idea an author is trying to get across. Therefore, you can use the same techniques you use with main idea questions to address most questions about an author's point of view. Alternatively, in narrative passages, questions about point of view might refer to the narrator's point of view, such as first person vs. third person. A point of view question might ask "What position does the author take in this debate?" or "From whose perspective is this story narrated?" It might also ask you to complete a sentence, such as "We can assume that the author of this passage agrees that..."

Questions on Figurative Language

An author uses figurative language to draw comparisons, enhance descriptions, or create a deeper meaning. In short, the term "figurative language" describes language that is meant to communicate without being taken literally. It often makes a comparison, creates an image, or otherwise highlights a fundamental quality about a being, object, or situation. Questions about figurative language can pop up anywhere, but they're especially common following poetry and literary passages, so it's important to practice looking for figurative language when reading such passages. Here are some common types of figurative language you might see on the SSAT and ISEE.

COMMON TYPES OF FIGURATIVE LANGUAGE

Term	Definition	Examples
Simile	A comparison between two objects or ideas using *like* or *as*.	• The lighthouse beacon was **as** bright **as** the sun. • My bedroom looks **like** a landfill.
Metaphor	A comparison in which the literal use of a phrase about an object or idea stands in as an analogy for another object or idea; usually uses a form of *is*.	• My math teacher **is** a monster! • Some say I **am** a shark in the courtroom. • That restaurant has always **been** a ghost town.
Hyperbole	An overtly exaggerated statement for figurative effect.	• I'm so hungry that I could **eat a horse**! • The **entire galaxy** stops to listen to her stories.
Imagery	Using vivid descriptions to create an image in a reader's mind, often involving adjectives, adverbs, and references to the five senses.	• The sun's **warm, bright** rays came **bursting** through the window as she **quickly** drew the **heavy velvet** curtain. • I **felt goosebumps** as a **biting cold whooshed across my skin**—my **clumsy** brother had left the door open for the **blustering winter wind** to **whip back** in.
Irony	When an author says something that is the opposite of what they mean or that involves a contradiction between expectation and reality. In literary texts, it can also be situations that create irony for a character.	• A character in a play tells their new friend Morgan that they wish they could speak to their brother, but the audience knows that Morgan is their brother in disguise. • A marriage counselor files for divorce. • A character in a story freezes to death in the desert.
Personification	When an object or animal is given human-like characteristics or abilities.	• I'm so tired that **my bed is calling me.** • The **ocean swallowed** the tiny ship whole. • **My cat** always **flirts** with visitors.

A question about figurative language might point out one of these figurative devices and ask you about it, or it might point to a line number and ask you to identify the type of figurative language used. The best way to prepare for these questions is to practice identifying figurative language in other texts you read, such as poems and novels, so that it's easier to spot figurative devices when they appear on the exam.

Test Yourself 5: Style, Tone, and Language Use

Directions: Read the passage below and then answer the four questions that follow, which address the author's tone/mood, style, or use of figurative language. After you've selected each answer, read the answer explanations to check yourself.

THE SLAVE MOTHER

Heard you that shriek? It rose
  So wildly on the air,
It seem'd as if a burden'd heart
  Was breaking in despair.

Saw you those hands so sadly clasped—
  The bowed and feeble head—
The shuddering of that fragile form—
  That look of grief and dread?

Saw you the sad, imploring eye?
  Its every glance was pain,
As if a storm of agony
  Were sweeping through the brain.

She is a mother pale with fear,
  Her boy clings to her side,
And in her kyrtle vainly tries
  His trembling form to hide.

He is not hers, although she bore
  For him a mother's pains;
He is not hers, although her blood
  Is coursing through his veins!

He is not hers, for cruel hands
  May rudely tear apart
The only wreath of household love
  That binds her breaking heart.

His love has been a joyous light
  That o'er her pathway smiled,
A fountain gushing ever new,
  Amid life's desert wild.

His lightest word has been a tone
  Of music round her heart,
Their lives a streamlet blent in one—
  Oh, Father! must they part?

They tear him from her circling arms,
  Her last and fond embrace.
Oh! never more may her sad eyes
  Gaze on his mournful face.

No marvel, then, these bitter shrieks
  Disturb the listening air:
She is a mother, and her heart
  Is breaking in despair.

—Frances Ellen Watkins Harper
(1854)

Questions

1. Of the following, the word that *best* describes the mood of the poem is
   A. sentimental.
   B. heartbroken.
   C. hopeful.
   D. anxious.
   E. thoughtful.

2. The poem is narrated from the point of view of
   A. someone who hears a crying mother.
   B. a mother.
   C. a baby.
   D. a slave owner.
   E. a pet.

3. Consider stanza 7:

   "His love has been a joyous light
     That o'er her pathway smiled,
   A fountain gushing ever new,
     Amid life's desert wild."

   This stanza is a good example of the author's use of
   A. metaphor.
   B. simile.
   C. hyperbole.
   D. irony.
   E. synecdoche.

4. Which of the following quotations *best* shows the author using personification?
   A. "The shuddering of that fragile form" from stanza 2
   B. "As if a storm of agony/ Were sweeping through the brain" from stanza 3
   C. "Her boy clings to her side" from stanza 4
   D. "He is not hers, although she bore/ For him a mother's pains" from stanza 5
   E. "That o'er her pathway smiled" from stanza 7

Answer Key and Explanations

1. **The correct answer is B.** The poem describes an enslaved woman who is wailing in distress after her baby has been taken from her arms, presumably to be sold to another slave owner. The mood of the poem expresses her despair and heartbreak, so *heartbroken* is a fitting description. Neither *anxious* (choice D) nor *thoughtful* (choice E) are apt descriptions of the mood, while *sentimental* (choice A) and *hopeful* (choice C) suggest the opposite of how the poem reads.

2. **The correct answer is A.** Hints throughout the poem tell us that the poem's narrator is someone hearing the cries of the slave mother. For instance, stanza 1 asks the reader "Heard you that shriek?" and stanza 10 mentions that "bitter shrieks/ Disturb the listening air." There is no evidence to support any of the other options as narrator.

3. **The correct answer is A.** This stanza contains examples of metaphor, personification, and imagery, only one of which is offered as an answer choice. You can narrow it down to metaphor (choice A) and simile (choice B) if you recognize that a comparison is being made. Since you do not see the words *like* or *as* being used to make the comparison, you can eliminate simile as an option.

4. **The correct answer is E.** Remember that personification involves an object or animal engaging in human-like behavior. Since neither love nor light can smile, choice E is your best answer, but you would need to return back to the poem to check for context and confirm. Choice B may seem like a possible answer but remember that "sweeping through" is a common phrase to describe the movement of storms, not necessarily personification.

Questions on Organization and Logic

A passage's organization includes how the information in the passage is arranged and whether that arrangement is logical. It is also about the transition between ideas and how smoothly those transitions are executed. An organized passage will follow a logical train of thought, using transitions and topic sentences when moving between ideas to guide the reader and show how all are related to an overall purpose or main idea. Disorganized passages, on the other hand, tend to jump around between topics without providing adequate transitions or integrating new topics into the context of older ones. You can trust that each of the passages you read on the SSAT or ISEE exams will be organized, but you should be prepared to answer questions about *how* the author chose to organize the passage.

The term *logic* refers to a reasonable way of thinking about something that makes sense. Logical ideas are organized, direct, ordered, and readily accessible to a reader with reasonable knowledge of the topic. By contrast, ideas are illogical if they are disorganized, jumbled, confusing, or unreasonable. All the passages you'll read on your exam should be logical, understandable, and clear. As with questions about organization, you will be tested less on whether the passage is logical or not and more on what logic it uses to justify its claims or ideas. It's up to you to decipher how each passage is organized, how the author has logically arranged their ideas, and how the author might logically build on what is already written if they were to do so.

Organization and logic questions might give you line numbers and ask you to choose how a particular section is organized. Questions might read something like "Which option best describes the organization of lines 6–12?" or "Why does the author begin with the example in paragraph 1?" Questions might also ask you to describe the organizational strategy of an entire

QUESTIONS TO ASK YOURSELF: ORGANIZATION AND LOGIC

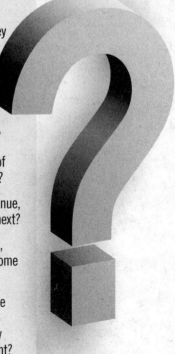

- How are the ideas in this passage arranged—are they in order of importance, time, or a different pattern?

- Does the author use transitions and topic sentences that help guide me through their argument?

- How does the organization of the passage affect its logic?

- If the passage were to continue, what might logically come next?

- If the passage is an excerpt, what might have logically come before it?

- Has the author cited credible sources or otherwise demonstrated the credibility of their research or argument?

passage: "This passage is organized in _____ order." The answer might be time order (known as chronological order), step-by-step order, in order of importance, in physical order (known as spatial order), or something else. Still other questions might ask you about hypothetical writing that isn't included, such as "Which of the following would make a logical topic for a hypothetical paragraph 5?" In each case, you're being asked to identify why the author constructed their passage the way they did and how they might expand on it, if they were to do so.

As we mentioned in the section on main idea questions, you may also be asked how the author's purpose relates to the organization of a passage, such as in questions like "What is the purpose of paragraph 3?" While a question like this does require you to understand the author's purpose, it is also asking you to figure out how the placement of that particular paragraph logically relates to ideas that came before and after it. Similarly, you might be asked what sort of information could be added to a passage that would logically match its current organization, such as in a question like "What would be a logical topic for a hypothetical new paragraph between paragraphs 1 and 2?" or "Which of the following facts would best support the author's purpose?"

One other type of organization question involves the author's use of research, quotations from experts, and facts. When authors include information like this, they are doing so to show that they are credible sources who have used credible research to make their claims. This type of construction is often called an "appeal to credibility." You may be asked a question like, "In which of the paragraphs does the author appeal to a credible source?" This and any other questions related to credibility tend to fall under the umbrella of organization and logic.

Scan this QR code to learn more about signal words.

TIP

Don't forget that both the SSAT and ISEE allow you to make notes in your test booklet! When using active reading strategies, taking basic notes and jotting down key words to later remember where answers to questions might be will save you a lot of time and energy. Remember that you can also do so on the actual questions to help visually remind you what is being asked.

Test Yourself 6: Organization and Logic

Directions: Read the passage below and then answer the four questions that follow, which address the author's organization and logic. After you've selected each answer, read the answer explanations to check yourself.

Sometimes referred to as the Godmother of Rock n' Roll, Sister Rosetta Tharpe is an example of a Black woman who shaped history but didn't end up as famous as most of her male contemporaries. Born in Cotton Plant, Arkansas, she was the daughter of Willis Atkins and Katie Bell Nubin Atkins, a mandolin-playing singer who was also an evangelist for the Church of God in Christ. As a result of her mother's influence, Tharpe's early musical inspiration came primarily from gospel music. To aid in her mother's efforts, Tharpe began singing and playing the guitar as young as four years old.

By the time Tharpe was six years old, she was performing regularly with her mother and was adept at combining secular music styles with the gospel styles popular in religious music. While she was a gifted singer, it was Tharpe's virtuoso skill on the guitar that from such a young age paved her path to fame. Not only could Tharpe easily find various chords and tones, but she was also able to manipulate the strings to produce individual notes, melodies, and riffs, as well as combine chords unexpectedly to produce new sounds. Very few women played guitar at the time, let alone young Black women, so Tharpe was something of an anomaly. Her experimentation with the capabilities of the guitar as an instrument proved foundational to rock n' roll music as a genre.

Over the years, Tharpe gathered new influences from sources like blues music and other musicians such as the pianist Arizona Dranes, the gospel bluesman Thomas A. Dorsey, and jazz musicians Cab Calloway and Lucky Millinder. She integrated sounds and styles from her various influences into her own work, creating a hybrid sound that would set the stage for later developments in rock n' roll and other musical genres. When Tharpe was eventually signed to Decca Records in 1938, it didn't take long for her to become a sensation. To avoid alienating her divergent fan bases, Tharpe would record gospel music for the religious crowd and more up-tempo songs for her growing (and largely white) secular audience. She continued to find success this way for the rest of her career, which ended with her death in 1973.

Questions

1. The author's purpose in paragraph 1 is to

   A. talk about Sister Rosetta Tharpe's musical influences.

   B. clarify how Sister Rosetta Tharpe's talents developed by singing in the church gospel choir.

   C. introduce rock n' roll music as a genre.

   D. offer background on Sister Rosetta Tharpe's early childhood.

   E. discuss the events that led to Sister Rosetta Tharpe's death.

2. The author's logic for mentioning other musicians in paragraph 3 is to

   A. name other artists who influenced Tharpe's sound.

   B. explain which artists posed the greatest amount of competition to Tharpe.

   C. mention other artists to whom Tharpe has been compared.

   D. talk about other musicians who followed in Tharpe's footsteps.

   E. list other musicians who got their start in gospel music.

3. The author wants to add a fourth paragraph. What would be a logical topic for this hypothetical paragraph 4?

A. Distinctive guitar sounds of Sister Rosetta Tharpe's era

B. How Sister Rosetta Tharpe influenced music before her death

C. How Sister Rosetta Tharpe continued to influence music after her death

D. The long-term influence of gospel music on popular music

E. A description of exactly how Sister Rosetta Tharpe produced some of her more unique sounds

4. This passage is organized

A. to provide step-by-step information.

B. according to relevance of topic.

C. by order of importance.

D. in spatial order.

E. in chronological order.

Answer Key and Explanations

1. **The correct answer is D.** The first paragraph offers background on Sister Rosetta Tharpe's parents and her early childhood.

2. **The correct answer is A.** The key word in choice A is *influence*, as it appears in the relevant sentence in paragraph 3: "Over the years, Tharpe gathered new influences from sources like blues music and other musicians such as the pianist Arizona Dranes, the gospel bluesman Thomas A. Dorsey, and jazz musicians Cab Calloway and Lucky Millinder."

3. **The correct answer is C.** Since paragraph 3 ends by mentioning Sister Rosetta Tharpe's death in 1973, the most logical next move would be to discuss how she continued to influence music after her death. All the other topics would be better suited to other sections of the passage if they were to be inserted.

4. **The correct answer is E.** Since the passage starts with Sister Rosetta Tharpe's birth and ends with her death, it is organized in chronological order.

NOTES

Questions on Opinion and Argument

While the specific categories tested by SSAT and ISEE don't mention opinion and argument explicitly, understanding both will help you address questions related to the main idea, supporting details, inferences, and the organization and logic of a passage. When an author tells their own beliefs, viewpoints, or judgments, they are expressing an opinion. When an author takes a side in a debate, presents a plausible perspective on a researched subject, or tries to convince you to agree with their opinion, they are making an argument. If an author is making an argument, you should be able to identify the argument and how the author organizes it as well as any support they give for that argument, such as related facts or examples. It's important when reading passages for this exam (or anything else) to decide if what you're reading is fact or opinion as it can inform how you respond.

A question dealing with opinion might ask you, "Which of these choices best expresses the author's opinion?" Or you might be asked the main idea or author's purpose with "expressing an opinion" as one of the possible answer choices. For argument questions, you might be presented with several arguments and asked, "Which of these options best summarizes the author's argument in this passage?" Argument and opinion aren't a question category unto themselves so much as a key factor that could affect any of the question types you have already practiced in this section.

QUESTIONS TO ASK YOURSELF: OPINION AND ARGUMENT

- Is this passage fact or opinion?
- What is the author's opinion and why?
- What is the author's argument?
- What strategies does the author use to convince me to agree with the argument?
- Is the author sticking to their own ideas or are they supporting their thoughts with outside information or sources?
- From whose perspective is the author speaking and to which intended audience?
- Does the author seem to have any bias that might cloud the logic of their argument?

 ALERT

A statement being true doesn't necessarily mean it's a correct answer. Make sure that the answer choice you mark answers the question that is asked. Several answer choices might be true, but only one will be the answer to the question.

Test Yourself 7: Opinion and Argument

Teenagers today are not receiving adequate educations in financial literacy, and it is having an undue impact on their adult lives. On top of that, common advice given to teenagers encourages them to embark on risky financial endeavors that they are too young to fully understand. An 18-year-old is not even considered responsible enough to purchase alcohol, yet our culture believes they have the wherewithal to make a sound and informed decision concerning five-figure loans. If the culture isn't going to change to be less financially predatory toward young people, then school curricula must change to incorporate a far greater degree of financial literacy training before students graduate high school.

Besides it simply being the ethical thing to do in today's world, there are numerous benefits for young people who learn financial literacy starting in high school or earlier. Knowing how to make money, save money, and make wise financial decisions is empowering for teens, allowing them to feel like they're in control of their financial futures. Furthermore, not providing this type of education leaves young people anxious and ill-equipped. As Geoffrey Bellamy notes in his book *Guiding Teens Toward Financial Success*, when young people don't receive financial literacy education, "they struggle to maintain good credit scores, are unable to save enough money to buy a home or prepare for retirement, and have no idea how to invest." Equipping teens with financial literacy ensures they enter the world with more confidence and avoid falling into bad habits that will be harder to break when they're in a financial hole later. This can protect them, too, such as by making it easier for them to keep a savings fund for emergencies and making them aware of common financial pitfalls, such as gambling and pyramid schemes.

Questions

1. The author's main argument in this passage is that

   A. financial literacy training should begin in early adulthood.

   B. young people deserve more financial literacy training before they graduate high school.

   C. teenagers are usually bad with money.

   D. it's becoming harder and harder to save money.

   E. young people aren't receiving enough education about credit scores.

2. With which of the following statements would the author likely agree?

   A. No one should ever take out student loans.

   B. Credit scores are an unfair way to determine who deserves loans.

   C. Teenagers should not have to pay taxes until age 18.

   D. More companies should offer insurance plans to young employees.

   E. High school students should be taught how to financially plan for their retirement.

3. Which quotation from the passage best expresses the author's argument?

   A. "…common advice given to teenagers encourages them to embark on risky financial endeavors…" (Paragraph 1)

   B. "…school curricula must change to incorporate a far greater degree of financial literacy training…" (Paragraph 1)

   C. "Knowing how to make money, save money, and make wise financial decisions is empowering…" (Paragraph 2)

   D. "Furthermore, not providing this type of education leaves young people anxious and ill-equipped." (Paragraph 2)

   E. "This can protect them, too, such as by making it easier for them to keep a savings fund for emergencies…" (Paragraph 2)

4. If the author were to add one of the following statements from Bellamy's book to the passage, which would *least* support the author's argument?

   A. Studies show that a quarter of teens lack basic financial skills.

   B. The average teen spent more than $2,000 in 2020.

   C. 3 in 4 teens admit to not feeling confident about money.

   D. The average American adult pays more than $575 in late fees and similar charges per year.

   E. 3 in 5 parents admit that talking to their teen(s) about money makes them uncomfortable.

Answer Key and Explanations

1. **The correct answer is B.** As is often the case with argumentative passages like this one, the author summarizes their argument in the final sentence of the first paragraph: "If the culture isn't going to change to be less financially predatory toward young people, then school curricula must change to incorporate a far greater degree of financial literacy training before students graduate high school."

2. **The correct answer is E.** Since the author's main idea is that young people should get more financial literacy education before they graduate high school, you can infer that the author would agree with the idea of teaching high school students how to start planning for their eventual retirement.

3. **The correct answer is B.** The second quotation comes from the author's thesis statement, which is a type of statement that summarizes an author's argument.

4. **The correct answer is D.** All the examples given concern financial literacy, but only one talks about adults instead of teens. Since the passage is focused more on teens than adults, it would be the least relevant support for the author's argument.

BRINGING YOUR READING SKILLS TOGETHER

You now know all the reading comprehension topics that are likely to be covered in reading questions for the SSAT or ISEE. As a reminder, these include the following:

- Author's Main Idea
- Author's Purpose
- Supporting Details
- Vocabulary in Context
- Making Inferences
- Author's Tone/Mood and Style
- Use of Figurative Language

- Organization and Logic of Passage
- Determining Opinion and/or Argument

On the next page, you'll find an example reading passage with a graphic illustration of how different parts of the passage relate to the six reading question categories on the SSAT and ISEE. Keep in mind that you might get a question on the exam that doesn't seem to fall into any of these categories, but don't panic! If you're reading actively for understanding, you can tackle any reading comprehension question that is thrown at you. Rest assured that the information you need to answer a question will always be found in the passage, so rely on the reading comprehension abilities you've built to find the right answer.

Example Reading Passage with Sample Questions

Directions: Read the passage and note how the numbered sections relate to the numbered sample questions on the opposite page. The numbers are there to help you identify how different types of questions relate to a single passage and where in the passage you would find the answer. Try to answer the questions for yourself. Then, check your answers against the answer key. As a challenge, imagine yourself in the role of an editor for this book. What sort of explanations would you write to show how and why the correct answers are correct?.

Sometimes, you can knock a vocabulary question out before you even begin reading by previewing the sentence that contains it.

Note that previewing the first and last sentence of the first and last paragraphs first would allow you to answer at least two questions before even reading the full passage!

Michelangelo Buonarroti's *David* is arguably the most famous statue in the world. Michelangelo sculpted the 17 ft. biblical figure from marble between **①** 1501 and 1504 to grace the Pallazo Vecchio, a public square near some government buildings. **②** Today, a replica stands in its initial location and Michelangelo's original is featured at the Galleria dell'Academia in Florence, Italy.

③ In David's left hand, the figure carries a sling reminiscent of the biblical story in which he slays a giant. This detail means that Michelangelo was likely picturing David as a left-handed person. However, art historians **④** note that it is David's right hand that presents a bigger mystery. First, it seems oversized compared to the otherwise proportionate statue. Second, the fingers appear to be curled around a mystery object. Art historians note that the veins in the right hand are prominent, suggesting that whatever David is holding, he's clutching it tightly.

There is some speculation that the oversized structure of the right hand **⑤** is purely symbolic and meant to remind viewers of David having a "strong hand" in his later years as a king. Others suggest it could be as simple as David holding the stone that he will use to slay a foe with his sling. Still others suggest he could be holding a second weapon entirely. Whatever the **⑥** case may be, there is no way of knowing what exactly Michelangelo imagined David gripping in his right hand, so the answer remains one of the art world's greatest mysteries.

1 INFERENCES

From paragraph 1, we can infer that

A. in the 16th century, all Italian art was required to have a religious context.

B. it took more than a decade to sculpt *David*.

C. *David* was not considered a masterpiece of sculpture until it was moved to a museum.

D. Michelangelo was not regarded well as an artist until long after his death.

E. the government in Michelangelo's time was at least somewhat tied to the Christian church.

2 SUPPORTING DETAILS

Where is the original *David* located today?

A. Museo di Michelangelo

B. Pallazo Vecchio

C. Galleria dell' Academia

D. Sistine Chapel

E. Pallazo Michelangelo

3 VOCABULARY

As used in paragraph 2, the underlined term *reminiscent* most nearly means

A. bashful.

B. elusive.

C. critical.

D. mindful.

E. remindful.

4 ORGANIZATION & LOGIC

The author's purpose in paragraph 2 is to

A. amuse the reader with an anecdote.

B. critique Michelangelo's artistic execution.

C. narrate Michelangelo's creative process.

D. clarify a prominent reason that art historians still speculate about the statue.

E. summarize recent findings about the importance of the statue.

5 STYLE, TONE, & LANGUAGE USE

The author's use of the phrase "strong hand" in paragraph 3 figuratively references the idea that David might have been a(n)

A. firm, decisive leader.

B. renowned athlete.

C. impulsive, hot-headed warrior.

D. celebrated artist.

E. naïve, immature monarch.

6 MAIN IDEA

The main idea of this passage is that

A. *David* is the most important statue of all time.

B. art historians remain divided as to what the David figure is holding in his right hand.

C. art historians determined that the David figure is holding a weapon in his left hand.

D. *David* is a proportionately oversized work, and its size reflects its symbolic meanings.

E. *David* may not have been made by Michelangelo at all.

ANSWER KEY

1. E   **2.** C   **3.** E   **4.** D   **5.** A   **6.** B

SUMMING IT UP

- The reading comprehension section on the SSAT will have 40 questions spread across 8–10 reading passages of about 200–400 words. You're allowed 40 minutes to complete it, which means you only have about 4–5 minutes per passage and question set.

- The reading comprehension section on the ISEE will have 36 questions spread across 6 reading passages of about 200–400 words. You're allowed 35 minutes to complete it, which means you only have about 5–6 minutes per passage and question set.

- The questions you will encounter on the reading comprehension section could be about:

  - Main Idea
  - Author's Purpose
  - Supporting Details for Main Idea
  - Vocabulary in Context
  - Making Inferences
  - Determining Style, Tone, and Mood
  - Author's Use of Figurative Language
  - Author's Organization and Logic
  - Determining Opinions and Arguments

- Use active strategies for quick reading like skim and scan, previewing first and last sentences, and making mental notes of the location of relevant details while reading to save time when you need to refer back to answer questions.

- Quickly scan questions for relevant key words before reading a passage.

- When possible, start with passages that interest you since you'll be able to get through those quicker and have a better chance of getting questions right.

- Pay attention to what the passage isn't saying. You might be asked to infer or predict something that isn't directly stated.

KNOWLEDGE CHECK

READING COMPREHENSION

40 Questions—40 Minutes

> **Directions:** Below, you will find 9 passages and a total of 40 questions. Read the passages and then decide which of the responses is the best answer to each question. Circle the letter that appears before your answer. Afterwards, check your responses using the answer key with answer explanations.

Questions 1–4 refer to the following passage.

In a world where the effects of climate change are already apparent, it's high time that Americans reconsider what's important to them in a front yard. Do they want an expanse of green grass that's hard to maintain without straining local water supplies, using harsh chemicals to fertilize or combat weeds, and taking up valuable real estate that could be used on denser housing models? Or do they want to reimagine what a "lawn" could be, such as by embracing more ecological friendly options like using native plants, employing creative rock landscaping, or planting gardens to grow vegetables for the community or flowers to help pollinators thrive? The possibilities are endless, so why are Americans so attached to their green lawns?

There are a lot of downsides to traditional grass lawns. For one, all the chemicals and fertilizers people use to keep them green don't stay put; instead, sprinklers and rainwater make them run off lawns and into sewers, where they end up polluting streams, rivers, lakes, and the ocean, wreaking havoc on the local ecosystem. Those same chemicals can also harm pets, such as by seeping into their paws when they hang out in the yard. Lawns are also typically unused or rarely used spaces, yet every house having one makes it harder for municipalities to create enough housing for increasing populations. Add to that the amount of water that keeping lawns green uses up and you have a serious problem. According to the Environmental Protection Agency, as much as 30% of the average American household's water use goes to the lawn alone. If you cut out the grass lawn, you're also saving thousands of gallons of water a year.

It is <u>imperative</u> that people consider more eco-friendly alternatives to the traditional grass lawn. One alternative involves mowing less often (or not at all) to allow native grasses and plants to be restored. This effect is all the better when homeowners plant noninvasive local plants that thrive in the climate. Similarly, turning some of the turf into planting ground for edible plants is a way to make more economical use of lawn space, especially if you plant things that might help others in your community, like fruit trees. Another method is xeriscaping, which is a fancy term for landscaping that requires little to no water. This often involves using hardy desert plants like succulents within rock arrangements to create a visually appealing lawn with minimal or no grass. Traditional lawns just aren't worth it when so many eco-friendly alternatives exist.

1. As used in paragraph 3, the underlined word *imperative* most nearly means

   A. ignorant.

   B. wise.

   C. crucial.

   D. unimportant.

   E. dangerous.

2. Which of the following statements *best* expresses the author's point of view?

   A. New houses should be built without space for a front lawn.

   B. Americans should adopt more eco-friendly alternatives to grass lawns.

   C. Americans are not using their water resources efficiently.

   D. Grass lawns are a useful way to protect the environment.

   E. People should plant more native grasses that do not need to be maintained.

3. What would be the best title for this passage?

   A. "Ecological Alternatives to Traditional Grass Lawns"

   B. "The Problem with Grass"

   C. "Why Americans Care About Grass Lawns"

   D. "What is a Lawn?"

   E. "Grass Lawns"

4. Based on the passage, which of the following is *not* a social or ecological concern associated with green grass lawns?

   A. Grass lawns use up a significant amount of water.

   B. Fertilizers and other lawn chemicals can hurt pets.

   C. Runoff from lawns pollutes streams and rivers.

   D. Lawns take up space that could be used for more housing.

   E. Fertilizers and other lawn chemicals can pollute the air.

Questions 5–8 refer to the following passage.

Rather than an idyllic place for specters to cohabitate, a "ghost town" is a town that has long since been left abandoned or uninhabited. While buildings and other artefacts remain as proof of the life that once lit up the streets, ghost towns are generally empty, decaying, and proverbially returning to nature. There are roughly 3,800 ghost towns in the United States alone, many of which exist because they were founded during gold rushes or periods of thriving industrial development, then abandoned when those industries became no longer <u>lucrative</u> or necessary.

   Increasingly, tourists in the US find themselves compelled to visit these once thriving little towns, in no small part thanks to the eerie stories that often accompany them. For instance, an entire million acre stretch in New Jersey known as Pine Barrens is home to several ghost towns that used to support colonial industry, but which now house overgrown forests and a folkloric half-man, half-animal beast known as the Jersey Devil who is said to be responsible for livestock deaths in the area. Many ghost towns are also rumored to have literal ghosts. For instance, while Thurmond, West Virginia, was once renowned as the home of the hotel that hosted the world's longest poker game, it's now known as the ghost town where all the buildings are haunted.

Other ghost towns are compelling due to the stories they tell about their pasts. Specifically, many famous ghost towns retain traces of the mining boom, such as Ashcroft, Animas Forks, and St. Elmo in Colorado, Terlingua in Texas, and Bodie in California. Though relics now, the buildings in these towns speak to a prosperity that once was. Centralia, Pennsylvania, is unsettling for some because of the coal fire that has been burning in its underground mining tunnels for more than 50 years, while Independence, Colorado, is considered an especially beautiful old mining town, having been built at an elevation of 11,000 feet in the Rocky Mountains.

5. As used in paragraph 1, the underlined word *lucrative* most nearly means

    A. profitable.

    B. expensive.

    C. habitable.

    D. safe.

    E. interesting.

6. What would be an appropriate title for this passage?

    A. "The History of American Mining"

    B. "Ghost Towns of the United States"

    C. "What Happened after the Gold Rush?"

    D. "Colorado's Ghost Towns"

    E. "Mining Towns of the American West"

7. Based on the information in the passage, we can infer that

    A. most ghost towns were abandoned for financial reasons.

    B. industry is not as important now as it once was.

    C. each of the 50 states in the US probably has at least one ghost town.

    D. tourists like ghost towns because they are not overly commercialized.

    E. America once had many more small towns than it does now.

8. Which of the following ghost towns is *not* in Colorado?

    A. Independence

    B. Animas Forks

    C. St. Elmo

    D. Terlingua

    E. Ashcroft

Questions 9–11 refer to the following passage.

In many old Japanese and Chinese books mention is made of a famous story about this incense,—a story of the Chinese Emperor Wu, of the Han dynasty. When the Emperor had lost his beautiful favorite, the Lady Li, he sorrowed so much that fears were entertained for his reason. But all efforts made to divert his mind from the thought of her proved unavailing. One day he ordered some Spirit-Recalling-Incense to be procured, that he might summon her from the dead. His counsellors prayed him to forego his purpose, declaring that the vision could only intensify his grief. But he gave no heed to their advice, and himself performed the rite,—kindling the incense, and keeping his mind fixed upon the memory of the Lady Li. Presently, within the thick blue smoke arising from the incense, the outline, of a feminine form became visible. It defined, took tints of life, slowly became <u>luminous</u>, and the Emperor recognized the form of his beloved. At first the apparition was faint; but it soon became distinct as a living person and seemed with each moment to grow more beautiful. The Emperor whispered to the vision, but received no answer. He called aloud, and the presence made no sign. Then unable to control himself, he approached the censer. But the instant that he touched the smoke, the phantom trembled and vanished.

—Excerpt from *In Ghostly Japan,* by Lafcadio Hearn (1899)

9. As used in the passage, the underlined term *luminous* most nearly means

   A. blurry.

   B. vivid.

   C. dark.

   D. red colored.

   E. odorous.

10. The "apparition" that appeared in the incense smoke was in the shape of

   A. Emperor Wu.

   B. Lady Li.

   C. a dragon.

   D. Emperor Wu's mother.

   E. Emperor Wu's daughter.

11. The passage states that Emperor Wu's counsellors "prayed him to forego his purpose, declaring that the vision could only intensify his grief." From this, we can infer that Emperor Wu was grieving about

   A. losing a war.

   B. the end of his reign.

   C. the beauty of magic.

   D. the death of Lady Li.

   E. the death of his father.

Questions 12–15 refer to the following passage.

In March 2018, writer Richard Grant published an article entitled "Do Trees Talk to Each Other?" in *Smithsonian Magazine*. The article offers a narrative of Grant's conversations with Peter Wohlleben, a German forester and author of the 2018 bestselling book *The Hidden Life of Trees: What They Feel, How They Communicate*. While Wohlleben was not the first person to make discoveries about tree communication, the article notes that he was "the first writer to convey its amazements to a general audience." Now, scientific studies from universities around the world are confirming theories that Wohlleben had only suspected before, which as Grant summarizes, boil down to the idea that "trees are far more alert, social, sophisticated—and even intelligent—than we thought."

Throughout the article, Grant recounts Wohlleben demonstrating these concepts in nature itself. For instance, Wohlleben takes Grant to a pair of beech trees and shows that their leaves avoid intruding on each other's space. Grant quotes Wohlleben saying, "These two are old friends. They are very considerate in sharing the sunlight, and their root systems are closely connected. In cases like this, when one dies, the other usually dies soon afterward, because they are dependent on each other." Instead of trees being isolated individuals, as scientists long thought, the article says new evidence points toward an opposite truth. Trees are communal, participating in communicative activities like sharing water and nutrients, using root networks to send distress signals to one another about unfavorable conditions like disease, pests, or drought, and even keeping old stumps alive after a tree has fallen. Wohlleben even pushes his theory into the realm of personification, emphasizing how mother trees have been known to "suckle their young" by sending sugar to their roots to stimulate healthy growth.

The article goes on to discuss how trees have certain senses we have previously only associated with animals. Consider the sense of smell; if trees can detect scents through their leaves, what is that if not smelling? The article also notes that they can detect caterpillar saliva, effectively a sense of taste, and release pheromones to lure parasitic wasps to attack pests, proving they also have senses of danger and a system for self-defense. So, do trees communicate with each other? Based on this article, it would seem that Grant, Wohlleben, and the ecological community as a whole are in agreement that the answer is *yes*.

Citation: Grant, Richard. 2018. Review of *Do Trees Talk to Each Other? Smithsonian Magazine*, March 2018. https://www.smithsonianmag.com/science-nature/the-whispering-trees-180968084/.

12. This passage is in the style of a(n)

A. biography.

B. autobiography.

C. summary.

D. critique.

E. personal narrative.

13. The author's overall purpose in writing this passage is to

A. praise Peter Wohlleben for his scientific findings.

B. critique Richard Grant for his scientific findings.

C. disprove Richard Grant's 2018 news article.

D. analyze Peter Wohlleben's scientific discoveries.

E. highlight the most important information from Richard Grant's 2018 news article.

14. The purpose of paragraph 2 is to

   A. theorize new ways for humans to communicate with trees.

   B. educate the reader about how climate change affects trees.

   C. persuade the reader to care more about ecological concerns that affect trees.

   D. list the different examples Wohlleben gave Grant that demonstrate trees being communicative.

   E. debate whether the findings Wohlleben showed Grant truly prove that trees communicate.

15. Which of the following is *not* an example the passage gave of trees being intelligent?

   A. Mother trees feeding sugar to their saplings

   B. Detecting scents through their leaves

   C. Sending nutrients to keep stumps that should be dead alive

   D. Sending signals to warn each other of drought conditions

   E. Branches from different trees intertwining as they grow

Questions 16–19 refer to the following passage.

What makes a painting a painting, and what makes a photograph a photograph? If you've ever seen works by the contemporary German artist Gerhard Richter, then you'll know that the answer to that question isn't as straightforward as it seems.

Richter was born in 1932 in Dresden, Germany. His interest in art blossomed following the acquisition of a simple plate camera as a Christmas gift in early childhood. To learn how to develop the pictures he took, Richter befriended a local camera shop owner. After that, his love of art grew and never stopped growing. He continued to develop his eye for art through all the cultural changes happening around him, most notably the re-designation of the eastern part of Germany as the German Democratic Republic, or East Germany, following the aftermath of WWII. While this cultural shift came with many social struggles, living in East Germany made it possible for Richter to access art materials that had once been banned under Nazi rule, allowing him to develop a unique set of art history references that would appear in his later work.

After acquiring formal training in painting through his teen years and early adulthood, Richter became fascinated with the interplay between abstract art and photorealism. More specifically, he was interested in blurring the lines between photographs and paintings—what would it mean if you could make a painting that looked just like a photograph? How would people know it was a painting? Would it matter that it was a painting and not a photograph if people couldn't tell the difference? Questions like these drove Richter to experiment. He created abstract but realistic oil paintings meant to look exactly like motion-blurred or unfocused photographs in hopes of convincing viewers to grapple with these same questions.

Richter's most famous works include portrait studies he did of his children, experimental installations that examine the interplay of light and panes of glass, and the aforementioned series of blurred, realistic photograph paintings, a style now associated with Richter and oft replicated by artists inspired by him. Today, Richter is regarded as one of Germany's finest contemporary artists. He has been celebrated by museums all over the world, including the Museum of Modern Art in New York City, which in 2002 hosted a major retrospective of Richter's work entitled "Forty Years of Painting."

16. The author's purpose in paragraph 1 is to

   A. set up a critique of Gerhard Richter's art.

   B. introduce the topic by discussing Gerhard Richter's personal biography.

   C. pose a rhetorical question that helps introduce the main idea.

   D. transition from earlier writing to a new topic.

   E. define what makes a piece of art abstract.

17. Gerhard Richter's love of art began with a

   A. painting class.

   B. trip to East Germany.

   C. book on art banned by Nazis.

   D. Christmas gift.

   E. meeting with a local camera shop owner.

18. As used in paragraph 3, the underlined term *grapple* most nearly means to

   A. agree.

   B. reject.

   C. avoid.

   D. deal.

   E. forget.

19. From the passage, we can infer that

   A. other artists besides Richter have made paintings that are supposed to look like photographs.

   B. Richter no longer works as a painter.

   C. Richter's paintings are some of the most expensive in the world.

   D. Richter is most popular in New York City.

   E. Richter's next exhibition will involve sculptures and museum installations.

Questions 20–24 refer to the following passage.

The Nehiyawak, more commonly known to English speakers as the Cree people, are the largest group of <u>indigenous</u> peoples in Canada. The Cree First Nations includes numerous subsets of Cree people groups, most of whom can be divided into Woodland Cree, who live in the forests of eastern and central Canada, and Plains Cree in the northern Great Plains of western Canada. There are also the Swampy Cree, Moose Cree, and James Bay Cree, among other subgroups; the English term "Cree" was given to those who shared a common language and does not necessarily tell you about the tribe with which a person identifies or the areas in which their ancestors have traditionally lived.

More than 350,000 people in Canada identify as having Cree ancestry. There are also a few pockets of Cree in the United States, such as on the Rocky Boy Indian Reservation in Montana. Of those with Cree ancestry, only about 96,000 still speak the language. Consequently, efforts are being made to preserve the Cree language, alongside many other indigenous languages, so that they won't be lost to the ravages of time. For instance, members of the James Bay Cree community founded an annual language symposium in 2018, and local governments in Cree communities have passed resolutions to support the preservation of language and culture by investing in community education on the topic.

Young people with Cree backgrounds are also working in their own way to protect the history of their people. For instance, there are numerous influencers on platforms like TikTok, Twitter, and Instagram who are working to inform their followers about their culture. A common message among them is the idea that indigenous culture isn't a relic of the past but rather a living, breathing aspect of their identities. They want to remind people that they exist and are still contributing their unique perspectives on art, culture, politics, and society to the world. By sharing traditional costumes, music, and dances as well as speaking on their experiences, these young influencers show that the Cree First Nations are still and always have been an integral part of Canadian life.

20. As used in paragraph 1, the underlined word *indigenous* most nearly means

A. foreign.

B. native.

C. hunting.

D. nomadic.

E. industrious.

21. Which statement best summarizes the main idea of this passage?

A. The Woodlands Cree and Plains Cree are two very different groups.

B. The Cree language is complicated, so fewer people are speaking it than once did.

C. Today, there are fewer Cree than there once were.

D. The Cree First Nations are one of the largest indigenous groups in Canada, and efforts are being made to preserve their language and culture.

E. The Cree are one of many Canadian First Nations, all of which have unique cultural traditions.

22. Which of the following is *not* a Cree subgroup mentioned in the passage?

    A. Moose Cree

    B. Woodlands Cree

    C. Plains Cree

    D. Swampy Cree

    E. Rocky Cree

23. The passage's tone is

    A. educational.

    B. cautionary.

    C. intimate.

    D. whimsical.

    E. sympathetic.

24. Say the author wanted to include a new paragraph between paragraphs 2 and 3. What would be the most logical topic for this hypothetical new paragraph?

    A. An argument for investing more money into indigenous cultural preservation

    B. An analysis of how Cree census data have changed over the past 50 years

    C. Examples of contemporary Cree artists using their art to preserve Cree culture and language

    D. Examples of Cree hunting techniques

    E. Historical facts about the Cree in Canada

Questions 25–30 refer to the following passage.

The Berlin Wall was built during the height of the Cold War, which was a period of tension between communist and democratic world powers. At that time, the city of Berlin was divided into two parts that sat in two different countries—East Germany and West Germany. East Germany, also known as the German Democratic Republic, had a Soviet-style communist government, and West Germany, also known as the Federal Republic of Germany, had a democratic government. Between 1949 and 1961, more than 2 million people escaped from East Berlin to the western parts of Germany to be free from what was effectively an oppressive and invasive socialist dictatorship. This created a so-called "brain drain," meaning those with educations and specialized skills were leaving the country en masse. As a result, the Berlin Wall was built practically overnight on August 13, 1961, to prevent East Germans from escaping East Berlin.

The wall was an imposing landmark. It was built of concrete right in the middle of the city and topped with barbed wire. It had a strip of "no man's land" in the center that was patrolled by attack dogs and included land mines and massive barriers. During the 28 years that armed guards watched over the wall, more than 100,000 East German citizens tried to escape using such innovative methods as digging tunnels, ziplining, performing suitcase contortion, and even flying hot air balloons. Tragically, more than 600 were not successful and lost their lives while attempting to escape.

Then, in 1989, all of that changed. Social unrest had been building for months in response to invasive spying by the East German secret police, known as the Stasi, as well as long wait times for domestic goods, and the government's threats of increasing violence against protesters. The East German government hoped that loosening travel restrictions would help ease this unrest, so they planned to start offering citizens more freedoms over the course of a year. However, in a televised press conference on November 9, 1989, upon being asked when East Germans would finally be able to travel to the other side of the Berlin Wall, a government official named Günter Schabowski mistakenly replied, "As far as I know, effective immediately…without delay."

That very same night, thousands of East Germans flooded the six border crossings of the Berlin Wall. The border guards, who had no idea what had just been broadcast on national television, were overwhelmed by the size of the crowds and <u>flummoxed</u> as to what to do. One crossing, Bornholmer Strasse, was located on a bridge. So many people gathered on this bridge that officials worried it would collapse; they were forced to open the gates and let the East Germans pour into West Berlin. Once the gates were opened, it wasn't long before citizens and government alike started dismantling the wall, and less than a year later, in October 1990, Germany was reunited as one country.

25. As used in paragraph 4, the underlined term *flummoxed* most nearly means

   A. angered.

   B. anxious.

   C. confused.

   D. disorganized.

   E. yelled at.

26. According to the author, what caused the opening of the Berlin Wall?

   A. Large crowds following a mistaken announcement

   B. Loosened border restrictions in neighboring countries

   C. The Cold War between the Soviet Union and the United States

   D. Striking workers in Poland

   E. A panel of party officials decided to switch to a more democratic system of governance

27. Which of the following was *not* a type of deterrent used to keep people from crossing the Berlin Wall?

   A. Armed guards

   B. Grenades

   C. Attack dogs

   D. Barbed wire

   E. Large barriers

28. Which term best describes the tone of the passage?

   A. Unassuming

   B. Wearied

   C. Sensationalistic

   D. Humorous

   E. Direct

29. Which statement can you infer is true based on the passage?

A. The building of the Berlin Wall led to the Cold War.

B. The Berlin Wall was necessary to protect West Germany from communism.

C. The number of skilled and educated citizens fleeing East Germany throughout the 1950s led to the erection of the Berlin Wall in 1961.

D. Ronald Reagan helped negotiate the fall of the Berlin Wall.

E. Those who died fleeing the Berlin Wall had no other choice.

30. Bornholmer Strasse was the first crossing opened because

A. the guards there had heard the announcement made by Günter Schabowski.

B. more people gathered there than at any other crossing.

C. the East German government planned for it to be the first crossing to open.

D. officials were worried about the infrastructure of the Bornholmer Strasse bridge.

E. the guards at Bornholmer Strasse had sympathy for the citizens' pleas.

Questions 31–35 refer to the following passage.

Picture this: You're a young, established revolutionary poet in the Soviet Union during Stalin's reign, living through a period that will later be called the "Great Terror" or "Great Purge" by historians. During this period, anyone who speaks out against Stalin or the atrocities they've witnessed is rounded up and sent to harsh labor camps in Siberia called *gulags*. As a poet, you know the importance of words for preserving history, but it's too dangerous to write your ideas down—someone might find them and report you, which would essentially be a death sentence. What would you do?

This is the exact dilemma Anna Akhmatova found herself in during the Great Purge between 1936 and 1938 when as many as 750,000 people were executed and another million were <u>interred</u> in gulags by Stalin's Soviet government. Akhmatova knew she was being closely watched by secret police because she was a known political agitator; her own husband had been framed and killed, and her son had been arrested and tortured at various points. All eyes were on her, so even a single scrap of paper containing a single critical line would have been enough for Akhmatova to end up facing execution.

So, what did Akhmatova do to make sure she and her poetry survived this period? She never kept a single written word. Instead, Akhmatova would create lines of poetry on paper, memorize them, then burn the scraps of paper. She regularly recited the parts she had already memorized so she could keep building on the poem over time. Akhmatova titled the poem "Requiem," and it became one of the only surviving pieces of Russian literature written about Stalin's Great Purge while it was occurring.

To safeguard the poem, Akhmatova wasn't the only person who memorized "Requiem." She wanted to be sure that it wouldn't be lost if she was indeed killed, so Akhmatova gathered some of her closest friends and had them memorize the poem as well. After Stalin's death, "Requiem" became one of the first examples of what's called *samizdat*, meaning self-published works. Works of samizdat literature like "Requiem" were published and distributed by dissidents in secret—in this way, Akhmatova was eventually able to make her perspective on what really happened during the Great Purge widely known.

31. The author's purpose in paragraph 1 is to

    A. offer background on the history of the Soviet Union before the Great Purge.

    B. tell a story to help the reader understand the conditions under which Akhmatova wrote "Requiem."

    C. explain who Anna Akhmatova was and why she was important.

    D. clarify why writers didn't approve of Stalin.

    E. educate the reader about the origins of samizdat poetry like "Requiem."

32. As used in paragraph 2, the underlined term *interred* most nearly means

    A. executed.

    B. interrogated.

    C. evaluated.

    D. imprisoned.

    E. investigated.

33. Approximately how many people were executed or interred in gulags during Stalin's Great Terror?

    A. 750,000

    B. 1,000,000

    C. 1,750,000

    D. No one knows.

    E. The passage does not provide this information.

34. Which of the following terms describes the author's style in this passage?

    A. Journalistic

    B. Vague

    C. Learned

    D. Pejorative

    E. Abstract

35. Which is the best title for this passage?

    A. "Women Writers in Stalin's Soviet Union"

    B. "Why is Poetry Important to History?"

    C. "A Biography of Anna Akhmatova"

    D. "Samizdat Literature of the Soviet Union"

    E. "Anna Akhmatova's 'Requiem' and the Great Purge"

Questions 36–40 refer to the following passage.

When Rosalind Franklin was born into a well-known Jewish family in Notting Hill, London, on July 25, 1920, her parents likely had no idea how pioneering a scientist she would go on to become. Nor could they have had an inkling that their daughter would pass away of ovarian cancer at the heartbreakingly young age of 37. However, Franklin knew that she wanted to be a scientist as early as age 15 and dedicated herself to her studies so vociferously that she made numerous paradigm-shifting scientific discoveries over the course of her tragically short life.

Franklin's most groundbreaking discovery was that of the structure of DNA. Having acquired skills in both x-ray diffraction and crystallography, she applied this knowledge to her study of DNA fibers. This was a pioneering move as no one else had thought to use x-ray diffraction in this way before. In the process, Franklin managed to take a photograph that played a pivotal role in scientists' early understanding of DNA structure. Specifically, Franklin determined that DNA had a dry form, known as the A form, and a wet form, known as the B form. The photograph Franklin took, known as Photograph 51, showed the B form clearly enough to help solidify this new knowledge about DNA, but getting it also meant Franklin was exposed to more than 100 hours of x-ray radiation. While there is no definitive proof, many speculate that Franklin's radiation exposure ultimately played a role in her developing terminal cancer at such a young age.

Frustratingly, as is the case with many women in science, it took many years for the scientific community to give Franklin the recognition she deserved. Drawing on her research, other scientists tried to claim her discoveries as their own. For instance, a colleague of Franklin's named Maurice Wilkins shared Photograph 51 with another scientist, James Watson, without Franklin's permission. Wilkins and Watson, along with scientist Francis Crick, went on to use the information gleaned from the photograph as the basis of their own famous DNA model. Effectively, this meant they published groundbreaking knowledge from Franklin's discovery without affording her proper credit beyond a measly footnote. It wasn't until many years later that this intellectual theft was recognized by the wider scientific community and scientific history properly <u>amended</u> to restore credit to Franklin.

36. The author's style can most accurately be described as

A. ornate.

B. incoherent.

C. argumentative.

D. autobiographical.

E. biographical.

37. We can infer from this passage that Rosalind Franklin

A. would have quit science had she survived cancer.

B. disliked science until she was 15 years old.

C. sued Wilkins and Watson for plagiarizing her work.

D. died of ovarian cancer caused by her exposure to radiation.

E. was not the only woman to ever have her scientific discoveries claimed by a man.

38. Photograph 51 was important to the scientific community because it

    A. was the first photograph taken with x-ray diffraction.

    B. required 100 hours of radiation exposure to get it.

    C. helped confirm Franklin's findings about the structure of DNA.

    D. was the only photograph taken during Franklin's experiments.

    E. required a unique developing process involving crystallography.

39. The author's purpose in paragraph 3 is to

    A. highlight how the men Franklin worked with took credit for her discoveries.

    B. critique Franklin for not protecting her intellectual property better.

    C. argue against the narrative that Franklin had her work stolen.

    D. enumerate the problems women face in the sciences.

    E. discredit the findings published by Wilkins, Watson, and Crick.

40. As used in paragraph 3, the underlined word *amended* most nearly means

    A. punished.

    B. modified.

    C. erased.

    D. disturbed.

    E. forgotten.

ANSWER KEY AND EXPLANATIONS

1. C	9. B	17. D	25. C	33. C
2. B	10. B	18. D	26. A	34. C
3. A	11. D	19. A	27. B	35. E
4. E	12. C	20. B	28. E	36. E
5. A	13. E	21. D	29. C	37. E
6. B	14. D	22. E	30. D	38. C
7. C	15. E	23. A	31. B	39. A
8. D	16. C	24. C	32. D	40. B

1. **The correct answer is C.** The word *imperative* means "crucial, vital, or necessary."

2. **The correct answer is B.** The author's point of view is their position on the topic they are discussing. Since this is an argumentative passage, the author's point of view is their argument. In this passage, the author argues that more Americans should create eco-friendly lawn spaces instead of using traditional grass sod.

3. **The correct answer is A.** A passage's title should summarize its main idea. "Ecological Alternatives to Traditional Grass Lawns" encompasses this passage's main idea. "Why Americans Care About Lawns" (choice C) and "What is a Lawn?" (choice D) do not reflect the passage's main idea while "The Problem with Grass" (choice B) and "Grass Lawns" (choice E) are both too vague.

4. **The correct answer is E.** While it is possible that some studies have shown a correlation between fertilizer use and air pollution, it is not mentioned in this passage.

5. **The correct answer is A.** Something that is lucrative is profitable.

6. **The correct answer is B.** The most appropriate title for this passage is "Ghost Towns of the United States." "The History of American Mining" (choice A) and "What Happened after the Gold Rush?" (choice C) are both inaccurate reflections of the passage's main idea. "Colorado's Ghost Towns" (choice D) and "Mining Towns of the American West" (choice E) are too specific to encompass the broader main topic, which focuses on mining towns all over the US.

7. **The correct answer is C.** Remember, for an inference to be logical and valid, it must be a reasonable conclusion one could draw from the details given. The only answer that satisfies that criterion is choice C. That's because the passage states that there are at least 3,800 ghost towns in the US, so it would be reasonable to infer that each of the 50 states is likely to have at least one.

8. **The correct answer is D.** Paragraph 3 states that Terlingua is a ghost town in Texas.

9. **The correct answer is B.** The word *luminous* means "vivid, lustrous, brilliant, or shining with light."

10. **The correct answer is B.** The text says that the emperor gazed into the incense smoke and "fixed upon the memory of the Lady Li" and then he "recognized the form of his beloved," who earlier in the passage was identified as Lady Li.

11. **The correct answer is D.** We are told that "when the Emperor had lost his beautiful favorite, the Lady Li, he sorrowed so much that fears were entertained for his reason" and that he procured the incense to "summon her from the dead," so we can infer that the grief his counsellors were worried about concerned the death of Lady Li.

12. **The correct answer is C.** The author states multiple times that they are summarizing the

information found in a March 2018 *Smithsonian Magazine* article by Richard Grant entitled "Do Trees Talk to Each Other?"

13. **The correct answer is E.** Since this passage is a summary, it does what most summaries are intended to do, which is highlight the most important information from a given source. The author's purpose in this summary passage is to highlight the most important information from Richard Grant's 2018 news article.

14. **The correct answer is D.** The purpose of paragraph 2 is to list all the different examples of tree communication that Wohlleben gave Grant while he was writing the article.

15. **The correct answer is E.** While it's possible that some trees grow so close to one another that their branches do intertwine, it is not one of the examples of tree communication given in the passage. The passage does mention root systems growing together as an example, but that is not the same as branches.

16. **The correct answer is C.** If you know that the first sentence "What makes a painting a painting, and what makes a photograph a photograph?" is a rhetorical question, then you likely spotted that the purpose of paragraph 1 is to pose a rhetorical question that helps introduce the main idea. If you didn't, you could also find your correct answer through a process of elimination. You know that paragraph 1 is being used as an introduction, so you can first eliminate any options that do not reflect an introduction (choices D and E). You can eliminate choice A because there is no attempt to critique Richter's art in the passage. While the passage does discuss Richter's personal biography, it does so in paragraph 2, so choice B can be eliminated. By process of elimination, you are left with choice C as the correct answer.

17. **The correct answer is D.** Paragraph 2 directly states that Richter's love of art "blossomed following the acquisition of a simple plate camera as a Christmas gift in early childhood."

18. **The correct answer is D.** When considering the context of the word identified in a vocabulary question, you'll sometimes find a grammatical hint in the surrounding words. Here, the underlined verb *grapple* is followed by the preposition *with*, so you can eliminate any answer option (choices B, C, and E) that includes a verb form that doesn't flow together logically with that preposition. From there, you have a 50/50 chance of being correct. Logically, it would make more sense for Richter's art to make people "deal with" questions rather than "agree with" questions, so choice D is the correct word choice.

19. **The correct answer is A.** Paragraph 4 states that paintings made to look like photographs reflect "a style now associated with Richter and oft replicated by artists inspired by him." Therefore, if other artists are trying to replicate (meaning "copy") Richter's style, then there are other artists who have made paintings that are supposed to look like photographs. Choices B and C can't be supported by the passage. Choices D and E mention key words from the passage but do not logically relate to the main idea.

20. **The correct answer is B.** The term *indigenous* refers to people, animals, or plants that are native to or were the first to inhabit a given place.

21. **The correct answer is D.** The main idea of this passage is that the Cree First Nations are widespread throughout Canada and that efforts are being made to preserve their language and culture.

22. **The correct answer is E.** While the passage does mention that there are Cree people living on the Rocky Boy Indian Reservation in Montana, there is no mention of Rocky Cree.

23. **The correct answer is A.** The author uses an educational tone in this passage. Other terms to describe the tone of the passage include *formal*, *direct*, *informative*, and *impartial*.

24. **The correct answer is C.** Paragraph 2 mentions efforts to preserve Cree language, and paragraph 3 discusses how young people are using social media to share Cree culture with the world. Of

the options given, the most logical paragraph that would fit between these two paragraphs is one that provides examples of how contemporary Cree artists are using their art to preserve Cree culture and language.

25. **The correct answer is C.** Synonyms for *flummoxed* include the words *confused*, *bewildered*, and *perplexed*. In paragraph 4, where the word *flummoxed* appears, the passage states: "The border guards, who had no idea what had just been broadcast on national television, were overwhelmed by the size of the crowds and flummoxed as to what to do." If the guards were both overwhelmed and didn't have enough information to know why it was happening or what to do, it would be safe to assume that they were confused. Furthermore, there are no contextual details to support the conclusion that they were angered (choice A) or disorganized (choice D). While they might have been anxious (choice B) and it's possible they were being yelled at (choice E), your job is to find the best answer for each question. Given the context, *confused* is the most accurate and specific answer.

26. **The correct answer is A.** This cause-and-effect question asks you to identify the factor that caused border guards to open the crossings in the Berlin Wall. To answer it, reread the sections that describe the opening of the wall. Paragraphs 3 and 4 discuss how a mistaken TV announcement by a government official led to crowds of East Germans swarming the border crossings. These crowds are what caused the border to open; soon after, the wall was dismantled.

27. **The correct answer is B.** Close reading reveals that grenades are never mentioned in the passage. However, land mines are, so if this question fooled you, make sure you're reading carefully and not confusing terms.

28. **The correct answer is E.** The author uses a direct, objective, fact-based tone. *Unassuming* (choice A) and *wearied* (choice B) point to an emotional tone, which is not present here. The author shows no attempt to be humorous (choice D) and the term *sensationalistic* (choice C) means "inaccurate,

exaggerated, or distasteful," which doesn't fit this passage.

29. **The correct answer is C.** The first paragraph mentions the idea of a "brain drain," which is when educated and skilled citizens move away from a place in large numbers. When so many East German citizens were leaving that officials worried about this issue, they put up the Berlin Wall in response. Choice A does not make sense, as the Cold War had already started when the Berlin Wall was erected. Choice B is tricky because it reverses a concept from the passage; rather than the wall being erected to protect West Germany from communism, the East Germans built it to keep their citizens in and Western ideas out. Ronald Reagan (choice D) is not mentioned at all. While it's possible that those fleeing East Germany felt they had no other choice, you do not have enough information from this passage to make that inference, so choice E cannot be correct.

30. **The correct answer is D.** This detail question is also a sneaky vocabulary question, since it relies on your understanding of the word *infrastructure*, meaning "the physical structure and organization of a particular facility or system." In this case, the passage discusses how the number of people gathered on the bridge at Bornholmer Strasse caused officials to worry about a collapse, forcing them to go along with the crowd's wishes. The passage specifically states that the guards had not heard Schabowski's announcement and that the opening did not go according to plan, so you can eliminate choices A and C. It may be possible that more people were gathered at Bornholmer Strasse than any other crossing (choice B) and that the guards had sympathy for the people gathered (choice E), but neither conclusion is supported by the details given in the passage.

31. **The correct answer is B.** In the first paragraph, the author uses a storytelling device to ask the reader to imagine themselves in the same position Akhmatova would have found herself when she wrote "Requiem." If a question asks about a specific paragraph, you can ignore any answer that

comes from the passage but isn't addressed in that paragraph, such as choice E, which more appropriately describes aspects of paragraph 4. You can also eliminate any answer that doesn't match the purpose of the passage overall; for instance, this passage never addresses the history of the Soviet Union prior to the Great Purge (choice A). You may be able to infer from the passage who Anna Akhmatova was and why she was important (choice C) or why writers like Akhmatova likely did not approve of Stalin (choice D), but that is not the purpose of the first paragraph.

32. **The correct answer is D.** To inter someone means to imprison them.

33. **The correct answer is C.** This is both a supporting detail and inference question. The number you need is not stated directly in the passage, but two of your distractors are: 750,000 (choice A) and 1,000,000 (choice B), which in the passage is written simply as "million." The reason an exam asks a question like this is to see if you were reading the relevant sentence closely enough to comprehend its implications. The relevant sentence from paragraph 2 states: "This is the exact dilemma Anna Akhmatova found herself in during the Great Purge between 1936 and 1938 when as many as 750,000 people were executed and another million were interred in gulags by Stalin's Soviet government." Therefore, to understand how to answer the question, you'll first need to recognize that "Great Purge" and "Great Terror" are terms that refer to the same event, as stated in paragraph 1. Then, to find the number who were "executed or interred," as your question states, you'll need to make an inference by adding the two quantities offered in the reading together. $1,000,000 + 750,000 = 1,750,000$. Yes, it may look like a math question, but notice that the math itself is very simple and relates directly to your reading comprehension. Exam questions that don't look like reading questions can still always be answered using close reading of the question and relevant portions of the passage.

34. **The correct answer is C.** It is not uncommon for questions about tone or style to also disguise themselves as vocabulary questions. If an author uses a learned style, that means they are fitting in a lot of information and demonstrating great knowledge of the topic. Informative writing often uses a learned style. Knowing what the other terms mean can help you use a process of elimination if you aren't sure which term is correct. Since this passage is straightforward, it's not vague (choice B) or abstract (choice E), both of which are antonyms of *straightforward*. *Pejorative* (choice D) means "critical," which is not the case here; if anything, the author's style includes word choices that suggest they praise Akhmatova's efforts. The term *journalistic* relates to *journalism* and refers to something written in the style of a news article. While it's possible this passage might appear in a newspaper or online journal, it's not typical of news writing, and *journalistic* is not as specific a description of the author's style as *learned*. Always choose the best answer if more than one seems possible.

35. **The correct answer is E.** Remember, questions that ask for a passage's best title are simply main idea/author's purpose questions. If you have figured out that the author's purpose in this passage is to talk about Anna Akhmatova's "Requiem" and how it came about during the Great Purge, then it becomes clear that "Anna Akhmatova's 'Requiem' and the Great Purge" is the best possible title. "Why is Poetry Important to History?" (choice B) and "Samizdat Literature of the Soviet Union" (choice D) both relate to the passage but do not express the main idea. While we learn about Akhmatova, the reader is not given the type of background information traditional of a biography (choice C). Akhmatova is an important woman writer of the Stalin era, but you would expect a passage entitled "Women Writers in Stalin's Soviet Union" (choice A) to discuss more than just one writer.

36. **The correct answer is E.** The passage focuses on talking about someone's life, so you can narrow your options to autobiographical (choice D) and biographical (choice E). Since the passage wasn't written by Franklin herself, it can't be autobiographical.

37. **The correct answer is E.** At the beginning of paragraph 3, the author states: "Frustratingly, as is the case with many women in science, it took many years for the scientific community to give Franklin the recognition she deserved." While the author doesn't state so in those exact words, you can infer from their statement that Franklin is not the only woman in history to have had this happen.

38. **The correct answer is C.** As paragraph 2 states, "The photograph Franklin took, known as Photograph 51, showed the B form clearly enough to help solidify this new knowledge about DNA." The same sentence does later go on to mention that getting the photograph required 100 hours of radiation exposure (choice B), but that would not be why the scientific community considered Photograph 51 important. Remember to read questions closely.

39. **The correct answer is A.** The author's purpose in paragraph 3 is to highlight how the men Franklin worked with took credit for her discoveries. While the author does point out that this is a problem faced by women in science, choice D is incorrect because listing those problems is not the purpose of the paragraph. Choice E might have thrown you if you mistook the word *discredit* to mean something like "criticized" when in fact it means "disprove," which the author does not do—Wilkins, Watson, and Crick may well have published accurate information, but the problem is that they used Franklin's discovery without her permission. The passage does the opposite of choice C, since it argues that Franklin's work was stolen. There is no attempt to critique Franklin (choice B) in the passage.

40. **The correct answer is B.** To amend is to modify, revise, or change.

PART IV
QUANTITATIVE AND NONVERBAL SKILLS

CHAPTER

Basic Mathematics

BASIC MATHEMATICS

OVERVIEW

Whether you love it or hate it, math is always a part of your life. Sometimes, you might feel as though you are just not good at math or that you're not a math person. While it may not be your favorite subject, sometimes, you just have to figure out which parts of math you enjoy. Other times, it might be a matter of needing to review some fundamental concepts so that you can feel more confident and prepared going into more advanced mathematics. It's important that you get comfortable with math because you will find mathematics questions on all scholastic aptitude and achievement tests,

SSAT   ISEE

including most high school entrance exams. On the SSAT, math questions are covered in the Quantitative (Math) section. On the ISEE, math questions are covered in the Quantitative Reasoning and the Mathematics Achievement sections.

In the sections that follow, we have condensed eight years of mathematics classes into a comprehensive review that touches on most topics covered in the exams. If you find that you're having difficulties with a specific topic, talk with a teacher or refer to your mathematics textbooks. The five chapters in Part IV will help most by illuminating what you *don't* know so you can focus some of your test-prep time on reinforcing your skills in problem areas. The explanations that accompany the mathematics exercises can help you understand the processes involved in finding the correct answers. For extra practice, complete the Test Yourself exercises and Knowledge Checks in each of these chapters. Work through the exercises carefully, and pay close attention to your accuracy and speed as you work. Note which problems are difficult as well as those that

are easy for you. After you complete each chapter, you'll know exactly which areas you need to strengthen.

First, we'll look at math symbols and types of numbers, including whole numbers and signed numbers. We'll also discuss properties and how the order of operations should guide your calculations. Then, we'll focus on decimals, fractions, and percentages and how to convert between them. Finally, we'll cover ratios, proportions, probability, and measurement conversions to illustrate some real-world applications of the concepts we've discussed here.

MATH SYMBOLS

Math is a language, with terms, meanings, structure, and symbols. To succeed at math, you need to understand the language. Often, the symbols used in equations can be the biggest challenge, so we'll start there. Some, if not all, of these symbols are already familiar to you, but it's worth reviewing the symbols that go beyond addition and subtraction. We've included a list of math symbols and their meanings for easy reference.

MATH SYMBOLS			
Symbol	**Meaning**	**Function**	**Example**
+	Plus sign	Addition	$5 + 3 = 8$
−	Minus sign	Subtraction	$5 - 3 = 2$
×	Times sign	Multiplication	$5 \times 3 = 15$
·	Multiplication dot	Multiplication	$5 \cdot 3 = 15$
÷	Division	Division	$10 \div 5 = 2$
/	Division slash	Division	$10/5 = 2$
·	Period	Decimal point	$5.3, 7.25$
%	Percent	$5\% = 5/100 = 0.05$	$0.5 = 50\%$ $1.25 = 125\%$

MATH SYMBOLS			
Symbol	**Meaning**	**Function**	**Example**
<	Strict inequality	Less than	$3 < 5$
≤	Inequality	Less than or equal to	$5 \leq 5, 4 \leq 5$
>	Strict inequality	Greater than	$5 > 3$
≥	Inequality	Greater than or equal to	$5 \geq 5, 5 \geq 4$
( )	Parentheses	Solve within first	$3 + (2 + 1) + 2 = 3 + 3 + 2 = 8$
[ ]	Brackets	Solve within first	$3 + [2 + 1] + 2 = 3 + 3 + 2 = 8$
x^y	Power	Exponent	$3^2 = 3 \times 3 = 9$ $3^3 = 3 \times 3 \times 3 = 27$
√	Square root	$\sqrt{a} \cdot \sqrt{a} = a$	$\sqrt{9} = 3, \sqrt{16} = 4$
π	Pi constant	Ratio between the circumference of a circle and its diameter	$c = \pi \times d$ $\pi = \dfrac{c}{d}$
∠	Angle	Formed by two rays	$\angle CDE = 45°$
∡	Measured angle	Formed by two rays	$\angle DEF = 60°$
∟	Right angle	Right angle = 90°	$a = 90°$
°	Degree	A circle = 360°, ½ = 180°	$a = 45°$
!	Factorial	$n! = 1 \times 2 \times 3 \times 4 \times ... \times n$	$4! = 1 \times 2 \times 3 \times 4 = 24$

TYPES OF NUMBERS

In math, various terms exist to describe the array of numbers used for counting and calculations. The ability to distinguish between whole numbers, integers, and rational and irrational numbers can keep you from selecting incorrect answer choices on your exam.

Whole Numbers and Integers

Starting with one of the most basic terms, whole numbers are simply numbers that are not decimals or fractions. They are always positive and include zero. An integer is any whole number not only including zero but also negative numbers—excluding negative decimals and fractions.

Some examples of whole numbers are as follows:

$$1, 2, 3, 50, 75, 100$$

Some examples of integers are as follows:

$$0, 1, 3, 42, 197, -2, -30, -212$$

Some examples of numbers that are NOT integers:

$$\frac{3}{4}, 0.14, -11.3, 56.0035$$

Rational and Irrational Numbers

A rational number is any number that results from dividing two integers. For example, $\frac{1}{3}, \frac{3}{5}, -\frac{7}{3}$ are all rational numbers. That means any number that has a terminating or repeating decimal, including no decimal, is rational. Here are some examples of rational numbers and what makes them so:

$$1 = \frac{1}{1} = \frac{2}{2} = \frac{-5}{-5} = \frac{0.354}{0.354} = \frac{10,000}{10,000}$$

$$-2 = \frac{-2}{1} = \frac{14}{-7} = \frac{-10}{5} = \frac{-40,000}{20,000}$$

$$5.25 = \frac{5.25}{1} = \frac{-10.5}{-2} = \frac{21}{4} = \frac{525,000}{100,000}$$

$$0.\overline{3} = \frac{1}{3} = \frac{30}{90} = \frac{400}{1,200}$$

 NOTE

A line over a decimal means that it is a repeating decimal that goes on forever, as in $0.\overline{3} = 0.3333333...$

The term *rational* is derived from *ratio*. In other words, any rational number is essentially the ratio of one integer to another or one integer divided by another integer. Each of these examples is expressed as a ratio. $\frac{-5}{-5}$ is equivalent to 1, just as $\frac{14}{-7}$ is equivalent to –2. The third example, 5.25, is a terminating decimal, so it is a rational number. The fourth example, $0.\overline{3}$, is a repeating decimal, so it can also be expressed as a ratio. We'll talk a bit more about ratios later on in this chapter.

Irrational numbers are numbers that have nonterminating, nonrepeating decimals. The most widely known irrational number is pi (π), or 3.141592653589793238462643383279 and on and on. The following are other irrational numbers:

$$\sqrt{2} = 1.41421356237...$$
$$\sqrt{3} = 1.73205080756...$$

Signed Numbers

We'll use a number line to talk about signed numbers. The number line exists on both sides of zero. Each positive number to the right of zero has a negative counterpart to the left of zero. The number line below shows the location of some pairs of numbers (+4, –4; +2, –2; +1, –1).

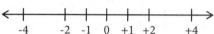

Because each number of a pair is located the same distance from zero (though in different directions), each has the same absolute value. Absolute value is symbolized by placing two vertical bars—one on each side of the number.

$$|+4| = |-4| = 4$$

The absolute value of +4 equals the absolute value of –4. Both are equivalent to 4. If you think of absolute value as the distance from zero, regardless of direction, it makes sense. The absolute value of any number, positive or negative, is expressed as a positive number.

Addition of Signed Numbers

When we add two oppositely signed numbers having the same absolute value, the sum is zero.

$$(+10) + (-10) = 0$$
$$(-1.5) + (+1.5) = 0$$
$$(-0.010) + (+0.010) = 0$$
$$\left(+\frac{3}{4}\right) + \left(-\frac{3}{4}\right) = 0$$

If one of the two oppositely signed numbers is greater in absolute value, the sum is equal to the amount of that excess and carries the same sign as the number having the greater absolute value.

$$(+2) + (-1) = +1$$
$$(+8) + (-9) = -1$$
$$(-2.5) + (+2.0) = -0.5$$
$$\left(-\frac{3}{4}\right) + \left(+\frac{1}{2}\right) = -\frac{1}{4}$$

Subtraction of Signed Numbers

Subtraction is the operation that finds the difference between two numbers, including the difference between signed numbers. When subtracting signed numbers, it can be helpful to refer to a number line.

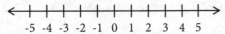

-5 -4 -3 -2 -1 0 1 2 3 4 5

For example, if we wish to subtract +2 from +5, we can use the number line to see that the difference is +3. We give the sign to the difference that represents the direction we are moving along the number line from the number being subtracted to the number from which you are subtracting. In this case, because we are subtracting +2 from +5, we count three units in a positive direction from +2 to +5 on the number line.

When subtracting signed numbers:

- The distance between the two numbers gives you the absolute value of the difference.
- The direction you move from the number being subtracted to get to the number from which you are subtracting gives you the sign of the difference.

EXAMPLES:

Subtract −3 from +5.

Solution:

Distance on the number line between −3 and +5 is 8 units.

Direction is from negative to positive, a positive direction.

Answer is +8.

Subtract −6 from −8.

Solution:

Distance on number line between −6 and −8 is 2 units.

Direction is from −6 to −8, a negative direction.

Answer is −2.

Subtract +1.30 from −2.70.

Solution:

Distance between +1.30 and −2.70 on the number line is 4.0.

Direction is from +1.30 to −2.70, a negative direction.

Answer is −4.0.

A quick way to subtract signed numbers accurately involves placing the numbers in columns, reversing the sign of the number being subtracted and then adding the two. In other words, change the sign of the number being subtracted and follow the rules for addition.

 TIP

To easily subtract signed numbers, change the sign of the number being subtracted and follow the rules for addition.

EXAMPLES:

Subtract +26 from +15.

Solution:

$$+15 = +15$$
$$- +26 = -26$$
$$= -11$$

Subtract −35 from +10.

Solution:

$$+10 = +10$$
$$- -35 = +35$$
$$= +45$$

Notice that in each of the examples, we found the correct answer by reversing the sign of the number being subtracted and then adding.

Multiplication of Signed Numbers

Signed numbers are multiplied as any other numbers would be, with the following exceptions:

1. The product of two negative numbers is positive.

$$(-3) \times (-6) = +18$$

2. The product of two positive numbers is positive.

$$(+3.05) \times (+6) = +18.30$$

3. The product of a negative and positive number is negative.

$$\left(+4\frac{1}{2}\right) \times (-3) = -13\frac{1}{2}$$
$$(+1) \times (-1) \times (+1) = -1$$

 TIP

In multiplication, if the signs are the same, the product is positive.

$$+ \cdot + = +$$
$$- \cdot - = +$$

If the signs are different, the product is negative.

$$+ \cdot - = -$$

Division of Signed Numbers

As with multiplication, the division of signed numbers requires you to observe three simple rules:

1. When dividing a positive number by a negative number, the result is negative.

$$(+6) \div (-3) = -2$$

2. When dividing a negative number by a positive number, the result is negative.

$$(-6) \div (+3) = -2$$

3. When dividing a negative number by a negative number or a positive number by a positive number, the result is positive.

$$(-6) \div (-3) = +2$$
$$(+6) \div (+3) = +2$$

MEAN, MEDIAN, AND MODE

Now that we've covered the types of numbers you'll encounter in math problems, let's take a look at some of the applications and uses of numbers in different real-world contexts. Statistics, for instance, is all about numerical data. Have you ever had a teacher ask the class how many students did their homework every day last month? That is a statistic. Out of the 26 students in the class, eight of them did all their homework last month. When you have a set of data points, like how often each student did homework over that month,

To learn more about finding the mean, scan this QR code.

you would have a data set of 26 numbers—one for each student—that is written as:

{1, 2, 3, 4, 5, 6, 7, 8, 9, 10, 11, 12, 13, 14, 15, 16, 17, 18, 19, 20, 21, 22, 23, 24, 25, 26}

Notice that the data points are between those squiggly brackets (which is the actual name for those, though they are generally referred to as *brackets*). Now, imagine that data set was made up of 26 random numbers. That could easily become confusing, especially when you have one hundred pieces of data, or 1,000, or 50,000. This is where the central tendency terms come in handy; they can help you organize, summarize, and describe the data in front of you. There are three central tendency terms you'll likely encounter on your exam: mean, median, and mode.

Mean

The first term, mean, may be the one you are most familiar with, as it's another word for average. Average means "typical" or "middle," which is exactly what the mean is. You find the mean by adding the numbers in the set of data, then dividing by the number of terms in that set. In the example above, you would find the mean by adding the data together $(1 + 2 + 3 + 4 + ...)$ and dividing that sum by the number of data points in the set.

$$\frac{351}{26} = 13.5$$

Your average then is 13.5. You can do this with any data set, and you do not have to put all the data points in order. Just add, then divide.

Median

Median is another method to help make sense of a data set. Unlike the mean, the median is looking for the middle number in your data set, and not the average, although the two may be very close or even equal. To find the median, you must put all the data points in order.

{7, 8, 9, 10, 11}

In this data set, the median, or the number that is in the middle, is 9. If you have an odd number of digits or data points, put them in order and find the one right in the middle.

Now, let's use the data set from earlier:

{1, 2, 3, 4, 5, 6, 7, 8, 9, 10, 11, 12, 13, 14, 15, 16, 17, 18, 19, 20, 21, 22, 23, 24, 25, 26}

You already know the median is the digit that appears right in the middle of the data set. In this case though, we have an even number of data points, and that means the median is two digits. If you have two numbers as the median, take those two and find the mean of the two. That is, when you have two numbers as the median, then the mean is exactly in the middle. For this data set, the median is {13, 14}.

$$13 + 14 = 27 \qquad 27 \div 2 = 13.5$$

The mean of those two numbers is 13.5, which is the median for the larger data set.

Mode

Mode is a bit different from the previous two. While the mean seeks the average of a data set and the median seeks the middle digit in a data set when it's written in order, the mode is the piece of data that shows up most often in a data set.

To learn more about median and mode, scan this QR code.

Let's take a data set where 26 students estimated how many hours per day they spend on social media. That would be written out as {5, 7, 8, 1, 4, 2, 5, 3, 9, 6, 5, 6, 5, 5, 4, 1, 7, 8, 2, 9, 2, 8, 5, 7, 4, 0}. That's a mess, so just like we did for finding the median, let's put this in order:

{0, 1, 1, 2, 2, 2, 3, 4, 4, 4, 5, 5, 5, 5, 5, 5, 6, 6, 7, 7, 7, 8, 8, 8, 9, 9}

Now, count how many times each number comes up.

0 = 1

1 = 2

2 = 3

3 = 1

4 = 3

5 = 6

6 = 2

7 = 3

8 = 3

9 = 2

Looking at this information, we see that the number 5 appears six times. That means the mode of that data set is 5. When would this be helpful information? If you want to show a trend (like hours spent on social media), knowing which value appears most frequently tells you which is the most popular. In this case, five hours a day on social media is the most common occurrence in the data set.

Let's find the mode for another set of data: This time, we'll examine how many pages each student reads at home every night. Your data set is {3, 3, 4, 4, 4, 5, 5, 7, 7, 7, 8, 8, 9, 11, 11, 12, 12, 12, 12, 12, 12, 12, 17, 23}. Counting the frequency for each number in the set, 12 is the number that occurs most often, meaning more students read 12 pages each night than any other amount.

Another practical application would be if you have several kinds of trading cards that you're hoping to sell. If you keep track of which kind of trading card sells the most, that's the mode. Looking at the mode would tell you which cards are purchased most often and which ones don't sell as well. If this becomes your business, knowing which trading cards sell the best can help you know what to keep in stock more often and what to stock less often.

Test Yourself 1

Find the mean, median, and mode for the number set provided. The answers will follow.

{37, 46, 49, 11, 40, 32, 3, 39, 6, 47, 40, 4, 35}

1. Mean =

2. Median =

3. Mode =

{31, 1, 20, 43, 21, 39, 31, 25, 31, 9, 28, 36, 28, 18, 12, 21, 29, 41, 28, 27, 31}

4. Mean =

5. Median =

6. Mode =

{12, 22, 7, 35, 3, 30, 12, 7, 13, 24, 12, 1, 11, 3, 17, 15}

7. Mean =

8. Median =

9. Mode =

Answers:

1. 29.92

2. 37

3. 40

4. 26.19

5. 28

6. 31

7. 14

8. 12

9. 12

PROPERTIES

When studying math, it's important to understand how properties describe the behavior of numbers in certain situations. Properties in math are rules that have been proven over time. Knowing properties can help simplify the process of solving problems because you can count on the fact that certain things will always be true. Become thoroughly familiar with the rules in this section, and commit to memory as many properties and rules as possible.

Here's a list of properties, with definitions and examples. You may need to refer back to this section as we get into more advanced math, like solving algebraic equations.

- **Commutative Property:** in addition and multiplication, order does not affect outcome.
  - $7 + 8 = 8 + 7$
  - $3 \times 5 = 5 \times 3$
  - $2(6) = 6(2)$

- **Distributive Property:** given an equation, $a(b + c)$, you can distribute the value a to the values inside the parentheses.
  - $7(2 + 8) = 7 \times 2 + 7 \times 8 = 14 + 56 = 70$

- **Associative Property:** in addition and multiplication, changing how numbers are grouped will not change the result.
  - $2(5 \times 4) = 5(2 \times 4) = 4(2 \times 5)$
  - $3 + (5 + 2) = 2 + (3 + 5) = 5 + (2 + 3)$

- **Identity Property:** any number added to zero will not change; any number multiplied by 1 will not change.
  - $15 + 0 = 15$
  - $15 \times 1 = 15$

- **Reflexive Property:** a number is always equal to itself.
  - $a = a$
  - $2 = 2$
  - $\pi = \pi$

- **Symmetric Property:** if $a = b$, then $b = a$.
  - If $x = 10$, then $10 = x$

- **Transitive Property:** if $a = b$ and $b = c$, then $a = c$.
  - If $a = b$ and $b = 3 + 4$, then $a = 3 + 4$

- **Substitution Property:** if $a = b$, then a can be substituted for b.
  - If $a = 7$ and $b = 7$, then $a + 3 = 10$ and $b + 3 = 10$

- **Additive Identity:** any variable added to zero will remain unchanged.
  - $x + 0 = x$

- **Multiplicative Property of Zero:** any number multiplied by zero equals zero.
  - $1 \times 0 = 0$
  - $4,962 \times 0 = 0$

- **Multiplicative Inverse:** any number multiplied by its reciprocal will equal 1.
  - $2 \times \dfrac{1}{2} = 1$
  - $2 \times \dfrac{1}{12} = 1$

ORDER OF OPERATIONS

One of the most important things to know when solving math problems is where to start. You will often encounter problems that have a series of operations to perform. Fortunately, there are rules to explain what goes first. We call these rules the order of operations. The order of operations ensures that, by solving operations in this order, you'll always be able to arrive at the same correct solution. At this stage of mathematics, there are only four rules to know. They are as follows:

1. Solve operations within parentheses first.

2. Solve operations with exponents and square roots next.

3. Solve multiplication and division from left to right.

4. Solve addition and subtraction from left to right.

TIP

Remember your order of operations with the acronym **PEMDAS:**

P Parentheses

E Exponents (and Square Roots)

M Multiplication

D Division

A Addition

S Subtraction

Some students use the mnemonic device "**P**lease **e**xcuse **m**y **d**ear **A**unt **S**ally."

These rules inform where you should start when solving a math problem. In short, solve anything in parentheses first, going from hardest to easiest. As you go through problems using the order of operations, carefully follow each step to make sure you don't skip a step or forget anything along the way.

Let's look at a few examples.

- $(7 \times 2) + (8 - 2) = (14) + (6) = 20$ (Solve within the parentheses before adding)

- $4^3 + (5 + 1) =$ (Parentheses first)

  $4^3 + 6 = 64 + 6$ (Exponent, then addition)

- $6 - 8 \div 2 + 3 =$ (No multiplication, so start with division)

  $6 - 4 + 3 = 5$ (Addition and subtraction from left to right)

- $\sqrt{81} \times 5^2 - 45 \div 9 + 14 =$ (No parentheses, so start with exponents and square roots)

  $9 \times 25 - 45 \div 9 + 14 =$ (Now solve multiplication and division from left to right)

  $225 - 5 + 14 = 234$ (Now solve addition and subtraction from left to right)

We just demonstrated the order of operations discussed here. As you go through these chapters on mathematics, you will come across other rules concerning order of operations. Refer back to this section as needed.

Test Yourself 2

Put the following equations into standard form. The answers will follow.

1. $(8 \times 2) + (9 - 2) - \sqrt{144} \div 2^2$
2. $10 + 5^2 - (7 \times 3) + 1$
3. $\sqrt{9} \div 1 + (6^2 \div 4) - 10$
4. $10 \times 3 + (11 - 2) \div 3$
5. $4^3 + 6 - (4 \times 7) \div 2$

Answers:

1. 20
2. 15
3. 2
4. 33
5. 56

Scan this QR code to watch a video about the order of operations.

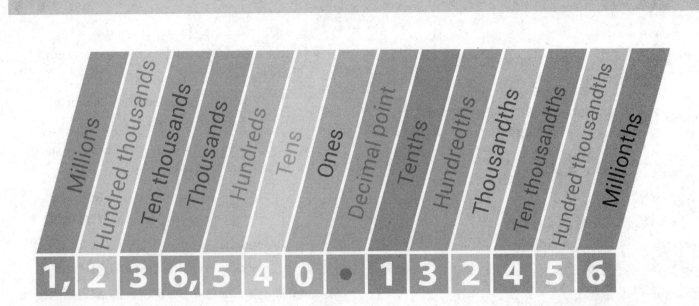

DECIMALS

So far, we've talked extensively about whole numbers and integers, but in math, you'll frequently be working with parts of numbers in the form of decimals, fractions, and percentages. First, we'll address decimals, and then we'll move on to fractions and percentages.

When a number is written in decimal form, everything to the left of the decimal point is a whole number, and everything to the right of the decimal point represents a part of the whole (a tenth, hundredth, thousandth, and so on). If you can count money or make change, then you already have experience with decimals. The most important step when writing decimals is placing the decimal point. The whole system is based on its location. The chart shows places for the number 1,236,540.132456.

Place value refers to the specific value of a digit in a decimal number. For example, in the decimal number 1,236,540.132456:

The digit 1 is in the "millions" place.

The digit 2 is in the "hundred thousands" place.

The digit 3 is in the "ten thousands" place.

The digit 6 is in the "thousands" place.

The digit 5 is in the "hundreds" place.

The digit 4 is in the "tens" place.

The digit 0 is in the "ones" place.

The digit 1 is in the "tenths" place.

The digit 3 is in the "hundredths" place.

The digit 2 is in the "thousandths" place.

The digit 4 is in the "ten thousandths" place.

The digit 5 is in the "hundred thousandths" place.

The digit 6 is in the "millionths" place.

As such, you could express the numbers to the left of the decimal point as $1,000,000 + 200,000 + 36,000 + 500 + 40 + 0$. You could express the numbers to the right of the decimal point as

$$\frac{1}{10} + \frac{3}{100} + \frac{2}{1000} + \frac{4}{10,000} + \frac{5}{100,000} + \frac{6}{1,000,000}.$$

Adding zeros to the end of a decimal number does not change its value. For example, the decimal number 0.5 is the same as 0.50 or 0.5000. But adding a zero to the front (the left) of the number will change the number's value. For example, 0.5 means "five tenths," but 0.05 means "five hundredths."

When adding or subtracting decimals, you need to keep the decimal points in line. After you have lined up the decimal points, proceed with the problem the same way as with whole numbers while maintaining the location of the decimal point.

EXAMPLES:

Add 36.08 + 745 + 4.362 + 58.6 + 0.0061.

Solution:

$$
\begin{array}{r}
36.08 \\
745. \\
4.362 \\
58.6 \\
+\quad 0.0061 \\
\hline
844.0481
\end{array}
$$

To keep track of the decimal places, you can also fill in the spaces with zeros.

$$
\begin{array}{r}
036.0800 \\
745.0000 \\
004.3620 \\
058.6000 \\
+\quad 000.0061 \\
\hline
844.0481
\end{array}
$$

Subtract 7.928 from 82.1.

Solution:

$$
\begin{array}{r}
82.1 \\
-\quad 7.928 \\
\hline
74.172
\end{array}
\quad\text{or}\quad
\begin{array}{r}
82.100 \\
-\quad 7.928 \\
\hline
74.172
\end{array}
$$

When multiplying decimals, ignore the decimal points until you reach the product. The placement of the decimal point depends on the sum of the places to the right of the decimal point in both the multiplier and number being multiplied.

$$
\begin{array}{r}
1.482 \quad \text{(3 places to the right of decimal point)} \\
\times\ 0.16 \quad \text{(2 places to the right of decimal point)} \\
\hline
8892 \\
14820 \\
\hline
0.23712 \quad \text{(5 places to the right of decimal point)}
\end{array}
$$

You cannot divide by a decimal because a decimal itself is a ratio. If the divisor is a decimal, you must move the decimal point to the right until the divisor becomes a whole number. Count the number of spaces you moved the decimal point in the divisor to the right, and move the decimal point in the dividend (the number being divided) the same number of spaces to the right. The decimal point in the answer should be directly above the decimal point in the dividend.

$$
0.06\overline{)4.212} \quad\Rightarrow\quad 70.2
$$

In the example above, the decimal point moves two spaces to the right.

Test Yourself 3

Write the answers to the following problems in the space provided. The answers will follow.

1. $1.52 + 0.389 + 42.9 =$
2. $84 - 1.9 =$
3. $18 \div 0.3 =$
4. $1.5 \times 0.9 =$
5. $7.55 \div 5 =$

Answers:

1. 44.809
2. 82.1
3. 60
4. 1.35
5. 1.51

To watch a video about decimals, scan this QR code.

FACTORS AND MULTIPLES

Before we can start working with fractions, we need to understand factors and multiples. A factor is a number that can be divided into a whole number evenly without leaving a remainder. The factors of any integer include 1 as well as the integer itself. Figuring out whether one number is a factor of another requires you to divide that number by another number. For example, to determine what numbers are factors of 4, we would divide 4 by the numbers in question: 1, 2, and 4 all divide into 4 evenly, without a remainder. In contrast, 3 is not a factor of 4 because when you divide 4 by 3 you do not end up with a whole number: $4 \div 3 = 1\frac{1}{3}$. Because 3 cannot be divided evenly into 4, it is not a factor of 4.

Keep in mind these two basic rules about factors:

1. Complementing factors are multiples. If f is a factor of n, then n is a multiple of f. For example, 8 is a multiple of 2 for the same reason that 2 is a factor of 8: because $8 \div 2 = 4$, which is an integer.

2. A prime number is a positive integer that is divisible by only two positive integers: itself and 1. Zero (0) and 1 are not considered prime numbers; 2 is the first prime number. Here are all the prime numbers less than 50:

   2 3 5 7
   11 13 17 19
   23 29
   31 37
   41 43 47

As you can see, factors, multiples, and divisibility are different aspects of the same concept.

Greatest Common Factor

In order to solve problems with fractions, you'll need to be able to determine the greatest common factor. The term greatest common factor (or GCF) refers to the largest number that can be factored into two numbers cleanly (that is, without a remainder). For example, the greatest common factor of 10 and 15 is 5. For 10 and 20, the GCF is 10. How did we get those answers? Let's look at a pair of numbers.

EXAMPLE:

Find the GCF for (12, 8)

Solution:

Factors for 12: 1, 2, 3, 4, 6, 12

Factors for 8: 1, 2, 4, 8

The common factors—the factors common to both sets of numbers—for 12 and 8 are 1, 2, and 4. The greatest (largest) of the group is 4, so that's your answer.

Divisibility Rules

RULE 1:

Any integer is a factor of itself.

RULE 2:

1 and −1 are factors of all integers (except 0).

RULE 3:

The integer zero (0) has no factors and is not a factor of any integer.

RULE 4:

A positive integer's largest factor (other than itself) will never be greater than one half the value of the integer.

EXAMPLE:

Find the GCF for (28, 56)

Solution:

Factors for 28: 1, 2, 4, 7, 14, 28

Factors for 56: 1, 2, 4, 7, 14, 28, 56

The greatest common factor the two numbers share is 28, which is your answer.

 TIP

Don't be confused by the term "Greatest Common Divisor," as a divisor and a factor have the same meaning. They are both numbers that can divide into something.

There may be number pairs, like (7, 13), that don't have anything other than 1 in common. When this happens, the numbers are relatively prime. Remember that a prime number is a number that is only divisible by itself and 1.

What about problems with more than two numbers to factor? That just means you add another group of factors to choose from.

EXAMPLE:

Find the GCF for (28, 56, 84)

Solution:

Factors for 28: 1, 2, 4, 7, 14, 28

Factors for 56: 1, 2, 4, 7, 14, 28, 56

Factors for 84: 1, 2, 3, 4, 6, 7, 12, 14, 21, 28, 42, 84

The greatest common factor the three numbers share is still 28, which is your answer.

Test Yourself 4

Find the greatest common factor for each group of numbers. The answers will follow.

1. (20, 75)
2. (14, 35)
3. (5, 13)
4. (30, 150)
5. (12, 78)
6. (13, 117)
7. (15, 25)
8. (6, 21)
9. (4, 12)
10. (24, 64)

Answers:

1. 5
2. 7
3. 1
4. 30
5. 6
6. 13
7. 5
8. 3
9. 4
10. 8

 Scan this **QR** code for more information on how to find the greatest common factor and least common multiple.

Least Common Multiple

In addition to using the greatest common factor, solving problems with fractions will also require you to find the least common multiple. The least common multiple (LCM) is the smallest whole number into which each number in the list divides evenly. For example, the GCF of {18, 36, 63} is 9, and the LCM of {18, 36, 63} is 504.

Both factors and multiples will be essential for simplifying and converting fractions; however, factors are used much more frequently than multiples, as you are usually aiming to simplify fractions. Finding the least common multiple is helpful when you need to add or subtract fractions with different denominators, as you'll need each to have the same denominator in order to add them together. However, you will likely use the greatest common factor to reduce or simplify the end result.

FRACTIONS

A fraction is a part of a whole. For instance, there are 10 dimes in each dollar, so one dime is one-tenth of a dollar—one of ten equal parts. The fraction to represent one-tenth is written $\frac{1}{10}$. The top number of a fraction is called the numerator, and the bottom number is called the denominator. The denominator tells you how many equal parts the object or number is divided into, and the numerator tells how many of those parts we are concerned with.

$$\frac{3}{4} \leftarrow \text{numerator} \rightarrow \frac{7}{8}$$
$$\phantom{\frac{3}{4}} \leftarrow \text{denominator} \rightarrow$$

A proper fraction is one in which the numerator is less than the denominator. An improper fraction is one in which the numerator is the same as or greater than the denominator. $\frac{3}{5}$ is a proper fraction, but $\frac{5}{3}$ is an improper fraction. Sometimes, you will see a whole number and a fraction together. This is called a mixed number. $2\frac{3}{5}$ is an example of a mixed number.

Let's look at a few examples of how to express parts of a whole as fractions.

EXAMPLE:

Divide a baseball game, a football game, and a hockey game into convenient numbers of parts. Write a fraction to answer each equation.

1. If a pitcher played two innings, how much of the whole baseball game did he play?
2. If a quarterback played three quarters of a football game, how much of the whole game did he play?
3. If a goalie played two periods of a hockey game, how much of the whole game did he play?

Solution 1:

A baseball game has nine parts (each an inning). The pitcher pitched two innings. Therefore, he played $\frac{2}{9}$ of the game. The denominator represents the nine parts the game is divided into; the numerator represents the two parts we are concerned with.

Solution 2:

Similarly, there are four quarters in a football game, and a quarterback playing three of those quarters plays in $\frac{3}{4}$ of the game.

Solution 3:

There are three periods in hockey, and the goalie played in two of them. Therefore, he played in $\frac{2}{3}$ of the game.

Reciprocals

When working with fractions (or any numbers), you may need to find a fraction's reciprocal. Finding a reciprocal comes down to flipping something over. Defined, a reciprocal is $\frac{1}{x}$ where x is the number in question. For example, the reciprocal of $5 = \frac{1}{5}$ or 0.2 as a decimal. Let's see a few more.

$$17 = \frac{1}{17}$$

$$100 = \frac{1}{100}$$

$$42 = \frac{1}{42}$$

One thing to think about with a whole number is that 17 is the same as $\frac{17}{1}$. Keep that in mind not only with reciprocals but any time you have a mix of whole numbers and fractions.

Finding the reciprocal of a fraction requires flipping the numerator and denominator. For example, to find the reciprocal of $\frac{4}{5}$, you flip the fraction over to get $\frac{5}{4}$. Let's look at a few more examples.

Scan this QR code to watch a video about fractions.

$$\frac{1}{8} = \frac{8}{1} = 8$$

$$\frac{2}{10} = \frac{10}{2} = 5$$

$$\frac{1}{0.25} = \frac{0.25}{1} = 0.25$$

The rule of thumb with reciprocals is to divide by one for whole numbers and to flip the numerator and denominator for fractions.

Test Yourself 5

Write the reciprocals to the following problems in the space provided. The answers will follow.

1. $72 =$
2. $\frac{1}{2} =$
3. $0.65 =$
4. $\frac{3}{36} =$
5. $-6 =$

Answers:

1. $\frac{1}{72}$
2. 2
3. $\frac{20}{13}$
4. 12
5. $\frac{1}{-6}$

Equivalent Fractions

Fractions having different denominators and numerators might represent the same amount. These are equivalent fractions.

For example, divide the following circle into two equal parts. Write a fraction to indicate how much of the circle is shaded.

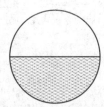

$$\frac{1 \text{ shaded}}{2 \text{ parts}} = \frac{1}{2} \text{ of the circle is shaded.}$$

The circle below is divided into four equal parts. Write a fraction to indicate how much of the circle is shaded.

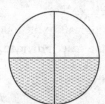

$$\frac{2 \text{ shaded}}{4 \text{ parts}} = \frac{2}{4} \text{ of the circle is shaded.}$$

This circle is divided into eight equal parts. Write a fraction to indicate how much of the circle is shaded.

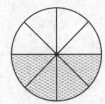

$$\frac{4 \text{ shaded}}{8 \text{ parts}} = \frac{4}{8} \text{ of the circle is shaded.}$$

In each circle, the same amount was shaded. This shows that there is more than one way to indicate one half of something.

The fractions $\frac{1}{2}$, $\frac{2}{4}$, and $\frac{4}{8}$ that you wrote are *equivalent fractions* because they all represent the same

amount. Notice that the denominator is twice as large as the numerator in every case. Any fraction you write that has a denominator that is exactly twice as large as the numerator will be equivalent to $\frac{1}{2}$.

Write other fractions equivalent to $\frac{1}{2}$.

Solution:

Any fraction that has a denominator that is twice as large as the numerator: $\frac{3}{6}, \frac{5}{10}, \frac{6}{12}, \frac{32}{64}$, etc.

Write other fractions equivalent to $\frac{1}{4}$.

Solution:

Any fraction that has a denominator that is four times as large as the numerator: $\frac{2}{8}, \frac{4}{16}, \frac{5}{20}, \frac{15}{60}$, etc.

Write other fractions equivalent to $\frac{2}{3}$.

Solution:

Any fraction that has a denominator that is one and one-half times as large as the numerator: $\frac{4}{6}, \frac{10}{15}, \frac{14}{21}, \frac{16}{24}$, etc.

When you cannot divide the numerator and denominator of a fraction evenly by the same whole number (other than 1), the fraction is in its simplest form. In the examples above, $\frac{1}{2}$, $\frac{1}{4}$, and $\frac{2}{3}$ are in their simplest forms. To write equivalent fractions where the numerator is not 1 requires one more step.

EXAMPLE:

What is the equivalent fraction for $\frac{4}{5}$ using 10 as a denominator?

Solution:

Each $\frac{1}{5}$ is equivalent to $\frac{2}{10}$; therefore, $\frac{4}{5}$ is equivalent to $\frac{8}{10}$.

The quickest way to find an equivalent fraction is to divide the denominator of the fraction you want by the denominator you know. Take the result and multiply it by the numerator of the fraction you know. This becomes the numerator of the equivalent fraction.

EXAMPLES:

Rename $\frac{3}{8}$ as an equivalent fraction having 16 as a denominator.

Solution:

$$\frac{3}{8} = \frac{6}{16} \quad (16 \div 8 = 2; 2 \times 3 = 6)$$

Rename $\frac{3}{4}$ as equivalent fractions having 8, 12, 24, and 32 as denominators.

Solution:

$$\frac{3}{4} = \frac{6}{8} \quad (8 \div 4 = 2; 2 \times 3 = 6)$$

$$\frac{3}{4} = \frac{9}{12} \quad (12 \div 4 = 3; 3 \times 3 = 9)$$

$$\frac{3}{4} = \frac{18}{24} \quad (24 \div 4 = 6; 6 \times 3 = 18)$$

$$\frac{3}{4} = \frac{24}{32} \quad (32 \div 4 = 8; 8 \times 3 = 24)$$

Simplifying Fractions

A fraction can be simplified to its lowest terms if its numerator and denominator share a common factor. Here are a few simple examples:

$$\frac{6}{9} = \frac{(3)(2)}{(3)(3)} = \frac{2}{3}$$

(you can "cancel" or factor out the common factor 3)

$$\frac{21}{35} = \frac{(7)(3)}{(7)(5)} = \frac{3}{5}$$

(you can factor out the common factor 7)

Before you perform any operation with a fraction, always check to see if you can simplify it first. By reducing a fraction to its lowest terms, you will also simplify whatever operation you perform on it.

Mixed Numbers and Improper Fractions

As noted earlier, a mixed number consists of a whole number along with a simple fraction. The number $4\frac{2}{3}$ is an example of a mixed number. Before combining fractions, you might need to convert mixed numbers to improper fractions. Recall that an improper fraction is a fraction where the numerator is larger than the denominator. To convert, follow these three steps:

1. Multiply the denominator of the fraction by the whole number.

2. Add the product to the numerator of the fraction.

3. Place the sum over the denominator of the fraction.

For example, here's how to convert the mixed number $4\frac{2}{3}$ to an improper fraction:

$$4\frac{2}{3} = \frac{(3)(4) + 2}{3} = \frac{14}{3}$$

To add or subtract mixed numbers, you can convert each one to an improper fraction, then find their lowest common denominator and combine them. Alternatively, you can add together the whole numbers, and add together the fractions separately. To perform multiple operations, always perform multiplication and division before you perform addition and subtraction.

A fraction that has a numerator greater than the denominator is an improper fraction. Examples of improper fractions include $\frac{3}{2}$, $\frac{12}{7}$, and $\frac{9}{5}$. Improper fractions can also be in their simplest forms when the numerator and denominator cannot be divided evenly by a number other than 1.

Improper fractions can be represented as mixed numbers and vice versa. Below are a few examples of how to rename a mixed number as an improper fraction.

EXAMPLE:

Rename $2\frac{1}{4}$ as an improper fraction.

Solution:

The whole number 2 contains 8 fourths. Add $\frac{1}{4}$ to it to write the equivalent fraction $\frac{9}{4}$.

Another way to solve this problem is to multiply the denominator of the fraction by the whole number and add the numerator.

EXAMPLE:

Rename $2\frac{1}{4}$ as an improper fraction.

Solution:

$4 \times 2 = 8 + 1 = 9$; combined with the denominator, the result is $\frac{9}{4}$.

To rename an improper fraction as a mixed number, proceed backward.

EXAMPLE:

Rename $\frac{9}{4}$ as a mixed number.

Solution:

Divide the numerator by the denominator and use the remainder (R) as the fraction numerator:

$9 \div 4 = 2$ R1 or $9 \div 4 = 2\frac{1}{4}$.

Adding and Subtracting Fractions

To add fractions with the same denominators, add the numerators and keep the common denominator.

EXAMPLE:

Add $\frac{1}{4} + \frac{3}{4} + \frac{3}{4}$.

Solution:

When the denominators are the same, add the numerators to arrive at the answer, $\frac{7}{4}$, or simplify $1\frac{3}{4}$.

To find the difference between two fractions with the same denominators, subtract the numerators, leaving the denominators alone.

EXAMPLE:

Find the difference between $\frac{7}{8}$ and $\frac{3}{8}$.

Solution:

$\frac{7}{8} - \frac{3}{8} = \frac{4}{8}$ simplified, $\frac{4}{8} = \frac{1}{2}$.

To add or subtract fractions with different denominators, you must first find the lowest common denominator, also known as the least common multiple. A common denominator is a number that can be divided by the denominators of all the fractions in the problem without a remainder. Finding the lowest common denominator is important to ensure that you have the simplest fraction. As you go through the upcoming exercises, review the section on factors and multiples to understand how to find the lowest common denominator.

EXAMPLES:

Find a common denominator for $\frac{1}{4}$ and $\frac{1}{3}$.

Solution:

Multiply the denominators to get $4 \times 3 = 12$.

12 can be divided by both 4 and 3:

$\frac{1}{4}$ is equivalent to $\frac{3}{12}$

$\frac{1}{3}$ is equivalent to $\frac{4}{12}$

We can now add the fractions because we have written equivalent fractions with a common denominator.

Therefore:

$$\frac{3}{12} + \frac{4}{12} = \frac{7}{12}$$

$$\frac{1}{4} + \frac{1}{3} = \frac{7}{12}$$

Seven-twelfths is in its simplest form because 7 and 12 do not have a whole number (other than 1) by which they are both divisible.

Add $\frac{3}{8}, \frac{5}{6}, \frac{1}{4}$, and $\frac{2}{3}$.

Solution:

Find a number into which all denominators will divide evenly. For 8, 6, 4, and 3, the lowest common denominator is 24. Now convert each fraction to an equivalent fraction having a denominator of 24:

$$\frac{3}{8} = \frac{9}{24} \quad (24 \div 8 = 3; \ 3 \times 3 = 9)$$

$$\frac{5}{6} = \frac{20}{24} \quad (24 \div 6 = 4; \ 4 \times 5 = 20)$$

$$\frac{1}{4} = \frac{6}{24} \quad (24 \div 4 = 6; \ 6 \times 1 = 6)$$

$$\frac{2}{3} = \frac{16}{24} \quad (24 \div 3 = 8; \ 8 \times 2 = 16)$$

Now add the fractions:

$$\frac{9}{24} + \frac{20}{24} + \frac{6}{24} + \frac{16}{24} = \frac{51}{24}$$

The answer, $\frac{51}{24}$, is an improperfraction. To rename the answer to a mixed number, divide the numerator by the denominator and express the remainder as a fraction.

$$\frac{51}{24} = 51 \div 24 = 2\frac{3}{24} = 2\frac{1}{8}$$

Multiplying and Dividing Fractions

When multiplying fractions, multiply numerators by numerators and denominators by denominators.

$$\frac{3}{5} \times \frac{4}{7} \times \frac{1}{5} = \frac{3 \times 4 \times 1}{5 \times 7 \times 5} = \frac{12}{175}$$

Try to work with numbers that are as small as possible. You can make numbers smaller by dividing out common factors. Do this by dividing the numerator of any one fraction and the denominator of any one fraction by the same number.

$$\frac{\overset{1}{\cancel{3}}}{\underset{2}{\cancel{4}}} \times \frac{\overset{1}{\cancel{2}}}{\underset{3}{\cancel{9}}} = \frac{1 \times 1}{2 \times 3} = \frac{1}{6}$$

In this case, we divided the numerator of the first fraction and the denominator of the second fraction by 3, while the denominator of the first fraction and the numerator of the second fraction were divided by 2.

To divide by a fraction, multiply by the reciprocal of the divisor.

$$\frac{3}{16} \div \frac{1}{8} = \frac{3}{\underset{2}{\cancel{16}}} \times \frac{\overset{1}{\cancel{8}}}{1} = \frac{3}{2} = 1\frac{1}{2}$$

Test Yourself 6

Divide out common factors wherever possible and express your answers in the simplest form. The answers will follow.

1. $\dfrac{4}{5} \times \dfrac{3}{6} =$

2. $\dfrac{2}{4} \times \dfrac{8}{12} \times \dfrac{7}{1} =$

3. $\dfrac{3}{4} \div \dfrac{3}{8} =$

4. $\dfrac{5}{2} \div \dfrac{3}{6} =$

5. $\dfrac{8}{9} \times \dfrac{3}{4} \times \dfrac{1}{2} =$

Answers:

1. $\dfrac{2}{5}$

2. $2\dfrac{1}{3}$

3. 2

4. 5

5. $\dfrac{1}{3}$

PERCENTAGES

A percentage (%) is a fraction or decimal number written in a different form. The decimal number 0.25 is written as 25%. A percentage expressed as a fraction is the number divided by 100. The last syllable of the word *percent*, *-cent*, is the name we give to one hundredth of a dollar. Think of the word *century*, which is 100 years. Both share the root *cent*. As an example, there are 100 cents in a dollar. One percent of $1.00, then, is one cent. Using decimal notation, we can write one cent as $0.01, five cents as $0.05, twenty-five cents as $0.25, and so forth. Instead of saying that 25 cents is equal to 25 hundredths of a dollar, we use the word percent.

The information in this section will help you understand the relationship between decimals, fractions, and percentages and convert numbers from one form to another.

Converting Between Decimals, Fractions, and Percentages

1. To change a decimal to a percentage, add the % sign and multiply by 100.

   Example: $0.25 = 0.25\% \times 100 = 25\%$

2. The fraction bar in a fraction means "divided by." To change a fraction to a decimal, follow through on the division.

   Example: $\dfrac{4}{5} = 4 \div 5 = 0.8$

3. To change a fraction to a percentage, multiply by 100 and add the percent sign (%).

   Example: $\dfrac{1}{4} \times 100 = 25\%$

4. To change a percentage to a decimal, remove the percent sign (%) and divide the number by 100.

   Example: $25\% = \dfrac{25}{100} = 0.25$

5. To change a percentage to a fraction, remove the % sign and use that number as your numerator, with 100 as your denominator.

   Example: $25\% = \dfrac{25}{100} = \dfrac{1}{4}$

Percentage is not limited to comparing other numbers to 100. You can divide any number into hundredths and talk about percentage.

EXAMPLE:

Find 1% of 200.

Solution:

1% of 200 is 1/100, or 0.01, of 200.
Using decimal notation, we can calculate one percent of 200 by multiplying 200 by 0.01:

$$200 \times 0.01 = 2$$

Similarly, we can find a percentage of any number we choose by multiplying it by the correct decimal notation. For example:

Five percent of 50: $0.05 \times 50 = 2.5$

Three percent of 150: $0.03 \times 150 = 4.5$

Ten percent of 60: $0.10 \times 60 = 6$

Not all percentage measurements are between one percent and 100 percent. You might need to consider less than one percent of something, especially if that something is very large.

For example, if you were handed a book 1,000 pages long and told to read one percent of it in five minutes, how much would you have to read?

$$1000 \times 0.01 = 10 \text{ pages}$$

Quite an assignment! You might bargain to read one half of one percent or one-tenth of one percent in the five minutes allotted to you.

Using decimal notation, we write one-tenth of one percent as 0.001, the decimal number for one thousandth. If you remember that a percent is one hundredth of

something, you can see that one tenth of that percent is equivalent to one thousandth of the whole.

In percent notation, one tenth of one percent is 0.1%. On high school entrance exams, students often mistakenly think that 0.1% is equal to 0.1. As you know, 0.1% is equal to 0.001.

Here are some common percentage and fractional equivalents you should remember:

- Ten percent (10%) is one tenth $\left(\dfrac{1}{10} \right)$ or 0.10.

- Twelve and one-half percent (12.5%) is one eighth $\left(\dfrac{1}{8} \right)$ or 0.125.

- Twenty percent (20%) is one fifth $\left(\dfrac{1}{5} \right)$ or 0.20.

- Twenty-five percent (25%) is one quarter $\left(\dfrac{1}{4} \right)$ or 0.25.

- Thirty-three and one-third percent $\left(33\dfrac{1}{3}\% \right)$ is one third $\left(\dfrac{1}{3} \right)$ or $0.\overline{333}$.

- Fifty percent (50%) is one half $\left(\dfrac{1}{2} \right)$ or 0.50.

- Sixty-six and two-thirds percent $\left(66\dfrac{2}{3}\% \right)$ is two thirds $\left(\dfrac{2}{3} \right)$ or $0.\overline{666}$.

 TIP

When multiplying by percentages, students frequently mix up 0.1 and 0.1%. If you are trying to find 0.1% of something, you must multiply by 0.001, not 0.1, to get the correct answer.

Scan this QR code to learn more about percentage problems.

Test Yourself 7

Rename each fraction, first as a decimal and then as a percent. The answers will follow.

1. $\dfrac{2}{4} =$
2. $\dfrac{7}{8} =$
3. $\dfrac{5}{6} =$
4. $\dfrac{3}{4} =$
5. $\dfrac{2}{3} =$

6. $\dfrac{3}{5} =$
7. $\dfrac{4}{10} =$
8. $\dfrac{1}{4} =$
9. $\dfrac{2}{5} =$
10. $\dfrac{1}{8} =$

Answers:

1. $0.5 = 50\%$
2. $0.875 = 87\dfrac{1}{2}\%$
3. $0.833 = 83\dfrac{1}{3}\%$
4. $0.75 = 75\%$
5. $0.666 = 66\dfrac{2}{3}\%$
6. $0.60 = 60\%$
7. $0.40 = 40\%$
8. $0.25 = 25\%$
9. $0.40 = 40\%$
10. $0.125 = 12\dfrac{1}{2}\%$

Percentages over 100%

Sometimes, we are concerned with more than 100% of something. When things are growing, or increasing in size or amount, we may want to compare their new size to the size they once were. For example, suppose we measured the heights of three plants to be 6 inches, 9 inches, and 12 inches one week and discover a week later that the first plant is still 6 inches tall, but the second and third ones are now 18 inches tall.

The 6-inch plant grew zero percent because it didn't grow at all. The second plant added 100% to its size. It doubled in height. The third plant added 50% to its height.

We can also say:

The first plant is 100% of its original height.

The second plant grew to 200% of its original height.

The third plant grew to 150% of its original height.

Solving Percentage Problems

A question involving percentages might involve one of these three tasks:

- Finding the percentage of a number
- Finding a number when a percentage is given
- Finding what percentage one number is of another

Regardless of the task, three distinct values are involved: the part, the whole, and the percentage. Often, the problem will give you two of the three numbers, and your job is to find the missing value. To work with percentages, use the following formula:

$$\text{percentage} = \frac{\text{part}}{\text{whole}} \times 100$$

Once again, knowing any two of those values allows you to determine the third.

Finding the Percentage

30 is what percent of 50?

In this question, 50 is the whole, and 30 is the part. Your task is to find the missing percent:

$$\text{percentage} = \frac{30}{50} \times 100$$
$$= 60\%$$

Finding the Part

What number is 25% of 80?

In this question, 80 is the whole, and 25 is the percentage. Your task is to find the part:

$$25\% = \frac{\text{part}}{80} \times 100$$

In this situation, it can be helpful to change the percentage into its decimal form (.25), which then lets you drop the 100 from the equation or to represent the percentage as a fraction, in this case $\frac{25}{100}$. That gives us a new form of the equation:

$$\frac{25}{100} = \frac{\text{part}}{80}$$

To solve for the missing part, cross multiply 25 with 80 and 100 with the missing part. That yields the following:

$$100(\text{part}) = 25(80)$$
$$100(\text{part}) = 2000$$
$$\text{part} = \frac{2000}{100}$$
$$\text{part} = 20$$

25% of 80 is 20. Because of the values used, there are any number of ways you could have come to that solution faster, such as by simplifying the left fraction to $\frac{1}{4}$ or calculating $80 \div 4$ or $80 \times .25$, but it's important that you see the full process. Let's look at how you can streamline your work in the next example.

Finding the Whole

75% of what number is 150?

In this question, 150 is the part, and 75 is the percentage. Your task is to find the whole. Here's the streamlined equation:

$$\frac{75}{100} = \frac{150}{\text{whole}}$$

Here, you can simplify the fraction on the left to $\frac{3}{4}$ and then cross multiply:

$$\frac{3}{4} = \frac{150}{\text{whole}}$$
$$\text{whole}(3) = 150(4)$$

Then, multiply the two diagonally situated numbers you know: $150 \times 4 = 600$. Finally, divide 600 by 3, which equals 200. 75% of 200 is 150.

$$\text{whole} = 200$$

Percent Increase and Decrease

You've likely encountered the concept of percent change with investment interest, sales tax, and discount pricing. Percent change always relates to the value before the change.

 **TIP**

You can find a percentage with the following equation:

$percentage = \left(\dfrac{part}{whole} \right) \times 100$. That equation can be flipped around algebraically to find

that $part = whole \times \left(\dfrac{percentage}{100} \right)$ or $whole = part \div \left(\dfrac{percentage}{100} \right)$.

Here are two examples:

> 10 increased by what percent is 12?
>
> The amount of the increase is 2.
>
> Compare the change (2) to the original number (10).
>
> The change in percent is $\frac{2}{10}$, or 20%.

Example:

> 12 decreased by what percent is 10?
>
> The amount of the decrease is 2.
>
> Compare the change (2) to the original number (12).
>
> The change is $\frac{2}{12}$, or $\frac{1}{6}$ (or 16.66%).

Notice that the percent increase from 10 to 12 (20%) is not the same as the percent decrease from 12 to 10 (16.66%). That's because the original number (before the change) is different in the two questions.

Percent-change problems typically involve tax, interest, profit, discount, or weight. In handling these problems, you might need to calculate more than one percent change.

Let's look at an example problem.

EXAMPLE:

A computer originally priced at $500 is discounted by 10%, then by another 10%. What is the price of the computer after the second discount, to the nearest dollar?

- **A.** $400
- **B.** $405
- **C.** $425
- **D.** $450
- **E.** $465

Solution:

The correct answer is B. After the first 10% discount, the price was $450 ($500 minus 10% of $500). After the second discount, which is calculated based on the $450 price, the price of the computer is $405 ($450 minus 10% of $450).

RATIOS AND PROPORTIONS

A ratio expresses proportion or comparative size—the size of one quantity relative to the size of another. Write a ratio by placing a colon (:) between the two numbers. Read the colon as the word "to." For example, read the ratio 3:5 as "3 to 5." As with fractions, you can reduce ratios to lowest terms by canceling common factors. For example, given a menagerie of 28 pets that includes 12 cats and 16 dogs:

The ratio of cats to dogs is 12:16, or 3:4 ("3 to 4").

The ratio of dogs to cats is 16:12, or 4:3 ("4 to 3").

The ratio of cats to the total number of pets is 12:28, or 3:7 ("3 to 7").

The ratio of dogs to the total number of pets is 16:28, or 4:7 ("4 to 7").

Another way to think about a ratio is as a fraction. A proportion is an equation relating two ratios; it is expressed by equating two fractions, say $\frac{1}{2} = \frac{4}{8}$. Another way of saying that two ratios (or fractions) are equivalent is to say that they are *proportionate*. For example, the ratio 12:16 is proportionate to the ratio 3:4. Similarly, the fraction $\frac{12}{16}$ is proportionate to the fraction $\frac{3}{4}$.

Proportions are formulated when one ratio is known and one of the two quantities in an equivalent ratio is unknown. They arise when changing units of measurement or scaling up a ratio, like in a recipe, among other applications. Since you can express any ratio as a fraction, you can set two equivalent ratios (also called proportionate ratios) equal to each other as fractions. The ratio 16:28 is proportionate to the ratio 4:7 because $\frac{16}{28} = \frac{4}{7}$.

If one of the four terms is missing from the equation (the proportion), you can solve for the missing term using the same method that you learned for solving percent problems:

1. Simplify the known fraction, if possible.
2. Cross-multiply the numbers you know.
3. Divide the product by the third number you know.

For example, if the ratio 10:15 is proportionate to 14:*x*, you can find the missing number by first setting up the following proportion:

$$\frac{10}{15} = \frac{14}{x}$$

Reading the ratio 10:15 as a fraction, simplify it to $\frac{2}{3}$.

$$\frac{2}{3} = \frac{14}{x}$$

Then, cross multiply the numbers you know: $3 \times 14 = 42$. Finally, divide by the third number you know: $42 \div 2 = 21$. The ratio 10:15 is equivalent to the ratio 14:21.

You'll often encounter proportion problems as word problems. Word problems will require you to parse out the numbers and then set up the ratios so that they are proportionate in order to solve for the missing term. Let's look at a sample problem.

EXAMPLE:

Suppose there are 2 hockey sticks for every 5 pucks in the storage locker room. If the last count was 60 pucks, how many hockey sticks are in the storage room?

Solution:

Let *h* denote the number of hockey sticks in the storage room. Here, we know that there are 2 hockey sticks for every 5 pucks. We know that there's a total of 60 pucks, but we don't know how many hockey sticks there are. However, because the number of hockey sticks is proportional to the number of pucks, we can scale up the ratio we do know to solve for the number of hockey sticks.

Set up the proportion as follows:

$$\frac{2}{5} = \frac{h}{60}$$
$$5h = 120$$
$$h = 24$$

Test Yourself 9

Write each problem as a ratio. The answers will follow.

1. If Imani can read 10 pages in 15 minutes, how long does it take her to read 40 pages?

2. At an elementary school, there are 17 students to every 1 teacher. There are a total of 425 students. How many teachers are there?

3. At an aquarium, there are 14 penguins for every 2 octopi. If there are 8 octopi, how many penguins are there?

4. The local grocery store has three times as many cashiers as janitors. If there are 21 cashiers, how many janitors are there?

5. For every day of rain in Los Angeles, there are 7 days of sunshine. If there were 315 days of sunshine, how many days of rain were there?

Answers:

1. 60 minutes
2. 25 teachers
3. 56 penguins
4. 7 janitors
5. 45 days of rain

PROBABILITY

Probability refers to the statistical chances of an event occurring (or not occurring). By definition, probability ranges from 0 to 1. Probability is never negative, and it is never greater than 1.

Here's the basic formula for determining probability:

$$\text{Probability} = \frac{\text{number of desired outcomes}}{\text{total possible outcomes}}$$

Probability can be expressed as a fraction, a percent, or a decimal number.

Determining Probability (Single Event)

Probability plays an integral role in games of chance. In the throw of a single die, for example, the probability of rolling a 5 is "one in six," or $\frac{1}{6}$, or 16.66%. Of course, the probability of rolling any other number is the same. A standard deck of 52 playing cards contains 12 face cards. The probability of selecting a face card from a full deck is $\frac{12}{52}$ or $\frac{3}{13}$. The probability of selecting a queen from a full deck is $\frac{1}{13}$.

Determining Probability (Two Events)

To determine probability involving two or more events, you must distinguish probabilities involving independent events from an event that is dependent on another one.

Two events are independent if neither event affects the probability that the other will occur. The events may involve the random selection of one object from *each of two or more groups*. Or they may involve the random selection of one object from a group, then *replacing* it and selecting again (as in a "second round" or "another turn" of a game).

In either scenario, to find the probability of two events BOTH occurring, multiply together their individual probabilities:

probability of event 1 occurring
×
probability of event 2 occurring
=
probability of both events occurring

For example, assume that you randomly select one letter from each of two sets: {A, B} and {C, D, E}. The probability of selecting A and C $= \frac{1}{2} \times \frac{1}{3} = \frac{1}{6}$.

To calculate the probability that two events will NOT both occur, subtract the probability of both events occurring from 1.

EXAMPLE:

If you randomly select one candy from a jar containing two cherry candies, two licorice candies, and one peppermint candy, what is the probability of selecting a cherry candy?

A. $\frac{1}{6}$

B. $\frac{1}{3}$

C. $\frac{2}{5}$

D. $\frac{3}{5}$

E. $\frac{7}{10}$

The correct answer is C. There are two ways among five possible occurrences that a cherry candy will be selected. Thus, the probability of selecting a cherry candy is $\frac{2}{5}$.

For dependent probability, two distinct events might be related in that one event affects the probability of the other one occurring—for example, randomly selecting one object from a group, then selecting a second object from the same group without replacing the first selection. Removing one object from the group increases the odds of selecting any particular object from those that remain.

For example, assume that you randomly select one letter from the set {A, B, C, D}. Then, from the remaining three letters, you select another letter. What is the probability of selecting both A and B? To answer this question, you need to consider each of the two selections separately.

In the first selection, the probability of selecting either A or B is $\frac{2}{4}$. But the probability of selecting the second of the two is $\frac{1}{3}$. Why? Because after the first selection, only *three* letters remain from which to select. Since the question asks for the chances of selecting both A and B (as opposed to either one), multiply the two individual probabilities: $\frac{2}{4} \times \frac{1}{3} = \frac{2}{12}$, or $\frac{1}{6}$.

A gaming die is a cube with numbers 1–6 on its faces, each number on a different face. In a roll of two gaming dice, what is the probability that the two numbers facing up will total 12?

A. $\dfrac{1}{64}$

B. $\dfrac{1}{36}$

C. $\dfrac{1}{12}$

D. $\dfrac{1}{9}$

E. $\dfrac{1}{6}$

The correct answer is B. The only two-number combination on the dice that can total 12 is 6 + 6. The probability of rolling 6 on both dice is $\dfrac{1}{6} \times \dfrac{1}{6} = \dfrac{1}{36}$.

MEASUREMENT CONVERSIONS

A common real-world application of ratios and proportions is converting measurements from one form to another. While the US has its own standard system of measurement, most of the world uses the metric system. As you've probably noticed, some things are commonly expressed in standard units, like miles per hour in speed limits or two cups of flour in a recipe. If you run track or cross country, you've probably tried a 100-meter dash or a 5K, which are metric units. Because we see both systems used in different parts of daily life, it's helpful to know how to convert between the two systems.

Measurement conversions are also helpful when you want to convert from one unit of measurement to another within the same system. For example, you wouldn't say that you've walked 5,280 feet to the grocery store. Instead, you would express that distance as a mile, since there are 5,280 feet in a mile. Conceptually, we can better understand longer distances in terms of

larger units rather than smaller units. If you're solving a problem and you notice that the figure could be more efficiently expressed in a different unit, you'll want to convert that figure to the most practical unit.

On the exam, you might be expected to know certain common conversions. For example, knowing how many feet are in a yard or a mile would be advantageous. You should also know how many cups are in a pint, pints in a quart, quarts in a gallon, and so on. Similarly, knowing that the metric system operates on powers of ten will allow you to quickly convert from millimeters to meters or from meters to kilometers. Some conversions, however, are less intuitive, especially when going from the US system to the metric system and vice versa. For example, converting from Fahrenheit to Celsius when discussing temperature requires you to memorize the formula: $(F - 32) \times 5 \div 9 = C$. In more complex conversions, you'll likely be given the necessary conversion factors. Here, we'll cover the basics for how to perform common unit conversions.

METRIC SYSTEM MEASUREMENTS		
Prefix	Power	Meaning
kilo	10^3	1,000
hecto	10^2	100
deca	10^1	10
Base Unit	10^0	1
deci	10^{-1}	0.1
centi	10^{-2}	0.01
milli	10^{-3}	0.001
micro	10^{-6}	0.000001
nano	10^{-9}	0.000000001

Let's start with the metric system. Since the metric system is based on powers of 10, converting units expressed in the metric system is a matter of appropriately moving the decimal point. For example, 300 cm = 3 m because 1 cm = 10^{-2} m. The exponent indicates the number of decimal places we're working with and whether those places are bigger than one or smaller than one. Positive

exponents indicate big numbers greater than one, while negative exponents indicate much smaller parts of numbers that are less than one. (We'll cover this concept in more detail in the next chapter.) In this case, therefore, multiplying both sides by 300 yields the result.

Likewise, $400\,dm = 40\,m$ since $1\,dm = 10^{-1}\,m$. In both cases, note that the conversion only involved moving the decimal point to the *left* the number of places indicated by the power without the negative sign (2 and 1, respectively). This is always true when converting a unit lower on the table to one higher up. The exact opposite is true if you are converting a unit higher on the table to one lower. For instance, $2\,km = 200\,hm$ because $1\,km = 100\,hm$.

Converting units in the US customary system is slightly more involved only because the units are not based on powers of 10. Here, the key is to set up products of fractions that show the original units canceling and the new units remaining in the final product. For example, to convert 3.5 feet to inches, we use the conversion factor 1 foot = 12 inches in the following computation:

$$3.5\text{ feet} = \frac{3.5\text{ feet}}{1} \times \frac{12\text{ inches}}{1\text{ foot}} = \frac{3.5\text{ feet}}{1} \times \frac{12\text{ inches}}{1\text{ foot}} = (3.5) \times (12)\text{ inches} = 42\text{ inches}$$

This works because the fraction $\frac{12\text{ inches}}{1\text{ foot}} = 1$.

Here's a list of common conversions for reference:

- 1 foot = 12 inches
- 1 yard = 3 feet = 36 inches
- 1 mile = 5,280 feet
- 1 lb. = 16 oz
- 1 ton = 2,000 lb.

- 1 gallon = 4 quarts = 16 cups
- 1 cup = 8 ounces

Converting units of speed involves making *two* conversions—one for the numerator and one for the denominator. For example, to convert 85 miles per hour to *feet per minute*, we use the conversion factors 1 mile = 5,280 feet and 1 hour = 60 minutes and perform the following computation:

$$\frac{85\text{ miles}}{1\text{ hour}} = \frac{85\text{ miles}}{1\text{ hour}} \times \frac{5,280\text{ feet}}{1\text{ mile}} \times \frac{1\text{ hour}}{60\text{ minutes}} = \frac{85 \times 5,280}{60}\text{ feet per minute}$$

You can also convert between the metric and US systems, but you will need to use established conversion factors (like $1\,m \approx 3.28$ feet) to do so. In this case, you'll likely be given the necessary conversion factors.

Test Yourself 10

Solve each conversion problem. The answers will follow.

1. Keisha's doctor says she should be drinking 11.5 cups of water per day. How many ounces of water should she drink per day?

2. Haziel is 5 feet, 8 inches tall. How tall is she in inches?

3. Angel's dad drives 15 miles to work one way. What is the length of his commute in feet?

4. Ian's dog weighed in at 67 pounds at the vet. What is the dog's weight in ounces?

5. Afi's hair is 400 millimeters long. How long is her hair in meters?

Answers:

1. 92 ounces
2. 68 inches
3. 158,400 feet
4. 1,072 ounces
5. 0.4 meters

SUMMING IT UP

- If you are having difficulties with any mathematics topic, talk with a teacher or refer to any of your math textbooks.

- Use the exercises in this chapter to determine what you DON'T know well and concentrate your study on those areas.

- Review the math symbols covered in this chapter so that you're prepared when you encounter them in math problems.

- Know the different types of numbers: whole numbers, integers, rational numbers, irrational numbers, and signed numbers.

- Using central tendency terms—mean, median, and mode—can help you summarize and describe a set of data.

- Properties describe how numbers behave in consistent and predictable ways, which simplifies the process of solving math problems. These will be especially important for solving algebraic equations.

- When solving equations, use the mnemonic device "Please excuse my dear Aunt Sally" to remember the order of operations:

  - Parentheses
  - Exponents (and Square Roots)
  - Multiplication
  - Division
  - Addition
  - Subtraction

- Decimals represent parts of numbers. Everything to the left of a decimal point is a whole number and everything to the right of a decimal point represents a part of the whole.

- A factor is a number that can be divided into a whole number evenly without leaving a remainder. Multiples are similar to factors in that they are whole numbers into which a number can be divided evenly. Being able to determine the greatest common factor and least common multiple of a set of numbers is important for solving problems with fractions.

- A fraction is a part of a whole and consists of both a numerator and a denominator. Proper fractions are those in which the numerator is smaller than the denominator and improper fractions are those in which the numerator is greater than the denominator.

- Percentages are fractions or decimals written in a different form. They represent parts of numbers, and you can convert between percentages, fractions, and decimals. Percentage problems may require you to find the percentage, the part, the whole, or the percent increase or decrease.

- Ratios express the size of one quantity relative to the size of another. Proportions are equations relating two ratios, expressed by equating two fractions.

- Questions centered on probability may ask you to calculate the odds of performing a certain task by dividing the number of ways it could happen by the total number of possible outcomes. Similar questions might require you to identify patterns and determine relationships to anticipate the next item in a series.

- Make sure you are familiar with common, everyday conversions, like feet to a mile, ounces in a pound, quarts in a gallon, etc. Also, remember that the metric system is based on powers of 10, which should simplify the process of conversions. For conversions between the US system and the metric system, you will likely be given the conversion factors on the exam.

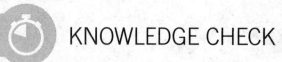

KNOWLEDGE CHECK

BASIC MATHEMATICS

50 Questions—40 Minutes

> **Directions:** In the following questions, work out each problem and mark the letter that corresponds to the correct answer. The answers will follow.

1. $(-12) + (+4) =$

   A. -16

   B. -8

   C. -3

   D. $+8$

   E. $+16$

2. $(-22) - (-18) =$

   A. -40

   B. -30

   C. -4

   D. $+6$

   E. $+13$

3. Adam scored 84, 65, 76, 76, 92, 75, and 85 on his math tests. What was his median grade?

   A. 75

   B. 76

   C. 78

   D. 80

   E. 84

4. Six children sold the following numbers of boxes of cookies: 42, 35, 28, 30, 24, 27. What was the mean number of boxes sold?

   A. 26

   B. 29

   C. 30

   D. 31

   E. 32

5. In the expression, $166 \div 42 + (17 \times 2) - 7^2$, what operation will you perform first to simplify?

   A. $166 \div 42$

   B. $42 + (17 \times 2)$

   C. -7^2

   D. 17×2

   E. $42 + 17$

6. $6 \times 4 \div 8 + 8^2 \div 2 - 5 =$

   A. -30

   B. 20

   C. 24

   D. 28

   E. 30

7. $(17 - 10 \div 5) + 6 \times 3$

   A. 0

   B. 14

   C. 33

   D. 40

   E. 42

8. $144 \div 12 + (-4 + 1) \times -10 =$

   A. -42

   B. 9

   C. 36

   D. 40

   E. 42

9. $(6 \times 10 \div 15) - (3^2 + 12) =$

   A. −35

   B. −15

   C. 5

   D. 12

   E. 14

10. $-2(64 \div 2^3) + 10 - 3^2 =$

    A. −15

    B. −5

    C. 10

    D. 15

    E. 20

11. $3.41 + 5.6 + 0.873 =$

    A. 4.843

    B. 9.883

    C. 15.264

    D. 16.863

    E. 17.743

12. $3.7\overline{)2,339.86}$

    A. 62.34

    B. 63.24

    C. 632.4

    D. 634.4

    E. 642.3

13. $\$59.60 \div \$0.40 =$

    A. 0.149

    B. 1.49

    C. 14.9

    D. 19.4

    E. 149

14. $0.3 \times 0.08 =$

    A. 0.0024

    B. 0.024

    C. 0.240

    D. 2.40

    E. 24.0

15. The greatest common factor of 24 and 12 is

    A. 2

    B. 4

    C. 6

    D. 12

    E. 16

16. The greatest common factor of 10 and 25 is

    A. 2

    B. 5

    C. 10

    D. 15

    E. 25

17. The greatest common factor of 6 and 9 is

    A. 2

    B. 3

    C. 6

    D. 9

    E. 18

18. The least common multiple of 4 and 14 is

    A. 14

    B. 16

    C. 28

    D. 42

    E. 56

19. $\frac{8}{15} \times \frac{3}{4} =$

A. $\frac{1}{5}$

B. $\frac{3}{10}$

C. $\frac{2}{5}$

D. $\frac{3}{5}$

E. $\frac{4}{5}$

20. $\frac{3}{4} + \frac{3}{8} =$

A. $\frac{7}{8}$

B. $\frac{8}{9}$

C. $1\frac{1}{8}$

D. $1\frac{3}{8}$

E. $1\frac{1}{2}$

21. $45,286$

    $\times \quad 4\frac{1}{5}$

    _____

A. $190,021\frac{1}{5}$

B. $190,201\frac{1}{5}$

C. $190,202\frac{2}{5}$

D. $190,204\frac{1}{5}$

E. $190,234$

22. $4\frac{1}{3} \overline{)\frac{1}{4}}$

A. $\frac{3}{52}$

B. $\frac{5}{52}$

C. $\frac{12}{52}$

D. $\frac{20}{52}$

E. $17\frac{1}{3}$

23. $\frac{1}{9} \times \frac{2}{3} \times \frac{7}{8} =$

A. $\frac{6}{108}$

B. $\frac{7}{108}$

C. $\frac{12}{52}$

D. $\frac{15}{52}$

E. $\frac{14}{27}$

24. $8\frac{1}{6}$

    $-5\frac{2}{3}$

    _____

A. 2

B. $2\frac{1}{3}$

C. $2\frac{1}{2}$

D. $3\frac{1}{6}$

E. $3\frac{2}{3}$

25.

$$3\frac{1}{4}$$
$$4\frac{1}{8}$$
$$+\,4\frac{1}{2}$$

A. $11\frac{5}{8}$

B. $11\frac{3}{4}$

C. $11\frac{7}{8}$

D. 12

E. $12\frac{1}{4}$

26. $5\frac{1}{4} \times 2\frac{2}{7} =$

A. $10\frac{3}{28}$

B. 11

C. $11\frac{4}{7}$

D. $11\frac{5}{28}$

E. 12

27. $\frac{3}{4}\overline{\smash{\big)}\,\frac{9}{16}}$

A. $\frac{27}{64}$

B. $\frac{7}{16}$

C. $\frac{5}{8}$

D. $\frac{3}{4}$

E. $\frac{1}{2}$

28.

$$10\frac{2}{3}$$
$$-\,9\frac{1}{2}$$

A. $\frac{13}{32}$

B. $1\frac{1}{6}$

C. $1\frac{1}{3}$

D. $1\frac{1}{2}$

E. $1\frac{3}{4}$

29. 10% of 32 =

A. 3

B. 3.2

C. 3.5

D. 4

E. 4.2

30. 8 is 25% of what number?

A. 16

B. 24

C. 32

D. 40

E. 48

31. 12 is what percent of 24?

A. 12%

B. 24%

C. 30%

D. 50%

E. 60%

32. 20% of 360 =

    A. 72

    B. 75

    C. 80

    D. 90

    E. 100

33. 5 is what percent of 60?

    A. 8%

    B. $8\frac{1}{3}$%

    C. $8\frac{2}{3}$%

    D. $8\frac{3}{4}$%

    E. 9%

34. A smartphone originally priced at $1,200 is discounted by 10%, then by another 10%. What is the price of the smartphone after the second discount, to the nearest dollar?

    A. $960

    B. $965

    C. $972

    D. $978

    E. $980

35. A library contains 600 books on arts and crafts. If this is 2% of the total number of books on the shelves, how many books does the library own?

    A. 12,000

    B. 30,000

    C. 40,000

    D. 60,000

    E. 100,000

36. During a sale, the price of a computer was discounted from $750 to $600. By what percent was the price decreased?

    A. 15%

    B. 20%

    C. 22%

    D. 25%

    E. 30%

37. Maurice sold 24 health club memberships this week. If he sold 18 club memberships last week, his sales this week are what percent higher than his sales last week?

    A. 18%

    B. 24%

    C. 25%

    D. $33\frac{1}{3}$%

    E. 36%

38. Duncan purchases $500 worth of cryptocurrency. The cryptocurrency's value rises by 20% during the first week, but then falls by 20% during the following week. What is the net percent change in the cryptocurrency's value?

    A. The value remains the same.

    B. The value increases by 2%.

    C. The value increases by 4%.

    D. The value decreases by 4%.

    E. The value decreases by 1%.

39. A recipe for 6 quarts of punch calls for $\frac{3}{4}$ cups of sugar. How much sugar is needed for 9 quarts of punch?

A. $\frac{5}{8}$ of a cup

B. $\frac{7}{8}$ of a cup

C. $1\frac{1}{8}$ cups

D. 2 cups

E. $2\frac{1}{4}$ cups

40. A house plan uses the scale $\frac{1}{4}$ inch = 1 foot, and in the drawing the living room is 7 inches long. If the scale changes to 1 inch = 1 foot, what will the length of the living room be in the new drawing?

A. 18 inches

B. 28 inches

C. 30 inches

D. 32 inches

E. 36 inches

41. The scale of a certain map is 4 inches = 32 miles. The number of inches that would represent 80 miles is

A. 8

B. 10

C. 12

D. 14

E. 16

42. A recipe calls for $1\frac{1}{2}$ cups of sugar. It is necessary to make eight times the recipe for a holiday supper. If 2 cups of sugar equal 1 pound, how many pounds of sugar will be needed to make the recipe?

A. 4

B. 6

C. 8

D. 10

E. 12

43. Suppose you roll a fair 6-sided die three times in succession and record the result each time. What is the probability that you do *not* roll three 5s?

A. $\frac{1}{216}$

B. $\frac{101}{216}$

C. $\frac{125}{216}$

D. $\frac{35}{36}$

E. $\frac{215}{216}$

44. A recipe calls for basil, thyme, and oregano in a ratio of 4:2:3. If 12 ounces of oregano are used, how much basil is used?

A. 12 ounces

B. 14 ounces

C. 16 ounces

D. 18 ounces

E. 20 ounces

45. A vase contains 14 carnations and 11 daisies. If two flowers are selected at random without replacement, what is the probability of selecting two daisies?

A. $\frac{11}{25} \times \frac{10}{25}$

B. $\frac{11}{25} \times \frac{11}{25}$

C. $\frac{11}{14} \times \frac{10}{14}$

D. $\frac{11}{25} \times \frac{10}{24}$

E. $\frac{11}{25} \times \frac{11}{24}$

46. How many yards of ribbon will it take to make 45 badges if each badge uses 4 inches of ribbon?

A. 5

B. 9

C. 11

D. 12

E. 15

47. If an inch of wire costs $0.20, how much will 5.25 feet of wire cost?

A. $0.87

B. $2.40

C. $12.60

D. $16.40

E. $63.00

48. A bag of sugar weighs 2.5 kg. What is its weight in grams?

A. 2.5 grams

B. 25 grams

C. 250 grams

D. 2,500 grams

E. 25,000 grams

49. A car is driving 60 mph. What is the speed of the car in feet per minute?

A. 4,000

B. 4,500

C. 5,000

D. 5,280

E. 6,000

50. If one pound equals 16 ounces, how many pounds are in 820 ounces?

A. $48\frac{1}{2}$

B. $51\frac{1}{4}$

C. $52\frac{1}{2}$

D. 54

E. $56\frac{1}{2}$

ANSWER KEY AND EXPLANATIONS

1. B	11. B	21. B	31. D	41. B
2. C	12. C	22. A	32. A	42. B
3. B	13. E	23. B	33. B	43. E
4. D	14. B	24. C	34. C	44. C
5. D	15. D	25. C	35. B	45. D
6. E	16. B	26. E	36. B	46. A
7. C	17. B	27. D	37. D	47. C
8. E	18. C	28. B	38. D	48. D
9. A	19. C	29. B	39. C	49. D
10. A	20. C	30. C	40. B	50. B

1. **The correct answer is B.** When adding two numbers of unlike sign, subtract and assign the sign of the larger number.

2. **The correct answer is C.** Minus negative becomes plus positive. The problem then reads:

$$(-22) + (+18) = -4$$

3. **The correct answer is B.** Rewrite these 7 scores in order from least to greatest: 65, 75, 76, 76, 84, 85, 92. The median, or middle value, is 76.

4. **The correct answer is D.** To find the mean, add all the numbers and divide the sum by the number of terms.

$$42 + 35 + 28 + 30 + 24 + 27 = 186$$
$$186 \div 6 = 31$$

5. **The correct answer is D.** Remember PEMDAS, the mnemonic device for remembering the order of operations, and you will know that the first step is to solve what is inside the parentheses first. 17 × 2 is the expression inside the parentheses, so it is the first thing you should solve.

6. **The correct answer is E.** Remember the order of operations as you solve the problem:

$$6 \times 4 \div 8 + 8^2 \div 2 - 5$$
$$6 \times 4 \div 8 + 64 \div 2 - 5$$
$$24 \div 8 + 64 \div 2 - 5$$
$$3 + 64 \div 2 - 5$$
$$3 + 32 - 5$$
$$35 - 5$$
$$= 30$$

7. **The correct answer is C.** Remember the order of operations as you work through the problem:

$$(17 - 10 \div 5) + 6 \times 3$$
$$(17 - 2) + 6 \times 3$$
$$15 + 6 \times 3$$
$$15 + 18$$
$$= 33$$

8. **The correct answer is E.** Remember the order of operations as you solve the problem:

$$144 \div 12 + (-4 + 1) \times -10$$
$$144 \div 12 + (-3) \times -10$$
$$12 + (-3) \times -10$$
$$12 + 30$$
$$= 42$$

9. **The correct answer is A.** Remember the order of operations as you work through the problem:

$$(6 \times 10 \div 15) - (3^3 + 12)$$
$$(6 \times 10 \div 15) - (27 + 12)$$
$$(60 \div 15) - (27 + 12)$$
$$4 - (27 + 12)$$
$$4 - (39)$$
$$= -35$$

10. **The correct answer is A.** Remember the order of operations as you proceed through the problem:

$$-2(64 \div 2^3) + (10 - 3^2) =$$
$$-2(64 \div 8) + (10 - 9)$$
$$-2(8) + (10 - 9)$$
$$-16 + (10 - 9)$$
$$-16 + 1$$
$$= -15$$

11. **The correct answer is B.**

$$\begin{array}{r} 3.410 \\ 5.600 \\ + 0.873 \\ \hline 9.883 \end{array}$$

12. **The correct answer is C.**

$$\begin{array}{r} 63\,2.39 \approx 632.4 \\ 3.7\overline{)2339.8\,60} \\ \underline{222} \\ 119 \\ \underline{111} \\ 88 \\ 74 \\ \hline 146 \\ \underline{111} \\ 350 \\ \underline{333} \\ \overline{17} \end{array}$$

13. **The correct answer is E.**

$$\begin{array}{r} 1\,49 \\ 0.40\overline{)59.60} \\ \underline{40} \\ \overline{19}\,6 \\ \underline{16}\,0 \\ \overline{3}\,60 \\ 3\,60 \end{array}$$

14. **The correct answer is B.** First multiply 8 and 3, then add up the spaces to the right of the decimal to solve. $0.3 \times 0.08 = 0.024$.

15. **The correct answer is D.** The greatest number by which both 12 and 24 can be divided is 12.

16. **The correct answer is B.** The greatest number by which both 10 and 25 can be divided is 5.

17. **The correct answer is B.** The greatest number by which both 6 and 9 can be divided is 3.

18. **The correct answer is C.** The lowest multiple that both 4 and 14 share is 28.

19. **The correct answer is C.**

$$\frac{\cancel{8}^2}{\cancel{15}_5} \times \frac{\cancel{3}^1}{\cancel{4}_1} = \frac{2}{5}$$

20. **The correct answer is C.**

$$\begin{array}{r} \dfrac{3}{4} = \dfrac{6}{8} \\ + \dfrac{3}{8} = \dfrac{3}{8} \\ \hline \dfrac{9}{8} = 1\dfrac{1}{8} \end{array}$$

21. **The correct answer is B.**

$$\frac{1}{5} = 0.20$$

$$\begin{array}{r} 45{,}286 \\ \times \quad 4.20 \\ \hline 905{,}720 \\ 181{,}144 \\ \hline 190{,}201.20 = 190{,}201\dfrac{1}{5} \end{array}$$

22. **The correct answer is A.**

$$\frac{1}{4} \div 4\frac{1}{3} = \frac{1}{4} \div \frac{13}{3} = \frac{1}{4} \times \frac{3}{13} = \frac{3}{52}$$

23. **The correct answer is B.**

$$\frac{1}{9} \times \frac{\cancel{2}^1}{3} \times \frac{7}{\cancel{8}_4} = \frac{7}{108}$$

24. **The correct answer is C.**

$$8\frac{1}{6} = 7\frac{7}{6}$$
$$-5\frac{2}{3} = 5\frac{4}{6}$$
$$\overline{\phantom{-5\frac{2}{3}}\,2\frac{3}{6} = 2\frac{1}{2}}$$

25. The correct answer is C.

$$3\frac{1}{4} = 3\frac{2}{8}$$
$$4\frac{1}{8} = 4\frac{1}{8}$$
$$+\ 4\frac{1}{2} = 4\frac{4}{8}$$
$$\overline{\qquad 11\frac{7}{8}}$$

26. The correct answer is E.

$$5\frac{1}{4} \times 2\frac{2}{7} = \frac{^3\cancel{21}}{\cancel{4}_1} \times \frac{^4\cancel{16}}{\cancel{7}_1} = \frac{12}{1} = 12$$

27. The correct answer is D.

$$\frac{9}{16} \div \frac{3}{4} = \frac{^3\cancel{9}}{\cancel{16}_4} \times \frac{^1\cancel{4}}{\cancel{3}_1} = \frac{3}{4}$$

28. The correct answer is B.

$$10\frac{2}{3} = 10\frac{4}{6}$$
$$-\ 9\frac{1}{2} = 9\frac{3}{6}$$
$$\overline{\qquad 1\frac{1}{6}}$$

29. The correct answer is B. Convert 10% to a decimal, 0.10, and multiply the total amount by the decimal to find the answer: $32 \times 0.10 = 3.2$.

30. The correct answer is C. Remember that you can't divide by a decimal, so if the divisor is a decimal, you must move the decimal point to the right until the divisor becomes a whole number. As such, we must first divide 8 by 25: $8 \div 25 = 0.32$. Then, move the decimal point two places to the right, which gives you 32.

31. The correct answer is D. If we express our part and our whole as a fraction, 12 would be the numerator and 24 would be the denominator. In this form, we can see that 12 is a common factor, and we can convert our simplest fraction to a percentage: $\frac{12}{24} = \frac{1}{2} \times 100 = 50\%$.

32. The correct answer is A. Start by converting the percentage to a decimal: 0.20. Then, multiply 360 by the decimal: $360 \times 0.20 = 72$.

33. The correct answer is B. If we express our part and our whole as a fraction, 5 would be the numerator and 60 would be the denominator. In this form, we can see that 5 is a common factor, so we can simplify the fraction to $\frac{1}{12}$. We can then convert this fraction to a percentage by multiplying by 100: $\frac{1}{12} \times 100 = 8.33\%$ or $8\frac{1}{3}\%$.

34. The correct answer is C. After the first 10% discount, the price was $1,080 ($1,200 minus 10% of $1,200). After the second discount, which is calculated based on the $1,080 price, the price of the smartphone is $972 ($1,080 minus 10% of $1,080).

35. The correct answer is B. The library has 30,000 volumes. If 600 books is 2% of the library's total collection, we can set up a proportion problem to solve for the whole:

$$\frac{2}{100} = \frac{600}{x}$$
$$2x = 60,000$$
$$x = 30,000$$

36. The correct answer is B. The total discount was $150, so we need to determine what percentage of the original price, $750, that $150 is. We can set up a proportion that allows us to find the percentage:

$$\frac{x}{100} = \frac{150}{750}$$
$$750x = 150(100)$$
$$750x = 15000$$
$$\frac{750x}{750} = \frac{15000}{750}$$
$$x = 20$$

37. The correct answer is D. The original number is 18, and the difference between the two numbers is $24 - 18 = 6$, which is $\frac{1}{3}$ of the original number, or $33\frac{1}{3}\%$.

38. The correct answer is D. First, the cryptocurrency rises by 20% ($0.2 \times \$500 = \$100$), so the value is: $500 + $100 = $600. Then, it falls by 20% ($0.2 \times$

$600 = $120), so the final value is: $600 – $120 = $480. The difference from the original price is: $500 – $480 = $20. Knowing the difference, set up a proportion problem to determine the percentage of decrease:

$$\frac{20}{500} = \frac{x}{100}$$
$$2000 = 500x$$
$$\frac{2000}{500} = \frac{500x}{500}$$
$$4 = x$$

39. **The correct answer is C.** First, find out how much sugar one quart of punch needs.

$$\frac{3}{4} \text{ cups} \div 6 = \frac{3}{4} \div \frac{6}{1} = \frac{1\cancel{3}}{4} \times \frac{1}{\cancel{6}_2} = \frac{1}{8}$$

For 9 quarts of punch:

$$9 \times \frac{1}{8} = \frac{9}{8} = 1\frac{1}{8}$$

40. **The correct answer is B.** $\frac{1}{4}$ inch = 1 foot, so 1 inch = 4 foot and the living room is 7 × 4 = 28 feet long. When the scale changes to 1 inch = 1 foot, the 28-foot living room will be 28 inches on the new drawing.

41. **The correct answer is B.** 4 inches = 32 miles; therefore, 1 inch = 32 ÷ 4 = 8 miles. 80 miles would be represented by 10 inches.

42. **The correct answer is B.**

$1\frac{1}{2}$ cups sugar × 8 = 12 cups sugar

12 cups ÷ 2 cups per pound = 6 pounds of sugar

43. **The correct answer is E.** The three rolls are independent of each other, and each has 6 possible outcomes. As such, there are (6)(6)(6) = 216 possible three-roll outcomes. There is only one way to get all 5s. The probability of NOT getting three 5s is $\frac{215}{216}$.

44. **The correct answer is C.** Basil and oregano have a part-to-part ratio of 4:3. Set up a proportion to solve for the amount of basil needed:

$$\frac{4}{3} = \frac{x}{12}$$
$$48 = 3x$$
$$\frac{48}{3} = \frac{3x}{3}$$
$$16 = x$$

45. **The correct answer is D.** There are 11 daisies of 25 flowers total that could be chosen in the first selection, so the probability of selecting a daisy is $\frac{11}{25}$. Once this flower is removed, there are 24 remaining in the vase, 10 of which are daisies. The probability of choosing a second daisy is $\frac{10}{24}$. Since the selections are performed in succession, we multiply the probabilities. Therefore, the probability of randomly selecting two daisies is $\frac{11}{25} \times \frac{10}{24}$.

46. **The correct answer is A.** 45 badges × 4 inches each = 180 inches needed. There are 36 inches in one yard. 180 inches ÷ 36 = 5 yards of ribbon needed.

47. **The correct answer is C.** If 1 inch of wire costs $0.20, 1 foot costs 12($0.20) = $2.40. Therefore, 5.25 feet of wire cost ($2.40)(5.25) = $12.60.

48. **The correct answer is D.** Remember that the prefix *kilo* means 1,000, so a kilogram is a thousand grams. Accordingly, 2.5 kilograms is 2,500 grams.

49. **The correct answer is D.** Because the car is traveling 60 mph, you know that the car is traveling 1 mile per minute, as there are 60 minutes in an hour. Since you already know that 1 mile is 5,280 feet, you have the answer: 5,280 feet per minute.

50. **The correct answer is B.** Set up a proportion to calculate this conversion problem:

$$\frac{1 \text{ lb.}}{16 \text{ oz.}} = \frac{x}{820 \text{ oz.}}$$
$$820 = 16x$$
$$\frac{820}{16} = \frac{16x}{16}$$
$$51\frac{1}{4} = x$$

NOTES

CHAPTER

Algebra

ALGEBRA

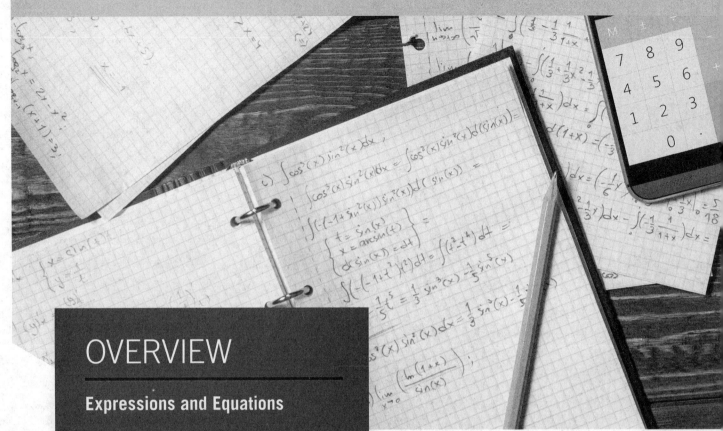

OVERVIEW

SSAT   ISEE

If you are finishing the eighth grade this year, you might not have had a formal algebra class yet. However, you may be familiar with algebraic terms and expressions, and you have probably solved simple equations. Algebra is essentially the manipulation of mathematical symbols in order to find unknown information. Algebraic thinking is essential for understanding how both numbers and variables can be used together, allowing you to logically solve real-world problems.

This chapter will review the skills you have acquired so far and will show you the kinds of questions you can expect to find on the SSAT and ISEE. First, we'll explore the different forms of expressions and equations, both manipulating and solving for variables.

Then, we'll look at two common applications of algebra in the form of word problems.

EXPRESSIONS AND EQUATIONS

Fundamentally, algebra is the manipulation of mathematical symbols. More than likely, your familiarity with the field stems from solving for unknowns by applying various rules and procedures. First, we'll discuss how to put an equation into standard form and how to use other types of notation, like scientific notation, factorials, and polynomials. Then, we'll cover the basics of how to solve an equation, work with systems of equations, analyze functions, and use matrices.

So far, you've already seen plenty of expressions: at least two values with some math operator used between them. Algebraic expressions, however, are usually used to form equations, which set two expressions equal to one another. When we're talking about algebraic expressions, know that a term is any coefficient, variable, or combination of a coefficient and a variable. In equations, at least one of the terms will be a variable—a letter such as x or y that represents a number that can *vary*. It does not need an exponent, but if it has one, it must be a non-negative exponent. A coefficient is the number that multiplies with a variable, such as the 2 in $2y$.

Standard Form

Standard form is something you've been using since you learned how to write numbers. Write the number one hundred: 100. That is standard form—the usual way you'd write a number. In addition to being the way you've written numbers all your life, standard form is also an agreed-upon method of writing an expression. The standard form for equations has a couple of rules you need to know.

1. Always set an equation $= 0$
   Example: $x = 7$ should have everything on the left of the equal sign, and 0 on the right:
   $x - 7 = 0$ is standard form
2. Work from the highest exponent
   Example: $7x^3 + 3x^6 - 5 + 4x^2$ should start with the highest exponent: $3x^6 + 7x^3 + 4x^2 - 5$

Writing equations in standard form makes it easier to locate information because it is presented in a consistent order. When an equation is in standard form, you'll know what to expect and how to proceed with isolating and solving for the variable.

Test Yourself 1

Put the following equations into standard form. The answers will follow.

1. $x + 7 = 49$
2. $x = 4y$
3. $ab = 14c$
4. $4x^3 + 17x^5 - 2 - 4x^9 = -12$
5. $3x + 4y + 5 = 17 + x$

Answers:

1. $x - 42 = 0$
2. $x - 4y = 0$
3. $ab - 14c = 0$
4. $-4x^9 + 17x^5 + 4x^3 + 10 = 0$
5. $2x + 4y - 12 = 0$

Evaluating Expressions

You know that expressions can have terms, coefficients, variables, and exponents. When putting expressions into standard form, often, you'll be simplifying the expression. Expressions can be simplified by combining like terms. Like terms must have the same variable (or lack thereof) and the same power (e.g., 3 and 4, $3x$ and x, $4y^7$ and $253y^7$). Sometimes, though, you'll not only be given an expression but also a value that can be substituted in for a variable to evaluate the expression. For instance, if you were told to evaluate the expression $4x^2 + 3x$ when $x = 3$, you would substitute 3 for each instance of x.

Evaluate $\frac{3}{4}x - \frac{5}{6}$ at $x = -2$.

To solve, replace every occurrence of the variable with the number and simplify the arithmetic expression using the order of operations:

$$\frac{3}{4}(-2) - \frac{5}{6} = -\frac{3}{2} - \frac{5}{6} = -\frac{9}{6} - \frac{5}{6} = -\frac{14}{6} = -\frac{7}{3}$$

Linear Expressions

A **linear expression** has the form $Ax + B$, where A and B are real numbers. They can be added and subtracted by combining like terms. For example:

$$\left(\frac{2}{3}x - \frac{3}{4}\right) + \left(\frac{1}{6}x + \frac{5}{12}\right) = \left(\frac{2}{3}x + \frac{1}{6}x\right) + \left(-\frac{3}{4} + \frac{5}{12}\right)$$

$$= \left(\frac{4}{6}x + \frac{1}{6}x\right) + \left(-\frac{9}{12} + \frac{5}{12}\right)$$

$$= \frac{5}{6}x - \frac{4}{12}$$

$$= \frac{5}{6}x - \frac{1}{3}$$

Using the distributive property, we can also multiply a linear expression by a single term:

$$1.4(0.3x - 1.4) = 1.4(0.3x) - 1.4(1.4) = 0.42x - 1.96$$

Using the distributive property twice in succession enables us to multiply two linear expressions.

Sometimes, you will need to formulate a linear expression as part of solving a word problem. You simply need to look for key words and interpret accordingly. The following table shows some examples.

REAL-WORLD LINEAR EXPRESSIONS	
Scenario	**Linear Expression**
One cable is two-thirds the length of one half of another piece.	Let x represent the length of the second piece. The word *of* means multiply, so the length of the cable is $\frac{2}{3}\left(\frac{1}{2}x\right)$.
Katie is three years older than twice her sister's age.	Let x be Katie's sister's age (in years). Then, Katie's age is $(2x+3)$ years.
The length of a rectangle is one meter more than one fourth the width.	Let w be the width of the rectangle (in meters). Then, the length is $\left(1 + \frac{1}{4}w\right)$ meters.

Exponents and Expressions with Radicals

The term exponent refers to the number of times that a number (referred to as the base number) is multiplied by itself. In the exponential number 2^4, the base number is 2 and the exponent is 4. The value of 2^4 can be written as follows: $2^4 = 2 \times 2 \times 2 \times 2 = 16$. An exponent is also referred to as a power. You can express the exponential number 2^4 as "2 to the 4th power."

The inverse of an exponent is the root of a number. The radical sign signifies a square root and looks like this: $\sqrt{}$. Here's an example of a square root:

$2 = \sqrt{4}$ (the square root of 4)

because 2×2 (or 2^2) is 4;

additionally, $\sqrt{4} = 4^{\frac{1}{2}}$

Rules for Exponents

A variety of rules exist for working with exponents with different operations. Use the following table as a guide.

RULES FOR EXPONENTS	
Product	$a^m a^n = a^{m+n}$
Product of a power	$(a^m)^n = a^{mn}$
Quotient to a power	$\left(\dfrac{a}{b} \right)^n = \dfrac{a^n}{b^n}$
Quotient	$\dfrac{a^m}{a^n} = a^{m-n}$
Zero exponent	$a^0 = 1$
Negative exponent	$a^{-n} = \dfrac{1}{a^n}$
Inversion	$\left(\dfrac{a}{b} \right)^{-n} = \left(\dfrac{b}{a} \right)^n$
Fractional powers	$a^{\frac{m}{n}} = \sqrt[n]{a^m}$

EXAMPLE:

Simplify the expression: $\left(\dfrac{x^2 y^4}{x^{-1} y} \right)^{-2}$

Here, apply the rules for exponents within the parentheses and then apply the −2 power. Note that a variable with no exponent is assumed to have an exponent of 1:

$$\left(\frac{x^2 y^4}{x^{-1} y} \right)^{-2} = \left(x^{2-(-1)} y^{4-1} \right)^{-2} = \left(x^3 y^3 \right)^{-2} = x^{-6} y^{-6} = \frac{1}{x^6 y^6}$$

Fractional Exponents and Roots

Fractional exponents follow the same rules as other exponents. However, fractional exponents can also be written as roots (radicals). Remember, the square root of a number n is a number that you "square" (multiply it by itself, or raise to the power of 2), to obtain n. Let's look at another example of a square root:

$$4 = \sqrt{16} \text{ (the square root of 16)}$$
$$\text{because } 4 \times 4 \text{ (or } 4^2) = 16$$

The cube root of a number n is a number that you raise to the power of 3 (multiply by itself twice) to obtain n. You determine higher roots (for example, the "fourth root") in the same way. Except for square roots, the radical sign will indicate the root to be taken. See the following example:

$$2 = \sqrt[3]{8} \text{ (the cube root of 8)}$$
$$\text{because } 2 \times 2 \times 2 \text{ (or } 2^3) \text{ is 8}$$

$$2 = \sqrt[4]{16} \text{ (the fourth root of 16)}$$
$$\text{because } 2 \times 2 \times 2 \times 2 \text{ (or } 2^4) \text{ is 16}$$

EXAMPLE:

Simplify the expression $\dfrac{x^{\frac{1}{2}} y^2}{x^{\frac{2}{3}} y^{\frac{1}{2}}}$. Write your answer as a radical expression.

First, apply the rules for exponents. Then, apply the rule that $x^{\frac{m}{n}} = \sqrt[n]{x^m}$:

$$\frac{x^{\frac{1}{2}} y^2}{x^{\frac{2}{3}} y^{\frac{1}{2}}} = x^{\frac{1}{2} - \frac{2}{3}} y^{2 - \frac{1}{2}} = x^{-\frac{1}{6}} y^{\frac{3}{2}} = \frac{y^{\frac{3}{2}}}{x^{\frac{1}{6}}} = \frac{\sqrt{y^3}}{\sqrt[6]{x}}$$

This expression can be simplified further. Since $y^3 = y \cdot y^2$ and $\sqrt{y^2} = y$, we can write the following:

$$\frac{\sqrt{y^3}}{\sqrt[6]{x}} = \frac{\sqrt{y y^2}}{\sqrt[6]{x}} = \frac{y\sqrt{y}}{\sqrt[6]{x}}$$

You can simplify these radical expressions anytime this occurs. The following image provides useful rules, some of which overlap with those for exponents, for working with radical expressions.

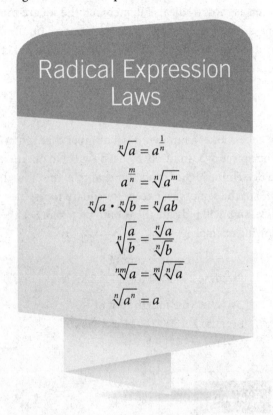

Radical Expression Laws

$$\sqrt[n]{a} = a^{\frac{1}{n}}$$

$$a^{\frac{m}{n}} = \sqrt[n]{a^m}$$

$$\sqrt[n]{a} \cdot \sqrt[n]{b} = \sqrt[n]{ab}$$

$$\sqrt[n]{\frac{a}{b}} = \frac{\sqrt[n]{a}}{\sqrt[n]{b}}$$

$$\sqrt[nm]{a} = \sqrt[m]{\sqrt[n]{a}}$$

$$\sqrt[n]{a^n} = a$$

These rules are demonstrated by the following example.

EXAMPLE:

Simplify the radical $\sqrt[4]{x^6 y^4}$.

Remember, $\sqrt[n]{a^n} = a$. By factoring out x^2 and rearranging, we can pull out xy:

$$\sqrt[4]{x^6 y^4} = \sqrt[4]{\left(x^4 y^4\right)\left(x^2\right)}$$

$$= \sqrt[4]{\left(xy\right)^4 \left(x^2\right)}$$

$$= \sqrt[4]{\left(xy\right)^4} \sqrt[4]{x^2}$$

$$= (xy)(x^{\frac{1}{2}})$$

$$= xy\sqrt{x}$$

Scientific Notation

While standard form helps to present information in a predictable way, it is not as useful for equations with extremely large or small numbers. Instead, you will want to use scientific notation, a system for writing extremely large or extremely small numbers more efficiently. For example, the number 380,000,000 is written in standard form. However, writing all of those zeros over and over again can be time consuming. In scientific notation, an integer or decimal number between 1 and 10 is written to the power of 10, which eliminates the need to include all those zeros. We can use scientific notation to express 380,000,000 as 3.8×10^8. Ultimately, scientific notation makes working with very large and small numbers more manageable and convenient.

To explain how we used scientific notation to write 380,000,000 as 3.8×10^8, let's work backwards. First, we start with a value between 1 and 10. In this case, we are using 3.8, the first non-zero digits of the larger value.

To go from 3.8 to 380,000,000, you need to shift the decimal 8 places to the right. The number of places to the right of the decimal point is expressed as the exponent in scientific notation. Here, the exponent is 8. In contrast, a negative exponent would signify a fractional number, since we would be moving that many decimal places to the left instead of the right. Now that we know the exponent is 8, we can write our very large number in scientific notation: 3.8×10^8.

Here are some more examples of how to write numbers in scientific notation.

EXAMPLES:

Write 4 million in scientific notation.

Solution:
$$4,000,000$$

Move the decimal point to the left six times to get to a number between 1 and 10.
$$4.000000$$

Multiply 4 by 10 to the power of the number of zeros to the right of the decimal point.
$$4 \times 10^6$$

Write 735 trillion in scientific notation.

Solution:
$$735,000,000,000,000$$

Move the decimal to get a number between 1 and 10.
$$7.35000000000000$$

Multiply 7.35 by 10 to the number of digits to the right of the decimal point.
$$7.35 \times 10^{14}$$

Write 32,570,000,000 in scientific notation.

Solution:

Move the decimal point to the right until you have a number between 1 and 10.
$$3.2570000000$$

Multiply by 10 to the power of the number of digits to the right of the decimal point.
$$3.257 \times 10^{10}$$

You can also use scientific notation to write out very small numbers like 0.00000000000092. To use scientific notation to express very small numbers, you are moving the decimal point to the right to get a value between 1 and 10 and your exponent is negative.

$$9.2 \times 10^{-13}$$

When the number is negative, be sure to make the scientific notation negative.

EXAMPLES:

$-42,000,000$

Solution:
-4.2×10^7

-0.00000000065

Solution:
-6.5×10^{-10}

Scan this QR code to learn more about scientific notation.

TIP

Moving the decimal point to the left gives a positive exponent. Moving the decimal to the right gives a negative exponent. Whether the number itself is positive or negative, the exponent's sign does not change.

Test Yourself 2

Write the following numbers in scientific notation. The answers will follow.

1. 20,000,000,000
2. 5,150,000,000,000,000,000
3. 3,420
4. 0.00000008
5. −0.0000000000005

Answers:

1. 2×10^{10}
2. 5.15×10^{18}
3. 3.42×10^3
4. 8×10^{-8}
5. -5×10^{-13}

Factorials

Like scientific notation, factorials are a type of notation used to more efficiently present information. Factorials denote when to multiply an integer by all the integers that come before it on a number line. To indicate a factorial, you would use the integer in question followed by an exclamation point:

$$5! = 5 \times 4 \times 3 \times 2 \times 1 = 120$$

In this example, we break down five factorial. Let's solve the example:

$$5 \times 4 = 20$$
$$20 \times 3 = 60$$
$$60 \times 2 = 120$$
$$120 \times 1 = 120$$

Let's try a few questions.

EXAMPLES:

$3! =$

Solution:

Write out the factorial and solve:

$$3 \times 2 \times 1 = 6$$

$4! =$

Solution:

Write out the factorial and solve:

$$4 \times 3 \times 2 \times 1 = 12 \times 2 = 24$$

To watch a video about factorials, scan this QR code.

EXAMPLES:

8! =

Solution:

Write out the factorial:

$8 \times 7 \times 6 \times 5 \times 4 \times 3 \times 2 \times 1 =$

Multiply pairs and solve:

$56 \times 30 \times 12 \times 2 =$

$1,680 \times 24 = 40,320$

10! =

Solution:

Write out the factorial and solve (again, multiply paired numbers):

$10 \times 9 \times 8 \times 7 \times 6 \times 5 \times 4 \times 3 \times 2 \times 1 =$

$90 \times 56 \times 30 \times 12 \times 2 = 3,628,800$

When adding factorials, it's not enough to add the numbers. Rather, you need to solve the factorials, then add those numbers together to make a new factorial.

You will notice the answer is not written as a factorial. Remember, solving a factorial does not itself create a new factorial. Let's look at some examples.

EXAMPLES:

2! + 3! =

Solution:

Solve each factorial

$(2 \times 1) + (3 \times 2 \times 1) =$

$2 + 6 = 8$

7! + 4! =

Solution:

$(7 \times 6 \times 5 \times 4 \times 3 \times 2 \times 1) + (4 \times 3 \times 2 \times 1) =$

$5,040 + 24 = 5,064$

The order in which you solve two factorials matters. Using the previous example, watch what happens when we first add the two factorials, then solve.

EXAMPLE:

$7! + 4! \neq 11!$

Solution:

$11! = 11 \times 10 \times 9 \times 8 \times 7 \times 6 \times 5 \times 4 \times 3 \times 2 \times 1 = 39,916,800$

That's a big difference, so remember to solve the factorials before adding. Fortunately, the same rule applies for subtraction, multiplication, and division. As such, you can put this step at the top of the order of operations discussed in the previous chapter. Here are some sample problems.

EXAMPLE:

4! – 3! =

Solution:

$(4 \times 3 \times 2 \times 1) - (3 \times 2 \times 1) =$

$24 - 6 = 18$

 TIP

Whenever you see a factorial in a problem, solve it first.

$6! \times 2! =$

Solution:

$(6 \times 5 \times 4 \times 3 \times 2 \times 1) \times (2 \times 1) =$

$$720 \times 2 = 1{,}440$$

$$\frac{6!}{4!} = \frac{6 \times 5 \times 4 \times 3 \times 2 \times 1}{4 \times 3 \times 2 \times 1}$$

Fortunately, we have common factors in the numerator and denominator.

$$\frac{6 \times 5 \times \cancel{4 \times 3 \times 2 \times 1}}{\cancel{4 \times 3 \times 2 \times 1}} =$$

$$6 \times 5 = 30$$

Test Yourself 3

Write the answers to the following problems in the space provided. The answers will follow.

1. $9! =$
2. $3! + 7! =$
3. $6! - 3! =$
4. $3! \times 7! =$
5. $7! \div 4! =$

Answers:

1. 362,880
2. 5,046
3. 714
4. 30,240
5. 210

Polynomials

A polynomial is an expression made up of terms with non-negative exponents. Here are some examples of different types of polynomials:

$$x^4 \times 14x^3 + 15x - 7$$
$$7x + 2 + 2x^2$$
$$14 + 3y$$
$$x$$
$$12$$

Let's look at a term from one of the earlier expressions: $14x^3$. We have a coefficient (14), a variable (x), and an exponent (^{3}). If you wanted to read this out loud, you'd say, "fourteen x to the third power" or "fourteen x cubed." Take a look at that full polynomial again.

$$x^4 \times 14x^3 + 15x - 7$$

This polynomial has four terms: x^4, $14x^3$, $15x$, and -7. Let's look at another polynomial from the earlier example:

$$7x + 2 + 2x^2$$

This polynomial has three terms, so you could call it a trinomial. From that list, $14 + 3y$ is a binomial because it has two terms. The last two expressions are monomials because they each have one term.

Writing Polynomials in Standard Form

You'll see many polynomials written in the standard form:

$$Ax^2 + Bx + C$$

A and B represent coefficients, C is a constant, and x represents the variable. The following are some examples of polynomials in standard form:

$$x^2 + 7x + 12$$
$$2x^3 - 18x^2 + 6x - 54$$
$$x^2 - 9$$

For larger polynomials, the standard form is to write the equation starting with the largest exponent as seen in the second example above and the following:

$$y^7 - 4y^3 + y^2 + 14y + 70$$

In this example, you start with y^7, or y to the seventh power. The next term is $-4y^3$, followed by y^2, $14y$, and finally 70.

Simplifying Polynomials

Simplifying polynomials means organizing and combining like terms to make a polynomial as easy to read as possible. This includes putting a polynomial into standard form. Let's look at a sample polynomial that has not been simplified:

$$2x + 4x^2 - 13 + 7x - x^2 + x - 3$$

To simplify, first gather like terms:

$$4x^2 - x^2 + 2x + 7x + x - 13 - 3$$

Then, combine like terms:
$$4x^2 - x^2 = 3x^2$$
$$2x + 7x + x = 10x$$
$$-13 - 3 = -16$$

Finally, write out the expression in standard form:

$$3x^2 + 10x - 16$$

This is much easier to read—and make sense of—than the original expression.

Adding and Subtracting Polynomials

If you have two polynomials and you want to combine them through addition or subtraction, the steps are similar to what you've done already. Let's take a look:

$$(11x^2 + 14 + 3x) + (-3x^2 + 2x + 6)$$

The first step, because you have two polynomials inside of parentheses connected by addition, is to remove the parentheses:

$$11x^2 + 14 + 3x + -3x^2 + 2x + 6$$

From here, gather terms and simplify:

$$11x^2 - 3x^2 + 3x + 2x + 14 + 6$$

The resulting polynomial is:

$$8x^2 + 5x + 20$$

Let's look at the same polynomial but instead focus on subtraction. The process is essentially the same except that you need to pay careful attention to number signs.

$$(11x^2 + 14 + 3x) - (-3x^2 + 2x + 6)$$

Now that you're subtracting one polynomial from the other, remove the parentheses and distribute the negative sign to the terms inside the second set of parentheses:

$$(11x^2 + 14 + 3x) + (3x^2 - 2x - 6)$$

Now, remove the parentheses, gather like terms and combine to simplify:

$$11x^2 + 14 + 3x + 3x^2 - 2x - 6$$

$$11x^2 + 3x^2 + 3x - 2x + 14 - 6$$

$$14x^2 + x + 8$$

Multiplying Monomials

Remember that a monomial is a polynomial with only one term. For example, $7x$ is a monomial. So is $2y^2$ and $1{,}784{,}921t^{45}$. Multiplying monomials gives us the chance to combine two terms that are not alike, such as $3x^2$ and $6x^4$. Let's review multiplying exponents:

$$3x^2(6x^4)$$

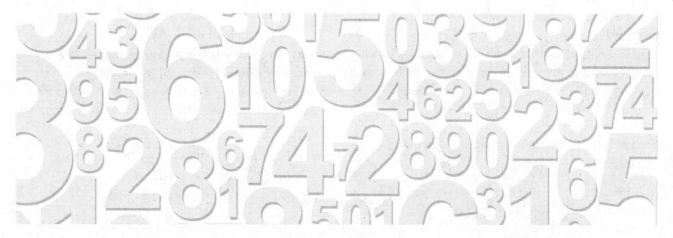

As with any polynomial equation, it's easier to solve after simplifying. With two monomials, break each monomial into its component parts:

$$3 \times 6 \text{ and } x^2 \times x^4$$

The first portion requires standard multiplication:

$$3 \times 6 = 18.$$

As for the exponents, when you are asked to multiply, remember that if they have the same base, you will add the exponents. Therefore, $3x^2 \times 6x^4 = 18x^6$.

Multiplying a Polynomial and a Monomial

When multiplying a polynomial and a monomial, distribution is the key. Here's a sample problem:

$$2(x^2 + 7x + 4)$$

The first step is to distribute the 2 to the terms in the trinomial:

$$(2 \times x^2) + (2 \times 7x) + (2 \times 4)$$

Finish multiplying and add the terms together to present the polynomial in standard form:

$$2x^2 + 14x + 8$$

Note that even though you can factor 2 out of each term, $2x^2 + 14x + 8$ is the simplified answer. Factoring out the 2 would bring us back to the original monomial and polynomial of $2(x^2 + 7x + 4)$.

Multiplying Binomials

Let's start with a problem with two binomials:

$$(4x + 3)(2x + 9)$$

These binomials need to be multiplied together. To multiply binomials, you'll use a process called FOIL. FOIL is a mnemonic that stands for First, Outer, Inner, Last. It describes the order in which you multiply terms. Let's apply it to the previous pair of binomials:

$$(4x + 3)(2x + 9)$$

Start with the first terms: $4x$ and $2x$. Multiply them together:

$$4x \bullet 2x = 8x^2$$

Then multiply the outer terms: $4x$ and 9:

$$4x \bullet 9 = 36x$$

Continue following FOIL. Next, multiply the inner terms:

$$3 \bullet 2x = 6x$$

Finally, multiply the last terms and combine:

$$3 \bullet 9 = 27$$

$$8x^2 + 36x + 6x + 27$$

$$8x^2 + 42x + 27$$

While you could have also used standard distribution to multiply the polynomial, tracking what you've multiplied can become challenging, especially as the number of terms in your polynomials grows. The mnemonic FOIL serves to remind you of the distributive property of multiplication.

Factoring Trinomials

Factoring a trinomial is essentially the same as multiplying binomials, but in reverse. Let's look at the standard form of a trinomial and an example:

$$Ax^2 + Bx + C$$
$$x^2 + 5x + 6$$

When factoring a trinomial, the goal is to build two binomials that when FOILed recreate the trinomial. Here's what you will see:

$$x^2 + 5x + 6 = (x + a)(x + b)$$

Let's expand the right side of this equation:

$$x^2 + 5x + 6 = (x + a)(x + b)$$
$$= x^2 + ax + bx + ab$$
$$= x^2 + (a + b)x + ab$$

What you see here is true for any trinomials that can be factored. You're looking for the values of a and b that multiply to make the C term of the standard form but also add up to the B term. In the example, ab must equal 6 and $a + b$ must equal 5.

We start by factoring the constant, 6.

$$6 : 6 \times 1$$
$$: 3 \times 2$$

Now, $6 \times 1 = 6$ but $6 + 1 = 7$. Try another pair of factors. What about 3×2?

$$3 \times 2 = 6$$
$$3 + 2 = 5$$

The numbers look correct, but test it to be sure.

$$a = 3,\ b = 2$$
$$x^2 + 5x + 6 = (x + a)(x + b)$$
$$= (x + 3)(x + 2)$$
$$= (x)(x) + (x)(2) + (3)(x) + (3)(2)$$
$$= x^2 + 2x + 3x + 6$$
$$= x^2 + 5x + 6$$

Our original trinomial was $x^2 + 5x + 6$, so $(x + 2)$ $(x + 3)$ would suffice as an answer. If the trinomial was set equal to 0, you would then solve for the roots (where the trinomial would intersect the x-axis if graphed) and the algebra would yield -2 and -3.

Let's look at another example. What if you are told to factor the following trinomial?

$$5x^2 + 35x + 50$$

To start, look to see if there are any common factors among 5, 35, and 50. The greatest common factor of these three numbers is 5. So, factor out a 5 from each term:

$$5(x^2 + 7x + 10)$$

From here, factor the trinomial like you did in the first example:

$$5(x^2 + 7x + 10) = (x + a)\ (x + b)$$
$$a + b = 7$$
$$ab = 10$$

We can factor 10 as 10 and 1 or 5 and 2. We need the factors to add to 7. Of the factors of the C term, only 5 and 2 add to 7. Substitute 5 and 2 for the a and b terms and you have your answer:

$$5(x + 5)\ (x + 2)$$

Solving an Equation Using the Four Basic Operations

Now that we've discussed the different forms of notation you'll encounter in algebra problems, let's move on to equations. To find the value of a variable (such as x), you must solve the equation. To solve any equation containing only one variable, your goal is always the same: isolate the variable on one side of the equation. To accomplish this, you may need to perform one or more of the following operations on both sides, depending on the equation:

- Add or subtract the same term on both sides.
- Multiply or divide both sides by the same term.
- Clear fractions by cross-multiplication.
- Clear radicals by raising both sides to the same power (exponent).

Whatever operation you perform on one side of an equation you must also perform on the other side. Otherwise, the two sides will not be equal. Performing any of these operations on *both* sides does not change the equality; it just restates the equation in a different form.

To isolate the variable and solve an equation, you'll need to know the properties we covered in the previous chapter, specifically the distributive, commutative, associative, and identity properties. Knowing these will be critical to solving algebra problems. If your memory is a bit fuzzy on what these are, review them and make sure that you fully understand what they look like in practice before moving on to solving equations.

To find the value of the variable (to solve for x), you may need to either add a term to both sides of the equation or subtract a term from both sides. Here is an example of adding the same number to both sides:

$$x - 2 = 5$$
$$x - 2 + 2 = 5 + 2$$
$$x = 7$$

This next example subtracts the same number from both sides of the following equation:

$$\frac{3}{2} - x = 12$$

The objective is to isolate the variable x. To do this, like terms must be combined.

$$\frac{3}{2} - \frac{3}{2} - x = 12 - \frac{3}{2}$$

$$-x = 10\frac{1}{2} \text{ (divide by } -1 \text{ to make the variable positive)}$$

$$x = -10\frac{1}{2}$$

Note that in the first example, you simply added 2 to both sides to isolate the x variable. In this second example, solving for x first required you to subtract the fraction from both sides. You then needed to divide both sides of the equation by –1 to make the variable positive.

Let's look at some examples of equations where we need to multiply or divide both sides of the equation by the same term in order to isolate the variable.

Multiplying both sides by the same number:

$$\frac{x}{2} = 14$$

$$2 \cdot \frac{x}{2} = 14 \cdot 2$$

$$x = 28$$

Dividing both sides by the same number:

$$3x = 18$$

$$\frac{3x}{3} = \frac{18}{3}$$

$$x = 6$$

The first system isolates x by multiplying both sides by 2. The second system isolates x by dividing both sides by 3. If the variable appears on both sides of the equation, first perform whatever operation is required to position the variable on just one side—either the left or the right. The next system positions both x-terms on the left side by subtracting $2x$ from both sides:

$$16 - x = 9 + 2x$$

$$16 - x - 2x = 9 + 2x - 2x$$

$$16 - 3x = 9$$

Now that x appears on just one side, the next step is to isolate it by subtracting 16 from both sides and then dividing both sides by –3:

$$16 - 3x = 9$$

$$16 - 16 - 3x = 9 - 16$$

$$-3x = -7$$

$$\frac{-3x}{-3} = \frac{-7}{-3}$$

$$x = \frac{7}{3}$$

Let's look at an example question similar to what you will see on the actual exam.

EXAMPLE:

For what value of x does $2x - 6$ equal $x - 9$?

Solution:

First, write the verbal description as the equation $2x - 6 = x - 9$. Then, position both x-terms on the same side. To place them both on the left side, subtract x from both sides. Then, combine x-terms:

$$2x - 6 - x = 9 - x$$

$$x - 6 = -9$$

Finally, isolate x by adding 6 to both sides:

$$x - 6 = -9 + 6$$

$$x = -3$$

Equations with fractional coefficients are solved in the same way as those with integer coefficients—don't be intimidated because they look more complex! Just treat them as you would any rational expression. Let's walk through a couple of examples.

EXAMPLES:

Solve for x:

$$\frac{2}{3}x - \frac{3}{2} = 3 - \frac{5}{6}x$$

Solution:

Gather the x-terms on the left side and constant terms on the right. Then, proceed as follows:

$$\frac{2}{3}x - \frac{3}{2} = 3 - \frac{5}{6}x$$

$$\frac{2}{3}x + \frac{5}{6}x = 3 + \frac{3}{2}$$

Find a common denominator for the fractions on the left side to make it easier to work with them.

$$\frac{4}{6}x + \frac{5}{6}x = \frac{9}{2}$$

$$\frac{9}{6}x = \frac{9}{2}$$

Then, divide both sides by $\frac{9}{6}$ to isolate x and solve.

$$\frac{9}{6}x \div \frac{9}{6} = \frac{9}{2} \div \frac{9}{6}$$

$$x = 3$$

Solve for x:

$$\frac{3}{4}\left(\frac{9}{2} - 2x\right) - 3\left(\frac{4}{3}x + 2\right) = -1$$

Solution:

This example may look complicated, but it is just testing your knowledge of working with rational expressions. First, apply the distributive property to simplify the left side. Then, take the constant terms to the right side and solve as follows:

$$\frac{3}{4}\left(\frac{9}{2} - 2x\right) - 3\left(\frac{4}{3}x + 2\right) = -1$$

$$\frac{27}{8} - \frac{3}{2}x - 4x - 6 = -1$$

$$\left(-\frac{3}{2} - 4\right)x = -1 + 6 - \frac{27}{8}$$

$$-\frac{11}{2}x = \frac{13}{8}$$

$$x = -\frac{2}{11}\left(\frac{13}{8}\right)$$

$$x = -\frac{13}{44}$$

Scan this QR code to watch a video about working with variables.

Systems of Equations

In the preceding section, you examined linear equations with only one variable. Now we will consider linear equations with two variables (x and y) of the form $Ax + By = C$, where A, B, and C are real numbers. The left side of the equation is called a linear combination of x and y. Before, you were able to find the value of the variable by isolating it on one side of the equation. This is not so, however, for a linear equation with two (or more) different variables. Consider the following equation, which contains two variables:

$$x + 3 = y + 1$$

What is the value of x? It depends on the value of y. Similarly, the value of y depends on the value of x. Without more information about either x or y, you simply cannot find the other value. However, you *can* express x in terms of y, and you can express y in terms of x:

$$x = y - 2$$
$$y = x + 2$$

Since these equations were previously set equal to each other, you cannot solve for either x or y. You can only solve for either variable in terms of the other variable.

Look at another example: $4x - 9 = \frac{3}{2}y$.

Solve for x in terms of y:

$$4x = \frac{3}{2}y + 9$$
$$x = \frac{3}{8}y + \frac{9}{4}$$

Solve for y in terms of x:

$$\frac{4x - 9}{\frac{3}{2}} = y$$
$$\frac{2}{3}(4x - 9) = y$$
$$\frac{8}{3}x - 6 = y$$

To determine numerical values of x and y, you need a system of two linear equations with the same two variables. Given this system, there are two different methods for finding the values of the two variables: the substitution method and the elimination or combination method.

The Substitution Method

To solve a system of two equations using the substitution method, follow these steps:

- In *either* equation isolate one variable (for example: x) on one side.
- Substitute the expression that equals x in place of x in the other equation.
- Solve that equation for y.
- Now that you know the value of y, plug it into *either* equation to find the value of x.

Consider these two equations:

$$\text{Equation A: } x = 4y$$
$$\text{Equation B: } x - y = 1$$

In equation B, substitute $4y$ for x, and then solve for y:

$$4y - y = 1$$
$$3y = 1$$
$$y = \frac{1}{3}$$

To find x, substitute $\frac{1}{3}$ for y into either equation. The value of x will be the same in either equation.

$$\text{Equation A: } x = 4\left(\frac{1}{3}\right) = \frac{4}{3}$$
$$\text{Equation B: } x - \frac{1}{3} = 1; \ x = \frac{4}{3}$$

The Elimination Method

Another way to solve for two variables in a system of two equations is with the elimination method, sometimes called combination. Here are the steps:

- Align the two equations by listing the same variables and other terms in the same order. Place one equation above the other.
- Make the coefficient of *either* variable the same in both equations (you can disregard the sign) by multiplying every term in one of the equations.
- Add or subtract one equation from the other to eliminate one variable.

Consider these two equations:

$$\text{Equation A: } x = 3 + 3y$$
$$\text{Equation B: } 2x + y = 4$$

In equation A, subtract $3y$ from both sides, so that all terms in the two equations "line up":

Equation A: $x - 3y = 3$

Equation B: $2x + y = 4$

To solve for y, multiply each term in Equation A by 2, so that the x-coefficient is the same in both equations:

Equation A: $2x - 6y = 6$

Equation B: $2x + y = 4$

Subtract Equation B from Equation A, thereby eliminating x, and then isolate y on one side of the equation:

$$\begin{array}{r} 2x - 6y = 6 \\ -2x + y = 4 \\ \hline 0x - 7y = 2 \\ -7y = 2 \\ y = \dfrac{2}{7} \end{array}$$

To solve for x, you can now substitute in the value of y into either equation to solve.

Which Method Should You Use?

Which method you should use, substitution or elimination, depends on what the starting system looks like. To understand this point, look at this system of two equations:

$$\frac{2}{5}p + q = 3q - 10$$
$$q = 10 - p$$

Notice that the second equation is already set up nicely for the substitution method. But you could use elimination instead; you'd need to rearrange the terms in both the equations first:

$$\frac{2}{5}p - 2q = -10$$
$$p + q = 10$$

Now, look at the following system:

$$3x + 4y = -8$$
$$x - 2y = \frac{1}{2}$$

Notice that the x-term and y-term already line up here. Also notice that it's easy to match the coefficients of either x or y: multiply both sides of the second equation by either 3 or 2. This system is an ideal candidate for elimination. To appreciate this point, try using substitution instead. You'll discover that it takes far more number crunching.

In short, to solve a system of two linear equations with two variables, use elimination if you can quickly and easily eliminate one of the variables. Otherwise, use substitution.

FUNCTIONS

In a function or functional relationship, the value of one variable depends upon the value of, or is "a function of," another variable. In mathematics, the relationship is expressed in the form $y = f(x)$—where y is a function of x.

To find the value of the function for any value of x, simply substitute the x-value for x wherever it appears in the function. In the following function, for example, the function of 2 is 14, and the function of −3 is 4.

$$f(x) = x^2 + 3x + 4$$
$$f(2) = 2^2 + 3(2) + 4 = 4 + 6 + 4 = 14$$
$$f(-3) = (-3)^2 + 3(-3) + 4 = 9 - 9 + 4 = 4$$

Determine the function of a variable expression the same way—just substitute the expression for x throughout the function. Using the function above, here is how you would find $f(2 + a)$:

$$f(2 + a) = (2 + a)^2 + 3(2 + a) - 4$$
$$= 4 + 4a + a^2 + 6 + 3a - 4$$
$$= a^2 + 7a + 6$$

A function is a relationship between two quantities. It can be expressed using a table of values, a formula, or a graph. Its domain is the set of inputs (x-values) that can be substituted in for the variable and produce a meaningful output (y-values). A function can have only *one output* for each input. The following are examples of relationships between two variables that are NOT functions.

x	-1	2	-1	1	1	3	0
y	4	1	3	2	3	4	1

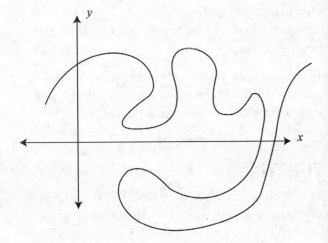

LOGARITHMS

Logarithms express the relationship that $y = \log_b a \Leftrightarrow b^y = a$. For instance, how many 2s do you need to multiply together to get 16? If you write this in exponential and logarithmic forms, you have $2^x = 16 \Leftrightarrow x = \log_2 16$. You need $2 \times 2 \times 2 \times 2$ or four 2s. Thus, you have $2^4 = 16 \Leftrightarrow 4 = \log_2 16$. When both sides of an exponential equation do not share a common base, however, you will take the log of both sides instead.

When you see *e*, remember that it is a special constant with an approximate value of 2.7182818. Its corresponding logarithm is called the natural log and is written as ln(*x*). Further, if there is no base on the log (the *b* in the earlier equations), it is assumed to be 10.

Here's an example where both sides of the exponential equation lack a common base.

EXAMPLE:

Solve: $4(3^{3x}) = 5$.

Isolate the exponential term:

$$4(3^{3x}) = 5$$

$$3^{3x} = \frac{5}{4}$$

Take log base 3 of both sides and solve:

$$\log_3(3^{3x}) = \log_3\left(\frac{5}{4}\right)$$

$$3x = \log_3\left(\frac{5}{4}\right)$$

$$x = \frac{1}{3}\log_3\left(\frac{5}{4}\right)$$

The solution is typically left in this form.

When working with logarithms, you may find the following rules helpful:

Log Rules

$$\log_b b^M = M$$

$$b^{\log_b M} = M$$

$$\log_b(MN) = \log_b M + \log_b N$$

$$\log_b\left(\frac{M}{N}\right) = \log_b M - \log_b N$$

$$\log_b(M^p) = p\log_b(M)$$

EXAMPLE:

Solve: $\log(-3x) - \log(2x + 4) = 1$

Use the log rules to isolate the log term. Then, take both sides to the 10th power since this is assumed to be base 10:

$$\log(-3x) - \log(2x + 4) = 1$$
$$\log\left(\frac{-3x}{2x+4}\right) = 1$$
$$10^{\log\left(\frac{-3x}{2x+4}\right)} = 10^1$$
$$\frac{-3x}{2x+4} = 10$$
$$10(2x+4) = -3x$$
$$20x + 40 = -3x$$
$$23x = -40$$
$$x = \frac{-40}{23} = -\frac{40}{23}$$

Let's look at an example with the natural log.

EXAMPLE:

Simplify: $\ln\left(\dfrac{10}{x^e}\right)$

Use the log rules for division to rewrite the log. The exponent on the second natural log then becomes a coefficient for the term:

$$\ln\left(\frac{10}{x^e}\right) = \ln 10 - \ln x^e$$
$$= \ln 10 - e\ln x$$

MATRICES

Matrices are rectangular arrays of numbers (or variables) that are organized into r rows by c columns. If a matrix A has r rows and c columns, we say A is an $r \times c$ (read "r by c") matrix. A matrix is written by listing all of its entries in an array, enclosed by brackets. Here are some examples:

$$\underbrace{\begin{bmatrix} a & b \\ c & d \end{bmatrix}}_{2 \cdot 2 \text{ matrix}} \quad \underbrace{\begin{bmatrix} 1 & -2 & 3 \\ 1 & 0 & 2 \\ 5 & 2 & 1 \end{bmatrix}}_{3 \cdot 3 \text{ matrix}} \quad \underbrace{\begin{bmatrix} 1 \\ 3 \\ 2 \\ 1 \end{bmatrix}}_{4 \cdot 1 \text{ matrix}}$$

The following is a $[3 \times 2]$ matrix (said "three by two"). Notice that it has 3 rows and 2 columns:

$$\begin{bmatrix} 1 & A \\ 2 & B \\ 3 & C \end{bmatrix}$$

The basic arithmetic operations involving matrices are performed "component-wise," which means you need to pay attention to each entry's position in a matrix. The following is a list of the basic operations on 2×2 matrices. (All letters stand for real numbers.)

Adding and Subtracting Matrices

Only matrices with the same dimensions may be added and subtracted. Perform the addition or subtraction on the corresponding entries:

$$\begin{bmatrix} 1 & A \\ 2 & B \\ 3 & C \end{bmatrix} + \begin{bmatrix} 10 & 4A \\ 11 & 5B \\ 12 & 6C \end{bmatrix} = \begin{bmatrix} 11 & 5A \\ 13 & 6B \\ 15 & 7C \end{bmatrix}$$

Here's an example of adding and subtracting that also relies on some basic algebra:

What is the value of w in terms of x?

$$\begin{bmatrix} 1 & 4 & 8x+6 \\ 2 & 5 & 7 \end{bmatrix} + \begin{bmatrix} -3 & 9 & w \\ 12 & 6 & 13 \end{bmatrix} = \begin{bmatrix} -2 & 13 & -2x-4 \\ 14 & 11 & 20 \end{bmatrix}$$

Add the corresponding entries on the left and set them equal to the sum on the right. Then, solve for w in terms of x:

$$8x + 6 + w = -2x - 4$$
$$w = -2x - 8x - 4 - 6$$
$$w = -10x - 10$$

Term/Operation	Definition
$Equality : \begin{bmatrix} a & b \\ c & d \end{bmatrix} = \begin{bmatrix} e & f \\ g & h \end{bmatrix}$	$\begin{bmatrix} a & b \\ c & d \end{bmatrix} = \begin{bmatrix} e & f \\ g & h \end{bmatrix}$ whenever $\underbrace{a = e,\ b = f,\ c = g,\ d = h}_{\text{corresponding entries are equal}}$
$Sum : \begin{bmatrix} a & b \\ c & d \end{bmatrix} + \begin{bmatrix} e & f \\ g & h \end{bmatrix}$	$\begin{bmatrix} a & b \\ c & d \end{bmatrix} + \begin{bmatrix} e & f \\ g & h \end{bmatrix} = \begin{bmatrix} a+e & b+f \\ c+g & d+h \end{bmatrix}$ In words, add corresponding entries to get the sum.
$Difference : \begin{bmatrix} a & b \\ c & d \end{bmatrix} - \begin{bmatrix} e & f \\ g & h \end{bmatrix}$	$\begin{bmatrix} a & b \\ c & d \end{bmatrix} - \begin{bmatrix} e & f \\ g & h \end{bmatrix} = \begin{bmatrix} a-e & b-f \\ c-g & d-h \end{bmatrix}$ In words, subtract corresponding entries to get the difference.
$Scalar\ Multiplication : k \begin{bmatrix} a & b \\ c & d \end{bmatrix}$	$k \begin{bmatrix} a & b \\ c & d \end{bmatrix} = \begin{bmatrix} ka & kb \\ kc & kd \end{bmatrix}$ In words, multiply all entries by the constant k.

Scalar Multiplication

Scalar multiplication is when a single multiple is multiplied to every entry in a matrix.

$$\text{Find } -\frac{1}{2}A \text{ if } A = \begin{bmatrix} 18 & -6 \\ -2 & 11 \end{bmatrix}$$

$$-\frac{1}{2}A = \begin{bmatrix} -\frac{1}{2} \cdot (18) & -\frac{1}{2} \cdot (-6) \\ -\frac{1}{2} \cdot (-2) & -\frac{1}{2} \cdot (11) \end{bmatrix} = \begin{bmatrix} -9 & 3 \\ 1 & -5.5 \end{bmatrix}$$

Matrix Multiplication

Matrix multiplication is much more involved than scalar multiplication. To multiply matrices, you will need to match up the 1st, 2nd, *n*th *rows* of the first matrix with the corresponding 1st, 2nd, *n*th *columns* of the second matrix. Then, you must multiply each entry in the *n*th *row* of the first matrix by each corresponding entry in the *n*th *column* of the second matrix. Then, the sum of these products will be the entry for the product in the resulting matrix. Matrices can only be multiplied if the number of columns in the first matrix is the same as the number of rows in the second matrix.

For instance, a 2 by 3 matrix could be multiplied by a 3 by 5 matrix but not another 2 by 3 matrix. Look at the example here:

$$\begin{bmatrix} A & B & C \\ W & X & Y \end{bmatrix} \begin{bmatrix} 1 & 4 \\ 2 & 5 \\ 3 & 6 \end{bmatrix} = \begin{bmatrix} (1A + 2B + 3C) & (4A + 5B + 6C) \\ (1W + 2X + 3Y) & (4W + 5X + 6Y) \end{bmatrix}$$

Notice that the top entry in the first column of the product matrix is (1A + 2B + 3C). This was the result of mapping the first *row* of the first matrix $\begin{bmatrix} A & B & C \end{bmatrix}$ onto the first *column* of the second matrix $\begin{bmatrix} 1 \\ 2 \\ 3 \end{bmatrix}$.

The entries matched up as follows: A corresponded with 1, B corresponded with 2, and C corresponded with 3. Therefore, to find the product of $\begin{bmatrix} A & B & C \end{bmatrix}$ and $\begin{bmatrix} 1 \\ 2 \\ 3 \end{bmatrix}$, we multiplied A by 1, B by 2, and C by 3, and the sum of these products was (1A + 2B + 3C).

DISTANCE, RATE, AND TIME PROBLEMS

On the SSAT and ISEE, you might be presented with word problems that require you to parse out relevant information and set up an equation to solve for one or more variables. An incredibly common real-world application of equations can be seen in the formula used for calculating distance, rate, and time. The skills we've discussed here and in the last chapter, especially fractions, should prepare you for these problems, but we're going to break down each type of word problem below.

The basic formula used in solving problems for distance is $D = RT$ (Distance = Rate × Time).

Use this formula when you know rate (speed) and time.

To find rate, use $R = \dfrac{D}{T}$ (Rate = Distance ÷ Time).

To find time, use $T = \dfrac{D}{R}$ (Time = Distance ÷ Rate).

Let's look at an example.

EXAMPLE:

A driver is traveling from Denver, Colorado, to Laramie, Wyoming. The distance between these two cities is 128 miles. If the driver goes straight there without stopping and drives at a rate of 60 mph the entire time, how long will it take to get to Laramie?

Solution:

Here, we are given two of the variables we need: rate and distance. This means we need to solve for time. To solve for time, we'll use $T = \dfrac{D}{R}$ and plug in the values we know. We know that the driver is traveling at a rate of 60 mph. We also know that the drive is 128 miles total.

If we plug the values into our formula, we get $T = \dfrac{128}{60}$. If we divide 128 miles by 60 mph, we get 2.13 hours. Note that this isn't the same as 2 hours and 13 minutes, but we generally know that it will take the driver a little over 2 hours to make the drive.

Depending on how this problem might be set up on the exam and what the answer choices are, you might want to take the extra step of calculating this figure to the minute just to be extra sure that you have the right answer. To calculate the exact number of minutes in 2.13 hours, we need to set up a proportion problem:

$$\frac{2.13\,\text{hrs}}{1\,\text{hr}} = \frac{x}{60\,\text{min}}$$

Here, we set 1 hour equal to 60 minutes, and we've set 2.13 hours equal to x minutes. Now, we can set up an equation by cross-multiplying:

$$2.13(60) = x$$

$x = 127.8$ minutes, which is about 2 hours and 8 minutes

Let's look at a more complex example.

EXAMPLE:

Two hikers start walking from the city line at different times. The second hiker, whose speed is 4 miles per hour, starts 2 hours after the first hiker, whose speed is 3 miles per hour. Determine the amount of time and distance that will pass before the second hiker catches up with the first.

Solution 1:

The first hiker has a 2-hour head start and is walking at a rate of 3 miles per hour. This means that Hiker 1 is 6 miles from the city line when Hiker 2 starts.

$$\text{Rate} \times \text{Time} = \text{Distance}$$

Subtracting 3 miles per hour from 4 miles per hour gives us 1 mile per hour, or the difference in the rates of speed of the two hikers. In other words, Hiker 2 gains 1 mile on Hiker 1 in every hour.

Because there is a 6-mile difference to cut down, and this difference is cut down at a rate of 1 mile every hour, Hiker 2 will need 6 hours to overtake Hiker 1. In this time, Hiker 2 will have traveled $4 \times 6 = 24$ miles. Hiker 1 will have been walking 8 hours, which, when factoring in the 2-hour head start, computes as $8 \times 3 = 24$ miles.

Solution 2:

One excellent way to solve word problems is to organize all of the data in a chart. For distance problems, make columns for Rate, Time, and Distance and separate lines for each moving object. In the problem about the two hikers, the chart technique works like this:

Step 1: Draw the chart.

	Rate	$\times$	Time	$=$	Distance
Hiker 1					
Hiker 2					

Step 2: Since the problem states that Hiker 1 is traveling at 3 miles per hour and Hiker 2 is traveling at 4 miles per hour, enter these two figures in the Rate column.

	Rate	$\times$	Time	$=$	Distance
Hiker 1	3 mph				
Hiker 2	4 mph				

Step 3: The problem does not tell us how long each hiker traveled, but it does say that Hiker 1 started 2 hours before Hiker 2. Therefore, if we use the unknown x to represent the number of hours Hiker 2 traveled, we can set Hiker 1's time as $x + 2$. Enter these two figures in the Time column.

	Rate	$\times$	Time	$=$	Distance
Hiker 1	3 mph	$x + 2$			
Hiker 2	4 mph	x			

Step 4: Using the formula $D = R \times T$, we can easily find each hiker's distance by multiplying the figures for rate and time already in the chart.

For Hiker 1: $3(x + 2) = 3x + 6$

For Hiker 2: $4(x) = 4x$

	Rate	$\times$	Time	$=$	Distance
Hiker 1	3 mph	$x + 2$	$3x + 6$		
Hiker 2	4 mph	x	$4x$		

Step 5: When the two hikers meet, each will have covered the same distance. Using this information, we can set up an equation:

Distance covered by Hiker 1		Distance covered by Hiker 2
$3x + 6$	$=$	$4x$

Solving this equation for x, we find that $x = 6$. This means that Hiker 1 has walked for $6 + 2 = 8$ hours when Hiker 2 catches up.

Step 6: Because Hiker 1 started 2 hours earlier than Hiker 2, Hiker 2 will have walked for 6 hours to catch up to Hiker 1.

Step 7: Using this information, we can determine that Hiker 1 walked 8 hours at 3 miles per hour to cover 24 miles. Hiker 2 walked for 6 hours at 4 miles per hour to cover the same 24 miles.

Let's try one more example.

EXAMPLE:

The same two hikers start walking toward each other along a road connecting two cities that are 60 miles apart. Their speeds are the same as in the preceding example, 3 and 4 miles per hour, respectively. How much time will elapse before they meet?

Solution 1:

In each hour of travel toward each other, the hikers will cut down a distance equal to the sum of their speeds, $3 + 4 = 7$ miles per hour. To meet, they must cut down 60 miles, and at 7 miles per hour, this would be:

$$\frac{D}{R} = T \quad \text{or} \quad \frac{60}{7} = 8\frac{4}{7} \text{ hours}$$

Solution 2:

In this problem, we know that the distance traveled by Hiker 1 plus the distance traveled by Hiker 2 equals 60 miles. We also know that the two hikers will have been traveling for the same length of time when they meet. Therefore, we set up an equation to represent this information and solve for x to find the time that will have elapsed before the two hikers meet:

$$3x + 4x = 60$$
$$7x = 60$$
$$x = 8\frac{4}{7}$$

The problem might also have asked: "How much distance must the slower hiker cover before the two hikers meet?" In such a case, we should go through the same steps plus one additional step:

The time consumed before meeting was $8\frac{4}{7}$ hours. To find the distance covered by the slower hiker, we multiply Hiker 1's rate by the time elapsed:

$$R \times T = D \qquad 3 \times 8\frac{4}{7} = 25\frac{5}{7}$$

Test Yourself 5

Solve the following problems. The answers and explanations will follow.

1. A sailor on leave drove to Yosemite Park from home at 60 miles per hour. On the trip home, the sailor's rate was 10 miles per hour less, and the trip took 1 hour longer. How far is the sailor's home from the park?

2. Two cars leave a restaurant at the same time and travel along a straight highway in opposite directions. At the end of 3 hours, they are 300 miles apart. Find the rate of the slower car if one car travels at a rate 20 miles per hour faster than the other.

Answers:

1. The correct answer is 300 miles.

	Rate ×	Time =	Distance
Going	60 mph	x	$60x$
Return	50 mph	$x + 1$	$50x + 50$

Let x = time of trip at 60 mph.

The distances are equal.

$$60x = 50x + 50$$

$$10x = 50$$

$$x = 5$$

$R \times T = D$; 60 mph × 5 hours = 300 miles

2. The correct answer is 40 miles per hour.

	Rate	×	Time	=	Distance
Slow Car	x		3		$3x$
Fast Car	$x + 20$		3		$3x + 60$

Let x = rate of slower car.

$$3x + 60 \leftarrow 300 \text{ miles} \rightarrow 3x$$

$$3x + 3x + 60 = 300$$

$$6x = 240 \text{ mph}$$

$$x = 40 \text{ mph}$$

To learn more about rate problems, scan this QR code.

WORK PROBLEMS

Another type of problem you might encounter is a work problem. The aim of a work problem is to predict how long it will take to complete a job if the number of workers increases or decreases. Work problems may also involve determining how fast pipes can fill or empty tanks. In solving pipe and tank problems, you must think of the pipes as workers.

In most work problems, a job is broken into several parts, each representing a fractional portion of the entire job. For each part represented, the numerator should represent the time actually spent working, while the denominator should represent the total time the worker needs to do the job alone. The sum of all the individual fractions must be 1 if the job is completed. The easiest way to understand this procedure is to carefully study the examples that follow. By following the step-by-step solutions, you will learn how to make your own fractions to solve the practice problems that follow and the problems you may find on your exam.

EXAMPLE:

If A does a job in 6 days, and B does the same job in 3 days, how long will it take the two of them, working together, to do the job?

Solution:

Step 1: Write the fractions as follows.

$$\frac{\text{Time actually spent}}{\text{Time needed to do entire job alone}} \quad \overset{A}{\frac{x}{6 \text{ days}}} + \overset{B}{\frac{x}{3 \text{ days}}} = 1$$

The variable x represents the amount of time each worker will work when both work together. The number 1 represents the completed job.

Step 2: Multiply all the terms by the same number (in this case, 6) in order to clear the fractions and work with whole numbers.

$$x + 2x = 6$$

Step 3: Solve for x.

$$3x = 6$$

$$x = 2 \text{ days}$$

Working together, A and B will get the job done in 2 days.

EXAMPLE:

A and B, working together, do a job in $4\frac{1}{4}$ days. If B works alone, B can do the job in 10 days. How long would it take A to do the job working alone?

Solution:

Step 1: Write the fractions as follows.

$$\frac{\text{Time actually spent}}{\text{Time needed to do entire job alone}} \quad \overset{A}{\underset{x \text{ days}}{\frac{4.5 \text{ days}}{x \text{ days}}}} + \overset{B}{\underset{10 \text{ days}}{\frac{4.5 \text{ days}}{10 \text{ days}}}} = 1$$

Step 2: Multiply all the terms by $10x$ to clear the fractions.

$$45 + 4.5x = 10x$$

Step 3: Solve for x.

$$45 = 5.5x$$

$$x = 8\frac{2}{11} \text{ or } 8.18 \text{ days}$$

It would take A nearly $8\frac{2}{11}$ days to do the job alone.

EXAMPLE:

One pipe can fill a pool in 20 minutes, a second pipe can fill the pool in 30 minutes, and a third pipe can fill it in 10 minutes. How long would it take the three pipes together to fill the pool?

Solution:

Step 1: Treat the pipes as workers and write the fractions as follows:

$$\frac{\text{Time actually spent}}{\text{Time needed to do entire job alone}} \quad \overset{A}{\underset{20 \text{ min.}}{\frac{x}{20 \text{ min.}}}} + \overset{B}{\underset{30 \text{ min.}}{\frac{x}{30 \text{ min.}}}} + \overset{C}{\underset{10 \text{ min.}}{\frac{x}{10 \text{ min.}}}} = 1$$

Step 2: Multiply all terms by 60 to clear the fractions.

$$3x + 2x + 6x = 60$$

Step 3: Solve for x.

$$11x = 60$$

$$x = 5\frac{5}{11} \text{ min}$$

If the water flows from all three pipes at once, it will take $5\frac{5}{11}$ minutes to fill the pool.

EXAMPLE:

If A can do a job in 6 days that B can do in $5\frac{1}{2}$ days and C can do in $2\frac{1}{5}$ days, how long would the job take if A, B, and C were working together?

Solution:

Step 1: This example is similar to the first example we presented in this section. While the number of workers is greater, the procedure to solve the problem is the same.

$$\frac{\text{Time actually spent}}{\text{Time needed to do entire job alone}} \quad \overset{A}{\underset{6 \text{ days}}{\frac{x}{}}} + \overset{B}{\underset{5.5 \text{ days}}{\frac{x}{}}} + \overset{C}{\underset{2.2 \text{ days}}{\frac{x}{}}} = 1$$

Convert all the decimals to fractions:

$$\frac{x}{6} + \frac{2x}{11} + \frac{5x}{11} = 1$$

Remember that 1 represents the completed job regardless of the number of days involved.

Step 2: Multiply all terms by 66 to clear the fractions.

$$11x + 12x + 30x = 66$$

Step 3: Solve for x.

$$53x = 66$$

$$x = 1.245 \text{ days}$$

A, B, and C all working together at their usual rates would get the job done in about $1\frac{1}{4}$ days.

Test Yourself 6

Solve the following work problems. Answers and explanations will follow.

1. John can complete a paper route in 20 minutes. Steve can complete the same route in 30 minutes. How long will it take them to complete the route if they work together?

2. Mr. Powell can mow his lawn twice as fast as his son Rick can. Together they do the job in 20 minutes. How many minutes would it take Mr. Powell to do the job alone?

Answers:

1. **The correct answer is 12 minutes.**

$$\frac{\text{Time actually spent}}{\text{Time needed to do entire job alone}} \quad \overset{\text{John}}{\underset{20}{\frac{x}{}}} + \overset{\text{Steve}}{\underset{30}{\frac{x}{}}} = 1$$

Multiply all terms by 60 to clear the fractions.

$$3x + 2x = 60$$

$$5x = 60$$

$$x = 12$$

2. **The correct answer is 30 minutes.**

It takes Mr. Powell x minutes to mow the lawn. Rick alone will take twice as long or $2x$ minutes.

$$\frac{\text{Time actually spent}}{\text{Time needed to do entire job alone}} \quad \overset{\text{Mr. Powell}}{\underset{x}{\frac{20}{}}} + \overset{\text{Rick}}{\underset{2x}{\frac{20}{}}} = 1$$

Multiply all terms by $2x$ to clear the fractions.

$$40 + 20 = 2x$$

$$60 = 2x$$

$$x = 30 \text{ minutes}$$

SUMMING IT UP

- Review the properties of mathematics covered in the previous chapter, as these will be important for knowing how to isolate the variable in an equation.
- Knowing how to put an equation into standard form, along with other types of notation like scientific notation, factorials, and polynomials, is essential for being able to solve equations.
- Polynomials are expressions comprising terms with non-negative exponents and are usually written in a standard form: $Ax^2 + Bx + C$.
- To isolate the variable and solve an equation, you might need to perform one of four basic operations:

  1. Add or subtract the same term on both sides.
  2. Multiply or divide both sides by the same term.
  3. Clear fractions by cross-multiplication.
  4. Clear radicals by raising both sides to the same power (exponent).

- Systems of equations can be solved using either the substitution or elimination method.
- Functions represent a relationship in which each input (x) has a unique output (y).
- To solve problems for distance, rate, or time, remember the formula $D = RT$ (Distance = Rate × Time). This formula can be used and rearranged to solve for any of the variables, as long as you know the other two.
- Functions represent a relationship in which each input (x) has a unique output (y).
- Logarithms express the relationship that $y = \log a <> b^y = a$.
- Matrices are rectangular arrays of numbers that can have standard operations applied. They have r rows and c columns.
- To solve work problems, remember that you'll need to set up fractions that reflect the relationship of different parts: The numerator should represent the time actually spent working, while the denominator should represent the total time the worker needs to do the job alone. The sum of all the individual fractions must be 1 if the job is completed.

KNOWLEDGE CHECK

ALGEBRA

35 Questions—28 Minutes

Directions: In the following questions, work out each problem on scratch paper or in the margins. Then, mark the letter that corresponds to the correct answer.

---

1. Solve the following problem for b:
   $5b + 3 = 4b + 19$

   A. 4

   B. 10

   C. 12

   D. 16

   E. 20

2. Solve the equation for y:
   $3(2y + 4) = 8y$

   A. 2

   B. 3

   C. 4

   D. 6

   E. 8

3. Solve for x:
   $\dfrac{x}{2} + 3 = 15$

   A. 18

   B. 20

   C. 22

   D. 22

   E. 24

4. If $y + 2 > 10$, then y must be

   A. smaller than 10.

   B. smaller than 8.

   C. smaller than 2.

   D. greater than 8.

   E. equal to 0.

5. Solve the following for x:
   $\dfrac{4}{x+5} = \dfrac{5}{x+7}$

   A. −1

   B. 0

   C. 3

   D. 4

   E. 5

6. If $x - y = 5$ and $x + 3y = 21$, what is the value of y?

   A. 4

   B. 5

   C. 6

   D. 8

   E. 9

7. Solve for x:

$5(2x - 1) = 4(3x - 2)$

A. $\dfrac{13}{2}$

B. $\dfrac{1}{2}$

C. $\dfrac{3}{2}$

D. 1

E. 3

8. $9.87 \times 10^{-1} =$

A. 0.00987

B. 0.0987

C. 0.987

D. 98.7

E. 9,870

9. $4,400,000 =$

A. 4.4×10^{-2}

B. 4.4×10^{3}

C. 4.4×10^{4}

D. 4.4×10^{5}

E. 4.4×10^{6}

10. $0.000623 =$

A. 6.23×10^{-4}

B. 6.23×10^{-3}

C. 6.23×10^{-2}

D. 6.23×10^{4}

E. 6.23×10^{5}

11. $6! - 5! =$

A. 8

B. 6!

C. $19 \times 18 \times 17 \times 16 \times 15 \times 14$

D. 120

E. 600

12. $30 \times 4! =$

A. 8

B. $19 \times 18 \times 17 \times 16 \times 15 \times 14$

C. 640

D. 6!

E. 360

13. $19! \div 13! =$

A. 8

B. 6!

C. $19 \times 18 \times 17 \times 16 \times 15 \times 14$

D. 500

E. 7!

14. Put this equation into standard form: $ab = 2c$

A. $ab - 2c = 0$

B. $ab + 2c = 0$

C. $2a + 2b + 2c = 0$

D. $2abc = 0$

E. $ab = 2c$

15. Put this equation into standard form:
$2x + 3y + 4 = 12$

A. $24x - 36y + 48 = 0$

B. $2x - 3y = 8$

C. $2x + 3y - 8 = 0$

D. $2x - 3y + 8 = 0$

E. $2x + 3y + 4 = 12$

16. Put this equation into standard form: $x - 10 = 24$

A. $x = 34$

B. $0 = x - 34$

C. $x - 10 - 24 = 0$

D. $x - 34 = 0$

E. $x - 10 = 24$

17. Put this equation into standard form: $2y = -x$

    A. $-2y - x = 0$

    B. $2y = -x$

    C. $y = \dfrac{-x}{2}$

    D. $2y + x = 0$

    E. $2y = -x$

18. Put this equation into standard form:
    $2x^3 + 5x^4 + 7x^5 + 12 = -13$

    A. $2x^3 + 5x^4 + 7x^5 - 1 = 0$

    B. $7x^5 + 5x^4 + 2x^3 - 1 = 0$

    C. $7x^5 + 2x^3 + 5x^4 - 1 = 0$

    D. $-1 - 7x^5 + 5x^4 + 2x^3 = 0$

    E. $7x^5 + 5x^4 + 2x^3 + 25 = 0$

19. Put this equation into standard form:
    $4x + 3y + 2 = 13 + x$

    A. $3x - 11 = -3y$

    B. $3x + 3y - 11 = 0$

    C. $3x + 3y + 11 = 0$

    D. $3x + 11 = 3y$

    E. $4x + 3y + 2 = 13 + x$

20. One boy skied the length of a 4.6-mile trail in just under 14 minutes. His average speed was approximately

    A. 15 miles per hour.

    B. 20 miles per hour.

    C. 25 miles per hour.

    D. 30 miles per hour.

    E. 35 miles per hour.

21. Three workers of about equal efficiency were assigned to work on a car. One worker worked on the car full time but was always assisted by one of the other workers. The work took 4 weeks to complete. If the full-time worker needed to complete the job alone, how many weeks would the car have been in the shop?

    A. 2 weeks

    B. 4 weeks

    C. 6 weeks

    D. 7 weeks

    E. 8 weeks

22. If a plane travels 1,000 miles in 5 hours 30 minutes, what is its average speed in miles per hour?

    A. $181\dfrac{9}{11}$

    B. $191\dfrac{1}{5}$

    C. 200

    D. 215

    E. 230

23. Two cars start from the same point at the same time. One drives north at 20 miles an hour, and the other drives south on the same straight road at 36 miles an hour. How many miles apart are they after 30 minutes?

    A. Fewer than 10

    B. Between 10 and 20

    C. Between 20 and 30

    D. Between 30 and 40

    E. Between 40 and 50

24. Two cars are 550 miles apart and traveling toward each other on the same road. If one travels at 50 miles per hour, the other travels at 60 miles per hour, and they both leave at 1:00 p.m., what time will they meet?

   A. 4:00 p.m.

   B. 4:30 p.m.

   C. 5:00 p.m.

   D. 5:45 p.m.

   E. 6:00 p.m.

25. If a vehicle is to complete a 20-mile trip at an average rate of 30 miles per hour, it must complete the trip in

   A. 20 minutes.

   B. 30 minutes.

   C. 40 minutes.

   D. 50 minutes.

   E. 60 minutes.

26. Solve for y: $4y + 3 = -9$

   A. -12

   B. -8

   C. -3

   D. -1.5

   E. 0

27. If $f(x) = 2 - x(1 - x)$, compute $f(-3)$.

   A. -10

   B. -4

   C. 2

   D. 14

   E. 16

28. Solve for x: $\sqrt[3]{2x + 5} = -5$

   A. -65

   B. -60

   C. 10

   D. 15

   E. 60

29. Factor completely: $4x^2 - 169$

   A. $(4x - 13)(x + 13)$

   B. $(2x - 13)^2$

   C. $(2x - 169)(2x + 1)$

   D. $(2x - 13)(2x + 13)$

   E. $(4x - 13)(2x + 13)$

30. The property tax for a house costing $252,000 is $4,200. At this rate, what would be the property tax for a house costing D dollars?

   A. $D + 60$ dollars

   B. $\dfrac{60}{D}$ dollars

   C. $\dfrac{D}{60}$ dollars

   D. $60D$ dollars

   E. D^{60} dollars

31. Two times the sum of three and a number is equal to ten less than six times that number. What is the number?

   A. -1

   B. $\dfrac{13}{4}$

   C. 4

   D. 12

   E. -4

32. Solve for z: $\dfrac{\frac{1}{w} + z}{2 + z} = \dfrac{3}{w}$

   A. $z = \dfrac{5}{w-3}$

   B. $z = \dfrac{7}{w+3}$

   C. $z = \dfrac{5}{w+3}$

   D. $z = \dfrac{5}{w-3}$

   E. $z = \dfrac{7}{3-w}$

33. Which of the following expressions is equivalent to $\dfrac{x^3 \left(x^2 y^3\right)^3}{x^5 y}$?

   A. $x^{13}y^8$

   B. $x^6 y^{26}$

   C. $x^{\frac{9}{5}} y^9$

   D. $x^4 y^8$

   E. $x^8 y^4$

34. Scott and Micah play racquetball twice a week. So far, Micah has won 13 of 22 matches. Which equation can be used to determine the number of matches, z, Micah must win consecutively to improve his winning percentage to 90%?

   A. $\dfrac{13 + z}{22 + z} = 0.90$

   B. $\dfrac{13 + z}{22} = 0.90$

   C. $\dfrac{z}{22 + z} = 0.90$

   D. $\dfrac{13}{22 + z} = 0.90$

   E. $\dfrac{22 + z}{13} = 0.90$

35. If $f(x) = 2x - 3x^2$, then what is $f(x + 1)$?

   A. $-3x^2 + 4x + 2$

   B. $-3x^2 - 2x - 1$

   C. $-3x^2 + 2x - 1$

   D. $-3x^2 + 2x + 1$

   E. $-3x^2 - 4x - 1$

ANSWER KEY AND EXPLANATIONS

1. D	6. A	11. E	16. D	21. E	26. C	31. C
2. D	7. C	12. D	17. D	22. A	27. D	32. A
3. E	8. C	13. C	18. E	23. C	28. A	33. D
4. D	9. E	14. A	19. B	24. E	29. D	34. A
5. C	10. A	15. C	20. B	25. C	30. C	35. E

1. **The correct answer is D.** Separate variables on one side and numbers on the other. Remember to always do the same thing to both sides of the equation:

$$5b + 3 = 4b + 19$$
$$5b + 3 - 3 = 4b + 19 - 3$$
$$5b = 4b + 16$$
$$5b - 4b = 4b + 16 - 4b$$
$$b = 16$$

2. **The correct answer is D.** First, we can distribute the 3 in order to simplify the equation:

$$3(2y + 4) = 8y$$
$$6y + 12 = 8y$$

Then, we can isolate the variable and divide both sides by 2:

$$12 = 2y$$
$$y = 6$$

3. **The correct answer is E.**

$$\frac{x}{2} + 3 = 15$$
$$\frac{x}{2} = 15 - 3$$
$$\frac{x}{2} = 12$$
$$x = 12 \cdot 2$$
$$x = 24$$

4. **The correct answer is D.**

$$y + 2 > 10$$
$$y > 10 - 2$$
$$y > 8$$

5. **The correct answer is C.** Solve the proportion for x in the following manner:

$$5(x + 5) = 4(x + 7)$$
$$5x + 25 = 4x + 28$$
$$5x - 4x = 28 - 25$$
$$x = 3$$

6. **The correct answer is A.** The question asks for the value of y, so solve the first equation for x:

$$x - y = 5$$
$$x - y + y = 5 + y$$
$$x = 5 + y$$

Now, replace x in the second equation with this result, and solve the second equation for y:

$$x + 3y = 21$$
$$(5 + y) + 3y = 21$$
$$5 + 4y = 21$$
$$5 + 4y - 5 = 21 - 5$$
$$4y = 16$$
$$\frac{4y}{4} = \frac{16}{4}$$
$$y = 4$$

7. **The correct answer is C.** First, distribute the 5 on the left side of the equation and the 4 on the right side of the equation:

$$5(2x - 1) = 4(3x - 2)$$
$$10x - 5 = 12x - 8$$

Then, subtract $10x$ from both sides, and add 8 to both sides.

$$10x - 5 = 12x - 8$$
$$-5 = 2x - 8$$
$$3 = 2x$$

Finally, divide each side by 2:

$$\frac{3}{2} = \frac{2x}{2}$$
$$\frac{3}{2} = x$$

8. **The correct answer is C.** Since the exponent is −1, move the decimal point to the left one place: $9.87 \times 10^{-1} = 0.987$.

9. **The correct answer is E.** To put 4,400,000 in scientific notation, move the decimal six places to the left: 4.4×10^6.

10. **The correct answer is A.** Since 0.000623 is a very small number, we move the decimal place in 6.23 to the left four places, so our exponent is negative: 6.23×10^{-4}.

11. **The correct answer is E.** $6! = 6 \times 5 \times 4 \times 3 \times 2 \times 1 = 720$. $5! = 5 \times 4 \times 3 \times 2 \times 1 = 120$. Therefore, $6! - 5! = 600$.

12. **The correct answer is D.** 30 is equal to 6×5, and $4! = 4 \times 3 \times 2 \times 1$. Therefore, the whole expression becomes $6 \times 5 \times 4 \times 3 \times 2 \times 1$, which is the same as $6!$

13. **The correct answer is C.** When you write this as a fraction and expand the terms, $13!$ cancels out of both the top and bottom. This leaves all of the numbers that are in the top but not in the bottom: $19 \times 18 \times 17 \times 16 \times 15 \times 14$.

14. **The correct answer is A.** To put the equation in standard form, you must set the equation to 0 by subtracting $2c$ from both sides: $ab - 2c = 0$

15. **The correct answer is C.** Set the equation to zero by subtracting 12 from both sides, giving you $2x + 3y - 8 = 0$.

16. **The correct answer is D.** You might be tempted to solve this equation, but remember that you are being asked to put the equation into standard form. To do so, subtract 24 from both sides, and you'll end up with $x - 34 = 0$.

17. **The correct answer is D.** In order to set the equation to 0, you must add x to both sides. This will get you $2y + x = 0$.

18. **The correct answer is E.** First, in order to set the equation to zero, you must add 13 to both sides. Then, you must arrange the exponents from greatest to smallest. This gives you $7x^5 + 5x^4 + 2x^3 + 25 = 0$.

19. **The correct answer is B.** Subtract x from both sides, which gives you $3x$ on the left side. Then, subtract 13 from both sides, and you'll end up with $3x + 3y - 11 = 0$.

20. **The correct answer is B.** The formula for determining rate is $\frac{D}{T}$. The distance skied is 4.6 miles. The time, just under 14 minutes, is approximately 0.25 hour.

$$4.6 \div 0.25 = 18.4 \text{ miles per hour}$$

Because the boy skied the distance in slightly less than 0.25 hour, his average speed was very close to 20 miles per hour.

21. **The correct answer is E.** You do not have to calculate this problem. If you read carefully, you will see that 2 workers worked full time and the work took 4 weeks. If only one worker (half the number) had worked, the job would have taken twice the time or 8 weeks.

22. **The correct answer is A.**

5 hours, 30 minutes $= 5\frac{1}{2}$ hours

1,000 miles $\div 5\frac{1}{2}$ hours $= 1,000 \div \frac{11}{2} =$

$1,000 \times \frac{2}{11} = 181\frac{9}{11}$ miles per hour

23. The correct answer is C. One car went 20 mph for $\frac{1}{2}$ hour = 10 miles. The other went 36 mph for $\frac{1}{2}$ hour = 18 miles. Because they went in opposite directions, add the two distances to find the total number of miles apart: $10 + 18 = 28$.

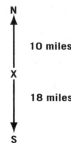

N

10 miles

X

18 miles

S

24. The correct answer is E. The cars are traveling toward each other, so the distance between them is being reduced at 60 + 50 or 110 miles per hour. At a rate of 110 miles per hour, 550 miles will be covered in 5 hours. If both cars left at 1:00 p.m., they should meet at 6:00 p.m.

25. The correct answer is C. Note that a 20-mile trip at 60 mph (which is 1 mile per minute) would take 20 minutes. Because the vehicle is traveling half as fast (30 miles per hour), the 20-mile trip should take twice as long or 40 minutes.

26. The correct answer is C. Subtract 3 from both sides and then divide by 4:

$$4y + 3 = -9$$
$$4y = -12$$
$$y = -3$$

Choice A is incorrect because –12 is equal to $4y$. In the first step, you should subtract 3, not add it, so –8 (choice B) is incorrect. In the second step, you should divide by 4, not add it to both sides, so –1.5 (choice D) is not correct either. Choice E does not reflect the values given.

27. The correct answer is D. Substitute in –3 for x and simplify using the order of operations:

$$f(-3) = 2 - (-3)(1 - (-3))$$
$$= 2 + 3(1 + 3)$$
$$= 2 + 3(4)$$
$$= 2 + 12$$
$$= 14$$

28. The correct answer is A. Cube sides to get rid of the radical, and then solve for x as you would any linear equation:

$$\sqrt[3]{2x + 5} = -5$$
$$2x + 5 = (-5)^3$$
$$2x + 5 = -125$$
$$2x = -130$$
$$x = -65$$

29. The correct answer is D. This is a difference of squares, since it can be written in the form $(2x)^2 - 13^2$. This factors as $(2x - 13)(2x + 13)$. The other choices are incorrect because while the squared term and constant terms are correct, each of them when multiplied out has a middle term not present in the original expression.

30. The correct answer is C. Let x be the amount of property tax for a house costing D dollars. Set up the proportion $\frac{252,000}{4,200} = \frac{D}{x}$. Solving for x yields $x = \frac{4,200D}{252,000} = \frac{D}{60}$ dollars.

31. The correct answer is C. Translating the sentence into symbols yields the following equation, where x is the unknown number:

$$2(x + 3) = 6x - 10.$$

Solve for x, as follows:

$$2(x + 3) = 6x - 10$$
$$2x + 6 = 6x - 10$$
$$16 = 4x$$
$$4 = x$$

Choice A is incorrect because to solve an equation of the form $az + b = c$, subtract b from both sides, do not add it. Choice B is incorrect because when translating the sentence into symbols, you incorrectly interpreted the phrase "two times the sum of three and a number" as $2x + 3$; it should be $2(x + 3)$. Choice D is incorrect because to solve an equation of the form $az = b$, divide both sides by a, do not subtract it from both sides. Choice E changes the sign for the solution.

32. **The correct answer is A.** First, cross-multiply. Then, simplify each side using the distributive property and isolate z, as follows:

$$\frac{\frac{1}{w} + z}{2 + z} = \frac{3}{w}$$

$$\left(\frac{1}{w} + z\right)w = 3(2 + z)$$

$$1 + wz = 6 + 3z$$

$$wz - 3z = 5$$

$$z(w - 3) = 5$$

$$z = \frac{5}{w - 3}$$

The other choices are incorrect due to errors when solving equations of the form $x + a = b$ and $ax = b$.

33. **The correct answer is D.** Apply the exponent rules, as follows:

$$\frac{x^3\left(x^2 y^3\right)^3}{x^5 y} = \frac{x^3 x^{2 \cdot 3} y^{3 \cdot 3}}{x^5 y}$$

$$= \frac{x^3 x^6 y^9}{x^5 y}$$

$$= \frac{x^{3+6} y^9}{x^5 y}$$

$$= \frac{x^9 y^9}{x^5 y}$$

$$= x^{9-5} y^{9-1}$$

$$= x^4 y^8$$

34. **The correct answer is A.** Let z be the number of matches Micah needs to win consecutively to raise his winning percentage to 90%. Then, after playing these z matches, he will have won

$13 + z$ out of $22 + z$ matches played. This yields the ratio $\frac{13 + z}{22 + z}$, which must equal 0.90. This yields the equation $\frac{13 + z}{22 + z} = 0.90$.

35. **The correct answer is E.** Substitute $x + 1$ for x in the function $f(x) = 2x - 3x^2$ and simplify:

$$f(x + 1) = 2(x + 1) - 3(x + 1)^2$$

$$= 2x + 2 - 3\left(x^2 + 2x + 1\right)$$

$$= 2x + 2 - 3x^2 - 6x - 3$$

$$= -3x^2 - 4x - 1$$

CHAPTER

Geometry

GEOMETRY

OVERVIEW

SSAT   ISEE

Roughly translated from Greek as "to measure the earth," geometry deals with the properties of figures and space. Its real-world applications are practically everywhere, ranging from fine arts and classical architecture to intricate LEGO sculpture art and video animation, from cooking to space travel, and from interior design to criminal forensic re-creations. Objects can fit together and work together because of the compatibility and predictability of their shapes. Geometry is the math that makes sure they fit and work together.

Geometry questions focus your attention on matters of distance, shape, and size of geometric figures—whether lines, angles, or solids. First, we'll discuss how to find the area and perimeter of plane figures and the volume of solid figures. Next, we'll cover the different types of angles as well as the relationships between pairs of angles. Then, we'll take a deeper dive into polygons and their traits. Finally, we'll provide a basic overview of coordinate geometry, which involves plotting and identifying ccoordinates on a grid, as well as lines and distances.

PERIMETER, AREA, AND VOLUME

In geometry problems, you'll be asked to find the perimeter, area, and volume of various geometric figures. Before we dive into these concepts, you should know the difference between plane figures and solid figures, which encompass the shapes of most everyday objects. Plane figures are flat, two-dimensional figures that have both length and width. Examples of these include triangles, squares, rectangles, circles, and a variety of other shapes. Solid figures are figures that have both length and width but also possess a third dimension: depth, also referred to as height. Examples of solid figures include cubes, spheres, pyramids, and so on.

There are formulas unique to each figure to help you determine its perimeter, area, or volume. First, we'll cover how to determine the perimeter of a plane figure. Next, we'll explain how to determine the area of a plane figure. Finally, we'll examine how to determine the volume of three-dimensional solid figures.

Perimeter of Plane Figures

The perimeter of a plane figure is the distance around the outside. To find the perimeter of a polygon (a plane figure bounded by line segments), add the lengths of the sides. When you are using a formula to determine the perimeter of a specific shape, the formula will be adjusted to account for the unique features of that shape, but generally, finding perimeter involves adding up the distance of its sides or the outer edges.

First, we'll discuss how to find the perimeter of quadrilaterals, shapes that have four sides. A rectangle is a type of quadrilateral, and in rectangles, opposite sides are equal. The longer side is considered the length of the rectangle, while the shorter side is considered the width. To find the perimeter of a rectangle, you would use the formula $2(l + w)$. In this formula, you're adding up the values for two of the four sides and then doubling it to arrive at the perimeter of a rectangle. You can also add up the lengths of all the sides, since opposite sides are equal, and arrive at the same result.

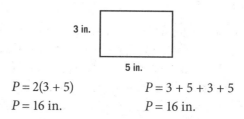

$$P = 2(3 + 5) \qquad P = 3 + 5 + 3 + 5$$
$$P = 16 \text{ in.} \qquad P = 16 \text{ in.}$$

A square is also a type of quadrilateral, but it has four sides of equal length. As such, finding the perimeter of a square only requires you to know the length of one side. The formula for finding the perimeter of a square is $P = 4s$.

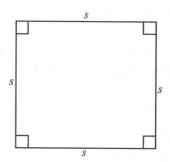

In this square, we're shown that each side is 5 inches. To find the perimeter, we either multiply the length of one side by four or add the lengths of each side.

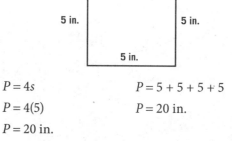

$$P = 4s \qquad P = 5 + 5 + 5 + 5$$
$$P = 4(5) \qquad P = 20 \text{ in.}$$
$$P = 20 \text{ in.}$$

A triangle is a three-sided shape. All triangles share a few universal properties:

- The base of a triangle is always perpendicular to its height.
- The sum of the lengths of any two sides of a triangle must be larger than the length of its third side.
- The measures of the three angles in any triangle must be 180°.

We'll elaborate on some of these concepts later on when we discuss finding the area of a triangle and working with angles.

Finding the perimeter of a triangle requires you to add up the lengths of its sides. Unlike other shapes, there is no formula involved in determining the perimeter of a triangle. In the triangle shown, we're given the length of each of its sides, which we can add up to determine the perimeter.

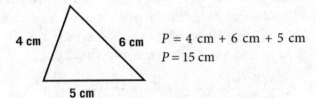

$P = 4\text{ cm} + 6\text{ cm} + 5\text{ cm}$
$P = 15\text{ cm}$

A circle is a perfectly round figure. Every circle is named by a point labeled at its center. In the figure shown, the circle has a center point O. This refers to circle O.

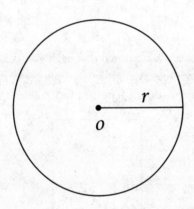

Extending from point O is a line that reaches to the edge of the circle. This line is called the radius of the circle. (The plural of radius is radii.) A circle's radius is represented by the lowercase letter r.

The radius is important because it is used in many circle measurements. Therefore, you need to know what a radius is—and be able to distinguish it from the second key component of a circle, the diameter.

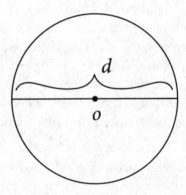

A diameter is essentially twice the length of a radius because it runs through the center of the circle and touches two points on the circle's edge. A circle's diameter is represented by the lowercase letter d.

The perimeter of a circle is called the circumference. The formula for the circumference of a circle is πd or $2\pi r$. Pi (π) is a mathematical value equal to approximately 3.14, or $\frac{22}{7}$. It is the ratio of a circle's circumference to its diameter, so pi (π) is frequently used in calculations involving circles.

 NOTE -------------------------------------

Many different lines can run across a circle and touch two points on its edge, but only those that run through the circle's center are diameters. All of a circle's diameters have equal length, and, because they all run through the center point, they are the longest possible lines on the circle.

The formulas for finding the circumference of a circle are both equivalent. However, depending on what information you are given about a circle, one formula might be more useful. For example, if you are given the diameter of a circle, you would use the πd formula, in which d stands for diameter. If you only know the radius, then you would plug in the length of the radius in $2\pi r$. Because the radius of a circle is always half of its diameter, both of these formulas are equivalent.

In the example shown, we're given the radius of the circle: 3 feet. To find the circumference, plug the radius into the $2\pi r$ formula and calculate.

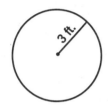

$$C = 2 \times 3 \text{ ft.} \times \pi = 6\pi \text{ ft.}$$

Perimeter problems on the exam will likely ask you to apply these formulas to a real-world context. For example, you might be asked to find the perimeter of a given space, or you might be asked to determine the length of one side if you know the length of another side of a shape. Alternatively, you could be given a shape that looks unfamiliar but actually comprises other shapes, like rectangles or squares, or has pieces cut out of it. In these scenarios, you can still use what you know about finding the perimeter—like the fact that opposite sides are always equal in rectangles—to answer the question. Knowing the formulas for finding the perimeter of the shapes we've covered will help you prepare for different scenarios you might encounter on the exams. We've included a table that provides an overview of the different shapes and their corresponding perimeter formulas.

Scan this QR code for a video on circles.

PERIMETER FORMULAS FOR PLANE FIGURES

Plane Figure	Illustration	Formula
Rectangle		$P = 2(l + w)$
Square		$P = 4s$
Triangle		Add up the three lengths of the triangle.
Circle		$P = 2\pi r = \pi d$

Area of Plane Figures

While perimeter is the distance around a figure, area measures the space inside a figure, the space a plane figure occupies. Because you are multiplying a unit by itself, you are squaring the unit. Therefore, area is always measured in square units. Like perimeter, the formulas for finding the area of different shapes vary depending on the shape's features. While finding the perimeter of a figure requires you to add sides together or to multiply sides by 2 or 4, finding the area requires you to multiply one side by another side.

To find the area of a rectangle, multiply the length of the rectangle by its width.

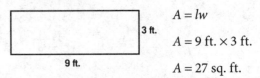

$$A = lw$$
$$A = 9 \text{ ft.} \times 3 \text{ ft.}$$
$$A = 27 \text{ sq. ft.}$$

Notice that the area is expressed in square feet. This is because we multiplied feet by feet, thereby arriving at square feet (or feet squared).

Recall that four sides of a square are the same length. You find the area of a square by squaring the length of one side, which is the same as multiplying the square's length by its width.

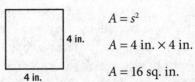

$$A = s^2$$
$$A = 4 \text{ in.} \times 4 \text{ in.}$$
$$A = 16 \text{ sq. in.}$$

Remember that the base of a triangle is always perpendicular to its height. The base is the bottom of the triangle. The height of a triangle is the length of the segment from the base to the vertex (corner) opposite of the base. To find the area of a triangle, multiply the base by the height. Then, multiply by one half, which is equivalent to dividing by 2.

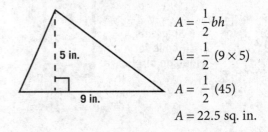

$$A = \frac{1}{2}bh$$
$$A = \frac{1}{2}(9 \times 5)$$
$$A = \frac{1}{2}(45)$$
$$A = 22.5 \text{ sq. in.}$$

Test Yourself 1

1. Find the perimeter.

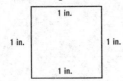

2. Find the perimeter.

3. Find the perimeter.

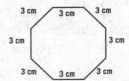

4. Find the circumference.

5. Find the perimeter.

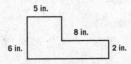

Answers:

1. $P = 1 + 1 + 1 + 1 = 4$ inches

2. $P = 8 + 8 + 6 = 22$ feet

3. $P = 3 + 3 + 3 + 3 + 3 + 3 + 3 + 3$
   $P = 24$ centimeters

4. $C = 2\pi r$
   $C = 2 \times \pi \times 7$
   $C = 14\pi$ centimeters

5. $P = 6 + 5 + (6 - 2) + 8 + 2 + (8 + 5)$
   $P = 38$ inches

Don't confuse the two formulas for calculating the circumference and the area of circles. A good way to keep them straight is to remember the square in πr^2. It should remind you that area must be in square units.

For circles, remember the difference between radius and diameter: A radius is a line that extends from the center of the circle to the edge of the circle. A diameter runs through the center of the circle and touches two points on the circle's edge. The diameter is always twice the length of the radius.

You find the area of a circle by squaring the radius and multiplying it by π. You may leave the area in terms of pi unless you are told what value to assign π.

$$A = \pi r^2$$
$$A = \pi(4 \text{ cm})^2$$
$$A = 16\pi \text{ sq. cm}$$

Like perimeter questions, area questions will likely be situated within a real-world application. For example, you might be asked to determine the area of a space based on its perimeter or vice versa, or you might need to figure out how much paint or carpeting is required to cover a specific area. Remember that area is always expressed in square units, and do your best to differentiate between area and perimeter formulas for a given shape. If you accidentally use a perimeter formula to determine area or vice versa, you'll find yourself confused when none of the answer options match your calculation. Here, we've included a table of plane figures and their corresponding area formulas.

AREA FORMULAS FOR PLANE FIGURES

Plane Figure	Illustration	Formula
Rectangle		$A = lw$
Square		$A = s^2$
Triangle		$A = \frac{1}{2}bh$
Circle		$A = \pi r^2$

Test Yourself 2

Find the area of each figure. The answers will follow.

1.
4 ft.
8 ft.

2.
8 in.
7 in.

3.
1 mi.

4.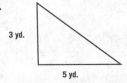
3 yd.
5 yd.

5.
2 cm

6.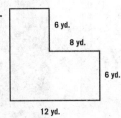
6 yd.
8 yd.
6 yd.
12 yd.

7.
3 yd.
8 yd.
10 yd.

8.
6 ft.

9.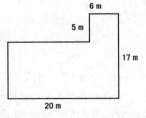
2 ft.
26 ft.

10.
6 m
5 m
17 m
20 m

Answers:

1. $A = lw$

$A = 8 \times 4 = 32$ sq. ft.

2. $A = \frac{1}{2}bh$

$A = \frac{1}{2}(7 \times 8)$

$A = \frac{1}{2}(56) = 28$ sq. in.

3. $A = s^2$

$A = 1^2 = 1$ sq. mi.

4. $A = \frac{1}{2}bh$

$A = \frac{1}{2}(5 \times 3)$

$A = \frac{1}{2}(15) = 7\frac{1}{2}$ sq. yd.

5. $A = \pi r^2$

$A = \pi 2^2$

$A = 4\pi$ sq. cm

6. $A = lw$

$A = 12 \times 6 + (12 - 8) \times 6$

$A = 12 \times 6 + 4 \times 6$

$A = 72 \times 24 = 96$ sq. yd.

7. $A = lw$

$A = 10 \times 8 = 80$ sq. yd.

$A = \frac{1}{2}bh$

$A = \frac{1}{2}(10 \times 3) = \frac{1}{2}(30)$

$A = 15$ sq. yd.

$80 + 15 = 95$ sq. yd.

8. $A = \pi r^2$

$A = \pi 6^2$

$A = 36\pi$ sq. ft.

9. $A = \frac{1}{2}bh$

$A = \frac{1}{2}(26 \times 2) = \frac{1}{2}(52)$

$A = 26$ sq. ft.

10. $A = lw$

$A = 6 \times 5 + 20 \times (17 - 5)$

$A = 6 \times 5 + 20 \times 12$

$A = 30 + 240 = 270$ sq. m

A cube is the three-dimensional version of a square. The volume of a cube is the cube of one side—the measurement of one side to the third power.

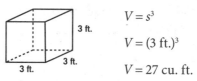

$$V = s^3$$
$$V = (3 \text{ ft.})^3$$
$$V = 27 \text{ cu. ft.}$$

A cylinder is the three-dimensional version of a circle, and it resembles a tube. In calculating its volume, use the formula for finding the area of circle but also multiply by height, since the shape has a third dimension. The height is the distance between the top and bottom circles. In other words, the volume of a cylinder is the area of the circular base (πr^2) times the height.

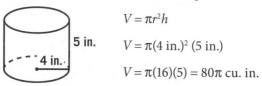

$$V = \pi r^2 h$$
$$V = \pi (4 \text{ in.})^2 \,(5 \text{ in.})$$
$$V = \pi (16)(5) = 80\pi \text{ cu. in.}$$

When encountering volume problems on the exam, prepare for questions that ask you to calculate the volume of everyday objects, typically containers like a can or a box. We've included a table with the volume formulas for the shapes we've covered here.

Volume of Solid Figures

Plane figures are two-dimensional, so you can only determine their perimeter and their area. Solid figures, however, have a third dimension, which gives them depth. As such, you can find their volume, or the measure of the space within a figure considering these three dimensions. Like perimeter and area, the formula for volume varies depending on the shape of the figure, but generally, it is each of its dimensions—the length, width, and height (depth) of the figure—multiplied together.

When discussing the volume of solid figures, you'll likely encounter the term base, which refers to the face on which the figure rests—the area of the two-dimensional version of the figure. Although area is calculated differently depending on the solid, the formula for finding a shape's volume is generally its area formula times its height. Volume is always expressed in cubic units because you are multiplying a unit by itself twice.

A rectangular solid is the three-dimensional version of a rectangle. The volume of a rectangular solid is length × width × height.

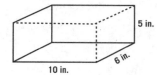

$$V = lwh$$
$$V = (10 \text{ in.})\,(6 \text{ in.})\,(5 \text{ in.})$$
$$V = 300 \text{ cu. in.}$$

VOLUME FORMULAS FOR SOLID FIGURES		
Plane Figure	**Illustration**	**Formula**
Rectangular Solid		$V = lwh$
Cube		$V = s^3$
Cylinder		$V = \pi r^2 h$

Cones and Pyramids

Two other three-dimensional figures you might encounter: the cone and the square pyramid (a four-sided pyramid with a square base). Both are shown below, along with their volume formulas:

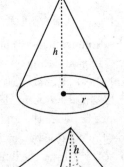

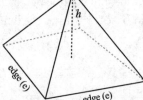

Volume of a cone: $\frac{1}{3} \pi \times \text{radius}^2 \times \text{height}$

Volume of a square pyramid: $\frac{1}{3} \times (\text{base edge})^2 \times \text{height}$

Notice that the volume of a cone is simply one-third that of a right cylinder, and that the volume of a square pyramid is simply one-third that of a rectangular prism.

EXAMPLE:

What is the volume of a pyramid with a height of 24 feet and a square base that measures 10 feet on each side?

   A. 240 cubic feet
   B. 480 cubic feet
   C. 760 cubic feet
   D. 800 cubic feet
   E. 840 cubic feet

The volume of the pyramid $= \frac{1}{3} \times \text{edge}^2 \times$ height $= \frac{1}{3} \times 100 \times 24 = 800$ cubic feet. **The correct answer is D.**

Spheres

The sphere is the final three-dimensional figure you could encounter.

The volume and surface area of a sphere with radius r are given by the following formulas:

Volume $= \frac{4}{3} \pi r^3$

Surface Area $= 4\pi r^2$

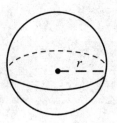

EXAMPLE:

What is the volume of a sphere with a surface area of 100π square meters?

   A. $\frac{100}{3} \pi$ cubic meters
   B. 166π cubic meters
   C. $\frac{500}{3} \pi$ cubic meters
   D. 250π cubic meters
   E. 500π cubic meters

We must determine the radius to compute the volume. Using the formula for the surface area enables us to do this:

$$4\pi r^2 = 100\pi$$
$$r^2 = 25$$
$$r = 5$$

So the volume of the sphere is
$\frac{4}{3} \pi \times 5^3 = \frac{4}{3} \pi \times 125 = \frac{500}{3} \pi$ cubic meters.
The correct answer is C.

Test Yourself 3

Find the volume of each figure. The answers will follow.

1.

2.

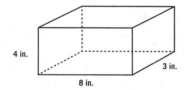

3.

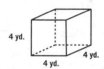

Answers:

1. $V = \pi r^2 h$
   $V = \pi \times 2^2 \times 6$
   $V = \pi \times 4 \times 6$
   $V = 24\pi$ cubic inches

2. $V = lwh$
   $V = 8 \times 3 \times 4$
   $V = 96$ cubic inches

3. $V = s^3$
   $V = 4 \times 4 \times 4$
   $V = 64$ cubic yards

ANGLES

Angles are classified according to their "size" measured using degrees. Angles are usually named by letters, and the notation ($m\angle A$) is used to denote the measure of angle A. The line that extends in only one direction from a point is called a ray. Lines, rays, or line segments meet at a point called the vertex.

The sum of angles and the types of angles you're working with will vary. For the shapes we covered in the previous section, the sum of the angles are as follows:

The sum of the angles of a triangle is 180°.

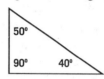

The sum of the angles of a rectangle is 360°.

90°	90°
90°	90°

The sum of the angles of a circle is 360°.

The sum of the angles of a polygon of n sides is $(n - 2)180°$.

$$(8 - 2)(180°) = 6 \times 180° = 1{,}080°$$

Knowing the different types of angles and the relationships between them will be important for solving geometry questions on the exam. Use the angle terminology table to help you navigate these terms.

Let's look at a few examples to better understand the relationships between pairs of angles and how different angles are formed by intersecting lines. We'll start with a right angle.

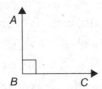

The name of this angle is ∠*ABC*. Notice the small square in the corner where lines *AB* and *BC* intersect. This square indicates that this is a right angle, which means that m∠*ABC* = 90°. When two lines meet to form a right angle, they are said to be perpendicular to each other, as indicated by the symbol ⊥. Therefore, $\overrightarrow{BA} \perp \overrightarrow{BC}$.

An angle that measures less than 90° is called an acute angle. An angle that measures more than 90° but less than 180° is called an obtuse angle.

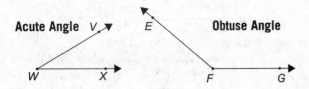

A straight angle measures 180°. ∠*XYZ* in the following figure is a straight angle.

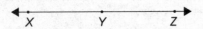

Two or more angles whose measures add up to 180° are called supplementary. In the next figure, ∠*DEG* forms a straight line and therefore measures 180°. ∠*DEF* and ∠*FEG* are supplementary angles; their measures add up to 180°.

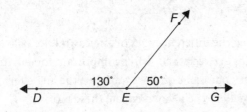

ANGLE TERMINOLOGY	
Term	**Definition**
Acute Angle	An angle with measure between 0 and 90 degrees.
Right Angle	An angle with measure of 90 degrees.
Obtuse Angle	An angle with measure between 90 and 180 degrees.
Straight Angle	An angle with measure of 180 degrees.
Complementary Angles	Two angles with measures that add up to 90 degrees.
Supplementary Angles	Two angles with measures that add up to 180 degrees.
Congruent Angles	Two angles with the same measure.
Vertical Angles	A pair of opposite angles formed by intersecting lines.
Adjacent Angles	Two angles that have a common side and a common vertex but do not overlap in any way.

Two angles are called complementary angles when their measurements add up to 90° (a right angle). In the next figure, m∠*ABC* = 90°. ∠*ABE* and ∠*CBE* are complementary because their measurements add up to 90°. You also know that m∠*ABD* = 90° because ∠*ABD* and ∠*ABC* are adjacent angles and combine to form a straight line, which measures 180°.

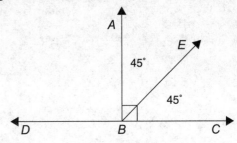

Test Yourself 4

Identify the size of the unlabeled angle in each figure. The answers will follow.

1.

2.

3.

4.
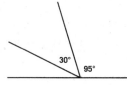

5.

6.
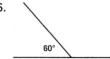

7.

8.

Answers:

1. 80°	5. 140°
2. 240°	6. 120°
3. 90°	7. 180°
4. 55°	8. 50°

In geometry, the set of points that makes up a flat surface is referred to as a plane. When two lines in the same plane never meet, no matter how far they are extended, they are called parallel lines and are indicated by the symbol ∥. If two parallel lines are intersected by a third line, eight angles are formed. A line that intersects two parallel lines is called a transversal. If a transversal intersects two parallel lines perpendicularly (at a 90° angle), all eight angles that are formed are right angles (90°). Otherwise, some angles are acute, while others are obtuse. This figure illustrates parallel lines intersected by a transversal line:

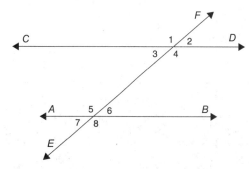

As noted earlier, angles that are equal in degree measure are called congruent angles (the symbol ≅ indicates congruency). In the figure, you can see that eight angles have been formed. The four acute angles (∠2, ∠3, ∠6, and ∠7) are congruent, and the four obtuse angles (∠1, ∠4, ∠5, and ∠8) are also congruent. Each pair of angles that are opposite each other in relation to a vertex (for example, ∠2 and ∠3) are called vertical angles. Vertical angles are always congruent.

Four angles formed by two intersecting lines add up to 360° in measure. In the same figure, m∠1 + m∠2 + m∠3 + m∠4 = 360°. (The same holds true for angles 5, 6, 7, and 8.) In the figure, the measure of any one of the four acute angles plus the measure of any obtuse angle equals 180°. If you know the measure of any one

Scan this QR code for a video on lines and angles.

Rules about angles formed by intersecting lines

VERTICAL ANGLES:

Vertical angles (angles across the vertex from each other and formed by the same two lines) are equal in degree measure or congruent (≅). In other words, they're the same size.

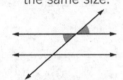

ADJACENT ANGLES:

If adjacent angles combine to form a straight line, their degree measures total 180. In fact, a straight line is actually a 180° angle.

PERPENDICULAR LINES:

If two lines are perpendicular (⊥) to each other, they intersect at right (90°) angles.

THE SUM OF ANGLES:

The sum of all angles formed by the intersection of two (or more) lines at the same point is 360°, regardless of how many angles are involved.

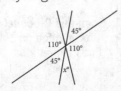

angle, you can determine the measure of all seven other angles. For example, if m∠2 = 30°, then ∠3, ∠6, and ∠7 each measures 30° as well, while ∠1, ∠4, ∠5, and ∠8 each measures 150°.

A geometry question might involve nothing more than intersecting lines and the angles they form. To handle this type of question, remember the four basic rules about angles formed by intersecting lines.

MORE ABOUT POLYGONS

Polygons include all two-dimensional figures formed only by line segments. Two key points about polygons to remember are these two reciprocal rules:

- If all angles of a polygon are congruent (equal in degree measure), then all sides are congruent (equal in length).
- If all sides of a polygon are congruent (equal in length), then all angles are congruent (equal in degree measure).

A polygon in which all sides are congruent and all angles are congruent is called a regular polygon.

Earlier, you saw that you can use the following formula to determine the sum of all interior angles of *any* polygon with angles that each measure less than 180° (n = number of sides):

$$(n - 2)(180°) = \text{sum of interior angles}$$

For regular polygons, the average angle size is also the size of every angle. But for *any* polygon (except for those with an angle exceeding 180°), you can find the average angle size by dividing the sum of the angles by the number of sides. One way to shortcut the math is to memorize the angle sums and averages for polygons with three to eight sides:

3 sides: $(3 - 2)(180°) = 180° \div 3 = 60°$

4 sides: $(4 - 2)(180°) = 360° \div 4 = 90°$

5 sides: $(5 - 2)(180°) = 540° \div 5 = 108°$

6 sides: $(6 - 2)(180°) = 720° \div 6 = 120°$

7 sides: $(7 - 2)(180°) = 900° \div 7 = 129°$

8 sides: $(8 - 2)(180°) = 1,080° \div 8 = 135°$

EXAMPLE:

The measures of a polygon's interior angles total
$(n - 2)(180°)$, where n = number of sides. If four
of the interior angles of a five-sided polygon
measure 100° each, what is the measure of the
fifth interior angle?

    A. 40°

    B. 60°

    C. 90°

    D. 140°

    E. 160°

The total number of degrees in the polygon = $(5 - 2)(180°) = 540°$. The four known angles total
400°, so the fifth angle must be 140°. **The correct answer is D.**

Triangles

Remember that a triangle is three-sided shape and that
all triangles, regardless of shape or size, share the following four properties:

- **Length of the sides:** Each side is shorter than the
  sum of the lengths of the other two sides.

- **Angle measures:** The measures of the three interior angles total 180°.

- **Angles and opposite sides:** Comparative angle
  sizes correspond to the comparative lengths of
  the sides opposite those angles. For example, a
  triangle's largest angle is opposite its longest side.
  (The sides opposite two congruent angles are also
  congruent.)

- **Area:** The area of any triangle is equal to one-
  half the product of its base and its height (or
  "altitude"): Area = $\frac{1}{2}$ × base × height. You can use
  any side as the base to calculate area.

The next figure shows three particular types of
triangles.

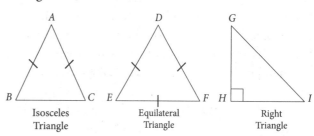

| Isosceles Triangle | Equilateral Triangle | Right Triangle |

An isosceles triangle is one in which two sides (and two
angles) are congruent. In the figure above, ∠B and ∠C
are congruent, and the sides opposite those two angles,
$\overline{AB}$ and $\overline{AC}$, are congruent. In an equilateral triangle,
all three angles are congruent, and all three sides are
congruent. In a right triangle, one angle is a right angle,
and the other two angles are acute angles. The longest
side of a right triangle (in this case, $\overline{GI}$) is called the
hypotenuse.

EXAMPLE:

The length of one side of a certain triangular
floor space is 12 feet. Which of the
following CANNOT be the lengths of the other
two sides?

    A. 1 foot and 12 feet

    B. 8 feet and 4 feet

    C. 12 feet and 13 feet

    D. 16 feet and 14 feet

    E. 16 feet and 10 feet

The length of any two sides combined must be
greater than the length of the third side. **The
correct answer is B.**

Right Triangles and the Pythagorean Theorem

In a right triangle, one angle measures 90° and each of the other two angles measures less than 90°. The Pythagorean theorem involves the relationship among the sides of any right triangle and can be expressed by the equation $a^2 + b^2 = c^2$. As shown in the next figure, the letters a and b represent the lengths of the two legs (the two shortest sides) that form the right angle, and c is the length of the hypotenuse (the longest side, opposite the right angle).

Pythagorean theorem: $a^2 + b^2 = c^2$

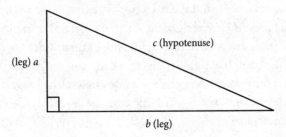

For any right triangle, if you know the length of two sides, you can determine the length of the third side by applying the Pythagorean theorem. Study the following two examples:

EXAMPLE:

If the two shortest sides (the legs) of a right triangle are 2 and 3 inches in length, then the length of the triangle's third side (the hypotenuse) is $\sqrt{13}$ inches:

$$a^2 + b^2 = c^2$$
$$2^2 + 3^2 = c^2$$
$$4 + 9 = c^2$$
$$13 = c^2$$
$$\sqrt{13} = c^2$$

EXAMPLE:

In a right triangle, one angle measures 90°. If the hypotenuse of a right triangle is c and one leg of the triangle is a, what is the length of the third side in terms of a and c?

- **A.** $\sqrt{a^2 + c^2}$
- **B.** $\dfrac{a + c}{2}$
- **C.** $\sqrt{a \times c}$
- **D.** $\sqrt{c^2 - a^2}$
- **E.** $\sqrt{a^2 - c^2}$

Use the Pythagorean theorem to determine the length of the third side, which is the other leg of the triangle. Call the length of the third side b. The Pythagorean theorem says that $a^2 + b^2 = c^2$. Solve for b:

$$b^2 = c^2 - a^2$$
$$b = \sqrt{c^2 - a^2}$$

The correct answer is D.

Isosceles and Equilateral Triangles

An *isosceles* triangle has the following special properties:

- Two of the sides are congruent (equal in length).
- The two angles opposite the two congruent sides are congruent (equal in size or degree measure).

If you know any *two* angle measures of a triangle, you can determine whether the triangle is isosceles. Subtract the two angle measures you know from 180. If the result equals one of the other two measures, then the triangle is isosceles. For example:

- If two of the angles are 55° and 70°, then the third angle must be 55° (180 − 55 − 70 = 55). The triangle is isosceles, and the two sides opposite the two 55° angles are congruent.

- If two of the angles are 80° and 20°, then the third angle must be 80° (180 − 80 − 20 = 80). The triangle is isosceles, and the two sides opposite the two 80° angles are congruent.

In any isosceles triangle, lines bisecting the triangle's three angles each bisect its opposite side. The line bisecting the angle connecting the two congruent angles divides the triangle into two congruent right triangles.

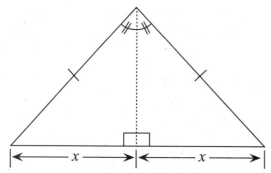

So if you know the lengths of all three sides of an isosceles triangle, you can determine the area of the triangle by applying the Pythagorean theorem.

All equilateral triangles share the following three properties:

- All three sides are congruent (equal in length).
- The measure of each angle is 60°.
- Area $= \dfrac{s^2\sqrt{3}}{4}$ ($s =$ any side)

As shown in the following diagram, any line bisecting one of the 60° angles divides an equilateral triangle into two right triangles with angle measures of 30°, 60°, and 90° (one of the Pythagorean angle triplets). Accordingly, the side ratio for each smaller triangle is $1{:}\sqrt{3}{:}2$. The area of this equilateral triangle is $\dfrac{1}{2}(2)\sqrt{3}$, or $\sqrt{3}$.

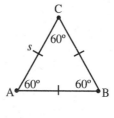
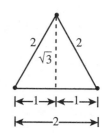

Congruency and Similarity

Two geometric figures that have the same size and shape are said to be **congruent**. The symbol for congruency is $\cong$. Two angles are congruent if their degree measure (size) is the same. Two line segments are congruent if they are equal in length. Two triangles are congruent if the angle measures and sides are all identical in size. (The same applies to figures with more than three sides.)

If a two-dimensional geometric figure, such as a triangle or rectangle, has exactly the same shape as another one, then the two figures are similar. Similar figures share the same angle measures, and their sides are proportionate (though not the same length).

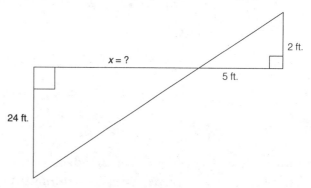

These two triangles are similar. They share an angle and both have right angles. Thus, their third angles must be equal. Because their angles are equal, their sides must be proportional. The ratio 2:5 is the same as 24:x. By creating a proportion, you can solve for x and find the missing side length as 60 ft.

CIRCLES

Earlier in this chapter, you learned about the key features of circles. Let's review those now before exploring some additional characteristics of the shape:

- **Circumference:** The distance around the circle (the same as "perimeter," but the word "circumference" applies only to circles, ovals, and other curved figures)

- **Radius:** The distance from a circle's center to any point along the circle's circumference

- **Diameter:** The greatest distance from one point to another on the circle's circumference (twice the length of the radius)

- **Chord:** A line segment connecting two points on the circle's circumference (a circle's longest possible chord is its diameter, passing through the circle's center)

As noted previously, a circle's diameter is twice the length of its radius. The next figure shows a circle with radius 6 and diameter 12.

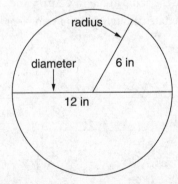

During the test, you'll apply one, or possibly both, of two basic formulas involving circles (r = radius, d = diameter):

Circumference = $2\pi r$, or πd

Area = πr^2

Recall that the value of π is approximately 3.14. A close fractional approximation of π is $\frac{22}{7}$.

With the circumference and area formulas, all you need is one value—area, circumference, diameter, or radius—and you can determine all the others. Referring to the circle shown above:

Given a circle with a diameter of 12:

$$radius = 6$$
$$circumference = 12\pi$$
$$area = \pi(6)^2 = 36\pi$$

For the test, you won't need to work with a value of π any more precise than 3.14 or $\frac{22}{7}$. In fact, you might be able to answer a circle question using the symbol π itself, without approximating its value.

EXAMPLES:

If a circle with radius r has an area of 4 square feet, what is the area of a circle whose radius is $3r$?

- **A.** 6π square feet
- **B.** 36 square feet
- **C.** 12π square feet
- **D.** 48 square feet
- **E.** 60 square feet

The area of a circle with radius $r = \pi r^2$, which is given as 4. The area of a circle with radius $3r = \pi(3r)^2 = 9\pi r^2$. Since $\pi r^2 = 4$, the area of a circle with radius $3r = (9)(4) = 36$. **The correct answer is B.**

If a circle's circumference is 10 centimeters, what is the area of the circle?

- **A.** $\frac{25}{\pi}$ cm^2
- **B.** 5π cm^2
- **C.** 22.5 cm^2
- **D.** 25 cm^2
- **E.** 28 cm^2

First, determine the circle's radius. Applying the circumference formula $C = 2\pi r$, solve for r:

$$10 = 2\pi r$$
$$\frac{5}{\pi} = r$$

Then, apply the area formula, with $\frac{5}{\pi}$ as the value of r:

$$A = \pi\left(\frac{5}{\pi}\right)^2$$

$$= \pi\left(\frac{25}{\pi^2}\right)$$

$$= \frac{25}{\pi^2} \cdot \frac{\pi}{1}$$

$$= \frac{25}{\pi}$$

The correct answer is A.

Arcs and Degree Measures of a Circle

An arc is a segment of a circle's circumference. A minor arc is the shortest arc connecting two points on a circle's circumference. For example, in the figure shown, minor arc $\overset{\frown}{AB}$ is the one formed by the 60° angle from the circle's center (O).

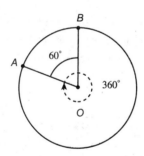

A circle, by definition, contains a total of 360°. The length of an arc relative to the circle's circumference is directly proportionate to the arc's degree measure as a fraction of the circle's total degree measure of 360°.

For example, in the preceding figure, minor arc $\overset{\frown}{AB}$ accounts for $\frac{60}{360}$, or $\frac{1}{6}$, of the circle's circumference. An arc of a circle can be defined either as a length (a portion of the circle's circumference) or as a degree measure. In the preceding figure, $\overset{\frown}{AB} = 60°$. If the circumference is 12π, then the length of minor arc $\overset{\frown}{AB}$ is $\frac{1}{6}$ of 12π, or 2π.

EXAMPLE:

Circle O has diameters $\overline{DB}$ and $\overline{AC}$, as shown in the figure below.

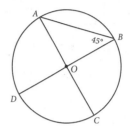

If the circumference of circle O is 12 inches, what is the length of minor arc $\overset{\frown}{BC}$?

A. 3 inches

B. $\frac{13}{4}$ inches

C. $\frac{11}{3}$ inches

D. 4 inches

E. 5 inches

Since $\overline{AO}$ and $\overline{BO}$ are both radii, $\triangle AOB$ is isosceles, and therefore m$\angle BAO = 45°$. It follows that m$\angle AOB = 90°$. That 90° angle accounts for $\frac{1}{4}$ of the circle's 360°. Accordingly, minor arc $\overset{\frown}{BC}$ must account for $\frac{1}{4}$ of the circle's 12-inch circumference, or 3 inches. **The correct answer is A.**

Circles and Tangent Lines

A circle is tangent to a line (or line segment) if the two intersect at one and only one point (called the point of tangency). Here's the key rule to remember about tangents: A line that is tangent to a circle is *always* perpendicular to the line passing through the circle's center and the point of tangency.

The figure shows a circle with center O inscribed in a square. Point P is one of four points of tangency. By definition, $\overline{OP} \perp \overline{AB}$.

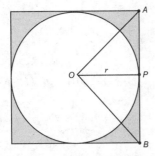

Also, notice the following relationships between the circle in the preceding figure and the inscribing square (r = radius):

Each side of the square is $2r$ in length.

The square's area is $(2r)^2$, or $4r^2$.

EXAMPLE:

Two parallel lines are tangent to the same circle. What is the shortest distance between the two lines?

   A. The circle's radius

   B. The circle's diameter

   C. The circle's circumference

   D. The product of the circle's radius and π

   E. The product of the circle's diameter and π

The two lines are both perpendicular to a chord that is the circle's diameter. Thus, the shortest distance between them is that diameter. **The correct answer is B.**

To learn more about coordinate geometry, scan this QR code.

COORDINATE GEOMETRY

Finding points on a plane is the study of coordinate geometry. A grid is commonly used to do this. The grid is divided into four sections. Each section is called a quadrant. The two number lines that divide the grid into quadrants are called the x-axis (the horizontal axis) and the y-axis (the vertical axis). The center of the grid, where the two axes meet, is called the origin. Any point on the plane has two coordinates that indicate its location relative to the axes. The points that are drawn on the grid are identified by ordered pairs. In ordered pairs, the x-coordinate is always written first. The ordered pair for the origin, in the middle of the grid, is (0, 0).

The quadrants of a grid are named in counterclockwise order, beginning with the first quadrant in the upper right corner. For any point in the first quadrant, the coordinates are positive. The quadrant in the top left is called the second quadrant. For any point in the second quadrant, the x-coordinate is negative but the y-coordinate is positive. The quadrant in the lower left is called the third quadrant. In the third quadrant, both coordinates are negative. The quadrant in the lower right is called the fourth quadrant, and in the fourth quadrant, the x-coordinate is positive, and the y-coordinate is negative.

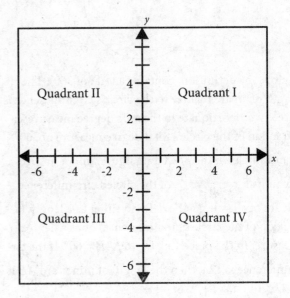

On the following graph, the *x*-coordinate of point A is 3. The *y*-coordinate of point A is 2. The coordinates of point A are given by the ordered pair (3, 2). Point B has coordinates (–1, 4). Point C has coordinates (–4, –3). Point D has coordinates (2, –3).

To graph (4, –2), locate 4 on the *x*-axis, then move –2 spaces vertically (2 spaces down, since the number is negative) to find the given point.

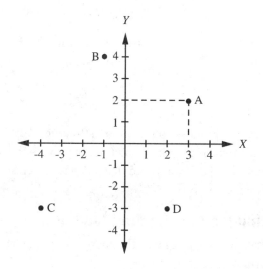

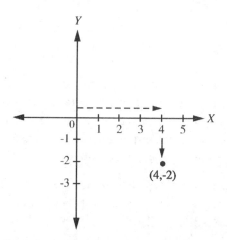

To graph a point whose coordinates are given, first locate the *x*-coordinate on the *x*-axis, then from that position move vertically the number of spaces indicated by the *y*-coordinate.

Ordered pairs, just like the origin, can have 0 for their *x*- or *y*- coordinate. Any point on the *y*-axis has 0 as its *x*-coordinate. Any point on the *x*-axis has 0 as its *y*-coordinate.

Finding the Distance Between Two Points

Finding the distance between two points that are directly horizontal or vertical from each other is simply a matter of counting the number of squares that separate the points. In the next grid, for example, the distance between points $A\,(2, 3)$ and $B\,(7, 3)$ is 5. The distance between points $C\,(2, 1)$ and $D\,(2, -4)$ is also 5.

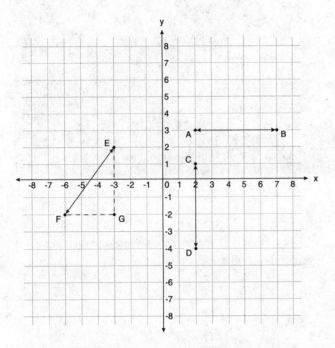

If you are asked to find the distance between two points that are not directly horizontal or vertical from each other, you can use the Pythagorean theorem. For example, to find the distance between points E and F on the preceding grid, follow these steps:

- Draw a right triangle in which $\overline{EF}$ is the hypotenuse (as shown by the broken lines on the preceding grid).
- Determine the distance between E and G. That distance is 4. This is the length of one leg of right triangle EFG.
- Determine the distance between F and G. That distance is 3. This is the length of the other leg of a right triangle EFG.

Apply the Pythagorean theorem to find the hypotenuse of $\triangle EFG$, which is the distance between E and F:

$$4^2 + 3^2 = c^2$$
$$16 + 9 = c^2$$
$$25 = c^2$$
$$5 = c$$

In applying the Pythagorean theorem to the coordinate grid, you may want to use the formula for determining the distance between two points, which is a more specific way of expressing the theorem.

Distance between points =

$$\left(x_2 - x_1\right)^2 + \left(y_2 - y_1\right)^2 \text{, where the two points are}$$

$$\left(x_1, y_1\right) \text{ and } \left(x_2, y_2\right)$$

Apply this formula to the preceding example, and you obtain the same result:

$$\sqrt{\left(-6 - (-3)\right)^2 + \left(-2 - 2\right)^2} = \sqrt{\left(-3\right)^2 + \left(-4\right)^2} = \sqrt{9 + 16} = \sqrt{25} = 5$$

Finding the Midpoint of a Line Segment

To find the coordinates of the midpoint (M) of a line segment, simply average the two endpoints' x-values and y-values:

$$x_M = \frac{x_1 + x_2}{2} \text{ and } y_M = \frac{y_1 + y_2}{2}$$

The midpoint formula is often used to find these coordinates:

$$M = \left(\frac{x_1 + x_2}{2}, \frac{y_1 + y_2}{2}\right)$$

A question might simply ask you to find the midpoint between two given points. Or, it might provide the midpoint and one endpoint, and then ask you to determine the other endpoint.

Defining a Line on the Plane

You can define any line on the coordinate plane by the following general equation:

$$y = mx + b$$

In this equation:

- The variable m is the slope of the line.
- The variable b is the line's y-intercept (where the line crosses the y-axis).
- The variables x and y are the coordinates of any point on the line. Any (x, y) pair defining a point on the line can substitute for the variables x and y.

Think of the slope of a line as a fraction in which the numerator indicates the vertical change from one point to another on the line (moving left to right) corresponding to a given horizontal change, which the fraction's denominator indicates. The common term used for this fraction is rise over run.

You can determine the slope of a line from any two pairs of (x, y) coordinates. In general, if (x_1, y_1) and (x_2, y_2) lie on the same line, calculate the line's slope according to the following formula:

$$\text{slope } (m) = \frac{y_2 - y_1}{x_2 - x_1}$$

In applying the formula, be sure to subtract corresponding values. For example, a careless test taker calculating the slope might subtract y_1 from y_2 but subtract x_2 from x_1. Also be sure to calculate rise over run, and not run over rise.

A question might ask you to identify the slope of a line defined by a given equation, in which case you simply put the equation in the form $y = mx + b$, then identify the m-term. Or, it might ask you to determine the equation of a line, or just the line's slope (m) or y-intercept (b), given the coordinates of two points on the line.

For example, suppose that the following points lie on the same line.

x	2	5	–1	–3
y	1	$-\frac{7}{2}$	$\frac{11}{2}$	$\frac{17}{2}$

Since the points lie on the same line, you can use any pair of points to determine the slope. For convenience, use the first two:

$$m = \frac{y_2 - y_1}{x_2 - x_1} = \frac{-\frac{7}{2} - 1}{5 - 2} = \frac{-\frac{9}{2}}{3} = \frac{9}{2} \cdot \frac{1}{3} = -\frac{3}{2}$$

EXAMPLE:

On the coordinate plane, what is the slope of the line defined by the two points $P(2, 1)$ and $Q(-3, 4)$?

A. $-\frac{5}{3}$

B. -1

C. $-\frac{3}{5}$

D. $\frac{1}{3}$

E. 1

Apply the slope formula:

$$\text{slope } (m) = \frac{4 - 1}{-3 - 2} = \frac{3}{-5}, \text{ or } -\frac{3}{5}$$

The correct answer is C.

Finding the Equation of a Line on the Plane

Let's say you are asked to find the equation of the line with slope $-\frac{2}{3}$ that passes through the point $(-1, -3)$.

The most efficient approach is to use the point-slope equation of the line. Precisely, a line with slope m passing through the point (x_1, y_1) has the equation $y - y_1 = m(x - x_1)$. Using the given information yields the equation $y - (-3) = -\frac{2}{3}(x - (-1))$. This can be simplified in different ways.

Slope-intercept form:

$$y + 3 = -\frac{2}{3}(x + 1)$$
$$y = -\frac{2}{3}x - \frac{11}{3}$$

Standard form:

$$2x + 3y = -11$$

You can also write the equation of a line when given 2 points on that line. For example, if you know the line passes through the points (2, –5) and (4, –1), first, determine the slope of the line:

$$m = \frac{-1-(-5)}{4-2} = \frac{-1+5}{2} = \frac{4}{2} = 2$$

Now, use the point-slope formula of a line to write the equation. You can use either of the two points—the equation will be the same. Using (2, –5) yields $y - (-5) = 2(x - 2)$ or equivalently, $y = 2x - 9$.

Two lines are parallel if they have the same slope, while they are perpendicular if the product of their slopes is –1. For instance, the line $y = 3x - 1$ is parallel to $y = 3x + 4$ because they both have slope 3. Similarly, the line $y = -2x + 3$ is perpendicular to $y = \frac{1}{2}x - 1$ because the product of their slopes is $(-2)\left(\frac{1}{2}\right) = -1$.

Say you are given the line $2x - 4y = 1$ and you know it passes through the origin. How do you find a line parallel to this given line?

First, find the slope of the given line by putting the equation into slope-intercept form; doing so yields $y = \frac{1}{2}x - \frac{1}{4}$. So the slope is $\frac{1}{2}$. Since parallel lines have the same slope, this is the slope of the line whose equation we seek. Using the point-slope formula for the equation of a line with this slope and the point (0, 0) yields $y = \frac{1}{2}x$.

Graphing a Line on the Plane

You can graph a line on the coordinate plane if you know the coordinates of any two points on the line. Just plot the two points, and then draw a line connecting them. You can also graph a line from one point on the line if you also know either the line's slope or its y-intercept.

A question might ask you to recognize the value of a line's slope (m) based on a graph of the line. If the graph identifies the precise coordinates of two points, you can determine the line's precise slope (and the entire equation of the line). Even without any precise coordinates, you can still estimate the line's slope based on its appearance.

Lines that slope upward from left to right:

- A line sloping *upward* from left to right has a positive slope (m).
- A line with a slope of 1 slopes upward from left to right at a 45° angle in relation to the x-axis.
- A line with a fractional slope between 0 and 1 slopes upward from left to right but at less than a 45° angle in relation to the x-axis.
- A line with a slope greater than 1 slopes upward from left to right at more than a 45° angle in relation to the x-axis.

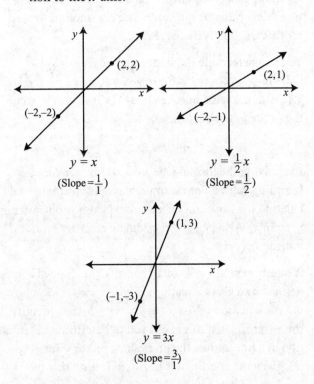

Lines that slope downward from left to right:

- A line sloping *downward* from left to right has a negative slope (m).
- A line with a slope of –1 slopes downward from left to right at a 45° angle in relation to the x-axis.
- A line with a fractional slope between 0 and –1 slopes downward from left to right but at less than a 45° angle in relation to the x-axis.
- A line with a slope less than –1 (for example, –2) slopes downward from left to right at more than a 45° angle in relation to the x-axis.

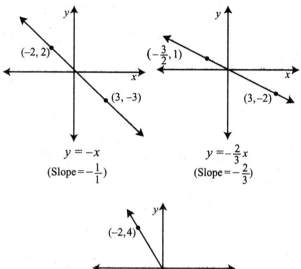

$y = -x$
(Slope $= -\frac{1}{1}$)

$y = -\frac{2}{3}x$
(Slope $= -\frac{2}{3}$)

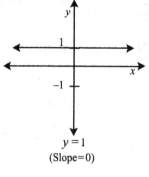

$y = 1$
(Slope $= 0$)

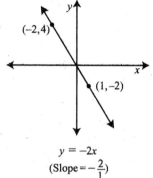

$y = -2x$
(Slope $= -\frac{2}{1}$)

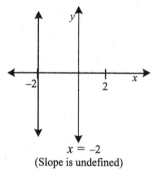

$x = -2$
(Slope is undefined)

Horizontal and vertical lines:

- A horizontal line has a slope of zero ($m = 0$, and $mx = 0$).

- A vertical line has either an undefined or an indeterminate slope (the fraction's denominator is 0), so the m-term in the equation is ignored.

SUMMING IT UP

- Know the difference between perimeter, area, and volume.

  - Perimeter is the distance around the outside of a shape.

  - Area measures the space inside a two-dimensional plane figure, like a rectangle or circle.

  - Volume measures the space inside a three-dimensional solid figure, like a cube or a cylinder, and is the product of the figure's area and its height.

- Memorize the formulas for determining perimeter, area, and base, as these may not be given to you on the test.

- Angles are measured in degrees. Lines, rays, or line segments form angles and meet at a point called the vertex. Know the different types of angles—right, obtuse, acute, and straight angles—as well as the relationships formed between pairs of angles—complementary, supplementary, congruent, vertical, and adjacent angles.

- To solve for the hypotenuse of a right triangle, use the Pythagorean theorem ($a^2 + b^2 + c^2$).

- Coordinate geometry requires you to find points on a plane. On the exam, you may be required to graph the points of an ordered pair or to determine the value of an ordered pair using the x- and y-coordinates plotted on a graph.

- To calculate the slope of a line on a graph, use the slope-intercept equation: $y = mx + b$, where m is the slope and b is the point where the line crosses the y-axis. Any point on the line can be substituted in for the values of x and y.

GEOMETRY

35 Questions—28 Minutes

Directions: In the following questions, work out each problem and mark the letter that corresponds to the correct answer. The answers will follow.

1. Suppose two sides of a triangle measure 4 cm and 8 cm and that the perimeter of the triangle is 17 cm. What is the length of the triangle's third side?

   A. 4 cm

   B. 5 cm

   C. 8 cm

   D. 10 cm

   E. 12 cm

2. Two rectangular boards, each measuring 7 feet by 5 feet, are placed together to make one large panel. How much shorter will the perimeter be if the two long sides are placed together than if the two short sides are placed together?

   A. 2 feet

   B. 4 feet

   C. 6 feet

   D. 8 feet

   E. 10 feet

3. Nine square tiles, each with an area of 25 square centimeters, have been arranged to form a larger square. What is the perimeter of the large square?

   A. 60 centimeters

   B. 75 centimeters

   C. 100 centimeters

   D. 150 centimeters

   E. 220 centimeters

4. What is the circumference of a circle with radius 9?

   A. 6π

   B. 9π

   C. 18π

   D. 27π

   E. 81π

5. What is the area of this triangle?

   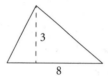

   A. 5

   B. 11

   C. 12

   D. 20

   E. 24

6. A square has an area of 49 square inches. The number of inches in its perimeter is

   A. 7.

   B. 14.

   C. 28.

   D. 49.

   E. 98.

7. If circle *F* has an area of 36π, what is its diameter?

    A. 6

    B. 12

    C. 36

    D. 54

    E. 72

8. A roll of carpeting will cover 224 square feet of floor space. How many rolls are needed to carpet a room 36' × 8' and another 24' × 9'?

    A. 2.25

    B. 2.50

    C. 4.25

    D. 4.50

    E. 5

9. What is the volume of this cylinder?

    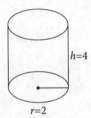

    A. 8π

    B. 16

    C. 16π

    D. 32

    E. 32π

10. What is the volume of a cube with a side of length 5 in.?

    A. 25 in.³

    B. 125 in.³

    C. 150 in.³

    D. 225 in.³

    E. 250 in.³

11. The number of cubic feet of soil needed for a flower box 3 feet long, 8 inches wide, and 1 foot deep is

    A. 2

    B. 3

    C. $4\frac{2}{3}$

    D. 12

    E. 24

12. The formula for the volume of a cylinder is $V = \pi r^2 h$. What is the volume of a cylinder with a radius of 5 ft. and a height of 3 ft.?

    A. 15π ft.³

    B. 45π ft.³

    C. 60π ft.³

    D. 65π ft.³

    E. 75π ft.³

13. If *a* + *b* = 200°, and *c* + *d* + *e* + *f* = 140°, what is the number of degrees in angle *g*?

    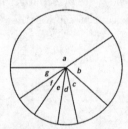

    A. 10°

    B. 20°

    C. 30°

    D. 45°

    E. 50°

14. In this figure, what is the value of $a + b$?

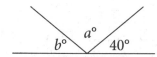

A. 60

B. 90

C. 120

D. 140

E. 150

15. Find the value of x in this figure:

A. 60

B. 85

C. 90

D. 100

E. 110

16. What is the measure of $\angle A$?

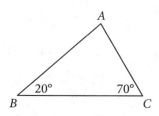

A. 20°

B. 50°

C. 70°

D. 80°

E. 90°

17. In the figure shown, line l is perpendicular to line m. One angle formed by line l and line q has a measure of 130°, as shown. What is the degree measure of a?

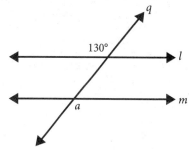

A. 25°

B. 65°

C. 130°

D. 155°

E. 160°

18. Lines RS and TU intersect at point V. If angle RVT has a measure of 35°, what is the measure of angle SVU?

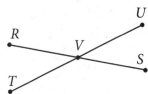

A. 35°

B. 45°

C. 60°

D. 70°

E. 145°

19. In triangle *ABC*, what is the value of *x*?

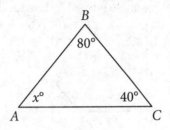

A. 40

B. 60

C. 80

D. 100

E. 120

20. What is the value of *x* in the diagram below?

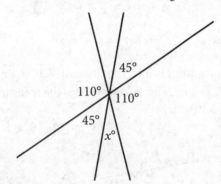

A. 25

B. 45

C. 70

D. 90

E. 100

21. Which point shown below corresponds to (8, 3)?

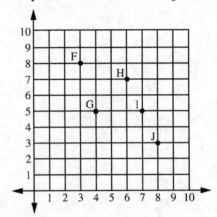

A. Point F

B. Point G

C. Point H

D. Point I

E. Point J

22. What are the coordinates of point M?

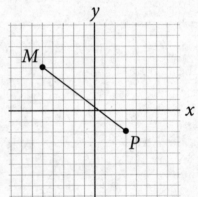

A. (5, 4)

B. (−5, 4)

C. (5, −4)

D. (−5, −4)

E. (4, 5)

23. What are the coordinates of point *P*?

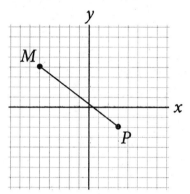

A. (3, 2)

B. (−3, 2)

C. (3, −2)

D. (−3, −2)

E. (2, 3)

24. Points A, B, C, D, and E are shown on the coordinate plane. Which point is located at (4, −3)?

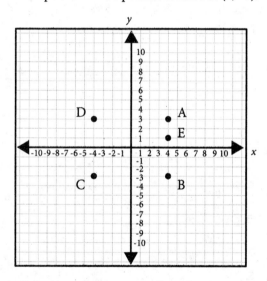

A. Point *A*

B. Point *B*

C. Point *C*

D. Point *D*

E. Point *E*

25. Which statement about the figure is true?

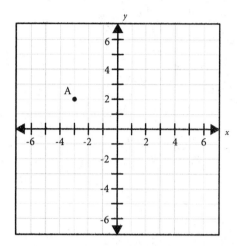

A. The coordinates of point A are (−3, −2).

B. The coordinates of point A are (3, 2).

C. Point A is located in quadrant I.

D. Point A is located in quadrant II.

E. Point A is located in quadrant IV.

26. Assume that *l* is parallel to *m*. Find the value of *y*.

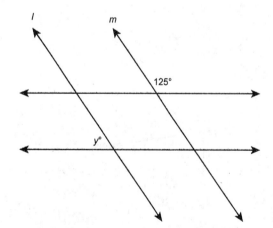

A. 45°

B. 55°

C. 90°

D. 125°

E. 135°

27. Find z:

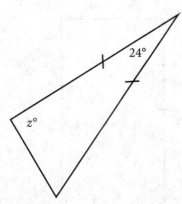

A. 24

B. 78

C. 90

D. 156

E. 180

28. What is the equation of the graphed line?

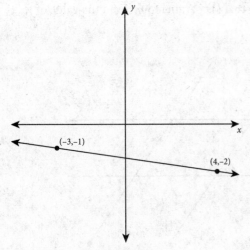

A. $x + 7y = -10$

B. $2x + 47 = -21$

C. $y + 7x = -22$

D. $y + 3x = -10$

E. $-x + 3y = 10$

29. What is the area of the following parallelogram?

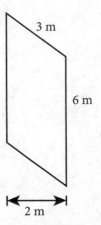

A. 6 square meters

B. 11 square meters

C. 12 square meters

D. 18 square meters

E. 24 square meters

30. Which of the following expressions is equivalent to y?

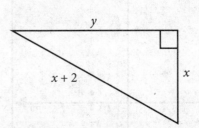

A. $2\sqrt{x+1}$

B. $4x+4$

C. 2

D. $\sqrt{2x^2 + 4x + 4}$

E. $2x$

31. The surface area of a cube is 13.5 square inches. What is its volume?

A. 4.5 cubic inches

B. 1.5 cubic inches

C. 3.375 cubic inches

D. 2.25 cubic inches

E. 1 cubic inch

32. What is the measure of the largest angle in the following triangle?

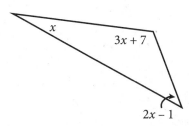

A. 29

B. 57

C. 94

D. 117

E. 123

33. What is the equation of the line passing through the points (0,-3) and (-6, 0)?

A. $y = -\dfrac{1}{2}x - 3$

B. $y = -\dfrac{1}{2}x - 6$

C. $y = -2x - 6$

D. $y = -2x - 3$

E. $x = -2y - 3$

34. The sides of a square have a length of x inches. If they are decreased by 30%, what is the perimeter of the resulting square?

A. 0.49x inches

B. 0.70x inches

C. 1.20x inches

D. 2.80x inches

E. 3.00x inches

35. What is the circumference of a circle with an area of $\sqrt{\pi}$ square centimeters?

A. $\dfrac{1}{\pi^{\frac{1}{4}}}$ centimeters

B. $2\pi^{\frac{1}{2}}$ centimeters

C. $2\pi^{\frac{5}{4}}$ centimeters

D. $2\pi^{\frac{1}{4}}$ centimeters

E. $2\pi^{\frac{3}{4}}$ centimeters

ANSWER KEY AND EXPLANATIONS

1. B	6. C	11. A	16. E	21. E	26. B	31. C
2. B	7. B	12. E	17. C	22. B	27. B	32. C
3. A	8. A	13. B	18. A	23. C	28. A	33. A
4. C	9. C	14. D	19. B	24. B	29. C	34. D
5. C	10. B	15. B	20. A	25. D	30. A	35. E

1. **The correct answer is B.** The perimeter of a triangle is the sum of the lengths of its sides. Since the perimeter is given and we know the lengths of two sides, we can assign the missing side a length of x and solve as follows:

$$P = x + y + z$$
$$17 = x + 4 + 8$$
$$17 = x + 12$$
$$5 = x$$

2. **The correct answer is B.** Perimeter of a rectangle $= 2l + 2w$. If the two long sides are together, the perimeter will be $7 + 5 + 5 + 7 + 5 + 5 = 34$.

If the two short sides are together, the perimeter will be $5 + 7 + 7 + 5 + 7 + 7 = 38$.

Therefore, $38 - 34 = 4$ feet shorter.

3. **The correct answer is A.** The side of each square equals $\sqrt{25}$ or 5 cm. Aligned to form a large square, the tiles form three rows and three columns, each column and row with side $5 \times 3 = 15$. The perimeter $= 15 \times 4 = 60$.

4. **The correct answer is C.** The formula for the circumference of a circle is $C = 2\pi r$, so the circumference of a circle with radius 9 is $C = 2\pi(9) = 18\pi$.

5. **The correct answer is C.** This triangle includes a height, 3, and a base, 8. The height given corresponds to the base, since the height starts at the corner opposite the base and stretches down to the base. Apply the formula for the area of a triangle.

$$A = \frac{1}{2}bh$$
$$= \frac{1}{2}(8)(3)$$
$$= \frac{1}{2}(24)$$
$$= 12$$

6. **The correct answer is C.**

Area of a square $= s^2$

$49 = 7^2$

One side $= 7$ inches

$P = 4s$

$P = 4 \times 7'' = 28$ inches

7. **The correct answer is B.** We know that $A = \pi r^2$, where r represents the radius. In this problem, we're given the area, so we can plug it into the formula and solve for r:

$$36\pi = \pi r^2$$
$$\frac{36\pi}{\pi} = \frac{\pi r^2}{\pi}$$
$$36 = r^2$$
$$6 = r$$

The radius equals 6, so the diameter must equal 6×2, or 12.

8. **The correct answer is A.**

First room:

36 ft. x 8 ft. = 288 sq. ft.

Second room:

24 ft. x 9 ft. = 216 sq. ft.

Both rooms:

288 + 216 = 504 sq. ft.

If each roll will cover 224 square feet, then 2.25 rolls (504 ÷ 224) are needed.

9. **The correct answer is C.** First, find the area of the base by using the formula for the area of a circle. Since the radius is 2, the area of the base is:

$$A = \pi r^2$$
$$= \pi(2)^2$$
$$= 4\pi$$

Now, find the volume of the cylinder by multiplying the area of the base times the height:

$$4\pi \times 4 = 16\pi$$

10. **The correct answer is B.** The formula for the volume of a cube is s^3, in which s is the length of a side of the cube. Therefore, the volume of a cube with a side of 5 in. in length equals 5^3, which equals $5 \times 5 \times 5$, or 125 in³.

11. **The correct answer is A.** Rename 8 in. as $\frac{2}{3}$ ft. so that all measurements are in the same unit. Then multiply $l \times w \times h$.

$$3 \text{ ft.} \times \frac{2}{3} \text{ft.} \times 1 \text{ ft.} = 2 \text{ cubic ft.}$$

12. **The correct answer is E.** You've been given the formula for a cylinder, so the only thing to do is to be sure you plug the values in all the right places. You've been asked for the volume, V, and you've been given the radius ($r = 5$) and the height ($h = 3$). Plug in those values and solve for V:

$$V = \pi r^2 h$$
$$= \pi(5^2)3$$
$$= \pi(25)(3)$$
$$= 75\pi$$

13. **The correct answer is B.** The sum of the angles of a circle equals 360°. Angles a through f total 340°. Angle g must be 20°.

14. **The correct answer is D.** In this question, we are presented with supplementary angles, angles that form a straight line. We know that the measures of angles lying on a straight line add up to 180°. Thus:

$$a + b + 40° = 180°$$
$$a + b = 180° - 40°$$
$$a + b = 140°$$

15. **The correct answer is B.** The sum of the interior angles of any quadrilateral equals 360°. In this case, we are given the measures of three interior angles, and are asked to find the measure of the fourth angle:

$$360° = 110° + 90° + 75° + x$$
$$360° = 275° + x$$
$$360° - 275° = 275° - 275 + x$$
$$85° = x$$

16. **The correct answer is E.** To answer this question, it's important to remember that the sum of the measures of the angles inside a triangle always equals 180°. In this case,

$$\angle A + 70° + 20° = 180°$$
$$\angle A + 90° = 180°$$
$$\angle A = 180° - 90°$$
$$= 90°$$

17. **The correct answer is C.** Lines l and m are parallel, and line q intersects these two parallel lines, so it is a transversal. Recall that certain angles are congruent when two parallel lines are intersected by a transversal. In this case, the obtuse angle that measures 130° and the angle with the measure of a degrees are congruent. Therefore, you know it measures 130°.

18. **The correct answer is A.** Vertical angles, formed when two lines intersect each other, are always equal to each other. Angles RVT and SVU are vertical angles, so their measures are equal. Therefore, if angle RVT has a measure of 35°, the measure of angle SVU is 35° as well.

19. **The correct answer is B.** The sum of the measures of the interior angles of a triangle is 180°. Therefore, $x = 180 - 80 - 40 = 60$.

20. **The correct answer is A.** The angle between the 110° angle and the 45° angle forms a vertical angle with the $x°$ angle and its measure is therefore equal

to $x°$. The three angles form a straight line, so the sum of their measures is 180°. As such, $x + 45 + 110 = 180$, so that $x = 25$.

21. **The correct answer is E.** In reading a graph, always read along the horizontal axis first. The point that corresponds to the coordinates (8, 3) is point J.

22. **The correct answer is B.** When a point is in quadrant II, the x-coordinate is negative and the y-coordinate is positive. Therefore, the coordinates of point M are (−5, 4).

23. **The correct answer is C.** When a point is in quadrant IV, the x-coordinate is positive and the y-coordinate is negative. Therefore, the coordinates of point P are (3, −2).

24. **The correct answer is B.** The ordered pair (x, y) gives the location of a point. Starting at the origin, (0, 0), the x-coordinate tells you the number of units to move to the right (if it's positive) or to the left (if it's negative). The y-coordinate tells you the number of units to move up (if it's positive) or down (if it's negative). Therefore, the point (4, −3) is 4 units to the right and 3 units down from the origin. Point B is located at (4, −3).

25. **The correct answer is D.** The quadrants are named in counterclockwise order beginning with quadrant I in the upper right corner. Point A is located in quadrant II.

26. **The correct answer is B.** The angles adjacent to the one labeled as 125° each measure 55° because they are supplementary angles. Because l is parallel to m, the angle labeled as y is the corresponding angle to one whose measure is 55°, so it also measures 55°.

27. **The correct answer is B.** Angles opposite the congruent sides of an isosceles triangle are congruent. Using this fact, together with the fact that the sum of the three angles in a triangle is 180°, yields the equation $z + z + 24 = 180$. Solve for z, as follows:

$$z + z + 24 = 180$$
$$2z + 24 = 180$$
$$2z = 156$$
$$z = 78$$

28. **The correct answer is A.** The slope of the line is:

$$m = \frac{-1 - (-2)}{-3 - 4}$$
$$= \frac{-1 + 2}{-7}$$
$$= -\frac{1}{7}$$

Using the point-slope form of the equation of a line, namely $y - y_1 = m(x - x_1)$ with the point $(x_1, y_1) = (-3, -1)$ yields

$$y - (-1) = -\frac{1}{7}(x - (-3))$$
$$y + 1 = -\frac{1}{7}(x + 3)$$
$$-7(y + 1) = x + 3$$
$$-7y - 7 = x + 3$$
$$x + 7y = -10$$

29. **The correct answer is C.** The height and base used in the area formula for a parallelogram must be perpendicular. Using 2 m for the height and 6 m for the base, we conclude the area is (2 m)(6 m) = 12 square meters.

30. **The correct answer is A.** Use the Pythagorean theorem:

$$y^2 + x^2 = (x + 2)^2$$
$$y^2 + x^2 = x^2 + 4x + 4$$
$$y^2 = 4x + 4$$
$$y = \sqrt{4x + 4}$$

This can be simplified further to $2\sqrt{x + 1}$

31. **The correct answer is C.** Let e be the edge of the cube. The surface area is $6e^2 = 13.5$. Solve for e:

$$6e^2 = 13.5$$
$$e^2 = 2.25$$
$$e = \sqrt{2.25} = 1.5$$

So the volume is $e^3 = (1.5)^3 = 3.375$ cubic inches.

32. **The correct answer is C.** The sum of the three angles in a triangle is 180°. Using this fact yields the following:

$$x + (2x - 1) + (3x + 7) = 180$$
$$6x + 6 = 180$$
$$6x = 174$$
$$x = 29$$

So the three angles are 29°, 57°, and 94°.

33. **The correct answer is A.** The slope of the line is $m = \dfrac{-3 - 0}{0 - (-6)} = -\dfrac{1}{2}$. Since the y-intercept is $(0, -3)$, we know that b in the slope-intercept form for the equation of a line, which is $y = mx + b$, is -3. So the equation is $y = -\dfrac{1}{2}x - 3$.

34. **The correct answer is D.** The new side (after the reduction) has length $x - 0.30x = 0.70x$. So the perimeter of the new square is $4(0.70x) = 2.8x$ inches.

35. **The correct answer is E.** Using the area formula for a circle yields the equation $\pi r^2 = \sqrt{\pi}$, where r is the radius. Solve for r:

$$\pi r^2 = \sqrt{\pi}$$
$$r^2 = \frac{\sqrt{\pi}}{\pi} = \frac{1}{\sqrt{\pi}}$$
$$r = \sqrt{\frac{1}{\sqrt{\pi}}} = \left(\frac{1}{\pi^{1/2}}\right)^{1/2}$$
$$r = \frac{1}{\pi^{1/4}}$$

So the circumference is $2\pi\left(\dfrac{1}{\pi^{1/4}}\right) = 2\pi^{3/4}$ centimeters.

CHAPTER

Quantitative Ability

QUANTITATIVE ABILITY

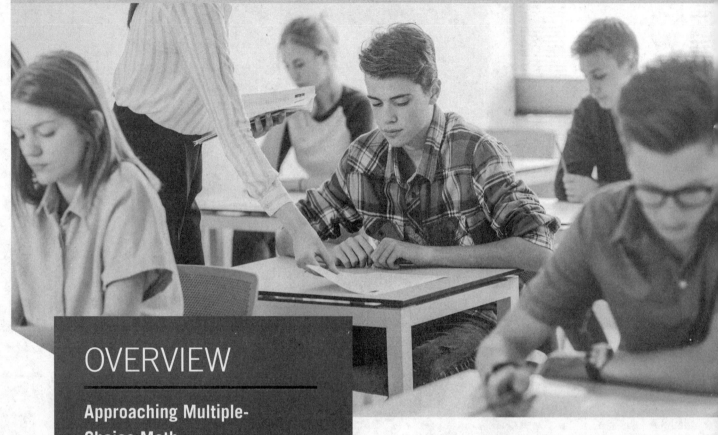

OVERVIEW

Approaching Multiple-Choice Math

Understanding Multiple-Choice Quantitative Ability Questions

Strategies for Multiple-Choice Quantitative Ability Questions

Summing It Up

Knowledge Check: Quantitative Ability

Answer Key and Explanations

SSAT   ISEE

APPROACHING MULTIPLE-CHOICE MATH

How can one kind of quantitative ability question possibly be easier than another? Well, multiple-choice math is typically easier than more open-ended exam questions. Since it's multiple choice, the correct answer is always on the page in front of you. That means even if you are estimating, you'll be able to narrow down the choices and improve your guessing odds.

Some multiple-choice questions require no calculation at all; the correct answer is based upon your grasp of the concepts introduced by the question. Some questions are straight calculations; others are presented in the form of word problems. Some include graphs, charts, or tables that you will be asked to interpret. All the questions have either four (ISEE) or five (SSAT) answer choices. These choices are arranged in order by size from smallest to largest or from largest to smallest.

UNDERSTANDING MULTIPLE-CHOICE QUANTITATIVE ABILITY QUESTIONS

Although it sounds quite official, the phrase "quantitative ability" is really just a fancy way to say "math." In a literal sense, it refers to your ability to make sense of questions involving quantities or numbers. Keeping that in mind, consider using the following steps to tackle the math problems you'll find on your test.

Five Steps for Multiple-Choice Math: Getting It Right

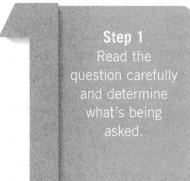

Step 1
Read the question carefully and determine what's being asked.

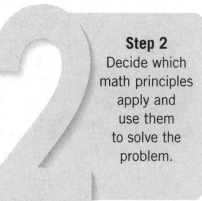

Step 2
Decide which math principles apply and use them to solve the problem.

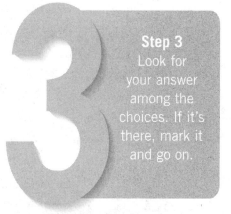

Step 3
Look for your answer among the choices. If it's there, mark it and go on.

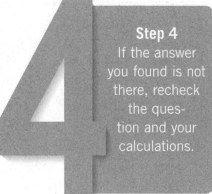

Step 4
If the answer you found is not there, recheck the question and your calculations.

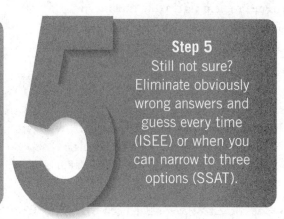

Step 5
Still not sure? Eliminate obviously wrong answers and guess every time (ISEE) or when you can narrow to three options (SSAT).

Now, let's try out these steps on a couple of multiple-choice math questions. Note that while you will always have to do the first three steps, you shouldn't need to do steps 4 and 5 unless you don't get a result doing the first three steps.

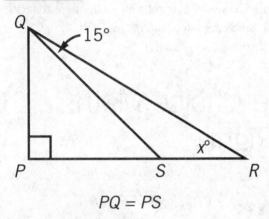

$$PQ = PS$$

In the figure above, $x =$

    A. 15°

    B. 30°

    C. 40°

    D. 60°

    E. 75°

Step 1: The problem asks you to find the measure of one angle of right triangle *PQR*.

Step 2: Two math principles apply: (1) the sum of the measures, in degrees, of the angles of a triangle is 180°, and (2) 45°-45°-90° right triangles have certain special properties. Because $PQ = PS$, triangle *PQS* is a 45°-45°-90° right triangle. Therefore, angle $PQS = 45°$ and angle $PQR = 45° + 15° = 60°$. Therefore, angle $x = 180° - 90° - 60° = 30°$.

Step 3: The correct answer is B. Since we have already found the correct answer, there is no reason to continue on to steps 4 and 5.

EXAMPLE:

If x and y are negative numbers, which of the following is negative?

    A. xy

    B. $(xy)^2$

    C. $(x - y)^2$

    D. $x + y$

    E. $\dfrac{x}{y}$

Step 1: The problem asks you to pick an answer choice that is a negative number.

Step 2: The principles that apply are those governing operations with signed numbers. Because x and y are negative, both choices A and E must be positive. As for choices B and C, as long as neither x nor y is zero, those expressions must be positive. (Any number other than zero squared gives a positive result.) Choice D, however, is negative because it represents the sum of two negative numbers. If you have trouble working with letters, try substituting easy numbers for x and y in each choice.

Step 3: By applying the rules governing signed numbers to each answer choice, you can determine that choices A, B, C, and E can only be positive numbers. Therefore, the correct answer must be choice D. Again, you would only need to complete steps 4 and 5 if your initial calculations don't yield a result.

STRATEGIES FOR MULTIPLE-CHOICE QUANTITATIVE ABILITY QUESTIONS

Some of these strategies you've heard before, and some will be new to you. Whatever the case, read them, learn them, love them. They will help you.

Not All Questions Will Be the Same Level of Difficulty

Not all tests arrange math questions by order of difficulty, but the SSAT often has. On exams that do so, questions will go from easy to hard as you work toward the end. In these cases, the first third of the questions are easy, the middle third are average but harder, and the final third get more and more difficult. Other times, difficult questions will be mixed in with easy and medium difficulty questions. Take a look at these three examples that get progressively harder. Don't solve them yet (you'll be doing that in a couple of minutes), just get an idea of how the level of difficulty changes from Question 1 to Question 2 to Question 3.

EXAMPLES:

1. If $x - 2 = 5$, then $x =$

   A. -10

   B. -3

   C. $\dfrac{5}{2}$

   D. 3

   E. 7

2. How many integers constitute x in the equation $-7 < 2x < -5$?

   A. None

   B. One

   C. Two

   D. Three

   E. Indefinite number

3. In a set of 5 books, no two of which have the same number of pages, the longest book has 150 pages and the shortest book has 130 pages. If x pages is the average (arithmetic mean) of the number of pages in the 5-book set, which of the following best indicates all possible values of x and only possible values of x?

   A. $130 < x < 150$

   B. $131 < x < 149$

   C. $133 < x < 145$

   D. $134 < x < 145$

   E. $135 < x < 145$

Can you see the difference? Unless you struggle a lot with math, you can probably do Question 1 easily. For Question 2, you might have to work a little harder and do some quick calculations on scratch paper, but it shouldn't be too hard. Question 3, by contrast, may cause you to wince a little before jumping into some heavy-duty thinking, but it can still be done. Having an awareness of the likelihood of a progression of difficulty on the SSAT and a range of difficulty on the ISEE will make you better prepared for when hard questions pop up.

 TIP

Look for shortcuts. Math problems test your math reasoning, not your ability to make endless calculations. If you find yourself calculating too much, you've probably missed a shortcut that would have made your work easier.

Easy Questions Usually Have Easy Answers; Difficult Questions Usually Don't

This tip may seem obvious, but it's important to remember in the heat of an exam. The easy questions are straightforward and don't have any hidden tricks. The obvious answer is almost always the correct answer. Test makers include these easier questions to balance out the time it will take you to complete harder ones. For Question 1 in the last section, the answer is indeed choice E.

When you hit the difficult stuff, you have to think harder. The information is not straightforward, and the answers aren't as obvious. A lot of times, on more difficult questions, what seems like the easy answer will be wrong since it's a distractor designed to catch those who make certain common mistakes. If you don't believe it, let's take a closer look at Question 3 again:

EXAMPLE:

3. In a set of 5 books, no two of which have the same number of pages, the longest book has 150 pages and the shortest book has 130 pages. If x pages is the average (arithmetic mean) of the number of pages in the 5-book set, which of the following best indicates all possible values of x and only possible values of x?

    A. $130 < x < 150$

    B. $131 < x < 149$

    C. $133 < x < 145$

    D. $134 < x < 145$

    E. $135 < x < 145$

Yes, this question is difficult mostly because the process you have to use to find the solution is difficult. Let's start by eliminating answer choices. Choice A can't be right. While it contains the same numbers that were already mentioned in the problem and might therefore

fool someone looking for an "easy" answer, you are more discerning! On close analysis, all choice A says is that the shortest book is 130 pages, the longest book is 150 pages, and the average is between 130 and 150. You already know this from the question, so it's unlikely to be your answer.

Choice B illustrates the reasoning that "no two books have the same number of pages, so the average must be one page more than the shortest book and one page less than the longest." While more plausible than Choice A, this is once again an answer that requires you to do very little actual math, so it is also unlikely to be the answer.

Now, let's skip to the correct answer, which is choice E, and find out how we got there. First, you want to find the minimum value for x, so you assume that the other three books contain 131, 132, and 133 pages. So, the average would be:

$$\frac{130 + 131 + 132 + 133 + 150}{5} = \frac{676}{5} = 135.2$$

So, x must be more than 135. Now assume that the other three books contain 149, 148, and 147 pages. The average length of all five books would be:

$$\frac{150 + 149 + 148 + 147 + 130}{5} = \frac{724}{5} = 144.8$$

Then, x would be greater than 135 but less than 145.

When Guessing at Hard Questions, You Can Toss Out Easy Answers

Now that you know the difficult questions won't have easy or obvious answers, use a guessing strategy. When you don't have much of a clue about a difficult question, scan the answer choices and eliminate the ones that seem easy or obvious, such as any that just restate the information in the question. Once you've eliminated any distractors designed to lead you astray, you have a better shot of guessing correctly from your remaining answer options.

Questions of Average Difficulty Won't Have Trick Answers

Let's look again at Question 2:

> **EXAMPLE:**
>
> 2. How many integers constitute x in the equation $-7 < 2x < -5$?
>
>   **A.** None
>
>   **B.** One
>
>   **C.** Two
>
>   **D.** Three
>
>   **E.** Indefinite number

This is a bit more difficult than Question 1, but it's still straightforward. There is only one integer between -7 and -5, and that's -6. There's also only one value for integer x so that $2x$ equals -6, and that is -3 because $2(-3) = -6$. So, choice B is the correct answer. Trust your judgment and your reasoning; no tricks here.

It's Smart to Test Answer Choices

Every standard multiple-choice math problem includes four (ISEE) or five (SSAT) answer choices. One of them has to be correct; the others are wrong. This means that it's always possible to solve a problem by testing each of the answer choices. Just plug each choice into the problem, and sooner or later, you'll find the one that works! Testing answer choices can often be a much easier and surer way of solving a problem than attempting a lengthy calculation. Do keep in mind that this is a lengthier way of solving equations than other methods, so you wouldn't want to do it for every question or you'll risk running out of time. However, this technique is there when you need it.

When Testing Answer Choices, It's Smart to Start Near the Middle

Remember, the answer is somewhere right in front of you. If you test all the answer choices, you'll find the right one. However, the smart place to start is always as close to the middle as possible. Why? Because the quantities in the choices are always arranged in order, either from smallest to largest or the other way around. If you start at the middle and it's too large, you'll just have to concentrate on the smaller choices. In doing so, you'll have knocked off some wrong choices in a heartbeat. Let's give it a "test" run, so to speak. Consider the following question.

> **EXAMPLE:**
>
> If a rectangle has sides of $2x$ and $3x$ and an area of 24, what is the value of x?
>
>   **A.** 2
>
>   **B.** 3
>
>   **C.** 4
>
>   **D.** 5
>
>   **E.** 6

You know that one of these answers is right. Start in the middle by testing choice C and assuming that $x = 4$. In this case, the sides would have lengths $2(4) = 8$ and $3(4) = 12$, and the rectangle would have an area of $8 \times 12 = 96$. Because 96 is larger than 24 (the area in the question), start working with the smaller answer choices. You can eliminate choices D and E automatically since they will both yield an area larger than 96. When you plug 3 into the equation, you get $2(3) = 6$ and $3(3) = 9$ and $6 \times 9 = 54$, which is still too large. After calculating only two of the five answer options, you've already managed to find the correct answer: choice A. Double check your answer by plugging it into the equation to make sure it works: $2(2) = 4$ and $3(2) = 6$ and $4 \times 6 = 24$, so it does!

Now let's try testing answer choices with a more difficult question:

EXAMPLE:

A farmer, Heidi, raises chickens and cows. If her animals have a total of 120 heads and a total of 300 feet, how many chickens does the farmer have?

    A. 50 chickens

    B. 60 chickens

    C. 70 chickens

    D. 80 chickens

    E. 90 chickens

Once again, we'll start in the middle with choice C. If Heidi has 70 chickens, she has 50 cows. (You know the farmer has 120 animals because each animal has only one head, right?) So now you're talking about $70 \times 2 = 140$ chicken feet and $50 \times 4 = 200$ cow feet, for a grand total of 340 animal feet. Well, that's more than the 300 animal feet in the question. To try another, let's logically assume that Heidi has more chickens and fewer cows (cows have more feet than chickens do). Give choice D—80—a try. Test $80 \times 2 = 160$ and $40 \times 4 = 160$; your total is 320 feet, which is closer but not quite right. The only answer left is choice E, and that's the correct one. Of course, you want to check your work to be sure: $90 \times 2 = 180$ and $30 \times 4 = 120$ and the total is . . . 300!

It's Often Easier to Work with Numbers than with Letters

Because numbers are more meaningful than letters, try plugging them into equations and formulas in place of variables. This technique can make problems much easier to solve. Here are some examples.

EXAMPLE:

If $x - 4$ is 2 greater than y, then $x + 5$ is how much greater than y?

    A. 1

    B. 3

    C. 7

    D. 9

    E. 11

Choose any value for x. Let's say you decide to make $x = 4$. All right, $4 - 4 = 0$, and 0 is 2 greater than y. So $y = -2$. If $x = 4$, then $x + 5 = 4 + 5 = 9$, and so $x + 5$ is 11 more than y. Therefore, the correct answer is choice E. Try the same technique with the following example.

EXAMPLE:

The unit cost of pens is the same regardless of how many pens are purchased. If the cost of p pens is d dollars, what is the cost, in dollars, of x pens?

    A. xd

    B. xpd

    C. $\dfrac{xd}{p}$

    D. $\dfrac{xp}{d}$

    E. $\dfrac{pd}{x}$

Time to plug in some real numbers.

Say that four pens (p) cost $2 ($d$), so each pen would cost 50 cents. And say that you only need one pen (x), so you're spending only $0.50. Then, $p = 4$, $d = 2$, and $x = 1$, and the right answer would be 0.5. Now, start using these numbers with the answer choices:

A. $xd = (1)(2) = 2$

B. $xpd = (1)(4)(2) = 8$

C. $\dfrac{xd}{p} = \dfrac{(1)(2)}{4} = 0.5$ there it is.

D. $\dfrac{xp}{d} = \dfrac{(1)(4)}{2} = 2$

E. $\dfrac{pd}{x} = \dfrac{(4)(2)}{1} = 8$

If a question asks for an odd integer or an even integer, go ahead and pick any odd or even integer you like.

It's Okay to Write in Your Test Booklet, So Use It for Scratch Work

The test booklet is yours, so feel free to use it for your scratch work. Also, go ahead and mark up any diagrams with length or angle information; it helps. If you need to remember a particular equation, feel free to jot it down in the margins. That said, don't waste time trying to redraw diagrams; it's just not worth it.

A Reality Check Can Help You Eliminate Answers That Can't Possibly Be Right

Knowing whether your calculations should produce a number that's larger or smaller than the quantity you started with can point you toward the right answer. It's also an effective way of eliminating wrong answers.

Here's an example.

EXAMPLE:

Using his bike, Daryl can complete a paper route in 20 minutes. Jennifer, who walks the route, can complete it in 30 minutes. How long will it take the two kids to complete the route if they work together, one starting at each end of the route?

A. 8 minutes

B. 12 minutes

C. 20 minutes

D. 30 minutes

E. 45 minutes

You can immediately see that choices C, D, and E are impossible because the two kids working together will have to complete the job in less time than either one of them working alone. In fact, the correct answer is choice B, 12 minutes.

	Jennifer	Daryl
Time spent working together	x	x
Time needed to do entire job alone	20	30

$$\frac{x}{20} + \frac{x}{30} = 1$$

Multiply by 60 to clear fractions:

$$3x + 2x = 60$$
$$5x = 60$$
$$x = 12$$

Your Eye Is a Good Estimator

Unless you see a note specifically telling you that a figure is not drawn to scale, you can assume it is. That means you can sometimes solve a problem just by looking at the picture and estimating the answer. Consider the following example.

EXAMPLE:

In the rectangle *PQRS* shown, *TU* and *WV* are parallel to *SR*. If *PS* = 6, *UV* = 1, and *PR* (not shown) = 10, what is the area of rectangle *TUVW* ?

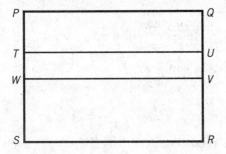

- **A.** 8
- **B.** 12
- **C.** 16
- **D.** 24
- **E.** 32

 TIP

Circle what's asked. For multiple-choice math questions, circle what's being asked so that you don't pick a wrong answer by mistake. That way, for example, you won't pick an answer that gives a perimeter when the question asks for an area.

If Some Questions Always Give You Trouble, Save Them for Last

Occasionally, particularly as standardized tests adopt online versions of their traditional paper exams, you won't be allowed to skip around and will have to do questions in the order they are presented to you. However, sometimes you have wiggle room to skip questions that stump you and come back to them later. If you find questions that you know will be challenging for you to solve, save them for last. They will take up a lot of your time, and you can use that time to do more of the easier questions.

To solve the problem, you will need to find the length of *TU*. You can do this by using the Pythagorean theorem. The triangle *PSR* has sides of 6 and 10, so *SR* = 8. Because *TU* = *SR*, *TU* = 8, so the area of the small rectangle is equal to 1 × 8 = 8.

As an alternative, you could simply estimate the length of *TU*. *TU* appears to be longer than *PS* (6), and *TU* must be shorter than *PR* (10). Therefore, *TU* appears to be approximately 8 and the area must be approximately 1 × 8 = 8. Is that sufficiently accurate to get the right answer? Look at the choices. Choice A is 8, and it's the only choice that is even close to 8.

SUMMING IT UP

- "Quantitative Ability" is just a fancy way to say "math."

- With multiple-choice questions, the correct answer is always on the page in front of you. So even if you're estimating, you'll be able to narrow down the choices.

- Some multiple-choice questions require no calculations—the correct answer is based on how well you know the concepts in the question.

- Some multiple-choice questions include graphs, charts, or tables for you to interpret.

- The answer choices are generally arranged in order by size from smallest to largest or from largest to smallest.

- All tests contain a variety of easy, medium-difficulty, and hard questions. On some tests (like the SSAT), the questions may even be arranged in ascending order from easiest to hardest.

- Always eliminate obviously wrong answers to give yourself a better shot at selecting a correct answer, even when guessing.

- For multiple-choice math questions, circle what's being asked so you don't pick a wrong answer by mistake. For example, you won't pick an answer that gives a perimeter when the question asks for an area.

KNOWLEDGE CHECK

QUANTITATIVE ABILITY

20 Questions—15 Minutes

Directions: Following each problem in this section, there are five suggested answers. Work each problem in your head or in the space provided (there will be space for scratchwork in your test booklet). Then, look at the five suggested answers and decide which is best. Circle the letter that appears before your answer.

1. A gas tank is $\frac{1}{3}$ empty. When full, the tank holds 18 gallons. How many gallons are in the tank now?

   A. 3
   B. 6
   C. 8
   D. 12
   E. 18

2. Which of the following is the least?

   A. $\frac{1}{4} + \frac{2}{3}$
   B. $\frac{3}{4} - \frac{1}{3}$
   C. $\frac{1}{12} \div \frac{1}{3}$
   D. $\frac{3}{4} \times \frac{1}{3}$
   E. $\frac{1}{12} \times 2$

3. If the sum of x and $x + 3$ is greater than 20, which is a possible value for x?

   A. −10
   B. −8
   C. −2
   D. 8
   E. 10

4. If a square has a perimeter of 88, what is the length of each side?

   A. 4
   B. 11
   C. 22
   D. 44
   E. 110

5. If a set R contains four positive integers whose average is 9, what is the greatest number set R could contain?

   A. 4
   B. 9
   C. 24
   D. 33
   E. 36

6. Which of the following is *not* a multiple of 4?

   A. 20
   B. 30
   C. 36
   D. 44
   E. 96

Questions 7 and 8 refer to the following definition:

For all real numbers m, $*m = 10m - 10$.

7. $*7 =$

   A. 70

   B. 60

   C. 17

   D. 7

   E. 0

8. If $*m = 120$, then $m =$

   A. 11

   B. 12

   C. 13

   D. 120

   E. 130

9. At the grocery store, an item that usually sells for $9 is on sale for $6. What approximate discount does that represent?

   A. 10%

   B. 25%

   C. 33%

   D. 50%

   E. 66%

10. In Linda's golf club, 8 of the 12 members are right-handed. What is the ratio of left-handed members to right-handed members?

    A. 1:2

    B. 2:1

    C. 2:3

    D. 3:4

    E. 4:3

11. The sum of five consecutive positive integers is 35. What is the square of the greatest of these integers?

    A. 5

    B. 9

    C. 25

    D. 81

    E. 100

12. $2^2 \times 2^3 \times 2^3 =$

    A. 2^4

    B. 2^6

    C. 2^8

    D. 2^{10}

    E. 2^{18}

13. If the area of a square is $100s^2$, what is the length of one side of the square?

    A. $100s^2$

    B. $10s^2$

    C. $100s$

    D. $10s$

    E. 10

14. If 10 books cost d dollars, how many books can be purchased for 4 dollars?

    A. $\dfrac{4d}{10}$

    B. $40d$

    C. $\dfrac{d}{40}$

    D. $\dfrac{40}{d}$

    E. $\dfrac{10d}{4}$

15. If *g* is an even integer, *h* is an odd integer, and *j* is the product of *g* and *h*, which of the following must be true?

    A. *j* is a fraction.

    B. *j* is an odd integer.

    C. *j* is divisible by 2.

    D. *j* is between *g* and *h*.

    E. *j* is greater than 0.

16. If a class of 6 students has an average grade of 78 before a seventh student joins, what must the seventh student get as a grade in order to raise the class average to 80?

    A. 80

    B. 84

    C. 88

    D. 92

    E. 96

17. If 6 is a factor of a certain number, what must be factors of that number?

    A. 1, 2, 3, and 6

    B. 2 and 3 only

    C. 6 only

    D. 2 and 6 only

    E. 1, 2, and 3

18.

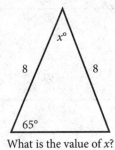

What is the value of *x*?

    A. 8

    B. 30

    C. 50

    D. 65

    E. 70

19. For an item of what price does 40% off equal a $2.00 discount?

    A. $4.00

    B. $5.00

    C. $10.00

    D. $40.00

    E. $80.00

20. On Monday, Gerri ate $\frac{1}{4}$ of an apple pie. On Tuesday, she ate $\frac{1}{2}$ of what was left of the pie. What fraction of the entire pie did Gerri eat in total?

    A. $\frac{3}{8}$

    B. $\frac{1}{2}$

    C. $\frac{5}{8}$

    D. $\frac{3}{4}$

    E. $\frac{7}{8}$

ANSWER KEY AND EXPLANATIONS

1. D	**5.** D	**9.** C	**13.** D	**17.** A
2. E	**6.** B	**10.** A	**14.** D	**18.** C
3. E	**7.** B	**11.** D	**15.** C	**19.** B
4. C	**8.** C	**12.** C	**16.** D	**20.** C

1. **The correct answer is D.** If the tank is $\frac{1}{3}$ empty, it must be $\frac{2}{3}$ full. $\frac{2}{3}$ of the total capacity of 18 gallons is 12.

2. **The correct answer is E.** The value of choice A is $\frac{11}{12}$; the value of choice B is $\frac{5}{12}$; the value of choice C is $\frac{1}{4}$ or $\frac{3}{12}$; the value of choice D is $\frac{1}{4}$ or $\frac{3}{12}$; and the value of choice E is $\frac{1}{6}$ or $\frac{2}{12}$. Therefore, choice E has the least value.

3. **The correct answer is E.** If $x + (x + 3) > 20$, then $2x > 17$. So $x > 8.5$. The only answer that is appropriate is 10.

4. **The correct answer is C.** The perimeter of a square is found by summing the lengths of each side. Because the lengths are equal on a square, you can multiply one side by 4 to get the perimeter. Therefore, $4s = 88$, so $s = 22$.

5. **The correct answer is D.** To find the greatest value of the four, assume the remaining three values are the least possible positive integer, 1. The average then is $\frac{1+1+1+x}{4} = 9$. Solve for x. $3 + x = 36$, so $x = 33$.

6. **The correct answer is B.** Multiples of 4 include: 4, 8, 12, 16, 20, 24, 28, 32, 36, 40, 44, etc. Comparing these with the answers provided, notice that the number 30 is not a multiple of 4.

7. **The correct answer is B.** Substitute 7 for m.
$$*7 = 10(7) - 10 = 70 - 10 = 60.$$

8. **The correct answer is C.** If $*m = 10m - 10$ and $*m = 120$, then $10m - 10 = 120$. Solve for m:
$$10m = 130$$
$$m = 13$$

9. **The correct answer is C.** The total discounted amount is $3 or ($9 – $6).

The original amount × the discounted percent = the total discounted amount.

$9 × discounted percent = $3.
The discounted percent $= \frac{3}{9} = \frac{1}{3} \approx 33\%$.

10. **The correct answer is A.** The number of left-handed members is equal to 12 – 8, or 4. The ratio of left-handers to right-handers is 4:8, which simplifies to 1:2.

11. **The correct answer is D.** Let the five consecutive integers be:
$$x, x + 1, x + 2, x + 3, \text{ and } x + 4$$
Then:
$$x + x + 1 + x + 2 + x + 3 + x + 4 = 35$$
$$5x + 10 = 35$$
$$5x = 25$$
$$x = 5$$
Since the least of the five integers is 5, the greatest is 5 + 4, or 9. $9^2 = 81$.

12. **The correct answer is C.** When multiplying like values raised to a power, add the exponents.
$$2^2 \times 2^3 \times 2^3 = 2^{2+3+3} = 2^8$$

13. **The correct answer is D.** The area of a square is equal to the (length of the side)^2, or L^2.
$$100s^2 = L^2$$
$$\sqrt{100s^2} = \sqrt{L^2}$$
$$10s = L$$

14. **The correct answer is D.** Set up a ratio for this problem and solve.

Let x represent the number of books purchased with 4 dollars:

$$\frac{10}{d} = \frac{x}{4}$$

Now use cross-multiplication and solve as follows:

$$\frac{10}{d} = \frac{x}{4}$$
$$10 \cdot 4 = d \cdot x$$
$$\frac{40}{d} = x$$

15. **The correct answer is C.** Since integers can be both positive and negative, and the product of a positive and negative integer is always negative, choice E must be false. Looking further at the answers, notice that choices B and C are opposites of one another. Therefore, one of those must be true and the other false. Substitute two numbers for g and h and see which of the two is true. If $g = -4$ and $h = 5$, then:

$$g \times h = -4 \times 5 = -20$$

Since –20 is even, choice C is correct.

16. **The correct answer is D.** The sum of the first six grades is $78 \times 6 = 468$. (To find the average grade of 78, divide the sum of the six grades by 6.)

The average with seven students is:

$$468 + x = 80 \cdot 7$$
$$468 + x = 560$$
$$x = 92$$

17. **The correct answer is A.** All factors of 6 are factors of the number. The factors of 6 are:

$$1 \times 6$$
$$2 \times 3$$

18. **The correct answer is C.** Since this is an isosceles triangle, the angles opposite the congruent sides are also congruent. The sum of the angles in a triangle equal 180°. So $65° + 65° + x° = 180°$ and $x = 50°$.

19. **The correct answer is B.**

Let p equal the price of the item.

Price × Discount Rate = Discount Amount

$$p \times 40\% = \$2.00$$
$$p \times 0.40 = 2.00$$
$$p = \frac{2.00}{0.40} = 5$$

20. **The correct answer is C.** On Monday, $\frac{1}{4}$ of the pie was eaten. On Tuesday, there was $\frac{3}{4}$ of the pie left.

$$\frac{1}{2} \times \frac{3}{4} = \frac{3}{8} \text{ and } \frac{1}{4} + \frac{3}{8} = \frac{5}{8}$$

NOTES

CHAPTER

Quantitative Comparisons

QUANTITATIVE COMPARISONS

OVERVIEW

SSAT   ISEE

UNDERSTANDING QUANTITATIVE COMPARISONS

Quantitative comparisons, which only appear on the ISEE, are not quite as out there as they might look at first glance. You can recognize quantitative comparison questions easily because they look very different from other math questions. Each one presents two quantities side by side for comparison—one in Column A and the other in Column B. Your task is to consider the two quantities and then choose the correct answer from choices A through D, which for these questions will always read as follows:

A. The quantity in Column A is greater.

B. The quantity in Column B is greater.

C. The two quantities are equal.

D. The relationship cannot be determined from the information given

There are some helpful things to remember about these types of questions. First, the answer choices are always the same, so this type of question is predictable. Second, you don't actually have to solve a problem. Rather than testing your calculating skills, these questions analyze your knowledge of mathematical principals. Third, sometimes you'll be provided a diagram or other information to assist you in your task. Generally, this information will be centered above the comparison boxes.

APPROACHING QUANTITATIVE COMPARISONS

In short, the best way to solve quantitative comparisons is to use your estimating and comparison skills. Additionally, you can practice following the four steps laid out here to help you tackle these questions. Once you get used to following the steps and working with the answer choices, you'll start to pick up speed when moving through these types of questions, which can help you save time on a timed exam like the ISEE.

Four Steps for Quantitative Comparisons: Getting It Right

1

Memorize the answer choices.

Don't just learn the directions; try to memorize the answer choices. (Remember, they are always the same.) Then, you can save time because you won't need to refer to them for every question.

2

For each question, compare the two quantities.

Even though there are two quantities in each question, deal with one at a time. If there is extra information above the two quantities, see how each quantity relates to the given information. Then, do any figuring you need to do, which shouldn't be much.

3

Consider all possibilities for any variables.

Try to address any unknowns. Think what would happen if special numbers such as 0, negative numbers, or fractions were to be put into play.

4

Choose your answer.

You shouldn't have to do involved calculations to get to the answer. If you find yourself calculating endlessly, you've probably missed the mathematical principle the question is asking about.

Let's consider these steps in terms of a few sample quantitative comparison questions.

EXAMPLE:

The price of a pound of cheese increased from $2 to $2.50.

Column A	Column B
The percent increase in the price of cheese	25%

Step 1: Let's assume that you have memorized the answer choices already. However, they're always right there in front of you if you need a reminder.

Step 2: The centered information tells you that cheese increased in price from $2 to $2.50 per pound. Column A asks for the percent increase, which is $\frac{\$0.50}{\$2} = 25\%$. Column B requires no calculation, and it's equal to Column A.

Step 3: There are no variables to consider here, so go on to Step 4.

Step 4: Since the two columns are equal, the answer is choice C. Mark choice C on the answer sheet.

EXAMPLE:

Column A	Column B
$x^2 + y^2$	$(x + y)^2$

Step 1: Review the answer choices if you haven't quite memorized them yet.

Step 2: The expression in Column B is $(x + y)^2 = x^2 + 2xy + y^2$. This is the same as the expression in Column A with the addition of the middle term $2xy$.

Step 3: The terms x and y are variables that can be positive, negative, or zero. For example, if x were 1 and y were 2, Column A would be $1^2 + 2^2 = 5$ and Column B would be $(1 + 2)^2 = 9$. The correct answer would then be choice B. But if x were -1 and y were 2, Column A would be $(-1)^2 + 2^2 = 5$ and Column B would be $(-1 + 2)^2 = 1^2 = 1$. This time the correct answer would be choice A.

Step 4: Any time more than one answer can be true for a comparison—as is the case here—then the answer to that question must be choice D, "the relationship cannot be determined from the information given." Mark choice D on the answer sheet.

Remember that many quantitative comparisons can be solved without doing any calculating at all. In many cases, you should be able to arrive at the correct answer simply by applying your knowledge of basic math rules and principles. The correct answer in the following examples can be found without performing a single calculation.

 TIP

Variables stay constant. A variable that appears in both columns has the same meaning in each column.

EXAMPLES:

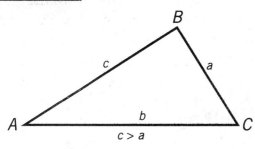

$c > a$

	Column A	Column B
1.	$\angle A$	$\angle C$
2.	$\angle A$	$\angle B$
3.	$a + b$	c

1. If two sides of a triangle are unequal, the angles opposite them are unequal, and the larger angle is opposite the longer side. So, the answer for this question is choice B.

2. Because we can't really tell whether a or b is greater, we can't tell which angle is greater, so choice D is the correct answer.

3. The sum of any two sides of a triangle must always be greater than the length of the third side. The only answer for this question is choice A.

ALERT

Figures can be deceiving. If a figure carries a warning that it is not drawn to scale, don't depend on estimating or measuring to help you solve the problem.

STRATEGIES FOR QUANTITATIVE COMPARISONS

Quantitative comparisons may look complex, but if you come at them from the right angle, you can streamline the answering process.

A Comparison Is Forever

In quantitative comparisons, choice A is correct only if the quantity is *always* greater than that in Column B. The reverse is true of choice B; it must *always* be greater than the information in Column A. If you choose C, it means that the two quantities are *always* equal. The condition must hold true regardless of what number you plug in for a variable.

Quantitative Comparisons Are Not about Calculating

If you find yourself calculating up a storm on a quantitative comparison, you've probably missed the boat. There's sure to be a simpler, shorter way to solve the problem. Find a way to reduce the amount of actual math you need to do. The following examples illustrate this concept.

EXAMPLE:

Column A	Column B
$31 \times 32 \times 33 \times 34 \times 35$	$32 \times 33 \times 34 \times 35 \times 36$

You don't have to do any calculations to get the answer. If you calculated, you would be comparing the product of five consecutive integers when all you really need to recognize is that the integers in Column B are larger. Therefore, the product of those numbers must, because of the principles of mathematics (i.e., the very thing questions like this are supposed to test your knowledge of), be greater than the product of those in Column A. So, the correct answer is B, and you didn't have to multiply a thing.

The formula for the volume of a right circular cylinder is $V = \pi r^2 h$.

Column A	Column B
The volume of a right circular cylinder with $r = 3$ and $h = 6$	The volume of a right circular cylinder with $r = 6$ and $h = 3$

Because the equations in the columns seem complex for this question, you might think that this is a case where you need to complete complicated calculations to find the volume of each cylinder. But remember, these questions are about your understanding of mathematical *principles*, so you likely don't! You have enough information here to complete the calculations rather simply:

Volume $A = \pi(3^2)(6) = (3.14)(3)(3)(6)$

Volume $B = \pi(6^2)(3) = (3.14)(6)(6)(3)$

Since you're doing the same operation for both formulas—multiplying by 3.14—that action cancels out. The problem then shifts to the other factors: Which is larger, $(3^2)(6)$ or $(6^2)(3)$? At this point, you should be able to see that the second one is larger. If you still need to take it another step, multiply $(3^2)(6) = (9)(6) = 54$ and then $(6^2)(3) = (36)(3)$. At this point, you don't even need to finish since this number will surely be larger than 54, but if you did take it a step further, you'd know that $(36)(3) = 108$.

If the Math Is Not Difficult, You Should Do It

In cases where the math in each column is simple enough to calculate it quickly, do so, as this will make it crystal clear which answer is correct.

Column A	Column B
$(0.6)(0.6)$	$\dfrac{36}{100}$

The correct answer is C. Do this simple math and you've got a guaranteed correct answer. They both equal 0.36, so your choice is C.

When the Centered Information Has Unknowns, Solve for the Unknowns

You can't do much with unknown information, so you'll need to solve for the unknowns in order to make headway.

$$3x = 12$$

$$4y = 20$$

Column A	Column B
x	y

The correct answer is B. You need to know what each of the unknowns is, so you must solve for both. Once you do, your answer should be clear.

First, solve for column A: $\dfrac{3x}{3} = \dfrac{12}{3}$, so $x = 4$.

Then, solve for column B: $\dfrac{4y}{4} = \dfrac{20}{4}$, so $y = 5$,

making the correct answer choice B.

It Pays to Simplify

Taking a few moments to simplify equations will remove guesswork.

EXAMPLE:

Column A	Column B
$\dfrac{(8)(45)(17)}{(462)(8)}$	$\dfrac{(17)(9)(42)}{(231)(16)}$

The correct answer is B. There are a couple of things to notice here that will help you simplify the problem. First, both denominators are really the same: 462 is 231 × 2, so the denominators become (231)(2)(8). Next, the (17)'s in both numerators cancel each other out. Now, all you must do is figure out the results of (8)(45) and (9)(42), compare, and mark the correct answer, which is choice B since the quantity in Column B is greater.

You Can Simplify by Adding or Subtracting the Same Value in Each Column

Remember this simple rule to make seemingly complicated equations less intimidating.

EXAMPLE:

Column A	Column B
$4x + 5$	$3x + 6$

The correct answer is D. You might not see how easy this is to simplify right away, so we'll show you. The first thing you do is subtract 5 from both sides. The result is $4x$ and $3x + 1$. Now, by subtracting $3x$ from both sides, you end up with x and 1. Since you don't know what x is, you can't know if it is larger or smaller than 1. That's why choice D is the correct answer: the relationship cannot be determined from the information given.

You Can Simplify by Multiplying or Dividing Each Side by the Same Positive Number

Again, this is an example of when doing the same thing to both sides of the column can help you find that information you need.

EXAMPLE:

Column A	Column B
$9^{99} - 9^{98}$	9^{98}

You begin to simplify by dividing both sides by 9^{98}.

Column A	Column B
$\dfrac{9^{99} - 9^{98}}{9^{98}}$	$\dfrac{9^{98}}{9^{98}}$
$9^1 - 9^0$	9^0
$9 - 1$	1
8	1

The correct answer is A. This proves that the quantity in Column A is larger, even though you haven't solved for the exact quantity.

Remember to Consider All the Possibilities

When there are unknowns in the quantities being compared, remember to consider all possibilities for what those unknowns might be. For example, an unknown might be 1, 0, a fraction, or a negative number. In each of these cases, the number has special properties that will affect your calculations. Alternatively, unless otherwise stated, two unknowns could even be equal. In the next few sections, you'll find examples of the different ways to deal with unknowns.

An Unknown Might Be a Zero

Zero has special properties that come into play when you plug it in for an unknown.

EXAMPLES:

$$x > 0, y > 0, z = 0$$

Column A	Column B
$3z(2x + 5y)$	$3x(2z + 5y)$

The correct answer is B. If $z = 0$, then $3z = 0$ and the product of Column A is 0. In Column B, though, $2z = 0$, so it comes out of the expression. The product will be $(3x)(5y)$, which will be a positive number.

$$x < 0, y > 0, z = 0$$

Column A	Column B
$3z(2x + 5y)$	$3x(z + 5y)$

The correct answer is A. Again, the product of Column A is 0, because $3z$ still equals 0. The change comes in Column B. Because x is less than 0, $3x$ will be negative and $5y$ will be positive, so the product will be a negative number.

An Unknown Might Be a Negative Number

When dealing with unknowns, remember how negative numbers will affect the quantities in each column.

EXAMPLE:

$$3x = 4y$$

Column A	Column B
x	y

The correct answer is D. Don't assume that choice A is the correct answer just because if x and y are positive, x is greater than y. What if x and y are negative, as in $3(-4) = 4(-3)$? In that case, y is greater than x. And if x and y are both zero, both columns are equal. Since you have no way of knowing what the values are, the correct answer is D.

An Unknown Might Be a Fraction

Don't assume that an unknown is a whole number! It could be a fraction.

EXAMPLE:

$$x > 0 \text{ and } x \neq 1$$

Column A	Column B
x^2	x

The correct answer is D. If x is larger than 1, then x^2 is larger than x. But if x is between 0 and 1—a fraction—then x^2 is smaller than x.

Fractions Can Play Tricks

Remember that a proper fraction raised to a positive power is smaller than the fraction itself.

Column A	Column B
$\dfrac{27}{41}$	$\left(\dfrac{27}{41}\right)^{15}$

The correct answer is A. If you keep the math principle in mind, you don't even have to think about doing these calculations. Since each successive multiplication would result in a smaller fraction, Column A will always be larger than Column B, so your answer is choice A.

 TIP

Need an easy way to remember the answer choices for quantitative comparisons? Just keep this key in mind:

A. = A is bigger

B. = B is bigger

C. = Columns are equal

D. = Determination impossible

In Quantitative Comparisons, Figures Are Not Necessarily Drawn to Scale

Usually, your test will indicate if a figure is not drawn to scale. If so, you can't assume that you'll be able to visually estimate quantities.

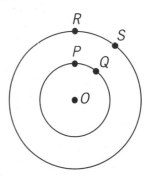

Minor arcs *PQ* and *RS* have equal length and each circle has center *O*.

NOTE: Figure not drawn to scale.

Column A	Column B
Degree measure of angle *POQ*	Degree measure of angle *ROS*

In the figure, angles *POQ* and *ROS* seem to be equal, but remember the warning. You're told that the figure is not drawn to scale, so don't be fooled.

The correct answer is A. You can prove this by the figure below that *is* drawn to scale.

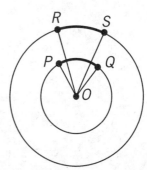

Plugging in Numbers Can Help

If you're stuck on a comparison with unknowns, try substituting numbers. Choose the numbers at random and plug them into the equations. Do this with three different substitutions and see if there is any consistent result. It's not a guarantee, but it's worth a shot if you're stumped.

Strategic Guessing Can Raise Your Score

When all else fails, call up your guessing skills. Here's how you can tip the scales in your favor, even if it's only a little bit:

- If a comparison involves only numbers without any unknowns, chances are that you'll be able to figure out the quantities and make a comparison. So, in this situation, don't guess choice D.

- If the comparison *does* contain an unknown or a figure, as a last resort guess choice D.

SUMMING IT UP

- Remember these steps as you work through the questions in this section:
    1. Memorize the answer choices.
    2. Compare the quantities in Column A and Column B.
    3. Consider all possibilities for any variables.
    4. Choose your answer.

- The quantitative comparison questions usually require less reading and computation than the standard multiple-choice questions.

- You may not actually have to solve the problem; you just need to determine which expression, if any, is greater—or if there is not enough information to determine the relationship.

- Quantitative comparison questions often require you to simplify equations.

- When dealing with variables, remember that unknowns can also be a zero, a negative number, or a fraction.

KNOWLEDGE CHECK

QUANTITATIVE COMPARISONS

15 Questions—15 Minutes

Directions: For each of the following questions, two quantities are given—one in Column A, the other in Column B. Compare the two quantities and write your answer in the margin as follows:

A. The quantity in Column A is greater.

B. The quantity in Column B is greater.

C. The two quantities are equal.

D. The relationship cannot be determined from the information given.

1. $a > 0$

                             $x > 0$

Column A	Column B
$a - x$	$a + x$

2.

Column A	Column B
The average of 18, 20, 22, 24	The average of 17, 19, 21, 23

3.

Column A	Column B
5% of 34	The number 34 is 5% of

4. $s = 1$

                             $t = 3$

                             $a = -2$

Column A	Column B
$[5a(4t)]^3$	$[4a(5s)]^2$

5.

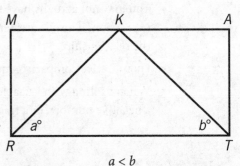

$a < b$

Column A	Column B
KR	KT

6. $4 > x > -3$

Column A	Column B
$\dfrac{x}{3}$	$\dfrac{3}{x}$

7.

Column A	Column B
$\dfrac{2}{3} + \dfrac{3}{7}$	$\dfrac{16}{21} - \dfrac{3}{7}$

8.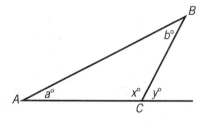

$$a > b$$
$$x < a + b$$

Column A	Column B
$a + b$	y

9. y = an odd integer

Column A	Column B
The numerical value of y^2	The numerical value of y^3

10.

Column A	Column B
$(8 + 6) \div [3 - 7(2)]$	$(6 + 8) \div [2 - 7(3)]$

11.

Column A	Column B
three fourths of $\dfrac{9}{9}$	$\dfrac{9}{9} \times \dfrac{3}{4}$

12.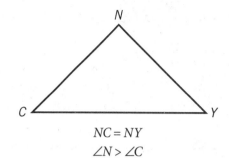

$$NC = NY$$
$$\angle N > \angle C$$

Column A	Column B
NC	CY

13.

Column A	Column B
A given chord in a given circle	The radius of the same circle

14.

Column A	Column B
$\dfrac{1}{\sqrt{9}}$	$\dfrac{1}{3}$

15.

Column A	Column B
$5\left(\dfrac{2}{3}\right)$	$\left(\dfrac{5}{3}\right)2$

ANSWER KEY AND EXPLANATIONS

1. B	**4.** B	**7.** A	**10.** B	**13.** D
2. A	**5.** A	**8.** C	**11.** C	**14.** C
3. B	**6.** D	**9.** D	**12.** B	**15.** C

1. **The correct answer is B.** The given information, $a > 0$ and $x > 0$, informs us that both a and x are positive numbers. The sum of two positive numbers is always greater than their difference.

2. **The correct answer is A.** The numbers in Column A are respectively larger than the numbers in Column B; therefore, their average must be greater.

3. **The correct answer is B.**

$$\frac{5}{100} = \frac{x}{34}$$
$$100x = 170$$
$$x = 1.7$$

$$\frac{5}{100} = \frac{34}{x}$$
$$5x = 3,400$$
$$x = 680$$

4. **The correct answer is B.**

$$\left[5a(4t)\right]^3 = \left[-10(12)\right]^3$$
$$= (-120)^3$$
$$= \text{negative answer}$$
$$\left[4a(5s)\right]^2 = \left[-8(5)\right]^2$$
$$= (-40)^2$$
$$= \text{positive answer}$$

A positive product is greater than a negative one.

5. **The correct answer is A.**

$$b > a$$
$$\therefore KR > KT \quad \text{(in a triangle, the greater side lies opposite the greater angle)}$$

6. **The correct answer is D.** Because x could be any integer from -3 to 4, the values of the fractions are impossible to determine.

7. **The correct answer is A.**

$$\frac{2}{3} + \frac{3}{7} = \frac{14}{21} + \frac{9}{21}$$
$$= \frac{23}{21}$$

$$\frac{16}{21} - \frac{3}{7} = \frac{16}{21} - \frac{9}{21}$$
$$= \frac{7}{21}$$

8. **The correct answer is C.**

$y = a + b$ (an exterior angle of a triangle is equal to the sum of the two interior remote angles)

9. **The correct answer is D.** There is not enough information, as y could equal 1, which would make both quantities equal; or y could be greater than 1, which would make y^3 greater than y^2. If y were a negative integer, then y^2 would be greater than y^3.

10. **The correct answer is B.**

$$(8+6) \div \left[3 - 7(2)\right]$$
$$= 14 \div -11$$
$$= \frac{14}{-11}$$

$$(6+8) \div \left[2 - 7(3)\right]$$
$$= 14 \div -19$$
$$= \frac{14}{-19}$$

11. **The correct answer is C.**

$$\frac{3}{4} \times \frac{9}{9} = \frac{3}{4} \qquad\qquad \frac{9}{9} \times \frac{3}{4} = \frac{3}{4}$$

12. **The correct answer is B.**

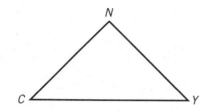

$NC = NY$ (given)

$\angle C = \angle Y$ (angles opposite equal sides are equal)

$\angle N > \angle C$ (given)

$\angle C > \angle Y$ (substitution)

$CY > NC$ (the greater side lies opposite the greater angle)

13. **The correct answer is D.** The radius could be less than, equal to, or greater than the chord.

14. **The correct answer is C.**

$$\frac{1}{\sqrt{9}} = \frac{1}{3}$$

15. **The correct answer is C.**

$$5\left(\frac{2}{3}\right) = \frac{5}{1} \times \frac{2}{3} = \frac{10}{3} \qquad\qquad \left(\frac{5}{3}\right)2 = \frac{5}{3} \times \frac{2}{1} = \frac{10}{3}$$

PART V
STRATEGIES FOR WRITING ESSAYS

CHAPTER

Essay Writing

ESSAY WRITING

OVERVIEW

The Essay Exam

Strategies to Improve Your Writing

Sample Prompts

Sample Essays

Summing It Up

SSAT   ISEE

THE ESSAY EXAM

This chapter focuses on strategies that will help you with the essay portion of the SSAT and ISEE. On both exams, the essay section is not scored. However, the essay is still important because it will be sent along with your score to any school that requires an SSAT or ISEE exam. While not receiving a grade for the essay takes some of the pressure off you as a test taker, you'll still want to focus on making the most of the time allotted. Even though this section of the exam is not graded, you still need some practice to hone your writing skills. At the end of this chapter, you'll find some practice prompts and sample essays to look over.

Neither exam tests your knowledge of writing mechanics directly. In other words, you won't be asked questions that specifically test topics like grammar, spelling, and capitalization. However, the writing sample you

submit will be used by schools to evaluate your over-all abilities as a writer. The essay tests far more than mechanics—it shows your ability to organize and convey your thoughts as well as your ability to develop your writing in a way that makes sense to a reader. It will give the school an overall impression of your maturity and power of self-expression. Understanding and utilizing appropriate writing mechanics can thus help assure that you make a positive impression on schools.

Both the ISEE and SSAT will give you a traditional essay prompt. There are two basic types of essay prompts. Here is an example of the first type.

EXAMPLE:

> **Directions:** Write a legible, coherent, and organized essay on the following topic.

Write about a time that you changed your mind about something you previously believed. What did you change your mind about and what made you change it? How did the experience affect your outlook?

This type of essay prompt is simple, relatively open-ended, and more common on the ISEE, though it might also pop up on the SSAT. It offers a personal topic as well as some related questions to consider. You are then expected to write a coherent essay on the given topic. You have a lot of freedom with this type of topic, as you can write about almost anything so long as you can make it fit the prompt, so you have freedom to show off your personality a bit.

Another type of common essay prompt looks something like the following example.

EXAMPLE:

> **Directions:** Read the topic, plan your writing, and write a legible, coherent essay on the paper provided.

High schools should reduce the school week to four days and allow students to pursue extra-curricular activities and/or part-time jobs on Fridays to build life experience.

Do you agree or disagree with this statement? Support your position with examples from your own experience, the experiences of others, current events, or your own existing knowledge.

For this type of prompt, which is more common on the SSAT, you are expected to write an essay in which you take a position for or against a particular topic. It is important to understand that it doesn't matter what stance you take; rather, it matters how well you coherently and directly support your argument. The best essays articulate specific reasons for the position taken.

 ALERT

Writing prompts emphasize that your writing should be legible (meaning "readable") because potential schools cannot evaluate it unless they can read your handwriting. If you're taking the exam on paper, take the time to write neatly enough to be understood.

The SSAT varies its approach to the writing sample from year to year. Sometimes, you'll be given two essay options, but other times, the SSAT will integrate a creative writing option. To prepare you for all possibilities, this book includes both types of prompts. If you are given the creative writing prompt and choose to write on it, your goal will be to write a story that uses the given prompt sentence as its first line. Prompts will look something like the following example.

EXAMPLE:

> **Directions:** Read the two prompts.

A: I stood there with my mouth hanging open because I couldn't believe my eyes.

B: The sun seemed brighter that morning than in the days prior.

Plan and write a legible, coherent story using one of these two statements as the first sentence. Be sure your story has a clear beginning, middle, and end.

The structure of a story is very different than that of an essay, but what is being evaluated will be the same. In both cases, you'll want to make sure that your writing has a clear beginning, middle, and end, but this is especially important with stories. Whether you write a story or an essay, evaluators will still focus on how well you express yourself in writing and how effectively you incorporate strong writing mechanics.

STRATEGIES TO IMPROVE YOUR WRITING

In addition to understanding writing mechanics, which we will discuss in the next chapter, it's important to understand how to organize your writing. Written communication starts with the sentence. A group of related sentences forms a paragraph. A series of connected paragraphs becomes a composition. The first step in improving your writing is to know what makes a good sentence. From there, you can decide how to combine those sentences into a logical and complete paragraph. Several strong paragraphs together will lead to a composition that is both clear and effective. At each step of the way, you're building onto what you've already written to develop a reasonable, logical train of thought.

Improving Sentences

A sentence must have a subject and an action word or verb. In addition, a sentence must express a complete thought. You can improve your sentences by adding in details while making sure they are still grammatically correct.

EXAMPLE:

Short Sentences:

Bob walks.

The dog swam.

Each of the sentences above are complete because they have a subject (Bob, the dog) who completes a verb (walks, swam). Add details to make these sentences more descriptive. For example, adding an adverb to each sentence gives a clearer picture of the action.

EXAMPLE:

Improved Sentences:

Bob walks briskly.

The dog swam rapidly.

Adding details that tell more about the subject or the verb can make these same two sentences even more interesting. For example, adding in a prepositional phrase places the action in context.

EXAMPLE:

Good Sentences:

Bob walks briskly down the road.

The dog swam rapidly across the pool.

The addition of another phrase at either the beginning or the end of these sentences provides an even clearer picture of the subjects and their actions.

EXAMPLE:

Better Sentences:

In a hurry to get to school on time, Bob walks briskly down the road.

The dog swam rapidly across the pool to fetch the tennis ball.

The more you can practice writing clear, descriptive sentences, the better you will become at writing them. Expanding your vocabulary so that you have a wide range of words from which to choose will enrich your descriptive powers as well.

Using a Thesis Statement

A thesis statement usually isn't necessary if you're writing a story, but if you're writing an essay, you can use a thesis statement to organize and ground your writing. Typically, a thesis statement is a single sentence that summarizes your argument. While you can put it in a few different places, it tends to make the most sense to place it at the end of your first paragraph. A reader should be able to tell what the main idea and purpose of your essay is just by reading the thesis statement.

Here are three examples of thesis statements on a similar topic:

- Despite the high costs associated with transit, more cities need to invest in high-speed rails and other forms of transportation infrastructure that aren't centered on individual vehicles.

- Those who support investing in high-speed rail note that development of this type of infrastructure leads to fewer emissions, increased transportation revenue, and reduced traffic.

- It is imperative that cities invest in high-speed rail infrastructure to reduce both traffic congestion and vehicle-based emissions.

While each of these thesis statements is similar, they point to different organizational structures for essays. For instance, the first one sets the writer up to discuss "other forms of transportation infrastructure" besides just high-speed rail, while the latter two set the writer up to discuss the specific issues mentioned in the thesis, like reduced traffic and emissions.

 TIP

Write your thesis statement first when planning your essay. Then, when your essay is finished, revisit your thesis statement to make sure it reflects the actual argument you wrote. If it doesn't, modify it so it does (rather than trying to change the entire essay to fit the old thesis statement).

A good thesis statement is specific, concise, and argumentative. To be specific, a thesis statement must not leave the reader with any questions as to what will be discussed. Take a look at the difference between the following thesis statements.

EXAMPLE:

Not Specific: Albert Einstein is an important figure because of his many discoveries.

Specific: Albert Einstein's most influential scientific discoveries include the general theory of relativity, the photoelectric effect, and Brownian motion.

The statement that is too vague leaves the reader with questions such as "An important figure to whom or in what?" and "Which discoveries?" The second, more specific thesis statement makes it clear that the argument will be about three specific scientific discoveries Einstein made. Furthermore, because this particular specific thesis statement is also divided, it previews the organization an essay might follow. In this case, the first body paragraph could be about the general theory of relativity, the second about the photoelectric effect, and the third about Brownian motion, allowing the writer to conclude by showing the relationship between the three.

 TIP

Using a "divided" statement in parallel structure is a good way to preview the topics of your body paragraphs within your thesis statement.

To be concise, a thesis statement should say exactly what it needs to say in as few words as possible without sacrificing meaning. Wordy thesis statements that try to fit in too much information can typically be reduced by eliminating any details that are not necessary to understanding the argument. Let's take a look at a wordy thesis statement and see how being concise can improve the statement's clarity and meaning.

EXAMPLE:

Not Concise: Because many people, especially children who are unable to vaccinate as well as those who have compromised immune systems such as cancer patients, cannot get vaccinations on their own in order to have their own immunity, it is necessary for other members of the community, especially healthy adults who do not have a host of health concerns to worry about, to make sure they are vaccinated in hopes that a great enough percentage of the population is vaccinated and herd immunity can happen.

Concise: Because some portions of the population are unable to vaccinate, it is important that those who can vaccinate follow through so that communities can achieve herd immunity.

A statement that is too wordy offers a lot of extra information that is not necessary for understanding the basic premise of the argument. The sentences that follow the thesis are a more appropriate place to address the extra information. The introduction, where the thesis is usually found, should stick to the most important tenets of the overall argument.

To be argumentative, a thesis statement must offer the reader the ability to agree or disagree with the position taken in the thesis statement. That doesn't necessarily mean that a reader is likely to react one way or another, only that it is possible for them to do so. If the thesis statement simply offers an already known fact or reiterates common knowledge, it is not making an argument. Let's take a look at the difference between the two types of statements in the following example.

Not Argumentative: In this novel, the author tells a fictional story about a young athlete.

Argumentative: In this novel, the author uses the fictional story of a young athlete as an allegory for adolescence.

In the nonargumentative statement, there is nothing to agree or disagree with—you can assume that a fictional novel about a young athlete does, in fact, tell a fictional story about a young athlete. There is nothing the author is arguing except for that which is already known, so the thesis statement does nothing to set up the information that should follow. In the argumentative example, you get a clear picture of what the writer plans to argue, which is that the novel can be considered an allegory for adolescence. A reader could, in theory, agree or disagree about the novel being an allegory for adolescence, so the thesis statement is argumentative.

Using Topic Sentences and Transitions

Transitions are necessary for guiding your reader through your writing. In essays, topic sentences are a particular type of transition that can help signal for your reader how different elements of your essay are knit together thematically. Think of a topic sentence as a mini thesis statement that occurs at the start of each paragraph. The purpose of the topic sentence is to offer a clear picture of what will be argued in that paragraph, often by referencing what came before to show how the two topics are linked. Let's take a look at an example transition sentence.

EXAMPLE:

While some believe that hemp plants should be grown for medicinal and industrial uses, others believe that the potential drug-related abuses of the crop outweigh the benefits of mass cultivation.

This topic sentence refers back to what was likely discussed in the paragraph before (the medicinal and industrial uses of hemp and why some support cultivating the crop) while also showing what is likely to come in the new paragraph (information on why hemp critics are concerned about drug-related abuse of the plant). When writing an essay, you'll want to have a topic sentence at the beginning of each new body paragraph.

Both topic sentences and story transitions often require using some form of transition word or phrase. Transition words and phrases are those that help you effectively transition between ideas. Often, these transition words or phrases will come at the start of a sentence, but that is not always the case. The following table details common transitions, their purpose, and examples of their usage. As a writing exercise, try making your own example sentences with the words and phrases given.

COMMON TRANSITION WORDS AND PHRASES		
Purpose of Transition	**Example Words**	**Example Sentences**
To introduce new ideas or add to/agree with topics that have already been introduced	<ul><li>additionally</li><li>coupled with</li><li>equally important</li><li>first, second, third, etc.</li><li>further</li><li>furthermore</li><li>in addition (to)</li><li>likewise</li><li>moreover</li><li>similarly</li></ul>	<ul><li>**First**, one must understand how the structure of DNA affects genetics.</li><li>**Furthermore**, these same observations were noted at another dig site 20 km away.</li><li>The question of municipal water usage is **equally important** to the discussion of local conservation efforts.</li></ul>
To communicate the writer's opposition to or a limit placed upon a given idea or phrase	<ul><li>as much as</li><li>by contrast</li><li>conversely</li><li>despite</li><li>notwithstanding</li><li>on the contrary</li><li>on the other hand</li><li>that said</li><li>while</li></ul>	<ul><li>**Despite** new evidence, Dr. Galins's theory remains prevalent in the field.</li><li>The question of parental input is, **conversely**, overemphasized in research on childhood literacy development.</li><li>**As much as** Sushmita had hoped to sleep in, the birds noisily nesting outside her window had other plans.</li></ul>
To show a cause-and-effect relationship or communicate the conditions that influence a circumstance or idea	<ul><li>as a result</li><li>as long as</li><li>because (of)</li><li>consequently</li><li>due to</li><li>hence</li><li>in case (of)</li><li>in effect</li><li>since</li><li>then</li><li>therefore</li><li>thus</li><li>unless</li><li>whenever</li><li>while</li></ul>	<ul><li>I am going fishing later, **hence** the tackle box and gear.</li><li>**Consequently**, commuters were unable to reliably predict what time the trains would arrive.</li><li>Tina was upset **because of** the letters she'd found in her brother's drawer.</li><li>**Therefore**, it's important for schools to invest adequate funds into arts and music programs.</li><li>The school board, in the **meantime**, is gathering community feedback on the matter.</li></ul>

COMMON TRANSITION WORDS AND PHRASES

Purpose of Transition	Example Words	Example Sentences
To set up an example, fact, piece of evidence, or other form of support for another concept	<ul><li>by all means</li><li>by no means</li><li>especially</li><li>explicitly</li><li>for this reason</li><li>indeed</li><li>in fact</li><li>in other words</li><li>markedly</li><li>notably</li><li>significantly</li><li>to clarify</li><li>to elaborate</li><li>to reiterate</li></ul>	<ul><li>The new model of the car is **by all means** a notable improvement on prior models.</li><li>**In other words,** those who wish to master a new skill should expect to devote numerous hours to being amateurish at first.</li><li>**Indeed,** Portugal was the first European nation to get actively involved in the Transatlantic slave trade.</li></ul>
To communicate the time at which an event occurred or the timing of one event in relation to another	<ul><li>after</li><li>all of a sudden</li><li>at present</li><li>at the moment</li><li>at the time</li><li>before</li><li>frequently</li><li>in the meantime</li><li>momentarily</li><li>now</li><li>occasionally</li><li>often</li><li>once</li><li>once upon a time</li><li>seldomly</li><li>suddenly</li><li>then</li><li>today</li></ul>	<ul><li>I was distracted, **momentarily,** by a high-pitched shriek emitting from the far-off woods.</li><li>**Today,** the James Webb Space Telescope is known for producing the clearest images of far-off galaxies.</li><li>**All of a sudden,** the doorbell rang.</li><li>The school board, **in the meantime,** is gathering community feedback on the matter.</li></ul>

COMMON TRANSITION WORDS AND PHRASES

Purpose of Transition	Example Words	Example Sentences
To help the writer communicate a conclusion or final idea on a topic	• all in all • altogether • effectively • in any event • in conclusion • in effect • in either case • in essence • in summary • nevertheless • nonetheless • to conclude • to summarize • to sum up	• **In any event**, the festival proved a success despite the weather issues and a series of unfortunate technical mishaps. • **Altogether**, there are numerous factors that contribute to a feeling of loneliness, not all of them psychological. • This means that the industry as it once was is, **effectively**, over.

Improving Paragraphs

A paragraph is a group of sentences that develops one main idea. In essays, as we discussed in the previous section, this main idea or topic is usually stated in a topic sentence at the start of the paragraph. The rest of the paragraph then provides details or clarifies the topic by offering specific examples or analysis. In stories, paragraph breaks usually occur when the author introduces new dialogue or when there is a shift in events, ideas, or tone. There are no rules for determining the length of a paragraph. However, it is a good idea to make most paragraphs in an essay at least three sentences long. In a story, you have more creative control over the lengths of paragraphs, but this is still a good basic rule to follow. One exception concerns dialogue—make a paragraph break each time you start a new line of dialogue in a story. Here, we'll cover not only how to develop a paragraph for an essay in which you make and support an argument but also how to develop a paragraph for a story.

Example of an Essay Paragraph Developed by Examples

EXAMPLE:

Intramural sports are a valuable part of the high school curriculum. A sports program provides a constructive outlet for the energy that has been stored up during the school day. For teens with a lot of spare time on their hands, practice sessions or games take up the time that might otherwise be spent looking for trouble. Tossing a basketball around the gym provides an acceptable alternative to tossing rocks at streetlights or other forms of mischief.

Each sentence in this paragraph provides a specific example of the value of intramural sports.

Example of a Story Paragraph Developed by Details

EXAMPLE:

The man opened the door cautiously and slipped quietly into the crowded waiting room. He was dressed in a clean but well-worn overcoat and bright red sneakers that had seen better days. On his head was a black knitted cap, pulled down to cover his forehead and ears.

Every sentence in this paragraph provides additional details about the topic—the man and his appearance.

Connecting Paragraphs

When you end a paragraph and start a new one, this indicates a change. Start a new paragraph to show a change in:

- The time, the place, or the action in a story
- The mood or point of view in a description
- Ideas or steps in an explanation

- Speakers in a conversation
- Subtopic or focus in a larger argument

Just as you must provide for an orderly flow of sentences within a paragraph, you must also provide for a logical transition from paragraph to paragraph in any composition, whether fictional (like a story) or not (like an essay).

The three most common ways of connecting paragraphs are:

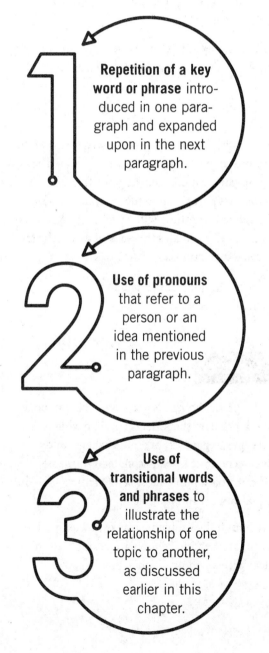

Repetition of a key word or phrase introduced in one paragraph and expanded upon in the next paragraph.

Use of pronouns that refer to a person or an idea mentioned in the previous paragraph.

Use of transitional words and phrases to illustrate the relationship of one topic to another, as discussed earlier in this chapter.

Connected by Repetition of a Key Word

> **EXAMPLE:**
>
> Last summer our whole family piled into the car and drove to Disney World in Florida. Although we had heard about the amusement park from friends who had already been there, this would be our first experience at a Disney park. We were all eager to get there, but we really did not know what to **expect**.
>
> Our first day at Disney World went beyond any **expectations** we might have had …

These paragraphs are connected using forms of the same word. *Expect* in paragraph 1 is repeated as *expectations* in paragraph 2, allowing one thought to flow from the first paragraph to the second. The second paragraph will continue with specific things the family did at Disney World and the ways in which the trip exceeded expectations.

Example of Paragraphs Connected by Transitional Words

> **EXAMPLE:**
>
> Teenage alcoholism is a serious problem today. It is a problem that affects young people of all types, regardless of ethnic background or socioeconomic level. Alcoholism shows no discrimination in choosing its victims—it is an equal-opportunity problem.
>
> **Although** the problem is far from being solved, both families and schools are taking steps to deal with alcoholism among teens.

These paragraphs are connected by the use of the transitional word *although* and the repetition of the key word *problem*. The second paragraph will continue by detailing some of the steps that are being taken to combat alcoholism.

Make Sure a Story Has a Beginning, Middle, and End

If you are writing a story on the SSAT exam instead of an essay, you will likely have to follow slightly different writing conditions than those outlined for essays. The most important thing to keep in mind is the idea of a beginning, middle, and end. Make sure you set the scene for your story, introduce characters, then have rising action leading to a climax and a resolution to the story after the climax.

SAMPLE PROMPTS

This page contains samples of both types of essay prompts. In a few pages, you'll also find a creative writing sample prompt. Try practicing your writing skills using the guidance we've presented in this chapter in response to one or more of these prompts. Remember, the essay exam is a sample of your writing abilities, so you want to make sure it is an accurate reflection of your skills. You should have enough space in this book to try one of each type of prompt, but feel free to practice as many prompts as you want using scratch paper.

Directions: Write a legible, coherent, and organized essay on one of the following topic(s).

1. Write about a time when you didn't meet a standard or goal that you set for yourself. What happened, and what did you learn from the experience?

2. Write about a time when you had to advocate for yourself. How did you go about asking for what you needed, and what was the end result?

3. Write about what it means to be a leader. What qualities or experiences should someone have to be an effective leader, and why?

4. What is the biggest challenge facing your community? What are the consequences of this problem, and what are some potential solutions?

Directions: Read the topics, select one, plan your writing, and write a legible, coherent essay in which you take a position agreeing or disagreeing with the statement. Support your position with examples from your own experiences, the experiences of others, current events, or your own existing knowledge.

1. Dress codes unfairly target students, especially girls. Middle schools and high schools should get rid of dress codes and trust that students will dress appropriately for class.

2. It is unfair for teachers to penalize students for late work. Students should be allowed to turn in work late for any reason, provided they get the work in during that grading term.

3. With so many unreliable sources on the internet, it can be hard for teenagers to figure out which is true and what is not. High schools should teach information literacy courses to help students identify credible sources and fact-check information they come across on the internet.

4. You can't truly know who you are until you see how you respond under pressure. Only high-stress situations like emergencies and deadlines allow a person to show their true colors.

5. It's better to have loved and lost than to have never loved at all. Heartbreak is difficult, but it's better than not knowing what might have happened if you showed someone how much you care for them.

6. Experience is more valuable than natural talent. Those who must work hard to gain knowledge or talent develop a more sophisticated understanding than those who are naturally good at things.

Directions: Read the statements, select one, then plan and write a legible, coherent story using the statement as your first sentence. Be sure your story has a clear beginning, middle, and end.

1. It seemed like the rain would never stop.

2. "Look out!" he shouted, breaking the silence.

3. I could feel the sweat dripping down my forehead as I answered the phone.

4. The floor creaked as they made their way toward the back door.

5. The woman blinked twice, trying to figure out what she was looking at.

6. That night, the stars seemed to shine brighter than they ever had before.

SAMPLE ESSAYS

Here, we've included sample essays in response to one of each kind of prompt. In the first two, pay attention to the use of thesis statements, paragraph structure, topic sentences, and transitions. In the last sample, note how the story has a clear beginning, middle, and end.

EXAMPLE:

Sample Essay 1

Write about what it means to be a leader. What qualities or experiences should someone have to be an effective leader, and why?

Being a leader means being willing to make hard decisions that no one else wants to make. It's hard to be a leader, and a lot of times, it can be hard to figure out who is a good leader and who just wants to be in charge. To be an effective leader, you have to listen and support the people you are leading and communicate with people to help them improve.

It's important for leaders to listen to the people they are responsible for. In my job, I have a great supervisor, who listens to all my concerns and answers my questions when they come up. He can't always give me the answer or the solution that I want, but at least I always know why he makes a decision. This makes it easier for me to follow his directions and take his advice at work. I feel like he really listens to me when I think something could be done better or more productively and he takes my feedback into consideration. A good leader is able to encourage people and support them as they grow.

Good leaders also have to communicate well to help people grow and improve. Sometimes, they need to deliver bad news or prepare team members for a change in how things are done. In my theater club at school, Ms. Porter, our faculty advisor, gives direction and advice to students who are struggling with certain lines or songs. It can be hard for students to hear that they're not doing a good job with something, but they also appreciate that Ms. Porter is trying to help them do the best they can do. These conversations can be hard to have, but a good leader will be prepared and will communicate directly and honestly with the people they're leading.

Being a leader can be a tough job, but some people are really good at listening and communicating with others to help them grow and become better in their roles. These leaders can motivate people to try harder and to seek out help when they need it. Good leaders can also teach and train people so that they do the best they can. Overall, it's hard to be a leader, but someone with these qualities will probably succeed as a leader wherever they want to help and support others.

EXAMPLE:

Sample Essay 2

Dress codes unfairly target students, especially girls. Middle schools and high schools should get rid of dress codes and trust that students will dress appropriately for class.

Do you agree or disagree with this statement? Support your position with examples from your own experience, the experiences of others, current events, or your own existing knowledge.

Dress codes have been used by schools to enforce outdated views on what it means to dress appropriately for school. I agree that schools should get rid of dress codes because they are not realistic and unfairly target students, especially girls. Instead, schools should trust that students know how to dress appropriately and in a way that is comfortable for them while they learn in class.

Dress codes unfairly target girls and don't take into consideration how clothes fit on different body types. For example, girls at my school who are tall often have a hard time finding shorts that cover enough of their thighs so that they don't get a dress code violation. It's unfair to enforce rules about the length of shorts, skirts, or dresses when the same dress will fit differently on someone who is 5'2" vs. someone who is 5'10". This is also true for girls who have trouble finding shirts that cover their chest and shoulders. Because dress codes don't take into account different body types and sizes, they should not be used or enforced at all.

Dress codes also don't consider what clothes are fashionable and can be found in stores. Sometimes, when I go back-to-school shopping with my mom, there are only crop tops and short shorts. This can make it hard for me to find clothes that follow the school dress code. If I can't find any shirts that cover my stomach, then I have to look at T-shirts or dresses instead, which can be more expensive, less comfortable for me, or even harder to find. If you add in that some kids cannot afford to always replace their clothes when they start to fit differently, you could also argue that dress codes don't consider people's economic situation for clothes shopping either.

If schools are meant to be places where students can learn, then students should be able to wear whatever they are most comfortable learning in. For some students, that might be crop tops and short shorts. For other students, it might be sweat pants and T-shirts. Considering how unfairly dress codes are enforced, they should be gotten rid of altogether.

Sample Essay 3

Prompt: "Look out!" he shouted, breaking the silence.

Plan and write a legible, coherent story using the statement as the first sentence. Be sure your story has a clear beginning, middle, and end.

"Look out!" he shouted, breaking the silence.

All the students looked up, only to see a huge raccoon fall from the ceiling.

"Is that… a raccoon?!" shouted Stephanie.

"It is!" shouted Jorge. "Run!"

The students scurried away from their desks and out the door of the classroom only to find the hallways filled with more raccoons than they had ever seen in their lives.

"They're everywhere!" screamed Xioanan.

"Where do we go?!" asked Kenan.

"The bathrooms!" a teacher exclaimed. "Get to the bathrooms!"

The students piled up in the bathrooms, trying to escape from the sneaky little animals that filled their school.

"Why are there raccoons everywhere?" Tia asked, assuming someone would know.

Once the frightened students had all made it into the bathrooms, Stephanie slowly pulled open the door to take a look at the hallway. The raccoons were frantic and couldn't figure out where they were. They were searching for an exit but couldn't find one.

Stephanie slowly shut the bathroom door and started to pull the flute out of her backpack.

"What are you doing?" asked Tia.

"I'm going to try and be the Pied Piper of Raccoons." Stephanie replied casually.

"You're what?" inquired Xiaonan with a shocked look.

"I think if they hear my music, they'll follow me, and I can lead them out the school doors. Like that story from German class."

"That's ridiculous—what if they bite you?" said Tia.

"They won't bite me. I think they'll sense that I'm trying to help them."

"I hope you're up to date on your rabies shots!" Xiaonan joked.

Stephanie opened the bathroom door again and started to walk out. Then, she slowly lifted the flute up to her lips and started to blow. She played the only song she knew how to play—"Twinkle Twinkle Little Star."

The raccoons immediately froze, their beady eyes locked in her direction.

Stephanie started skipping toward the main entrance of the school. The raccoons weren't moving. She stopped playing, and all the raccoons tilted their heads, confused as to what she was doing. But Stephanie was undeterred. She picked up right where she left off and started playing again.

This time, the raccoons began to follow her. They almost seemed to be stepping in rhythm with the music. Slowly but surely, Stephanie repeated her song and led the raccoons to the school doors. She kicked open the doors and never stopped playing. The raccoons realized they were free and ran into the street, grinding traffic to a halt.

Stephanie did it—she was the Pied Piper of Raccoons.

As she turned back around to go back into the school, she bumped into Brock, a senior who seemed to be a holding a raccoon in a cage with his left hand.

Stephanie froze. "Why do you have a raccoon?"

Brock laughed. "Don't tell anyone, but me and the guys are going to pull off the best senior prank yet. We're going to drop raccoons into classrooms from the ceiling! It'll be hilarious."

Stephanie held the door open for Brock, gesturing at the hoard of raccoons in the street in front of the school. "Looks like you missed your cue."

SUMMING IT UP

- Both the SSAT and ISEE include an essay section that will be treated like a writing sample by schools to which you apply with your test results. As such, it's important to familiarize yourself with the types of writing on the exam so that you're prepared to do your best in this section.

- There are many ways to improve your writing, including using thesis statements and topic sentences, strengthening sentences with details, and using transitions between paragraphs.

- Practice writing your own essays in response to the sample prompts included in this chapter. The more you practice, the better prepared you will be on the exam.

CHAPTER

Writing Mechanics

WRITING MECHANICS

OVERVIEW

Grammar

Sentence Structure and Formation

Punctuation

Capitalization

Spelling

Summing It Up

As covered in the last chapter, both the SSAT and ISEE will have an essay component. While the essay section is unscored, it's still important to do your best, as the essay is an opportunity for you to showcase your skills to the schools that receive your exam scores. Knowing the mechanics of writing is essential to doing well on the essay portion, so while writing mechanics isn't tested directly on either exam, you'll want to study up so that you can communicate your ideas clearly and effectively in writing. In this chapter, we'll cover the basics of writing mechanics, including grammar, sentence structure and formation, punctuation, capitalization, and spelling. As with Chapter 16: Essay Writing, there will be no Knowledge Check for this chapter, but there will be plenty of examples and explanations along the way.

SSAT   ISEE

The mechanics of writing include grammar, sentence structure and formation (including word choice), punctuation, capitalization, and spelling. Each work together to produce writing that communicates effectively, is readily understandable to the average reader, and follows the conventions of the language in which it is written. It is important to understand and practice these elements of writing if you want to do well on your essay, which effectively works as a writing sample for schools to which you are applying using your SSAT or ISEE results. When you compose your writing, pay attention to "big picture" ideas like organization, clarity, and content, but also pay attention to the smaller details like writing mechanics. Being able to convey your ideas with correct and proper English usage and in a logical, organized manner demonstrates your expressive abilities.

GRAMMAR

The rules of grammar govern the ways in which parts of speech are organized in a sentence. There are rules concerning word endings, word order, and which words may be used together. You must know the parts of speech to follow the rules of grammar.

PARTS OF SPEECH		
Type	**Definition**	**Examples**
Noun	A person, place, thing, or idea	teacher, city, desk, democracy
Pronoun	Substitute for a noun	he, she, they, ours, those
Adjective	Describes a noun	warm, quick, tall, blue
Verb	Expresses action or a state of being	yell, interpret, feel, are
Adverb	Modifies a verb, an adjective, or another adverb	fast, slowly, friendly, well
Conjunction	Joins words, sentences, and phrases	for, and, nor, but, or, yet, so
Preposition	Shows position in time or space	in, during, after, behind

Nouns

A noun is a person, place, thing, or idea. There are different kinds of nouns:

- **Common nouns** are general, such as house, person, street, or city.
- **Proper nouns** are specific, such as White House, Fernando, Main Street, or New York.
- **Collective nouns** denote a group of people or things. They often look singular (e.g., team, crowd, organization, Congress).

To learn more about nouns and verbs, scan this QR code.

Nouns have cases:

- A noun is in the **nominative** case when it is the subject of the sentence.

> **EXAMPLE:**
>
> *Roberto* joined the band.

- A noun is in the **objective** case when it is the direct object, indirect object, or object of the preposition.

> **EXAMPLES:**
>
> **Direct object:** She built a *treehouse*.
>
> **Indirect object:** Joel sent a message to *Marco*.
>
> **Object of the preposition:** The fairies danced around *Jasmine*.

- **Possessive** case is the form that shows possession.

> **EXAMPLE:**
>
> The *queen's* crown was filled with rubies.

Pronouns

A pronoun is a substitute for a noun. The antecedent of the pronoun is the noun that the pronoun replaces. A pronoun must agree with its antecedent in gender, person, and number. There are several kinds of pronouns:

- **Demonstrative pronoun:** this, that, these, those
- **Indefinite pronoun:** all, any, nobody

- **Interrogative pronoun:** who, which, what
- **Personal pronoun:** I, you, we, me, him, her, us, they

Adjectives

An adjective describes a noun. Adjectives can answer questions like:

- Which one?
- What kind?
- How many?

There are three uses of adjectives:

- A **noun modifier** is usually placed directly before the noun it describes.

> **EXAMPLE:**
>
> He is a *tall* man.

- A **predicate adjective** follows a linking verb and modifies the subject.

> **EXAMPLES:**
>
> She is *happy*.
>
> I feel *terrible*.

- An **article** or **noun marker** points to a noun. The articles are *the*, *a*, and *an*.

> **EXAMPLE:**
>
> *The* teacher took *a* vacation to *an* island.

Verbs

A verb expresses action or a state of being. There are four major kinds of verbs: transitive, intransitive, linking, and auxiliary or helping verbs.

- **Transitive verbs** are action verbs and always have a direct object. In other words, there's something receiving the action of a transitive verb.

EXAMPLES:

The dog *broke* her tooth.

The teacher *discussed* the effects of the Black Death during the Middle Ages.

- **Intransitive verbs** are action verbs with no direct object. Some verbs can be either transitive or intransitive depending on their usage.

EXAMPLES:

The vase *broke*.

Miguel *cried*.

- **Linking verbs** indicate a state of being and have no action. These verbs serve to link the subject to additional descriptive information. Examples include *is, are, was, were, be, been, am, smell, taste, feel, look, seem, become,* and *appear.* Sometimes, the verbs listed here can be linking, auxiliary, or action verbs depending on their usage.

EXAMPLES:

I *am* here.

He *looks* nervous.

She *is* sick.

The food *tasted* delicious.

- **Auxiliary** or **helping verbs** are used with an infinitive or participle to create a verb phrase. Auxiliary verbs always need a primary verb to function. Examples of auxiliary verbs include all forms of the verbs *to be, to have, to do,* and *to keep,* as well as *can, could, may, might, must, ought to, shall, will, would,* and *should.*

EXAMPLES:

I *am having* a glass of water.

She *might go* to the store.

Alex *should study* harder.

For more information on adjectives and adverbs, scan this QR code.

Adverbs

An adverb modifies a verb, an adjective, or another adverb and can answer questions like:

- Why?
- How?
- Where?
- When?
- To what degree?

Adverbs should not be used to modify nouns. Many adverbs are easy to identify because they end in -*ly*. But there are other adverbs that do not have this ending.

> **EXAMPLES:**
>
> He *quickly* jumped over the hole.
>
> I am doing *well*.
>
> The water swirled *clockwise* down the drain.

Conjunctions

A conjunction joins words, sentences, and phrases. The best way to remember the conjunctions is with the acronym FANBOYS. This stands for: <u>f</u>or, <u>a</u>nd, <u>n</u>or, <u>b</u>ut, <u>o</u>r, <u>y</u>et, <u>s</u>o.

> **EXAMPLES:**
>
> She *and* I went to the park.
>
> I wanted to play video games, *but* my mom said it was time to leave.
>
> Neither Jin *nor* his children wanted to move to the new city.

 TIP

For coordinating conjunctions, remember the acronym **FANBOYS**:

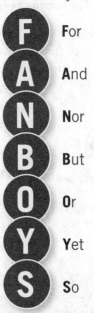

For

And

Nor

But

Or

Yet

So

Conjunctions connect ideas together. If you're using a comma to separate two complete sentences, you also need one of the FANBOYS.

Prepositions

A preposition shows position in time or space. Common prepositions are words like *around*, *in*, *over*, *under*, *during*, *after*, and *behind*. A preposition starts a prepositional phrase that usually shows the relationship between a noun or pronoun and the rest of the information in the sentence.

> **EXAMPLES:**
>
> The dog sleeps *under the bed*.
>
> She stood up *during the presentation*.
>
> *After the meeting*, Dr. Masamba changed her policy.

SENTENCE STRUCTURE AND FORMATION

Understanding the parts of speech is fundamental to good writing, but so is understanding how to combine them to form effective sentences. Word choice is related, since the words you choose to fulfill different parts of speech within a sentence have an impact on what the sentence communicates and how.

There are four different kinds of sentence structures in English:

1. **Simple sentence:** an independent clause
2. **Compound sentence:** two independent clauses joined together
3. **Complex sentence:** an independent clause and at least one dependent clause
4. **Compound-complex sentence:** at least two independent clauses and one dependent clause

Compound, complex, and compound-complex sentences can technically have as many clauses as you want, as long as they are connected and punctuated correctly.

Fragments

Every sentence must have a subject (something to do the action) and a verb or predicate (the action), which combine to express a complete idea. When all those items are present, you get an independent clause (another way of saying "a complete sentence"). A group of words that is missing one of these elements is called a sentence fragment or an incomplete sentence. If a group of words has a subject and verb but doesn't express a complete thought, it's a dependent clause.

There are two ways to correct incomplete sentences.

1 Add the fragment to the sentence that precedes it.

 Incorrect: Zoologists and wildlife biologists study animals and other wildlife. Including how they interact with their ecosystems.

 Correct: Zoologists and wildlife biologists study animals and other wildlife, including how they interact with their ecosystems.

 Explanation: The fragment is added to the sentence that precedes it by inserting a comma.

CLAUSES AND SENTENCE STRUCTURE

Term	Definition	Examples
Independent clause	A complete sentence	• Maureen gets up early to feed her cats. • I slept well on the airplane. • Our family visited the ruins on the beach in Tulum.
Dependent clause	Words that include a subject and verb, but which do not express a complete thought; can complete a sentence when combined with an independent clause	• Because it is already noon. • When Aunt Colleen arrives. • Better than my neighbor can.
Sentence fragment	An incomplete sentence; missing either a verb/action word or a subject	• In the city. • A really great time. • Was late but then helped out.

2

Add the fragment to the sentence that follows.

Incorrect: By studying animal behaviors. Wildlife biologists seek to understand how animals interact with their ecosystems.

Correct: Wildlife biologists seeks to understand how animals interact with their ecosystems by studying animal behaviors.

Explanation: The fragment is turned into a prepositional phrase that modifies the rest of the sentence. (The fragment now serves as a prepositional phrase that modifies the rest of the sentence.)

3

Add a subject and verb to the fragment.

Incorrect: Considerable time studying animals in their natural habitats.

Correct: Wildlife biologists may spend considerable time studying animals in their natural habitats.

Explanation: A subject (*wildlife biologists*) and verb (*may spend*) are added to the fragment.

Run-Ons and Comma Splices

Complete sentences must be separated by a period, a comma and a coordinating conjunction, or a semicolon. A run-on sentence occurs when a writer fails to use either end-stop punctuation to divide complete thoughts or suitable conjunctions to join two ideas. When two independent clauses are joined only by a comma, you have an error called a comma splice.

The following rules will help you avoid and fix run-on sentences and comma splices.

1

Divide the sentence using periods.

Incorrect: Zoologists need a bachelor's degree for entry-level positions a master's degree or Ph.D. is often needed for advancement.

Correct: Zoologists need a bachelor's degree for entry-level positions. A master's degree or Ph.D. is often needed for advancement.

Explanation: Inserting a period between *positions* and *A* corrects the run-on sentence by creating two independent clauses.

2

Create a compound sentence by joining independent clauses using a coordinating conjunction such as *and*, *but*, or *so*.

Incorrect: Zoologists need a bachelor's degree for entry-level positions, a master's degree is often needed for advancement.

Correct: Zoologists need a bachelor's degree for entry-level positions, but a master's degree is often needed for advancement.

Explanation: Adding a comma and the coordinating conjunction *but* eliminates the comma splice and connects the two independent clauses correctly. (Remember that a comma is required when you use a coordinating conjunction to join two independent clauses.)

Scan this QR code to learn more about forming complex sentences.

3

Create a complex sentence by adding a subordinating conjunction—such as *because*, *although*, or *while*—making one of the independent clauses a dependent clause.

❌ Incorrect: Zoologists need only a bachelor's degree for entry-level positions a master's degree is often needed for advancement.

✓ Correct (option 1): Zoologists need only a bachelor's degree for entry-level positions although a master's degree is often needed for advancement.

ℹ Explanation: Adding the conjunction *although* between the two independent clauses corrects the run-on sentence by changing the second clause to a dependent clause and creating a complex sentence. Note: In general, commas are not required when the dependent clause follows the independent clause.

✓ Correct (option 2): Although a master's degree is often needed for advancement, zoologists need only a bachelor's degree for entry-level positions.

ℹ Explanation: Adding the conjunction *although* and moving the second independent clause corrects the run-on sentence by changing the first clause to a dependent clause and creating a complex sentence. Note: Commas are required when the dependent clause precedes the independent clause.

4

Use a semicolon when ideas are closely related in meaning.

❌ Incorrect: Zoologists and wildlife biologists study how animals and other wildlife interact with their ecosystems, these scientists work in offices, laboratories, or outdoors.

✓ Correct: Zoologists and wildlife biologists study how animals and other wildlife interact with their ecosystems; these scientists work in offices, laboratories, or outdoors.

ℹ Explanation: Inserting a semicolon between the two independent clauses corrects the comma splice and creates a compound sentence.

Coordination and Subordination

Coordinating and subordinating conjunctions are used to join phrases and clauses and form compound and complex sentences.

COMMON CONJUNCTIONS	
Coordinating conjunctions	**Subordinating conjunctions**
for, and, nor, but, or, yet, so	after, although, as, as if, because, before, even if, even though, if, if only, rather than, since, that, though, unless, until, when, where, whereas, wherever, whether, which, while

To learn more about subjects and predicates, scan this QR code.

Basic Rule of Coordinating Conjunctions

Coordinating conjunctions are used to add items to a list and join independent clauses to make compound sentences. With items in a list, the last item in the list should be preceded by a coordinating conjunction.

 Independent clauses: There was a Treaty of Paris signed in 1763. There was also one signed in 1783. There was another signed in 1919.

 Joined: There were Treaties of Paris signed in 1763, 1783, and 1919.

When two clauses are joined, if the second remains an independent clause, a comma must be used before the coordinating conjunction. The coordinating conjunction signals that each clause carries the same weight while also creating a relationship between the ideas (additive, contrasting, or causal).

 Independent clauses: There was a Treaty of Paris signed in 1763. There was also one signed in 1783.

 Joined: There was a Treaty of Paris signed in 1763, but there was another Treaty of Paris signed in 1783.

Basic Rule of Subordinating Conjunctions

Subordinating conjunctions are added to an independent clause to make it a dependent clause.

A dependent clause establishes a place, a time, a reason, a condition, a concession, or a comparison for the independent clause—some form of extra information that clarifies the action of the independent clause. Dependent clauses have a subject and a verb but don't express

a complete though. Due to the presence of a subordinating conjunction, the clause needs (or *depends* on) an independent clause to be grammatically correct. This also means that dependent clauses are subordinate to the information in the independent clause—meaning they're less important (offering extra information) and

 TIP

Remember that an independent clause is just a complete sentence. It has a subject and a verb and expresses a complete thought.

preceded by a subordinating conjunction. Dependent clauses can come before or after an independent clause, but if they're before, they must be separated from the independent clause by a comma. Review the list of subordinating conjunctions to identify dependent clauses more quickly. Let's look at some examples of subordinating conjunctions used to create dependent clauses.

 Independent clauses: A tax on imported goods from another country is called a tariff. A tax on imported goods from another country to protect a home industry is called a protective tariff.

 Joined: A tax on imported goods from another country is called a tariff while a tax on imported goods from another country to protect a home industry is called a protective tariff.

Here, the subordinating conjunction *while* was added to the second independent clause. The resulting dependent clause is then joined to the end of the first independent clause without using any punctuation.

A subordinating conjunction can also be used at the beginning of a sentence. The resulting dependent clause must be joined to an independent clause and separated by a comma.

 Independent clauses: A tax on imported goods from another country is called a tariff. A tax on imported goods from another country to protect a home industry is called a protective tariff.

 Joined: While a tax on imported goods from another country is called a tariff, a tax on imported goods from another country to protect a home industry is called a protective tariff.

Modifier Placement

A modifier is a word, phrase, or clause that adds detail to a sentence. To avoid confusion, modifiers should be placed as close as possible to the things they modify. Examples of different modifiers are underlined in the following examples.

 Example: <u>Within the field of marine biology</u>, employment is <u>highly</u> competitive.

Explanation: The phrase "within the field of marine biology" modifies the subject of the sentence, which is *employment*. The word *highly* modifies our understanding of the competitive nature of finding employment.

 Example: The <u>abundant</u> supply of <u>marine</u> scientists far exceeds the demands, and the number of <u>federal</u> and <u>state</u> <u>government</u> jobs is <u>limited</u>.

Explanation: *Abundant* modifies *supply. Marine* modifies *scientists. Federal, state, government,* and *limited* modify our understanding of *jobs.*

To learn more about modifier placement, scan this QR code.

When the subject of a modifier is unclear or is not included in the sentence, it is considered a dangling modifier.

 Incorrect: Not realizing that the job title of marine biologist rarely exists, *marine biology* is a term recognized by most people. (What is the first phrase modifying?)

 Possible revision: Not realizing that the job title of marine biologist rarely exists, most people recognize the term *marine biology.*

Misplaced modifiers occur when a modifier is poorly placed and doesn't express the writer's intent accurately.

 Incorrect: The term *marine biologist* is used to almost describe all of the disciplines and jobs that deal with the study of marine life, not just those that deal with the physical properties of the sea.

 Possible revision: The term *marine biologist* is used to describe almost all of the disciplines and jobs that deal with the study of marine life, not just those that deal with the physical properties of the sea.

Parallel Structure

Parallel structure is the repetition of a grammatical form within a sentence. When things are parallel, they are moving in the same direction. Parallel structure is a hallmark of effective writing and is often used to emphasize ideas and present compared items in an equal light. Coordinating conjunctions are often used in parallel constructions.

 Nonparallel structure: As a child, George Washington Carver enjoyed reading, learned about plants, and he made art.

 Parallel structure: As a child, George Washington Carver enjoyed reading, learning about plants, and making art.

In the first sentence, "George Washington Carver enjoyed reading" leads the reader to expect that the next items in the list will also be gerunds, verbs that end in -*ing*. However, the next items in the list are not in the same form: the phrase "learned about plants" is in the past tense, while the phrase "he made art" is an independent clause. To resolve the issue with parallel structure, we need to pick one form of the word and stick to it. The easiest and most concise fix is to change the last two items to gerunds to match the first item, *reading*.

Issues with parallel structure are most noticeable in lists of things. It's important to remember that parallel structure applies to other parts of speech as well. To be grammatically correct, items that are being compared should be the same part of speech and used correctly in the structure of the sentence. For essay writing purposes, parallel structure is especially effective in divided thesis statements, wherein the author expresses their primary argument in a single statement at the end of their first paragraph, using parallel structure to present the main elements of their argument.

Verb Tense

Use the same verb tense whenever possible within a sentence or paragraph. Do not shift from one tense to another unless there is a valid reason for doing so.

 Incorrect: The Magna Carta *was* signed in 1215 by King John of England and *has been* the first document of its kind to limit the power of the British monarchy.

 Correct: The Magna Carta *was* signed in 1215 by King John of England and *was* the first document of its kind to limit the power of the British monarchy.

Naturally, different verb tenses have different forms, but you will see some overlap. For example, even though the sentences "He was tall" and "He was running" both use the verb *was*, the former is a simple past tense verb while the latter is called the past progressive and has a helping verb attached to the word *running*. Complete verbs can be individual words or consist of a helping verb (often a form of *to be, to have,* or *to do*) and a main verb or a participle.

 ALERT

Different verb tenses have different forms, and there may be some overlap. Use your best judgment to decide which verb tense best captures your intended meaning.

When to Use the Perfect Tenses

Use *present perfect* for an action begun in the past and extended to the present.

 1

 Example: Scientists at NASA *have seen* an alarming increase in the accumulation of greenhouse gases.

Explanation: In this case, *scientists at NASA saw* would be incorrect. What they *have seen* (present perfect) began in the past and extends to the present.

Use *past perfect* for an action begun and completed in the past before some other past action.

 2

 Example: Despite their preparations, Lewis and Clark *had never encountered* the kinds of challenges that awaited them before their expedition.

Explanation: In this case, *never encountered* would be incorrect. The action *had never encountered* (past perfect) is used because it is referring to events prior to their expedition.

Use *future perfect* for an action begun at any time and completed in the future.

Example: When the American astronauts arrive, the Russian cosmonauts *will have been* on the International Space Station for six months.

Explanation: In this case, although both actions occur in the future, the Russian cosmonauts *will have been* on the space station before the American astronauts *arrive*. When there are two future actions, the action completed first is expressed in the future perfect tense.

Knowing when to choose between the simple (past, present, and future) and perfect tenses can be challenging because they can have similar effects on the meaning of the sentence. When choosing the appropriate verb tense, provide other contextual information within the sentence to help clarify your intended meaning.

Tenses: Common Verbs

Refer to the following chart to familiarize yourself with some common verbs and their tenses.

COMMON VERBS AND THEIR TENSES						
Infinitive	Present	Past	Future	Present Perfect	Past Perfect	Future Perfect
to ask	ask	asked	will ask	have asked	had asked	will have asked
to be	am	was	will be	have been	had been	will have been
to become	become	became	will become	have become	had become	will have become
to begin	begin	began	will begin	have begun	had begun	will have begun
to come	come	came	will come	have come	had come	will have come
to do	do	did	will do	have done	had done	will have done
to eat	eat	ate	will eat	have eaten	had eaten	will have eaten
to feel	feel	felt	will feel	have felt	had felt	will have felt
to find	find	found	will find	have found	had found	will have found
to get	get	got	will get	have gotten	had gotten	will have gotten
to give	give	gave	will give	have given	had given	will have given
to go	go	went	will go	have gone	had gone	will have gone
to grow	grow	grew	will grow	have grown	had grown	will have grown
to have	have	had	will have	have had	had had	will have had
to hear	hear	heard	will hear	have heard	had heard	will have heard
to hide	hide	hid	will hide	have hidden	had hidden	will have hidden

COMMON VERBS AND THEIR TENSES						
Infinitive	**Present**	**Past**	**Future**	**Present Perfect**	**Past Perfect**	**Future Perfect**
to keep	keep	kept	will keep	have kept	had kept	will have kept
to know	know	knew	will know	have known	had known	will have known
to leave	leave	left	will leave	have left	had left	will have left
to like	like	liked	will like	have liked	had liked	will have liked
to look	look	looked	will look	have looked	had looked	will have looked
to make	make	made	will make	have made	had made	will have made
to meet	meet	met	will meet	have met	had met	will have met
to put	put	put	will put	have put	had put	will have put
to say	say	said	will say	have said	had said	will have said
to see	see	saw	will see	have seen	had seen	will have seen
to sleep	sleep	slept	will sleep	have slept	had slept	will have slept
to speak	speak	spoke	will speak	have spoken	had spoken	will have spoken
to study	study	studied	will study	have studied	had studied	will have studied
to take	take	took	will take	have taken	had taken	will have taken
to think	think	thought	will think	have thought	had thought	will have thought
to walk	walk	walked	will walk	have walked	had walked	will have walked
to want	want	wanted	will want	have wanted	had wanted	will have wanted
to work	work	worked	will work	have worked	had worked	will have worked
to write	write	wrote	will write	have written	had written	will have written

*Note: For consistency, all verbs are conjugated in the first-person singular.

Word Choice

Word choice means using words in English correctly and effectively. Many English words are easily confused and misused because they have similar spellings, sounds, or meanings. Using the wrong word can have a negative effect on the clarity of your writing, so it's important to know some of the most commonly confused words and how to use them correctly. It's also important to build your vocabulary, such as by using the techniques discussed in Chapter 10: Reading Comprehension. Doing so affords you a wider variety of words from which to choose when writing.

Words that are homophones are pronounced the same but mean different things. For example, I might be *bored* in class, but I'm not *board* in class. *Bored* means to be dissatisfied with a tedious task while *board* means a piece of wood. Even though these words sound alike, their meanings are quite different.

There are also some words that don't have similar spellings or pronunciations, but it can still be difficult to decide which word to use. For example, when do you use *good* and when do you use *well*? *Good* is an adjective and describes a noun while *well* is an adverb that describes a verb. For example, I did *well* on the exam, but this pizza is *good*!

Here is a list of commonly misused words and examples of how to use them correctly.

accede—to agree with.
We shall *accede* to your request for more evidence.

concede—to yield, but not necessarily in agreement.
To avoid delay, we shall *concede* that more evidence is necessary.

exceed—to be more than.
Federal expenditures now *exceed* federal income.

addition—the act or process of adding.
In *addition* to a dictionary, she always used a thesaurus.

edition—a printing of a publication.
The first *edition* of Shakespeare's plays appeared in 1623.

breath—an intake of air.
Before you dive in, take a very deep *breath*.

breathe—to draw in and release air.
It is difficult to *breathe* under water.

breadth—width.
The *breadth* and length of a square are equal.

amount—applies to quantities that cannot be counted one by one.
The review provided a vast *amount* of data.

number—applies to quantities that can be counted one by one.
The farmer delivered a *number* of fruits.

cite—quote or give credit.
He was fond of *citing* from the Scriptures.

sight—vision or looks.
The *sight* of the wreck was appalling.

site—a place for a building or web page.
The school board seeks a new school *site*.

complement—a completing part.
Her wit was a *complement* to her beauty.

compliment—expression of admiration.
He *complimented* her sense of humor.

access—availability.
The lawyer was given *access* to the grand jury records.

excess—more than.
The lab work revealed *excess* fluid.

accept—(v) take an offer.
The draft board will *accept* all seniors as volunteers before graduation.

except—(prep) excluding.
All students *except* seniors will be called.

affect—(v) to influence.
Your education will *affect* your future.

effect—(n) a result.
The *effect* of the last war is still being felt.

adverse—unfavorable.
He took the *adverse* decision in poor taste.

averse—disliking.
Many students are *averse* to criticism by their classmates.

coarse—vulgar or harsh.
We were shunned because of his *coarse* behavior.

course—a path or study.
The ship took its usual *course*.
I am taking an English *course*.

cent—a coin.
One *cent* isn't enough to buy anything.

scent—an odor.
The *scent* of roses is pleasing.

sent—past tense of send.
We were *sent* to the rear of the balcony.

decent—suitable.
The *decent* thing to do is to admit your fault.

descent—going down.
The *descent* into the cave was treacherous.

dissent—disagreement.
Two of the nine justices filed a *dissenting* opinion.

---

their—belonging to them.
We took *their* books home.

there—in that place.
Your books are over *there*.

they're—contraction for "they are."
They're going to the park.

---

principal—(adj.) chief or main; (n) leader; (n) a sum placed at interest.

His *principal* supporters were enraged.

The school *principal* asked for test scores.

Her payment was applied as interest on the *principal*.

principle—a fundamental truth or belief.
Humility was the guiding *principle* of Buddha's life.

---

conscience—sense of right.
His *conscience* prevented him from selfishness.

conscientious—faithful.
We all depend on him because he is *conscientious*.

conscious—aware.
The injured woman was completely *conscious*.

---

desert—an arid area.
The Sahara is a world-famous *desert*.

dessert—the final course of a meal.
We had gelato for *dessert*.

capital—the city.
Paris is the *capital* of France.

capitol—the building.
We visited the *capitol* building on the tour.

---

can—able to.
I *can* lift this chair over my head.

may—implies permission.
You *may* leave after you finish your work.

---

precede—to come before.
The other symptoms *precede* a fever.

proceed—to go ahead.
We can then *proceed* with our diagnosis.

---

former—the first of two.
The *former* half of the book was in prose.

latter—the second of two.
The *latter* half of the book was in poetry.

---

its—belonging to "it."
The house lost *its* roof.

it's—contraction for "it is."
It's an exposed house now.

---

two—the numeral 2.
There are *two* sides to every story.

to—in the direction of.
We shall go *to* school.

too—more than or also.
The weather is *too* hot.

Other things to consider related to word choice include using impactful adjectives, adverbs, and verbs to convey your ideas, avoiding repeating the same word over and over, especially if the word is a cliché like *good* or *interesting*, and making sure you understand the exact definition of the words you are using.

PUNCTUATION

Like the other conventions of good writing, punctuation helps you communicate more effectively. Punctuation includes commas, semicolons, em dashes, parentheses, colons, and apostrophes, among other punctuation marks. Here, we'll prioritize the most important punctuation to remember for your essay section.

The Comma

We use commas for a lot of things, but focus on separating the following:

- Independent clauses that are connected by a coordinating conjunction
- Introductory clauses and phrases
- Dependent and independent clauses
- Items in a series
- Nonessential and parenthetical elements
- Coordinate adjectives

Let's look at some examples:

- To separate independent clauses connected by a coordinating conjunction

EXAMPLE:

Toni Morrison's first novel, *The Bluest Eye*, was published in 1970, and it received a rave review from *The New York Times*.

- To set off introductory clauses and phrases

EXAMPLE:

The year after winning her Nobel Prize, Toni Morrison published the novel *Jazz*.

- To separate a leading dependent clause from an independent clause

EXAMPLE:

While she was praised for her writing style and range of emotion, Toni Morrison was also celebrated for the attention she drew to racial tension in the past and present of the United States.

- To separate three or more items in a list

EXAMPLE:

In a span of 15 years, Toni Morrison won a National Book Critics Circle Award, the Pulitzer Prize, and the Nobel Prize for Literature.

If you pay attention to punctuation, it's likely you've noticed that not everyone puts the serial or Oxford comma before the *and* when separating three or more items in a list. In recent years, a lot of writing (especially online) has ignored the serial comma, but its absence or presence can affect what a sentence means. In 2018, a missing Oxford comma in a Maine labor law cost a dairy company in the state $5 million dollars in a lawsuit with its employees. Increasingly, using the Oxford comma is considered preferable punctuation.

- To separate nonessential and parenthetical elements from the main clause

EXAMPLES:

Toni Morrison, who won the Nobel Prize in Literature in 1993, was a Professor Emeritus at Princeton University.

Last night, Toni Morrison began her lecture, titled "The Future of Time: Literature and Diminished Expectations," with a meditation on the nature of time and the human perception of progress.

- To separate coordinate adjectives that precede the noun they describe

EXAMPLE:

Toni Morrison was rumored to be a fun, entertaining speaker.

When you have at least two adjectives describing a noun (e.g., "The tall, funny man" or "The cold and windy weather"), try separating the adjectives with a comma when their order can be reversed or when the conjunction *and* can be placed between them while still preserving the meaning of the phrase. If reversing the order or adding *and* disrupts the meaning of the phrase (e.g., "The giant hockey players" as "The hockey giant players" or "The giant and hockey players"), no comma is needed.

The Semicolon

A semicolon may be used to separate two complete ideas (independent clauses) in a sentence when the two ideas have a close relationship and are *not* connected with a coordinating conjunction.

EXAMPLE:

"Inalienable rights" are basic human rights that many believe cannot and should not be given up or taken away; life, liberty, and the pursuit of happiness are some of those rights.

The semicolon is often used between independent clauses connected by conjunctive adverbs such as *consequently, therefore, also, furthermore, for example, however, nevertheless, still, yet, moreover,* and *otherwise.*

 TIP

Nonessential and parenthetical elements (commas, parentheses, or em dashes) provide extra information that is not necessary for the meaning or grammatical correctness of a sentence. While each of these punctuation marks serves a similar purpose, the difference between them is one of emphasis.

EXAMPLE:

In 1867, critics thought William H. Seward foolish for buying the largely unexplored territory of Alaska for the astronomical price of $7 million; however, history has proven that it was an inspired purchase.

A word of caution: Do not use the semicolon between an independent clause and a phrase or subordinate clause.

 Incorrect: While eating ice cream for dessert; Clarence and Undine discussed their next business venture.

 Correct: While eating ice cream for dessert, Clarence and Undine discussed their next business venture.

Similar to serial commas, semicolons are used to separate items in a list when the items themselves contain commas.

EXAMPLE:

Some kinds of biologists study specific species of animals. For example, cetologists study marine mammals, such as whales and dolphins; entomologists study insects, such as beetles and butterflies; and ichthyologists study wild fish, such as sharks and lungfish.

The Em Dash

Em dashes are used to set off parenthetical material that you want to emphasize. Dashes interrupt the flow of your sentence, thereby calling attention to the information they contain. An em dash always precedes the nonessential information, so the aside must start later in the sentence.

EXAMPLES:

Many consider Toni Morrison—winner of both the Pulitzer and Nobel Prizes in Literature—to be one of the greatest writers of her generation.

Benjamin Franklin's many intellectual pursuits—from printmaking to politics—exemplify his eclectic personality.

Em dashes can also be used to rename a nearby noun. Typically, a comma would be used to set off this information, but since it includes commas already, use an em dash.

EXAMPLE:

Benjamin Franklin—a printer, writer, inventor, and statesman—was the son of a soap maker.

An em dash also indicates a list, a restatement, an amplification, or a dramatic shift in tone or thought.

EXAMPLE:

Eager to write for his brother's newspaper, young Benjamin began submitting letters to the editor under the pseudonym Silence Dogood—they were a hit!

Parentheses

Just like commas and em dashes, parentheses separate nonessential (also called nonrestrictive or parenthetical) elements from the rest of the sentence. Parentheses indicate that the enclosed information is less important or more tangential to the surrounding sentence. Parentheses must always come in pairs.

EXAMPLES:

Toni Morrison's novel *Beloved* (1987) was made into a movie in 1998.

While at Princeton, Toni Morrison (the writer) established a special creative workshop for writers and performances called the Princeton Atelier.

The Colon

The colon is used to precede a list, a long quotation, or a statement that illustrates or clarifies the earlier information. A colon can only be used after an independent clause.

EXAMPLES:

There are only three nations that have successfully landed spacecraft on the moon: the Soviet Union, the United States, and China.

In the United States, there are three branches of government: the Executive, the Legislative, and the Judicial.

Only use colons after independent clauses. Most commonly, that means that you won't use colons after a verb. Further, no introductory or connecting information should occur before or after a colon, such as *and* or *including*.

 Incorrect: The Louisiana Purchase included territory that would become: Montana, South Dakota, Nebraska, Kansas, Oklahoma, Arkansas, Louisiana, and Missouri.

 Correct: The Louisiana Purchase included territory that would become many of today's states: Montana, South Dakota, Nebraska, Kansas, Oklahoma, Arkansas, Louisiana, and Missouri.

The Apostrophe

Apostrophes usually serve one of two purposes:

1

To indicate the possessive case *of nouns*: If the noun does not end in *s*—whether singular or plural—add an *'s*; if the noun ends in *s*, simply add the *'*.

 Example 1: The impact of Allen Ginsberg's poem "Howl" on the cultural landscape of the United States cannot be overstated.

 Example 2: A car's headlights are typically wired in parallel so that if one burns out the other will keep functioning.

 Example 3: The women's club sponsored many charity events.

 Example 4: Charles Mingus' skill as a jazz musician is widely recognized.

2

To indicate a *contraction*—the omission of one or more letters: Place the apostrophe exactly where the missing letters occur.

 Examples:

can't = cannot

it's = it is

we're = we are

 ALERT

Do not use apostrophes with possessive pronouns such as *yours*, *hers*, *ours*, *theirs*, and *whose*, which indicate possession already.

End-of-Sentence Punctuation

There are three types of punctuation used to end a sentence: the period, the question mark, and the exclamation mark.

1 A period is used at the end of a sentence that makes a statement.

Example: In 1620, the Pilgrims in Plymouth signed the Mayflower Compact.

2 A question mark is used after a direct question. A period is used after an indirect question.

Direct Question: Were *The Federalist Papers* written by James Madison, John Jay, or Alexander Hamilton?

Indirect Question: Professor Mahin wanted to know if you knew who wrote *The Federalist Papers*.

3 An exclamation mark is used after an expression that shows strong emotion or issues a command. It may follow a word, a phrase, or a sentence.

Example: Koko the gorilla knew more than 1,000 sign-language signs and could communicate with humans. Amazing!

Unnecessary Punctuation

Unnecessary punctuation can break a sentence into confusing and illogical fragments. Here are some common mistakes to look out for.

- Don't use a comma alone to connect independent clauses. This is called a comma splice.

Incorrect: Toni Morrison grew up in an integrated neighborhood, she did not become fully aware of racial divisions until she was in her teens.

Possible revision: Toni Morrison grew up in an integrated neighborhood and did not become fully aware of racial divisions until she was in her teens.

- Don't use a comma between compound elements that are not independent clauses.

Incorrect: In 1998, Oprah Winfrey, and Danny Glover starred in a film adaptation of Morrison's novel *Beloved*.

Possible revision: In 1998, Oprah Winfrey and Danny Glover starred in a film adaptation of Morrison's novel *Beloved*.

- Do not use an apostrophe when making a noun plural.

Incorrect: In 2006, *The New York Times Book Review* named *Beloved* the best American novel published in the last 25 year's.

Possible revision: In 2006, *The New York Times Book Review* named *Beloved* the best American novel published in the last 25 years.

CAPITALIZATION

Capitalization is important because it helps set apart proper nouns and titles from other words in a sentence. As an English skill, capitalization signals familiarity with the conventions of the language and adds clarity to written texts. Some rules, like the one governing that the first word of a sentence be capitalized, are likely already very familiar to you. To help you understand some of the logic behind why things are capitalized, we've grouped capitalization rules into a few categories: title case, proper nouns, proper titles and honorifics, and general capitalization rules. This section includes a sample email that applies the capitalization rules we cover here. As you go through this section, take note of the rationale behind why certain things are capitalized and look for opportunities to identify these rules being used in real-word contexts. Use the reference tables included in this section to determine which rules are trickiest for you so that you can build skills accordingly. One good way to practice is writing your own examples for each capitalization rule.

Title Case

There are numerous capitalization rules that specifically apply to title case. By title case, we mean the way that words should be presented to readers when they are part of a given title for something, like a book, movie, newspaper article, or anything else that receives a title. The following table lists the rules that govern title case according to the *Chicago Manual of Style*. Another common way to do title case is to capitalize every word in a title. On your essay, there is no set standard, so just make sure you are consistent.

TITLE CASE	
Rule	**Examples**
The first word, last word, and any major word in the title should be capitalized. Major words are typically considered nouns, pronouns, verbs, adjectives, adverbs, and some conjunctions.	• *A Midsummer Night's Dream* • "Missing Lawyer Found" • *Stranger Things* • *Mario Kart 8*
All prepositions remain lowercase in titles unless they are the first or last word of the title, regardless of the length of the preposition.	• *The Legend of Zelda* • *The Fault in Our Stars* • "Track Team Preps with Extra Practices for Tournament against Shaded Lake" • "Across the Universe" by The Beatles
Most conjunctions and articles also remain lowercase in titles, including *the, an, a, to, as, and, but, for, or,* and *nor*. As with prepositions, you can ignore this rule if it's the first or last word in the title.	• *Tristan and Isolde* • *The Good, the Bad, and the Ugly* • "A History of Aeronautics" • *But I'm Just a Kid!*
Title case should be used for subtitles and headlines. Email subject lines are also generally written in title case (as if they were headlines).	• *Frankenstein: The Modern Prometheus* • *Black Beauty: The Autobiography of a Horse* • "New Medicine Deemed Effective for Patients with Chronic Asthma" • Subject: Regarding the Vote on School Uniforms

Proper Nouns

Proper nouns are the most common place where capitalization is used. In English, no matter where in the sentence a proper noun is placed, it is always capitalized. Proper nouns can be identified by the way they take a general noun (*cat, school*) and give it a specific name (*Giorgio, Mountain View High School*), so you may also hear them called "proper names."

PROPER NOUNS	
Rule	**Examples**
Always capitalize a person or other being's proper name. This includes any initials and hyphenated names. Some have names that require more than one capital letter.	• Barack Obama • Beyoncé Knowles-Carter • Michael J. Fox • This is my hamster, Mochi. • McKenzie O'Connell
In addition to the names of people, always capitalize the proper names of buildings, events (including holidays), places, words formed by referencing places, organizations, documents, individual deities, or anything else that can be represented by a specific name.	• Empire State Building • Sundance Film Festival • Valentine's Day • Brazil • Brazilian • World Wildlife Fund • US Constitution • Shiva
If a proper noun gets long or contains prepositions, title case is often used. It is also not uncommon for such proper nouns to be represented by chosen acronyms, which also require capitalization.	• Centers for Disease Control and Prevention (CDC) • Museum of Modern Art (MoMA) • American Society for the Prevention of Cruelty to Animals (ASPCA)
The pronoun *I* is treated like a proper noun—it always gets capitalized no matter where it falls in the sentence, including within contractions.	• I went to the farmer's market. • Max will be here soon, so I need help. • I think I'm just tired.
A noun or adjective that is not regularly capitalized should still be capitalized when it is used as part of a proper name.	• Have you met Uncle Casimiro? • This is my Grandma Velma. • Can Nurse Rick do it? • My truck's nickname is Big Betty.

Proper Titles and Honorifics

If a person, group, or document can be referred to with a particular title, capitalization should be used. In these cases, you treat the title as if it were a proper noun. However, if the term does not apply to something or someone specific, then it should remain lowercased. Consider the following examples:

Amadou is the best man for the job. → I am the Best Man in Amadou's wedding.

I want to become a professor. → I asked Professor Smith-Loewen for an essay extension.

They haven't spoken to the senators. → Senator Hasad and Senator O'Brien wrote the bill.

Our club needs a constitution. → The Constitution grants everyone certain rights.

Capitalization Model

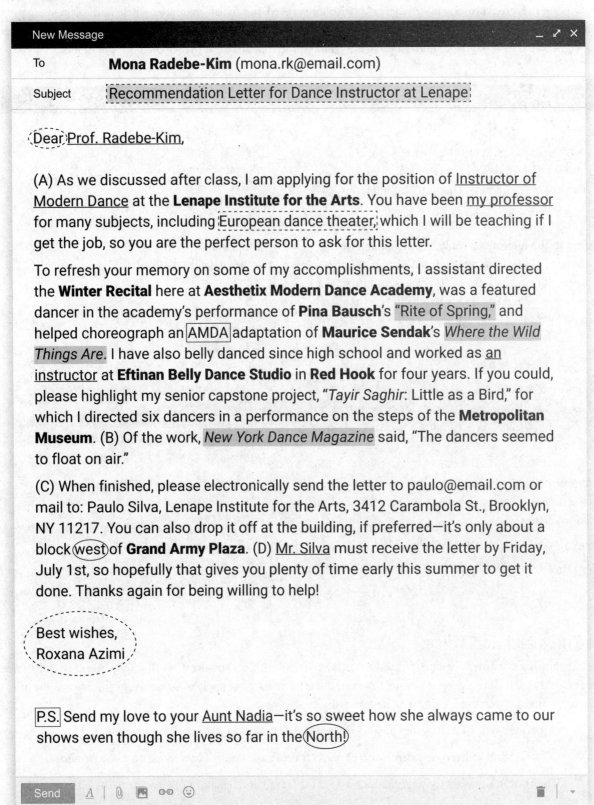

New Message   _ ⤢ ✕

To   **Mona Radebe-Kim** (mona.rk@email.com)

Subject   Recommendation Letter for Dance Instructor at Lenape

Dear Prof. Radebe-Kim,

(A) As we discussed after class, I am applying for the position of Instructor of Modern Dance at the **Lenape Institute for the Arts**. You have been my professor for many subjects, including European dance theater, which I will be teaching if I get the job, so you are the perfect person to ask for this letter.

To refresh your memory on some of my accomplishments, I assistant directed the **Winter Recital** here at **Aesthetix Modern Dance Academy**, was a featured dancer in the academy's performance of **Pina Bausch**'s "Rite of Spring," and helped choreograph an AMDA adaptation of **Maurice Sendak**'s *Where the Wild Things Are*. I have also belly danced since high school and worked as an instructor at **Eftinan Belly Dance Studio** in **Red Hook** for four years. If you could, please highlight my senior capstone project, "*Tayir Saghir*: Little as a Bird," for which I directed six dancers in a performance on the steps of the **Metropolitan Museum**. (B) Of the work, *New York Dance Magazine* said, "The dancers seemed to float on air."

(C) When finished, please electronically send the letter to paulo@email.com or mail to: Paulo Silva, Lenape Institute for the Arts, 3412 Carambola St., Brooklyn, NY 11217. You can also drop it off at the building, if preferred—it's only about a block west of **Grand Army Plaza**. (D) Mr. Silva must receive the letter by Friday, July 1st, so hopefully that gives you plenty of time early this summer to get it done. Thanks again for being willing to help!

Best wishes,
Roxana Azimi

P.S. Send my love to your Aunt Nadia—it's so sweet how she always came to our shows even though she lives so far in the North!

Send   A   ◰   🖼   🔗   ☺   🗑   ▾

Title Case

In titles and subtitles, one should follow title case rules by capitalizing the first and last word of any title or subtitle as well as any important words. Prepositions and most conjunctions should remain lowercase.

Proper Names

Proper names of events, buildings, people, places, and organizations all require capitalization. As with title case, words like *for* and *the* can remain lowercase (Lenape Institute for the Arts). For hyphenated names, both names should be capitalized (Radebe-Kim). Note: General nouns (senior capstone project, performance) don't get capitalized, but proper names or titles given for such nouns ("*Tayir Saghir*: Little as a Bird", Winter Recital) do.

Titles for People

If a title applies to a specific person, it should be capitalized (Prof. Radebe-Kim). If the word is being used more generally, it should not be (my professor). Likewise, official job titles (Instructor of Modern Dance) should be capitalized when referring to a specific position or person but not when used more generally (an instructor). You should also capitalize a word that would not normally be capitalized if it acts like a title in a person's proper name (Aunt Nadia).

◯	If the points of the compass refer to a specific place, they are capitalized; however, when used to give directions, they are not.
▭	In acronyms and most abbreviations, like P.S., one should always use capital letters.
▯	School subjects don't require capitalization unless they refer to specific languages or place names.
◯	When opening and closing a letter, capitalize the first word and any titles or proper nouns.
▭	Many formal subject lines follow title case, just like headlines do.

(A) Capitalize the first letter of any complete sentence, including the sentence that immediately follows your salutation. You also always capitalize *I* when it stands alone.

(B) If a quotation is a complete sentence, the first word inside the quotation should be capitalized.

(C) The city, state, and any street or building names should all be capitalized when formatting an address.

(D) Days of the week, months of the year, and holidays all need to be capitalized, but seasons do not.

General Capitalization Rules

Other rules cannot be grouped together as neatly yet still represent important capitalization situations that one should learn.

GENERAL CAPITALIZATION RULES	
Rule	**Examples**
Capitalize the first word of a complete sentence, including the first sentence that comes after a greeting in a letter.	• Kelsie is a good friend. • We hate mushroom soup! • Are those for the party?
Capitalize the first word of a quotation if it contains a complete sentence. However, if the quoted material is not a complete sentence, do NOT capitalize the first word (unless it's a proper noun).	• Ms. Neff said, "Please turn in your essays." • When the firefighter asked, "Are you hurt?" I was still in shock. • My mom said she needed to "have a think" about the situation. • These so-called "appleheads" are devoted fans of Fifi's Candy Apples. • When I asked Andre his favorite player, he said "Steph Curry."
Capitalize days of the week and months of the year, but do NOT capitalize the seasons.	• I'll see you next Wednesday. • My birthday is in June. • He'll fly out at the end of the summer. • The first day of winter is in December.
Points of the compass are capitalized when they refer to a specific place. When they are used as directions, they should remain lowercased.	• Head north on Monstera Ave., then the park is on the east side of the road. • Is there anything due west of here? • My grandpa is from the South.
The only school subjects that are regularly capitalized are languages and specific place names used as modifiers.	• Next year, I am taking German, biology, African dance, ancient philosophy, and English composition. • Does this book cover religion generally or East Asian religions specifically?
Acronyms and certain abbreviations are generally represented by capital letters.	• P.S. I love you! • I work at NASA. • The CDC recommends yearly flu shots. • Gia had to get a CT scan.
When opening a letter, capitalize the first and last words in the salutation. Remember to also capitalize any proper nouns or titles.	• Dear Dr. Hensley, • My dear Sir, • To Prof. Stanley on his Birthday:
When closing a letter, capitalize only the first word in the complimentary closing.	• Respectfully yours, • To your continued success, • Until we meet again,

SPELLING

Like capitalization, understanding spelling typically requires learning several rules. Additionally, spelling seems to be one of those skills that comes naturally to some, while others (regardless of intelligence level) may struggle more to pick it up. That said, as with capitalization, we have broken these rules into a series of categories to help you make sense of them. Then, you will have the opportunity to spellcheck an example email so you can apply your new understanding of these rules in context. We also encourage you to look in the dictionary for the spelling of words you encounter in your daily life as you practice for your essay—the more words with which you familiarize yourself, the better! Since some of these tips or rules will seem more familiar than others, remember to maximize your study time by concentrating first on those that seem less familiar.

TIP

When writing your essay, make sure to save yourself a bit of time at the end to proofread for errors in spelling, grammar, and capitalization!

Tips for Improving Your Spelling Skills

You can improve your spelling by keeping a list of words that you spell incorrectly or need to look up repeatedly. Add to this list whenever you find a word you can't spell. Set aside a few minutes to study spelling and write down each word correctly ten times. You can also type the words, but physically writing it out gives you time to concentrate on the spelling and apply it to memory. Let your hands get used to the feeling of spelling a difficult word correctly. Let your eye become accustomed to seeing a difficult word spelled correctly. Ask someone to read your list aloud to you on occasion and try writing

them correctly or spelling them aloud. Frequent self-testing of problematic words should help you learn the correct spellings. On the day before the test, carefully read back over your list to refresh your memory.

Another way to improve your spelling is to develop mnemonic devices. A mnemonic device is a private clue that you create to help you remember something. For example, if you have trouble spelling the word *friend*, you might find it helpful to remember the sentence, "A friend is true to the *end*." This little sentence will help you remember to place the *i* before the *e*. If you have trouble distinguishing between *here* and *hear*, try a sentence like, "To listen is to *hear* with an *ear*." If you confuse the spellings *principle* and *principal*, remember (whether you believe it or not), "The princiPAL is your PAL." And finally, this cute mnemonic device might help you spell "misspells" correctly: "*Miss Pells* never *misspells*." When you have trouble spelling a word, try to invent your own mnemonic device to help you out during the essay portion of the exam.

Finally, you can use the list of 100 commonly misspelled words at the end of this section to familiarize yourself with their correct spellings in advance of your exam.

TIP

If spelling is difficult for you, don't be discouraged. Many intelligent and creative people have had problems spelling, including highly regarded authors such as Agatha Christie, Ernest Hemingway, and Jane Austen. You can improve your spelling by using a dictionary each time you encounter a word you don't know and by testing yourself on words you often misspell.

Spelling Rules

While there are many spelling rules, they can be divided based on which kinds of situations govern them; for instance, many rules concern what kind of suffix is affixed to the end of a word. Unfortunately, since English is tricky and borrows a lot from other languages, there are also exceptions to many of the rules. To help you identify exceptions, we have included them with the examples when relevant.

Rules Related to Suffixes and Word Endings

A suffix describes a set of letters added to the end of all or part of a base word to create a new word. For instance, the suffix *-ical*, meaning "possessing the form of," can be added to base words like *method*, *magic*, and *nonsense* to make the words *methodical*, *magical*, and *nonsensical*. The table that follows contains spelling rules that pertain to suffixes and word endings.

RULES RELATED TO SUFFIXES AND WORD ENDINGS		
Rule	**Exceptions (if applicable)**	**Examples**
If a word ends in a *y* preceded by a vowel, keep the *y* when adding a suffix.	N/A	• day → days • attorney → attorneys • journey → journeyed • play → playing
If a word ends in a *y* preceded by a consonant, change the *y* to an *i* before adding a suffix.	To avoid creating a double *i*, retain the *y* when adding the suffixes *-ing* and *-ish*.	• silly → silliest • try → tries, tried, trying • fly → flying, flier • baby → babyish
If a word ends in a silent *e*, then the *e* is dropped before any suffix that begins with a vowel.	To retain the soft sounds of *c* and *g*, words ending in *ce* and *ge* often (but not always) retain *e* before the suffixes *-able* and *-ous*. Other exceptions: *canoeing, dyeing, acreage, mileage, rideable*	• dance → dancing • locate → location • use → using, usable • notice → noticeable • courage → courageous
Generally, retain a silent *e* before any suffix that begins with a consonant.	Some exceptions include the words *truly, duly, argument, wholly,* and *ninth.*	• care → careless, careful • late → lately • whole → wholesome • waste → wasteful • bore → boredom
One-syllable words that end in a single consonant preceded by a single vowel double the final consonant before any suffix beginning with a vowel, including *-y*.	Note that if the final consonant is preceded by two vowels, this rule doesn't apply. need → needing, needy	• drop → dropped, dropper • swim → swimmer, swimmingly • fit → fitted, fitting • mud → muddy, muddier • cut → cutting, cuttable

RULES RELATED TO SUFFIXES AND WORD ENDINGS

Rule	Exceptions (if applicable)	Examples
A word with two or more syllables that accents the last syllable and ends in a single consonant preceded by a single vowel doubles the final consonant before any suffix beginning with a vowel.	Remember, this rule does not apply if the accent is not on the last syllable. enter → entered, entering exhibit → exhibition	• begin → beginner • admit → admittance • control → controlling • commit → committed
A word ending in -er or -ur that is accented on the last syllable will double the r in the past tense. However, if the accent falls before the last syllable, the r will not be doubled.	N/A	• occur → occurred • prefer → preferred • transfer → transferred • answer → answered • offer → offered • differ → differed
When pluralizing a word that ends with a consonant and y, change the y into an i and then add -es	N/A	• lady → ladies • canary → canaries • jelly → jellies • curry → curries
When adding the suffix -full to the end of a noun, drop the final l.	In the rare case when adding -full to a word that is not a noun, keep the final l. over → overfull	• wonder → wonderful • event → eventful • hope → hopeful
To pluralize a word, add -s. However, if it ends in -s, -sh, -ch, -x, or -z, spell it with an -es suffix.	N/A	• duck → ducks • meal → meals • box → boxes • crash → crashes

TIP

One great way to improve your vocabulary and practice skills like spelling and capitalization is to look for computer games or apps that test these skills. When you "gamify" learning, you also make it more interactive, which means you're more likely to build skills quickly.

Rules Related to Prefixes and Word Beginnings

There are fewer rules governing prefixes, but they are still important to know. A prefix is a set of letters added to the beginning of all or part of a base word to create a new word. For instance, the prefix *de-*, meaning "away from, off, or down" can be added to words like *escalate*, *activate*, and *sensitize* to make *deescalate*, *deactivate*, and *desensitize*. The following table lists the spelling rules that pertain to prefixes and word beginnings.

RULES RELATED TO PREFIXES AND WORD BEGINNINGS	
Rule	**Examples**
When *over-* is used as a prefix, the result is one word, not two.	• overcast • overcharge • overhear
All words with the prefix *self-* should be hyphenated.	• self-taught • self-control • self-defense
In general, prefixes will not change how a word is spelled. Simply attach the prefix to the word without a space between.	• anti + body → antibody • hyper + active → hyperactive • sub + marine → submarine
When attaching a prefix to a proper noun, add a hyphen before the proper noun.	• The pre-World War II landscape was different. • The protesters expressed anti-Walmart sentiments.
Some prefixes may create double letters—this is fine, and the double letter should be retained.	• un + necessary → unnecessary • mis + spell → misspell • re + education → reeducation

Rules Related to Grammar and Meaning

Some rules that pertain to spelling are also related to grammar, punctuation, and meaning. For instance, when two or more words sound the same but are spelled differently, misspelling them can also impact the grammatical correctness of one's sentence and make it unclear. Therefore, while it is important to memorize these rules for grammar purposes, thinking of them as spelling rules may also help you remember which form of a word to use and when.

RULES RELATED TO GRAMMAR AND MEANING	
Rule	**Examples**
Use *to* to show movement toward a particular location or reaching a particular state of being. Use *too* to mean "in addition," "also," or "to an excessive degree." Use *two* to represent the number 2.	• Are you going to the Billie Eilish concert? • No, I am too tired after such a long week. • Well, I still have two tickets, so if I give one to my friend, Tianna, maybe she can come too.

RULES RELATED TO GRAMMAR AND MEANING

Rule	Examples
Use *your* as the possessive form of *you*. Use *you're* as a contraction for *you are*.	• Who did your mother say was supposed to pick you up? • Dad, she said you're supposed to!
Who's is the contraction for *who is*. *Whose* is the possessive of *who*.	• Do you know who's ringing the doorbell? • It's probably the person whose car is parked in our driveway.
Its is the possessive of *it*. *It's* is the contraction for *it is*.	• Is that birthday card with its yellow envelope? • Yes, it's in the top drawer.
They're is the contraction for *they are*. *Their* is the possessive of *they*. *There* means *at that place*.	• They're going to put their books over there. • The honeymooners said they're going to drive their Porsche along the beach in Italy when they get there.
To lose something means to misplace it. *Lose* is a verb. If something is loose, then it is not tight or secure. *Loose* is an adjective.	• Did you lose your wallet? • Yes, unfortunately, I think that pocket of my backpack came loose on the train.
All right, meaning "everything's correct," is two words. *Alright* is a different word that means "okay" or "fine."	• The camp counselor asked me if I needed help or if I was alright, and I told him that the decorations for the party were all right.
All ready means "completely ready." *Already* means "prior to some specified time."	• By the time I was all ready to go to the play, the tickets had already sold out.
Altogether means "entirely." *All together* means "in sum" or "collectively."	• There are altogether too many people to seat in this room when we are all together on holidays.

Other Spelling Rules

There are a few other rules that cannot easily be categorized, so it's best to just learn them independently.

OTHER SPELLING RULES	
Rule	**Examples**
The letter *q* is essentially always followed by *u*. Note: There are exceptions to this rule, but they are so rare that they don't impact much except word games.	• quiz • bouquet • acquire • quick • equate
Numbers from twenty-one to ninety-nine include a hyphen when spelled out.	• Two hundred and twenty-two • Eighty-five • Three thousand and thirty-eight
Percent is never hyphenated (*per-cent*), but it may be written as one word (*percent*) or two (*per cent*).	• I am 100 percent certain that I'm right. • This chart represents 7 per cent of our annual budget.
The sound expressed as *oi* differs depending on where it's found. If it occurs in the middle of a word, use *oi*. If it occurs at the end of a word, use *oy*.	• foil • avoid • annoy • boy
Generally, to express the sound *ch* at the beginning of a word, you use *ch*. However, to express this sound at the end of a word, you usually (but not always!) use *tch*. Some exceptions: *much, tchotchke, coach, march, branch, starch*	• childish • champion • chatty • stretch • clutch • wristwatch

The "i before e except after c" Trap

This is one of the most common spelling rules that people know, but it's also one of the most misleading. While it is generally true that in most English words, an *i* will come before an *e* except when the two letters follow *c* (*piece, ceiling, receipt, deceive, mischief*), there are enough exceptions to this rule to make it a confusing one. For instance, words that create an *ay* sound (*neighbor, sleigh, weigh, reign*) do not tend to follow this rule, nor do words that use the Germanic *ei* vowel sound (*either, neither, feisty, heist, heights*). Still, others are simply run-of-the-mill exceptions, like *foreign, seizure, weird, species, leisure, albeit, glacier, cueing,* and *science,* to name just a few. You can still consider this a useful guideline if you have to make a guess when you aren't sure how to spell a word—just know that it won't apply when your neighbor Keith receives a beige sleigh from eight feisty, caffeinated weightlifters on a weird and heinous heist to seize foreign leisure goods for their sovereign heir.

100 Commonly Misspelled Words

Recognizing a word that commonly gets misspelled and devoting time to learning the right way to spell it is another way to accelerate your overall spelling skills. In the process, you may notice patterns in your misspellings that also make it easier to recognize when a word might be tricky for you.

To help you find words you might like to practice, we have compiled the following list of 100 commonly misspelled words. If you don't know the meaning of a word, take this opportunity to practice looking it up in the dictionary.

acceptable	exceed	license	questionnaire	schedule
accidental	exhilarate	maneuver	raspberry	separate
accommodate	existence	memento	receipt	sergeant
acquire	extreme	millennium	recommend	subpoena
amateur	foreign	miniature	reference	supersede
apparent	gauge	minuscule	refrigerator	surprise
atheist	grateful	mischievous	relevant	tableau
believe	guarantee	misspell	remembrance	tariff
calendar	harass	nauseous	rendezvous	threshold
camouflage	height	necessary	renowned	tongue
cantaloupe	hierarchy	neighbor	restaurant	vacuum
cemetery	humorous	noticeable	rhyme	weather
changeable	immediately	occasionally	rhythm	weird
collectible	independent	occurrence	ridiculous	welcome
colonel	indispensable	official		
column	inoculate	omitted		
commemorate	intelligence	pastime		
committed	irresistible	perseverance		
congratulations	jewelry	personnel		
conscience	judgment	playwright		
definitely	kernel	precede		
discipline	leisure	principal		
dumbbell	liaison	principle		
embarrass	library	privilege		

Test Yourself: Spelling

Directions: The following email contains 30 different spelling errors. See if you can identify all 30 and determine the correct spelling for each, as if you were proofreading Rocco's email. For an extra challenge, time yourself.

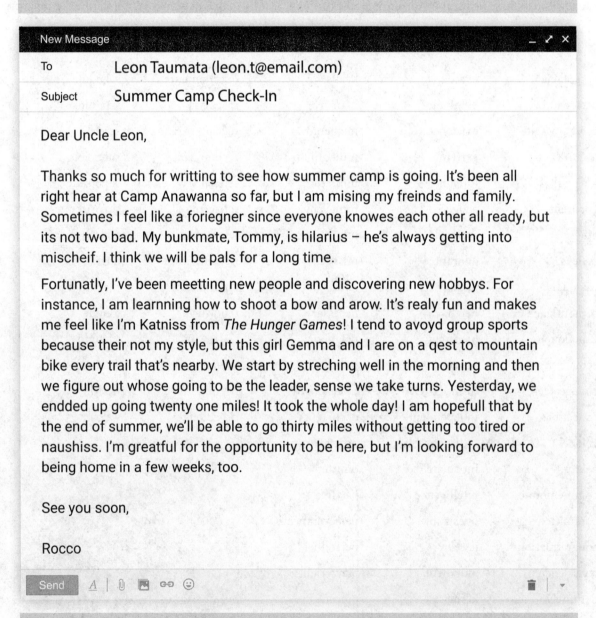

New Message   — ⤢ ✕

To   Leon Taumata (leon.t@email.com)

Subject   Summer Camp Check-In

Dear Uncle Leon,

Thanks so much for writting to see how summer camp is going. It's been all right hear at Camp Anawanna so far, but I am mising my freinds and family. Sometimes I feel like a foriegner since everyone knowes each other all ready, but its not two bad. My bunkmate, Tommy, is hilarius – he's always getting into mischeif. I think we will be pals for a long time.

Fortunatly, I've been meetting new people and discovering new hobbys. For instance, I am learnning how to shoot a bow and arow. It's realy fun and makes me feel like I'm Katniss from *The Hunger Games*! I tend to avoyd group sports because their not my style, but this girl Gemma and I are on a qest to mountain bike every trail that's nearby. We start by streching well in the morning and then we figure out whose going to be the leader, sense we take turns. Yesterday, we endded up going twenty one miles! It took the whole day! I am hopefull that by the end of summer, we'll be able to go thirty miles without getting too tired or naushiss. I'm greatful for the opportunity to be here, but I'm looking forward to being home in a few weeks, too.

See you soon,

Rocco

Send   A   📎   🖼   🔗   ☺   🗑   ▾

Answer Key: Here are the correct spellings of the incorrectly spelled words, presented in the order they appear within the email: writing, alright, here, missing, friends, foreigner, knows, already, it's, too, hilarious, mischief, fortunately, meeting, hobbies, learning, arrow, really, avoid, they're, quest, stretching, who's, since, ended, twenty-one, hopeful, nauseous, grateful.

SUMMING IT UP

- Neither the SSAT nor the ISEE test the mechanics of writing directly, but each exam includes an essay section that will be treated like a writing sample by schools to which you apply with your test results, so you'll want to use your best writing mechanics on this section.

- The mechanics of Standard English reviewed in this chapter are keys to good writing. When you utilize proper sentence structure, grammar, and punctuation, your writing is stronger, clearer, and more focused.

- Knowing the parts of speech is critical for understanding the conventions and rules of grammar:

  - A **noun** is a person, place, thing or idea.
  - A **pronoun** is a substitute for a noun.
  - An **adjective** describes a noun.
  - A **verb** expresses action or a state of being.
  - An **adverb** modifies a verb, an adjective, or another adverb.
  - A **conjunction** joins words, sentences, and phrases.
  - A **preposition** shows position in time or space.

- The following list summarizes the key conventions you need to remember to write effectively:

  - **Sentence Structure and Formation**

    - **Fragments:** Every sentence must have a subject and a verb and express a complete idea.
    - **Run-Ons and Comma Splices:** Connect complete sentences with proper punctuation.
    - **Combining Independent Clauses:** Use periods, a comma + FANBOYS, or a semicolon; you can also make an independent clause dependent with a subordinating conjunction to link sentences.
    - **Combining Dependent and Independent Clauses:** Place a comma after a dependent clause at the beginning of a sentence.
    - **Misplaced Modifiers:** Place modifiers (adjectives, adverbs, prepositional phrases) as close to the word they're modifying as possible.
    - **Parallel Structure:** Keep verbs and phrases in the same grammatical form when writing sentences.
    - **Verb Tense:** Keep consistent verb tense within sentences and paragraphs unless otherwise justified.

o **Punctuation**

- **Commas:** Separate independent clauses with a comma and FANBOYS; add a comma after an introductory phrase or leading subordinate clause; separate items in lists of three or more (including before the *and* before the final item); place commas around nonessential information to separate it from the main clause of a sentence.

- **Em dashes:** Indicate nonrestrictive or nonessential information with em dashes; these tangents, asides, and parenthetical statements follow em dashes and must be closed by another em dash—unless they finish the sentence.

- **Semicolons:** Separate related independent clauses and items in a list where the items have commas with a semicolon.

- **Colons:** Indicate the start of a list, a quotation, or emphasis with a colon; colons must be preceded by an independent clause.

- **Apostrophes:** Indicate possession with an *'s* (or just an apostrophe after a noun that ends in an *s*) or signal the contraction of two words into one (*they + are = they're*).

- **Parentheses:** Separate low-importance, nonessential information from the rest of the sentence with a pair of parentheses.

- **End-Stop Punctuation:** End statements and indirect questions with periods; use question marks to end direct questions; end statements that indicate strong emotion or commands with an exclamation point.

- Practice writing on your own to build skills in capitalization and spelling. Keep track of words that are hard for you to spell so that you can get used to writing them out. Try coming up with your own mnemonic devices to remember the words you struggle with most.

- Remember that there are general capitalization rules as well as specific rules for title case, pronouns, and titles and honorifics.

- Spelling rules can be divided based on which kinds of situations govern them: There are spelling rules for word endings and suffixes as well as word beginnings and prefixes. There are also spelling rules that are tied to principles of grammar and meaning. Oftentimes, there are exceptions to these rules based on the sound of a word or its origins. Learn these rules and be aware of any exceptions you might encounter.

- Capitalization, spelling, grammar, and punctuation are best understood in context, so make sure you can apply each rule to your own example sentences.

NOTES

PART VI
PRACTICE TESTS

CHAPTER

SSAT (UPPER LEVEL)
PRACTICE TEST

SSAT (UPPER LEVEL) PRACTICE TES

PRACTICE TEST

This practice test is designed to help you recognize your strengths and weaknesses. The questions cover information from all the different sections of the SSAT. Use the results to help guide and direct your study time.

>>

ANSWER SHEET: SSAT (UPPER LEVEL) PRACTICE TEST

Part I: Writing Sample

Lined pages provided within test.

Part II: Multiple Choice

Section 1: Quantitative (Math)

1. Ⓐ Ⓑ Ⓒ Ⓓ Ⓔ
2. Ⓐ Ⓑ Ⓒ Ⓓ Ⓔ
3. Ⓐ Ⓑ Ⓒ Ⓓ Ⓔ
4. Ⓐ Ⓑ Ⓒ Ⓓ Ⓔ
5. Ⓐ Ⓑ Ⓒ Ⓓ Ⓔ
6. Ⓐ Ⓑ Ⓒ Ⓓ Ⓔ
7. Ⓐ Ⓑ Ⓒ Ⓓ Ⓔ

8. Ⓐ Ⓑ Ⓒ Ⓓ Ⓔ
9. Ⓐ Ⓑ Ⓒ Ⓓ Ⓔ
10. Ⓐ Ⓑ Ⓒ Ⓓ Ⓔ
11. Ⓐ Ⓑ Ⓒ Ⓓ Ⓔ
12. Ⓐ Ⓑ Ⓒ Ⓓ Ⓔ
13. Ⓐ Ⓑ Ⓒ Ⓓ Ⓔ
14. Ⓐ Ⓑ Ⓒ Ⓓ Ⓔ

15. Ⓐ Ⓑ Ⓒ Ⓓ Ⓔ
16. Ⓐ Ⓑ Ⓒ Ⓓ Ⓔ
17. Ⓐ Ⓑ Ⓒ Ⓓ Ⓔ
18. Ⓐ Ⓑ Ⓒ Ⓓ Ⓔ
19. Ⓐ Ⓑ Ⓒ Ⓓ Ⓔ
20. Ⓐ Ⓑ Ⓒ Ⓓ Ⓔ
21. Ⓐ Ⓑ Ⓒ Ⓓ Ⓔ

22. Ⓐ Ⓑ Ⓒ Ⓓ Ⓔ
23. Ⓐ Ⓑ Ⓒ Ⓓ Ⓔ
24. Ⓐ Ⓑ Ⓒ Ⓓ Ⓔ
25. Ⓐ Ⓑ Ⓒ Ⓓ Ⓔ

Section 2: Reading

1. Ⓐ Ⓑ Ⓒ Ⓓ Ⓔ
2. Ⓐ Ⓑ Ⓒ Ⓓ Ⓔ
3. Ⓐ Ⓑ Ⓒ Ⓓ Ⓔ
4. Ⓐ Ⓑ Ⓒ Ⓓ Ⓔ
5. Ⓐ Ⓑ Ⓒ Ⓓ Ⓔ
6. Ⓐ Ⓑ Ⓒ Ⓓ Ⓔ
7. Ⓐ Ⓑ Ⓒ Ⓓ Ⓔ
8. Ⓐ Ⓑ Ⓒ Ⓓ Ⓔ
9. Ⓐ Ⓑ Ⓒ Ⓓ Ⓔ
10. Ⓐ Ⓑ Ⓒ Ⓓ Ⓔ

11. Ⓐ Ⓑ Ⓒ Ⓓ Ⓔ
12. Ⓐ Ⓑ Ⓒ Ⓓ Ⓔ
13. Ⓐ Ⓑ Ⓒ Ⓓ Ⓔ
14. Ⓐ Ⓑ Ⓒ Ⓓ Ⓔ
15. Ⓐ Ⓑ Ⓒ Ⓓ Ⓔ
16. Ⓐ Ⓑ Ⓒ Ⓓ Ⓔ
17. Ⓐ Ⓑ Ⓒ Ⓓ Ⓔ
18. Ⓐ Ⓑ Ⓒ Ⓓ Ⓔ
19. Ⓐ Ⓑ Ⓒ Ⓓ Ⓔ
20. Ⓐ Ⓑ Ⓒ Ⓓ Ⓔ

21. Ⓐ Ⓑ Ⓒ Ⓓ Ⓔ
22. Ⓐ Ⓑ Ⓒ Ⓓ Ⓔ
23. Ⓐ Ⓑ Ⓒ Ⓓ Ⓔ
24. Ⓐ Ⓑ Ⓒ Ⓓ Ⓔ
25. Ⓐ Ⓑ Ⓒ Ⓓ Ⓔ
26. Ⓐ Ⓑ Ⓒ Ⓓ Ⓔ
27. Ⓐ Ⓑ Ⓒ Ⓓ Ⓔ
28. Ⓐ Ⓑ Ⓒ Ⓓ Ⓔ
29. Ⓐ Ⓑ Ⓒ Ⓓ Ⓔ
30. Ⓐ Ⓑ Ⓒ Ⓓ Ⓔ

31. Ⓐ Ⓑ Ⓒ Ⓓ Ⓔ
32. Ⓐ Ⓑ Ⓒ Ⓓ Ⓔ
33. Ⓐ Ⓑ Ⓒ Ⓓ Ⓔ
34. Ⓐ Ⓑ Ⓒ Ⓓ Ⓔ
35. Ⓐ Ⓑ Ⓒ Ⓓ Ⓔ
36. Ⓐ Ⓑ Ⓒ Ⓓ Ⓔ
37. Ⓐ Ⓑ Ⓒ Ⓓ Ⓔ
38. Ⓐ Ⓑ Ⓒ Ⓓ Ⓔ
39. Ⓐ Ⓑ Ⓒ Ⓓ Ⓔ
40. Ⓐ Ⓑ Ⓒ Ⓓ Ⓔ

Section 3: Verbal

1. Ⓐ Ⓑ Ⓒ Ⓓ Ⓔ
2. Ⓐ Ⓑ Ⓒ Ⓓ Ⓔ
3. Ⓐ Ⓑ Ⓒ Ⓓ Ⓔ
4. Ⓐ Ⓑ Ⓒ Ⓓ Ⓔ
5. Ⓐ Ⓑ Ⓒ Ⓓ Ⓔ
6. Ⓐ Ⓑ Ⓒ Ⓓ Ⓔ
7. Ⓐ Ⓑ Ⓒ Ⓓ Ⓔ
8. Ⓐ Ⓑ Ⓒ Ⓓ Ⓔ
9. Ⓐ Ⓑ Ⓒ Ⓓ Ⓔ
10. Ⓐ Ⓑ Ⓒ Ⓓ Ⓔ
11. Ⓐ Ⓑ Ⓒ Ⓓ Ⓔ
12. Ⓐ Ⓑ Ⓒ Ⓓ Ⓔ
13. Ⓐ Ⓑ Ⓒ Ⓓ Ⓔ
14. Ⓐ Ⓑ Ⓒ Ⓓ Ⓔ
15. Ⓐ Ⓑ Ⓒ Ⓓ Ⓔ

16. Ⓐ Ⓑ Ⓒ Ⓓ Ⓔ
17. Ⓐ Ⓑ Ⓒ Ⓓ Ⓔ
18. Ⓐ Ⓑ Ⓒ Ⓓ Ⓔ
19. Ⓐ Ⓑ Ⓒ Ⓓ Ⓔ
20. Ⓐ Ⓑ Ⓒ Ⓓ Ⓔ
21. Ⓐ Ⓑ Ⓒ Ⓓ Ⓔ
22. Ⓐ Ⓑ Ⓒ Ⓓ Ⓔ
23. Ⓐ Ⓑ Ⓒ Ⓓ Ⓔ
24. Ⓐ Ⓑ Ⓒ Ⓓ Ⓔ
25. Ⓐ Ⓑ Ⓒ Ⓓ Ⓔ
26. Ⓐ Ⓑ Ⓒ Ⓓ Ⓔ
27. Ⓐ Ⓑ Ⓒ Ⓓ Ⓔ
28. Ⓐ Ⓑ Ⓒ Ⓓ Ⓔ
29. Ⓐ Ⓑ Ⓒ Ⓓ Ⓔ
30. Ⓐ Ⓑ Ⓒ Ⓓ Ⓔ

31. Ⓐ Ⓑ Ⓒ Ⓓ Ⓔ
32. Ⓐ Ⓑ Ⓒ Ⓓ Ⓔ
33. Ⓐ Ⓑ Ⓒ Ⓓ Ⓔ
34. Ⓐ Ⓑ Ⓒ Ⓓ Ⓔ
35. Ⓐ Ⓑ Ⓒ Ⓓ Ⓔ
36. Ⓐ Ⓑ Ⓒ Ⓓ Ⓔ
37. Ⓐ Ⓑ Ⓒ Ⓓ Ⓔ
38. Ⓐ Ⓑ Ⓒ Ⓓ Ⓔ
39. Ⓐ Ⓑ Ⓒ Ⓓ Ⓔ
40. Ⓐ Ⓑ Ⓒ Ⓓ Ⓔ
41. Ⓐ Ⓑ Ⓒ Ⓓ Ⓔ
42. Ⓐ Ⓑ Ⓒ Ⓓ Ⓔ
43. Ⓐ Ⓑ Ⓒ Ⓓ Ⓔ
44. Ⓐ Ⓑ Ⓒ Ⓓ Ⓔ
45. Ⓐ Ⓑ Ⓒ Ⓓ Ⓔ

46. Ⓐ Ⓑ Ⓒ Ⓓ Ⓔ
47. Ⓐ Ⓑ Ⓒ Ⓓ Ⓔ
48. Ⓐ Ⓑ Ⓒ Ⓓ Ⓔ
49. Ⓐ Ⓑ Ⓒ Ⓓ Ⓔ
50. Ⓐ Ⓑ Ⓒ Ⓓ Ⓔ
51. Ⓐ Ⓑ Ⓒ Ⓓ Ⓔ
52. Ⓐ Ⓑ Ⓒ Ⓓ Ⓔ
53. Ⓐ Ⓑ Ⓒ Ⓓ Ⓔ
54. Ⓐ Ⓑ Ⓒ Ⓓ Ⓔ
55. Ⓐ Ⓑ Ⓒ Ⓓ Ⓔ
56. Ⓐ Ⓑ Ⓒ Ⓓ Ⓔ
57. Ⓐ Ⓑ Ⓒ Ⓓ Ⓔ
58. Ⓐ Ⓑ Ⓒ Ⓓ Ⓔ
59. Ⓐ Ⓑ Ⓒ Ⓓ Ⓔ
60. Ⓐ Ⓑ Ⓒ Ⓓ Ⓔ

Section 4: Quantitative (Math)

1. Ⓐ Ⓑ Ⓒ Ⓓ Ⓔ
2. Ⓐ Ⓑ Ⓒ Ⓓ Ⓔ
3. Ⓐ Ⓑ Ⓒ Ⓓ Ⓔ
4. Ⓐ Ⓑ Ⓒ Ⓓ Ⓔ
5. Ⓐ Ⓑ Ⓒ Ⓓ Ⓔ
6. Ⓐ Ⓑ Ⓒ Ⓓ Ⓔ
7. Ⓐ Ⓑ Ⓒ Ⓓ Ⓔ

8. Ⓐ Ⓑ Ⓒ Ⓓ Ⓔ
9. Ⓐ Ⓑ Ⓒ Ⓓ Ⓔ
10. Ⓐ Ⓑ Ⓒ Ⓓ Ⓔ
11. Ⓐ Ⓑ Ⓒ Ⓓ Ⓔ
12. Ⓐ Ⓑ Ⓒ Ⓓ Ⓔ
13. Ⓐ Ⓑ Ⓒ Ⓓ Ⓔ
14. Ⓐ Ⓑ Ⓒ Ⓓ Ⓔ

15. Ⓐ Ⓑ Ⓒ Ⓓ Ⓔ
16. Ⓐ Ⓑ Ⓒ Ⓓ Ⓔ
17. Ⓐ Ⓑ Ⓒ Ⓓ Ⓔ
18. Ⓐ Ⓑ Ⓒ Ⓓ Ⓔ
19. Ⓐ Ⓑ Ⓒ Ⓓ Ⓔ
20. Ⓐ Ⓑ Ⓒ Ⓓ Ⓔ
21. Ⓐ Ⓑ Ⓒ Ⓓ Ⓔ

22. Ⓐ Ⓑ Ⓒ Ⓓ Ⓔ
23. Ⓐ Ⓑ Ⓒ Ⓓ Ⓔ
24. Ⓐ Ⓑ Ⓒ Ⓓ Ⓔ
25. Ⓐ Ⓑ Ⓒ Ⓓ Ⓔ

PART I: WRITING SAMPLE

25 Minutes

Directions: Read the topics, choose the one that interests you the most, and plan your essay or story before writing. Write a legible essay on the paper provided.

Topic A: Choose one of the following two statements, then write an essay that takes a position in relation to the statement. Whether you agree or disagree, support the position you take with examples from your own experience, the experiences of others, current events, or your own existing knowledge.

A: High schools should require students to maintain a certain grade point level to play on competitive sports teams or participate in competitive extracurricular activities.

B: The most important value to honor in a friendship is loyalty.

Topic B: Consider the following two statements.

A: When I woke up that morning, I knew things would be different.

B: They weren't expecting a knock at the door.

Write a story using one of these two statements as the first sentence. Be sure your story has a clear beginning, middle, and end.

PART II: MULTIPLE CHOICE

Section 1: Quantitative (Math)

25 Questions—30 Minutes

> **Directions:** Calculate the answer to each of the following questions. Select the answer choice that is best and mark the appropriate letter on your answer sheet

1. $\dfrac{3}{5} + 1.25 + 0.004 =$

   A. 1.750

   B. 1.854

   C. 1.9

   D. 2.25

   E. 2.35

2. Evaluate: $\dfrac{10^6}{10^3}$

   A. 1 billion

   B. 1 million

   C. 1,000

   D. 100

   E. 13

3. $71.4 \times 98.2 =$

   A. 4,011.38

   B. 5,321.48

   C. 6,921.38

   D. 7,011.48

   E. 8,231.48

4. $\dfrac{4\dfrac{2}{3} + \dfrac{1}{6}}{\dfrac{1}{3}} =$

   A. 9

   B. $10\dfrac{1}{3}$

   C. $12\dfrac{3}{24}$

   D. $14\dfrac{1}{2}$

   E. 23

5. $(0.25)^2 =$

   A. 0.00625

   B. 0.0625

   C. 0.625

   D. 1.625

   E. 16.25

6. $(3 + 1) + [(2 - 3) - (4 - 1)] =$

   A. 6

   B. 2

   C. 0

   D. –2

   E. –4

7. $10{,}001 - 8{,}093 =$

A. 1,908

B. 2,007

C. 2,108

D. 18,094

E. 20,007

8. The ratio of 3 quarts to 3 gallons is

A. 3:1

B. 1:4

C. 6:3

D. 4:1

E. 1:3

9. 10% of $\dfrac{1}{5}$ of $50 is

A. $100

B. $15

C. $10

D. $5

E. $1

10.
$$\begin{array}{llll} & 4 \text{ hours} & 12 \text{ minutes} & 10 \text{ sec.} \\ - & 2 \text{ hours} & 48 \text{ minutes} & 35 \text{ sec.} \\ \hline \end{array}$$

A. 2 hr. 23 min. 25 sec.

B. 2 hr. 12 min. 40 sec.

C. 1 hr. 23 min. 35 sec.

D. 1 hr. 23 min. 25 sec.

E. 1 hr. 12 min. 35 sec.

11. If we double the value of a and c in the fraction $\dfrac{ab}{c}$, the value of the fraction is

A. doubled.

B. tripled.

C. multiplied by 4.

D. halved.

E. unchanged.

12. What percentage of 220 is 24.2?

A. 909%

B. 99%

C. 40%

D. 27%

E. 11%

13. 98 reduced by $\dfrac{5}{7}$ is equivalent to

A. 28

B. 33

C. 66

D. 70

E. 85

14. How long should an object $6\dfrac{1}{2}$ feet long be drawn, if according to the scale, $\dfrac{1}{4}$ inch in the drawing equals 1 foot?

A. $1\dfrac{3}{4}$ inches

B. $1\dfrac{5}{8}$ inches

C. $\dfrac{7}{8}$ inches

D. $\dfrac{5}{8}$ inches

E. $\dfrac{17}{32}$ inches

15. $12\dfrac{1}{2} \div \dfrac{1}{2} + \dfrac{3}{2} \times 4 - 3 =$

A. 1

B. $4\dfrac{3}{4}$

C. 20

D. 28

E. $32\dfrac{1}{2}$

16. If $y + 2 > 10$, then y must be

    A. larger than 8.
    B. larger than 6.
    C. larger than 0.
    D. equal to 0.
    E. unknown.

17. The shadow of a man 6 feet tall is 12 feet long. How tall is a tree that casts a 50-foot shadow?

    A. 100'
    B. 50'
    C. 25'
    D. 15'
    E. 10'

18. In the fraction $\dfrac{1}{\triangle}$, $\triangle$ could be replaced by all of the following EXCEPT:

    A. 0
    B. 1
    C. 4.2
    D. 9
    E. 10

19. 0.0515×100 is equivalent to

    A. $5150 \div 100$
    B. 5.15×10
    C. $0.00515 \times 1,000$
    D. $510,000 \div 10$
    E. $5,150 \div 10,000$

20.

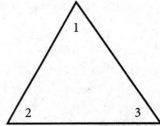

$m\angle 2 = 60°$

NOTE: *Figure not drawn to scale.*

Which of the following is true?

    A. $m\angle 1 + m\angle 3 > 180°$
    B. $m\angle 1 > m\angle 3$
    C. $m\angle 1 = m\angle 3$
    D. $m\angle 1 - m\angle 3 > m\angle 2$
    E. $m\angle 1 + m\angle 3 = 120°$

21. 45 is to _____ as 90 is to 0.45.

    A. 0.225
    B. 0.900
    C. 4.50
    D. 9.00
    E. 22.5

22. If $n = \sqrt{20}$, then

    A. $\sqrt{5} > n > \sqrt{3}$
    B. $3 > n > 2$
    C. $n = 4.5$
    D. $4 < n < 5$
    E. $n > 5$

23.

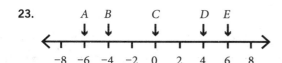

$$
\begin{array}{ccccccc}
A & B & & C & & D & E \\
\downarrow & \downarrow & & \downarrow & & \downarrow & \downarrow
\end{array}
$$

-8 -6 -4 -2 0 2 4 6 8

How would you move along the number line above to find the difference between 4 and –6?

A. From *E* to *B*

B. From *A* to *D*

C. From *B* to *D*

D. From *D* to *A*

E. From *B* to *E*

24. How many sixths are there in $\frac{4}{5}$?

A. $2\frac{3}{8}$

B. 3

C. $4\frac{4}{5}$

D. $5\frac{1}{5}$

E. 6

25. Four games drew an average of 36,500 people per game. If the attendance at the first three games was 32,000, 35,500, and 38,000, how many people attended the fourth game?

A. 36,500

B. 37,000

C. 39,000

D. 40,500

E. 43,000

END OF SECTION.
IF YOU HAVE ANY TIME LEFT, GO OVER YOUR WORK IN THIS SECTION ONLY.
DO NOT WORK IN ANY OTHER SECTION OF THE TEST.

Section 2: Reading Comprehension

40 Questions—40 Minutes

Directions: Read each passage carefully. Then decide which of the possible responses is the best answer to each question. Mark the appropriate space on your answer sheet.

Questions 1–5 refer to the following passage.

Most people think of an image when they hear the word *art*. Whether it's an elaborate oil painting, a thoughtful photograph, an intricate drawing, or even a sculpture, art is understandably most often considered the realm of the visual. This does not mean, of course, that no art exists outside of traditional visual art media and discourses. It does mean that conceptual artists like Jenny Holzer have free range to interrogate the idea of what art is by introducing elements that others might not think of as visual.

In Holzer's case, the two elements she plays with most in her conceptual artworks are text and the built environment. Specifically, Holzer is known for projecting written statements in a bold font onto buildings, posting messages as neon signage, integrating poetry into places where more official communication usually appears, or otherwise finding ways to introduce text into the spaces of everyday life. Holzer has also been known to display her signature alongside these works, creating an additional thoughtful play on the idea of the artist's signature as a type of visual representation that is both text and personal doodle.

Holzer also frequently explores art as social commentary. The content of her text-based works is usually commentary on human nature and everyday life. For instance, one famous work is called "By Your Response to Danger" (1980–1982). It is a bronze plaque that reads, "BY YOUR RESPONSE TO DANGER, IT IS EASY TO TELL HOW YOU HAVE LIVED AND WHAT HAS BEEN DONE TO YOU. YOU SHOW WHETHER YOU WANT TO STAY ALIVE, WHETHER YOU THINK YOU DESERVE TO, AND WHETHER YOU BELIEVE IT'S ANY GOOD TO ACT." Holzer's intentional use of capital letters is designed to make an impact, since capitals tend to affect readers more than traditional letters. The sense of danger or urgency one feels when looking at a message in all caps is reflected in Holzer's assertion that you can learn a lot about someone based on how they act when alerted to danger.

One of Holzer's go-to methods for her conceptual works is LED signs like those one would find throughout the architecture of everyday life. Other places her works have turned up include parking meters, T-shirts, billboards, placards, and anywhere else where one might find text. In every act, Holzer's goal is to get her viewer to pause and think about the visual messages we receive every day; what are their true contents, where are they <u>situated</u>, and how do we respond to them?

1. The main purpose of this passage is to

   A. explain what makes a piece of art "conceptual."

   B. offer an overview of Jenny Holzer as an artist.

   C. critique Jenny Holzer as an artist.

   D. discuss the merits of conceptual art.

   E. debate the value of art that appears outside museums.

2. In which of the following places can you infer you would be *least likely* to see a piece of Jenny Holzer's artwork?

 A. Hanging as an oil painting in a private art gallery

 B. Screen-printed onto a sweatshirt

 C. Graffitied on a subway car

 D. Painted into a parking spot

 E. Scrolling across an LED sign at the airport

3. Holzer's work "By Your Response to Danger" appeared

 A. on a billboard.

 B. on the side of a skyscraper.

 C. on a plaque.

 D. in a scrolling LED sign.

 E. in a greeting card.

4. The purpose of paragraph 3 is to

 A. argue for Holzer's superiority to other conceptual artists.

 B. illuminate Holzer's creative process.

 C. share how critics have traditionally received Holzer's works.

 D. introduce biographical information on Holzer.

 E. discuss one of Holzer's works as an example of how she uses art as social commentary.

5. As used in paragraph 4, the underlined term *situated* most nearly means

 A. remembered.

 B. erased.

 C. placed.

 D. removed.

 E. highlighted.

Questions 6–9 refer to the following passage.

In the animal kingdom, it's exceptionally common for like animals to group together. For every species in which individuals tend to keep to themselves, there are a handful of others (including humans) instinctively programmed to stick by kin. When animals group together, scientists generally come up with a special name to designate that group. These group names vary based on the name, characteristics, or public reception of the species in question.

Some of the names used to refer to groups of animals are more familiar than others. For instance, a group of deer, cows, sheep, or any other kind of cattle is generally referred to as a herd. Groups of dogs, wolves, and other animals with canine features are typically called a pack, as are groups of mules. Groups of swimming mammals are generally called pods, as is the case with dolphins and whales. The word colony is another common term for a group of animals; it can refer to a group of ants, bats, beavers, frogs, penguins, rabbits, rats, feral cats, and weasels, to name just a few.

Occasionally, scientists get creative when deciding what a group of animals should be called. Often, this takes the form of alliteration, such as in a flamboyance of flamingos, a caravan of camels, a wisdom of wombats, a coalition of cheetahs, a shiver of sharks, or a pandemonium of parrots. Other groups have dramatic names that <u>allude to</u> the unique characteristics of the species in question, as is the case with a quiver of cobras, a murder of crows, a thunder of hippopotami, a conspiracy of lemurs, or an ostentation of peacocks. Still other terms make the groups of animals sound sophisticated; who wouldn't want to learn some wisdom from a parliament of owls or witness the majesty of a convocation of eagles?

6. Groups of all the following animals are called colonies EXCEPT:

   A. Ants

   B. Weasels

   C. Penguins

   D. Flamingos

   E. Beavers

7. As used in paragraph 3, the underlined phrase "allude to" most nearly means to

   A. avoid.

   B. contradict.

   C. offer.

   D. disagree.

   E. hint at.

8. Which of the following animal group names figuratively communicates that the animal in question is considered scary?

   A. A parliament of owls

   B. A pandemonium of parrots

   C. A quiver of cobras

   D. A pod of dolphins

   E. An ostentation of peacocks

9. Based on the passage, why might you infer that a group of hippopotami is called a "thunder"?

   A. It refers to the scientific name *Hippopotami thunderia.*

   B. The sound of a group of hippopotami moving is probably a lot like thunder.

   C. The last name of the scientist who came up with the term is "Thunder."

   D. Everyone considers hippopotami scary like thunder.

   E. They aren't cattle, so they must have a different name than "herd."

Questions 10–13 refer to the following passage.

Shen Zhou was a Chinese artist who lived from 1427 to 1509 during the Ming dynasty. Because he was born into a wealthy family, Zhou did not have to worry about struggling for money, which allowed him to spend his days on creative pursuits like poetry, calligraphy, and painting. This freedom ensured that Zhou had the time and energy to explore numerous artistic styles across his long life, with the splendor of nature and the elegance of prior generations' art styles being his two most common subjects.

Zhou's landscapes are considered a revelation because they demonstrate an expertise and confidence that can only come from years of dedicated study. Even when working primarily with ink on paper, art historians note Zhou's skillful understanding of how to capture the qualities of light. Zhou tended to avoid being overly <u>ostentatious</u>, focusing instead on the subtleties of his subjects. One of his most famous works, a long handscroll entitled "Autumn Colors among Streams and Mountains," exhibits a sprawling landscape of delicate trees, rocks, and mountains elegantly rendered in textured brushstrokes.

Zhou was one of the most prominent members of an artistic group known as the Wu school. Named for Wu, the district in which most of the artists worked, this group of painters shared a desire to preserve and continue older artistic styles so that they wouldn't fall out of fashion. Part artist and part scholar, painters from the Wu School, like Zhou, were particularly interested in the highly expressive qualities that made these older styles seem more emotive than the more simplified and conservative painting styles that were popular during the Ming dynasty.

10. As used in paragraph 2, the underlined term *ostentatious* most nearly means

    A. extravagant.

    B. modest.

    C. bold.

    D. vibrant.

    E. technical.

11. All the following are mentioned as positive qualities of Zhou's art EXCEPT:

    A. Integration of older art techniques

    B. Aptitude with natural landscapes

    C. Highlighting the quality of light

    D. Textured, detailed brushstrokes

    E. Use of gold foil to create dimension

12. What would be a good title for this passage?

    A. "Art of the Ming Dynasty"

    B. "Shen Zhou and the Wu School"

    C. "Classical Chinese Landscapes"

    D. "Shen Zhou and Chinese History"

    E. "Natural Landscapes in Art History"

13. The genre of this passage can best be described as

    A. biographical.

    B. autobiographical.

    C. academic.

    D. persuasive.

    E. personal narrative.

Questions 14–19 refer to the following passage.

People didn't always use to stink this much. Or rather, they didn't always use to think they stunk this much. Tolerance of natural human body odor is largely a matter of individual perception, which tends to shift based on the cultural and environmental conditions one grows up in. What one culture considers normal, another might consider either offensively pungent or overly sanitized. Similar can be said about the amount of sweat that is considered normal for the body—people from hotter climates tend to tolerate the appearance of sweat more readily, for instance.

This is all to say that when a Cincinnati high school student named Edna Murphey set off in 1910 to market her father's antiperspirant invention as a solution for underarm sweat, she was marketing about a problem that didn't necessarily exist yet. In fact, her father hadn't created the substance for underarms at all but rather for his hands; as a surgeon, he wanted to keep sweat off his palms when operating. Edna, however, saw opportunity. She named the product Odorono, which when sounded out sounds like "Odor? Oh, no!," and began manufacturing it for sale after receiving an initial investment from her grandfather.

Murphey, and others who tried to peddle similar inventions in that era, faced pushback at the idea of handling issues like sweat and odor. As historian Juliann Silvulka of Tokyo's Waseda University clarified in a 2012 *Smithsonian Magazine* article, "This was still very much a Victorian society. Nobody talked about perspiration, or any other bodily functions, in public." When working door-to-door and attempting to get her product stocked in drugstores, Murphey mostly got brushed off, resulting in returned product and a useless amount of back stock.

However, Murphey was innovatively persistent and decided to sell her product at an exposition in Atlantic City in 1912. It was a hot, sweaty summer, so despite sales at her booth initially moving at a snail's pace, word got around that Odorono could cure any number of embarrassments associated with sweating too much in the summer sun. Despite numerous side effects associated with the product's acid-based chemistry, including discoloration and damage to clothing plus skin irritation and inflammation, Odorono sold successfully throughout the rest of the summer, allowing Murphey enough capital to become one of the earliest successful <u>purveyors</u> of antiperspirant. In the process, Murphey played a significant role in shifting American perceptions about perspiration and body odor such that, for better or worse (depending on who you ask), antiperspirant is a staple of American hygienic routines today.

Citation: Everts, Sarah. 2012. Review of *How Advertisers Convinced Americans They Smelled Bad. Smithsonian Magazine*, August 2, 2012. https://www.smithsonianmag.com/history/how-advertisers-convinced-americans-they-smelled-bad-12552404/.

14. As used in paragraph 4, the underlined word *purveyors* refers to people who

    A. perform experiments.

    B. sell products.

    C. manufacture products.

    D. conduct medical procedures.

    E. entertain crowds.

15. Which of the following would be the best title for this passage?

    A. "An Exposition in Atlantic City"

    B. "The Life of Edna Murphey"

    C. "Edna Murphey and the History of Antiperspirant"

    D. "Why Americans Think They Stink"

    E. "Victorian Views on Perspiration"

16. Who invented Odorono and why?

    A. Edna Murphey invented Odorono because she was embarrassed of underarm odor.

    B. Edna Murphey invented Odorono because her father hated sweating at work.

    C. Edna Murphey invented Odorono because she knew Americans would want a product to limit underarm sweat.

    D. Edna Murphey's father invented Odorono because he was embarrassed of sweating through his clothes in the summer.

    E. Edna Murphey's father invented Odorono to keep his hands from sweating when performing surgery.

17. What does the author mean by calling antiperspirant a "staple" of American hygiene at the end of paragraph 4?

    A. Antiperspirant is something everyone uses but that few people talk about.

    B. Antiperspirant is unnatural, and Americans should have never started using it.

    C. Americans like using antiperspirant more than people in other places do.

    D. Antiperspirant is considered a standard part of most Americans' daily routines.

    E. Too few brands sell antiperspirant for consumers today to truly have options.

18. We can infer from the passage that

    A. people in Atlantic City sweat more than people in other places.

    B. Edna Murphey's family didn't approve of her business ventures.

    C. Odorono was the first antiperspirant to ever sell 100,000 units.

    D. not all customers who bought Odorono were satisfied with the product.

    E. young entrepreneurs are uncommon.

19. Which paragraph demonstrates the author appealing to credibility by citing a reputable source?

    A. Paragraph 1

    B. Paragraph 2

    C. Paragraph 3

    D. Paragraph 4

    E. The author does not appeal to credibility.

Questions 20–24 refer to the following passage.

The world of fungi goes far beyond the portobello and shiitake mushrooms that most of us are more likely to encounter on a dinner plate than growing wild in the woods. The term "mushroom" describes fungus that has fruited and can release spores. There are roughly 14,000 species of mushrooms, also known as toadstools, described in nature so far, though some scientists suspect there could be millions more as of yet undiscovered. Of those thousands, as many as 20 are potentially lethal to humans while hundreds more are known to be poisonous. Still others are known to have medicinal qualities. There's so much to discover inside the weird, wide world of mushrooms!

Some mushroom species are known for their gruesome appearances. For instance, the bleeding tooth mushroom (*Hydnellum peckii*) initially resembles a white human tooth, then over time produces a blood-colored sap that gives it the eerie appearance for which it is named. Devil's fingers (*Clathrus archeri*) have the appearance of gnarled red and rotting flesh in the form of curling fingers. This strange fungus also lets off a stench of death in hopes of attracting insects to help it spread spores. Similarly, the mushroom known as dead man's fingers (*Xylaria polymorpha*) looks like a zombie hand reaching out from the ground.

Often, mushrooms are considered notable because of their beauty, such as the veiled lady mushroom (*Phallus indusiatus*), which produces a fragile net that drapes down over its cap like a bridal veil. Examples of vividly colorful mushrooms include the amethyst deceiver (*Laccaria amethystina*), a striking purple mushroom usually found in forests, the white-speckled red mushroom known as fly amanita (*Amanita muscaria*) often <u>depicted</u> in illustrated children's books, and the vibrant indigo milk cap (*Lactarius indigo*), which oozes a milky blue substance when you cut into it. There are also 80 different species of bioluminescent mushrooms that glow in the dark. Like the devil's fingers mushroom, such species have this adaptation to attract insects who can help the sporing process along.

20. The scientific name for the mushroom that is said to resemble a bride's veil is

   A. *Hydnellum peckii.*

   B. *Lactarius indigo.*

   C. *Clathrus archeri.*

   D. *Laccaria amethystine.*

   E. *Phallus indusiatus.*

21. As used in paragraph 3, the underlined term *depicted* most nearly means

   A. disposed of.

   B. decorated.

   C. discussed.

   D. shown.

   E. eaten.

22. It would be accurate to describe the tone of this passage as

   A. contemptuous.

   B. dispassionate.

   C. navel-gazing.

   D. enthusiastic.

   E. somber.

23. Of the following, which would *not* make a logical topic for a fourth paragraph?

   A. Mushrooms known for their medicinal purposes

   B. Mushrooms beloved for their use in cooking

   C. A description of how different cultures have celebrated mushrooms

   D. An explanation of which mushrooms are the most dangerous

   E. A short, fictional story about mushrooms

24. The main purpose of this passage is to

   A. talk about the historical background behind the word "mushroom."

   B. discuss the wide variety of mushrooms that exist in the world and provide examples of a few compelling species.

   C. analyze why mushrooms have been used for medicinal purposes.

   D. debate which mushroom is the most interesting species in the world.

   E. persuade the reader to add more mushrooms to their diet.

Questions 25–28 refer to the following passage.

A nomad is essentially a wanderer; it's a word for those who do not make their home in one permanent place. Many times, nomadic peoples have been living this way for years as a way to continuously find resources or match the ebbs and flows of seasons, weather patterns, and animal migration. There are many nomadic people groups still scattered across the world, including the Kochi of Afghanistan, the Pokot of Kenya and Uganda, the Nukak-Maku of Colombia, and the Sarakastsani of Greece, to name just a few.

One such group with a centuries long tradition of nomadic living are the Bedouin, primarily of Jordan, Iraq, and Syria, but also prominent in other areas throughout northern Africa and the Arabian Peninsula. Bedouins are particularly adapted to life in the desert, having a keen understanding of how to navigate the landscape and rely on sources of water along the way, such as the Nile in Egypt. Rather than being connected to one particular nation or culture, Bedouins are bonded by their shared nomadic tradition.

Bedouins predominantly live in tribes of animal herders, meaning that they move animals with them from place to place and raise them. This is often how the tribes earn their livelihood, as they sell food and wares related to their chosen form of animal stewardship wherever they go. However, not all Bedouin tribes raise the same animals; in fact, the species of animal that a tribe chooses to raise often dictates how they are classified by other Bedouin tribes and where they can choose to live. A nomadic tribe raising goats and sheep is likely to live somewhere like Syria or Iraq, whereas those who raise cattle do well in the southern part of the Arabia Peninsula, such as in Saudi Arabia. In the Sahara and other deserts, Bedouin camel tribes dominate.

Family is very important in Bedouin culture. Since tribes are not tied to plots of land, it is the tribal family unit that helps Bedouin establish a sense of place and belonging. Most of Bedouin life is organized around a patriarchal structure that includes large, extended families wherein the head of the family is often called the sheikh. While the sheikh <u>wields</u> a great deal of power in deciding matters for the tribe, other elders also often get a say in tribal matters, usually by creating a council.

25. Where are you *not* likely to find Bedouin encampments?

   A. Egypt

   B. Saudi Arabia

   C. Jordan

   D. South Africa

   E. Syria

26. If you met a Bedouin person who said that their family raised camels, you could infer that they have *most likely* lived in different parts of

   A. the Arabian Peninsula.

   B. Egypt.

   C. the Sahara Desert.

   D. Afghanistan.

   E. Iraq.

27. As used in paragraph 4, the underlined term *wields* most nearly means

   A. plays down.

   B. resists.

   C. wastes.

   D. uses.

   E. requires.

28. What would make the best title for this passage?

   A. "Nomadic Tribes"

   B. "Indigenous Peoples of Northern Africa"

   C. "Bedouin Culture"

   D. "Bedouin Family Structure"

   E. "The Role of Animal Husbandry in Bedouin Culture"

Questions 29–33 refer to the following passage.

The coffin was got out of its rough box and down on the snowy platform. The townspeople drew back enough to make room for it and then formed a close semicircle about it, looking curiously at the palm leaf which lay across the black cover. No one said anything. The baggage man stood by his truck, waiting to get at the trunks. The engine panted heavily, and the fireman dodged in and out among the wheels with his yellow torch and long oilcan, snapping the spindle boxes. The young Bostonian, one of the dead sculptor's pupils who had come with the body, looked about him helplessly. He turned to the banker, the only one of that black, <u>uneasy</u>, stoop-shouldered group who seemed enough of an individual to be addressed.

"None of Mr. Merrick's brothers are here?" he asked uncertainly.

The man with the red beard for the first time stepped up and joined the group. "No, they have not come yet; the family is scattered. The body will be taken directly to the house." He stooped and took hold of one of the handles of the coffin.

"Take the long hill road up, Thompson—it will be easier on the horses," called the liveryman as the undertaker snapped the door of the hearse and prepared to mount to the driver's seat.

Laird, the red-bearded lawyer, turned again to the stranger: "We didn't know whether there would be anyone with him or not," he explained. "It's a long walk, so you'd better go up in the hack." He pointed to a single, battered conveyance, but the young man replied stiffly: "Thank you, but I think I will go up with the hearse. If you don't object," turning to the undertaker, "I'll ride with you."

They clambered up over the wheels and drove off in the starlight up the long, white hill toward the town. The lamps in the still village were shining from under the low, snow-burdened roofs; and beyond, on every side, the plains reached out into emptiness, peaceful and wide as the soft sky itself, and wrapped in a tangible, white silence.

Excerpt from "The Sculptor's Funeral" by Willa Cather (1905)

29. As used in paragraph 1, the underlined term *uneasy* most nearly means

   A. troubled.

   B. unbothered.

   C. difficult.

   D. angry.

   E. calm.

30. From the final paragraph of the passage, we can infer that this story takes place during the

   A. beginning of summer.

   B. end of summer.

   C. harvest season.

   D. winter.

   E. first blooms of spring.

31. By saying that the family can't pick up the coffin because they are "scattered," the red-bearded man means that the family is

   A. too depressed to be up to the task.

   B. living in different places far from the town.

   C. mostly dead already.

   D. estranged from the dead sculptor.

   E. under criminal investigation for the sculptor's death.

32. The "stranger" mentioned in the story is the dead sculptor's

A. student.

B. brother.

C. lawyer.

D. son.

E. teacher.

33. The story is narrated from the point-of-view of

A. the lawyer, Laird.

B. Mr. Merrick.

C. a dead sculptor's ghost.

D. the author, Willa Cather.

E. an omniscient narrator.

Questions 34–37 refer to the following passage.

Despite being very similar celestial objects, scientists have long pondered why Neptune and Uranus appear to be different colors. The planets are similar sizes, composed of similar atmospheric gasses, and have similar masses. If given this information, a scientist would hypothesize that the two planets should look alike. However, Uranus has always appeared to be a much lighter shade of blue than Neptune. So, why the difference?

In 2022, scientists finally landed on a working theory that could explain the color difference. Namely, observations taken from three different telescopes (Gemini North, the Hubble Space Telescope, and the NASA Infrared Telescope Facility) allowed scientists to create models of the two planets' atmospheres. What scientists found is that Uranus has a much thicker version of a particular type of atmospheric haze that is found on both planets. Because this haze is so dense on Uranus, it tends to make the planet's color appear <u>blanched</u>, such that it reads more as a deep cyan or turquoise than a true blue, like Neptune. Researchers suspect that were it not for this whitening haze, both planets would indeed appear to be about the same shade of blue.

Scientists are excited about this finding because it shows how atmospheric models created from telescope observations can help address questions they have but cannot otherwise answer given our distance from the galaxy's most far-flung gas giants. They are hopeful that continued observation will yield even further insights about Uranus, Neptune, and the far edges of the Milky Way.

34. As used in paragraph 2, the underlined term *blanched* most nearly means

A. tinted with green.

B. blurry.

C. darkened.

D. paled.

E. brightened.

35. This passage is primarily about the

A. reason Neptune and Uranus appear the same color even though they aren't.

B. methods scientists used to determine why Neptune and Uranus are different colors.

C. techniques scientists deploy to observe distant planets.

D. differences between the chemical composition of Neptune and Uranus.

E. historical reasons scientists have been interested in Neptune and Uranus.

36. Gemini North is one of

   A. many black holes located near Uranus.

   B. numerous comets in Neptune's orbit.

   C. the moons of Uranus.

   D. the moons of Neptune.

   E. the telescopes scientists used to make atmospheric models of Neptune and Uranus.

37. The purpose of paragraph 2 is to

   A. introduce the scientists' original hypothesis about the planets' colors.

   B. explain why scientists now believe Neptune and Uranus are different colors and how they came to that conclusion.

   C. question the scientists' findings.

   D. explain the composition of Uranus and Neptune.

   E. clarify how telescopes can be used to conduct scientific experiments.

Questions 38–40 refer to the following passage.

Goffman's dramaturgical theory, or Goffman's dramaturgical model, is a sociological theory proposed by Erving Goffman in his 1959 book *The Presentation of Self in Everyday Life*. The term *dramaturgy*, which is usually associated with the world of theatre, means "the practice and theory of composing drama." Goffman borrowed from his study of the dramatic arts, saying that theatrical drama is a good metaphor for the way people play-act to present themselves a certain way to the rest of society.

   Social interactions then, in this model, are like scenes of dialogue in which the actors (humans in a society) are constantly acting and reacting to the norms and values communicated to them by others. Whether they follow those rules and norms or not is a matter of character, manner, and temperament, all of which are curated by the individual at both the conscious and subconscious levels to create a particular version of the self to present to society. One of the ways they do so is through a practice Goffman calls "impression management," during which the individual curates their behavior toward a particular favorable end. For instance, when a person gets dressed up and ensures that they look their best for a first date or interview, they're doing so in hopes of assuring themselves a good first impression.

38. Which of the following is an example of impression management?

   A. Two neighbors not interacting for years

   B. Using polite language when meeting your best friend's parents for the first time

   C. Recovering from a bad first impression by making a good joke

   D. Becoming too anxious about first impressions to act

   E. Responding to something someone says with a question of your own

39. When creating his theory, Goffman borrowed ideas from the field of

   A. literature.

   B. medicine.

   C. psychiatry.

   D. theatre.

   E. economics.

40. The main idea of Goffman's dramaturgical theory is that

    A. humans are like actors and society is like a stage.

    B. humans are not like actors because society is not a stage.

    C. humans are like directors and their relationships are the play.

    D. the theatrical world always reflects the real world.

    E. human behaviors cannot be adequately captured by the dramatic arts.

END OF SECTION.
IF YOU HAVE ANY TIME LEFT, GO OVER YOUR WORK IN THIS SECTION ONLY.
DO NOT WORK IN ANY OTHER SECTION OF THE TEST.

Section 3: Verbal

60 Questions—30 Minutes

The Verbal section consists of two different types of questions. There are directions for each type of question.

Directions: Each question shows a word in CAPITAL letters followed by five words or phrases. Choose the word or phrase whose meaning is most similar to the word in CAPITAL letters. Mark the appropriate space on your answer sheet.

1. AGENDA

   A. receipt

   B. agent

   C. combination

   D. correspondence

   E. schedule

2. CREDIBLE

   A. believable

   B. untrue

   C. correct

   D. suitable

   E. fortunate

3. PLACID

   A. explosive

   B. quiet

   C. public

   D. lenient

   E. crystalline

4. INTERVENE

   A. induce

   B. invert

   C. interfere

   D. solve

   E. intermediary

5. MUNDANE

   A. stupid

   B. extraordinary

   C. weekly

   D. immense

   E. common

6. DEHYDRATED

   A. airless

   B. deflated

   C. pointless

   D. worthless

   E. waterless

7. PREVALENT

   A. predating

   B. predominant

   C. preeminent

   D. prior

   E. predictive

8. SUCCINCT

   A. concise

   B. superfluous

   C. alert

   D. despicable

   E. fearful

9. NOCTURNAL
   A. by night
   B. by day
   C. revolving
   D. alternating
   E. frequent

10. EQUITABLE
    A. preferential
    B. fair
    C. unreasonable
    D. biased
    E. prejudiced

11. EXPEDITE
    A. hinder
    B. harm
    C. send
    D. hasten
    E. block

12. TURBULENT
    A. authentic
    B. tranquil
    C. tamed
    D. fatal
    E. violent

13. TENACIOUS
    A. timid
    B. thin
    C. unyielding
    D. divisive
    E. stranded

14. PERTINENT
    A. applicable
    B. prudent
    C. irreverent
    D. irrelevant
    E. truthful

15. DOGMATIC
    A. bovine
    B. canine
    C. opinionated
    D. individualistic
    E. traditional

16. UNSCRUPULOUS
    A. filthy
    B. honest
    C. austere
    D. unprincipled
    E. unresolved

17. WILY
    A. crooked
    B. narrow
    C. cunning
    D. blunt
    E. broken

18. BLATANT
    A. insipid
    B. obvious
    C. shining
    D. closed
    E. secret

SSAT (UPPER LEVEL) PRACTICE TEST

19. PRETEXT

   A. excuse

   B. reason

   C. preface

   D. fit

   E. doubt

20. ACUMEN

   A. beauty

   B. poise

   C. keenness

   D. illness

   E. courtesy

21. EVASION

   A. attack

   B. displeasure

   C. enjoyment

   D. avoidance

   E. fatigue

22. INDISPENSABLE

   A. incontrovertible

   B. essential

   C. impetuous

   D. ungovernable

   E. confused

23. OBLITERATE

   A. obligate

   B. subjugate

   C. exhibit

   D. maintain

   E. erase

24. AMIABLE

   A. allied

   B. disjointed

   C. indignant

   D. friendly

   E. introverted

25. WRITHE

   A. strangle

   B. topple

   C. trouble

   D. slide

   E. twist

26. ABATE

   A. diminish

   B. continue

   C. forego

   D. placate

   E. intimidate

27. ENDORSEMENT

   A. inscription

   B. approval

   C. standard

   D. editorial

   E. article

28. CONVERT

   A. reform

   B. predict

   C. weave

   D. transform

   E. translate

29. ERUDITE

    A. knowledgeable

    B. meddlesome

    C. eroded

    D. careless

    E. intrusion

30. ENDEAVOR

    A. expectation

    B. attempt

    C. tack

    D. necessity

    E. ability

Directions: The following questions ask you to find relationships between words. Read each question, then choose the answer that best completes the meaning of the sentence. Mark the appropriate space on your answer sheet.

SSAT (UPPER LEVEL) PRACTICE TEST

31. None is to little as never is to

    A. nothing.

    B. infrequently.

    C. negative.

    D. much.

    E. often.

32. Receive is to admit as settle is to

    A. resist.

    B. anger.

    C. remain.

    D. adjust.

    E. mediate.

33. Dishonesty is to distrust as

    A. violin is to bow.

    B. hand is to paper.

    C. money is to thief.

    D. strange is to odd.

    E. carelessness is to accident.

34. Sociologist is to group as

    A. psychologist is to individual.

    B. doctor is to nurse.

    C. children is to pediatrician.

    D. biologist is to frog.

    E. mathematician is to algebra.

35. Generous is to frugal as

    A. wasteful is to squander.

    B. philanthropist is to miser.

    C. tasteful is to garish.

    D. gratify is to desire.

    E. important is to nonessential.

36. Transparent is to translucent as

    A. water is to milk.

    B. glass is to crystal.

    C. translucent is to opaque.

    D. muddy is to clear.

    E. suspension is to mixture.

37. Discontent is to rebellion as

    A. friction is to spark.

    B. complacent is to revolt.

    C. success is to study.

    D. employment is to retirement.

    E. surgeon is to operation.

38. Beaker is to chemist as hammer is to

    A. nails.

    B. geologist.

    C. construction.

    D. architect.

    E. noise.

39. Follow is to lead as dependent is to

    A. subservient.

    B. supportive.

    C. child.

    D. autonomous.

    E. anonymous.

40. State is to country as country is to

    A. island.

    B. capitol.

    C. continent.

    D. planet.

    E. ocean.

41. Accelerator is to motion as

    A. catalyst is to change.

    B. inertia is to immobile.

    C. ignition is to speed.

    D. automobile is to vehicle.

    E. experiment is to hypothesis.

42. Probable is to certain as

    A. approach is to reproach.

    B. steady is to rocky.

    C. correct is to accurate.

    D. save is to record.

    E. plausible is to definite.

43. Obstruct is to impede as impenetrable is to

    A. impervious.

    B. hidden.

    C. merciful.

    D. porous.

    E. transparent.

44. Include is to omit as acknowledge is to

    A. notice.

    B. ignore.

    C. recognize.

    D. greet.

    E. know.

45. Nucleus is to electron as

    A. Earth is to satellite.

    B. Earth is to Sun.

    C. constellation is to Sun.

    D. neutron is to proton.

    E. atom is to neutron.

46. Sculptor is to statue as

    A. actor is to play.

    B. paint is to artist.

    C. composer is to music.

    D. orchestra is to conductor.

    E. programmer is to computer.

47. Dreary is to happy as

    A. light is to graceful.

    B. close is to narrow.

    C. dearth is to surplus.

    D. curtain is to play.

    E. interdict is to expect.

48. Allow is to restrict as

    A. gain is to success.

    B. seeing is to believing.

    C. heart is to soul.

    D. encourage is to prevent.

    E. terrible is to worse.

49. Interrupt is to speak as

    A. telephone is to telegraph.

    B. interfere is to assist.

    C. shout is to yell.

    D. intercede is to interfere.

    E. intrude is to enter.

50. Modesty is to arrogance as

    A. debility is to strength.

    B. cause is to purpose.

    C. hate is to emotion.

    D. finance is to poverty.

    E. agility is to stamina.

51. Adversity is to happiness as

    A. fear is to misfortune.

    B. solace is to sorrow.

    C. graduation is to superfluous.

    D. vehemence is to serenity.

    E. troublesome is to petulant.

52. Extortionist is to blackmail as

    A. kleptomaniac is to steal.

    B. criminal is to arrest.

    C. kidnapper is to crime.

    D. businessman is to profit.

    E. clerk is to stock.

53. Monsoon is to rain as

    A. hurricane is to destruction.

    B. tornado is to wind.

    C. sun is to spring.

    D. famine is to drought.

    E. morning is to dew.

54. Introspective is to withdrawn as

    A. hesitant is to hasty.

    B. quick is to feelings.

    C. introvert is to extrovert.

    D. import is to export.

    E. gregarious is to social.

55. Equator is to world as

    A. boundary is to country.

    B. capital is to state.

    C. fur is to animal.

    D. waist is to person.

    E. latitude is to longitude.

56. Superficial is to surface as

    A. probing is to deep.

    B. subway is to subterranean.

    C. crust is to Earth.

    D. tepid is to warm.

    E. internal is to external.

57. Stagnant is to pond as

    A. sandy is to river.

    B. noisy is to sheep.

    C. flowing is to stream.

    D. oceanic is to tide.

    E. tidal is to wave.

58. Sanctuary is to fortress as

    A. sanctum is to inner.

    B. shelter is to house.

    C. violent is to peaceful.

    D. guns is to fort.

    E. sanction is to assassinate.

59. Mentor is to professor as

    A. advisor is to counselor.

    B. child is to parent.

    C. learning is to teacher.

    D. mental is to physical.

    E. tooth is to dentist.

60. Lucid is to clear as

    A. sullen is to gloomy.

    B. furtive is to clever.

    C. potent is to weak.

    D. droll is to serious.

    E. pensive is to hanging.

END OF SECTION.
IF YOU HAVE ANY TIME LEFT, GO OVER YOUR WORK IN THIS SECTION ONLY.
DO NOT WORK IN ANY OTHER SECTION OF THE TEST.

Section 4: Quantitative (Math)

25 Questions—30 Minutes

> **Directions:** Each question below is followed by five possible answers. Select the one that is best and mark the appropriate letter on your answer sheet

1. In two days a point on the earth's equator rotates through an angle of approximately

   A. 90°.

   B. 180°.

   C. 360°.

   D. 480°.

   E. 720°.

2. Which of the following groups is arranged in order from smallest to largest?

   A. $\dfrac{3}{7}, \dfrac{11}{23}, \dfrac{15}{32}, \dfrac{1}{2}, \dfrac{9}{16}$

   B. $\dfrac{3}{7}, \dfrac{15}{23}, \dfrac{11}{23}, \dfrac{1}{2}, \dfrac{9}{16}$

   C. $\dfrac{11}{23}, \dfrac{3}{7}, \dfrac{15}{32}, \dfrac{1}{2}, \dfrac{9}{16}$

   D. $\dfrac{15}{32}, \dfrac{1}{2}, \dfrac{3}{7}, \dfrac{11}{23}, \dfrac{9}{16}$

   E. $\dfrac{1}{2}, \dfrac{5}{32}, \dfrac{3}{7}, \dfrac{11}{23}, \dfrac{9}{16}$

3. The rectangle below has a length twice as long as its width.

   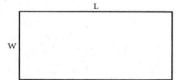

   If its width is *x*, its perimeter is

   A. 6

   B. $2x^2$

   C. $4x$

   D. $6x$

   E. $8x$

4. This square has a side of 1". The diagonal distance from one corner to another is

   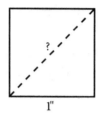

   A. 1 inch.

   B. $\sqrt{2}$ inches.

   C. $\sqrt{3}$ inches.

   D. 2 inches.

   E. 3 inches.

5. A plumber needs eight sections of pipe, each 3'2" long. If pipe is sold only by the 10' section, how many sections must the plumber buy?

   A. 1

   B. 2

   C. 3

   D. 4

   E. 5

6. The ratio of the area of the shaded part to the unshaded part is

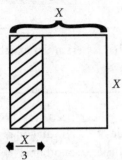

A. $x : \dfrac{x}{3}$

B. 2:1

C. 1:3

D. 1:2

E. 3:1

7. An airplane on a transatlantic flight took 4 hours 20 minutes to get from New York to its destination, a distance of 3,000 miles. However, to avoid a storm, the pilot went off course, adding a distance of 200 miles to the flight. Approximately how fast did the plane travel?

A. 640 mph

B. 710 mph

C. 738 mph

D. 750 mph

E. 772 mph

8. A photograph measuring 5" wide × 7" long must be reduced in size to fit a space 4 inches long in an advertising brochure. How wide must the space be so that the picture remains in proportion?

A. $1\dfrac{4}{7}$"

B. $2\dfrac{6}{7}$"

C. $4\dfrac{3}{5}$"

D. $5\dfrac{3}{5}$"

E. $8\dfrac{3}{4}$"

9. The total area of the shaded part of the figure is

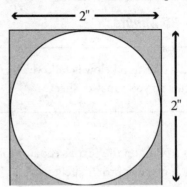

A. $\dfrac{2}{7}$ in.^{2}

B. $\dfrac{1}{2}$ in.^{2}

C. $\dfrac{6}{7}$ in.^{2}

D. $1\dfrac{3}{7}$ in.^{2}

E. $2\dfrac{1}{3}$ in.^{2}

10. A certain population of microbes grows according to the formula $P = A \times 2^n$, where P is the final size of the population, A is the initial size of the population, and n is the number of times the population reproduces itself. If each microbe reproduces itself every 20 minutes, how large would a population of only one microbe become after 4 hours?

A. 16

B. 64

C. 128

D. 1,028

E. 4,096

11. If x is a positive number and $y = \dfrac{1}{x}$, as x increases in value, what happens to y?

A. y increases.

B. y decreases.

C. y is unchanged.

D. y increases then decreases.

E. y decreases then increases.

12. A box was made in the form of a cube. If a second cubical box has inside dimensions three times those of the first box, how many times as much does it contain?

    A. 3
    B. 9
    C. 12
    D. 27
    E. 33

13. Mr. Azubo has a circular flower bed with a diameter of 4 feet. He wishes to increase the size of this bed so that it will have four times as much planting area. What must be the diameter of the new bed?

    A. 6 feet
    B. 8 feet
    C. 12 feet
    D. 16 feet
    E. 20 feet

14. A train left Albany for Buffalo, a distance of 290 miles, at 10:10 a.m. The train was scheduled to reach Buffalo at 3:45 p.m. If the average rate of the train on this trip was 50 mph, it arrived in Buffalo

    A. about 5 minutes early.
    B. on time.
    C. about 5 minutes late.
    D. about 13 minutes late.
    E. more than 15 minutes late.

15. If $3x - 2 = 13$, what is the value of $12x + 20$?

    A. 5
    B. 20
    C. 30
    D. 37
    E. 80

16. A bakery shop sold three kinds of mini cakes. The prices of these were 25¢, 30¢, and 35¢ per mini cake. The income from these sales was $36. If the number of each kind of mini cake sold was the same, how many were sold?

    A. 120
    B. 90
    C. 60
    D. 45
    E. 36

17. How many more 9" × 9" linoleum tiles than 1' × 1' tiles will it take to cover a 12' × 12' floor?

    A. 63
    B. 98
    C. 112
    D. 120
    E. 144

18. If p pumpkin seeds cost a farmer c cents, n seeds at the same rate will cost

    A. $\dfrac{pc}{n}$ cents.
    B. $\dfrac{cn}{p}$ cents.
    C. npc cents.
    D. $\dfrac{np}{c}$ cents.
    E. $n + p + c$ cents.

19. Which, if any, of the following statements is always true?

    A. If the numerator and denominator of a fraction are increased or decreased by the same amount, the value of the fraction is unchanged.

    B. If the numerator and denominator of a fraction are squared, the value of the fraction is unchanged.

    C. The square of any number is greater than that number.

    D. If unequal quantities are added to unequal quantities, the sums are unequal.

    E. None of the above

20. If the length and width of a rectangle are each doubled, by what percent is the area increased?

    A. 50%

    B. 75%

    C. 100%

    D. 300%

    E. 400%

21. If one pipe can fill a tank in $1\frac{1}{2}$ hours, and another can fill the same tank in 45 minutes, how long will it take for the two pipes to fill the tank together?

    A. $\frac{1}{3}$ hour

    B. $\frac{1}{2}$ hour

    C. $\frac{5}{6}$ hour

    D. 1 hour

    E. $1\frac{1}{2}$ hours

22. A baseball team has won 50 games out of 75 played. It has 45 games still to play. How many of these must the team win to make its record for the season 60%?

    A. 20

    B. 22

    C. 25

    D. 30

    E. 35

23. If 9 million barrels of oil are consumed daily in the United States, how many barrels are required to meet commercial and industrial needs?

DAILY OIL CONSUMPTION

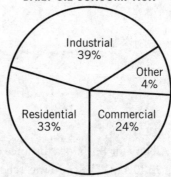

    A. 2,840,000

    B. 3,420,000

    C. 4,750,000

    D. 5,670,000

    E. 7,400,000

24. A real estate investor buys a house and lot for $440,000. He pays $12,500 to have it painted inside and out, $17,500 to fix the plumbing, and $10,000 for grading a driveway. At what price must he sell the property in order to make a 12% profit?

    A. $537,600

    B. $528,000

    C. $520,000

    D. $497,600

    E. $444,800

25. If $a = 1$, $b = 2$, $c = 3$, and $d = 5$, the value of
$\sqrt{b(d+a)-b(c+a)}$ is

A. 2

B. 3.5

C. 4

D. $\sqrt{20}$

E. 50

END OF SECTION.
IF YOU HAVE ANY TIME LEFT, GO OVER YOUR WORK IN THIS SECTION ONLY.
DO NOT WORK IN ANY OTHER SECTION OF THE TEST.

ANSWER KEYS AND EXPLANATIONS
Part I: Writing Sample

Below you will find examples of a well-written response for each prompt.

Topic A

I can understand why some schools require students to maintain their grades if they want to be in sports or clubs. It seems like a reasonable idea since a school's primary job is to educate students, not necessarily create star athletes. Activities are time consuming and cut into study time. At the same time, I do not think that students should be deprived of the benefits of club participation just because they are struggling in school. Therefore, if a student is kept out of sports or clubs due to their grades, they should also be given a tutor to help bring them up quickly.

The argument that students should keep up their grades if they want to be in clubs is worth listening to. Take sports, for example. Since they take up a lot of time, learning to take care of homework as well is a way for students to learn time management. By middle and high school, when kids are allowed to start playing sports at school, they should be building those skills up. At the same time, the grades of a few students might in fact suffer from sports participation if they are given an unreasonable number of practices, so coaches should think about how much they demand from student athletes, too.

Ultimately, when it comes to keeping up grades for extracurricular participation, I think that more students will work harder and will learn to manage time better if they are allowed to participate. If they are going to be kept from big events or tournaments, they should also be given extra study help to catch them up. Learning to organize time is an important lesson to be gained from school, but students are also young still and deserve second chances. Happy people tend to reach to meet expectations, and less capable students may even do better in school to prove that being in activities has had a positive impact on them. An equally good argument is that everyone must succeed at something. If a student who struggles in school can do well at sports or nurture a creative talent, maybe they will learn confidence they can use in class, too.

While the attitude that schoolwork comes first does make a good point, I think that permitting a student to participate in extracurricular activities and to develop a good self-image is more important. Schools should give extra help to students who are struggling to make sure everyone can participate equally.

Topic B

They weren't expecting a knock on the door. Huddled together in their secret hideout, the three friends thought they were far from where anyone could find them. They'd been coming here since they were in 3rd grade, when Kimmy first saw the worn-out door buried under the leaves. When they went down the stairs into the dark basement below, they found not ghosts and bats but beanbag chairs and an old TV. The TV didn't turn on anymore, but this is where they came to hang out and share secrets.

"Shh," Henry said, covering Omar's mouth. Kimmy, Omar, and Henry huddled together behind a big shelf with some old boardgames on it. The door creaked open. Kimmy, always the bravest one in the group, was the first to speak.

"Who's there?" she called out. At first there was no answer, just the flickering of a flashlight moving back and forth across the walls. You could almost hear the sound of the three kids' teeth chattering in their skulls as they shivered with fear. Right when Omar was about to scream and make a run for it, their eyes adjusted to the light enough for them to make out a face.

"Ranger Thompson?" Omar quietly inquired, "Is that you?"

"What are you kids doing down here?!" the ranger replied with a tone of surprise. "I knocked at the door because I heard a sound when I arrived and I thought it might be a squatter or worse, a wild animal. I certainly wouldn't want to run into a bear in the old bomb shelter!"

"So that's what this place is!" Henry exclaimed. They regaled Ranger Thompson with the story of how they'd found the place and how they'd been coming here for years to share stories or play the old board games on the shelves. In turn, Ranger Thompson told them all about how the shelter had been built in the 1950s for the rangers to hide in in the event of a nuclear war.

"Sometimes I like to come here for a bit of quiet myself, too, or to get out of the rain like today. I have no problem with you three doing so as long as you tell your parents where you are," Ranger Thompson said, reminding Kimmy that he would be over to go fishing with her dad that Saturday. "I have to get back to my ranger duties soon, but how about a round of Go Fish first?" The four sat down on the beanbags and played cards all afternoon until the rain had passed.

Part II: Multiple Choice

Section 1: Quantitative (Math)

1. B	6. C	11. E	16. A	21. A
2. C	7. A	12. E	17. C	22. D
3. D	8. B	13. A	18. A	23. B
4. D	9. E	14. B	19. C	24. C
5. B	10. C	15. D	20. E	25. D

1. **The correct answer is B.** Rename $\frac{3}{5}$ as a decimal, then solve.

$$\frac{3}{5} = 0.6$$

$$0.6 + 1.25 + 0.004 = 1.854$$

2. **The correct answer is C.**

$$\frac{10^6}{10^3} = 10^{6-3} = 1,000$$

or $10^6 = 1,000,000$ and $10^3 = 1,000$

Therefore, $1,000,000 \div 1,000 = 1,000$

3. **The correct answer is D.**

$$
\begin{array}{r}
71.4 \\
\times\ 98.2 \\
\hline
1,428 \\
5,712 \\
6,426 \\
\hline
7,011.48
\end{array}
$$

4. **The correct answer is D.** Simplify the numerator.

$$\frac{4\frac{2}{3}+\frac{1}{6}}{\frac{1}{3}} = \frac{4\frac{4}{6}+\frac{1}{6}}{\frac{1}{3}} = \frac{4\frac{5}{6}}{\frac{1}{3}}$$

Proceed as you would to divide any fraction:

$$4\frac{5}{6} \div \frac{1}{3} = \frac{29}{\cancel{6}_2} \times \frac{\cancel{3}^1}{1} = 14\frac{1}{2}$$

5. **The correct answer is B.**

$$(0.25)^2 = 0.25 \times 0.25 = 0.0625$$

6. **The correct answer is C.** Begin with the inner-most group and work outward:

$(3 + 1) + [(2 - 3) - (4 - 1)]$
$= (3 + 1) + [(-1) - (3)]$
$= (3 + 1) + [-1 - 3]$
$= (3 + 1) + [-4]$
$= 4 + [-4]$
$= 0$

7. **The correct answer is A.** In some cases, estimating is faster than calculating. Here, we can start by rounding to the nearest 100 and then subtracting. $10,000 - 8,100 = 1,900$. We don't even need to add back in the remainder to see that choice A is the correct answer.

8. **The correct answer is B.** 3 gallons contain 12 quarts. The ratio is 3 quarts:12 quarts, or in simplest form, 1:4.

9. **The correct answer is E.** One fifth of $50 is $10. Ten percent or $\frac{1}{10}$ of $10 is $1.

10. **The correct answer is C.** Borrow 1 minute from the minutes column, and 1 hour from the hours column. Then subtract:

	3 hr.	71 min.	70 sec.
–	2 hr.	48 min.	35 sec.
	1 hr.	23 min.	35 sec.

11. **The correct answer is E.** By doubling the size of one of the factors of the numerator and the size of the denominator, we do not change the value of the fraction. We are actually writing an equivalent

fraction. Try this with fractions having numerical values for the numerator and denominator.

12. **The correct answer is E.** This is a good problem for estimation. Note that 10% of 220 = 22. One percent of 220 = 2.2 and 24.2 = 22 (10 percent) + 2.2(1 percent). Or $\frac{24.2}{220} = 0.11$.

13. **The correct answer is A.** Be careful. This problem asks you to reduce 98 by $\frac{5}{7}$. In other words, find $\frac{2}{7}$ of 98.

$$98 \times \frac{2}{7} = \frac{\overset{14}{98}}{1} \times \frac{2}{\underset{1}{7}} = 28$$

14. **The correct answer is B.** Since 1 foot corresponds to $\frac{1}{4}$ inch in the drawing, the drawing should be $6\frac{1}{2} \times \frac{1}{4}$ inches long.

$$6\frac{1}{2} \times \frac{1}{4} = \frac{13}{2} \times \frac{1}{4}$$
$$= \frac{13}{8}$$
$$= 1\frac{5}{8} \text{ inches}$$

15. **The correct answer is D.** Bracket the multiplication and division operations from left to right. Then calculate.

$$\left[12\frac{1}{2} \div \frac{1}{2}\right] + \left[\frac{3}{2} \times 4\right] - 3$$
$$= [25] + [6] - 3$$
$$= 28$$

16. **The correct answer is A.**
Since $y + 2 > 10$, $y > 10 - 2$, or $y > 8$.

17. **The correct answer is C.** This is a simple proportion. A man casts a shadow twice as long as his height. Therefore, so does the tree. Thus, a tree that casts a shadow 50' long is 25' high.

18. **The correct answer is A.** The denominator of a fraction can never be equivalent to zero. Division by zero is undefined in mathematics.

19. **The correct answer is C.** $0.0515 \times 100 = 5.15$, and so does $0.00515 \times 1,000$. You should be able to do this problem by moving decimal points and not by multiplying out. To divide by 10, move the decimal point one place to the left. Move it two places to the left to divide by 100, three places to divide by 1,000, and so forth. To multiply by 10, 100, 1,000, and so forth, move the decimal point the corresponding number of places to the right.

20. **The correct answer is E.** Choices B, C, and D might be true in some cases, depending upon the exact measurements of $\angle 1$ and $\angle 3$. The only answer that is true no matter what the measures of $\angle 1$ and $\angle 3$ is the one in which their sum is equal to 120°.

21. **The correct answer is A.** This can be set up as a proportion where x is the unknown number:

$$\frac{45}{x} = \frac{90}{0.45}$$

This is a good problem for estimation. Study the numerators of the fractions and note that 45 is one half of 90. Therefore, the denominators of the fractions must have the same relationship. One half of 0.45 is 0.225.

22. **The correct answer is D.** The square root of 20 is less than the square root of 25, which is 5, and greater than the square root of 16, which is 4. Therefore, n is between 4 and 5.

23. **The correct answer is B.** To find the difference, we subtract −6 from 4 and move from −6 to 4, which is a distance of +10 units.

24. **The correct answer is C.** Simply divide $\frac{4}{5}$ by $\frac{1}{6}$ to find the answer.

$$\frac{4}{5} \div \frac{1}{6} = \frac{4}{5} \times \frac{1}{6} = \frac{24}{5} = 4\frac{4}{5}$$

25. **The correct answer is D.** Four games averaged 36,500 people per game. Thus, the total attendance for all four games was 146,000 people. The total attendance of the first three games was 105,500. Therefore, the fourth game attracted 40,500 people.

Section 2: Reading

1. B	9. B	17. D	25. D	33. E
2. A	10. A	18. D	26. C	34. D
3. C	11. E	19. C	27. D	35. B
4. E	12. B	20. E	28. C	36. E
5. C	13. A	21. D	29. A	37. D
6. D	14. B	22. D	30. D	38. B
7. E	15. C	23. E	31. B	39. D
8. C	16. E	24. B	32. A	40. A

1. **The correct answer is B.** Active reading should make it clear that the main purpose of the passage is to offer an overview of Jenny Holzer as an artist. Conceptual art isn't the primary focus of the passage, so you can eliminate choices A and D. There is no attempt to critique (choice C) or debate (choice E), either.

2. **The correct answer is A.** Paragraphs 2 and 4 both make it clear that Holzer most often chooses nontraditional places for her works. For instance, paragraph 4 states: "Other places her works have turned up include parking meters, t-shirts, billboards, placards, and anywhere else where one might find text." While it is true that some of Holzer's works have appeared in museums and galleries, your goal is to make an inference based on the text provided. Your most logical inference based on the information given is that Holzer's work is less likely to turn up in a traditional art space, like as an oil painting in a private art gallery, than in the nontraditional places listed. Tip: Even if you struggled with this question, you could also land on the right answer by considering which option was *least* like the others.

3. **The correct answer is C.** Paragraph 3 states that this work appeared on a bronze plaque.

4. **The correct answer is E.** In paragraph 3, the author discusses how Holzer is interested in social commentary and then gives details about Holzer's work "By Your Response to Danger" to support this assertion.

5. **The correct answer is C.** To situate something means to place it in a particular location or within a particular context.

6. **The correct answer is D.** Paragraph 3 states that a group of flamingos is called a flamboyance.

7. **The correct answer is E.** To allude to something means to suggest, draw attention to, or hint at it. Contextually, *allude to* is used here to discuss names for groups of animals that evoke the traits associated with those animals.

8. **The correct answer is C.** A group of cobras would likely make someone quiver with fear, so choice C is an example of figurative imagery in naming groups of animals.

9. **The correct answer is B.** In paragraph 1, the passage states that "group names vary based on the name, characteristics, or public reception of the species in question." Therefore, you need only locate an answer that has to do with the name, characteristics, or reception of hippopotami, meaning you can eliminate choices A and C right away. Choice E is also a weak choice since the passage already states that most animal groups get unique names, so it's not like the word *herd* is the only option. That leaves you with choices B and D; choice D is much vaguer and relies on an opinion, since not all people think hippopotami or thunder are scary. However, most people would agree that a group of hippopotami would be thunderously loud, so choice B is your best, most logical answer.

10. **The correct answer is A.** The word *ostentatious* means "extravagant, garish, over-the-top, or gaudy."

11. **The correct answer is E.** While the passage touches on each of the other traits, it never mentions Zhou using gold foil in his works.

12. **The correct answer is B.** Shen Zhou is the primary focus of this passage, so you can eliminate any answer that doesn't include his name (choices A, C, and E). Of the two remaining options, choice B focuses on a specific art movement (the Wu School) while choice D talks about art history more generally. Since the focus of paragraph 3 is on the Wu School, the most fitting title is "Shen Zhou and the Wu School."

13. **The correct answer is A.** This passage focuses primarily on Shen Zhou's life, so you can narrow your choices to biographical (choice A) and autobiographical (choice B). Since it's impossible for Zhou to have written the passage about himself, you know it's a biography, which is a story written about someone's life, rather than an autobiography, which is a story one writes about their own life.

14. **The correct answer is B.** Even if you're not sure what this term means, the context clues surrounding the word should make it clear that a purveyor (of a good) is someone who sells or does deals related to that particular good.

15. **The correct answer is C.** Edna Murphey and her role in changing American ideas about antiperspirant is the focus of this passage. The title that best encompasses this main idea is "Edna Murphey and the History of Antiperspirant."

16. **The correct answer is E.** This is a detail question that helps determine if you read closely. Paragraph 2 states: "[Edna's] father hadn't created the substance for underarms at all but rather for his hands; as a surgeon, he wanted to keep sweat off his palms when operating."

17. **The correct answer is D.** If something is a "staple" of something else, that's a figurative way of saying that something is a common, main, or primary item of something. Here, the author is saying that antiperspirant is one of a few main hygiene basics for most Americans.

18. **The correct answer is D.** Even if the passage doesn't say so directly, we can assume that if Odorono caused side effects like "discoloration and damage to clothing plus skin irritation and inflammation" and if early attempts to sell resulted in "returned product," then not everyone who bought Odorono early on was satisfied with their purchase.

19. **The correct answer is C.** In paragraph 3, the author cites a quotation from an article in *Smithsonian Magazine*, which is considered a reputable source for this type of information. Furthermore, the author notes that the quoted information comes from a professor and historian named Juliann Silvulka who works at Waseda University in Tokyo. Both pieces of information help the author demonstrate that their research while writing the passage was credible.

20. **The correct answer is E.** More commonly called the "veiled lady mushroom," the *Phallus indusiatus* is the mushroom that "produces a fragile net that drapes down over its cap like a bridal veil."

21. **The correct answer is D.** *Depicted* means "shown, illustrated, described, or outlined."

22. **The correct answer is D.** In this passage, the author's word and sentence structure choices reveal a great deal of enthusiasm for the topic of mushrooms. For instance, at the end of paragraph 1, you'll find an enthusiastic exclamation: "There's so much to discover inside the weird, wide world of mushrooms!" Other terms that might explain the tone of this passage include *informative, celebratory, appreciative,* and *light-hearted.*

23. **The correct answer is E.** This is an informative passage, so it would be most logical for the next paragraph to stick with the same tone and genre. A fictional story is the least suitable inclusion to an informative text.

24. **The correct answer is B.** When a question asks you the purpose of a passage, a quick way to eliminate some wrong answers is to look at the

active verb in each sentence. There is no attempt to analyze (choice C), debate (choice D), or persuade (choice E) in this text, so you can eliminate those options right away. Of the two remaining choices, there is nothing in the passage that discusses the etymology (meaning "historical background of a word") of the word *mushroom* (choice A).

25. **The correct answer is D.** Egypt (choice A), Saudi Arabia (choice B), Jordan (choice C), and Syria (choice E) are all mentioned in the passage. South Africa is not.

26. **The correct answer is C.** The purpose of paragraph 3 is to explain the different types of animal husbandry that different Bedouin tribes take part in. At the end of this paragraph, the passage states: "In the Sahara and other deserts, Bedouin camel tribes dominate." While this doesn't mean that your new Bedouin friend who says their family raised camels has for sure lived in the Sahara, the question is asking you to make an inference based on what is *most likely* according to the details you've been given.

27. **The correct answer is D.** To wield is to "use, exert, or maintain."

28. **The correct answer is C.** The best title for this passage is "Bedouin Culture." The first two titles, "Nomadic Tribes" (choice A) and "Indigenous Peoples of Northern Africa" (choice B) are too broad for a passage focused specifically on Bedouin tribes. The latter two titles, "Bedouin Family Structure" (choice D) and "The Role of Animal Husbandry in Bedouin Culture" (choice E) are too specific, since they focus only on the topics of paragraphs 3 and 4 respectively.

29. **The correct answer is A.** *Uneasy* means "troubled" or "feeling anxiety."

30. **The correct answer is D.** Context clues like "snow-burdened roofs" and plains that are "wrapped in a tangible, white silence" assure the reader that there is snow on the ground, so this story must take place in winter.

31. **The correct answer is B.** Saying that the sculptor's family is "scattered" is a way of saying that they are living in different places far from the town.

32. **The correct answer is A.** While identified as a stranger to the townspeople, paragraph 1 states that this person who came with the body is "one of the dead sculptor's pupils," meaning the sculptor's student.

33. **The correct answer is E.** This story is told from the perspective of an omniscient narrator. Laird (choice A) and Mr. Merrick (choice B) are both mentioned in the story, but neither are the narrator. While Willa Cather (choice D) is the author of the story, an author is different than a narrator. There is no evidence to suggest that the story is being narrated by the dead sculptor's ghost (choice C).

34. **The correct answer is D.** *Blanched* means "paled, lightened, or whitened, such as by extracting color."

35. **The correct answer is B.** The main idea of this passage is that while Neptune and Uranus have similar compositions, they appear different colors, and scientists have recently determined that the reason has to do with a particular haze on both planets being thicker on Uranus. The passage contradicts choices A and D, while choices C and E do not adequately encompass the passage's main idea.

36. **The correct answer is E.** Not only does the passage clearly state that Gemini North is one of three telescopes that scientists used to make atmospheric models of Neptune and Uranus, but also, none of the other options are mentioned in the passage.

37. **The correct answer is D.** The central paragraph of this brief, informative summary concerns how the scientists created atmospheric models that helped them determine why Neptune and Uranus are different colors, namely because a haze that appears on both planets is thicker on Uranus.

38. **The correct answer is B.** The passage notes that impression management involves any actions humans take to ensure they make a good impression on people. Adopting a more polite way of speaking around your best friend's parents when meeting them for the first time is an example of impression management, since it's a behavior you're engaging in with hope that your friend's parents will like you more.

39. **The correct answer is D.** The passage states that Goffman borrowed ideas from the "dramatic arts," which is another way of saying the theatre.

40. **The correct answer is A.** The passage states that "people play-act to present themselves a certain way to the rest of society." The idea that humans are actors and society is the stage is thus closest to the idea expressed in the passage.

Section 3: Verbal

1. E	11. D	21. D	31. B	41. A	51. D
2. A	12. E	22. B	32. C	42. E	52. A
3. B	13. C	23. E	33. E	43. A	53. B
4. C	14. A	24. D	34. A	44. B	54. E
5. E	15. C	25. E	35. B	45. A	55. D
6. E	16. D	26. A	36. C	46. C	56. A
7. B	17. C	27. B	37. A	47. C	57. C
8. A	18. B	28. D	38. B	48. D	58. B
9. A	19. A	29. A	39. D	49. E	59. A
10. B	20. C	30. B	40. C	50. A	60. A

1. **The correct answer is E.** The term *agenda* describes a "program of things to be done" or "schedule."

2. **The correct answer is A.** The adjective *credible* can be used to describe something plausible, reliable, or believable.

3. **The correct answer is B.** *Placid* means "tranquil, calm, or peaceful." The word *quiet* is most similar in meaning.

4. **The correct answer is C.** The verb *intervene* means to "come between two people or things to either interfere or positively influence."

5. **The correct answer is E.** *Mundane* can be used to describe something that is commonplace, earthly, or ordinary.

6. **The correct answer is E.** To dehydrate is to remove water, therefore *dehydrated* means "waterless or drained of water." The root *hydr-* refers to water, and the prefix *de-* is a negative prefix.

7. **The correct answer is B.** *Prevalent* means "widely existing, prevailing, or generally accepted." *Predominant* means "being most frequent or common."

8. **The correct answer is A.** *Succinct* means "brief," "to the point," or "said in as few words as necessary." In other words, concise.

9. **The correct answer is A.** Something that is nocturnal happens at night or is active at night.

10. **The correct answer is B.** *Equitable* means "fair and just." You should see the root *equal* in this word.

11. **The correct answer is D.** To expedite means to "speed up the action" or "send quickly."

12. **The correct answer is E.** *Turbulent* means "unruly or agitated." *Violent* is a synonym.

13. **The correct answer is C.** The term *tenacious* can mean either "persistent" or "holding on tightly." *Unyielding* has the closest meaning.

14. **The correct answer is A.** *Pertinent* is a synonym for *relevant.* To be relevant is to be applicable.

15. **The correct answer is C.** *Dogmatic* means either "dictatorial" or "staunchly opinionated."

16. **The correct answer is D.** An unscrupulous person is not restrained by ideas of right and wrong. To be unprincipled is to be unscrupulous.

17. **The correct answer is C.** The term *wily* means "sly or crafty." A cunning person is characterized by wiliness and trickery.

18. **The correct answer is B.** If someone is blatant, that means they are loud, obvious, or obtrusive.

19. **The correct answer is A.** A *pretext* is an excuse or a false reason (for an action).

20. The correct answer is C. *Acumen* describes "a keenness and quickness in understanding a concept or dealing with a situation."

21. The correct answer is D. *Evasion* is a synonym for *subterfuge* or *avoidance*.

22. The correct answer is B. The term *indispensable* means what it sounds like; it describes something or someone that cannot be dispensed with or who is essential.

23. The correct answer is E. The verb *obliterate* means "to destroy without leaving a trace."

24. The correct answer is D. The adjective *amiable* means "pleasant, friendly, and good-natured." Often, the Latin root *ami-* relates to the terms *friend* and *loved one*.

25. The correct answer is E. To writhe is to "twist, squirm, or contort, generally in discomfort."

26. The correct answer is A. The verb *abate* is a synonym for *diminish*.

27. The correct answer is B. An endorsement is a statement of approval.

28. The correct answer is D. The verb *convert* means "change from one form to another." *Transform* is a synonym.

29. The correct answer is A. The adjective *erudite* is a synonym for *learned, scholarly,* or *knowledgeable*.

30. The correct answer is B. The verb *endeavor* is a synonym for *attempt* or *try*.

31. The correct answer is B. The relationship of the terms is one of degree. *None* is the ultimate, the empty set, of *little; never* bears the same relationship to *infrequently*.

32. The correct answer is C. If you think in terms of a house, you can see that the terms on each side of the relationship are synonymous. You can *receive* a person into your home or *admit* the person. Once the person decides to *remain*, that person *settles* in.

33. The correct answer is E. Here the cause-and-effect relationship is clear. Recognized *dishonesty* leads to *distrust; carelessness* leads to *accidents*.

34. The correct answer is A. The relationship is that of actor to object. A sociologist studies groups; a psychologist studies individuals. The relationship of the children to the pediatrician is in reverse order.

35. The correct answer is B. The terms are antonyms. *Generous* is the opposite of *frugal*; a *philanthropist* is the opposite of a *miser*. The terms in choices C and E are also antonyms. When faced with questions in which the same relationship is maintained by a few choices, look for a relationship among all four terms. In this case, the theme among the choices is "money."

36. The correct answer is C. The relationship is one of degree. *Translucent* describes a level of light penetration denser than does *transparent*; one can see clearly through something that is transparent but something that is translucent will only allow light to be visible. Carrying on to the next degree, *opaque* is denser than *translucent*. Not even light can pass through something that is opaque. Choice A is incorrect because it skips a degree and jumps from transparent to opaque. Choice D reverses the order. Glass and crystal (choice B) may both be transparent.

37. The correct answer is A. This is a classic cause-and-effect relationship. Discontent leads to rebellion; friction creates a spark.

38. The correct answer is B. The relationship is that of worker to tool. A chemist uses a beaker in the laboratory; a geologist uses a hammer to chip at rocks in the field or laboratory. Avoid the "trap" of choice C. A hammer is certainly used in construction, but the relationship of the first two terms requires that a person be involved to complete the analogy.

39. The correct answer is D. The basis of the analogy is antonyms.

40. The correct answer is C. This is a part-to-whole analogy. A state is part of a country; a country is part of a continent.

41. **The correct answer is A.** This is a cause-and-effect analogy. An accelerator causes the motion of the car; a catalyst causes the chemical change.

42. **The correct answer is E.** The relationship is one of degree. *Probable* means something likely, but less likely than *certain; plausible* means possible but less likely than *definite*.

43. **The correct answer is A.** The relationship is one of true synonyms.

44. **The correct answer is B.** This analogy involves true antonyms.

45. **The correct answer is A.** The relationship is that of object to actor. The nucleus is the object that is orbited by an electron; Earth is the object that is orbited by a satellite. Choice B reverses the order of the relationship.

46. **The correct answer is C.** Here the relationship is that of actor to object. A sculptor creates a statue; a composer creates music. An actor performs in a play but does not create it. A programmer creates a program while working at a computer.

47. **The correct answer is C.** The analogy is based on an antonym relationship.

48. **The correct answer is D.** This analogy is also based on antonyms.

49. **The correct answer is E.** It is hard to categorize this relationship. One interrupts by speaking out of turn; one intrudes by entering out of turn. The relationship in choice B might be that of opposites.

50. **The correct answer is A.** The first two terms are true opposites. Only choice A offers true opposites. *Financial stability* is the opposite of *poverty*.

51. **The correct answer is D.** This analogy is best understood as a negative cause and effect. Adversity leads to a lack of happiness; vehemence leads to a lack of serenity.

52. **The correct answer is A.** The relationship is that of actor to action. An extortionist blackmails; a kleptomaniac steals.

53. **The correct answer is B.** This is a whole-to-part relationship. A monsoon is a major storm of which rain is a crucial component; a tornado is a major storm of which wind is a crucial component.

54. **The correct answer is E.** The relationship between the two sets of words is that the words in each half of the analogy are synonyms. Don't worry that the words in the first half are antonyms of the second. You aren't looking at how all four words relate to one another in this analogy, just at how the words in each half relate to one another.

55. **The correct answer is D.** You don't always have to categorize an analogy; sometimes, you just need to understand it. The equator is the midline that circles the world; the waist is the midline that circles a person.

56. **The correct answer is A.** On each side of the analogy, the first term is a characteristic of the second.

57. **The correct answer is C.** This analogy is based on characteristics of bodies of water. A pond may be stagnant; a stream is likely to flow. Sheep may be noisy but since there are two choices that involve characteristics, you must choose the one that is closest in other aspects to the first set of terms, that is, the one involving water.

58. **The correct answer is B.** This is a purposeful or functional relationship. A fortress gives sanctuary; a house gives shelter.

59. **The correct answer is A.** The terms are synonyms.

60. **The correct answer is A.** This analogy is based on synonyms. Choice E is incorrect because pensive means "thoughtful." If you made this choice, you were mistaking *pensive* for *pendant*, which does mean "hanging."

Section 4: Quantitative (Math)

1. E	6. D	11. B	16. A	21. B
2. B	7. C	12. D	17. C	22. B
3. D	8. B	13. B	18. B	23. D
4. B	9. C	14. D	19. E	24. A
5. C	10. E	15. E	20. D	25. A

1. **The correct answer is E.** Any point on the equator rotates the circumference of the earth once each day. Each revolution is an angle of 360°. In two days, two revolutions take place, 360° × 2 = 720°.

2. **The correct answer is B.** $\frac{3}{7}, \frac{15}{32}$, and $\frac{11}{23}$ are all less than $\frac{1}{2}$; $\frac{9}{16}$ is larger than $\frac{1}{2}$. Compare the size of fractions this way.

$$\frac{3}{7} \diagdown\diagup \frac{15}{32}$$

   Because the product of 7 and 15 is larger than the product of 32 and 3, $\frac{15}{32}$ will be found to be larger. Using the same method, $\frac{15}{32} < \frac{11}{23}$.

3. **The correct answer is D.** If the width is x, the length, which is twice as long, is $2x$. The perimeter is equal to the sum of the four sides:

$$2x + 2x + x + x = 6x$$

4. **The correct answer is B.** Use the Pythagorean theorem $c^2 = a^2 + b^2$ to find the length of the diagonal:

$$c^2 = 1^2 + 1^2$$
$$c^2 = 2$$
$$c = \sqrt{2}$$

5. **The correct answer is C.** Eight sections, each 3'2" long, is equivalent to 8 × 38" = 304".

   $304" = 25\frac{1}{3}$ feet; therefore, three 10-foot sections are needed.

6. **The correct answer is D.** The width of the shaded area is $\frac{1}{3}$ of the width of the square. Therefore, the area of the shaded part is $\frac{1}{3}$ the area of the whole square. The unshaded part is twice as large as the shaded part. The ratio of the shaded part to the unshaded, therefore, is 1:2.

7. **The correct answer is C.**

   If distance = rate × time, then rate = distance ÷ time.

   Total distance traveled is 3,200 miles.

   Total time is 4 hours 20 minutes.

   Rate = 3,200 miles ÷ 4 hours 20 minutes

   $$= 3{,}200 \text{ miles} \div 4\frac{1}{3} \text{ hours}$$

   = 738 mph, approximately

8. **The correct answer is B.** This is a simple proportion:

$$\frac{7}{4} = \frac{5}{x}$$

   x is the unknown width. Cross-multiply to solve:

$$\frac{7}{4} = \frac{5}{x}$$
$$7x = 20$$
$$x = \frac{20}{7} \text{ or } 2\frac{6}{7}"$$

9. **The correct answer is C.** Subtract the area of the circle from the area of the square to find the area of just the shaded part.

   Note that the diameter of the circle equals the width of the square.

   Area of square = s^2 = 4 sq. in.

   Area of circle = $\pi r^2 = \pi(1)^2 = \pi$ sq. in.

Area of square – Area of circle

$$= 4 \text{ sq. in.} - \frac{22}{7} \text{ sq. in.}$$

$$= \frac{6}{7} \text{ sq. in. or } \frac{6}{7} \text{ in.}^2$$

10. **The correct answer is E.** The population would reproduce 12 times in 4 hours. The size then is:

$$P = 1 \times 2^{12}$$
$$= 2 \times 2 \times 2 \times 2 \times 2 \times 2 \times 2 \times 2 \times 2 \times 2 \times 2 \times 2$$
$$= 4,096$$

11. **The correct answer is B.** The larger the number of the denominator of a fraction, the smaller the quantity represented. For example, $\frac{1}{4}$ represents a lesser quantity than $\frac{1}{2}$. Therefore, as x becomes greater, y becomes smaller.

12. **The correct answer is D.** If the second box has each dimension three times that of the first box, then its volume is $3 \times 3 \times 3 = 27$ times as great.

13. **The correct answer is B.** The area of the flower bed is 4π sq. ft. $(A = \pi r^2)$. The area of the new bed is to be four times as great, or 16π sq. ft. A bed with an area of 16π sq. ft. must have a diameter of 8' and a radius of 4' since $A = \pi r^2$.

14. **The correct answer is D.** Use the formula $D = R \times T$ to find the time it took to get to Buffalo:

time = distance ÷ rate

Travel time of trip was equal to 290 miles ÷ 50 mph.

Travel time $= 5\frac{4}{5}$ hours, or 5 hours 48 minutes.

Scheduled travel time was between 10:10 a.m. and 3:45 p.m., an interval of 5 hours 35 minutes.

Therefore, the train took about 13 minutes longer than scheduled.

15. **The correct answer is E.** Solve the equation for x:

$$3x - 2 = 13$$
$$3x = 15$$
$$x = 5$$

If $x = 5$, then $12x + 20 = 12(5) + 20 = 80$.

16. **The correct answer is A.** Since the number of each kind of cake sold was the same, we can say that the cakes sold for an average price of 30¢.

$$25¢ + 30¢ + 35¢ = 90¢ \div 3 = 30¢ \text{ per cake}$$

Divide the total sales income of $36 by 30¢ to find how many mini cakes were sold:

$$\$36 \div 0.30 = 120$$

17. **The correct answer is C.** A floor 12' × 12' is 144 sq. ft. in area and would require 144 tiles that are each 1 foot by 1 foot. Twelve tiles would be placed along the width and length of the room. If 9" tiles are used, it requires 16 of them placed end to end to cover the length of the room. Therefore, it requires 16 × 16 tiles to cover the floor, or 256 tiles. It requires 112 more 9" tiles than 12" tiles to cover the floor.

18. **The correct answer is B.** If p pumpkin seeds cost the farmer c cents, the cost of each seed is $\frac{c}{p}$ cents. To find the cost of n seeds, we multiply the cost of each times n:

$$\frac{c}{p} \times n = \frac{cn}{p}$$

19. **The correct answer is E.** If necessary, try each of the answers for yourself to see that each is false. Choice C is untrue for the number 1.

20. **The correct answer is D.** Think of a rectangle with the dimensions 1" by 2". Its area is 2 square inches. If we double each dimension to 2" by 4", the area becomes 8 square inches, which is four times the area of the first rectangle. This is equal to an increase of 300%.

21. **The correct answer is B.** The first pipe can fill the tank in $1\frac{1}{2}$, or $\frac{3}{2}$, hours; that is, it can do $\frac{2}{3}$ of the job in 1 hour. The second pipe can fill the tank in 45 minutes, or $\frac{3}{4}$ of an hour, or it can do $\frac{4}{3}$ of the job in 1 hour. Together, the pipes can complete $\frac{4}{3} + \frac{2}{3} = \frac{6}{3}$ of the job in 1 hour. $\frac{6}{3} = 2$, or twice the job in 1 hour. Therefore, together the 2 pipes could fill the tank in $\frac{1}{2}$ hour.

22. **The correct answer is B.** The whole season consists of 120 games. For a season record of 60%, the team must win 72 games. Since it has already won 50, it must win 22 more games out of those left.

23. **The correct answer is D.** Commercial and industrial needs total 63% of daily oil consumption. Since consumption is 9 million barrels, 63% of 9 million is 5,670,000 barrels.

24. **The correct answer is A.** Add the cost of the house, driveway, painting, and plumbing:

$440,000 + $12,500 + $17,500 + 10,000 = $480,000

If he wants to make a 12% profit when reselling the house, he should increase the total cost by 12% to find the new selling price:

12% of $480,000 = $57,600

$480,000 + $57,600 = $537,600

25. **The correct answer is A.** This is a problem that must be done carefully.

$$a = 1, b = 2, c = 3, d = 5$$

$$\sqrt{b(d+a)-b(c+a)}$$

$$=\sqrt{2(5+1)-2(3+1)}$$

$$=\sqrt{2(6)-2(4)}$$

$$=\sqrt{12-8}$$

$$=2$$

SCORE YOURSELF

Check your answers against the answer keys. Count the number of answers you got right and the number you got wrong.

SSAT SCORING		
Section	**No. Right**	**No. Wrong**
Quantitative (Math)		
Reading Comprehension		
Verbal		

Now calculate your raw scores:

Quantitative (Math): $(\underline{\hspace{2cm}}) - \left(\dfrac{1}{4}\right) (\underline{\hspace{2cm}}) = (\underline{\hspace{2cm}})$
 No. Right   No. Wrong   Raw Score

Reading Comprehension: $(\underline{\hspace{2cm}}) - \left(\dfrac{1}{4}\right) (\underline{\hspace{2cm}}) = (\underline{\hspace{2cm}})$
 No. Right   No. Wrong   Raw Score

Verbal: $(\underline{\hspace{2cm}}) - \left(\dfrac{1}{4}\right) (\underline{\hspace{2cm}}) = (\underline{\hspace{2cm}})$
 No. Right   No. Wrong   Raw Score

Now check your Raw Score against the conversion charts to get an idea of the range in which your test scores fall:

SSAT RAW SCORE CONVERSION CHART			
Raw Score	Quantitative (Math)	Reading Comprehension	Verbal
60			800
55			800
50	800		779
45	782		752
40	755	800	725
35	725	722	698
30	698	692	671
25	668	662	644
20	641	632	617
15	614	602	590
10	584	572	563
5	557	542	533
0	530	512	506
−5 or lower	500	500	500

Remember:

- The same exam is given to students in grades 8 through 11. You are not expected to know what you have not been taught.

- You will be compared only to students in your own grade. Use your scores to plan further study if you have time.

CHAPTER

ISEE (UPPER LEVEL)
PRACTICE TEST

ISEE (UPPER LEVEL) Practice Test

PRACTICE TEST

This practice test is designed to help you recognize your strengths and weaknesses. The questions cover information from all the different sections of the ISEE. Use the results to help guide and direct your study time.

ANSWER SHEET: ISEE (UPPER LEVEL) PRACTICE TEST

Section 1: Verbal Reasoning

1. Ⓐ Ⓑ Ⓒ Ⓓ
2. Ⓐ Ⓑ Ⓒ Ⓓ
3. Ⓐ Ⓑ Ⓒ Ⓓ
4. Ⓐ Ⓑ Ⓒ Ⓓ
5. Ⓐ Ⓑ Ⓒ Ⓓ
6. Ⓐ Ⓑ Ⓒ Ⓓ
7. Ⓐ Ⓑ Ⓒ Ⓓ
8. Ⓐ Ⓑ Ⓒ Ⓓ
9. Ⓐ Ⓑ Ⓒ Ⓓ
10. Ⓐ Ⓑ Ⓒ Ⓓ

11. Ⓐ Ⓑ Ⓒ Ⓓ
12. Ⓐ Ⓑ Ⓒ Ⓓ
13. Ⓐ Ⓑ Ⓒ Ⓓ
14. Ⓐ Ⓑ Ⓒ Ⓓ
15. Ⓐ Ⓑ Ⓒ Ⓓ
16. Ⓐ Ⓑ Ⓒ Ⓓ
17. Ⓐ Ⓑ Ⓒ Ⓓ
18. Ⓐ Ⓑ Ⓒ Ⓓ
19. Ⓐ Ⓑ Ⓒ Ⓓ
20. Ⓐ Ⓑ Ⓒ Ⓓ

21. Ⓐ Ⓑ Ⓒ Ⓓ
22. Ⓐ Ⓑ Ⓒ Ⓓ
23. Ⓐ Ⓑ Ⓒ Ⓓ
24. Ⓐ Ⓑ Ⓒ Ⓓ
25. Ⓐ Ⓑ Ⓒ Ⓓ
26. Ⓐ Ⓑ Ⓒ Ⓓ
27. Ⓐ Ⓑ Ⓒ Ⓓ
28. Ⓐ Ⓑ Ⓒ Ⓓ
29. Ⓐ Ⓑ Ⓒ Ⓓ
30. Ⓐ Ⓑ Ⓒ Ⓓ

31. Ⓐ Ⓑ Ⓒ Ⓓ
32. Ⓐ Ⓑ Ⓒ Ⓓ
33. Ⓐ Ⓑ Ⓒ Ⓓ
34. Ⓐ Ⓑ Ⓒ Ⓓ
35. Ⓐ Ⓑ Ⓒ Ⓓ
36. Ⓐ Ⓑ Ⓒ Ⓓ
37. Ⓐ Ⓑ Ⓒ Ⓓ
38. Ⓐ Ⓑ Ⓒ Ⓓ
39. Ⓐ Ⓑ Ⓒ Ⓓ
40. Ⓐ Ⓑ Ⓒ Ⓓ

Section 2: Quantitative Reasoning

1. Ⓐ Ⓑ Ⓒ Ⓓ
2. Ⓐ Ⓑ Ⓒ Ⓓ
3. Ⓐ Ⓑ Ⓒ Ⓓ
4. Ⓐ Ⓑ Ⓒ Ⓓ
5. Ⓐ Ⓑ Ⓒ Ⓓ
6. Ⓐ Ⓑ Ⓒ Ⓓ
7. Ⓐ Ⓑ Ⓒ Ⓓ
8. Ⓐ Ⓑ Ⓒ Ⓓ
9. Ⓐ Ⓑ Ⓒ Ⓓ
10. Ⓐ Ⓑ Ⓒ Ⓓ

11. Ⓐ Ⓑ Ⓒ Ⓓ
12. Ⓐ Ⓑ Ⓒ Ⓓ
13. Ⓐ Ⓑ Ⓒ Ⓓ
14. Ⓐ Ⓑ Ⓒ Ⓓ
15. Ⓐ Ⓑ Ⓒ Ⓓ
16. Ⓐ Ⓑ Ⓒ Ⓓ
17. Ⓐ Ⓑ Ⓒ Ⓓ
18. Ⓐ Ⓑ Ⓒ Ⓓ
19. Ⓐ Ⓑ Ⓒ Ⓓ
20. Ⓐ Ⓑ Ⓒ Ⓓ

21. Ⓐ Ⓑ Ⓒ Ⓓ
22. Ⓐ Ⓑ Ⓒ Ⓓ
23. Ⓐ Ⓑ Ⓒ Ⓓ
24. Ⓐ Ⓑ Ⓒ Ⓓ
25. Ⓐ Ⓑ Ⓒ Ⓓ
26. Ⓐ Ⓑ Ⓒ Ⓓ
27. Ⓐ Ⓑ Ⓒ Ⓓ
28. Ⓐ Ⓑ Ⓒ Ⓓ
29. Ⓐ Ⓑ Ⓒ Ⓓ
30. Ⓐ Ⓑ Ⓒ Ⓓ

31. Ⓐ Ⓑ Ⓒ Ⓓ
32. Ⓐ Ⓑ Ⓒ Ⓓ
33. Ⓐ Ⓑ Ⓒ Ⓓ
34. Ⓐ Ⓑ Ⓒ Ⓓ
35. Ⓐ Ⓑ Ⓒ Ⓓ
36. Ⓐ Ⓑ Ⓒ Ⓓ
37. Ⓐ Ⓑ Ⓒ Ⓓ

Section 3: Reading Comprehension

1. Ⓐ Ⓑ Ⓒ Ⓓ   9. Ⓐ Ⓑ Ⓒ Ⓓ   17. Ⓐ Ⓑ Ⓒ Ⓓ   25. Ⓐ Ⓑ Ⓒ Ⓓ   33. Ⓐ Ⓑ Ⓒ Ⓓ

2. Ⓐ Ⓑ Ⓒ Ⓓ   10. Ⓐ Ⓑ Ⓒ Ⓓ   18. Ⓐ Ⓑ Ⓒ Ⓓ   26. Ⓐ Ⓑ Ⓒ Ⓓ   34. Ⓐ Ⓑ Ⓒ Ⓓ

3. Ⓐ Ⓑ Ⓒ Ⓓ   11. Ⓐ Ⓑ Ⓒ Ⓓ   19. Ⓐ Ⓑ Ⓒ Ⓓ   27. Ⓐ Ⓑ Ⓒ Ⓓ   35. Ⓐ Ⓑ Ⓒ Ⓓ

4. Ⓐ Ⓑ Ⓒ Ⓓ   12. Ⓐ Ⓑ Ⓒ Ⓓ   20. Ⓐ Ⓑ Ⓒ Ⓓ   28. Ⓐ Ⓑ Ⓒ Ⓓ   36. Ⓐ Ⓑ Ⓒ Ⓓ

5. Ⓐ Ⓑ Ⓒ Ⓓ   13. Ⓐ Ⓑ Ⓒ Ⓓ   21. Ⓐ Ⓑ Ⓒ Ⓓ   29. Ⓐ Ⓑ Ⓒ Ⓓ

6. Ⓐ Ⓑ Ⓒ Ⓓ   14. Ⓐ Ⓑ Ⓒ Ⓓ   22. Ⓐ Ⓑ Ⓒ Ⓓ   30. Ⓐ Ⓑ Ⓒ Ⓓ

7. Ⓐ Ⓑ Ⓒ Ⓓ   15. Ⓐ Ⓑ Ⓒ Ⓓ   23. Ⓐ Ⓑ Ⓒ Ⓓ   31. Ⓐ Ⓑ Ⓒ Ⓓ

8. Ⓐ Ⓑ Ⓒ Ⓓ   16. Ⓐ Ⓑ Ⓒ Ⓓ   24. Ⓐ Ⓑ Ⓒ Ⓓ   32. Ⓐ Ⓑ Ⓒ Ⓓ

Section 4: Mathematics Achievement

1. Ⓐ Ⓑ Ⓒ Ⓓ   11. Ⓐ Ⓑ Ⓒ Ⓓ   21. Ⓐ Ⓑ Ⓒ Ⓓ   31. Ⓐ Ⓑ Ⓒ Ⓓ   41. Ⓐ Ⓑ Ⓒ Ⓓ

2. Ⓐ Ⓑ Ⓒ Ⓓ   12. Ⓐ Ⓑ Ⓒ Ⓓ   22. Ⓐ Ⓑ Ⓒ Ⓓ   32. Ⓐ Ⓑ Ⓒ Ⓓ   42. Ⓐ Ⓑ Ⓒ Ⓓ

3. Ⓐ Ⓑ Ⓒ Ⓓ   13. Ⓐ Ⓑ Ⓒ Ⓓ   23. Ⓐ Ⓑ Ⓒ Ⓓ   33. Ⓐ Ⓑ Ⓒ Ⓓ   43. Ⓐ Ⓑ Ⓒ Ⓓ

4. Ⓐ Ⓑ Ⓒ Ⓓ   14. Ⓐ Ⓑ Ⓒ Ⓓ   24. Ⓐ Ⓑ Ⓒ Ⓓ   34. Ⓐ Ⓑ Ⓒ Ⓓ   44. Ⓐ Ⓑ Ⓒ Ⓓ

5. Ⓐ Ⓑ Ⓒ Ⓓ   15. Ⓐ Ⓑ Ⓒ Ⓓ   25. Ⓐ Ⓑ Ⓒ Ⓓ   35. Ⓐ Ⓑ Ⓒ Ⓓ   45. Ⓐ Ⓑ Ⓒ Ⓓ

6. Ⓐ Ⓑ Ⓒ Ⓓ   16. Ⓐ Ⓑ Ⓒ Ⓓ   26. Ⓐ Ⓑ Ⓒ Ⓓ   36. Ⓐ Ⓑ Ⓒ Ⓓ   46. Ⓐ Ⓑ Ⓒ Ⓓ

7. Ⓐ Ⓑ Ⓒ Ⓓ   17. Ⓐ Ⓑ Ⓒ Ⓓ   27. Ⓐ Ⓑ Ⓒ Ⓓ   37. Ⓐ Ⓑ Ⓒ Ⓓ   47. Ⓐ Ⓑ Ⓒ Ⓓ

8. Ⓐ Ⓑ Ⓒ Ⓓ   18. Ⓐ Ⓑ Ⓒ Ⓓ   28. Ⓐ Ⓑ Ⓒ Ⓓ   38. Ⓐ Ⓑ Ⓒ Ⓓ

9. Ⓐ Ⓑ Ⓒ Ⓓ   19. Ⓐ Ⓑ Ⓒ Ⓓ   29. Ⓐ Ⓑ Ⓒ Ⓓ   39. Ⓐ Ⓑ Ⓒ Ⓓ

10. Ⓐ Ⓑ Ⓒ Ⓓ   20. Ⓐ Ⓑ Ⓒ Ⓓ   30. Ⓐ Ⓑ Ⓒ Ⓓ   40. Ⓐ Ⓑ Ⓒ Ⓓ

Section 5: Essay

Lined pages provided within test.

SECTION 1: VERBAL REASONING

40 Questions—20 Minutes

Directions: Each question in Part One consists of a word in captial letters followed by four answer choices. Select the one word that is most nearly the same in meaning as the word in captial letters.

---

1. IMPLIED

    A. acknowledged

    B. stated

    C. predicted

    D. hinted

2. FISCAL

    A. critical

    B. basic

    C. personal

    D. financial

3. STRINGENT

    A. demanding

    B. loud

    C. flexible

    D. clear

4. PERMEABLE

    A. penetrable

    B. durable

    C. unending

    D. allowable

5. SCRUPULOUS

    A. conscientious

    B. unprincipled

    C. intricate

    D. neurotic

6. STALEMATE

    A. pillar

    B. deadlock

    C. maneuver

    D. work slowdown

7. REDUNDANT

    A. concise

    B. reappearing

    C. superfluous

    D. lying down

8. SUPPLANT

    A. prune

    B. conquer

    C. uproot

    D. replace

9. COMMENSURATE

    A. identical

    B. of the same age

    C. proportionate

    D. measurable

10. ZENITH

    A. depths

    B. astronomical system

    C. peak

    D. solar system

11. SUCCOR

  A. assistance

  B. nurse

  C. vitality

  D. distress

12. DISPATCH

  A. omit mention of

  B. send out

  C. tear

  D. do without

13. PORTABLE

  A. drinkable

  B. convenient

  C. having wheels

  D. able to be carried

14. VERBOSE

  A. vague

  B. brief

  C. wordy

  D. verbal

15. SUBVERSIVE

  A. secret

  B. foreign

  C. evasive

  D. destructive

16. MALLEABLE

  A. changeable

  B. equalizing

  C. decisive

  D. progressing

17. PETTY

  A. lengthy

  B. communal

  C. small

  D. miscellaneous

18. INTREPID

  A. willing

  B. fanciful

  C. cowardly

  D. fearless

19. NEGOTIATE

  A. argue

  B. think

  C. speak

  D. bargain

20. STERILE

  A. antique

  B. germ-free

  C. unclean

  D. perishable

Directions: Each question in Part Two is made up of a sentence with one or two blanks. One blank indicates that one word is missing. Two blanks indicate that two words are missing. Each sentence is followed by four answer choices. Select the one word or pair of words that best completes the meaning of the sentence as a whole.

21. Undaunted by his many setbacks, Joshua _____.

    A. crumpled

    B. drew back

    C. canceled

    D. persevered

22. Nationwide, if college arts and science departments wish to attract new students, it will be necessary for them to undertake _____ measures.

    A. no

    B. puny

    C. innovative

    D. few

23. With less capital available and fewer deals being done, it has clearly become a(n) _____ market.

    A. heinous

    B. inflationary

    C. sellers'

    D. buyers'

24. The penalty for violating the law would _____ for multiple offenses.

    A. accede

    B. nullify

    C. diminish

    D. escalate

25. The hotel was a world-class _____ property and, thanks to recent refurbishing and clever marketing efforts, it is experiencing a _____.

    A. luxury ... renaissance

    B. communal ... withdrawal

    C. opulent ... decline

    D. decadent ... stalemate

26. Some colleges, rather than _____ students to take arts courses, simply force them.

    A. requiring

    B. enticing

    C. demanding

    D. allowing

27. Requiring _____ by the criminal to the victim would be a far better way of dealing with many lawbreakers than _____, she argued.

    A. punishment ... freedom

    B. imprisonment ... pardon

    C. restitution ... imprisonment

    D. mea culpa ... negligence

28. Knowledge gained from books without the benefit of practical experience is usually not so profitable in everyday work as the opposite, _____ without _____.

    A. culture ... manners

    B. experiments ... science

    C. experience ... scholarship

    D. learning ... knowing

29. To _____ some of its _____ over the huge increase in state insurance premiums for employees, the school district invited one insurance expert to speak at a recent board meeting.

    A. quell ... anxiety

    B. dispel ... myths

    C. aggravate ... nervousness

    D. foment ... trepidation

ISEE (UPPER LEVEL) PRACTICE TEST

30. While many people are indeed _____, poverty is _____ among the millions of older Americans who rely solely on Social Security.

   A. penurious ... rampant

   B. invalid ... abolished

   C. absolute ... widespread

   D. comfortable ... pervasive

31. An educator's _____ job is to teach students.

   A. primary

   B. only

   C. ostentatious

   D. ostensible

32. The candidate's inability to connect with middle-class voters was his greatest _____.

   A. virtue

   B. extinction

   C. shortcoming

   D. performance

33. Despite religious differences, the family _____ clashes by respecting each other's values.

   A. denied

   B. averted

   C. condescended

   D. declined

34. While marketing aimed at health-conscious consumers will _____ a restaurant change, it may also have an effect in supermarkets.

   A. denigrate

   B. cancel

   C. encourage

   D. emit

35. Despite the politician's overwhelming loss, she _____ her popularity with a small core of followers.

   A. revoked

   B. maintained

   C. restrained

   D. encouraged

36. The decision to seek therapeutic treatment is often provoked by a(n) _____, such as an arrest or a domestic dispute.

   A. dearth

   B. crisis

   C. enigma

   D. casualty

37. Knowing that any new business can _____, Tianna avoided investing in one even if the potential _____ was high.

   A. succeed ... down side

   B. reduce ... profit

   C. do well ... monies

   D. fail ... payoff

38. Because of the _____ caused by the flood, living conditions in the area have _____; many people have lost all their belongings.

   A. trepidation ... augmented

   B. morass ... careened

   C. devastation ... deteriorated

   D. vertigo ... ameliorated

39. The management is providing all needed building facilities to help the scientists _____ their research project.

   A. magnify

   B. discontinue

   C. relinquish

   D. implement

40. We can easily forgo a _____ we have never had, but once obtained it often is looked upon as being _____.

   A. requirement ... unusual

   B. gift ... useless

   C. comfort ... essential

   D. bonus ... unearned

END OF SECTION.
IF YOU HAVE ANY TIME LEFT, GO OVER YOUR WORK IN THIS SECTION ONLY.
DO NOT WORK IN ANY OTHER SECTION OF THE TEST.

SECTION 2: QUANTITATIVE REASONING

37 Questions—35 Minutes

Note: You may assume that all figures accompanying Quantitative Reasoning questions have been drawn as accurately as possible EXCEPT when it is specifically stated that a particular figure is not drawn to scale. Letters such as *x*, *y*, and *n* stand for real numbers. The Quantitative Reasoning Test includes two types of questions. There are separate directions for each type of question.

Directions: For questions 1–19, each question consists of a word problem followed by four answer choices. You may write in your test booklet; however, you may be able to solve many of these problems in your head. Next, look at the four answer choices given and select the best answer.

1. If the decimal point in a number is moved one place to the right, the number has been
   A. divided by 10.
   B. multiplied by 10.
   C. divided by 100.
   D. multiplied by 100.

2. What is the total number of degrees found in angles *A* and *C* in the triangle below?

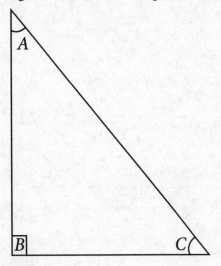

   A. 180°
   B. 100°
   C. 90°
   D. 75°

3. If $r + s = 3s$, then which expression is equal to *r*?
   A. *s*
   B. 2*s*
   C. 4*s*
   D. $3s^2$

4. Using exponents, write 329 in expanded form.
   A. $(3^2 \times 10) + (2 \times 10) + 9$
   B. $(3 \times 10^2) + (2 \times 10) + 9$
   C. $(3 \times 10^2) + (2 \times 10^2) + 9$
   D. $(3 \times 10^3) + (2 \times 10) + 9$

5. Find the circumference of a circle whose radius is 21 feet.
   A. 65.94 feet
   B. 132 feet
   C. 153 feet
   D. 1,769.4 feet

6. If $x > -4$, and $y < 2$, then $x \cap y$ includes
   A. −4, 0, 1, 2
   B. −2, −1, 1, 2
   C. 1, 2, 3, 4
   D. −3, −2, −1, 0, 1

7. $(6 \times 2) + (7 \times 3) = ?$

   A. $(6 \times 7) + (2 \times 3)$

   B. $(7 - 6) + (3 - 2)$

   C. $(7 \times 3) + (6 \times 2)$

   D. $(7 \times 3) \times (6 \times 2)$

8. Which of the following will substitute for x and make the statement below true?

   $56 - (7 - x) = 53$

   A. 4

   B. 3

   C. 2

   D. 1

9. An angle that is greater than 90° and less than 180° is a(n)

   A. acute angle.

   B. right angle.

   C. straight angle.

   D. obtuse angle.

10. What is the value of the expression $(2^2 + 4) + 2^2 (6 + 3)$?

    A. 21

    B. 35

    C. 44

    D. 56

11. $\dfrac{17}{30}$ is greater than

    A. $\dfrac{7}{8}$

    B. $\dfrac{9}{20}$

    C. $\dfrac{8}{11}$

    D. $\dfrac{20}{25}$

12. 1 centimeter equals what part of a meter?

    A. $\dfrac{1}{10}$

    B. $\dfrac{1}{100}$

    C. $\dfrac{1}{1,000}$

    D. $\dfrac{1}{10,000}$

13. What is the lowest common denominator for the fractions $\dfrac{3}{4}, \dfrac{6}{9}, \dfrac{8}{6}$, and $\dfrac{5}{12}$?

    A. 24

    B. 32

    C. 36

    D. 48

14. The set of common factors of 36 and 64 is

    A. {1, 2, 4}

    B. {1, 2, 3, 4}

    C. {1, 2, 4, 6, 18}

    D. {1, 2, 3, 4, 6}

15. If one angle of a triangle measures 115°, what is the sum of the other two angles?

    A. 245°

    B. 195°

    C. 75°

    D. 65°

16.

    $AB \cup BC =$

    A. $\overline{BD}$

    B. $\overline{BC}$

    C. $\overline{AD}$

    D. $\overline{AC}$

17. If a playing card is drawn from a standard deck, what are the chances it will be a 6?

 A. $\dfrac{1}{4}$

 B. $\dfrac{4}{13}$

 C. $\dfrac{1}{13}$

 D. $\dfrac{6}{52}$

18. The scale on a map is $\dfrac{1}{2}$" = 8 miles. If 2 towns are 28 miles apart, how many inches will separate them on a map?

 A. $1\dfrac{3}{4}$

 B. $1\dfrac{5}{8}$

 C. $1\dfrac{1}{2}$

 D. $1\dfrac{3}{8}$

19. A certain highway intersection has had A accidents over a 10-year period, resulting in B deaths. What is the yearly average death rate for the intersection?

 A. $A + B - 10$

 B. $\dfrac{B}{10}$

 C. $10 - \dfrac{A}{B}$

 D. $\dfrac{A}{10}$

ISEE (UPPER LEVEL) PRACTICE TEST

Directions: For questions 20–37, you are given quantitative comparisons between the quantities shown in Column A and Column B. Using the information given in each question, compare the quantity in Column A to the quantity in Column B, and choose one of these four answer choices:

A. The quantity in Column A is greater.

B. The quantity in Column B is greater.

C. The quantities are equal.

D. The relationship cannot be determined from the information given.

20. $x = -2$

Column A	Column B
$3x^2 + 2x - 1$	$x^3 + 2x^2 + 1$

21.

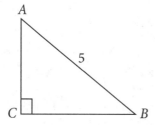

Column A	Column B
AC	BC

22.

Column A	Column B
$(16 \div 4) + (8 \times 2) - 8$	$(3 \times 4) + (10 \div 5) - 3$

23. A radio priced at $47.25 includes a 5% profit (based on cost).

Column A	Column B
$44.89	The original cost before profit

24. $a - b = -1$
               $-b - a = -3$

Column A	Column B
b	a

25. 25% of the 300 girls in the school have blonde hair.

Column A	Column B
The ratio of girls with blonde hair to those without blonde hair.	$\dfrac{1}{3}$

26.

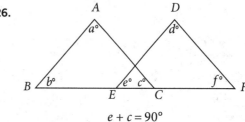

$e + c = 90°$

Column A	Column B
$b + a + d + f$	270

27.

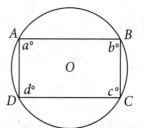

$ABCD$ is a parallelogram inscribed in circle O.

Column A	Column B
$a° + c°$	$b° + d°$

28.

Column A	Column B
Difference between $\dfrac{9}{8}$ and $\dfrac{3}{5}$	0.5

29.   A can do a job alone in 4 days.

B can do a job alone in 3 days.

Column A	Column B
The number of days it takes A and B working together to do the job	2 days

30. In a certain college, the ratio of the number of freshmen to the number of seniors is 3:1.

Column A	Column B
$\dfrac{1}{3}$	The ratio between the number of seniors and the total enrollment

31.

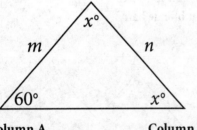

Column A	Column B
m	n

32. $a + b = x$
            $a - b = y$

Column A	Column B
x	y

33.

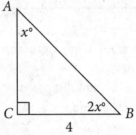

Column A	Column B
5	AB

34.

Column A	Column B
$\sqrt[3]{125}$	$\sqrt{25}$

35. $x > 0$

                              $y < 0$

Column A	Column B
$x - y$	$x + y$

36. During a store sale, a $43.50 radio can be purchased at a 15% discount.

Column A	Column B
The selling price of the radio with the discount	$36

37.

Column A	Column B
75% of $\dfrac{1}{2}$	50% of $\dfrac{3}{4}$

END OF SECTION.
IF YOU HAVE ANY TIME LEFT, GO OVER YOUR WORK IN THIS SECTION ONLY.
DO NOT WORK IN ANY OTHER SECTION OF THE TEST.

SECTION 3: READING COMPREHENSION

36 Questions—35 Minutes

Directions: Each passage is followed by six questions based on its content. Answer the questions following each passage on the basis of what is <u>stated</u> or <u>implied</u> in that passage. You may write in your test booklet.

Questions 1–6 refer to the following passage.

In the summer of 2021, during a mission to excavate sections of the ancient Mayan city, Palenque, archeologists found a partial visage of an ancient statue in which a chin, nose, and parted mouth are visible. In 2022, researchers from Mexico's National Institute of Anthropology and History (INAH) asserted that the partial statue shows the likeness of Hun Hunahpu, the Mayan god associated with maize.

Maize, or corn, is indigenous to the areas of Central America the Maya had inhabited. It was not only a staple of the Mayan diet but also a critical symbol of the Maya people's spiritual relationship with the earth. Perhaps most importantly, the Mayans believed that humankind itself had come from maize, since their creation folklore included the idea that humans had been <u>fashioned</u> by the gods using white and yellow corn. In short, maize was linked to virtually all aspects of Mesoamerican culture.

Because of the god's association with such an important resource, the Maya worshipped Hun Hunahpu devoutly. Beliefs associated with Hun Hunahpu include the idea that every autumn, when the harvest came, the god would be decapitated, only to be reborn when spring came. This deep connection to the cycle of life and death as well as the changing of the seasons meant both Hun Hunahpu and the maize with which they were associated were central to Mayan concepts of time itself.

The discovery of this partial statue in Palenque was momentous for researchers in that it is the first of its magnitude from the dig site. Archaeologists believe the stucco statue comes from the Late Classic Period, which would place its origin somewhere between 600 and 900 C.E. The statue was found in a preserved pond area likely devoted to Hun Hunahpu, who researchers identified based on the maize-like appearance of the statue's visible hair and the items discovered nearby the statue. The statue's head also appeared to be intentionally separated from the original statue's body, suggesting it depicted Hun Hunahpu in the decapitated state. Researchers also believe that the statue's placement was important; its gaze would have aligned with rows of maize at dawn and its orientation at the foot of a pond likely signified the deity's close relationship with the underworld.

1. As used in paragraph 2, the underlined term *fashioned* most nearly means

   A. illustrated.
   B. created.
   C. imagined.
   D. destroyed.

2. All the following statements are true of the Mayans' beliefs about Hun Hunahpu EXCEPT that the god

   A. would be decapitated every autumn.
   B. maintained a close relationship with the underworld.
   C. oversaw the wellbeing of maize crops.
   D. thrived in a water-based environment.

3. If this passage were a newspaper article, what would be the *most suitable* title for the article?

   A. "The History of Maize in Palenque"

   B. "Mayan Gods"

   C. "The Role of Hair in Mayan Worship"

   D. "New Archeological Findings on Hun Hunahpu, the Mayan God of Maize"

4. We can infer from the passage that

   A. Palenque was an important city in Mayan culture.

   B. the Mayans only ate maize.

   C. Hun Hunahpu was a violent god.

   D. archaeological digs are too expensive.

5. Which of the following pieces of information about Mayan culture would be the *most logical* addition to this passage?

   A. The Maya started cultivating maize seeds sometime around 2500 B.C.

   B. The concept of "zero" was invented by the Maya.

   C. There were at least 60 cities built by the Maya.

   D. Most of the buildings that archaeologists associate with the Maya were completed without metal tools.

6. The overall tone of this passage is

   A. dispassionate.

   B. intense.

   C. informative.

   D. jaded.

Questions 7–12 refer to the following passage.

SNOWY MOUNTAINS

Higher and still more high,
Palaces made for cloud,
Above the <u>dingy</u> city-roofs
Blue-white like angels with broad wings,
Pillars of the sky at rest
The mountains from the great plateau
Uprise.

But the world heeds them not;
They have been here now for too long a time.
The world makes war on them,
Tunnels their granite cliffs,
Splits down their shining sides,
<u>Plasters</u> their cliffs with soap-advertisements,
Destroys the lonely fragments of their peace.

Vaster and still more vast,
Peak after peak, pile after pile,
Wilderness still untamed,
To which the future is as was the past,
Barrier spread by Gods,
Sunning their shining foreheads,
Barrier broken down by those who do not need
The joy of time-resisting storm-worn stone,
The mountains swing along
The south horizon of the sky;
Welcoming with wide floors of blue-green ice
The mists that dance and drive before the sun.

—John Gould Fletcher (1922)

7. As used in the poem's first stanza, the underlined term *dingy* most nearly means

   A. drab.

   B. modern.

   C. floating.

   D. stunning.

8. In the final two lines of the poem, in stanza 3, who or what is doing the "welcoming"?

   A. The author, John Gould Fletcher

   B. The mountains

   C. Arctic birds

   D. The town at the foot of the mountain

9. Which of the following quotes shows personification?

   A. "Palaces made for cloud" from stanza 1

   B. "They have been here now for too long a time" from stanza 2

   C. "Peak after peak, pile after pile" from stanza 3

   D. "Sunning their shining foreheads" from stanza 3

10. As used in stanza 2, the underlined term *plasters* most nearly means

    A. covers.

    B. uncovers.

    C. illustrates.

    D. reconstructs.

11. The purpose of stanza 2 is to

    A. illustrate how the mountains change from morning to evening.

    B. illustrate how the mountains change from season to season.

    C. discuss how humans have positively impacted the mountain landscape.

    D. discuss how humans have negatively impacted the mountain landscape.

12. We can infer from stanza 2 that the speaker

    A. believes the expansion of human life into the natural world is necessary.

    B. believes human expansion into nature has been a detrimental thing.

    C. grew up at the base of the mountains being described.

    D. is seeing snow-capped mountains for the very first time.

Questions 13–18 refer to the following passage.

Back in 1992, Mae Jemison became the first African American woman to ever travel to space. Having trained as a doctor, engineer, and NASA astronaut, Jemison was more than ready for the job. In fact, it was the culmination of a dream she had had ever since she was a child, back when she used to idolize Lieutenant Uhura on *Star Trek*, who was played by an equally groundbreaking African American woman named Nichelle Nichols.

Despite the discrimination she experienced throughout her education, particularly later when she was often the only woman or African American student in some of her graduate school classes, Jemison pushed through to achieve her dreams. While completing her undergraduate education at Stanford University and later attending Cornell Medical School, Jemison also somehow found time to engage in charitable work. For instance, she led medical studies in Cuba and assisted at a refugee camp in Cambodia. After graduating, she spent two years with the Peace Corps working as a medical officer in Africa.

It wasn't until 1983, when Sally Ride became the first American woman in space, that Jemison truly set her sights on NASA. She applied a few times to the astronaut program before finally being accepted in 1987. After two years of <u>rigorous</u> training, Jemison was slated to join the STS-47 crew, who would head to space in 1992 aboard the space shuttle *Endeavour*.

Jemison retired from NASA in 1993, but her space adventures weren't over. After hearing about how inspired Jemison was by Lieutenant Uhura growing up and that she was such a huge fan of the show, actor LeVar Burton invited Jemison to be the first real-life astronaut to ever appear in an episode of *Star Trek: The Next Generation*. She also went on to create a summer camp for children interested in space and wrote a children's book about her own life story called *Find Where the Wind Goes* in 2001.

13. Nichelle Nichols was a famous

   A. astronaut.

   B. actress.

   C. engineer.

   D. doctor.

14. The primary purpose of this passage is to

   A. advocate for more women astronauts.

   B. discuss the barriers Black women face pursuing careers in medicine.

   C. offer a biographical summary of astronaut Mae Jemison's accomplishments.

   D. compare Sally Ride's and Mae Jemison's experiences at NASA.

15. As used in paragraph 3, the underlined term *rigorous* most nearly means

   A. tough.

   B. gentle.

   C. planned.

   D. unintentional.

16. We can infer from the passage that

   A. no Black women have been to space since Mae Jemison.

   B. it is easier to become an astronaut than a doctor.

   C. it takes more than a year for astronauts selected for a mission to prepare to go to space.

   D. philanthropy is an important part of becoming an astronaut.

17. The purpose of the final line in the passage is to

    A. summarize what Jemison has been doing since she retired.

    B. show how astronauts are important role models for children.

    C. discuss potential career paths for former astronauts.

    D. lament the end of the space shuttle program.

18. In paragraph 4, by saying "[Jemison's] space adventures weren't over" after her 1993 NASA retirement, the author is setting up the idea that

    A. she got cast to play Lieutenant Uhura.

    B. Jemison got to fulfill a further space-related dream by appearing on *Star Trek: The Next Generation*.

    C. she would eventually be placed on another NASA mission.

    D. Jemison was nostalgic for her time at NASA.

Questions 19–24 refer to the following passage.

It was July 1916 when Hugo Ball, Emmy Hennings, Tristan Tzara, Jean Arp, Sophie Taeuber-Arp, and a few others first gathered at the Cabaret Voltaire in Zurich, Switzerland. What began that night as a series of performances between friends would later evolve and come to be known as Dada, an art movement focused on not making "art" at all.

The evening of that first gathering, the group's de facto leader, Hugo Ball, who had conceived of the event, read from the *Dada Manifesto*. He declared, "Dada is a new tendency in art," and that "Dada comes from the dictionary. It is terribly simple. In French, it means 'hobby horse.' In German, it means 'good-bye,' 'Get off my back,' and 'Be seeing you sometime.' In Romanian, it means, 'Yes, indeed, you are right, that's it. But of course, yes, definitely right.'" What Ball was trying to say is that the word *dada* means both everything and nothing, or rather, that it can mean whatever it means to each person. If one person hears "dada" and thinks "father" and another hears it and thinks of the word "data," both are right.

This idea of coincidence, chance, and nonsense commingling with chaos and questions of meaning and meaninglessness was central to Dada art, as was the idea that people should question what makes something a piece of art to begin with. These ideas manifested as sound poems composed entirely of nonsense syllables, geometric masks meant to mimic ideas of primitivism from around the world, largely improvised dances that would later inspire much of the modern dance movement, and early experimental works of photography and cinema.

Later, in the New York iteration of Dada, Marcel Duchamp created what have become some of the most recognizable examples of Dada art. Generally referred to as "readymades," these were sculptures created from everyday objects. The first one Duchamp created involved a bicycle wheel mounted to a stool. The object had no use value since it could be used neither as a bicycle wheel nor a stool; its purpose was simply to exist as an art object. Duchamp later pushed this idea further by installing a urinal on the wall of a museum and signing it "R. Mutt 1917." This work, titled *Fountain*, toys with the question of what makes something art to begin with. Did Duchamp truly make a piece of art by doing something like jotting an artist's signature on a urinal and hanging it on the wall of a museum, or was it just a urinal with graffiti on it? Getting people to ask themselves this and similar questions was precisely the purpose of both the readymade and Dada art more generally.

19. By describing Hugo Ball as Dada's "de facto leader," the author of the passage most nearly means that

   A. different artists took turns leading the movement.

   B. no one was ever a leader in Dada.

   C. there was no official leader, but Hugo Ball took on the role unofficially.

   D. Hugo Ball had been elected to lead by the others.

20. We can infer from the passage that

   A. the Dada movement is dedicated to making art.

   B. Hugo Ball intended for the Dada movement to spread worldwide.

   C. Hugo Ball was most proud of his art piece titled *Fountain*.

   D. the Dada movement spread beyond its starting point in Zurich, Switzerland.

21. A readymade is a type of art that

   A. can be used in more than one way.

   B. is composed entirely of trash.

   C. invites the viewer to question whether it's really art.

   D. is composed entirely of nonsense syllables.

22. As an art movement, Dada was primarily interested in

   A. finding a way to notate ephemeral events, like improvisational dance.

   B. modernizing primitive sculpture and costumes.

   C. questions about the difference between photography and painting.

   D. chaos, chance, and the question of meaning vs. meaninglessness.

23. Let's say the author wants to add a new paragraph between paragraphs 2 and 3. Which of the following would be a logical topic for this hypothetical new paragraph?

   A. Surrealism in the work of Pablo Picasso

   B. Tristan Tzara's "Dada Manifesto 1918"

   C. The influence of Dada on Fluxus art in the 1960s

   D. The influence of Futurism and Expressionism on the creation of Dada

24. All the following terms adequately describe the author's tone in this passage EXCEPT:

   A. Pretentious

   B. Thoughtful

   C. Objective

   D. Impartial

Questions 25–30 refer to the following passage.

If you've been finding yourself feeling out of sorts, stressed, depressed, or even just like you're in a funk, you may have a helpful balm to soothe your troubles right at home. Increasingly, scientific studies are showing that tending to and being surrounded by houseplants can make a positive impact on a person's general outlook and mood.

   As Professor Mengmeng Gu of Texas A&M University tells the *Washington Post*, "Different properties of plants, such as how they look, smell, and feel, impact us in so many ways…They can feel good to the touch, make a space more fragrant, and please our eyes." Horticultural scientists like Gu have been analyzing the relationship between humans and houseplants for decades and have unearthed a series of powerful insights, most notably surrounding the way indoor plants can positively impact a person's frame of mind.

For one, the connection humans feel with plants seems to be primal and instinctual, not the least of reasons being that plants are oxygen-producers who feed on the carbon dioxide animals breathe out, a mutually beneficial relationship ingrained as one of the primary building blocks of biology itself. Beyond this fundamental connection, though, a concept known as the "biophilia hypothesis" asserts that when people inhabit environments cut off from natural elements like plants, they suffer as a result. This means that urban dwellers stuck in concrete jungles would do well to bring as many houseplants into their apartments as they like. The biophilia hypothesis even supports the idea that being in and around nature can aid human healing processes, both physically and psychologically.

Plants have a huge impact on our mood, too. One study showed that when young people spend time tending to plants, it had a repressing effect on signals of stress in their bodies, such as by reducing high blood pressure. Plants are also known to provide people with a sense of visual escape from their everyday lives. Imagine, for instance, that you're stuck in a dreary office environment and looking at a computer screen all day. Taking a few moments to admire the fern on your desk might then give you a moment of reprieve from the environment and provide a spot of tranquility. The smell, feel, and sight of plants have also all been shown to improve a person's overall <u>disposition</u>.

Citation: Das, Lala Tammoy. 2022. Review of *What Science Tells Us about the Mood-Boosting Effects of Indoor Plants. Washington Post*, June 6, 2022. https://www.washingtonpost.com/wellness/2022/06/06/how-houseplants-can-boost-your-mood/.

25. When the author says "you may have a helpful balm to soothe your troubles right at home" in paragraph 1, the "balm" is a figurative way of referring to

A. houseplants.

B. fresh-cut flowers.

C. planting a garden.

D. cooking with homegrown vegetables.

26. In which of the four paragraphs can you find the author appealing to credibility by citing an authority?

A. Paragraph 1

B. Paragraph 2

C. Paragraph 3

D. Paragraph 4

27. What is the main idea of this passage?

A. Taking care of houseplants is an expensive hobby.

B. People should spend more time enjoying the benefits of nature.

C. Houseplants can cure depression and other mental health disorders.

D. Studies have shown a positive correlation between taking care of houseplants and improved mood.

28. The biophilia hypothesis states that

A. when people are surrounded by plants, their mood improves.

B. when people are in environments that don't have plants, their mood suffers.

C. plants need to be around people to thrive.

D. plants don't do as well when sharing space with humans.

29. As used at the end of paragraph 4, the underlined term *disposition* most nearly means

A. temperament.

B. appearance.

C. sense of humor.

D. health.

30. We can infer from the passage that

A. the more plants a person has, the happier they are.

B. plants can cure diseases.

C. plants may be able to help alleviate sadness after a breakup.

D. certain plants are better at improving a person's mood.

Questions 31–36 refer to the following passage.

Most cultures have some form of ritual, ceremony, or festival meant to celebrate the joining of two people as long-term romantic mates. In the US, enduring customs around weddings include purchasing an engagement ring, tossing the bouquet, cutting the cake as a couple, having a first dance, or even making sure you have "something old, something new, something borrowed, and something blue" for good luck. The idea is that by partaking in these traditions, you are following in the footsteps of those who came before you and bringing good tidings to your new start as a married couple.

Outside the US, there are <u>myriad</u> other cultural wedding traditions. One common type involves rituals to ward off evil spirits. In Germany, ahead of a wedding, guests will throw porcelain dishes on the ground to scare off spirits during an evening called a "Polterabend." In Norway, brides believe that sporting elaborate gold and silver crowns with noisy charms and reflective accents does the trick. Armenian couples place lavash flatbread on their shoulders to keep the spirits at bay, while in Scotland, newlyweds are covered in molasses, feathers, grass, or anything else that's messy to make them less attractive to nefarious forces. It's also said that if an Irish bride wants to avoid being kidnapped by evil faeries, she must keep one foot on the dance floor during her entire first dance.

Other practices are about bringing good luck to the newlyweds. In China, this means hiring a woman to attend to the bride as she travels to the wedding. Venezuelan couples will sneak away before the reception is over; if they can do so without being caught, it's considered very fortuitous! In other cultures, good luck wedding rituals are loaded with symbolic meanings. For instance, in Wales, the bride will offer a cutting of myrtle from her own bouquet to each bridesmaid as a symbol of love.

Generating spending money for the newlyweds is another common cause for wedding rituals. In Spain, the groom's friends cut his tie into pieces and then auction the pieces off to make money for the couple. In Canada, the siblings of the newlyweds will perform a dance in colorful, whimsical socks while guests toss cash for the couple's honeymoon at them. Similarly, in Cuba, any man who requests a dance with the bride must pin some money for the honeymoon fund onto her dress.

31. As used in paragraph 2, the underlined term *myriad* most nearly means

    A. few.

    B. countless.

    C. rarely.

    D. often.

32. The passage mentions all the following types of wedding rituals EXCEPT:

    A. Good luck rituals

    B. Rituals to generate cash for the couple

    C. Rituals to ward off spirits

    D. Rituals to ensure long life

33. The author of this passage organizes their argument by grouping wedding customs according to

    A. how old they are.

    B. where in the world they're practiced.

    C. the purpose of the custom.

    D. who performs the custom.

34. Which of the following is the *most appropriate* title for this passage?

    A. "Wedding Customs from Around the World"

    B. "The Romance of Weddings"

    C. "Weddings Outside the US"

    D. "The History of Wedding Traditions"

35. We can infer from the passage that

    A. multiple cultures around the world have traditionally believed in the existence of evil spirits.

    B. wedding traditions are fairly homogeneous overall.

    C. people who get married always ask their wedding guests for money.

    D. wedding traditions are always religious in nature.

36. Of the following options, which term *best describes* the author's tone in this passage?

    A. Cautionary

    B. Critical

    C. Celebratory

    D. Compliant

END OF SECTION.
IF YOU HAVE ANY TIME LEFT, GO OVER YOUR WORK IN THIS SECTION ONLY.
DO NOT WORK IN ANY OTHER SECTION OF THE TEST.

SECTION 4: MATHEMATICS ACHIEVEMENT

47 Questions—40 Minutes

Directions: Each question is followed by four suggested answers. Read each question and then decide which one of the four suggested answers is best.

---

1. A recipe for 6 quarts of punch calls for $\frac{3}{4}$ cup of sugar. How much sugar is needed for 9 quarts of punch?

   A. $\frac{5}{8}$ cup

   B. $\frac{7}{8}$ cup

   C. $1\frac{1}{8}$ cups

   D. $2\frac{1}{4}$ cups

2. How many yards of ribbon will it take to make 45 badges if each badge uses 4 inches of ribbon?

   A. 5

   B. 9

   C. 11

   D. 15

3. As an employee at a clothing store, you are entitled to a 10% discount on all purchases. When the store has a sale, employees are also entitled to an additional 20% discount offered to all customers. What would you have to pay for a $60 jacket bought on a sale day?

   A. $6

   B. $10.80

   C. $36

   D. $43.20

4. A section of pavement that is 10 feet long and 8 feet wide contains how many square feet?

   A. 18 sq. ft.

   B. 80 sq. ft.

   C. 92 sq. ft.

   D. 800 sq. ft.

5. The decimal number 0.375 is equivalent to which of the following?

   A. $0.3\overline{75}$

   B. $0.\overline{3}$

   C. $\frac{6}{9}$

   D. $\frac{3}{8}$

6. A baseball team lost exactly 20% of the games it played last season. If the team lost 30 games, how many games did it play?

   A. 50

   B. 110

   C. 120

   D. 150

7. What is the value of x when $5x = 5 \times 4 \times 2 \times 0$?

   A. 8

   B. 6

   C. 1

   D. 0

8. A particular store has a 100% markup from wholesale to retail prices. A dress that costs $130 retail will cost how much wholesale?

   A. $260

   B. $100

   C. $90

   D. $65

9. The scale used on a blueprint is $\frac{1}{8}" = 1$ foot. If a room is actually $17' \times 22'$ how large will it be on the drawing?

   A. $1\frac{1}{8}" \times 2\frac{1}{4}"$

   B. $2\frac{1}{8}" \times 2\frac{3}{4}"$

   C. $2\frac{1}{2}" \times 3"$

   D. $2\frac{3}{4}" \times 3\frac{1}{8}"$

10. A roll of carpeting contains 90 square feet of carpet. How many rolls will be required to carpet a room $28' \times 20'$?

    A. $6\frac{2}{9}$

    B. 6

    C. $5\frac{8}{9}$

    D. $5\frac{3}{8}$

11. $100 - x = 5^2$. What is the value of x?

    A. 75

    B. 50

    C. 25

    D. 5

12. If $72x = 6y$, and $y = 2$, $x =$

    A. $\frac{1}{2}$

    B. $\frac{1}{6}$

    C. 6

    D. 12

13.   60 hr.   21 min.
    $-$ 5 hr.   37 min.
    _____

    A. 54 hr. 44 min.

    B. 54 hr. 84 min.

    C. 55 hr. 44 min.

    D. 55 hr. 84 min.

14. Which of the following represents one half of a certain number squared, minus 6?

    A. $6 = \frac{1}{2}x^2$

    B. $\frac{1}{2}x - 6$

    C. $\dfrac{x^2}{\frac{1}{2}} - 6$

    D. $\frac{1}{2}x^2 - 6$

15. A mixture contains 20 gallons of water and 5 gallons of nitric acid. If 10 more gallons of water are added, the part that is water is

    A. $\frac{1}{7}$

    B. $\frac{2}{9}$

    C. $\frac{1}{4}$

    D. $\frac{6}{7}$

16. Which is the longest time?

    A. $\frac{1}{24}$ of a day

    B. $1\frac{1}{2}$ hours

    C. 100 minutes

    D. $\frac{1}{30}$ of a month

17. What percentage of a circle graph would be represented by a portion having a right angle?

    A. 90%

    B. 45%

    C. 25%

    D. 20%

18. Which expression is equivalent to the expression $(z + 7)(z - 7)$?

    A. $z^2 - 49$

    B. $z^2 + 49$

    C. $z^2 - 14z - 49$

    D. $z^2 + 14z - 49$

19. Find the perimeter of a rectangle with the dimensions $115' \times 63'$.

    A. 7,245'

    B. 356'

    C. 187'

    D. 178'

20. $6.28 \times 1.003 =$

    A. 0.629884

    B. 6.29884

    C. 62.9442

    D. 629.884

21. Solve for x: $\dfrac{x^2}{2.5} = 10$.

    A. ± 5

    B. ± 10

    C. ± 20

    D. ± 25

22. If Mr. Green borrowed $2,000 at 12% simple interest for two years, what would the total interest charge be?

    A. $240

    B. $360

    C. $420

    D. $480

23. The pup tent shown is 3 feet wide and 2 feet high. Find its volume if it is 6 feet long.

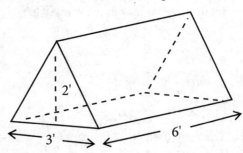

    A. 36 sq. ft.

    B. 18 cu. ft.

    C. 24 cu. ft.

    D. 36 cu. ft.

24. A board 30' long is cut into three unequal parts. The first is three times as long as the second. The third is twice as long as the first. How long is the longest piece?

    A. 6'

    B. 9'

    C. 12'

    D. 18'

25. A wine merchant has 32 gallons of wine worth $1.50 a gallon. If she wishes to reduce the price to $1.20 a gallon, how many gallons of water must she add?

    A. 10

    B. 9

    C. 8

    D. 7

26. Six is four more than $\dfrac{2}{3}$ of what number?

    A. 1

    B. 3

    C. 4

    D. 6

27. The winner of a race received $\frac{1}{3}$ of the total purse. The third-place finisher received one third of the winner's share. If the winner's share was $2,700, what was the total purse?

A. $8,100

B. $2,700

C. $1,800

D. $900

28. Two cars start toward each other along a straight road between two cities that are 450 miles apart. The speed of the first car is 35 mph, and that of the second is 48 mph. How much time will elapse before they meet?

A. 6.01 hours

B. 5.42 hours

C. 5.25 hours

D. 4.98 hours

29. A stock clerk had 600 brake pads on hand. He then issued $\frac{3}{8}$ of his supply of brake pads to Division X, $\frac{1}{4}$ to Division Y, and $\frac{1}{6}$ to Division Z. The number of brake pads remaining in stock is

A. 48

B. 125

C. 240

D. 475

30. One person can load a truck in 25 minutes, a second can load it in 50 minutes, and a third can load it in 10 minutes. How long would it take the three together to load the truck?

A. $5\frac{3}{11}$ minutes

B. $6\frac{1}{4}$ minutes

C. $8\frac{1}{3}$ minutes

D. 10 minutes

31. If $4x - y = 20$, and $2x + y = 28$, then $x =$

A. 24

B. 16

C. 8

D. 6

32. If $6 + x + y = 20$, and $x + y = k$, then $20 - k =$

A. 0

B. 6

C. 14

D. 20

33.

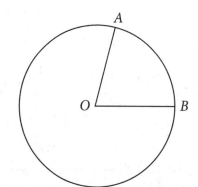

In the figure above, m$\angle AOB = 60°$. If O is the center of the circle, then minor arc AB is what part of the circumference of the circle?

A. $\frac{1}{2}$

B. $\frac{1}{3}$

C. $\frac{1}{6}$

D. $\frac{1}{8}$

34. If all P are S and no S are Q, it necessarily follows that

A. all Q are S.

B. all Q are P.

C. no P are Q.

D. no S are P.

35. *A* is older than *B*. With the passage of time the

    A. ratio of the ages of *A* and *B* remains unchanged.

    B. ratio of the ages of *A* and *B* increases.

    C. ratio of the ages of *A* and *B* decreases.

    D. difference in their ages varies.

36. From a temperature of 15°, a drop of 21° would result in a temperature of

    A. 36°

    B. −6°

    C. −30°

    D. −36°

37.

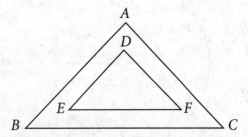

In the figure above, the sides of △*ABC* are respectively parallel to the sides of △*DEF*. If the complement of *A* is 40°, what is the complement of *D*?

    A. 20°

    B. 40°

    C. 50°

    D. 60°

38. A line of print in a magazine article contains an average of 6 words. There are 5 lines to the inch. If 8 inches are available for an article that contains 270 words, how must the article be changed?

    A. Add 30 words.

    B. Delete 30 words.

    C. Delete 40 words.

    D. Add 60 words.

39.

The area of triangle *R* is 3 times triangle *S*. The area of triangle *S* is 3 times triangle *T*. If the area of triangle *S* = 1, what is the sum of the areas of the three triangles?

    A. $2\dfrac{1}{3}$

    B. $3\dfrac{1}{3}$

    C. $4\dfrac{1}{3}$

    D. 6

40. If 5 pints of water are needed to water each square foot of lawn, the minimum gallons of water needed for a lawn 8′ × 12′ is

    A. 5

    B. 20

    C. 40

    D. 60

41. In the formula $l = p + prt$, what does *l* equal when $p = 500$, $r = 20\%$, and $t = 2$?

    A. 700

    B. 8,000

    C. 10,000

    D. 12,000

42. A car owner finds he needs 12 gallons of gas for each 120 miles he drives. If he has his carburetor adjusted, he will need only 80% as much gas. How many miles will 12 gallons of gas then last him?

    A. 90

    B. 96

    C. 150

    D. 160

43. What is the maximum number of books, each $\frac{1}{4}$ inch thick, that can be placed standing on a shelf that is 4 feet long?

   A. 16

   B. 48

   C. 96

   D. 192

44. In a bag, there are red, green, black, and white marbles. If there are 6 red, 8 green, 4 black, and 12 white, and one marble is to be selected at random, what is the probability it will be white?

   A. $\frac{1}{5}$

   B. $\frac{2}{5}$

   C. $\frac{2}{15}$

   D. $\frac{4}{15}$

45.

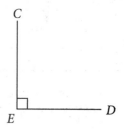

In the diagram above, $\overline{CE} \perp \overline{ED}$. If $CE = 7$ and $ED = 6$, what is the shortest distance from C to D?

   A. 6

   B. 7

   C. $\sqrt{85}$

   D. $4\sqrt{12}$

46. If $a = 3$, then $a^a \times a =$

   A. 9.

   B. 18.

   C. 51.

   D. 81.

47. $(3 + 2)(6 - 2)(7 + 1) = (4 + 4)(x)$. What is the value of x?

   A. $13 + 2$

   B. $14 + 4$

   C. $4 + 15$

   D. $8 + 12$

END OF SECTION.
IF YOU HAVE ANY TIME LEFT, GO OVER YOUR WORK IN THIS SECTION ONLY.
DO NOT WORK IN ANY OTHER SECTION OF THE TEST.

SECTION 5: ESSAY

30 Minutes

Directions: You will have 30 minutes to plan and write an essay on the following topic. Do not write on another topic. An essay on another topic is not acceptable.

The essay is designed to give you an opportunity to show how well you can write. You should try to express your thoughts clearly. How well you write is much more important than how much you write, but you need to say enough for a reader to understand what you mean.

You will probably want to write more than a short paragraph. You should also be aware that a copy of your essay will be sent to each school that will be receiving your test results. Please write or print so that your writing may be read by someone who is not familiar with your handwriting.

You may make notes and plan your essay. Allow enough time to copy the prompt onto the first two lines of your answer sheet. Please remember to write your response in blue or black pen. Again, you may use cursive writing or you may print.

Topic: Talk about one extracurricular activity in which you hope to participate in high school. Give reasons why you have chosen this activity.

ANSWER KEYS AND EXPLANATIONS

Section 1: Verbal Reasoning

1. D	9. C	17. C	25. A	33. B
2. D	10. C	18. D	26. B	34. C
3. A	11. A	19. D	27. C	35. B
4. A	12. B	20. B	28. C	36. B
5. A	13. D	21. D	29. A	37. D
6. B	14. C	22. C	30. D	38. C
7. C	15. D	23. D	31. A	39. D
8. D	16. A	24. D	32. C	40. C

1. **The correct answer is D.** The verb *imply* means "to indicate indirectly, to suggest, or to hint."

2. **The correct answer is D.** That which is fiscal has to do with money. *Financial* is a synonym for fiscal.

3. **The correct answer is A.** *Stringent* means "rigidly controlled, strict, or severe." The term *demanding* is closest in meaning.

4. **The correct answer is A.** That which is permeable can be penetrated, especially by fluids.

5. **The correct answer is A.** *Scrupulous* means "careful to do the right, proper, or correct thing in every detail." *Conscientious* means "meticulous" and "careful."

6. **The correct answer is B.** A stalemate is a deadlock or impasse.

7. **The correct answer is C.** *Redundant* means "more than necessary or superfluous."

8. **The correct answer is D.** To supplant is to "supersede" or "replace."

9. **The correct answer is C.** *Commensurate* means "proportionate."

10. **The correct answer is C.** The zenith is "the point directly overhead or the highest point." A peak is the highest point of a roof, hill, or mountain.

11. **The correct answer is A.** *Succor* is "aid, help, or relief." To provide assistance is to help.

12. **The correct answer is B.** To dispatch is to "send out quickly."

13. **The correct answer is D.** *Portable* means "easily moved or carried." The word meaning "drinkable" is *potable*.

14. **The correct answer is C.** *Verbose* means "containing too many words or long-winded."

15. **The correct answer is D.** *Subversive* means "seeking to overthrow or to destroy something established."

16. **The correct answer is A.** That which is malleable tends to be changeable.

17. **The correct answer is C.** *Petty* means "trivial, narrow, or small."

18. **The correct answer is D.** *Intrepid* means "bold, brave, and fearless."

19. **The correct answer is D.** To negotiate is to "make arrangements" or "bargain."

20. **The correct answer is B.** *Sterile* means "extremely clean, barren, or germ-free."

21. **The correct answer is D.** Since Joshua was undaunted (not discouraged) by his failures, a positive word is necessary. *Persevered* is the only positive word.

22. **The correct answer is C.** In order to attract students, innovative (new, novel) methods are necessary.

23. **The correct answer is D.** Since there is less money available and fewer business transactions are being conducted, buyers have the upper hand in how they spend their money.

24. **The correct answer is D.** Multiple offenses would require an increased penalty; therefore, *escalate* is the only correct choice.

25. **The correct answer is A.** All the adjectives describing the hotel are positive; therefore, a positive description is necessary.

26. **The correct answer is B.** The opposite of forcing students to take courses is enticing them to do so.

27. **The correct answer is C.** An innovative method of dealing with criminals is being suggested in contrast to the usual method, which is imprisonment.

28. **The correct answer is C.** The sentence mentions "knowledge gained without experience" and then asks for the opposite condition, which must be experience without scholarship.

29. **The correct answer is A.** By having an insurance expert discuss the changes, the school system was attempting to reduce, or quell, anxiety over those increased fees.

30. **The correct answer is D.** The first half of the sentence requires a word that contrasts with poverty (*comfortable*). The second word must show that poverty is widespread among older Americans.

31. **The correct answer is A.** An educator's job is to teach students, but that is not the educator's only job, just their primary job.

32. **The correct answer is C.** An inability to appeal to a certain voting group would be a shortcoming for a candidate.

33. **The correct answer is B.** The fact that the family respected one another means that they averted clashes.

34. **The correct answer is C.** Health-conscious marketing will encourage a change in consumer behavior, such as by influencing restaurant choice.

35. **The correct answer is B.** Although the politician lost the election, she maintained her popularity with some followers.

36. **The correct answer is B.** An arrest or domestic dispute is considered a serious crisis.

37. **The correct answer is D.** A negative word (*fail*) must be followed by a positive word (*payoff*).

38. **The correct answer is C.** A flood that destroys people's belongings causes devastation. Living conditions in the area can be said to have deteriorated (worsened).

39. **The correct answer is D.** The word *help* indicates the need for a positive word to complete this sentence. Therefore, you need consider only choices A and D. Of these two, *implement* (meaning put into action) is a better choice than *magnify* (meaning "to make larger").

40. **The correct answer is C.** The words required to complete the thought must be opposites. A comfort is something that is nice to have but we can do without, but once we have had that comfort for a while, we can no longer do without it, and it becomes a necessity (an essential).

Section 2: Quantitative Reasoning

1. B	9. D	17. C	25. C	33. B
2. C	10. C	18. A	26. C	34. C
3. B	11. B	19. B	27. C	35. A
4. B	12. B	20. A	28. A	36. A
5. B	13. C	21. D	29. B	37. C
6. D	14. A	22. A	30. A	
7. C	15. D	23. B	31. C	
8. A	16. D	24. A	32. D	

1. **The correct answer is B.** It is useful to know that you multiply and divide by 10, 100, 1,000, and so on, by moving the decimal point.

2. **The correct answer is C.** The sum of the angles of a triangle is 180°. Angle *B* is 90°. Angles *A* and *C*, therefore, must total 180° – 90°, or 90°.

3. **The correct answer is B.** To find the value of *r*, subtract *s* from both sides of the equation. This gives us $r = 3s - s$, or $r = 2s$.

4. **The correct answer is B.** $(3 \times 10^2) + (2 \times 10) + 9$. Choice A is 929 in expanded form. Choice C is 509 in expanded form. Choice D is 3,029.

5. **The correct answer is B.**

   Circumference = π × diameter

   Diameter = 2 × radius

   $$\pi = \frac{22}{7}$$

   Solve as follows:

   $$C = \pi \times 21 \times 2$$
   $$= 42 \times \pi$$
   $$= 42 \times \frac{22}{7}$$
   $$= 132'$$

   You can also estimate 40 × 3 and choose the closest answer.

6. **The correct answer is D.** The set {*x*, *y*} includes all those numbers larger than –4 and smaller than 2. Considering only whole numbers, this set includes –3, –2, –1, 0, 1.

7. **The correct answer is C.** Remember, order of operations matters. According to PEMDAS, the numbers inside the parentheses will be multiplied first, then the results will be added. So as long as the correct numbers are multiplied together first, the order in which numbers are added does not affect the sum. You don't need to calculate the answer if you understand how order of operations works.

8. **The correct answer is A.** We want the amount in the parentheses to be equal to 3. The value of *x* that will make the amount in parentheses equal to 3 is 4.

9. **The correct answer is D.** An obtuse angle is any angle that is greater than 90 degrees but less than 180 degrees. An acute angle (choice A) measures less than 90 degrees. A right angle (choice B) equals 90 degrees. A straight angle (choice C) measures 180 degrees.

10. **The correct answer is C.** Using the order of operations (PEMDAS), perform the calculations in parentheses first.

    $$(2^2 + 4) + 2^2 (6 + 3) = (2^2 + 4) + 2^2 (9)$$

    Next, perform the operations with exponents:

    $$(2^2 + 4) + 2^2 (9) = (4 + 4) + 4(9)$$
    $$= (8) + 4(9)$$

    Next, perform multiplication, followed by addition:

    $$(8) + 4(9) = (8) + 36$$
    $$= 44$$

11. **The correct answer is B.** Note that $\frac{17}{30}$ is slightly larger than $\frac{15}{30}$, or $\frac{1}{2}$. Choices A, C, and D are closer in value to 1 than to $\frac{1}{2}$.

12. **The correct answer is B.** 100 centimeters = 1 meter. Each centimeter is $\frac{1}{100}$ of a meter.

13. **The correct answer is C.** Find the LCM (least common multiple) of 4, 9, 6, and 12. 36 is the least common denominator.

14. **The correct answer is A.**

    The set of factors of 36 is:

    $\{1, 2, 3, 4, 6, 9, 12, 18, 36\}$

    The set of factors of 64 is:

    $\{1, 2, 4, 8, 16, 32, 64\}$

    The set of common factors is:

    $\{1, 2, 4\}$

15. **The correct answer is D.** The sum of the angles of a triangle is 180°. $180° - 115° = 65°$

16. **The correct answer is D.** The union of the two adjacent line segments creates one continuous line segment.

17. **The correct answer is C.** The 52 playing cards in a deck consist of 4 suits of 13 cards each. There is 1 six in each of the four suits, making the probability of drawing a six $\frac{4}{52}$, or $\frac{1}{13}$.

18. **The correct answer is A.** Every 8 miles is represented on the map by $\frac{1}{2}$ inch. $28 \div 8 = 3\frac{1}{2}$, so $3\frac{1}{2}$ half-inch units are needed to represent 28 miles.

    $$3\frac{1}{2} \times \frac{1}{2} = \frac{7}{2} \times \frac{1}{2} = \frac{7}{4} = 1\frac{3}{4}$$

    The following is an alternative way to solve:

    If $\frac{1}{2}" = 8$ miles, then $1" = 16$ miles. $28 \div 16 = 1\frac{3}{4}$, so $1\frac{3}{4}"$ are required to represent 28 miles.

19. **The correct answer is B.** The number of accidents is irrelevant to the question, so A has no place in the equation.

    B (total deaths) $\div$ 10 years $= \frac{B}{10}$ average deaths per year.

20. **The correct answer is A.**

    Column A solution:
    $$3x^2 + 2x - 1$$
    $$= 3(-2)^2 + 2(-2) - 1$$
    $$= 12 - 4 - 1$$
    $$= 7$$

    Column B solution:
    $$x^3 + 2x^2 + 1$$
    $$= (-2)^3 + 2(-2)^2 + 1$$
    $$= -8 + 8 + 1$$
    $$= 1$$

    Column A > Column B

21. **The correct answer is D.** The relationship between Column A and Column B cannot be determined from the information given.

22. **The correct answer is A.**

    Column A:
    $$(16 \div 4) + (8 \times 2) - 8$$
    $$= 4 + 16 - 8$$
    $$= 20 - 8$$
    $$= 12$$

    Column B:
    $$(3 \times 4) + (10 \div 5) - 3$$
    $$= 12 + 2 - 3$$
    $$= 14 - 3$$
    $$= 11$$

    Column A > Column B

23. **The correct answer is B.**

    Original Cost + Profit = Selling Price

    Let x = original cost

Then $x + 0.05(x) = \$47.25$

$1.05x = \$47.25$

$x = \$45$

$\$45 > \$44.89$

Column B > Column A

24. **The correct answer is A.**

Column A:
$$a - b = -1$$
$$-a - b = -3$$
$$-2b = -4$$
$$b = 2$$

Column B:
$$a - b = -1$$
$$a - (2) = -1$$
$$a = 1$$

Column A > Column B

25. **The correct answer is C.**

$0.25(300) = 75$ (girls with blond hair)

$300 - 75 = 225$ (girls without blond hair)

$$\frac{75}{225} = \frac{1}{3}$$

Column A = Column B

26. **The correct answer is C.** The sum of the angles of a triangle equals 180°.

$$a + b + c = 180$$
$$\text{and } d + e + f = 180$$
$$a + b + c + d + e + f = 360$$
$$\text{Also, } e + c = 90$$

Therefore, $a + b + d + f = 270$

Column A = Column B

27. **The correct answer is C.** A parallelogram inscribed in a circle is a rectangle. Therefore, all angles equal 90°.

Hence, $a + c = b + d$

Column A = Column B

28. **The correct answer is A.**

$$\frac{9}{8} = 1.125$$

$$\frac{3}{5} = 0.60$$

$$1.125 - 0.60 = 0.525$$

$$0.525 > 0.5$$

Column A > Column B

29. **The correct answer is B.** Let $x =$ the number of days A and B take working together.

A can do the job in 4 days; thus, A's rate is $\frac{1}{4}$.

B can do the job in 3 days; thus, B's rate is $\frac{1}{3}$.

$$\frac{x}{4} + \frac{x}{3} = 1$$

$$\frac{7x}{12} = 1$$

$$x = 1\frac{5}{7} \text{ days}$$

$$2 \text{ days} > 1\frac{5}{7} \text{ days}$$

Column B > Column A

30. **The correct answer is A.** The ratio between seniors and the total of seniors and freshmen is 1:4. The ratio between seniors and the total enrollment (including sophomores and juniors) would actually decrease. Therefore, Column A > Column B.

31. **The correct answer is C.** The sum of the three angles of a triangle equals 180°.

Thus:
$$x + x + 60° = 180°$$
$$2x = 120°$$
$$x = 60°$$

Therefore, the triangle is equilateral.

Hence, side $m =$ side n.

Column A = Column B

32. **The correct answer is D.** The relationship cannot be determined from the information given.

33. **The correct answer is B.** The sum of the angles of a triangle equals 180°.

Thus:

$$x + 2x + 90° = 180°$$
$$3x = 90°$$
$$x = 30°$$

Therefore, $\triangle ABC$ is a 30°-60°-90° right triangle. In a 30°-60°-90° right triangle, the hypotenuse is equal to twice the side opposite the 30° angle.

$AB = 8$

$8 > 5$

Column B > Column A

34. **The correct answer is C.**

$$\sqrt[3]{125} = 5 \text{ and } \sqrt{25} = 5$$

Column A = Column B

35. **The correct answer is A.**

$x > 0$, x is positive

$y < 0$, y is negative

Substitute some arbitrary figures of your choosing.

Column A:

If $y = -2$, then
$$x - y = 10 - (-2)$$
$$= 12$$

Column B:

If $y = 2$, then
$$x + y = 10 + (-2)$$
$$= 8$$

Column A > Column B

36. **The correct answer is A.**

$$15\% = 0.15$$
$$0.15(43.50) = 6.525$$
$$\$43.50 - 6.53 = 36.97$$
$$\$36.97 > \$36$$

Column A > Column B

37. **The correct answer is C.**

Column A:

$$75\% = \frac{3}{4}$$
$$\frac{3}{4}\left(\frac{1}{2}\right) = \frac{3}{8}$$

Column B:

$$50\% = \frac{1}{2}$$
$$\frac{1}{2}\left(\frac{3}{4}\right) = \frac{3}{8}$$

Column A = Column B

Section 3: Reading Comprehension

1. B	7. A	13. B	19. C	25. A	31. B
2. D	8. B	14. C	20. D	26. B	32. D
3. D	9. D	15. A	21. C	27. D	33. C
4. A	10. A	16. C	22. D	28. B	34. A
5. A	11. D	17. A	23. B	29. A	35. A
6. C	12. B	18. B	24. A	30. C	36. C

1. **The correct answer is B.** The word *fashioned* means "created, formed, or constructed."

2. **The correct answer is D.** While the statue was found in a preserved pond area, the passage does not suggest that Hun Hunahpu thrived in a water-based environment.

3. **The correct answer is D.** The focus of the passage is the recent archaeological discovery involving a partial statue of Hun Hunahpu. "Mayan Gods" (choice B) is too broad since the passage only focuses on Hun Hunahpu. While maize played an important role in Mayan culture, "The History of Maize in Palenque" (choice A) implies that the passage only focuses on maize, while its focus is primarily on the god of maize. Similarly, "The Role of Hair in Mayan Worship" (choice C) mistakes a small detail about the statue's hair for a main idea.

4. **The correct answer is A.** There are two facts from the passage that help you confirm this answer. One is that the statue of Hun Hunahpu and its placement at the foot of a pond were likely not random but instead coincided with an important gathering space for Maya people. Secondly, if researchers are particularly interested in what they might find at Palenque, then you can infer that they believe this city was important enough to have something worth finding when digging. Based on these details, we can infer that Palenque was an important city in Mayan culture.

5. **The correct answer is A.** Since the passage focuses extensively on the importance of maize in Mayan culture, additional context on the history of

maize cultivation would be relevant and helpful information.

6. **The correct answer is C.** The goal of the passage is to inform the reader of a recent, significant archaeological discovery.

7. **The correct answer is A.** The term *dingy* means "drab or dull."

8. **The correct answer is B.** The preceding lines "The mountains swing along / The south horizon of the sky" in stanza 3 indicate that the mountains are doing the welcoming.

9. **The correct answer is D.** Personification means attributing human characteristics to something, as in the mountains' "sunning their shining foreheads."

10. **The correct answer is A.** If one thing is plastered in another thing, that means it is completely covered in that thing. The closest synonym given for *plasters* is *covers*.

11. **The correct answer is D.** While the first and third stanzas focus on the wild and resilient beauty of the mountains, the second stanza illustrates how "the world makes war" on the mountains through industrial projects like mining ("Tunnels their granite cliffs / Splits down their shining sides") and advertising ("Plasters their cliffs with soap-advertisements").

12. **The correct answer is B.** The speaker's tone suggests that they are critical of human expansion into nature and believes it has been detrimental, meaning "harmful."

13. **The correct answer is B.** Nichelle Nichols was an actress who played Lieutenant Uhura on the TV show *Star Trek*.

14. **The correct answer is C.** The passage summarizes the life and achievements of Mae Jemison.

15. **The correct answer is A.** *Rigorous* most nearly means "tough, brutal, meticulous, or strict."

16. **The correct answer is C.** The passage states that Jemison was accepted to be a NASA astronaut in 1987, then spent two years in "rigorous training" before being selected for the STS-47 crew mission. Therefore, we can assume she was selected in 1989 and then finally went to space in 1992, meaning there were as many as four years between the selection process and her crew's trip.

17. **The correct answer is A.** The final line discusses what Jemison has been doing since she retired from NASA.

18. **The correct answer is B.** LeVar Burton invited Jemison, who was inspired by Nichelle Nichols on *Star Trek*, to be the first real astronaut to appear on *Star Trek: The Next Generation*.

19. **The correct answer is C.** The term *de facto* means "in fact" or "in effect." Contextually, what the author is trying to say is that there was no official leader of the Dada movement, but Hugo Ball arranged many of the first events, making him effectively the leader if not officially so.

20. **The correct answer is D.** As paragraph 4 illustrates, the Dada movement spread beyond Zurich to New York City. It was also prevalent in other world cities, such as Berlin and Paris.

21. **The correct answer is C.** As discussed in paragraph 4, the purpose of readymades, which are composed of everyday objects, is to encourage the viewer to question what constitutes art.

22. **The correct answer is D.** The passage provides examples of how chaos and meaninglessness were major themes of Dada art, as exemplified in sound poems, geometric masks, and improvised dances.

23. **The correct answer is B.** To understand what should come between paragraphs 2 and 3, your first step is to remind yourself of the topic of each. Paragraph 2 was focused on Hugo Ball's original manifesto, while paragraph 3 goes on to talk about some of the types of art that Dada popularized. It wouldn't make sense to refer to something that came before Dada here (choice D), nor would it make sense to reference something that comes after (choice C). In the passage, there is no mention of surrealism in relation to Dada (choice A). You can find your answer through this process of elimination, but the topic also confirms it. Since Tristan Tzara wrote a second Dada manifesto a few years after Hugo Ball did, it likely contains ideas that were central to the art movement as it expanded, and it would make sense to discuss that second manifesto after a paragraph that quotes the first one by Hugo Ball.

24. **The correct answer is A.** The passage is meant to provide information about the Dada movement. The word *pretentious* is not an adequate description because the author is not attempting to impress the reader with information about Dada or art itself.

25. **The correct answer is A.** A balm is something that is soothing or healing. In this passage, the focus is on houseplants and their role in creating a soothing environment for humans, so you can assume the metaphor refers to houseplants.

26. **The correct answer is B.** The author appeals to an authority on the subject of houseplants and mood when citing Professor Mengmeng Gu of Texas A&M University and mentioning that the quote in question came from a reputable news source, the *Washington Post*.

27. **The correct answer is D.** The passage explores how and why houseplants can improve mood. The passage does not mention the cost of keeping houseplants (choice A) nor does it advocate for spending more time in nature (choice B), though that could be inferred from some of the author's statements. While the passage discusses the impact of houseplants on mood, it does not delve into the subject of diseases or claim that plants can actually cure any ailments (choice C).

28. **The correct answer is B.** The biophilia hypothesis states that spending time in environments lacking greenery can negatively affect one's mood.

29. **The correct answer is A.** A person's disposition is their mood, frame-of-mind, temperament, or personality.

30. **The correct answer is C.** Because the passage tells us that houseplants can improve one's mood, a reader could reasonably infer that houseplants can help with negative feelings, like the sadness one experiences after a breakup.

31. **The correct answer is B.** The word *myriad* can be used in an adjectival or noun form to refer to something countless or extremely great in number.

32. **The correct answer is D.** The passage provides examples of good luck rituals (choice A), rituals for generating cash for the newlyweds (choice B), and rituals to ward off spirits (choice C) but does not provide any examples of rituals to ensure long life.

33. **The correct answer is C.** The passage groups the rituals covered according to the purpose of the ritual, first discussing those designed to ward off spirits, then those meant to bring good luck to the couple, and finally customs around raising funds for newlywed couples.

34. **The correct answer is A.** Since the passage focuses on common wedding customs in numerous countries, including Armenia, Norway, China, and more, the most fitting title is "Wedding Traditions from Around the World." Choice C, "Weddings Outside the US" might seem fitting, but paragraph 1 *does* discuss American wedding traditions, so it is not an effective title. The other titles are too broad and do not capture the specific focus of the passage.

35. **The correct answer is A.** Since the passage provides numerous examples of rituals for warding off spirits in countries across the world, we can assume that residents of multiple countries have traditionally believed in the existence of evil spirits.

36. **The correct answer is C.** The passage takes a celebratory look at the customs and rituals involved in weddings across the globe. The author does not caution against specific traditions (choice A), nor do they critique any of the customs presented (choice B). The term *compliant* (choice D), meaning "agreeable" or "acquiescent," makes no sense in the context of this passage.

Section 4: Mathematics Achievement

1. C	9. B	17. C	25. C	33. C	41. A
2. A	10. A	18. A	26. B	34. C	42. C
3. D	11. A	19. B	27. A	35. C	43. D
4. B	12. B	20. B	28. B	36. B	44. B
5. D	13. A	21. A	29. B	37. B	45. C
6. D	14. D	22. D	30. B	38. B	46. D
7. D	15. D	23. B	31. C	39. C	47. D
8. D	16. D	24. D	32. B	40. D	

1. **The correct answer is C.** First find out how much sugar is needed for one quart of punch:

$$\frac{3}{4} \text{ cup} \div 6 = \frac{3}{4} \times \frac{1}{6} = \frac{\cancel{3}^{1}}{4} \times \frac{1}{\cancel{6}_{2}} = \frac{1}{8}$$

For 9 quarts of punch, you need:

$$9 \times \frac{1}{8} = \frac{9}{8} = 1\frac{1}{8}$$

2. **The correct answer is A.** 45 badges × 4 inches each = 180 inches needed. There are 36 inches in one yard:

180 inches ÷ 36 = 5 yards of ribbon needed.

3. **The correct answer is D.**

$60 × 0.10 = $6 (employee discount)

$60 − $6 = $54

$54 × 0.20 = $10.80 (sale discount)

$54 − $10.80 = $43.20

4. **The correct answer is B.** Area equals length times width.

$A = l \times w$

$A = 10 \text{ ft.} \times 8 \text{ ft.}$

$A = 80 \text{ sq. ft.}$

5. **The correct answer is D.** The decimal number 0.375 is equivalent to the fraction $\frac{3}{8}$. The line over the decimal number indicates a repeating number that goes on forever, so choices A and B are incorrect.

6. **The correct answer is D.** 20% is the same as $\frac{1}{5}$, so 30 is $\frac{1}{5}$ of the games played. Therefore, the total number of games played must be 5(30) = 150. You could also have taken 20% of each answer choice to see which one yielded 30.

7. **The correct answer is D.** Any number multiplied by 0 equals 0. Since one multiplier on one side of the = sign is 0, the product on that side of the sign must be 0. The value on the other side of the = sign must also be 0.

$$5x = 5 \times 4 \times 2 \times 0$$
$$5x = 40 \times 0$$
$$5x = 0$$
$$x = 0$$

8. **The correct answer is D.** An item marked up 100% has a retail price twice the wholesale price. The dress now costs $130, which is twice $65.

9. **The correct answer is B.** The width of the room will be $17 \times \frac{1}{8}$", or $2\frac{1}{8}$". The length of the room will be $22 \times \frac{1}{8}$", or $2\frac{3}{4}$".

10. **The correct answer is A.** The room has an area of = 560 sq. ft.

Each roll of carpet can cover 90 sq. ft.

The number of rolls required is $560 \div 90 = 6\frac{2}{9}$ rolls.

11. **The correct answer is A.** To square a number, multiply it by itself.

$$100 - x = 5^2$$
$$100 - x = 5 \times 5$$
$$100 - x = 25$$
$$100 - 25 = x$$
$$75 = x$$

12. **The correct answer is B.**

If $y = 2$, then:

$$72x = 6(2)$$
$$72x = 12$$
$$x = \frac{1}{6}$$

13. **The correct answer is A.** Borrow 60 minutes and rewrite as follows:

$$\begin{array}{ll} 59 \text{ hr.} & 81 \text{ min.} \\ -5 \text{ hr.} & 37 \text{ min.} \\ \hline 54 \text{ hr.} & 44 \text{ min.} \end{array}$$

14. **The correct answer is D.** $\frac{1}{2}x^2 - 6$

15. **The correct answer is D.** Ten more gallons of water would bring the volume of the mixture to 30 gallons of water + 5 gallons of acid = 35 gallons. The part that is water is $\frac{30}{35}$, or $\frac{6}{7}$.

16. **The correct answer is D.** $\frac{1}{30}$ of a month is about one day.

17. **The correct answer is C.** A circle graph contains 360°, while a right angle contains 90°. A right angle, therefore, contains $\frac{1}{4}$, or 25%, of the circle.

18. **The correct answer is A.** To find the value of this expression, multiply the binomials using the FOIL method. Multiply the first, outer, inner, and last terms:

$$(z + 7)(z - 7) = z^2 - 7z + 7z - 49$$
$$= z^2 - 49$$

The $-7z$ and $+7z$ in the middle cancel each other out, and we are left with $z^2 - 49$.

19. **The correct answer is B.** The perimeter is the sum of the lengths of the four sides. A rectangle has two pairs of sides of equal length. The perimeter then is $(2 \times 115) + (2 \times 63) = 356$ feet.

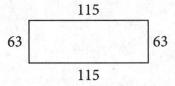

$$115 + 63 + 115 + 63 = 356$$

This is a good problem to solve by estimation. You can readily discard three of the possible answers without doing any calculation.

20. **The correct answer is B.** Don't bother to calculate here. Notice that your answer will be very close to 6×1. There is only one answer anywhere near that estimate.

21. **The correct answer is A.** The square of a number divided by 2.5 equals 10. The square of the number, then, equals 10 multiplied by 2.5.

$$x^2 = 10 \times 2.5$$
$$x^2 = 25$$
$$x = \pm 5$$

22. **The correct answer is D.** Each year, 12% is charged as interest. On $2,000, 12% interest is $2,000 \times 0.12 = 240. For two years, the amount is $240 \times 2 = 480.

23. **The correct answer is B.** Find the volume by finding the area of the triangular end and multiplying by the length.

$$A = \frac{1}{2}bh$$

The area of the triangular end is:

$$A = \frac{1}{2}(3)(2) = 3 \text{ sq. ft.}$$

Multiply 3 sq. ft. by the length to find the volume:

$$3 \text{ sq. ft.} \times 6 \text{ ft.} = 18 \text{ cu. ft.}$$

24. **The correct answer is D.** Note that the second piece is the shortest. We don't know its exact length, so call it x feet long. The first piece is three times as long as the second, or $3x$ feet long. The

third is twice as long as the first, or $6x$ feet long. All the pieces total $x + 3x + 6x = 10x$ feet. The board is 30 feet long, and the pieces are $10x$ feet long. $10x = 30$, so $x = 3$, which is the length of the shortest piece. The largest piece is six times the shortest, or 18 feet long.

25. **The correct answer is C.** We assume that the merchant wants to have the same total value of wine after reducing the price. She now has ($32 \times \$1.50$), or \$48 worth of wine. At \$1.20 per gallon, she would need 40 gallons to have \$48 worth. Therefore, she must add 8 gallons of water.

26. **The correct answer is B.** If six is four more than $\frac{2}{3}$ of a number, then $6 - 4$ equals $\frac{2}{3}$ of the number. Since $6 - 4 = 2$, we know that 2 is $\frac{2}{3}$ of the number, so the number is 3. Another way to solve this problem is to write an equation, and solve for x:

$$\frac{2}{3}x + 4 = 6$$
$$\frac{2}{3}x = 2$$
$$x = 3$$

27. **The correct answer is A.** You only need to read the first and third sentences of the problem. The information in the second sentence contains information not relevant to the problem.

The winner received $\frac{1}{3}$ of the total, or \$2,700. Thus, the total purse was $\$2,700 \times 3 = \$8,100$.

28. **The correct answer is B.** The distance between the cars is being reduced at a rate equal to the sum of their speeds. They are coming closer together at $35 + 48 = 83$ miles per hour. Since the distance between them was 450 miles, the time required for traveling is $450 \div 83 = 5.42$ hours. Remember that distance is the product of rate and time, or $d = rt$.

29. **The correct answer is B.** Of his total, he issued $\frac{3}{8} + \frac{1}{4} + \frac{1}{6} = \frac{19}{24}$, so he had $\frac{5}{24}$ brake pads remaining. His total in stock was 600. $600 \times \frac{5}{24} = 125$ brake pads remaining.

30. **The correct answer is B.** The first person can load $\frac{1}{25}$ of the truck in 1 minute. The second person can load $\frac{1}{50}$ of the truck in 1 minute. The third person can load $\frac{1}{10}$ of the truck in 1 minute. Together, they can load $\frac{1}{25} + \frac{1}{50} + \frac{1}{10}$ of the truck each minute.

$$\frac{1}{25} + \frac{1}{20} + \frac{1}{10} = \frac{2}{50} + \frac{1}{50} + \frac{5}{50}$$
$$= \frac{8}{50} = \frac{4}{25}$$

of the truck loaded per minute. The whole job then requires $\frac{25}{4}$ minutes, or $6\frac{1}{4}$ minutes.

31. **The correct answer is C.** This question requires some knowledge of algebra. The equations are "added." The y-term is eliminated, leaving only x.

$$4x - y = 20$$
$$+\ 2x + y = 28$$
$$\overline{6x = 48}$$
$$x = 8$$

32. **The correct answer is B.**

First, find the value for x plus y in the first equation:
$$6 + x + y = 20$$
$$x + y = 14$$
Since $x + y = k$, we know that $k = 14$. Now substitute for k and solve:
$$20 - 14 = 6$$

33. **The correct answer is C.** A circle is 360°.
$$60° \text{ is } \frac{1}{6} \text{ of } 360°.$$

34. **The correct answer is C.** Diagram to visually see the answer.

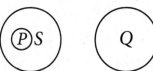

ANSWERS: ISEE (UPPER LEVEL) PRACTICE TEST

35. **The correct answer is C.** Pick a pair of ages and try for yourself. *A* is 4; *B* is 2; the ratio of their ages is 4 to 2, or 2 to 1. In two years, *A* is 6 and *B* is 4. The ratio of their ages is 6 to 4, or 3 to 2.

36. **The correct answer is B.**

$$15° - 21° = -6°$$

37. **The correct answer is B.** If the sides are parallel, the angles are congruent.

38. **The correct answer is B.**

6 words per line × 5 lines per inch

= 30 words per inch.

30 words per inch × 8 inches

= 240 words.

If the article has 270 words and there is space for only 240 words, then 30 words must be deleted.

39. **The correct answer is C.**

$$S = 1; \ R = 3 \times 1; \ T = \frac{1}{3}$$

$$1 + (3 \times 1) + \left(\frac{1}{3}\right) = 4\frac{1}{3}$$

40. **The correct answer is D.**

The lawn is 8' × 12' = 96 sq. ft.

96 × 5 = 480 pints of water needed

8 pts. in 1 gal.

480 ÷ 8 = 60 gallons needed

41. **The correct answer is A.**

$l = 500 + (500 \times 0.20 \times 2)$

$l = 500 + 200$

$l = 700$

42. **The correct answer is C.** Right now, he gets 120 mi. ÷ 12 gal. = 10 mpg. With 80% more efficiency, he will need 80% of 12, or 9.6 gal. to go 120 miles. He will then get 120 mi. ÷ 9.6 gal. = 12.5 mpg.

12 gal. × 12.5 mpg = 150 miles on 12 gal.

43. **The correct answer is D.**

4 feet = 48 inches

$$48 \div \frac{1}{4} = 48 \times 4 = 192 \text{ books}$$

44. **The correct answer is B.** There are 6 + 8 + 4 + 12 = 30 marbles.

$$12 \div 30 = 0.40 = \frac{2}{5}$$

45. **The correct answer is C.** $\overline{CD}$ is a hypotenuse, so use the Pythagorean Theorem:

$$CD = \sqrt{CE^2 + ED^2}$$
$$CD = \sqrt{7^2 + 6^2}$$
$$CD = \sqrt{49 + 36}$$
$$CD = \sqrt{85}$$

46. **The correct answer is D.**

$$3^3 \times 3 = 27 \times 3 = 81$$

47. **The correct answer is D.**

$$(3+2)(6-2)(7+1) = (4+4)(x)$$
$$(5)(4)(8) = 8x$$
$$160 = 8x$$
$$20 = x$$

The only two numbers that equal 20 among the answer choices given are 8 + 12.

Section 5: Essay

Example of a well-written essay.

When I enter high school, I plan to become an active member of the drama club. The drama club offers a variety of activities within one organization. In the course of a single year, a member of the drama club can get involved in acting, set building, lighting design, publicity, ticket sales, and much more. And because of the variety of activities, I expect to make friends with classmates with a variety of interests and abilities.

People involved with theater appear to have a lot of fun. While there may be some competition among stars, a production is generally a cooperative effort. Teamwork is key to making an amateur production appear to be professional. Even in kindergarten I got high marks from my teachers in "works and plays well with others," and I would like to carry this aspect of my personality into joining a cast and crew that creates theater.

Another reason for joining the drama club is that it will give me a chance to perform. I have always been a bit of a show-off. Being on stage will allow me to flaunt my skills without being criticized. I hope that my acting will contribute to successful productions along with my work as part of the behind-the-scenes crew.

Finally, any cooperative effort must be a social activity. There should be lots of give and take and conversation during preparations and rehearsals. And I do look forward to cast parties when the show closes. Drama club seems like the perfect extracurricular activity; I will have a good time while doing something worthwhile.

SCORE YOURSELF

Scores on the ISEE are determined by comparing each student's results against all other students in their grade level who took that particular test. A scaled score is then calculated. You can use the following calculations to determine how well you did on this diagnostic test, but keep in mind that when you take the actual test, your score might vary.

ISEE SCORING			
Test	Raw Score ÷ No. questions	× 100	= %
Synonyms	_____ ÷ 20	× 100 =	_____%
Sentence Completions	_____ ÷ 20	× 100 =	_____%
Total Verbal Ability	_____ ÷ 40	× 100 =	_____%
Multiple-Choice Quantitative	_____ ÷ 19	× 100 =	_____%
Quantitative Comparisons	_____ ÷ 18	× 100 =	_____%
Total Quantitative Ability	_____ ÷ 37	× 100 =	_____%
Reading Comprehension	_____ ÷ 36	× 100 =	_____%
Mathematics Achievement	_____ ÷ 47	× 100 =	_____%

Remember:

- Scores are not reported as percentages. A low percentage may translate to a respectable scaled score.
- The same test is given to students in grades 8 through 11. Unless you have finished high school, you have not been taught everything on the test. You are not expected to know what you have not been taught.
- You will be compared only to students in your own grade.
- Use your scores to plan further study if you have time.